AMERICAN FOREIGN
POLICY
AND POLITICAL
AMBITION

AMERICAN FOREIGN
POLICY
AND POLITICAL
AMBITION

JAMES LEE RAY
VANDERBILT UNIVERSITY

CQ PRESS

A Division of Congressional Quarterly Inc.
WASHINGTON, D.C.

CQ Press
1255 22nd Street, NW, Suite 400
Washington, DC 20037

Phone: 202-729-1900; toll-free, 1-866-4CQ-PRESS (1-866-427-7737)

Web: www.cqpress.com

Cover design: Marlyn Garcia, TGD
Composition: Alan Grimes
Photo credits:
DoD photo by Sgt. Rob Summitt, U.S. Army: 2
The Granger Collection: 12, 22
Reuters: 36, 62, 86
AP Images: 116, 152, 172, 194, 224, 254, 284, 316, 350

♾ The paper used in this publication exceeds the requirements of the American National Standard for Information Sciences—Permanence of Paper for Printed Library Materials, ANSI Z39.48-1992.

Printed and bound in the United States of America

11 10 09 08 07   1 2 3 4 5

Library of Congress Cataloging-in-Publication Data
Ray, James Lee.
  American foreign policy and political ambition / James Lee Ray.
      p. cm.
  Includes bibliographical references and index.
  ISBN 978-1-56802-832-3 (alk. paper)
 1. United States—Foreign relations. 2. United States—Foreign relations—Sources. 3. United States—Foreign relations—Philosophy. 4. Ambition—History. I. Title.

  E183.7.R35 2007
  327.73--dc22
                                                2007025859

TO CAM

TABLES

FIGURES

MAPS

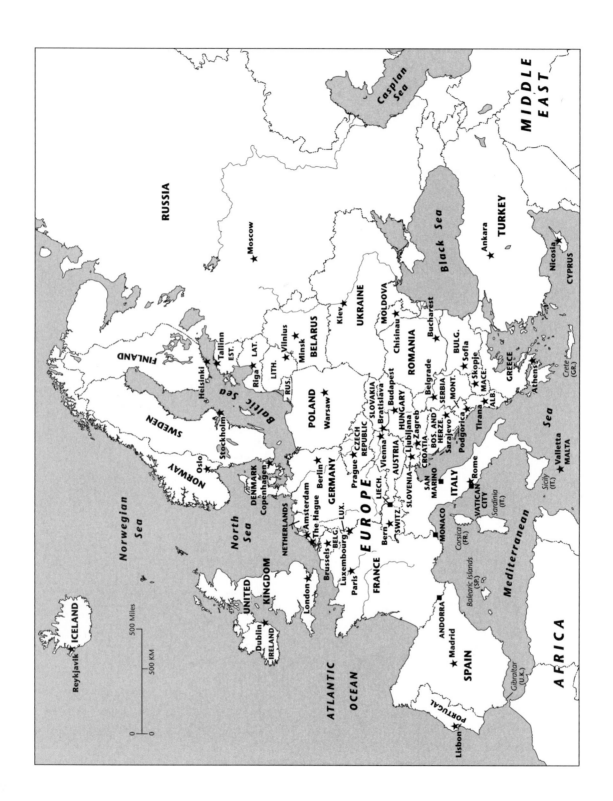

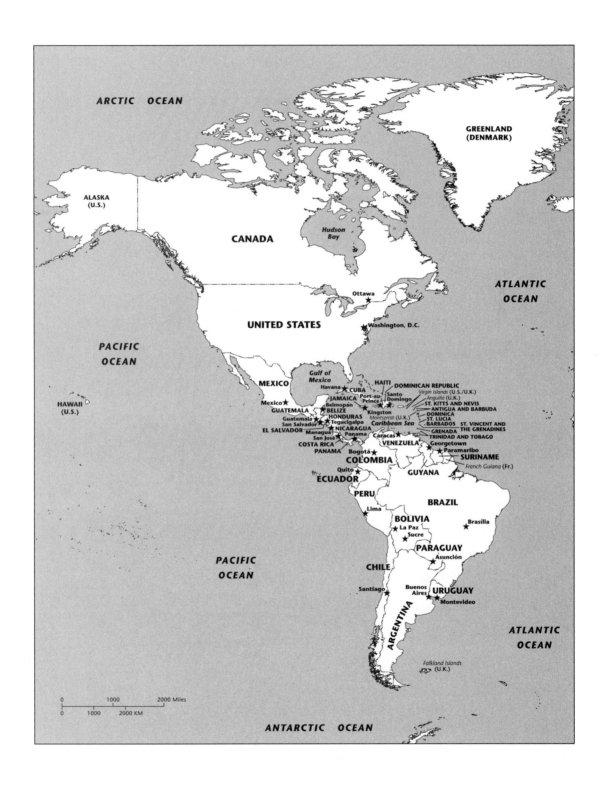

ARCTIC OCEAN

GREENLAND
(DENMARK)

ALASKA
(U.S.)

CANADA

Hudson
Bay

ATLANTIC
OCEAN

Ottawa ★

PACIFIC
OCEAN

UNITED STATES

★ Washington, D.C.

HAWAII
(U.S.)

Gulf of
Mexico

MEXICO

HAITI   DOMINICAN REPUBLIC
Havana   Virgin Islands (U.S./U.K.)
★ CUBA   Anguilla (U.K.)
Port-au-   Santo   ST. KITTS AND NEVIS
Prince   Domingo   ANTIGUA AND BARBUDA
JAMAICA   DOMINICA
BELIZE   ST. LUCIA
Belmopán   Montserrat (U.K.)   BARBADOS
HONDURAS   Kingston   ST. VINCENT AND
Caribbean Sea   THE GRENADINES
Tegucigalpa   GRENADA
NICARAGUA   TRINIDAD AND TOBAGO
Managua   Caracas ★
San José   Panama   VENEZUELA   Georgetown
★   ★   Paramaribo
COSTA RICA   ★   SURINAME
PANAMA   Bogotá ★   French Guiana (Fr.)
COLOMBIA   GUYANA
Quito ★
ECUADOR

Mexico ★
GUATEMALA
Guatemala ★
San Salvador ★
EL SALVADOR

PERU
Lima ★

BRAZIL

BOLIVIA
★ La Paz
★ Sucre

Brasília ★

PARAGUAY
Asunción ★

PACIFIC
OCEAN

CHILE

Santiago ★

Buenos
Aires   URUGUAY
★   ★ Montevideo

ATLANTIC
OCEAN

ARGENTINA

Falkland Islands
(U.K.)

0   1000   2000 Miles
0   1000   2000 KM

ANTARCTIC OCEAN

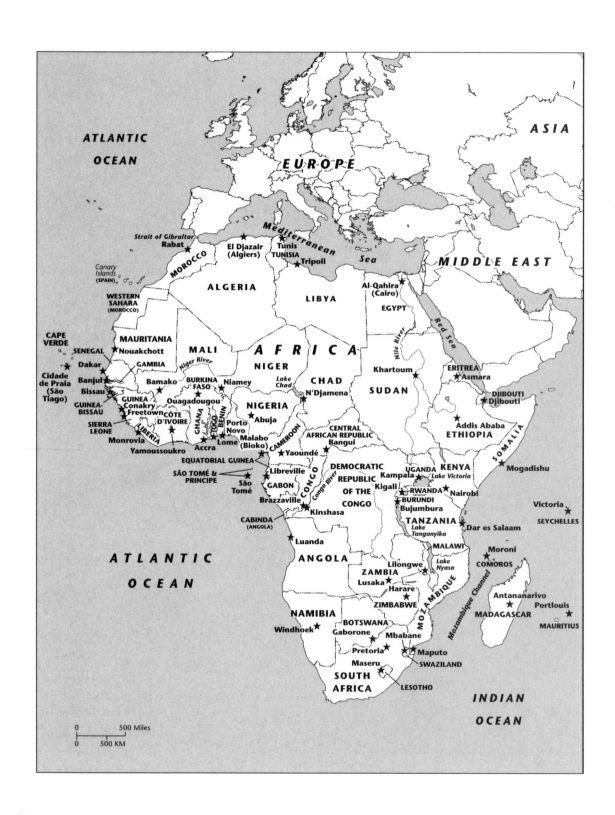

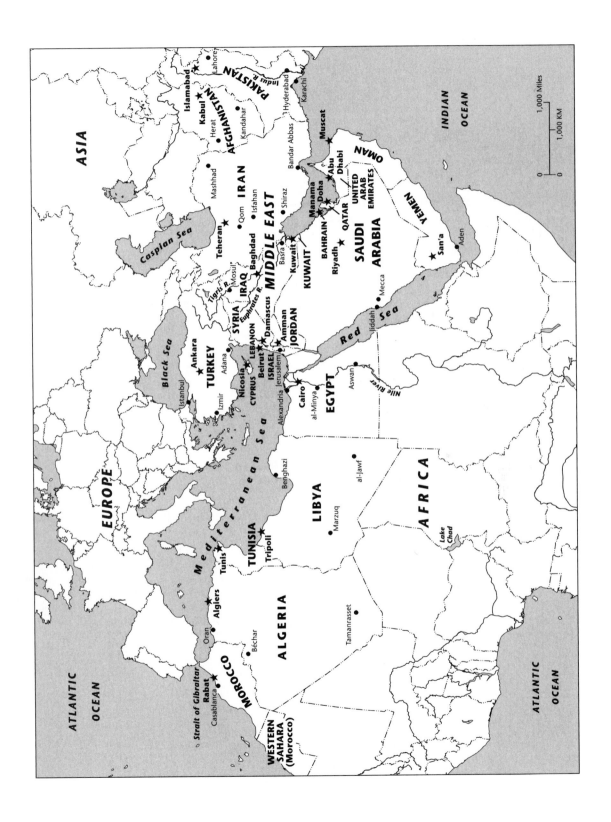

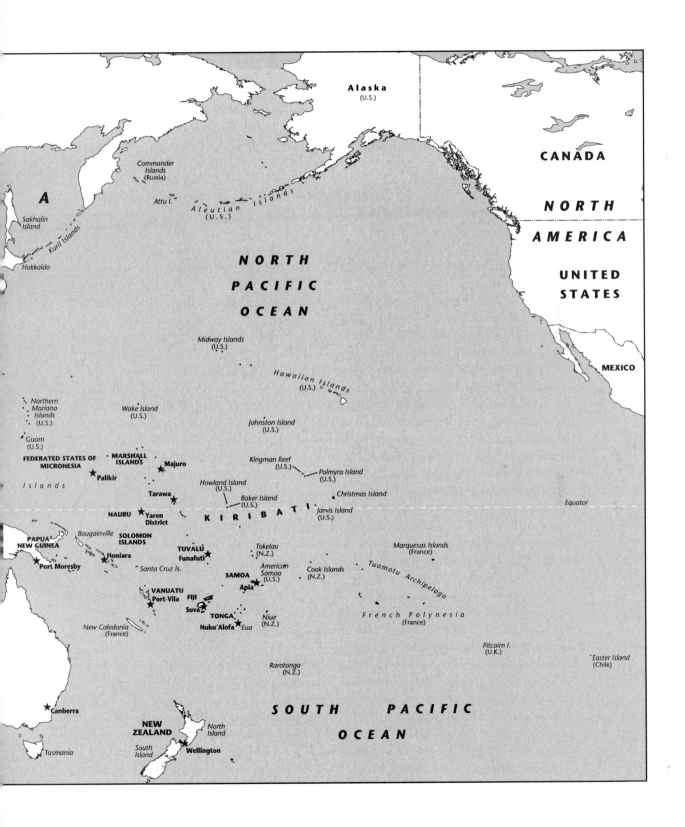

A

Sakhalin Island

Kuril Islands

Hokkaido

Commander Islands (Russia)

Attu I.

Aleutian Islands (U.S.)

Alaska (U.S.)

CANADA

NORTH

AMERICA

UNITED STATES

MEXICO

NORTH PACIFIC OCEAN

Midway Islands (U.S.)

Hawaiian Islands (U.S.)

Northern Mariana Islands (U.S.)

Wake Island (U.S.)

Johnston Island (U.S.)

Guam (U.S.)

FEDERATED STATES OF MICRONESIA

MARSHALL ISLANDS

Majuro

★ **Palikir**

Kingman Reef (U.S.)

Palmyra Island (U.S.)

Islands

Howland Island (U.S.)

Tarawa ★

Baker Island (U.S.)

Christmas Island

Equator

NAURU ★ **Yaren District**

K I R I B A T I

Jarvis Island (U.S.)

Bougainville

SOLOMON ISLANDS

PAPUA NEW GUINEA

Honiara

Port Moresby

Santa Cruz Is.

TUVALU **Funafuti** ★

Tokelau (N.Z.)

American Samoa (U.S.)

Cook Islands (N.Z.)

Marquesas Islands (France)

Tuamotu Archipelago

SAMOA

Apia ★

VANUATU

Port-Vila ★

FIJI

Suva

TONGA

Nuku'Alofa ★ *Eua*

Niue (N.Z.)

French Polynesia (France)

New Caledonia (France)

Pitcairn I. (U.K.)

Easter Island (Chile)

Rarotonga (N.Z.)

★ **Canberra**

NEW ZEALAND

North Island

SOUTH PACIFIC

OCEAN

Tasmania

South Island

Wellington

Understanding American foreign policy is difficult, to put it mildly. The United States is a large, complex country that has been one of the world's most powerful for many decades. Since its inception, the United States has dealt with so many issues of such magnitude—and the processes that have shaped foreign policy have involved so many millions of people—that to provide a fully comprehensive account would be beyond the capabilities of one person, or even a group of collaborating analysts. That does not mean we should throw our hands up in the air; nor should we settle for an unbalanced account. As counterintuitive as it may seem, the key to getting a grip on the complexity of the subject is to rely on simplifications, to come to terms with the theoretical approaches that help crystallize the overall dynamics of the field, and to use these simplifications and approaches to gain crucial insight rather than be exhausted by detail.

American Foreign Policy and Political Ambition is particularly attuned to the different theoretical approaches that analysts adopt as they attempt to understand and explain American foreign policies, including realist, liberal, radical, constructivist, and feminist approaches. While giving each of these respectful attention, this book lays claim to an explicit preference for a particular model and uses it throughout the book: rational political ambition theory. In a nutshell, this is the idea that what leaders of states primarily want is to retain their hold on power. In the context of foreign policy, this means that leaders are forced to pay as much or more attention to the concerns of their strongest domestic constituencies as they are to any other foreign leader or group when they are making foreign policy decisions. Many will recognize in this approach Machiavelli's classic advice to rulers regarding effective political tactics to deal with internal and external threats to their hold on power. In contemporary political science, however, the idea is based primarily on a model developed by Bruce Bueno de Mesquita, Alastair Smith, Randolph M. Siverson, and James D. Morrow, along with elements borrowed from R. J. Rummel, Alex Mintz, Helen Milner, Susan Shirk, and Robert Putnam. Rational political ambition theory also borrows from, and to some degree is built on, aspects of many other major analytical traditions, while deviating from all of them in other respects that will be made clear in the course of the discussion.

My primary intention is to ensure that the text's discussions about the history, processes, and issues involved in American foreign policy allow readers to understand the heart of each issue through the insights of rational political ambition theory. The chapter on early American foreign policy, for instance, shows how John Quincy Adams's refusal to issue the Monroe Doctrine jointly with the British while he was a candidate for president was informed by his desire to insulate himself against charges of being too pro-British, a factor that eventually enhanced his chances of winning the presidency. The discussion of current American foreign policy regarding Asia looks at how first the Clinton and then the Bush administrations made a key assumption that the United States would be able to maintain a peaceful relationship with a democratic China, but also shows how in domestic contexts both presidents had to position their attitudes toward China carefully. Even chapters that look at the basic institutions and processes of U.S. foreign policy consider rational political ambition theory. For instance, I look at how the State Department's power and influence are circumscribed by its limited contact with and influence over the selectorate. The book's theoretical approach is thus evident in every chapter, but used strategically where it most makes sense. I am clear about where other theoretical approaches may be brought to bear fruitfully in understanding certain problems and issues, and about where those approaches overlap with rational political ambition theory, since it pays to be ecumenical when one's primary goal is to further readers' understanding of the issues.

ABOUT THE CONTENT

The focus of the book is on American foreign policy since World War II. Nevertheless, it does briefly discuss the history of American foreign policy since the country's founding, especially to the extent that such historical analysis provides a background and basis helpful to an understanding of more contemporary foreign policy issues. The twenty-first century seems fraught with extraordinarily dangerous threats and formidable obstacles for the United States, but every decade has brought its own problems that seemed at the time to verge on the overwhelming.

Part 1 of *American Foreign Policy and Political Ambition* thus sets the stage for the historical and more recent contexts of American foreign policy, and also lays the necessary theoretical planks. Chapter 1 begins with an analysis of just how important the foreign policies of the United States have been in virtually every corner of the globe as well as in the lives of its own citizens, and the chapter starts to make the case for the salience of viewing foreign policy decision making from the viewpoint of rational political ambition theory.

Chapter 2 is devoted to an overview of the history of American foreign policy since the country's inception. It follows the rapid expansion of the United States from a loosely integrated set of colonies along the eastern seaboard of the North American continent to the shores of the Pacific Ocean, as well as its possibly surprising level of activity and foreign policy initiatives around the globe during the nineteenth century. It concludes with an analysis of American foreign policy in the first half of the twentieth century that deals in some detail with U.S. strategies for coping with both world wars. It points out how the cautious and belated fashion in which the United States entered these conflicts may well have been in part a function of its democratic political regime.

With the basic contexts for modern U.S. foreign policy in focus, Chapter 3 describes and evaluates several important analytical approaches to the field. Realism, liberalism, radicalism, constructivism, and rational political ambition theory receive special emphasis. Neoconservatism also is reviewed. The chapter emphasizes the extent to which rational political ambition theory rests on the central tenet that leaders of states primarily want to retain their hold on power. It also focuses on how this approach borrows from, but is still quite distinct from, previous approaches to the study of foreign policies and international politics.

The book's second part takes a close look at foreign policy inputs and processes. In Chapter 4, the focus shifts to political economy to examine the interaction between American foreign policy and domestic as well as global economic processes. The United States has had a dramatic global economic impact at least since the Great Depression, and the mistakes it made during the 1930s in dealing with that disaster created the post–World War II agenda. The global economic structure resting on the International Monetary Fund, the World Bank, and GATT worked well until the 1970s, when serious problems set in that created significant and persistent doubts about American economic leadership that lasted for some two decades. Those doubts were relieved during the 1990s, but currently American political leaders, far from acting in the "national interest," seem so immobilized by their short-run concerns about staying in power that they cannot deal effectively with looming crises regarding the long-range impact of such programs as Social Security, Medicare, and Medicaid, combined with mammoth defense expenditures, on the economic viability of the U.S. federal government.

Chapters 5 and 6 deal with the process of developing and carrying out American foreign policies. One crucial impact of public opinion involves the anticipation by the U.S. president of how the public will react to foreign policy initiatives, especially unsuccessful wars. American media create vivid impressions in the minds of government leaders about what the public is thinking as well as serve as tools that political leaders use to communicate with the public and special interest groups about foreign policy ventures. Interest groups have an important impact on foreign policies of special concern to them. Those groups and political parties have their greatest impact on foreign policies when their support seems especially essential to preserve the president's hold on power.

Formally speaking, the Department of State lies at the heart of the American foreign policy making process, but various factors and processes conspire to diminish its role, especially in more recent times, in its competition with the Department of Defense and intelligence agencies. This is partly because President George W. Bush tended to find the Defense Department, the National Security Administration, and the other various intelligence agencies more in touch with American political processes and more sensitive to his own political priorities. The Constitution issues an "invitation to struggle" over foreign policy to the Congress and the president, with presidents typically winning on most issues. Nevertheless, the role of Congress can be crucial, especially when presidents appear to have seriously mishandled important foreign policy crises.

Part 3 of the book turns to a close examination of the post–World War II era, with the previous discussions of history, inputs, processes, and rational political ambition theory in mind. The chapters in this section analyze in detail landmark issues in U.S. foreign policy having to do with the threat of Communism and show how different approaches to the study of foreign policy inform our understanding of those events. The beginning of the Cold War is the focus of Chapter 7, where I review the arguments that suggest that the Cold War was the fault primarily of either the United States or the Soviet Union. There are powerful arguments that the structure of the international system emerging out of World War II made a confrontation between the United States and the Soviet Union very likely. It was a confrontation foreseen at the beginning of the nineteenth century by Alexis de Tocqueville, who emphasized the fundamental differences between the domestic political and economic systems of the two states he saw as destined to become predominant.

Chapter 8 deals with one of the key confrontations of the Cold War, namely the U.S. war in Vietnam. The origins of the war are traced to events that took place in the 1950s, but this chapter emphasizes the fundamental impact of domestic political considerations on the process of escalation in the 1960s. It also evaluates the validity of the domino theory, the idea that served as another important motivating factor in light of the evidence that emerged at the conclusion of the war, and discusses its impact on subsequent American foreign policies.

Unique to this textbook, the chapters in Part 4 examine contemporary foreign policy concerns in each of the world's major regions: Europe, the Americas, sub-Saharan Africa, Asia, and the Middle East. Chapter 9 explores U.S.-European relations. Those relations have focused most intently on the North Atlantic Treaty Organization (NATO) and the European Union. Both have expanded recently. This chapter analyzes the costs and benefits of the expansion of these organizations.

Inter-American relations are the focus of Chapter 10, which discusses U.S. interventions in Central America and the Caribbean in the first decades of the twentieth century and the Good Neighbor Policy. In its review of U.S. foreign policy with respect to Latin America since World War II, it looks at the intervention in Guatemala in the early 1950s and the prolonged conflict between the United States and Fidel Castro's regime in Cuba. The Cuban Missile Crisis is portrayed as a particularly dramatic example of interstate interactions fueled by domestic political regimes focusing primarily on preserving their existence. It concludes with an analysis of U.S.-Mexican relations, and on the "pink tide" of leftist, mostly anti-American regimes coming to power in Latin America in the first decade of the twenty-first century.

U.S.-African relations serve as the main topic of Chapter 11. Africa has only rarely been an urgent foreign policy priority for the United States. Nevertheless, the importing of slaves in the eighteenth and nineteenth centuries created an important link between the United States and Africa, and the issue of slavery played a crucial role in the development and evolution of the United States in ways that reverberate to this day. The United States did become involved in an international campaign against apartheid in South Africa in the twentieth century, and it has intervened intermittently and half-heartedly in contemporary crises in such places as Somalia, Rwanda, and the Democratic Republic of the Congo (Zaire). However, the time and energy that the United States has devoted to foreign policy in Africa have tended to be restricted by the fact that most African Americans vote for Democratic candidates for president, regardless of what foreign policy stands they take. In addition, research shows that most African Americans feel that several domestic issues are more pressing than any international or foreign policy issues. These factors mean that there is a much smaller constituency advocating for African concerns, especially relative to the constituencies that back foreign policy in other regions.

U.S.-Asian relations, particularly with respect to China, may ultimately be the most important foreign policy issue of the twenty-first century. Chapter 12 points out that Asia now looks somewhat like Europe did at the beginning of the twentieth century, a troubling parallel given that in Europe that century led to tumult. The United States fought China in Korea in the 1950s, and China seems destined to become more powerful than the United States. Will that transition be peaceful? Will China and the United States cooperate in efforts to curb North Korea's nuclear ambitions? Will the United States be able to play a useful role in preventing armed conflict from erupting over the inflammatory issue regarding the future of Taiwan?

While Asia may ultimately become the top foreign policy priority for the United States, there is no doubt that the Middle East is currently the region of greatest concern to U.S.

foreign policy makers. Chapter 13 discusses the tension created by international political strategic calculations that suggest currying favor with Islamic regimes while domestic political considerations lead to consistent support for Israel. The attacks of 9/11 created new dynamics and issues in the Middle East, and it is possible that the domestic political pressures highlighted by rational political ambition theory led the United States to divert resources from the war in Afghanistan to an attack on Saddam Hussein's regime in Iraq.

Chapter 14 is the final chapter in *American Foreign Policy and Political Ambition,* and it deals with the future of U.S. foreign policy in part by going "back to the future," focusing on the demise of the Cold War between the United States and the Soviet Union and drawing parallels for current and future foreign policy strategies. It argues that Ronald Reagan apparently was concerned with international competitors to a degree that is unusual in the view of rational political ambition theory. The leading foreign policy makers of the George W. Bush administrations believed that Reagan's strategy for dealing with international competitors was eminently successful. They tried to emulate his strategies in their struggle with Islamic fundamentalism, with markedly less apparent success.

The United States faces a series of daunting problems in this century. But it has faced potentially catastrophic problems in almost every recent decade, and even though political ambition may lead political leaders to make choices that are dubious in light of the interests of the country, so far the United States has dealt with those potential crises with enough success to preserve and perhaps even reinforce its preeminent position in the global political system.

TEACHING AND LEARNING AIDS

In addition to the tried-and-true scholarly sources one would expect to see in a work on foreign policy, *American Foreign Policy and Political Ambition* relies on policy-oriented journals and papers as well as historical and serious journalistic works and the best materials available on the Internet. The text includes an extensive list of sources for students who wish to delve further into the literature on the subject. To help students with review, each chapter includes key terms in bold print, which are listed at the end of each chapter. A glossary is included at the back of the book. Chapters end with a recurring feature that highlights how rational political ambition theory intersects with the material under discussion. At the end of the text, readers will find a list of suggested readings and Web sites, organized by type and topic, that supplement in useful ways the information, arguments, and data provided in the chapters.

Adopters also can download a set of instructor's resources at college.cqpress.com/instructors-resources/Ray. This includes 350 multiple-choice, short-answer, and long-answer questions loaded in *Respondus* test generation software, a format compatible with most course management systems, including BlackBoard; a set of PowerPoint lecture slides for each chapter; and all of the graphics (including the maps) from the text.

ACKNOWLEDGMENTS

The primary specific academic inspiration for this book is Bruce Bueno de Mesquita, along with his colleagues Alastair Smith, Randy Siverson, and Jim Morrow. Were my friend and colleague Bruce Bueno de Mesquita to have written a textbook on U.S. foreign policy, it would have been very different. Nevertheless, although his ideas about foreign policies and international politics on occasion have seemed attractive to me because I encountered them in some form or other in previous sources, it was his research and writings (as well as personal conversations) that made the largest contribution to my thinking about this book.

J. David Singer has had a longer and even more profound influence on my views on the issues discussed in this book. He too would be reluctant to take responsibility for various aspects of my work as it appears here, but he came into my academic life at a crucial early stage, and without his mentoring I might never have reached the point where I could consider writing a book like this.

Bruce Cronin, City College of New York; Errol Henderson, Pennsylvania State University; Brian Lai, University of Iowa; John Owen, University of Virginia; Mark Souva, Florida State University; and Richard Stoll, Rice University, reviewed the project at various stages, and their reviews were unusually conscientious, insightful, and crafted with an obvious eye toward being as helpful as possible. That I did not take all of their advice in no way indicates that I was not grateful for every word of it.

Danny O'Donnell provided important and helpful research assistance at an early stage of this project. Luke Blaize developed all of the ancillary materials, including the test bank and PowerPoint slides on the instructor's resources Web site. Students in all of my courses over the years have taught me a lot; those I have had in my courses on American foreign policy in recent years have been especially helpful in the development and sorting through of the ideas on which this book is based.

I have more than a little experience on which to base my opinion that the staff of CQ Press is extraordinarily good at what it does. Brenda Carter and Charisse Kiino were both encouraging and helpfully critical in the process of getting the project off the ground. Lorna Notsch provided important assistance to me in the process of selecting and captioning photos and maps. Katharine Miller copyedited the text in a manner that was all at the same time precise, competent, penetrating, thorough, good-humored, and patient. Elise Frasier was editor for this project. The fact that she never seemed to doubt that I would finish the project, even when there were times when I began to wonder, was a significant factor that helped me to overcome the various unexpected obstacles that cropped up from time to time. She has an impressive ability to focus on important—even if minute—details, while at the same time never losing sight of the big picture and the fundamental purposes of the project.

Finally, my wife Cam provides me a firm base of support in the real world, which is indispensable to me in my attempts to deal with academic life (which is also real, of course, but in a different manner). She and my children Katherine, Justin, Alex, and Nicholas are never far from my mind, even when I might appear to be preoccupied with esoteric intellectual matters, which happens on occasion, or so I'm told.

LAYING THE FOUNDATIONS

The Importance, the History, and Competing Theories of American Foreign Policy

WHY SHOULD ANYONE CARE ABOUT AMERICAN FOREIGN POLICY? THE answer to this question may seem obvious, but chapter 1 elaborates on that answer in order to make the obvious quite unmistakable. The United States is—and arguably has been since at least the beginning of the twentieth century—the most powerful country in the world. Its foreign policies have had profound impacts around the globe for over one hundred years. Furthermore, the United States has interacted with its global environment, and has been so integrated with it, that its foreign policy decisions have had consistently dramatic effects on its own citizens.

Chapter 2 sketches in the basic historical background. Although this book as a whole focuses on American foreign policies and their effects since the end of the Second World War, understanding the policies of the contemporary era depends in part upon some familiarity with how the United States reached its position of preeminence at the beginning of the postwar era, which in turn requires knowledge of the nation's most important interactions with its peers, competitors, and enemies during the period from its birth in 1776 until 1945.

Part I ends with a survey of major theoretical approaches to the analysis of American foreign policy. This author favors an approach called "rational political ambition theory," but proselytizing on behalf of that approach is not the overriding priority of this book. Instead, as chapter 3 explains, the goals are to explore the role of theorizing in general in the process of studying American foreign policy and to cultivate an appreciation of the most important alternative theoretical frameworks that have been applied to the subject. The ultimate aim of this chapter—and of the rest of the book—is to encourage readers to develop their own theoretical commitments and to cultivate the habit of evaluating those commitments in a self-conscious fashion as they observe the unfolding of American foreign policies in coming decades.

CHAPTER **1**

THE IMPACTS OF AMERICAN FOREIGN POLICY

A READER OF THIS BOOK WHO IS TWENTY YEARS OLD WILL HAVE HEARD references to the United States as the "sole remaining superpower" almost all of his or her life. Perhaps the reader will have paid no attention. Nonetheless, it is true that, since the end of the Cold War in 1989 (or 1991), the United States has confronted no peer with anything like the power and influence that the Soviet Union once had. Just how powerful is the United States in the first decade of the twenty-first century?

One answer to that question can be found in table 1.1, which lists the "major powers"— the world's most important, influential, and powerful states, as defined by experienced and knowledgeable observers of global politics. That table, reflecting the proportion of various indicators of military-industrial resources held by each of these major powers, shows that, according to this comprehensive index of national capabilities, the United States is, indeed, the most powerful country in the world.

However, table 1.1 also suggests that China is almost as powerful as the United States, and that the coalition of Russia, Germany, and Japan could match the United States in military-industrial capabilities. So perhaps that comprehensive indicator does not accurately reflect the current status of the United States.

If we rely on an indicator more specifically focused on military power, for example, such as the annual military budgets reflected in figure 1.1, the United States is clearly predominant. According to the data in that figure, the United States spent almost as much on defense in the years 2004–2005 as did the rest of the world combined. Christopher Layne (2006, 41) asserts that "the sheer magnitude of the U.S. economy means that Washington is easily able to spend over $500 billion annually on defense," and that "this is more than the rest of the world combined spends on defense." And, of course, many of the most powerful states in the world are U.S. allies. States that were overtly hostile to the United States—such as Cuba, Iran, Libya,

The influence of the United States throughout the world is perhaps unprecedented in its scope and impact. Nevertheless, it has confronted substantial obstacles to achieving its goals in the war in Iraq. Here, a U.S. Army staff sergeant instructs an Iraqi soldier from the 8th Iraqi Army Division as part of the U.S. effort to enable the Iraqis to take the responsibility for their own security. In general, the U.S. effort to prepare Iraqis to create domestic peace and stability in the face of insurgent and sectarian violence has revealed that overwhelming military superiority will not necessarily allow the United States to bring democracy or political order even to those states whose formal military forces have been entirely subdued.

| TABLE 1.1 | Major Powers of the World Ranked According to Military-Industrial Capabilities, 2001 |

State	Index Score
United States	14.5
China	12.5
Russia	6.3
Japan	5.4
Germany	3.1
United Kingdom	2.3
France	2.3

Note: The index reflects each state's share of the world's total of overall population, urban population, iron/steel production, energy consumption, military personnel, and military expenditures.
Source: Bennett and Stam 2000.

North Korea, Sudan, and Syria—were outspent by the United States in 2005 by a ratio of 29 to 1. Even if potential enemies of the United States, such as Russia and China, are added to that list, all of their annual military budgets combined total only about 30 percent of the U.S. military budget (Shah 2006).

When one takes into account that the United States, which has only about 5 percent of the world's population, generates approximately 20 percent of its economic activity, and that American culture—in the form of TV programs, music, blue jeans, Coca Cola, McDonald's, books, movies, and computer software—exerts a pervasive influence throughout the world, it is clear that the United States plays a unique and influential role in contemporary global politics.

But it is a role that is not entirely new. According to the same comprehensive index of national capabilities on which table 1.1 is based, the United States was already the most powerful state in the world in the year 1900 (Ray and Kaarbo 2005, 117). It made its first appearance at the center of "great power" politics during World War I. At a time when the opposing coalitions were involved in what appeared to be an endless stalemate, the U.S. entry into the conflict provided a crucial addition to the capabilities of what became the winning side in the "war to end all wars."

The Treaty of Versailles that ended World War I was substantially shaped by U.S. President Woodrow Wilson. It was largely his influence that led that treaty to address in its very first articles the need for creation of a universal international organization, the League of Nations. Ironically, the United States subsequently refused to join the organization that it had been so instrumental in creating.

By that time, the United States was so important to the operation of the international system that its reticence about remaining involved in **great power politics** was itself a factor that

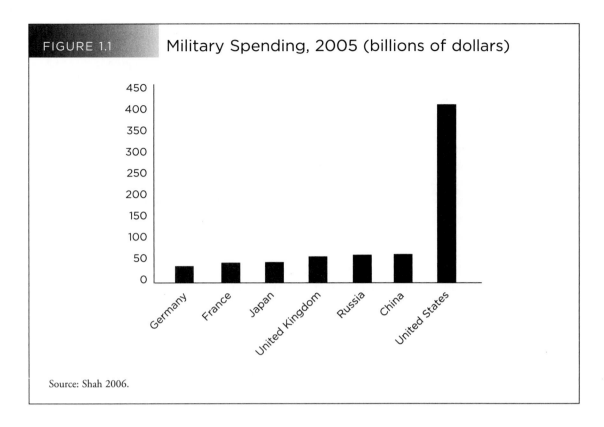

FIGURE 1.1   Military Spending, 2005 (billions of dollars)

Source: Shah 2006.

had a profound influence on the course of events. Robbed of support by the United States, the status quo powers were not sufficiently strong to defend the structure of the system set up after World War I, even though some of the best minds of the world had concentrated with great determination on setting up a system that would prevent repetition of the tragic consequences of that war. That structure was also undermined by the stock market crash in the United States in 1929 and the ensuing Great Depression, which soon became virtually a worldwide phenomenon. Then, in a process rather eerily reminiscent of World War I, all the other great powers of the world fought to a state of nearly complete exhaustion and depletion in World War II, only to have the United States once again enter the conflict belatedly and provide the pivotal increment of power to what became the winning side.

Ever since World War II—and certainly since the 1950s—the United States has, largely because of its foreign policies (as well as the economic activities of its corporations), exerted a profound and pervasive influence around the world. In fact, it is difficult to find a single country anywhere on the globe whose fate has not been substantially affected by U.S. foreign policies.

Chile, for example, is a relatively small country with a current population of some 16 million people, located on a thin strip of land along the Pacific coast of South America. Its capital, Santiago, is almost 5,000 miles from Washington, D.C. Yet, during the era of the President Kennedy's Alliance for Progress in Latin America in the 1960s, Chile became a focus of much attention and was lavished with huge amounts of foreign aid by the United States—especially as measured on a per capita basis. As the U.S. government had become keenly interested in its domestic politics, the election of a Socialist, Salvador Allende, to the presidency of Chile in 1970 evoked a series of hostile actions by the United States and by international organizations influenced by the United States. The Central Intelligence Agency (CIA) may even have played a key role in the coup that removed Allende from power, and killed him, in 1973. He was replaced by a military dictator, Augusto Pinochet, who, although best known for instituting a reign of terror, also introduced market-oriented policies that laid a basis for economic growth, which, according to some observers, continues to this day. The point here is not to resolve any of the controversial aspects of these developments, but to demonstrate that the political and economic history of Chile for approximately the past forty-five years cannot be understood without an appreciation of the substantial, even crucial, impacts of U.S. **foreign policy** on that small and distant country.

The Democratic Republic of the Congo, whose capital city, Kinshasa, is over 6,500 miles from Washington, D.C., was established as a Belgian colony in 1908, gained its independence in 1960, and came under the control of Joseph Mobutu in November 1965. This leader, who changed his own name to Mobutu Sese Seko, also changed the name of the country, to Zaire.

Chances are that most Americans would confidently tell you that the U.S. government has never paid any sustained attention to Zaire, landlocked thousands of miles away in the heart of sub-Saharan Africa. In fact, however, the CIA was instrumental in bringing Joseph Mobutu to power—aiding him in 1960, for example, in the overthrow of the elected leader, Patrice Lumumba, who was too favorably disposed to the Soviet Union for American tastes. As was noted in a July 1995 letter to Secretary of State Warren Christopher—signed by both Benjamin Gilman, the Republican chairman of the U.S. House of Representatives' International Relations Committee, and Lee Hamilton, the ranking Democratic member—the United States provided more than $1.5 billion in foreign aid to Mobutu in the decades following 1965. The letter goes on to point out that "during this time Mr. Mobutu was becoming one of the world's wealthiest individuals while the people of Zaire, a once-wealthy country, were pauperized" (Ayittey 2002).

Mobutu was finally thrown out of power by Laurent Kabila in 1997. In the years since that time, the country has been renamed again, and the Democratic Republic of the Congo has suffered from internal political strife, attracting the attention and occasional intervention by military troops of such foreign powers as Angola, Chad, Namibia, Sudan, Zimbabwe, Rwanda, and Uganda. By 2006, as the political and military conflict continued, some 4 million people were thought to have died in the previous eight or nine years—perhaps more from disease than from actual combat.

To blame the United States entirely for this incredibly ugly situation in the Democratic Republic of the Congo would be unfair. Nevertheless, its foreign policy was clearly responsible in important part for bringing Mobutu Sese Seko to power in Zaire and keeping him there for decades, even as he established a reputation as one of the most spectacularly corrupt dictators in the world.[a] Meanwhile, his country was reduced to such an impoverished and politically unstable status that it has suffered grievously ever since.

---

a. Having amassed a fortune of over $4 billion, Mobutu may well deserve a place in the "'Haul' of Fame" (Bueno de Mesquita et al. 2003, 167, 103).

On a happier note—in terms of its long-term impact, at any rate—U.S. intervention has also had an absolutely crucial impact on the development and fate of South Korea, whose capital, Seoul, lies almost 7,000 miles from Washington, D.C. South Korea came into being as a political entity in the first place because of an agreement between the Soviet Union and the United States as World War II came to a close. The two victorious powers agreed to accept the surrender of Japanese troops on the Korean peninsula in designated areas—the Soviets above and the United States below the 38th Parallel. Although, as Alexander DeConde (1963, 703) remarks, "the line corresponded to no geographical, economic, or social division in the Korean peninsula," it remains the dividing line between South Korea and North Korea to this day.

When North Korea sent more than 100,000 troops into South Korea in June of 1950, the United States, with the support of the United Nations, decided to resist the attack. More than 50,000 U.S. troops and around a million Korean soldiers were lost in the ensuing war, which ended with a cease-fire agreement in 1953. As of 2006, the United States maintained 37,000 troops in South Korea, "to help defend it from a potential conflict with North Korea under a bilateral defense treaty signed after the 1950–1953 Korean War" ("US To Move Troops...," 2006). In the 1950s, South Korea was the relatively impoverished sector of this bifurcated land; today, the GNP in South Korea is $20,400 per capita, while in North Korea it is $1,700.

Another participant in the Korean War of the early 1950s was the People's Republic of China. About 16 percent of the people in the world are citizens of China; its population is currently around 1.3 billion. Beijing, China's capital city, is almost 7,000 miles from Washington, D.C. Yet the United States was intimately involved in Chinese history throughout most of the twentieth century, beginning with its participation in the suppression of the Boxer Rebellion in 1900. Sun Yat-sen, who is often referred to as the father of his country, was born in China but raised in Honolulu, and he very early came under the influence of Western ideas and the ideals of American political leaders such as Thomas Jefferson and Abraham Lincoln. His successor, Chiang Kai-shek, led China into the Second World War, during which his regime received substantial support from the United States. And, since he received further U.S. assistance in his postwar struggle against the Communist leader Mao Zedong, the revolution that brought the Communist Party to power in China in 1949 was waged, in part, against the United States.

The United States refused to recognize "Red China" for decades after the Communist revolution, including the aftermath of the bloody Korean War, during which China lost some 900,000 soldiers. Relations improved in the early 1970s, however, and China's current economic boom is fueled in important part by a flood of Chinese exports to the United States. The Chinese also invest huge amounts in U.S. treasury bonds, thus helping the U.S. government to fund its massive annual budget deficits. In short, the fates of the United States and China, the largest country in the world, have long been tightly intertwined.

In light of China's imposing size and expanding economic importance, its substantial historical relationship with the United States is not surprising. But, for contrast, let us consider the fate of an obscure, out-of-the-way speck of land in the middle of the Pacific Ocean—namely, Guam.[b] Only about thirty miles long and four-to-nine miles wide, Guam lies almost precisely in the middle of nowhere—3,300 miles west of Hawaii, 1,500 miles east of the

---

b. Admittedly, this is not a totally random or haphazard choice.

Philippines, and 1,550 miles south of Japan. (As can be seen on the map on page xix, it is about 8,000 miles from Washington, D.C.) Its population is currently about 170,000. Surely, the unwary reader might presume, here is an isolated piece of real estate of no interest or connection to the United States or its foreign policies.

Guam's first known contact with the Western world occurred in 1521, when it was visited by Ferdinand Magellan. By 1565, it was formally claimed by Spain, and it remained in Spanish hands until the Spanish-American War in 1898, after which it was ceded to the United States and placed under the administration of the U.S. Navy. Japan took it over shortly after the invasion of Pearl Harbor, and the United States regained control in 1944.

At present, far from being a pristine place untouched by the pervasive American power and influence, it is, in fact, an unincorporated territory of the United States—and a focal point of interest for U.S. military planners (Halloran 2006). The air force is planning to revitalize its bases on Guam, at a cost of $2 billion; the Marine Corps is planning to re-deploy 8,000 marines from Okinawa in Japan to Guam; and the navy, having based three attack submarines in Guam, is now planning to send two more. All of these plans for modernization and upgrading of U.S. military facilities in Guam will cost an additional $10 billion over the next ten years. Way out in the middle of the vast Pacific Ocean, tiny little Guam, whose military bases are among the 702 American installations in 132 countries around the world, is now, in fact, a hub of vital activity in the U.S. war on terror!

Since, clearly, the impact of U.S. foreign policy around the world has been pervasive, understanding that impact is crucial for understanding political processes around the globe, within and among a substantial portion of existing states. But the impact of U.S. foreign policy decisions on Americans themselves has also been profound. A twenty-year-old reader of this book might have grandparents who were born in the 1920s, and who will have been about twenty years old themselves when the United States became involved in World War II—a major undertaking that significantly affected the lives of most of its citizens.

But the impacts of American foreign policy and of the interaction of the United States with its global environment in the years after World War II continued to be pervasive and profound. By 1950, the Soviet Union had successfully tested an atomic bomb, and Communists had taken over the most populous country in the world, China. Having expended tremendous amounts of time, energy, money, and blood to vanquish Nazism and Fascism, five short years later the United States faced a threat from a different kind of political extremism that in some ways seemed even more ominous. In short, the Cold War was under way.

In its earliest years, the Cold War was marked by an actual war in Korea. Americans were drafted and sent to fight and die in this distant Asian land, becoming involved also and directly against troops from Communist China. Even when that war was terminated by a cease-fire rather than a peace agreement, tensions remained high between the Communist powers and the United States. By successfully launching *Sputnik* in 1957—before the Americans could launch a satellite of their own—the Soviets proved that they had powerful ballistic missiles with a range that made it fairly simple, in principle, for them to attack virtually anywhere in the United States with nuclear weapons. And what could the United States do to protect itself? It could threaten to retaliate in-kind. Otherwise, every single American was basically defenseless against the possibility of being vaporized by immensely powerful nuclear weapons sitting atop Soviet ballistic missiles aimed at the United States.

Thus, Communism seemed a threat to the very existence of the United States, and American leaders, as well as much of the general public, felt it crucial to resist Soviet expansion on a very broad front, if not in every single place in the world into which these adversaries might try to extend their influence. Such thinking led the United States to become ever more deeply involved in the war in Vietnam. Military conscription, introduced during the World War II years, was still in place, and so young men were again drafted and sent off in significant numbers—500,000 by the late 1960s—to fight, and sometimes to die in a far-off Asian land.

Then, too, in the early 1960s, there was a frightening confrontation between the two superpowers over the Soviet attempt to place nuclear-tipped ballistic missiles in Cuba. (The Soviets may well have been tempted to do so by fears that the United States was about to attack Cuba, and, as we see in chapter 10, those fears may not have been entirely unfounded.) Also in the 1960s, American corporations accelerated the rate at which they were investing overseas, and Americans themselves found that goods from Europe, Asia, and Latin America were increasingly available for purchase in the United States.

By the 1970s, the Cold War was winding down, as was the war in Vietnam, and détente broke out between the Soviet Union and the United States. President Nixon visited China, the United States finally came to recognize the People's Republic, and global tensions between Communism and the "free world" diminished. Nevertheless, Americans were still profoundly affected by American foreign policy decisions, and by interactions between the United States and foreign countries. In 1973 Egypt attacked Israel, and during the ensuing crisis, the Organization of Petroleum Exporting Countries (OPEC) suspended shipments of oil to the United States. The price of a barrel of oil "skyrocketed" from $3 to $12 a barrel, and the country suddenly confronted a serious energy crisis. The twenty-year-old reader's parents probably have vivid memories of the 1970s as a time of rapidly escalating gasoline prices; by the end of the decade, the price of oil had increased again, from $12 to around $36 a barrel, resulting in serious shortages and forcing drivers to wait in long lines at gas stations in a desperate attempt to secure enough fuel to stay on the road. In creating this energy crisis, OPEC was, in part, retaliating against the United States for its consistent and generous support for Israel. In short, during the 1970s, the average American could not escape the consequences of U.S. foreign policy decisions, or the reactions by states outside the United States to those decisions.

In 1979 the Soviet Union invaded Afghanistan, which led to a rebirth of the Cold War. Ronald Reagan, who was elected president in the following year, proceeded to increase the defense budget of the United States in dramatic fashion, which—along with, beginning in 1982, the worst recession in the United States since World War II—produced record-breaking federal budget deficits. In fact, as measured in current dollars, U.S. federal budget deficits under Reagan were higher than all the deficits accumulated by all previous presidents.

At the same time, tensions between the United States and the Soviet Union escalated in a manner that deeply impressed, and depressed, many Americans, as well as many citizens of Western European states. During the 1970s, the Soviets had stationed new, intermediate-range missiles at sites on the western border of the Soviet Union. In response, the NATO member states, led by President Jimmy Carter, decided to install over 500 intermediate-range missiles in Western Europe. President Reagan's subsequent efforts to carry out this plan evoked massive peace demonstrations in favor of a nuclear freeze, in both the United States and

Western Europe. The new missiles were capable of reaching Moscow in a relatively short time, just as the Soviet missiles could quite rapidly threaten major cities in Western Europe. The two superpowers seemed poised on a knife edge, hurtling toward a possible nuclear war.

Instead, a new era of peaceful interaction unfolded in the second half of the 1980s, as the United States and the Soviet Union signed a peace treaty eliminating the category of intermediate-range missiles that had provoked so much tension in the preceding years. From 1982 until 1989, the United States enjoyed what was, up to that time, the longest period of economic growth during a time of peace in its history. American defense expenditures declined, and the threat of nuclear annihilation that had dangled over the heads of all Americans since the 1950s dissipated.

But, as had happened once before when the Cold War "ended" in the early 1970s, issues and threats from the Middle East soon replaced those from the Soviet Union, which disappeared altogether in 1991. Iraq's leader, Saddam Hussein, attacked and annexed Kuwait in 1990, leading to yet another spike in the price of oil. The United States mobilized, with the cooperation of many allies and the support of the UN Security Council, and in early 1991 drove Iraqi troops out of Kuwait, inflicting a devastating defeat on the Iraqi military. The price of oil dropped, and kept on dropping. Defense budgets again began to decrease, and the American economy, buoyed by cheap oil and shrinking federal budget deficits—which even turned into surpluses by the end of the decade—embarked upon a period of peacetime growth that was even longer than the 1980s' boom. To be sure, the United States, along with its NATO allies, became involved in another war, this one against Serbia in 1999. But this war's aim of ending Serbian atrocities in the province of Kosovo was accomplished without the death (by enemy fire, at any rate) of even a single American soldier.

Then came the terrorist attacks of September 11, 2001—the deadliest assault on the United States by a foreign enemy in its history. (A similar number of people died in the attack on Pearl Harbor in 1941, but Hawaii was not an incorporated part of the United States at the time.) Since that tragic day in 2001, which even readers as young as twenty will remember, debates over American foreign policy issues have dominated American political discourse. In the wake of the second Bush administration's retaliatory strikes against its proclaimed terrorist enemies, Americans have been fighting and dying virtually every day in Afghanistan and Iraq. Spending on defense has expanded dramatically, especially given that monies spent on "homeland security" are also aimed primarily at foreign enemies. Security concerns have transformed the experience of airline travel, and the prices of oil and gasoline have risen to new levels. Immigration, mostly from Mexico, has become a hot-button foreign policy issue, in part because of the fear that terrorists could infiltrate the United States through its long, porous southern border.

In short, for most of the past hundred years, and especially since World War II, U.S. foreign policy has had numerous profound impacts on virtually every region and country in the world. At the same time, American foreign policy decisions, their impacts on the global environment, and reactions to those decisions in other countries, have consistently had dramatic impacts inside the United States and on the lives of individual American citizens as well. This book is devoted to the description and analysis of crucial American foreign policies and decisions, with a focus on the post–World War II era. We will assess the forces leading to those policies and decisions, describe the goals toward which American foreign policy makers have striven, and analyze the impacts of those decisions, both on the foreign countries that have been their targets and on the United States. We will conduct this multifaceted analysis by means of an approach—**rational political ambition theory**—that focuses specifically on the interaction of factors internal to the United States and the foreign policies it has pursued.

This approach to foreign policy analysis differs from more traditional and orthodox approaches, which start with the basic assumption that states seek power (or security), by emphasizing instead the related but quite distinct axiom that *leaders of all states—and for our purposes here, the president of the United States in particular—seek primarily to stay in power.* Alternative approaches to foreign policy analysis will be described, and the views of their advocates on important trends, decisions, and policy impacts will be taken into account throughout the book. But the potential utility of rational political ambition theory will be a recurring theme.

In this opening chapter, we have mentioned such key events in the history of U.S. foreign policy as the Cuban missile crisis and the war in Vietnam. And we have described these events in a rather traditional way, focusing on the policies of the United States in those situations as mostly a result of, or a reaction to, geopolitical considerations and calculations meant to deal with international adversaries. But, as we shall see in the following chapters, such foreign policy decisions are *also* to an important extent fashioned in such a way as to increase the probability that the president of the United States will be able to retain power. In fact, on many occasions, the foreign policies of the United States may be more heavily influenced by domestic political factors than by the international political environment that is ostensibly their primary target.

The following chapters, then, focus on the interplay between domestic politics and foreign policies, and on the leaders who confront competitors in both the domestic and foreign realms as they attempt to deal with their counterparts in other countries and with the global environment of the United States in such a way as to maintain their own positions as leaders.

KEY CONCEPTS

foreign policy   6
great power politics   4
rational political ambition
    theory   11

CHAPTER

2

THE PAST AS PROLOGUE

American Foreign Policy
from the American Revolution
through World War II

THE UNITED STATES DECLARED ITS INDEPENDENCE FROM GREAT BRITAIN in July of 1776. Within four years of that provincial uprising, the American rebellion against British rule "had become a world war, waged not only in continental North America but at Gibraltar, in the English Channel, in India, and off the African coast..." (Morris 1972, 761). A popular myth holds that the United States remained mostly removed from international politics—a stance that is commonly thought of as **isolationism**—until the Germans at long last forced its hand in the second decade of the twentieth century. But, in fact, it can be argued that the United States has been deeply involved in world politics from the time of its birth, and in a consistently assertive manner.

Not only has the United States been deeply involved in global political struggles since its earliest days, but also, it has pursued mostly successful foreign policies over that period. Walter Mead (2001, xv) sums up the nation's rise to global dominance: "In a little more than two hundred years, the United States has grown from a handful of settlements on the Atlantic seaboard to become the most powerful country in the history of the world." The new Republic itself came into being in the course of an anticolonial war, during which the support of foreign allies was crucial. About 90 percent of the gunpowder used by the American rebels in the first two years of the Revolutionary War, for example, came from European allies. Once they had successfully achieved independence from Great Britain, the former colonies adopted the Articles of Confederation as their constitution. These Articles were flawed in many respects, but one of the most noticeable was in the area of foreign policy. As Alexander DeConde (1963, 51) notes: "Keenly aware of their country's impotence, some of America's leading statesmen argued that a respected foreign policy could be based only on a stronger national government." Thus, the United States owes its very Constitution, in important part, to its early struggles in dealing with foreign policy challenges.

Perhaps, then, the common impression that the United States concentrated almost solely on domestic politics and internal challenges over its first 150 years is unwarranted? Indeed,

Although the United States is typically thought to have remained aloof from international politics throughout most of the nineteenth century, its military forces were in fact quite active throughout much of the world. An early example depicted here involves naval combat between the USS *Constitution* and the HMS *Java* from Great Britain off the coast of Brazil on December 29, 1812.

the vast project of integrating the entire broad swath of the North American continent from the Atlantic seaboard to the Pacific coastline was itself an adventurous, expansive foreign policy enterprise. This expansion involved dealing not only (in brutal fashion) with the aboriginal inhabitants of North America, but also with the European powers who had staked claims to various parts of the land west of the original colonies, all the way to the Pacific Ocean. It also collided at one point with the concrete fact of Mexico's control of vast areas to the southwest. Only through notably aggressive military action did the territories that would form such states as Colorado, Texas, New Mexico, Arizona, and California come into U.S. possession. (See map 2.1 for the original political geography of the United States.)

Then, too, the United States was much more active all over the globe in the nineteenth century than might have been expected of a country taking to heart President George Washington's advice (1796) that it not only "steer clear of permanent alliances," but also "in regard to foreign nations … have with them as little political connection as possible." A 1993 report issued by the Department of the Navy on the "Instances of Use of United States Forces Abroad, 1798–1993" listed 234 such instances (Collier 1993). These incidents of international activism and **interventionism** by the United States started very early, and they never really let up. From 1798 to 1800, there was an undeclared naval war with France, and then, from 1801 to 1805, the First Barbary War, which involved sending two U.S. warships and several marines to Tripoli, in what is currently Libya. (Hostilities against the Barbary States resumed in 1815.)

The War of 1812 against Great Britain is well-known. Less familiar is the continuing U.S. military action over the course of the nineteenth century in faraway China, where American marines landed in Guangzhou province as early as 1843. U.S. troops returned to China twice in 1854, in 1855, and in some force in 1856.[a] They found themselves involved in China again in 1859, 1866, 1894–1895, 1898–1899, and then again in 1900, during the so-called Boxer Rebellion.[b]

In short, according to Mead (2001, 26), "during the period of American innocence and isolation, the United States had forces stationed on or near every major continent in the world; its navy was active in virtually every ocean, its troops saw combat on virtually every continent, and its foreign relations were in a perpetual state of crisis and turmoil." Is this isolationism?

In the meantime, the United States actively and persistently pursued a foreign policy based on deterring intervention and interference in the Western Hemisphere by outside foreign powers. Its aim, in terms familiar to traditional analysts of international politics, was to establish for itself a **sphere of influence**. The United States did not exactly win the War of 1812, but it did manage to stave off defeat at the hands of the British. This accomplishment created a kind of *modus vivendi* with the former colonial master that lasted to the end of the century, although the relationship was still often fraught with tension and threatened by numerous crises, even war scares.

---

a. "In 1843, American marines landed in Guangzhou (Canton) to protect Americans from Chinese mobs. They returned 13 years later and defeated five thousand Chinese troops in pitched battle" (Mead 2001, 25).

b. The U.S. military was also active in China during the twentieth century on a continuing, and recurring, basis; see Collier 1993 for a history of this two-century involvement.

THE PROCLAMATION OF THE MONROE DOCTRINE

One of the important turning points in that relationship came in the 1820s. By that time, many colonies in Latin America had achieved independence, but there was some fear that reactionary states in Europe might try to re-impose colonial control over South America. There was also some concern that the Russians might work their way down through Alaska to encroach upon the Oregon Territory. Because Great Britain and the United States had a common interest in preventing any of these other major powers from extending their influence into the Western Hemisphere, George Canning, the British foreign minister, suggested to the administration of James Monroe that the two governments issue a joint statement of opposition to intervention in Latin America by any third party.

John Quincy Adams, who was Monroe's secretary of state, is typically given credit for fashioning the ultimate response to the British proposal (Perkins 1927, 1963). In the end, Adams persuaded Monroe to deliver an anticolonialism declaration in the name of the United States alone, rather than jointly with Great Britain. In a speech to Congress on December 2, 1823, Monroe announced that "the American Continents, by the free and independent condition which they have assumed and maintain, are henceforth not to be considered as subjects for future colonization." Some, and perhaps most, historians believe that it was the perceived threat of foreign intervention in Latin America that led to promulgation of this defiant warning to other world powers, which came to be known as the **Monroe Doctrine**. Mead (2001, 200), for example, argues that "the fear of European dynastic adventures in Latin America was anything but fanciful."

At least one historian, however, believes that domestic politics was actually the determining factor in the process, thus adding this key event in the history of American foreign policy to the list of examples potentially supportive of the theoretical approach (rational political ambition theory) introduced in chapter 1. According to Ernest May (1975), the most important decision makers—President Monroe and Secretary of State Adams in particular—realized not only that foreign threats to intervene in Latin America were not entirely serious, but also that the British would act to prevent any such interventions regardless of what the United States did or did not do. However, Adams, who was, at the time, a candidate to succeed Monroe as president, felt vulnerable to charges by competing candidates that he was an Anglophile, more prone to cooperate with Great Britain than the national interests of the United States would indicate. So, mostly for his own political reasons—that is, to aid in his quest for personal political power—he successfully urged Monroe to turn down the British proposal for a joint declaration and to issue instead a unilateral prohibition of foreign intervention.

A typical historical interpretation of the significance of the Monroe Doctrine suggests that, to the extent it was meaningful at all, the British navy was the main enforcer.[c] This common idea may be another example of the general tendency to underestimate the energy and assertiveness of American foreign policy in the nineteenth century. Yet, as early as 1832, the United States had sent a fleet to the Falkland Islands, off the coast of Argentina. American

---

c. "[The United States] was a protégé of British sea power, and Great Britain was responsible for the protection of Latin American from the designs of other European powers, so far as they were restrained" (Atkins 1977, 93–94).

military forces were engaged in Haiti in 1799, 1800, and from 1817 to 1821. Prior to the Civil War, the United States was involved in military action in what became the Dominican Republic, in Cuba, in Puerto Rico, repeatedly in Argentina (after 1832, also in 1833, 1852, and 1853), and in Peru (1835–1836). And, after the Civil War (but before the Spanish-American War), American marines saw action in Cuba, Uruguay, Argentina, Chile, Colombia, and Haiti (Mead 2001, 24).

U.S. EXPANSION IN THE NINETEENTH CENTURY

While there is no doubt that it received some help from the British in successfully excluding foreign intervention and influence in the Western Hemisphere, the United States managed to establish control of the vast area that would constitute its contiguous forty-eight states almost entirely by its own devices. The original United States did, in fact, include some territories beyond the colonies that became the original thirteen states. Virginia, for example, owned the Northwest Territory, which encompassed the principal part of what would later be Ohio, the entire state of Indiana, and all of Illinois, Michigan, and Wisconsin. Virginia also owned at that time the tract that eventually became the state of Kentucky, while North Carolina owned the land later to be incorporated as Tennessee, and South Carolina and Georgia together owned what would be the states of Mississippi and Alabama.

The Louisiana Purchase

But west of those territories—and south, in Florida—were lands owned by European powers. Indeed, at the dawn of the nineteenth century, France owned such a huge tract of land in North America that it might have established a political entity capable of becoming a major competitor to the United States within the continent, or at least in the Western Hemisphere. In 1762 France had ceded the Louisiana Territory to Spain, but in the secret Treaty of San Ildefonso in 1800, the French reestablished their ownership. Napoleon Bonaparte, in fact, dreamed of establishing a great French empire in the New World. In this vision, Hispaniola—an island that ultimately was divided between the states of Haiti and the Dominican Republic—would be the heart of the empire, while Louisiana and the Mississippi River valley would serve as a center of supply for the island.

Instead, Napoleon faced a revolt in what would become Haiti, led by a former slave, Toussaint L'Ouverture. The French lost thousands of troops attempting to suppress this revolt, including their commander, Charles Leclerc, who was Napoleon's brother-in-law. Napoleon's initial reaction was to send another expeditionary force to restore control in Hispaniola and to establish a stronger position in Louisiana, particularly in New Orleans. But this plan failed, and by 1803 Napoleon was ready to abandon his dream of a significant French empire in North America, as he was becoming more concerned about an impending war with Great Britain.

Thus, it seemed a propitious moment for an American delegation led by President Thomas Jefferson's envoy, James Monroe, to purchase New Orleans, as well as western Florida. The French response, however, was to suggest that perhaps the United States would prefer to purchase the entire Louisiana Territory, which extended up the Mississippi River and west to the Rocky Mountains. After some haggling over the price, the Americans agreed to pay some $15 million for the 828,000 square miles of land—which was only some 60,000 square miles less than the whole of the United States at the time (Williams 1991, 368). Had the Jefferson administration not acted promptly on the French proposal, it might soon have had to contend with a British force that was planning to contest French control of Louisiana (DeConde 1963, 81). So, by means of the timely economic transaction known as the Louisiana Purchase, the United States both doubled its size and substantially diminished the influence of two potentially troublesome major power competitors within the North American continent.

The Acquisition of Florida

The U.S. government originally had the impression that it had acquired Florida as part of the Louisiana Purchase. Soon discovering that it was wrong on that point, it set about dealing with the problem in relatively short order. With the Mobile Act of 1804, Congress authorized President Jefferson to acquire West Florida. At first, Spain balked, and when Spain was taken over by Napoleon's France, Napoleon also resisted the takeover. However, the new U.S. president, James Madison, was enthusiastic about the unfinished project. American agents helped to foment rebellion in West Florida, leading to that territory's declaring its independence. In 1810 West Florida became part of the United States (DeConde 1963).

Still, East Florida remained in Spanish hands. In response to the looming possibility that this residual tract might pass from Spanish control into the hands of the British—even as war clouds gathered between the United States and Britain—the U.S. Congress passed a resolution asserting that the United States could not see "without serious inquietude" the transfer of Florida into the hands of a foreign power. This "no transfer" idea would remain a consistent part of U.S. policy regarding colonial holdings in the Western Hemisphere from this point onward.

Although Madison did not accomplish the takeover of East Florida during his presidency, the United States took steps in that direction by sending troops under General Andrew Jackson to invade the territory in 1818. President Monroe later officially restored Spanish control of the area but then pushed Spain to relinquish it. By the terms of the Onís-Adams Treaty of 1819, Spain officially ceded East Florida to the United States (see map 2.1), while also abandoning any claims to territory in the Northwest or Oregon territories. What Spain received in return was recognition of its sovereignty over Texas (U.S. Department of State 2003a).

Taking over Texas

Despite the recognition of Spanish sovereignty there, in 1821 Stephen F. Austin pressed for and obtained concessions from Spain allowing American homesteaders to settle in Texas. By 1830, there were some 25,000 American settlers in the territory. In the meantime, Texas had passed officially into the hands of independent Mexico, which soon took steps to solidify its control. For example, in 1829 the Mexicans abolished slavery in Texas, and in 1830 they ordered a stop to further migration into the territory. Six years later, Mexican military forces wiped out an American outpost at the Alamo in San Antonio, killing the defenders to the last man. However, in a subsequent battle, the commander of the Mexican troops, Antonio Lopez de Santa Ana, was captured, and soon thereafter, "the state of Texas was lost to the Mexican union" (Herring 1972, 306–307).

The United States recognized Texas as an independent nation in 1837, and there were those who wanted to see it remain so. As Gordon Connell-Smith (1974, 77) notes, "Texas was ... recognized by ... European powers including Britain and France. These two nations were eager to promote a treaty between Mexico and Texas on the basis of a pledge by the latter not to annex herself to the United States: in other words, to have an independent Texas as a buffer against further United States expansion." In short, the two most powerful states in the world were opposed to the idea of Texas becoming part of the United States.

Not all citizens of the United States were enthusiastic about the idea of annexation, either. DeConde (1963, 185) explains: "Abolitionists feared that Texas might add four or five slave states to the Union, and argued that the Texas revolution was part of a dark conspiracy by the slave power in the United States to gain more slave territory." Even so—and despite the Mexican government's warning that if the United States annexed Texas, it would mean war—the administration of President James K. Polk proceeded to do so anyway, in 1845.

In view of the threat by Mexico, Polk sent American troops to Texas under General Zachary Taylor. He also offered to purchase the territory that later became California and New Mexico, as well as some land that would have established the Rio Grande River as the boundary between Texas and Mexico. When Mexico refused this offer, Polk ordered Taylor to move his troops up to the Rio Grande. As Connell-Smith (1974, 79) comments: "This was a provocative step, for the Rio Grande had never been the boundary of Texas, and the recent United States offer in respect of it confirmed that at least it was in dispute."

When Mexican soldiers attacked the American troops, President Polk asserted in response that Mexico "has passed the boundary of the United States, has invaded our territory, and shed American blood on American soil." Abraham Lincoln, a young congressman from Illinois, then introduced a series of "spot resolutions," requesting that Polk specify the "spot" on American soil where American blood had been spilled (DeConde 1963, 200). Although the territory in question was not clearly American soil—after all, the United States had just offered to purchase it—a declaration of war against Mexico passed both the House and the Senate, and the war was on.

The ensuing battle turned out to be more lengthy and difficult than President Polk had anticipated. Still, by September of 1847, American marines had entered into Mexico City. Meanwhile, domestic opposition to the war was considerable; in the following year, in fact, the House of Representatives passed a resolution declaring that the war had been "unnecessarily and unconstitutionally begun by the President of the United States." By 1848, however, Mexico agreed to sign the Treaty of Guadalupe Hidalgo, which turned over to the United States not only the disputed tract between Texas and the Rio Grande, but also the territory known as the Mexican Cession, which would eventually become the states of California, Nevada, and Utah, as well as parts of New Mexico, Arizona, Wyoming, and Colorado.

Soon thereafter, a new dispute between the United States and Mexico arose over lands that now constitute the southern reaches of Arizona and New Mexico. "Under threats of force," the United States urged Mexico to sell this territory, and, ultimately, the Gadsden Purchase turned it over to the United States for about $20 million (DeConde 1963, 204–213; see map 2.1).

The Acquisition of the Oregon Territory

At about the same time that the U.S. border with its southern neighbor was being established, the burgeoning Republic's relationship with its neighbor to the north was also a matter of controversy. In 1840 a war scare arose in a boundary dispute between Maine and the Canadian province of New Brunswick. Both the Americans and the British rushed troops to the area for the "Aroostook War" (Mead 2001, 20), but no fighting ensued. Eventually, the troops departed, and in 1842 the Webster-Ashburton Agreement ended the dispute.

A much larger area at issue was the vast Oregon Territory that lay north of California. The United States and Great Britain established joint control by an official agreement in 1818, and they successfully limited Spanish and Russian claims to the territory in the ensuing years. American settlers streamed into the area, and by the 1840s, presidential candidate James K. Polk adopted as a campaign slogan the phrase "54 degrees and 40 minutes or fight." This rather oddly technical slogan urged that the United States should take over the entire Oregon Territory, up to its northern boundary with land claimed by the Russians (present-day Alaska).

However, once elected, President Polk became embroiled in the dispute that would lead to the Mexican-American War, and so he was actually inclined to be somewhat conciliatory in negotiating to divide up the Oregon Territory with Great Britain. The resulting treaty, signed in 1846, finally settled the border between the U.S. parcel and Canada at 49 degrees rather than 54. Acceptance of this lower boundary line disappointed some of Polk's more assertive, nationalistic supporters, but it proved to be a compromise with staying power (U.S. Department of State 2003c; see map 2.1).

The acquisition of the Oregon Territory thus contributed to a brief but quite spectacular period of expansion for the United States. After the 1819 annexation of Florida, the country consisted of about 1.8 million square miles of land. But between 1845 and 1853, it added Texas, the Oregon Territory, the Mexican Cession, and the Gadsden Purchase. So, by the final year of that period, the United States had grown to almost 3 million square miles—an increase of 67 percent in just eight years (Williams 1991).

THE FOREIGN POLITICS OF THE CIVIL WAR

Within the decade following that era of expansion, however, the United States came close to falling apart. The North industrialized more rapidly, creating economic interests divergent from those of the more agricultural South. But, as James McPherson (2002) explains, "What lay at the root of this separation? Slavery. It was the sole institution not shared by North and South. The peculiar institution *defined* the South."

Slavery certainly figured intensively in the history of the U.S. expansion from the Atlantic to the Pacific Coast. Southerners were particularly interested in acquiring territories to which the practice could be exported, calculating that adding new slaveholding states would augment

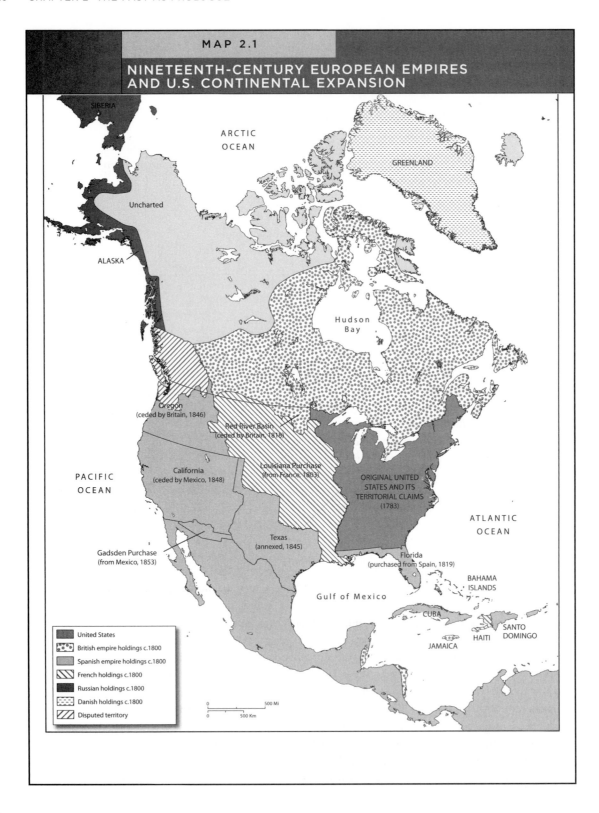

MAP 2.1

NINETEENTH-CENTURY EUROPEAN EMPIRES AND U.S. CONTINENTAL EXPANSION

SIBERIA

ARCTIC OCEAN

GREENLAND

Uncharted

ALASKA

Hudson Bay

PACIFIC OCEAN

Oregon
(ceded by Britain, 1846)

Red River Basin
(ceded by Britain, 1818)

Louisiana Purchase
(from France, 1803)

California
(ceded by Mexico, 1848)

ORIGINAL UNITED STATES AND ITS TERRITORIAL CLAIMS (1783)

ATLANTIC OCEAN

Gadsden Purchase
(from Mexico, 1853)

Texas
(annexed, 1845)

Florida
(purchased from Spain, 1819)

BAHAMA ISLANDS

Gulf of Mexico

CUBA

SANTO DOMINGO

HAITI

JAMAICA

United States
British empire holdings c.1800
Spanish empire holdings c.1800
French holdings c.1800
Russian holdings c.1800
Danish holdings c.1800
Disputed territory

0   500 Mi
0   500 Km

their region's ability to preserve its "peculiar institution." Political leaders in the South, for example, were enthusiastic about adding Texas to the Union, because they assumed that it would become a slaveholding state. In contrast, much of the enthusiasm for acquiring the Oregon Territory came from those who saw it as a counterweight to Texas—a place where slavery would be forbidden.

The Civil War provides yet another example of the tendency of foreign policy and international politics to play crucial roles in the development of the United States. France's Napoleon III, who, according to Mead (2001, 23), "openly sought the breakup of the United States and the independence of the South," took advantage of the conflict to establish a virtual colony in Mexico. French troops marched into Mexico City in 1863 and set up a regime under the Emperor Maximilian. This aggression was clearly a gross violation of the Monroe Doctrine, but the United States was too preoccupied with its internal struggle to resist the French incursion into North America, and Great Britain was either unwilling or unable to put an end to it.

The political leadership of the Confederacy apparently realized that one of its best hopes for survival lay in obtaining official recognition, as well as military support, from European states, especially Britain or France. Great Britain did immediately declare neutrality in 1861, recognizing the Confederacy as a government capable of fighting a war. However, the southerners' hopes of drawing more tangible support from the important European states were always stymied, in part, because of their association with slavery. The Union government deliberately exploited that weakness. President Abraham Lincoln issued the Emancipation Proclamation to solidify support for the war among abolitionist elements in the North, but he also intended it, in part, as a foreign policy tactic. In describing this ulterior motive, Mead (2002, 27) cites Lincoln's own reasoning: "'To proclaim emancipation would secure the sympathy of Europe and the whole civilized world.... No other step would be so potent to prevent foreign intervention,' wrote Lincoln in 1862."

Here we have a classic case of the consistent interaction between domestic and interstate politics that serves as an important theme of this book focusing on rational political ambition theory. Although the Civil War certainly reflects domestic politics at its most intense, one of the main concerns of both belligerents was the potential role of outsiders on the outcome of the war. Even as President Lincoln was intent on solidifying domestic support for the Union war effort, he was also quite attuned to the struggle for support in the international political arena. As we shall see repeatedly in the chapters that follow, some of the more important determinants of American foreign policy choices involve such domestic political inputs and calculations—especially those that have to do with preserving the power of the incumbent leaders. But also, as in the Emancipation Proclamation, foreign influences have a direct and important impact on domestic policy choices. Domestic and foreign politics, particularly from the point of view of the national leadership, form a seamless web, and their interrelationships are never very far from the minds of those national leaders.

In the aftermath of the Civil War, the government of the restored Union could turn its attention to another foreign policy problem, namely the French incursion into Mexico. Secretary of State William H. Seward gave "pointed advice" to the French to cease their support of Emperor Maximilian in Mexico, since "with the Civil War ended, [he was] free to act" (Herring 1972, 322). Napoleon III accordingly began to withdraw his troops, and also to cut

Foreign policy decisions often are made as much for their impact on domestic politics as for their effect on interstate relations. Conversely, domestic political decisions can be aimed in large part at a foreign audience. Here, President Lincoln and his cabinet, meeting on September 22, 1862, discuss adopting the Emancipation Proclamation, which had as one of its purposes making an impression on a European audience.

back on financial support for the Mexican regime. In 1867 Maximilian was taken prisoner by opposition elements in Mexico, and he was executed in June of that year.

FURTHER EXPANSION

Having survived the trauma of the Civil War, the United States promptly resumed the process of territorial expansion. Alaska came into its possession without any international opposition. Russia had established dominance over Alaska early in the eighteenth century, but, by the middle of the next century, the Russian government realized that it would have a difficult time retaining control of the territory. Suffering financial difficulties, it then offered to sell Alaska to the United States. The Civil War derailed those negotiations, but when that conflict came to a close, the Russians renewed their efforts. Secretary of State William Seward and Russia's minister to the United States, Baron Edouard de Stoeckl, met literally in the middle of the night on March 30, 1867, to negotiate the treaty calling for transfer of Alaska's 600,000 square miles from Russia to the United States for $7 million.

When news of the treaty became public, anti-administration newspapers in the United States complained that "Alaska's only products were icebergs and polar bears" (DeConde 1963, 273). Such ignorance about Alaska was so widespread, and general opposition to expansion sufficiently strong, that persuading the U.S. Senate to ratify the treaty with Russia was not easy. However, a one-vote majority ultimately agreed to accept the purchase, and the United States again expanded its territory—this time by 20 percent. Alaska became its forty-ninth state in 1959.

The acquisition of Hawaii was an even more contentious and difficult process. Both Britain and France had intervened in Hawaiian affairs early in the nineteenth century. In fact, by the 1840s, Britain seemed on the verge of a takeover attempt. Partly to forestall such incursions by foreign powers, the United States then strengthened its economic and political ties to the islands. As the sugar industry became particularly important, "U.S. sugar plantation owners from the United States came to dominate the economy and politics of the islands" (U.S. Department of State 2003b).

Coming to resent this political domination by immigrants from the United States, the native population rallied to the cause of Queen Lilioukalani, who was to be the last reigning monarch of Hawaii. In order to preserve "Hawaii for Hawaiians," the queen attempted in 1893 to impose a new constitution on the island, giving her extensive political powers. This step, however, led to a revolution and to establishment of a provisional government that was quickly recognized by the U.S. minister there, who then proceeded to order an American military intervention. Given this military support, the new government deposed Queen Lilioukalani and took steps to make Hawaii a U.S. territory.

The intervening election of President Grover Cleveland in 1894 almost derailed this process, however. Cleveland tried to restore the deposed queen to power, but the revolutionary government refused to step down. Instead, it proclaimed Hawaii an independent republic, which was immediately recognized by the United States. In 1895 Queen Liliuokalana was placed under house arrest.

President William McKinley, elected in 1896, negotiated a treaty with the new republic. In the atmosphere created by the Spanish-American War, which began in 1898, the Hawaiian port of Pearl Harbor was put to good use, and the U.S. Congress passed a joint resolution calling for the annexation of Hawaii. (Because of some anti-expansionist, anti-imperial sentiment in the Senate, it was unlikely that a formal treaty of annexation could have acquired the required two-thirds vote in that body.) Shortly thereafter, Hawaii became an American territory (Tate 1965), and in 1959 it was admitted as the fiftieth state.

THE DIFFERING FATES OF NORTH AND SOUTH AMERICA

By the end of the nineteenth century, therefore, the United States had completed its metamorphosis from a small band of rebellious colonies hugging the eastern coast of North America to a unified transcontinental federation ranging across four time zones, all the way to the Pacific

Ocean. In retrospect, there is an aura of inevitability about this expansion, aptly captured by the phrase **manifest destiny**, which was utilized as a political slogan in defense of policies meant to bring about this "destiny" throughout the century. But it was not, of course, predetermined that the huge portion of the North American continent ultimately designated the United States would emerge as one unified state. The creation of such a state met opposition from aboriginal inhabitants of the continent, as well as from European powers such as Britain, France, Spain, and, to some extent, Russia, not to mention the Mexicans. Yet by the end of the 1800s, a strong federal union in the form of the United States had come into being.

In order to better understand the emergence of the United States in North America, it is useful to consider the southern half of the so-called New World, asking why a similar process of integration and expansion did not take place there. In South America, in fact, a story that started out along the same lines eventually came to quite a different conclusion. By 1824, thanks to the Battle of Ayacucho in Peru, the Spanish colonies in South America had established their independence from the colonial master. Venezuela's Simón Bolívar, in particular, had hopes of uniting much of Spanish America in one republic, and Argentina's José de San Martín led a movement for independence in the southern cone of South America. Bolivar and San Martín met in 1822, while both were in the process of leading organized rebellions against Spain. Had these two revolutionary leaders then chosen to combine forces, the ultimate result might have been a federal republic much like the one growing to its north. Having achieved its independence from Portugal at about the same time, Brazil might have joined in as well, thus uniting virtually the entire continent in a United States of South America.[d]

But nothing of that sort occurred. South America today is divided into twelve independent states and one (French) territory, all of whose combined population is about 350 million, compared to the approximately 300 million people who live in the United States. The U.S. gross national product is about $10 trillion, while the largest gross national product in South America—that of Brazil—is about $1.3 trillion, and the combined GNPs of all the South American states amount to about $2.3 trillion. Since, again, the South American states together have a population that is nearly 50 million larger than that of the United States, the GNP per capita in South America is about $6,600, while in the United States it is about $36,300.[e] In short, the thirteen original colonies that became the United States have emerged as an economically and politically integrated, extraordinarily wealthy and powerful single state, while the Spanish (and Portuguese) colonies in South America, having achieved independence within about forty years after their northern neighbors did so, are still separated into a dozen separate, much poorer and much less politically potent states. How and why did this happen?

One possible explanation, offered by historians Howard J. Wiarda and Harvey F. Kline (1979a, 6), is that "geography has not always been kind to Latin America and has retarded efforts toward development and national integration." The Andes Mountains, running along

---

d. Admittedly, North America is also divided, as Mexico and Canada are not part of the United States. Canada, having a population of only 33 million, is a relatively minor exception to the integration of the North American federal union. Mexico, much larger, is located on the North American continent, but it was colonized by Spain and is culturally part of Latin America.

e. Such data are available from many sources. I relied on Coutsoukis 2003 to make these broad comparisons between the United States and the separate but combined states of South America.

the western side of the South American continent, have hindered economic and political integration. It certainly appears, for example, that Chile remains separate from Argentina because the Andes divide them geographically. Then, too, the huge Amazon rain forest at the heart of the continent may well have played a role in preventing the emergence of a United States of South America.

In the end, though, this geographic explanation of the different fates of the North and South American colonies is not entirely convincing. North America has its Rocky Mountains, which might have exerted at least as powerful a dis-integrating force as the Andes in South America. The vast, arid plains in the middle of the North American continent could also have placed barriers to economic and political integration that would be at least roughly analogous to those created by the South American rain forest.

The differing character, aims, and purposes of the colonizers in North and South America may offer a more convincing explanation for their divergent fates in modern times. Latin America was settled primarily by adventurers aiming to exploit the New World for the sake of the motherland (be it Spain or Portugal). In contrast, that portion of North America destined to become the United States was largely colonized by groups of people escaping from England—more intent upon making lives for themselves than upon maintaining an outpost for the sake of a colonial power. Spanish settlers, in particular, set up rigid, hierarchical societies that were based on slave labor by aboriginals in many cases. North Americans also came to depend on slave labor, but their societies were not so single-mindedly created as systems for the extraction of resources as were those in South America. These differences may well account for some of the contrasts in economic and political dynamism that have persisted in later centuries on the two continents.

Another important difference that helps to account for the contrasting political and economic fates of the colonies established on the two continents may have to do with the kinds and the numbers of native peoples that the colonizers found when they arrived in the New World. Wiarda and Kline (1979b, 16) describe the situation: "It has been estimated that, whereas the Indian population of North America numbered only 3 million at the time of European colonization and was organized generally in dispersed and small-sized tribes, the number of Indians in Latin America was about 30 million, many grouped into settled, large-scale civilizations." This is not to say that these aboriginal peoples were inherently inferior—in fact, it is perfectly possible to argue that their cultures were superior to those of the European settlers in many respects. However, their ways seemed incompatible with various economic, political, and social norms of the newcomers, and it would surely have been more difficult to create an integrated modern state if the colonizers had somehow to become unified and integrated while substantial populations of non-European, aboriginal peoples remained in their midst.

In the words of Wiarda and Kline (1979b, 16): "North America largely solved its Indian problem by either killing the Indians, or, later, confining them to reservations." In some areas of Latin America, however, there were too many of these native peoples to annihilate, so attempts were made to assimilate them instead. These efforts met with mixed success; in some states, such as Guatemala, Peru, and Bolivia, the aboriginal population remains large and is still unassimilated. In addition, divisive cultural gaps persist between some South American states in part because of disparities in their proportions of aboriginal inhabitants.

For example, about 55 percent of the Bolivian population is Amerindian, and another 30 percent is of mixed "white" and Amerindian ancestry. In Uruguay, in contrast, the Amerindian
portion of the population is "practically nonexistent." In detailing these demographic figures,
Photius Coutsoukis (2003) also reports that life expectancy in Uruguay is 76 years, the infant
mortality rate is 14.25 per 1000 live births, and the GNP per capita is $9,200, while in Bolivia
life expectancy is 64 years, the rate of infant mortality is 57.52 deaths per 1000 live births, and
the GNP per capita is $2,600. In Uruguay, 6 percent of the population lives below the offi-
cial poverty line; in Bolivia, the corresponding figure is 70 percent.

Again, the point here is not to assert a general inferiority of aboriginal culture or peoples—
indeed, it would be easier to see these data as evidence of heartless cruelty by their oppressors.
But the fact is that there are stark cultural, political, and economic differences between
Uruguay and Bolivia that are apparently related in various ways to the proportions of aboriginal inhabitants in the two states. And these differences would make it both awkward and difficult to integrate Uruguay and Bolivia into some kind of federal union. Efforts to unify the
United States have never faced such sharp cultural contrasts, and one reason for that may be
that North America has for centuries had much lower numbers of aboriginal inhabitants.

Another reason that the states of Spanish America have remained relatively unintegrated
and poor, compared to the United States, is that the South American continent was colonized
by Spain and Portugal, while the predominant settlers of the North American continent—
excepting Mexico—came from England. The social and political system that the Spanish and
the Portuguese exported to South America was, as we have already noted, relatively rigid and
hierarchical, while the British colonists were less focused on exploiting the wealth of their new
homeland for the benefit of the mother country. In the aggregate, the British settlers were
more self-reliant, individualistic, and economically efficient. At bottom, perhaps this difference reflects the fact that the Spanish and the Portuguese colonists were Catholic, while most
of those from Britain were Protestants.

In other words, perhaps it is possible to extend the thesis of Max Weber's *The Protestant
Ethic and the Spirit of Capitalism* (1904, 1958) to the New World. In its original form, Weber's
thesis served as an explanation of why capitalism had progressed earlier and more rapidly in
northwestern Europe than in southern Europe. The Catholic Church has always expressed a
certain skepticism, even suspicion, about capitalism that was missing in the Protestant states
of northwestern Europe. Then, too, the Catholic Church fought more vigorously, or at least
with more success, against the "scientific revolution" of the fifteenth, sixteenth, and seven-
teenth centuries than did Protestant churches. Perhaps, then, its colonization by members of
various Protestant sects helps to explain why the United States has been more thorough-going
in its commitment to market-oriented capitalism than the states of Latin America, and why it
now is relatively wealthier and better integrated than the states of Spanish and Portuguese
South America?

Wiarda and Kline (1979b) specifically reject this argument. In their view, it is not the
alleged economic vitality of Protestant culture as opposed to Catholic cultural conservatism
that accounts for the different fates of North and South America. Rather, it is the *timing* of
the Spanish and Portuguese colonizing effort in comparison to that of the British in North
America. The Spanish and Portuguese colonies were well established by 1570, decades earlier
than the founding of the British colonies in North America. Reflecting the intellectual climate

of its moment in history, the era of Spanish and Portuguese colonialism in South America was dominated by authoritarian political values, feudal economic notions, and hierarchical social systems. In contrast,

> by the seventeenth century, when colonial North America was effectively settled, the first steps toward limited representative government were already under way, and the Protestant Reformation had broken the monopoly of Catholic absolutism. . . . Economically, capitalism had begun to supersede . . . feudal . . . conceptions. Socially, a more pluralistic and predominantly middle-class society had come into existence. And intellectually, the revolution ushered in by Galileo and Newton had taken place. . . . (Wiarda and Kline 1979b, 22).

Obviously, our "thinking experiment" of comparing the political and economic evolution of British colonies in North America with that of the Spanish and Portuguese colonies in South America bears only a slight resemblance to a laboratory experiment. Interpreting the results of this experiment is, accordingly, a difficult task. But, especially in the context of this work focusing on American foreign policy, let us posit that another factor deserving of consideration in any attempt to explain the contrasting evolutionary paths of North and South America would be the successful, expansionary foreign policy of the entity that emerged from the original thirteen British colonies in North America. For example, the Revolutionary War might have failed had not the rebellious colonies attracted the support of foreign powers, especially France. Success in that war allowed the emergence of a "core" that might be an important part of the explanation of the expansion and integration of the United States.

In their study of the emergence of "amalgamated security communities"—by which they mean "the formal merger of two or more previously independent units into a single larger unit"—Karl Deutsch et al. (1966, 2) focus considerable attention on the United States as an exemplar. The integration and emergence of such amalgamated security communities, in the view of these authors, historically has seemed to depend crucially on the presence of "cores of strength." The "original thirteen colonies," according to Deutsch et al., "functioned . . . as a composite core in the integration of territories and states that were gradually added to the union in the West" (20).

No such core of strength existed in South America, however. Brazil might have played this role, but its Portuguese origins made it sufficiently distinct culturally that it could have unified its Spanish-speaking neighbors only through a process that would have been awkwardly dependent on brute force. No Spanish-American colony or set of colonies emerged as a core around which a United States of South America might have formed. In contrast, the thirteen British-based colonies to the north did form a core, and that core adopted a series of foreign policy strategies and tactics that successfully dealt with opposing forces in the form of aboriginal communities, the British, the French, the Spanish, the Mexicans—and to some minor extent, the Russians—to put together the continent-wide United States of (North) America.

FOREIGN POLICY CHALLENGES IN THE FIRST HALF OF THE TWENTIETH CENTURY

In terms of foreign policy, the twentieth century might be said to have begun for the United States with the Spanish-American War of 1898. The origins of the dispute arose in Cuba, a restless colony of Spain. Having lost something on the order of 100,000 soldiers suppressing a rebellion on the island in the 1860s and 1870s, the Spanish government was in no mood to tolerate continued unrest there. It sent General Valeriano Weyler to deal with the problem. He did so by setting up virtual concentration camps, where unsanitary conditions led to what estimates at the time claimed to be about 400,000 deaths, or a quarter of the population of Cuba (Offner 1992, 241). Although the actual number of fatalities probably was closer to 100,000, there is no quarreling with the fact that this awful situation inflamed public opinion in the United States. Indeed, the crisis leading to the Spanish-American War often serves as an example of an interstate confrontation in which public opinion played a key role (May 1961).

Other sources, however, argue that the Spanish-American War was fought on behalf of business interests who stood to gain economically from American **imperialism**. And in the end, many business interests did undoubtedly benefit—especially from the acquisition of the Philippine Islands, which was one result of the war. Nevertheless, according to Alexander DeConde (1963, 347), "business interests in the United States with few exceptions, opposed war." Until very late in the game, so did President McKinley, whose efforts to avoid war led his critics to argue that "McKinley's policy reflected self-interested economic considerations— an indication of the public realization that the business community generally opposed intervention in Cuba" (Trask 1981, 43). Some politicians, such as Theodore Roosevelt and Henry Cabot Lodge, as well as military analysts such as Alfred Thayer Mahan, believed that the American economy needed overseas markets, and they were generally in favor of the war. But the "one group decidedly reluctant to go to war was composed of big businessmen and financiers" (Keller 1991, 1015).

The final spark setting off this combustible situation was an explosion on the American battleship *Maine* in Havana harbor, killing almost three hundred people.[f] Even then, President McKinley was reluctant to give in to the pressures for war with Spain, but in the end, he acquiesced, because he felt that war was necessary if he wished to hold onto his position as president of the United States. According to John Offner (1992, ix), "In the final analysis, Republicans made war in Spain in order to keep control of Washington" (see also Trask 1981, 31). In other words, this was one of many instances in American history in which a key foreign policy decision by the U.S. government was fundamentally influenced—as would be anticipated by rational political ambition theory—by domestic political considerations, especially the leader's apprehension that the "wrong" decision could lead to his loss of power.[g]

In waging the Spanish-American War, the United States proved not only that it could defeat a European power—albeit a seriously declining one—but also that it was a state to be reckoned with by the entire international political system. In other words, it first gained recognition as a great power. John Mearsheimer's theoretical and historical analysis of great power politics (2001a, 41) leads him to conclude that "the best outcome a great power can hope for is to be a regional hegemon," and (in a chapter entitled "Great Powers in Action") that "powerful states ... seek regional hegemony whenever the possibility arises." The Monroe Doctrine

---

f. This explosion resulted, "it now seems clear, [from] spontaneous combustion in one of its magazines, not because of a Spanish or Cuban mine" (Keller 1991, 1015).

g. This discussion of the Spanish-American War relies extensively on my review of the war in Ray 1995.

in late September of 1918, when they "fought the greatest battle in American history to that point in the Meuse-Argonne campaign; it proved to be a major contribution to the Allied victory" (Coffman 1991, 830).

A major contribution it was, but it came only after the other major powers of the world had fought, over many prolonged, agonizing months and years, to a horrifically bloody standoff. The United States had stood by without serious involvement in the carnage until the spring and summer of 1918; the war was over by early November. In short, in the Great War that lasted almost four and one-half years, substantial American involvement in intense military conflict was limited to a little more than six months. As a result of the war, the Germans lost 1.8 million troops, Austria-Hungary suffered 1.2 million battle deaths, 1.7 million Russian soldiers lost their lives, the French Army lost 1.35 million troops, and the British—who had done a certain amount of holding back and waiting of their own—suffered somewhat less than 1 million battle fatalities. In strictly numerical terms, it is fair to say that the total of 126,000 American soldiers who died in World War I was, in relative terms, strikingly small (Small and Singer 1982, 89).

The next world war began in September 1939, when Hitler's Germany attacked Poland, but the United States showed no signs of becoming directly involved in this great conflict in 1939, in 1940, or through virtually all of 1941. It entered the war only after being attacked by Japan on December 7, 1941. Germany then immediately did President Roosevelt a great favor by declaring war on the United States; otherwise, it is not clear that Roosevelt could have used the attack at Pearl Harbor as a rationale for becoming deeply involved in the war in Europe. In the words of Stephen Ambrose and Douglas Brinkley (1997, 16), "Well into 1942, public-opinion polls revealed that Americans were more eager to strike back at the Japanese than [to] fight the Germans."

The United States, having been very cautious about entering the war at all, and declaring war on Japan only after it was attacked, was then very cautious about becoming involved in offensive military action on the European continent. But the pressure to launch an attack directly on Germany's western front became quite intense following June 22, 1941, when Hitler, in spite of the nonaggression pact he had signed with Stalin in 1939, launched a massive attack against the Soviet Union. In reaction to that attack, the logic of the strategic situation from the viewpoint of the United States was expressed by then–U.S. Senator Harry S. Truman: "If we see that Germany is winning we ought to help Russia and if Russia is winning we ought to help Germany and that way let them kill as many as possible…" (Catledge 1941, 7).

President Roosevelt had suggested to the Russians that the Allies might open up a western front against the Germans by 1942, but that year came and went, and so did all of 1943. D-Day, when the invasion of France was finally launched, did not come until June of 1944. By that time, the Germans and the Russians had fought the greatest military battle in history, and the Russians had beaten back the invasion by the Nazis at a tremendous cost in Russian lives.

Thus, in both world wars, the United States was slow to get involved; it entered those conflicts only after all the other major participants had suffered grievously and for prolonged periods of time; and it suffered, in comparison, relatively few battle casualties. (Also, no serious military conflict ever took place in the United States itself.) Not coincidentally, the United States emerged from both world wars as the most powerful state in the world.

Were American policies and strategies for dealing with the world wars based on cynical calculations designed to maximize the losses of every other state and minimize the losses of the United States? Probably not, on any sustained, deliberate basis in the minds of most leading American foreign policy decision makers, although Harry Truman's opportunistic opinion expressed in the wake of the 1941 Nazi invasion of the Soviet Union was surely not confined to him. Instead, American policy in those wars was rather clearly attributable, at least in part, to the democratic character of the domestic political system in the United States. The leaders of democracies are particularly prone to lose power in the wake of lost wars (Bueno de Mesquita and Siverson 1995; Bueno de Mesquita et al. 2003). It is probably not a coincidence, therefore, that democratic leaders tend to be relatively risk-averse and cautious when it comes to initiating military conflict. In short, they tend to initiate hostilities only against opponents whom they are likely to defeat. They also fight wars in a relatively efficient and effective manner (Reiter and Stam 2002; Bueno de Mesquita et al. 1999).

As mentioned earlier, President Wilson ran an election campaign in 1916 on a kind of "peace platform," and then led the country into World War I in the following year, while President Roosevelt promised in 1940 that he would not send American troops into foreign wars, and then took the country into war against Japan, Germany, and Italy in 1941. There were many reasons for the timing of these decisions, but one of them, according to Kurt Gaubatz (1991), may have been that democratic states tend not to take the initiative in military action when elections are close at hand. (Conversely, they are more likely to become involved in military conflict when scheduled elections are relatively distant in time.) And, of course, the United States emerged victorious in both world wars, for democratic states tend to win the wars in which they participate (Lake 1993; Bueno de Mesquita et al. 2003; Reiter and Stam 2002). In short, American policies, strategies, and behavior—and the political outcomes achieved—with respect to both world wars conform quite clearly to historical patterns governing the relationships of democratic states to enemies, potential enemies, and peer competitors in interstate conflict.[h]

CONCLUSION

In a prevalent stereotype, the United States started out as thirteen separate colonies that successfully united to gain freedom from their British colonial masters, and then formed a republic that devoted the first 130 years of its existence primarily to domestic affairs. Taking over the major part of the continent from the eastern seaboard to the Pacific Ocean is also often conceived of as primarily a domestic matter—after all, that land ultimately became part of the United States. According to this stereotype, this reclusive union became importantly involved in international politics only at the initiation of the Spanish-American War in 1898, and deeply intertwined in the global political system only when its hand was forced by the Germans in 1917. Immediately after that war (as this arguably misleading impression would have it), the United States thought better of this involvement and retreated into its historical

h. Furthermore, all these patterns regarding the foreign policies of democratic states conform clearly to the main theoretical basis of this book, to be introduced in chapter 3.

isolationism, until Japan put an end to this deeply ingrained instinct, perhaps forever, with its attack on Pearl Harbor.

In fact, the thirteen colonies that emerged as the United States were deeply involved in foreign policy issues and international politics from the beginning. The American Revolution might not have succeeded at all were it not for the successful courting of foreign support, primarily from the French. The new government then immediately became concerned about its constitution, the Articles of Confederation, mainly because it failed to provide a basis for the formulation of an effective foreign policy. The United States went to war with the most powerful state in the world in 1812, declared the Western Hemisphere off-limits to colonizers by 1823, and deployed its military forces on virtually every continent throughout the nineteenth century.

The United States almost fell apart during the Civil War, and several foreign powers were inclined to help that process along. During this struggle, France took advantage of the weakness of the Union by establishing a virtual colony in Mexico, on its southern border. But for the most part during the 1800s, even while its troops were engaged in China and in the Mediterranean, for example, the United States successfully contended with opposition from aboriginal peoples, the British, the French, the Spanish, the Russians, and the Mexicans and so managed to extend its federation from coast to coast. Increasingly, it came to dominate the Western Hemisphere, interpreting the Monroe Doctrine in ever more expansive and exclusive terms over the next hundred years. And then, in the twentieth century, it stood aside, judiciously perhaps, from the early fighting in both world wars, becoming involved in both conflicts only after all the other major powers had fought themselves to near-exhaustion, and then only to provide decisive, rather than intense and costly, assistance. As a result, the original thirteen colonies of 1776 emerged from World War II as the most powerful and wealthiest state in the world.

The rest of this book will be devoted primarily to analysis of foreign policy processes and issues in and for the United States during the post–World War II era.

KEY CONCEPTS

imperialism   28

interventionism   14

isolationism   13

manifest destiny   24

Monroe Doctrine   15

Roosevelt Corollary   29

sphere of influence   14

RATIONAL POLITICAL AMBITION AND ...
The EARLY HISTORY OF AMERICAN FOREIGN POLICY

LESSONS
LEARNED

☑ The declaration of the Monroe Doctrine in 1823 was a response in important part to international political considerations. But it was also affected by the domestic political calculations of Secretary of State John Adams, at the time a candidate to succeed James Monroe as president. As a presidential candidate, John Quincy Adams was vulnerable to the charge of being too pro-British. By refusing to issue the Monroe Declaration jointly with the British, Adams enhanced his chances of winning the presidency by demonstrating some independence from Great Britain.

☑ During the Civil War, President Lincoln was too absorbed in domestic problems to deal with the French when they occupied Mexico in 1863, thus violating the Monroe Doctrine. President Lincoln also issued the Emancipation Proclamation not only to solidify support for the war among abolitionist elements in the North, but also to win sympathy for the North's cause in Europe and elsewhere, thus exemplifying the continual interplay of domestic and international political calculations.

☑ President McKinley initiated the Spanish-American War in part as a response to Spain's actions and policies toward its colony Cuba. But he also apparently felt that a vigorous response to the Spanish during the developing crisis over Cuba was necessary in order to enhance his chances of winning the next presidential election.

CHAPTER **3**

ANALYZING MODERN AMERICAN FOREIGN POLICY

Competing Approaches

CHAPTER 2 FOCUSED ON BASIC HISTORICAL EVENTS AND PATTERNS IN American foreign policy. Writing that description of such a sprawling subject necessarily involved making a large number of choices, since no facts—certainly no set of historical facts—"speak for themselves." In principle, an ambitious analyst might embark on a project to describe, on a day-by-day basis, all important foreign policy events and fundamental trends taking place in the United States since July 4, 1776, but that would be foolish. Even assuming that such a project could be completed in the analyst's lifetime, nobody would be inclined to read such a comprehensive historical tome.

Therefore, choices must be made. And, an obvious initial question is: On what basis? It is impossible to consider all the events, persons, conflicts, economic factors, or ideological currents—to cite several, but by no means all, possible explanatory factors that might have had important and fundamental impacts on American foreign policy—nor is it possible to address every foreign policy outcome. So just which explanatory factors and outcomes *should* be taken into account?

The general answer is that one needs to adopt basic guidelines that specify which outcomes are most significant, and which factors may best explain those outcomes. At least as important, these guidelines must make it clear which outcomes and explanatory factors are *not* so important—meaning that they can be ignored, at least most of the time. In short, in order to understand American foreign policies, one needs to rely on theoretical approaches that provide bases for selecting the outcomes or impacts that should be addressed, as well as the explanatory factors that should be emphasized.

The main point of this chapter is to describe and begin to analyze the theoretical approaches that are currently most prevalent among those who think, speak, and write about American foreign policy. These theoretical approaches provide differing sets of lenses, so to speak, through which we will proceed to analyze events, trends, and patterns in American foreign policy in the rest of the book. Ideally, readers will formulate their own ideas about which

According to rational political ambition theory, political leaders such as George W. Bush make foreign policy decisions with both internal as well as international threats to their continuation in power in mind. Here, President Bush discusses the U.S. war on terrorism in his first State of the Union address in January 2002. The purpose of the war was not only to protect the United States from international enemies, but also to maintain Republican control of the White House and Congress.

guidelines are generally the most useful for understanding, explaining, and even making predictions about the contours, content, and impacts of American foreign policy.

This does not mean that readers are advised simply to adopt one of the approaches described in this chapter and, from that point on, to ignore all competing theoretical ideas. Well-informed, perceptive observers of American foreign policy will, on the contrary, be aware of differing interpretations of the behavior of American leaders, or of patterns in policies, and they will also compare the strengths and weaknesses of these theories. They may even ultimately change their minds about which approach is best suited to providing the clearest understanding of American foreign policy.

However, in this writer's view, it is a mistake to adopt a strictly neutral or indifferent attitude about competing theoretical approaches to American foreign policy. It is too easy to conclude: "Well, Theory A says one thing, Theory B says quite another, Theory C provides an interpretation quite different from those advocated by supporters of Theory A and Theory B. The truth probably lies somewhere in the middle." Such a passive, neutral approach is unlikely to maximize one's ability to understand and interpret events, trends, and patterns in American foreign policy. Progress toward developing a coherent, informed, and insightful view of this broad topic is more likely if one makes a commitment—even a tentative one—to a particular theoretical approach. Readers are encouraged, therefore, to develop a preference for one particular theoretical approach to American foreign policy, and to put that particular approach to the test repeatedly in observing, attempting to understand, and trying to anticipate developments in relationships between the United States and its counterparts in the international system. Interested observers of American foreign policy cannot expect, in other words, to develop a penetrating and comprehensive understanding of any theoretical approach to that topic without extended reliance on it, in a manner that will reveal both its strengths and its weaknesses.

At the same time, it is important to understand that it is much easier to categorize *theories* of American foreign policy than it is to classify most *theorists* who think, read, and write about the subject. The different theories can be separated from each other rather neatly; in their pristine forms, the contrasts between them are easy to see. But individual analysts, considering multiple topics, are unlikely to be quite so easy to sort out. Since most of them tend to be at least somewhat eclectic—and even inconsistent—attempts to pigeonhole them may well be frustrating. One practical solution to this problem is to develop a tolerance for unavoidable ambiguity.

REALISM: THE PREDOMINANT THEORY

It is widely agreed, at least among North American analysts of relationships among states in the global political system, that **realism** is the most important, widely adopted theoretical approach to foreign policies and international politics. Historically, the roots of this approach can be traced back at least to the English political theorist, Thomas Hobbes (most prominently in his book *Leviathan,* published in 1651), or to the Italian philosopher Niccoló Machiavelli (in his work *The Prince,* which was completed in 1513 but not published until 1532), or even to the writings of the ancient Greek historian Thucydides on the Peloponnesian War. That war between Athens and Sparta took place between 431 and 404 BC; Thucydides' account of it was published sometime after his death in approximately 400 BC.[a]

The prevalence of the realist approach to analyzing actions by and interactions among states can be seen in similar ideas from non-Western sources. Perhaps the oldest known treatise on international politics is the Chinese general Sun Tzu's *The Art of War*, written by around 500 BC. Its realist tone much resembles that of the *Arthasastra* (the "Science of Polity"), written by Kautilya for the first great Indian emperor, Chandragupta, around 300 BC. On this work, George Modelski (1964, 550) comments: "Kautilya's *Arthasastra* is above all, a manual of statecraft, a collection of rules which a king or administrator would be wise to follow *if he wishes to acquire and maintain power*. In inspiration it is therefore close to other digests of rules of statecraft and of advice to princes such as Sun Tzu's work on *The Art of War* or Niccoló Machiavelli's *The Prince*." [b]

Thus, the realist approach to international politics has ancient origins, widely scattered in many cultures throughout the world. But its most influential incarnation in modern times is *Politics among Nations* by Hans J. Morgenthau. First published in 1948, this seminal work had appeared in six different editions by 1985. It is still widely used in college classrooms, and its influence on the policymaking community in the United States continues to be obvious. The main thesis of *Politics among Nations* is that "statesmen think and act in terms of interest defined as power" (Morgenthau and Thompson 1985, 5).

The primary tenets of "realism" as an approach to international politics and foreign policy are summarized in figure 3.1. According to Robert Keohane (1983, 507), an authoritative source on this topic: "The three most fundamental Realist assumptions are: that the most important actors in world politics are territorially organized entities (city-states or modern states); that state behavior can be explained rationally; and that states seek power and calculate their interest in terms of power...."[c]

It may seem commonsensical, even banal, to say that **states** are the most important actors in world politics, and that they dominate international politics. The state in the modern sense, however, has not always been the dominant political entity; it is commonly asserted that the concept came into prominence with the Peace of Westphalia in 1648. Moreover, it is typically argued in contemporary times that states are decreasing in importance. So, the basic realist assumption that states are the most important actors is not, in fact, free of critics.

It is true that the belief in the preeminence of states has encountered important challenges in the post–World War II era. Early on, political scientist John Herz (1957) argued that, in the era of nuclear weapons and ballistic missiles, states could no longer perform their most basic and important function—that is, to provide basic physical security for their citizens—

---

a. In 1629, before writing *Leviathan*, Hobbes completed a translation of Thucydides' *The Peloponnesian War*.

b. Emphasis added. The crucial political implications of the italicized phrase should become clear by the end of this chapter.

c. The authoritative character of this statement derives from the fact that Keohane has served as president of both the American Political Science Association and the International Studies Association, as well as chair of the Department of Government at Harvard University; also, it appears in a volume published by the American Political Science Association, authoritatively entitled *Political Science: The State of the Discipline*.

| FIGURE 3.1 | The Basic Tenets of Realism |

- States are the most important actors.
- They can be treated as unitary actors.
- They act in the national interest, defined in terms of power.

and that therefore they would soon cease to be as important as they had been for hundreds of years. More recently, economic and technological developments have led many observers to conclude that states now are and increasingly will be challenged in their role as the predominant political entities in the global political system. For example, both **globalization**—the increasingly interdependent status of national economies—and the increasing strength of multinational corporations are seen as threats to the sovereignty of states (Strange 1996). The growing ease of communication between and among peoples in different states, and the speed of transportation between states, also seem to many to be increasing the permeability of national borders, subsequently decreasing the ability of governments to control their citizens. All of these factors may diminish the importance of states.

But, then, states have always had their critics and detractors. From the beginning, states have gotten into wars with each other. And from the beginning, these wars have led some observers to believe that there must be some better, more peaceful way to organize the global political system. According to F. H. Hinsley (1967, 13), "in modern history, war-prevention theories have increasingly been based on the argument that it is essential to establish some organization for regulating the relations of sovereign states; the first plans to use this argument naturally made their appearance in the early days of the modern states' system." Such ideas reached a peak of influence, naturally enough, after World War I, the bloodiest interstate war in history up to that time. But the failure of the League of Nations, which was created to avoid another catastrophe like World War I, severely damaged the credibility of the belief that the international system based on sovereign nation-states could be pacified through the creation of some influential, comprehensive, and universal international organization.

Nowadays, critics of the states system no longer see them being replaced or subordinated to a central, universal organization such as the League of Nations (or the United Nations). Instead, states now seem on the verge of being overwhelmed by the global technological and economic developments already mentioned, which appear to be beyond their control. Today's states may be losing authority to multinational corporations, to international organizations such as the International Monetary Fund and the World Bank, and to an ever-expanding list of nongovernmental organizations (NGOs), such as Amnesty International, Greenpeace, and Human Rights Watch. International economic intercourse cannot be managed by individual, separate states; environmental problems such as global warming supersede national boundaries; and when human rights violations on the scale of the 1994 genocide in Rwanda lead to the deaths of 800,000 people within a few weeks, the idea that the perpetrators of such slaughter should be able to hide behind state borders suggests that the concept of state sovereignty may be anachronistic.

Nevertheless, since states (and their governments) remain the most important type of political entity in the global political system, the realist assumption that they are the most important unit is, for the time being, almost certainly viable. The 9/11 attacks on the World Trade Center and the Pentagon had paradoxical effects on the viability of this assumption. These devastating terrorist strikes demonstrated the vulnerability of the most powerful state on earth to attack by a small number of determined operatives of al-Qaeda, a shadowy nongovernmental, transnational organization. But they also evoked a patriotic and nationalistic backlash in the United States, leading it to utilize its military force in far-flung places such as Afghanistan and Iraq.

But what of the second assumption in Keohane's list—that states are unitary, rational political actors? Surely this premise is so out of touch with reality as to be an initial step in the wrong direction for any attempt to understand foreign policies or international politics? Here it is important to recognize, however, that the world is too complicated to be understood without some degree of simplification. Theories reduce the world to basic essentials in order to make it intelligible; ideally, they are based on streamlined assumptions that are sufficiently valid to make the world more comprehensible than it would otherwise be, even though they do not provide an accurate or complete *description* of the world, or the events on which they focus.

Imagine that a person living in New York wants to drive to Detroit, and that he or she has been given a choice between two "theories," or models, purporting to explain how to do so. One of these models consists of a series of videotapes made in the course of a drive from New York to Detroit, by a car equipped with a video camera on its roof that taped every foot of the roads, streets, and highways along the way. The other model consists of one piece of paper on which some knowledgeable person has drawn a few more or less straight lines representing (in a highly abstract and simplified manner), the relevant interstate highways, labeled with their identifying numbers.

Which theory or model would our driver find more useful for achieving an effective understanding of the task of driving from New York to Detroit? Indisputably, the videotapes of every foot of highway to be traversed are more descriptively accurate; they contain a lot more information about the trip than the one piece of paper with the crude map. But, in fact, the videotapes are too exhaustively accurate, containing so much information as to be virtually useless for coming to grips with the task of driving from one city to the other. In order to make any use of them at all, one would have to watch all the tapes before embarking and then draw up a set of driving directions, if possible, from any route-marking data that could be gleaned from the hours of recorded scenery.

In contrast, the map model—the few lines on paper—leaves out all sorts of information about the territory to be negotiated between New York and Detroit. Such a schematic representation is not nearly as descriptively accurate of the territory to be negotiated as the hours of videotape; in other words, it constitutes an exceedingly simplified explanation of the task. But, if it is well done, it contains all the information that is *essential* for understanding the task, precisely because it has excluded a lot of the less crucial data provided by the videotapes.

In a roughly analogous fashion, the assumption that states are unitary actors is a drastic simplification of the "real world." To be sure, the foreign policies of states are, in part, the results of inputs from presidents, prime ministers, and dictators, each of whom is, in fact, an individual human being whose judgments are made in a process that at least approximates those that might be devised by unitary, rational actors. But foreign policies and the decisions on which they are based are also impacted by governmental bureaucracies, legislators, lobbyists, social groups, business interests, labor unions, college students, and churches, among other factors. And those complicated processes certainly do not always produce policies that can be described as "rational," no matter how straightforward or simple the definition of that term may be. Nevertheless, the assumption that states are rational—even though descriptively inaccurate or at least incomplete (like a road map)—may be sufficiently valid to allow interested observers to achieve a better understanding of foreign policies and interstate interactions than would be possible if one had to take into account exhaustive descriptions of foreign policy processes and the roles played in them by interest groups, bureaucracies, legislators, the media, and so on.

Finally, there is the basic realist assumption that the primary goal of states—their No. 1 priority most of the time—is power. In other words, according to realists, states make most foreign policy decisions with a view toward increasing their power. A variant of realism known as **neorealism** posits instead that states seek security above all (Waltz 1979), but this, too, is a severe simplification of reality, even an exaggeration. States typically seek many goals, such as economic benefits, glory, Olympic gold medals, and internal political stability. And which of those goals they give priority to varies along with changes in the identity of the leaders in charge of the governments of those states. To posit that "states seek power" is, in short, a descriptively inaccurate statement.

But many states—perhaps, especially, the larger and more powerful ones—certainly do consistently make power and/or security a high priority. At a minimum, most states, most of the time, clearly want to continue to exist, and they consistently devote a good deal of effort to maintaining their territorial integrity. Thus, the realist assumption that states consistently and perpetually seek power or security may well be a useful assumption on which to base theoretical analyses of the foreign policies of states and of the interactions among them.

LIBERALISM: THE MAIN ALTERNATIVE

The main alternative to realism as a theoretical approach to the analysis of American foreign policy is **liberalism**, the basic features of which are listed in figure 3.2. Liberals have much in common with realists. Many of them, in fact, would not deny the basic validity of the main realist assumptions—that states are the most important actors, and that it is useful to analyze them as unitary rational actors who consistently give high priority to national security concerns, power, and territorial integrity.

Liberals, in other words, differ from realists mainly on several points of emphasis. Although, as Michael Doyle acknowledges (1997, 206), "there is no canonical description of Liberalism," its roots can be traced back to such philosophers as John Locke, who posited individual human rights; Adam Smith, who believed in the pacifying effects of international trade; and Immanuel Kant, who emphasized the possibility of peaceful relationships among liberal states.

> ## FIGURE 3.2   The Basic Tenets of Liberalism
>
> • Domestic politics are important.
>
> • Economic goals are important.
>
> • International law and international organizations are relatively important.
>
> • Values, especially democratic values, are important.

Realism in its pristine, even rather extreme form, does not place much emphasis on the potential impact of domestic politics on foreign policies, or on interactions among states—for realists, a state is a state is a state, much as a rose is a rose is a rose.[d] Liberals are more prone to acknowledge important impacts of domestic political considerations on foreign policies and interstate interactions. And, whereas realists regard power, national security, and territorial integrity as the overriding foreign policy issues, liberals are more likely to see economic goals as potentially important. In other words, for liberals, "the agenda of interstate relationships consists of multiple issues that are not arranged in a clear or consistent hierarchy.... Military security does not consistently dominate the agenda" (Keohane and Nye 1989, 25). Liberals point out that, since life-and-death decisions, or decisions about peace and war, actually arise rather rarely for most states, a typical state's decision makers instead devote considerable attention to economic issues and problems, concerning themselves most often with matters such as tariffs, trade agreements, attracting foreign investment, and so on.

Similarly, whereas realists tend to think that international law and international organizations tend to have—and should have—only an ephemeral influence on the foreign policies of states, liberals believe that it would be desirable for these supranational authorities to be more influential. They also believe that realists tend to systematically underestimate both the influence and the potentially beneficial impacts of these external authorities. In the modern context, liberals in the United States tend to see international law, international organizations, and multilateralism in general as important avenues to the maintenance of American power over the long run. According to Joseph Nye, in a book subtitled "Why the World's Only Superpower Can't Go It Alone" (2002, 159), "the multilateralism of American preeminence is a key to its longevity, because it reduces the incentives for constructing alliances against us."

Finally, realists emphasize the differences between the contexts in which individual human beings interact with each other and the anarchic system within which states interact. In this system, there is no basis for the ethical and moral considerations that should and do play important roles in the lives of individuals. For state leaders, political success is an imperative that may well trump such traditional considerations in many situations. This does not mean that ethical and moral considerations are irrelevant for foreign policy makers, according to

---

d. "As an analytical matter, realism does not distinguish between 'good' states and 'bad' states.... In realist theory, all states are forced to seek the same goal: maximum relative power" (Mearsheimer 1994–1995, 48).

realists. It does mean that the actions of state leaders need to be judged by different criteria than those used to evaluate actions and interactions among individuals in a functioning domestic society with well-developed legislative and legal systems.

Liberals, however, hold that foreign policy decisions should be based, at least in part, on ethical considerations. It is particularly important to be attentive to the political as well as the moral value of democracy. Not even the most enthusiastically democratic state can afford to shun autocracies entirely, of course, for the machinations and contingencies of international politics may sometimes require it to cooperate with and support even tyrannical regimes. (The United States, for example, when confronting Hitler during World War II, provided substantial support to Joseph Stalin's Soviet Union; later, involved in Cold War competition with the Soviet Union, the United States formed a supportive tie with Mao Zedong's China.) But under normal circumstances, it is important for democratic states to provide foreign policy support to democratic regimes, and to do whatever is practical and possible to encourage the establishment of democratic political systems in states ruled by dictators. Liberals believe that democratic governments serve the needs of their constituents better, in the first place, and that they are more likely to have peaceful, cooperative relationships with each other than autocratic governments will have among themselves. Finally, democratic governments are particularly likely to have troubled relationships with autocratic governments, and vice versa.

NEOCONSERVATISM: A HYBRID?

In the wake of the 9/11 terrorist attacks, an approach to foreign policy and international politics known as **neoconservatism** suddenly seemed to take on fundamental importance in American foreign policy, although, by 2001, neoconservatives had actually been around for some time. Their roots can be traced back to former liberals, and even some Trotskyites, who became antagonized by what they considered the excesses of liberals and leftists during the 1960s. For example, Irving Kristol, who is often referred to as "the godfather of neoconservatism," had been a Trotskyite at the City College of New York in the 1930s, but by the late 1960s he had shifted to the right of the political spectrum.

Both realism and liberalism have their roots in traditional schools of political thought and, in more recent times, in academia. Neoconservatism, in contrast, was developed by public intellectuals such as Kristol, journalists such as Charles Krauthammer, and even policymakers such as Paul Wolfowitz, who served as a deputy secretary of defense from 2001 until 2005 and who is often referred to as the "key architect" of the second Bush administration's Iraq war ("Empire Builders" 2005). Neoconservatives clearly exerted significant influence on American leaders such as National Security Adviser and then Secretary of State Condoleezza Rice, Vice President Dick Cheney, and, most important, President George W. Bush in response to the attacks of 9/11. As David J. Rothkopf (2005, 39) puts it: "The neocons saw their opportunity to assert their case that diplomatic balancing acts in the Middle East had created danger for the United States, and that the time had come for stronger measures, whatever the cost."

From the point of view of realists, liberals, and most academic analysts of foreign policies and state interactions, "neo-conservatism" is more ideology than theory. It is probably true, of course, that academic analysts always tend to see themselves as objective, dispassionate, and independent observers who formulate theoretical notions and develop theoretical perspectives in an intellectual fashion, while disparaging those who disagree with them as more subjective, emotional, and overly influenced by passions and prejudices. Nevertheless, even though invidious comparisons between "theories" and "ideologies" may be consistently unfair to the latter, creating distinctions of questionable validity, there are important differences between analytical approaches to the understanding of events, and the more didactic guides or ideas that serve as the bases for prescriptions about foreign policies. Admittedly, prescriptive ideas about how foreign policies *ought* to be formulated must be based, if they are to be credible, on plausible (and theoretical) ideas about how the world works. Realists and liberals feel that they have more fully developed ideas of this sort, on which to base their prescriptions about how the world should be dealt with, while neoconservatives give relatively less attention to discovering how the world *is* and focus more on how it might most effectively be changed, or reformed.

So what do the "neocons" believe? One articulate advocate, Max Boot (2005), claims that "neocons combine the best of the two dominant strains of U.S. foreign policy thinking: Wilsonian idealism and Kissingerian realpolitik."[e] Boot (2004, 21) also explains that "the ambitious National Security Strategy that the [Bush] administration issued in September 2002—with its call for U.S. primacy, the promotion of democracy, and vigorous action, preemptive if necessary, to stop terrorism and weapons proliferation—was a quintessentially neoconservative document." Another well-known advocate of this particular approach to American foreign policy is Charles Krauthammer (2004, 17), who also emphasizes its potentially hybrid character by labeling it "democratic realism," which he describes in the following fashion:

> Targeted, focused, and limited, it intervenes not everywhere that freedom is threatened but only where it counts—in those regions where the defense or advancement of freedom is critical to success in the larger war against the existential enemy. That is how we fought the Cold War. The existential enemy then was Soviet communism. Today, it is Arab/Islamic radicalism.

Neoconservatism arguably first had a fundamental impact on American foreign policy during the presidency of Ronald Reagan. And a useful way to appreciate its impact on current American foreign policy is, as Krauthammer's analogy suggests, to see it as the theoretical framework for an attempt by the second Bush administration to duplicate, in its struggle against Islamic fundamentalism, what it regards as the spectacular success of the Reagan administration's confrontation with the Communist Bloc. Should its goals be achieved, the Middle East would be transformed in the wake of the Bush administration in much the same way that the Soviet Union and Eastern Europe were in the years immediately following Reagan's presidency.

While neoconservatism does combine aspects of realism with tenets of liberalism, it is important to understand that it also differs quite widely from its diverse roots. Realists have little patience with what they see as moralistic crusades advocated by neoconservatives to instill democracy in autocratic countries, just as liberals are put off by the neoconservatives' con-

---

e. This comment perhaps confirms that neoconservatism focuses on prescriptions; when it comes to more theoretical analyses of how the world actually works, it tends to borrow from previously existing approaches.

tempt for international organizations and international law, and by their willingness to engage in preemptive and unilateral military initiatives, even if for the admirable cause—with which, of course, they sympathize—of spreading democracy. As a result, both realists and liberals tended to be very skeptical about, and, in the aftermath, very critical of George W. Bush's war to depose Saddam Hussein.[f] How much influence neoconservatives will retain on the conduct of American foreign policy will be determined, certainly in the short run, by the outcome of that war in Iraq.

RADICAL AND TRADITIONAL LEFTIST APPROACHES

Karl Marx, clearly one of the most influential social scientists in history, devised a mode of political analysis that became critically important for the discussion of political forces in the modern era. Indeed, at one time Marx's approach may well have been the most important ideology/theory of politics in the world. His basic idea was that capitalism as a social-political system had inherently self-destructive tendencies.[g] The working class, in Marx's view, would become so numerous and so impoverished in advanced capitalist societies that it would inevitably rise up and overthrow capitalist systems. It would, in short, give birth to socialism, in which market forces would be brought under political control, to the benefit of everyone in the society except the small minority of capitalists.

By World War I, **Marxist theory** faced an obvious problem: the workers in advanced capitalist societies were not becoming progressively more impoverished. Nor were they showing any signs of uniting in opposition to capitalist societies in order to establish revolutionary, socialist regimes. Even so, Vladimir Lenin, an admirer of Marx, expected that the Social Democrats in Germany would refuse to support the government's war effort in August of 1914—that workers in the opposing bourgeois states would, instead, form a kind of united front against the machinations of their capitalist oppressors. And, as Kenneth Waltz (1959, 137) reports, when he was informed that the Social Democrats had, in fact, supported the German government at the onset of the war, Lenin "could explain it only as a plot of the capitalist press. It had, with obvious intent, wrongly reported the stand of the German socialists."

Eventually discovering that his suspicion of journalistic perfidy was wrong, Lenin soon devised another explanation for the behavior of workers and the German socialist party at the beginning of World War I. In *Imperialism: The Highest Stage of Capitalism,* he argued that the workers in industrialized societies had not risen up against their capitalist oppressors (and in fact were not experiencing the impoverishment that Marx had predicted for them), because they were, in effect, being bought off, bribed, or co-opted with the fruits of capitalist imperialism. Capitalists in the industrialized countries had found—overseas, in their colonies—another working class to exploit, and some portion of the profits from that exploitation was being used to derail working-class rebellion at home. Thus, by building on Marxist analysis,

---

f. "32 prominent international relations scholars, most of them realists, bought an ad in the *New York Times* to make their case against the Bush strategy" (Snyder 2003, 37). The ad appeared on September 26, 2002.

g. For an argument that there is in the Marxist critique of capitalism at least a hint of anti-Semitism, in spite of the fact that both of Marx's grandfathers were rabbis, see Carroll 2001, 403, 428–229.

FIGURE 3.3   The Basic Tenets of Radicalism

- Market forces are unjust.
- Conflict between rich and poor (individuals and states) is inevitable.
- Foreign policies of capitalist states are dominated by the capitalist class (and its interests).

Lenin developed what might be termed the quintessential **radical** approach to the analysis of foreign policies and international politics, the basic tenets of which are listed in figure 3.3.

According to those tenets, market forces—the operation of the free market—produce rampant inequality and injustice. The natural tendency of "free" markets, in other words, is to bring about a steadily increasing concentration of wealth in the capitalist classes. Inevitably, then, there will be fundamental, irresolvable conflicts of interest between the rich and the poor, both within individual states and between rich states and poor states. In the realm of global politics, the fundamental claims of radical analysis are that the foreign policies of capitalist states are based primarily on the economic interests of capitalists, and that all key foreign policy decisions of capitalist states can be understood only if that basic assumption is kept in mind.

Intriguingly, however, both Marx and Lenin thought that economic exploitation by capitalists from rich countries would ultimately benefit poor countries. Marx felt that no matter how greedy might be the motives of capitalist entrepreneurs in poor countries and colonies, they would play a vital role in bringing capitalism to those areas, and that this was a vital step down the road toward socialism. Also, according to Karl Deutsch (1974, 6),

> as Lenin pointed out, imperialism would bring about the *decay* of the metropolitan power. That is, as imperialism would eventually drive capital from the not very profitable investments in the home country into the more profitable investments in the colonies—since in the home country wages were higher in order to keep the labor aristocracy in a pleasant mood, while native labor out in the colonies was cheap—eventually the heavy industries would all end up in the colonies.

After World War II, this version of radicalism was, in turn, found to be inadequate by prominent **leftist** analysts. From their point of view, the expectation by both Marx and Lenin that capitalist penetration into the poorer regions of the world would bring advanced capitalism and wealth (even if unevenly distributed) to those regions was turning out to be mistaken. The explanation for the continued poverty in areas that had recently become independent politically, and were increasingly being incorporated into the capitalist world system, had to do, in the eyes of **dependency theorists**, with the fact that capitalist inroads in poor countries did not create the entrepreneurial class needed to provide the dynamic productive forces seen in the developed, industrialized countries.

Basically, the reason for this failure was that the capitalist class in developing countries was co-opted and corrupted—its primary loyalties tied to the economic interests of rich countries.

This meant that capitalists in poor countries typically made decisions and took actions that benefited themselves individually but, on the collective level, kept poor societies poor and resulted in great flows of wealth from poor states to rich states. The solution to this problem, in the view of most dependency theorists, was to cut economic and political ties between poor countries and rich countries, and to establish independent political and economic systems, featuring "strong states" and socialist economies (Cardoso and Faletto 1978; Dos Santos 1970; Frank 1967).

The application of radical ideas to U.S. foreign policy is straightforward. Most foreign policy decisions, in the eyes of radicals, are intended to benefit the free-market economic system of the United States and the capitalists who dominate it. The second Bush administration's war in Iraq, for example, was intended primarily to secure the oil that is necessary to keep the capitalist economy running smoothly and profitably, while the war in Afghanistan was tied to deposits of oil in nearby Central Asian countries. The war in Vietnam in the 1960s and 1970s was, likewise, motivated primarily by a fear that success by leftist guerrillas there would inspire rebel movements in an expanding list of developing countries, depriving the capitalist economy of the United States of necessary raw materials, lucrative markets, and profitable fields of investment. Radical analysts tend to agree with realists that American foreign policy leaders' professions about spreading democracy, protecting human rights, or other ethical, moral causes is cheap talk—intended, in important part, to obscure the real purposes behind American foreign policy.

MODERN, ANTI-ESTABLISHMENT APPROACHES

Marx thought that capitalism would naturally and inevitably impoverish the working class, which would eventually overthrow capitalist systems. By the time of World War I, Lenin had decided that this revolution would not happen because capitalist states were using the fruits of imperialism to mollify domestic working classes. Both Lenin and Marx believed that imperialism would ultimately bring progressive capitalism to poor countries. After World War II, dependency theorists decided that this prediction was not coming true, and that autarky, independence, and socialism were the best bets for poor countries attempting to break the cycle of poverty.

But, in the late 1980s and early 1990s, the Soviet Union fell apart, China abandoned Marxist orthodoxy, and the few remaining socialist states in the Third World (such as North Korea) looked like anything but the wave of the future. This collapse of the Communist model created a kind of vacuum on the radical end of the ideological spectrum. The result has been, depending on one's point of view, disarray among the most vigorous critics of mainstream approaches to foreign policy and international politics, or the emergence of a variety of imaginative, creative, and powerful "anti-establishment" voices and approaches.

For example, the proponents of **critical theory** (which has relatively clear ties to historical Marxist traditions) argue that the orthodox theories of foreign policy and international politics are products of, and serve the interests of, currently predominant states and their rulers. Critical theory, in contrast, "stands apart from the prevailing order of the world and asks how that order came about" (Cox 1986, 208). In short, critical theorists feel that they understand how the world works, and they place a high priority on changing it.

Postmodernists share the contempt of critical theorists for prevailing theoretical views and social orders. Their preferred mode of analysis has its roots in literary criticism. Postmodernism pays special attention to important texts and "discourses," or the rhetorical structure of conflicts between competing interests. Postmodern analysts, in other words, attempt to read between the lines of ideological and theoretical discussions, expositions, and debates in order to uncover their deeper meanings (Rosenau 1992).

Feminists are another anti-establishment source of theoretical approaches to foreign policies and international politics. Some of these critics adopt a recognizably Marxist approach, with an emphasis on issues of interest to women (Enloe 1989, 1993), while others adopt postmodern concepts (Peterson 1992; Sylvester 1994). Additional feminist voices add liberal notions to the "polyphonic chorus of female voices" (Elshtain 1987, 232–233).

Cutting across many of these theoretical divides is a basic controversy about whether or not women are essentially different from men. "Essentialists" believe that women are fundamentally different from men, and that they are capable of providing a beneficial impact on domestic and global political processes because of these differences. Women, in this view, tend to be more peaceful and less violent than men; they are also less individualistic and more tied to their social community (Goldstein 2001, 42). Probably a majority of feminists reject these ideas, believing instead that any ideological or behavioral differences that do exist between women and men are the result of socialization in patriarchal political systems.

One difference between men and women that is clearly important for the analysis of foreign policies and international politics has to do with the subordinate roles that women have played in politics of all kinds, domestic and international. Women everywhere and for all time, of course, have been relegated to relatively rare and minor roles in most political processes. In virtually all of the earliest democratic societies, for example, female citizens were allowed to vote only after decades of struggle and protest. And women's participation in one of the most crucial areas of foreign policy and international politics has always and everywhere been severely limited: "Virtually all human cultures to date have faced the possibility ... of war.... *In every known case, past and present,* cultures have met this challenge in a gender-based way, by assembling groups of fighters who were primarily, and usually exclusively male" (Goldstein 2001, 3–4; emphasis added).

In short, feminist analysts of foreign policies and international politics adopt a wide variety of theoretical approaches. They do have in common a worldview, as well as personal experiences, that are fundamentally different from those of the males who dominate both foreign-policy-making processes and international politics, as well as the academic and policy-oriented analyses of those fields and activities.

A final anti-establishment approach to foreign policies and international politics bears an uncertain relationship to its "out-of-the-mainstream" counterparts. **Social constructivists** clearly share their radical colleagues' skepticism about realism and liberalism—especially about the former. Ideas are clearly important to constructivists; on this point they share common ground with postmodernists, who emphasize the impact of discourse among political competitors and players. Constructivists believe that both realists and liberals tend to take the interests of political actors, such as states in the global political system, as a given. Both realists and liberals assume, for example, that states in an anarchical system value national security as a pressing priority and rely on military force more or less automatically as an important guarantor of that security.

But for constructivists, "anarchy is what states make of it" (Wendt 1992, 1999). In other words, there is no automatic link between the anarchical international system and national policies that seek power and security through the traditional policies of arms buildups, military alliances, and, if necessary, military action. On the contrary, states and their leaders develop interpretations about the meaning of anarchy in the course of interactions with each other. And these interactions may lead to very different, "un-realist" ideas about the meaning of anarchy. New norms may develop in the process of this interaction, and these norms can lead to a dramatically different kind of international politics.

To the extent that realism and liberalism do seem to describe and accurately predict the content of foreign policies and the course of international politics, it is mostly because realism dominates the discourse and the thinking of foreign policy makers. Social constructivists insist, however, that the world could be changed if only national leaders were to develop new ideas about how to deal with each other. In short, in the constructivist view, "human beings are free to change the world by a collective act of good will" (Fischer 1992, 430). Social constructivism thus might be labeled the "Why can't we just all get along?" approach to international politics. And the answer it provides to that key question is this: "We can, if we think we can."

RATIONAL POLITICAL AMBITION THEORY

The final theoretical approach to be discussed in this chapter is the one to which this author is most sympathetic. My preference does not mean, however, that the remaining chapters are to be devoted primarily to advocating this approach. On the contrary, more emphasis will be placed on providing sufficient information about various viewpoints to allow readers to make up their own minds about the validity or the relative utility of competing theories.

Rational political ambition theory is, to some extent, an amalgam of many of its predecessors, and yet it does not adopt a "middle of the road," or "least common denominator" strategy. It contradicts and remains distinct from all previous approaches on crucial points. Its basic tenets are shown in figure 3.4.

The roots of this approach can be traced back to Machiavelli (at least).[h] In his best-known work, *The Prince,* Machiavelli (1532/1996) offers advice to political rulers about how to keep themselves in power. One of his most important pronouncements is as follows:

> There are two things a prince must fear: internal subversion from his subjects; and external aggression by foreign powers. Against the latter, his defence lies in being well armed and having good allies.... [D]omestic affairs will always remain under control provided that relations with external powers are under control and if indeed they were not disturbed by a conspiracy.... He can adequately guard against this if he avoids being hated or scorned and keeps the people satisfied; this, as I have said above at length, is crucial. (59)

---

h. As noted earlier in this chapter, one respected authority in the field (Modelski 1964) holds that the classical realist, Kautilya, emphasized that his approach aimed at preserving the power of political leaders.

> ### FIGURE 3.4 — The Basic Tenets of Rational Political Ambition Theory
>
> - Political leaders of states want primarily to stay in power.
> - To stay in power, those leaders must deal with internal and external competitors.
> - Which (domestic and foreign) policies they choose to pursue depends fundamentally on the structure of their domestic political systems.
> - The foreign policies of states such as the United States are shaped in fundamental ways by their impact on political support for the president.
> - Additional actors and interest groups may have important impacts on foreign policies, but their influence will be maximized to the extent that they can either help leaders to stay in power or mount credible threats to their hold on power.

More contemporary analysts, in the manner of Machiavelli and other classical political theorists, begin with the assumption that leaders want to stay in power, focusing on the fact that, in order to do so, they must cope with both external and internal political competitors. These initial tenets point inescapably to the close relationship of domestic politics to both foreign policies and interactions among states—which is the starting point for rational political ambition theory. Helen Milner (1997, 3), for example, asserts that "domestic politics and international relations are inextricably intertwined." This point follows unavoidably from her conclusion that the chief executive of the modern state "wants to maximize her utility, which is assumed above all to depend on reelection.... I make the simplifying assumption that staying in office is the main goal of executives" (34).[i]

Similarly, the analysts who have developed the rational political ambition approach most fully assume that "everyone in a position of authority wants to keep that authority" (Bueno de Mesquita et al. 2003, 9). One of the main strengths of this approach is that it provides a basis for examining a state's domestic politics and its dealings with the international environment in an integrated, coherent fashion. For the purposes of analyzing American foreign policy, it highlights the importance of the president of the United States, assuming that the president is central to the foreign-policy-making process and that he makes all important foreign policy choices with a view toward keeping himself in power.

In other words, this approach emphasizes that, in the political realm, the U.S. president continually plays what Robert Putnam (1988) calls a "two-level game": on one level, he deals

---

i. By her reference to reelection, Milner makes it obvious that she focuses on democratic states. Rational political ambition theory, in general, deals with both democratic and autocratic states.

with his counterparts in other states; on the other level, he interacts with political supporters and competitors in the domestic political arena. Foreign policies are consistently fashioned by the president in such a way as to enhance his political power and influence in general—as well as the power and influence of the United States, as realists emphasize—but also to protect and increase his own influence and power within the domestic political system. But, especially in the case of a very powerful state such as the United States, the leader's future political fate is rarely if ever directly threatened by foreign competitors. So, Putnam says (457), "it is reasonable to presume, at least in the international case of two-level bargaining, that the [president] will normally give primacy to his domestic calculus, if a choice must be made, not least because his own incumbency often depends on his standing [on the domestic political level]."

The rational political ambition approach shares with realism the basic assumption that political actors tend to be self-interested. However, rather paradoxically, realism posits that policymakers tend to be self-sacrificial or altruistic when they make foreign policy decisions—that is, they base their choices on what is best for the *states* they lead. That is the clear implication of the idea that decision makers base their policy choices on the **national interest**. But, as I have argued elsewhere (Ray 1995, 39), from the point of view of rational political ambition theory, "the basic realist argument that foreign policy makers will make decisions that are in the 'national interest' has always implied a quite 'unrealistic' tendency of national leaders and foreign policy makers to be altruistic, self-abnegating, and self-sacrificial." It is more realistic in a generic sense, and more useful for the purposes of understanding foreign policy choices, to assume instead that political leaders will behave in ways that serve not so much the interests of the states they lead or those of their constituents, as their own primary goal of attaining and staying in office.

Rational political ambition theory also shares with realism the assumption that states are the most important actors in the global political system. It is, however, in fundamental disagreement with the idea that, for the purposes of analyzing the foreign policies of states or their interactions, one can assume that states are all essentially the same. It shares with liberalism the assumption, in other words, that for the purpose of understanding foreign policies and international politics, domestic politics and political structures are important.j

Of course, many types of analysts believe that domestic political factors play an important role in the formation of foreign policies. Liberals tend to assume that, especially in democratic states, the economic well-being of the state is a high priority for governments and their leaders, so those leaders pay special attention to various powerful economic interest groups when foreign policy decisions are made. Liberals are also inclined to disaggregate the state, emphasizing the impact of the media and different parts of the foreign-policy-making bureaucracy. Radicals, in contrast, emphasize the impact of capitalists, or business interests, on the process.

---

j. In this respect, the approach adopted here reflects, to some extent, the influence of a controversy among German historians over the impact of *innenpolitik* (domestic politics) on German foreign policy, especially in the years leading up to the First World War. See, especially, *Der Primat of Innenpolitik* by Eckart Kehr, published in English translation in Kehr 1965; and Fischer 1975. The latter discusses the tendency of some political leaders in Germany to see the possible oncoming war as "the deliverer from democracy and socialism."

(They also assume that if capitalists were eliminated as a class, as in socialist states, foreign policies in those states would be very different.)

Rational political ambition theory does not deny that the influence of various interest groups, or the media, or different foreign-policy-making bureaus, can be very important. But it takes all those forces and interests into account by focusing on their impact on the political fate of the executive political leadership in all states (not just democratic states). And it emphasizes the fundamental importance of structural features shared by all types of political systems. "Every country has fundamental institutional arrangements, or rules, that define interactions within its borders," among the most important of which are the rules that define "what constitutes a winning coalition," according to Bruce Bueno de Mesquita (2003, 381). And the characteristic of **winning coalitions** that has the greatest impact is quite stunning in its simplicity: in autocratic states, winning coalitions are relatively small, whereas in other—typically democratic—states, winning coalitions are relatively large. Thus, a fundamental argument based on rational political ambition theory is that democratic states, such as the United States, have foreign policies (and interactions among themselves) that are different in essential respects from those adopted by autocratic states.

Rational political ambition theory shares with radical approaches the idea that "class conflict" is an essential part of domestic political processes, and that it has an important impact on the outcomes of those processes. According to rational political ambition theory, however, the key conflict is not that between capitalists and the proletariat but rather that between the rulers and the ruled.[k] As R. J. Rummel (1976, 13, 93) puts it: "There are two *classes*: those who command and those who obey.... Positions within groups ... divide people into two classes: those who have the legitimate right to command, and those who are obligated to obey." In order to understand the foreign policies of states, therefore, rational political ambition theory focuses on the relationship between the rulers and the ruled.

The impact of that relationship on foreign policies (and on domestic politics as well) is shaped to an important extent by the size of the coalition that a political leader depends on to keep herself in power. Leaders of states such as the United States, where large winning coalitions must be held together in order to keep a leader in power, need to play two-level games that are very different from those played by leaders of states wherein small winning coalitions suffice to keep the leader in power. A leader who needs to maintain her support within a relatively large winning coalition—one-half the voting population in democracies such as the United States—cannot offer sizable private benefits, or individual payoffs, to each of the members of that coalition. She must concentrate instead on providing public goods, such as peace, or victories in wars (if they must be fought), or general economic prosperity. An autocratic leader, in contrast, needs to satisfy only a relatively small winning coalition that is typically composed of few enough members that it is possible to win or retain their support with various forms of corruption, direct payoffs in the form of government subsidies, and so on.

There is good evidence that, as a result, staying in power is easier for leaders of states with small winning coalitions. Over the past 200 years, for example, the average democratic leader

---

k. "I define class difference as between ruled and rulers. Classes ultimately form around the right of command, not private property, as for Marx" (Rummel 1977, 149).

has been in power for 3.7 years, while the average autocratic leader has stayed in power for 8.6 years. As Bueno de Mesquita (2003, 380) notes: "Autocratic leaders suffer relatively few punishments for creating famine, sickness and misery at home, or military defeat abroad. They seem relatively unconcerned with whether or not peace and prosperity are achieved." They can be thus unconcerned because neither economic misery at home nor even defeat in wars abroad will necessarily threaten their hold on power, as long as they can, in the wake of such problems, continue to provide payoffs and benefits to their relatively small winning coalitions.

Surely the size of winning coalitions is not the *only* structural feature of states that must be taken into account in order to understand the foreign policies of states, or their interactions? Milner (1997, 67) advocates viewing foreign policy processes as determined or dominated by the political executive, the legislature, and various interest groups. Bueno de Mesquita et al. (2003, 42) identify at least some of the main factors involving political forces inside the state but outside the winning coalition by focusing on interactions between the winning coalition and what they choose to refer to as the **selectorate**. The selectorate is the group of people within any political system "whose endowments include the qualities or characteristics institutionally required to choose the government's leadership and necessary for gaining access to private benefits doled out by the government's leadership."[1] The selectorate is also that set of people within a political system from whom members of the winning coalition can potentially be recruited.

This emphasis on the concept of a selectorate has attractive features. First, it provides a basis for discrimination among traditional categories of political systems, such as monarchies, autocracies, and democracies. Within the framework provided by Bueno de Mesquita et al. (2003), monarchies have small winning coalitions and small selectorates; modernizing autocracies or dictatorships have small winning coalitions but large selectorates; and democracies have both large winning coalitions and large selectorates. This pattern is especially important as a step toward recognition of fundamental differences among autocratic states. For example, the Soviet Union and Saudi Arabia were, before the demise of the former, both autocratic states, but they were obviously quite different autocratic systems. (Accordingly, on the Bueno de Mesquita et al. (2003) selectorate scale from 0 to 1, the Soviet Union receives a score of 1—meaning that is has a large selectorate, or that virtually 100 percent of its citizens are included—while Saudi Arabia is assigned a score of 0—indicating that it has a very small selectorate, including a number so small as to be not very different from 0 percent).

Furthermore, their focus on the relationship between the size of the winning coalition and the size of the selectorate allows Bueno de Mesquita et al. (2003) to arrive at some theoretically intriguing derivations from their basic framework. For example, they explain that in autocratic systems with small winning coalitions and large selectorates, members of the winning coalitions tend to be very loyal to incumbent political leaders. This loyalty originates in recognition of the high risk—defined in concrete terms by the ratio of the winning coalition to the selectorate—that a new winning coalition will exclude any given member of the current winning coalition altogether. In contrast, supporters of leaders in democratic states, where both

---

1. Writing on his own, Bueno de Mesquita (2003, 381) defines the selectorate as "the set of people in a country who have a legitimate say in the selection of government leadership and who have the possibility (however small) of becoming essential supporters of an incumbent leader."

the required winning coalition and the selectorate are large, tend to be relatively fickle. In the United States, for instance, if the incumbent government is to be replaced, the new ruling coalition must comprise 50 percent of the large selectorate, plus one vote. If the new winning coalition must be large, then any member of the current winning coalition has a fairly good chance of being included in it. In other words, if someone who voted for an incumbent Republican president becomes disaffected, he or she can easily become a member of a new winning coalition put together by the Democratic Party.

However, even though Bueno de Mesquita et al. (2003) have developed an operational measure of the size of selectorates in contemporary states, this rather precise index may hide some ambiguity in the concept. Indeed, this team of analysts acknowledge that they have borrowed the concept from Susan Shirk (1993), who created it in her analysis of the Communist regime in China. Shirk asserts that party leaders in Communist systems are chosen not by an electorate, but rather by a "selectorate," which she defines as a group within the Communist Party that has the effective power to choose leaders. In China, as well as in the Soviet Union before its demise, Shirk reports (71), "the communist party constitution grants formal authority to select party leaders to the Central Committee," and she goes on to observe that in 1987, the Chinese leader Hu Yaobang was fired by the Politburo.

In short, in Shirk's view, the "selectorate" in the Communist states of China and the Soviet Union is, or was, pretty small,[m] while in the view of Bueno de Mesquita et al. (2003), the selectorate in the Soviet Union was, and that in China is, very large—equivalent in size to that in democratic states, in fact. Obviously, determining which residents of a state have a formal or legitimate role in selecting its leadership is not a simple or straightforward matter. Thus, despite what Shirk says, Bueno de Mesquita and his colleagues conclude that the selectorate in the former Soviet Union was, like that in today's China, quite large, apparently because of the existence of universal suffrage in both states. And yet, these analysts acknowledge, the elections in those states were and are "rigged." Do such rigged elections confer a "legitimate"—or even a merely "formal"—right or role in the process leading to the selection of leaders?

R. J. Rummel (1975–1981) makes an extensive (though not widely recognized) attempt to develop a theory of interstate conflict. He divides political regimes into three categories—libertarian, authoritarian, and totalitarian—which are, in turn, based on three corresponding types of social systems—namely, exchange, authoritative, and coercive. These categories also differentiate between the autocratic systems of the Soviet Union or China, on the one hand, and that of Saudi Arabia, on the other, and they do so in a way that may be somewhat less ambiguous than the conceptualization based on determining the size of a selectorate. Still, Rummel's observation (1976, 307) that "the United States comprises a more libertarian system, but increasingly is oriented in the totalitarian direction" suggests (to this author, at any rate) that his categorization of political regimes is not free of ambiguities, either.

In the view of rational political ambition theory, the distinction between political systems with small or large winning coalitions is crucial to an understanding of the foreign policies of

---

m. Admittedly, Shirk does leave some room for interpretation on this point by acknowledging that, in both cases, the Central Committees were/are selected by party congresses. She also stipulates at one point, however, that the selectorate in China consists of 500 top party leaders; see Shirk 1993, 81.

states and their interactions. Almost as important is the issue of whether or not the political system has elections that result in the transfer of executive political power between independent political parties (Ray 1995). These two criteria distinguish in theoretically helpful ways between democratic and autocratic states. While there are different types of democratic states, as well—presidential versus parliamentary systems, for example—those distinctions are probably not, for our purpose, as significant as those between different types of autocratic systems, wherein the former Soviet Union and the current People's Republic of China exemplify the "modernizing" autocracy or dictatorship, while Saudi Arabia is perhaps the quintessential traditional autocratic system. The size of the selectorate in such states may be an indicator as precise and operational as any we now have for distinguishing between these two quite different types of autocratic systems.[n]

So, the U.S. president has a hold on power that is less secure than that of autocratic leaders in general and leads a political system in which it has been demonstrated repeatedly that elections can result in the transfer of executive power from one independent political party to another. Nevertheless, presidents do play a crucial role in the foreign policy process that may well have become more influential over the most recent decades in the history of the United States.

This is not to say that rational political ambition theory offers anything like a precise, unerring guide to which of several foreign policy options the president will make in the wide variety of contexts she may face. This shortcoming is, however, one that it shares with all other approaches to foreign policy and international politics. Realists, for example, assert that decision makers will base their decisions on the national interest, although that concept is notoriously difficult to define, either in the abstract or in regard to specific foreign policy options (Nincic 1992, 160–162). Indeed, even informed observers of foreign policy issues may conclude that every foreign policy option from unilateral, total disarmament to a preemptive, full-scale nuclear attack is in the national interest. Both realism and rational political ambition theory—and every other approach that I am aware of—are, in other words, too abstract and too general to provide specific guidance about which foreign policy options will be selected by the leading decision makers in a state like the United States.

Perhaps it may be possible to move to some greater degree of specificity, however, by borrowing a basic idea from what is known as the **poliheuristic** approach to foreign policy decision making.[o] As described by Alex Mintz (2004, 7), this approach clearly resonates with rational political ambition theory to the extent that it assumes that "policy makers are political actors whose self-interest in political survival is paramount." It also posits that foreign policy decision making typically occurs in a two-stage process. In the first stage, policymakers reject a whole set of alternatives as being too politically costly—as in posing too great a threat to their political survival, in the next presidential election in the case of the United States. In

---

n. Nevertheless, the fact that in 1999, according to the data provided by Bueno de Mesquita et al. (2003), the United States, China, and Kuwait all had selectorate scores of 1 (on a scale from 0 to 1) suggests that this particular indicator does not discriminate between types of autocratic systems, or even between democracies and autocracies as consistently or clearly as would be desirable.

o. This term alludes to the fact that foreign policy makers typically rely on many—hence the "poli"—heuristics, which are aids to learning or deciding, or "shortcuts" in the decision-making process. See Mintz 2004, 6.

the second stage, they consider the remaining alternatives according to criteria that are more rational, from the point of view of the state as a whole. In other words, having eliminated all options that seem too risky to their own individual political futures, these leaders then choose among the remaining alternatives according to each option's perceived relationship to the national interest.

Even these more specific tenets of rational political ambition theory will not, of course, generate specific or precise predictions about which foreign policy options will be selected in every situation. But they constitute, we can hope, a useful step in that direction.

CONCLUSION

The rational political ambition approach borrows from or is similar to realism in that it focuses on states as the most important entities. It differs from realism primarily in that it does not view the so-called national interest as the primary source of inspiration for foreign policies, generally speaking. Instead, it emphasizes the impact of all national leaders' desire to retain their positions of power. Rational political ambition theory shares with liberalism a belief in the centrality of domestic politics to any effort at understanding foreign policies of states or their interactions. But while liberalism takes quite a broad view of domestic political processes—dealing with the media, interest groups, and governmental bureaucracies, for example, as important sources of influence over foreign policy processes—rational political ambition theory takes all those groups and influences into account by assessing their impact on the continual effort by leaders to stay in power.

How does the rational political ambition approach relate to radicalism and other anti-establishment approaches to the analysis of foreign policy and interactions among states? One answer to that question is that it shares with those approaches a degree of skepticism about the realists' assumption that leading decision makers formulate policies with a view toward advancing the national interest. It also shares the radicals' skepticism regarding the sometimes implicit assumption made by liberals that leaders of states, or at least democratic states, have a natural or personal interest in the economic welfare of the societies or polities they lead. Instead, rational political ambition theorists believe that, when democratic leaders do take steps to improve or sustain economic growth in the societies they lead, they are acting on an instrumental rather than a fundamental aim. In other words, a growing economy—which may have little impact on the political fate of autocratic leaders—is important to leaders of democratic states because it can help to keep them in power (see Bueno de Mesquita and Root 2002).

Finally, rational political ambition theory shares with radical and anti-establishment approaches an emphasis on class conflict. Marx, of course, defined classes in terms of the ownership of property: capitalists own the major means of production, while the workers must survive by selling their labor power. For rational political ambition theory, though, class conflict focuses on the divide between the rulers and the ruled, whose different places within the structure of all political systems create clearly diverging interests. How the conflict between these opposing forces is resolved depends largely on the structure of the political system; specifically, and most importantly, the size of the winning coalitions needed to place and maintain leaders in power has a fundamental impact on relationships between the rulers and the ruled within all political systems. This conflict of interests and the structure of political systems also have crucial impacts on the policies, both domestic and foreign, that are adopted by leaders of states in their quest to establish and maintain themselves in leadership positions.

The chapters that follow will be devoted to the analysis of the foreign policies of the United States. Those chapters will refer consistently to the viewpoints of alternative approaches to the analysis of foreign policies in general and of interactions among states. In other words, our discussions of foreign policies will take into account the viewpoints of realists, liberals, and radicals, as well as current anti-establishment theoretical approaches. Most consistently, however, these chapters will analyze American foreign policies according to assumptions and guidelines provided by the rational political ambition approach.

KEY CONCEPTS

critical theory   48

dependency theorists   47

feminists   49

globalization   40

leftist   47

liberalism   42

Marxist theory   46

national interest   52

neoconservatism   44

neorealism   42

poliheuristic   56

postmodernists   49

radical   47

rational political ambition theory   50

realism   38

selectorate   54

social constructivists   49

states   39

winning coalitions   53

| RATIONAL POLITICAL AMBITION AND . . . | **LESSONS** |
| The ALTERNATIVE THEORIES OF AMERICAN FOREIGN POLICY | LEARNED |

☑ Rational political ambition theory is the author's preferred approach to the analysis of foreign politics and international politics. One central tenet of this theory is that the highest priority of political leaders is to attain and maintain their power.

☑ It shares with realism a focus on the importance of power, but emphasizes the political power of individual leaders instead of the power of states.

☑ It shares with liberalism an emphasis on the importance of domestic political processes to foreign policy making, but replaces liberalism's broader focus on groups and interests inside and outside the government with a concentration on the role of the president, and how that leader is affected by other actors and interest groups.

☑ It shares with radicalism an emphasis on "class conflict," not between capitalists and workers but rather between the rulers and the ruled.

PART 2

ECONOMICS, DOMESTIC POLITICAL PROCESSES, AND AMERICAN FOREIGN POLICY

THE UNITED STATES HAS ALMOST CERTAINLY HAD A LARGER IMPACT ON the global economy than any other state. But global economic forces are beyond the control of any single state, and those forces have had important impacts on American foreign policy as well. Part 2 examines the roles of economic issues and of domestic political factors, both outside and inside the government, as they relate to American foreign policy. The aim is to outline the general institutional background for foreign policy making before we begin to deal with the more specific issues, such as the twentieth-century contest with Communism and American foreign policies vis-à-vis the various geographic regions of the world, that will occupy the remainder of the book.

Chapter 4 focuses first on the profound impact of the lessons from the 1930s on the construction of the post–World War II global economic system, and on the role played by the United States in that reformed system. It deals with the various economic challenges and issues faced by the United States in the later decades of the twentieth century, and concludes with an analysis of the rather foreboding problems for the American economy that have emerged in the first decade of the twenty-first century.

Chapter 5 examines the impacts of public opinion and the media on American foreign policy processes, and then identifies the more important interest groups. It concludes with a review and comparison of the impacts of the two major political parties on American foreign policies.

Finally, chapter 6 focuses on the governmental agencies that are fundamental to the American foreign-policy-making process, including the State Department, the Defense Department, and the various intelligence agencies, as well as the relationship between Congress and the president when they grapple with foreign policy issues.

CHAPTER 4

ECONOMICS AND POLITICS

Globalization and American Foreign Policy

"HISTORY, ACCORDING TO KARL MARX, IS ECONOMICS IN ACTION...," remarked the historians Will and Ariel Durant (1968, 52). And, until the end of the Cold War, at any rate, Karl Marx was arguably the most influential social scientist who ever lived. Even in the post–Cold War era, Marx's ideas remain enormously influential. The basic Marxian proposition that economic processes and interests have a profound impact on political conflict and outcomes now evokes virtually unanimous assent. And the idea that economics drives politics in just about every conceivable context—from the global political system down to daily interactions in the office or even within the family—is one with obvious, powerful attraction.

The proposition that politics has a profound impact on economics is perhaps less pervasive among analysts in general, and among students of foreign policies and international politics in particular. But this notion is a useful complement to the more prevalent idea that economics determines politics, and a corrective to the rather common impression that *everything* about politics boils down to, or can be traced to its origins in, economic considerations. Joan Spero and Jeffrey Hart (2003,1) describe the relationship of these two forces from another angle: "Throughout history, governments have created international economic systems to regulate various aspects of their international economic interaction.... These systems are shaped by political factors such as the distribution of power among the players...." Thus, it is true that economic motives often explain political actions, but it is also true that political power and political goals have profound impacts on economic actions, interactions, and outcomes.

THE UNITED STATES IN THE WORLD ECONOMY: THE LESSONS OF THE 1930s

By 1900, the United States was generating nearly 25 percent of the world's manufacturing output (Kennedy 1987, 202). As Joseph Nye (2002, 36) puts it: "Before World War I and

The United States currently plays a key role in global economic processes and has had the world's largest domestic economy for at least a century. Here, a Chinese shopper considers her options at a Wal-Mart in Jinan, the capital city of Shandong Province. Wal-Mart currently has thirty-four stores with more than eighteen thousand employees in China.

again before World War II, the United States accounted for about a quarter of the world product, and it remains slightly above or below that level today." In short, the U.S. economy has been the world's largest and most productive for over one hundred years. As table 4.1 indicates, at the beginning of the twenty-first century, the economy of the United States was about three times larger than that of its closest industrialized competitor, Japan. As we will see later in this chapter, the Japanese economy has suffered serious problems in recent years, and, although China's economy is huge, its per capita income is roughly one-tenth that of the United States.

Because its economic system was so large and influential, the United States played a major role in leading the world into dire straits economically in the late 1920s and early 1930s. The U.S. stock market crash of 1929 was both an indication and an important cause of the Great Depression in the United States and beyond. And the nation's major policy response to this economic collapse was the Smoot-Hawley Tariff Act of 1930, which raised American tariffs to their highest level in history. According to Alexander DeConde (1963, 560): "Over a thousand economists had pleaded with the President not to sign the bill, pointing out that higher rates would hamper foreign exports, block collection of the war debts, invite foreign retaliation, and embitter foreign relations. The predictions proved true."

The depression brought prolonged economic pain to the United States and to every other major state in the world, and policymakers learned many important lessons from those agonizing years. Probably the most prominent lesson was that a dramatic increase in tariffs imposed by the United States produced retaliation in the form of high tariffs from its leading trading partners, a substantial decrease in trade, and prolonged economic stagnation. That dire image of the 1930s, which is accepted by most economists, is made all the more vivid by the associated idea that the economic stagnation of the depression years brought about World War II. Adolf Hitler, in other words, was a product of the Great Depression, which was, in turn, largely a product of protectionist measures adopted by the United States and other major states during the 1930s. Spero and Hart (2003, 67) spell out the lesson thus learned the hard way: "Protectionism and the disintegration of world trade in the 1930s created a common interest in an open trading order and a realization that states would have to cooperate to achieve and maintain that order."

The impact of American policy in the **tariff wars** had also been reinforced by U.S. policy choices in the area of international monetary exchange rates, which, in retrospect, were equally unfortunate. Great Britain's economic difficulties in the 1930s had driven it to abandon its commitment to the gold standard, which called for the Bank of England to sell gold in exchange for the British national currency. When the collapse of this pillar of the international gold standard led to a crisis in the form of great instability in international exchange rates, the League of Nations organized an international economic conference to devise some new system to stabilize exchange rates among the world's major currencies. President Franklin Roosevelt initially pledged to send a high-level delegation to this conference, which was scheduled for 1933. However, in response to *domestic* economic and political pressures (especially from the farm bloc), Roosevelt instead abruptly abandoned the gold standard and then deliberately reduced the foreign exchange value of the dollar. He took these actions in order to reduce the price of American commodities on international markets, which he hoped would boost American exports.

TABLE 4.1	The World's Largest National Economies	

State	2006 GDP (in $trillions)
United States	12.98
China	10.0
Japan	4.22
India	4.04
Germany	2.58

Source: U.S. Central Intelligence Agency, 2006 estimates, available at www.cia.gov/cia/publications/factbook/rankorder/2001rank.html (accessed January 29, 2007).

In retrospect—but even, one might argue, at the time—it should have been easy to predict what the response of American trading partners would be. They, too, devalued their currencies, just as they had increased their tariffs in response to the Smoot-Hawley tariffs. Competitive, **beggar-thy-neighbor devaluations** thus became a hallmark of international economic interactions in the 1930s. "The absence of a universally recognized mechanism for the convertibility of national currencies … prevented the recovery of world trade (which at the end of 1936 stood at 10 percent below its 1929 level)," explains William Keylor (1996, 134). In short, it is widely agreed that both the monetary policies and the trade policies adopted by the United States in the 1930s were disastrous.

APPLYING THE LESSONS OF THE 1930s: THE BRETTON WOODS SYSTEM

The world's political leaders gathered in Paris to put together the Treaty of Versailles, which officially ended World War I. President Woodrow Wilson attended this conference in person, becoming the first American president to visit a foreign country while in office (Keylor 1996, 72). The political leaders of the major countries of the world, and several less important ones, were determined to bring World War I to a close and to develop postwar policies to ensure that such a terrible catastrophe would never occur again. Unfortunately, their efforts failed in a way so spectacular as to be almost beyond belief. The Treaty of Versailles was signed in 1919; within twenty years, Europe was plunged into yet another world war that would prove even more destructive than the first.

Given this history, the political leaders of the victorious coalition in World War II were acutely aware of the potential importance of postwar agreements, settlements, and institutional innovations, and they particularly focused on avoiding the serious mistakes made in the aftermath of World War I. The international institutions they set up, especially those pertaining to international economic issues, clearly reflected the lessons of the 1930s.

The response of these postwar planners to the problems caused by competitive devaluations of exchange rates in the 1930s was a belief that some mechanism for dealing with relationships among the world's different national currencies would be crucial to the maintenance of stable international economic interactions in future. This concept may appear to be a minor technical matter on the surface, but, as we have seen, a common interpretation of the events of the 1930s is that the international community's inability to deal with erratic official exchange rates and competitive devaluations was a key to prolonging the economic agony of the Great Depression throughout most of the decade. In order to prevent a repetition of that agony, representatives of forty-four countries met in Bretton Woods, New Hampshire, in 1944 to create a new international economic system, which came to be called the **Bretton Woods system**.

One of the principal pillars of this new international economic order was to be a revised international monetary system. As Robert Gilpin (2001, 235) describes this new monetary system, "its fundamental principle was that exchange rates should be fixed in order to avoid the 'beggar-thy-neighbor' polices of the 1930s and the ensuing economic anarchy." Indeed, because they regarded the reliance on market mechanisms to determine international exchange rates in the 1930s as anarchic and disorderly, the participants at the Bretton Woods conference were determined to provide rational political guidance to shape the new international monetary system. They concluded, in other words, that "a fixed exchange rate was the most stable and conducive basis for trade" (Spero and Hart 2003, 14). Therefore, all the countries represented at Bretton Woods agreed to designate a specific value for their currencies in relationship to gold, and to maintain that value within a range of plus or minus 1 percent. They also pledged to preserve the convertibility of their separate currencies—that is, to make it possible for traders and investors to convert one national currency into another without great cost or uncertainty as to what exchange rates might be in place.

The organization set up to maintain this new monetary order was the International Monetary Fund (IMF). Its original function was to help its member states to maintain the official, fixed exchange rates that were assumed to be desirable. The IMF collected from its member states a pool of funds from which they could borrow if they ran into balance-of-payments problems. In other words, if market pressures should threaten to push the "real," or market, value of a member's currency below its official "pegged" value, that member state could borrow funds from the IMF to support that currency—that is, to buy it at the official pegged price. Theoretically, at least, such purchases eventually would bring the real value and the pegged value of the national currency in question into line with each other, and so the threatened member state would not have to resort to foreign exchange controls or devaluation (Keylor 1996, 265).

In the United States and elsewhere, after World War II, there was even more widespread agreement that protectionism and high tariffs had been disastrous in the 1930s than there was about the deleterious effects of disorderly exchange rates and competitive devaluations. It would be logical to conclude, then, that even more vigorous action might have been taken at Bretton Woods and beyond to prevent a repetition of that crisis of protectionism and competition in the area of tariffs. However, *domestic politics* in the United States played a key role in the process focusing on international efforts to assure **free trade**, thereby complicating that process considerably. There was, in fact, a proposal to create an International Trade

Organization (ITO) that was to be analogous to the International Monetary Fund; the charter of the organization was signed in Havana, Cuba, in 1947.

However, a series of opponents to this organization soon surfaced in the United States. Even after the sad experience of the 1930s, some powerful members of the Republican Party still feared that the proposed International Trade Organization would leave important economic interests in the United States unprotected (by tariffs). Some important proponents of free trade, meanwhile, felt that the charter for the ITO did not go far enough in the direction of lowering tariffs. Facing this atmosphere of internal dissension, the Truman administration delayed submission of the ITO charter to Congress for three years. Then, as Spero and Hart (2003, 68) explain, it "finally decided in 1950 that it would not submit the [ITO] Charter to Congress where it faced inevitable defeat. Once the United States withdrew, the charter was dead."

It seems strange—but is not at all atypical—that the solid agreement in the United States about the harmful impact of protectionism in the 1930s should be overwhelmed by domestic political pressures when it came to the fate of the ITO. In the end, however, the idea that the United States and the rest of the international community needed to do something substantial to prevent a repetition of the tariff wars of the 1930s did prevail. Although the International Trade Organization itself was killed, the Havana conference had produced procedural guidelines for dealing with issues of international trade, in the form of the General Agreement on Tariffs and Trade, or GATT.

This agreement was intended to foster free trade; its major focus was on encouraging its member states to abide by the **most-favored-nation principle**, which stipulates that "any advantage, favor, privilege, or immunity granted by any country shall be accorded immediately and unconditionally to the like product originating in or destined for the territories of all other contracting parties" (CIESIN Thematic Guides 2003). In short, although the name of this principle makes it sound as if it were aimed at extending special privileges, its purpose, in fact, is fostering nondiscrimination, or equal rather than privileged treatment. Originally it was meant to be only a paper agreement, but, following the demise of the ITO, GATT ultimately became a full-fledged organization. It was finally replaced in 1995 by the World Trade Organization (WTO), which took over GATT's functions, along with extended powers and responsibilities. The lessons of the 1930s, thus, did produce institutional innovations in the area of trade, as well as in monetary issues such as exchange rates. It just took several decades—nearly five, in fact—for the process to reach its ultimate, and perhaps logical, conclusion in the stabilization of international trade.

The other main international economic institution created at the meeting in Bretton Woods in 1944 was the International Bank for Reconstruction and Development, commonly known as the World Bank. As the formal name of the organization suggests, its original focus was on the reconstruction of states devastated by the Second World War. This organization, too, was based, to some extent, on the lessons of the 1930s, although less directly so, perhaps, than were the IMF and the ITO. The World Bank was apparently inspired, in part, by the idea that one of the lessons of the pre–World War II period was the importance of helping defeated countries to recover economically, so that they would not fall into the economic hard times that produced fascist governments not only in Germany, but in Italy and Japan as well.

The perceived original purpose of the bank was to make loans to finance reconstruction and development efforts, not so much with monies of its own, but through funds generated from the private sector with the help of guarantees that the World Bank would offer to lenders in order to lower their risks. Once the original task of funding reconstruction efforts in war-torn countries was completed, the bank began to focus instead on financing development projects in the poorer countries of the world. This evolution of the bank's mission had not been unforeseen at the time of the founding of the organization. On the contrary, the eminent British economist John Maynard Keynes, serving as an adviser to the British Treasury, specifically forecast, in a 1944 speech to the assembled delegates at Bretton Woods, that "although reconstruction would mainly occupy the bank in its early days ... it would later have another primary duty—to develop the resources and productive capacity of the world, with special attention to the less developed countries" (Porter 1944, 15).

Taken together, the IMF, GATT, and the World Bank are seen as the main pillars of the "liberal," or free-market-based, international economic order desired by the United States in the post–World War II era. In fact—from the perspective of a liberal "true believer," at any rate—these pillars represent something of a mixed bag. GATT was, in fact, focused on eliminating barriers to free-market processes and free trade. But the IMF was based specifically on the idea that it is undesirable to allow market processes to determine exchange rates for the world's different currencies; indeed, its mission was to allow political intervention to maintain stable exchange rates in the face of continual market pressures that might cause these exchange rates to fluctuate. And the World Bank was essentially a foreign-aid-dispensing organization, providing politically directed flows of capital into projects aimed at promoting economic growth and development in a manner that would likely be looked on with some skepticism by liberals. But there was no doubt, as World War II drew to a close, that the noncommunist world, at any rate, would have a new international economic system in place. As noted by Jeffrey Frieden and David A. Lake (1995, 14): "At its center were the three pillars of the Bretton Woods system ... all ... essentially designed by the United States and dependent on American support."

AMERICAN FOREIGN POLICY AND THE RESPONSIBILITIES OF THE HEGEMON

In stepping forward so vigorously to provide economic (and political) leadership in the wake of the Second World War—in distinct contrast to its more limited and unilateral approach after the First World War—the United States assumed the role of a **hegemon**, or leader in the international system. According to a prominent theoretical analysis focused originally, at least, on international economic processes, the presence of such a leader is an important prerequisite to maintaining the stability and efficiency of the global economic and political system.

Charles Kindleberger (1973, 1978) is the name most prominently associated with the basic idea of **hegemonic stability theory**—the notion that a free-trade, market-based global economic order requires a predominant and willing leader to preserve its stability.[a] Kindleberger

---

a. The term was actually coined by Robert Keohane (1980); Kindleberger (1986) himself prefers the simpler word *leadership* over *hegemony.* See also Lake 1993.

originally presented this idea as an explanation for the Great Depression, which, in his view, was largely the result of the inability of Great Britain to maintain its historic role as leader, and the unwillingness of the United States to step into that role as an alternative. Thus, the reluctance of the United States to provide vigorous leadership on economic issues in the global system was a key factor in prolonging the depression throughout the 1930s and allowing it to play a key role in producing the even greater tragedy of World War II. An obvious implication of this theory is that it was vital that the United States avoid this error the second time around, by providing the requisite hegemonic leadership after that war came to an end. The U.S. government at least acted as if it took these theoretical ideas about international economics and politics seriously.

The Bretton Woods system—based on the International Monetary Fund, GATT, and the World Bank, and launched in 1944—was impressive on paper. However, by 1947, the "Western economic system was on the verge of collapse" (Spero and Hart 2003, 15). According to Kindleberger (1973), the functions of a leader, or hegemon, in a liberal economic order include providing a "market for distress goods" and serving as a source of sufficient liquidity to keep the system afloat in times of emergency or financial panic. The United States stepped in to perform both of these functions in the late 1940s and early 1950s, launching the Marshall Plan, which provided some $17 billion in foreign aid to sixteen Western European countries. The impact of these funds was increased due to large U.S. military expenditures for the North Atlantic Treaty Organization (NATO). Perhaps most important, the United States allowed both its European and Japanese trading partners to run large balance-of-trade surpluses that resulted, in part, from discriminatory, protectionist measures against U.S. exports.

It would be reasonable to wonder why the United States would engage in what appears to be rather impressively altruistic behavior. Any analyst concerned with hegemonic stability theory would have special cause to wonder about this behavior in light of the fact that, according to Kindleberger (1973), states are "rational egoists"—primarily intent on maximizing their own welfare (see also Lake 1993, 462). The explanation for this apparent anomaly is that the actions taken by the United States in the short run were plausibly calculated to provide benefits to the United States in the long run. In other words, American political leaders anticipated that both Europe and Japan would eventually become important markets for American exports and lucrative fields for investment by American entrepreneurs. But neither Europe nor Japan would be able to offer such future economic benefits to the United States if their market economies were to collapse in the immediate aftermath of the war.

At least as important, and perhaps more so, was the fear that economic stagnation or chaos might create opportunities for Communism in either region. So, from about 1947 to the late 1950s, the United States pumped money into both Europe and Japan, and increased the impact of those monetary flows by allowing the development of substantial negative balances of trade. Arguably, this behavior—tolerating short-run costs for the sake of benefits that would emerge only after a prolonged period of time—reflected enlightened self-interest, but self-interested it certainly was.

Another function that a leader in a liberal economic order must serve, according to hegemonic stability theory, involves the need for a stable, trustworthy medium of exchange. "By 1947, it was clear that neither gold nor the pound could continue to serve as the world's money," say Spero and Hart (1993, 16), and so the United States and the dollar stepped into the breach. The dollar became the predominant reserve currency—that is, the currency most relied upon to settle international accounts. The standard established as the basis for the new international monetary order was that one ounce of gold would be equal to $35. All other currencies in the international system were to be measured against this standard, and ideally, the value of those currencies would fluctuate only marginally against it.

This standard implied that gold and the dollar were freely interchangeable. Any state possessing dollars and wanting gold could submit its dollar holdings to the U.S. government, which was committed by the norms of this international monetary order to provide the gold equivalent at the rate of $35 for each ounce of gold. Thus the United States fulfilled the basic hegemonic function for a liberal, open-market-based international economic system.

Throughout the 1950s and most of the 1960s, the new international economic order created after World War II worked pretty well, thus providing some supporting evidence for hegemonic stability theory. Europe and Japan, both ravaged by the horrors of war, recovered economically. The Soviet Union, China, and like-minded Communist states excluded themselves from this system, of course, but they were not crucial to the existence of a thriving, liberal, market-based global economy. Trade among the major free-market-oriented states grew substantially, tariffs were lowered, and there were increasing flows of investment among the richer states.

The poorer states of the world were, in many cases, achieving political independence during this period. Free trade was often denied to them, as richer countries such as the United States refused to lower their tariffs on important exports from developing countries, including agricultural products or textiles. More to the poor states' benefit, perhaps, was burgeoning competition between the United States and its allies, on the one hand, and the Communist states on the other, in the area of foreign aid. Some so-called Third World states, at least, played both ends against the middle starting in the 1950s, extracting generous amounts of assistance from one side or the other, or both. In general, however, with the United States firmly in the role of leader, the postwar liberal economic order entered the 1970s with a prosperous, stable appearance.

THE WAR IN VIETNAM AND THE END OF THE BRETTON WOODS SYSTEM

By the end of the 1950s, Western Europe and Japan were well on the way to economic recovery. That recovery had been a goal of the United States, but it was also the beginning of some major changes in the economic and political relationships between the United States and its most important allies in the Cold War. By 1960, for the first time, foreigners held dollars in amounts that exceeded the value of gold reserves held by the United States. Shortly afterward, the United States made its first commitment of troops to the war in Vietnam, which became increasingly expensive as the war expanded. According to Spero and Hart (2003, 24), "the Vietnam conflict, as well as the refusal of the Johnson administration to pay for both the war and its domestic social programs by increasing taxes, resulted in an increased dollar outflow to pay for military expenses and in rampant inflation caused by a growing budget deficit."

This analysis reflects a questionable, though quite common interpretation of important economic trends in the United States and in its relationship to the international economic system in the late 1960s. In retrospect, President Lyndon Johnson has somehow acquired a reputation as a free-spending liberal who insisted (in that typical, liberal profligate way) on having his cake and eating it, too—by simultaneously fighting a very expensive war in Vietnam *and* launching a series of elaborate social welfare programs that came to be known collectively as the Great Society. Since he reputedly insisted on doing all this without raising taxes, he is often alleged to have bequeathed to the U.S. government massive federal budget deficits.

This characterization of the Johnson presidency ultimately founders, however, as it encounters several awkward examples of contradictory evidence. For instance, when the U.S. federal government budget reported a surplus in 1998, it was the first such surplus realized since 1969; President Johnson, of course, left office in 1968, the year in which the fiscal 1969 budget was drafted. In other words, far from irresponsibly spending the U.S. government into massive budget deficits, Johnson actually left it with the last surplus to be achieved for three decades. In addition, the charge that President Johnson was unwilling to raise taxes to pay for his policies and programs simply ignores the 10 percent surcharge on the income tax that he pushed for and persuaded Congress to pass in 1968. Furthermore, Johnson had to accept painful compromises in order to get this increase: "Congress would not give him his 1968 surcharge until he agreed to cut $6 billion from non-defense programs" (Small 1999). Thus, much of what is said and written about the Johnson administration's policies, especially its fiscal policies, seems to be based more on stereotypes than on even a brief review of various key facts and figures. (Johnson's shaky reputation also reflects both the unwillingness of liberal analysts to forgive him for his Vietnam War policy, and conservative writers' visceral loathing for his ambitious social welfare programs.)

There were, of course, some economic problems related to the U.S. war in Vietnam. The war was at least partly responsible for a flood of American currency going overseas, which put increasing pressure on the value of the dollar, as the dollar holdings of foreigners increasingly outweighed the U.S. gold reserves that were, in theory, "backing" these dollars. Logically, the transference of lots of dollars overseas might seem likely to encourage an increase in American exports. But, instead—possibly because some American productive capacities were diverted to military purposes, thus necessitating the import of goods previously produced domestically—the American balance of trade became increasingly negative. That is, as the 1970s approached, Americans were importing more and exporting less. The substantial pressures created by the massive dollar holdings overseas and the growing trade imbalances contributed to the political anxieties that led to a fundamental modification of the Bretton Woods system in the early 1970s.

PRESIDENT NIXON REFORMS THE BRETTON WOODS SYSTEM

Richard Nixon won the 1968 presidential election in part because of his claim to have a "secret plan" to end the Vietnam War. In practice, his plan turned out to depend on "Vietnamizing" the war—that is, building up the South Vietnamese military to a point at which it could take on increasing and, ultimately, total responsibility for defending the South Vietnamese regime against its Communist opponents in both the southern and the northern parts of the country.

This plan certainly did not meet with immediate success. Nevertheless, by 1971, the future of the Nixon presidency seemed more threatened by economic problems than by continued frustration over the military quagmire in Vietnam. By the spring and summer of that year, "for the first time in the twentieth century, the United States showed a trade deficit" (Spero and Hart 2003, 24).[b] Perhaps the greatest source of U.S. economic vulnerability stemmed from the fact that by the summer of 1971, some $80 billion was held by foreign investors, while the U.S. stock of gold (mostly in Fort Knox) amounted to only $10 billion. Since the U.S. government was officially pledged to provide gold in return for dollars whenever dollar holders requested such an exchange, it was obviously vulnerable to pressure from those who might threaten to present large numbers of dollars for conversion to gold. (And, indeed, there were rumors at the time that France was using the threat of converting some of its dollar holdings into gold as a means of getting the United States to modify its policies with respect to the war in Vietnam.)

President Nixon, in response to this situation, tried to persuade allies such as West Germany and Japan to revalue their currencies. In other words, he wanted them to increase the value of the mark and the yen in relationship to the dollar, thus making American exports more affordable and so helping the United States to address its balance-of-trade difficulties. The United States at this juncture was in a uniquely powerful position as the hegemon of the international system—a position that, paradoxically, deprived it of options that were available to every other state in the system. Specifically, any other state faced with similar balance-of-trade difficulties could devalue its currency, thus making its exports less expensive and moving in the direction of a more favorable balance of trade. But, since the United States had accepted responsibility for maintaining the official standard (one ounce of gold = $35) against which all other currencies were measured, it alone could not devalue its currency.

Ultimately, this situation came to be seen as intolerable for the United States. Or, more precisely, it came to be seen as intolerable to the Nixon administration. On August 15, 1971, President Nixon made a dramatic announcement: the United States would no longer guarantee the convertibility of dollars and gold. In other words, from that point on, the United States would not abide by its long-standing pledge to provide an ounce of gold for every $35 that dollar holders wanted to convert. Analysts such as Joanne Gowa (1983) make it clear that this was, arguably, a rational strategy for the United States, because of its involvement in economic interaction and competition in the global economic system. It was a strategy that increased autonomy and flexibility for the United States.

But it was also yet another crucial American foreign policy decision (with global ramifications) that seems best explained by recognizing, as the rational political ambition approach does, that leaders of states place the highest priority on staying in power. This recognition does not mean that leaders are oblivious or indifferent to political and economic competition with their peers in the international system. But it certainly does imply that important foreign policy decisions, although most often explained by their authors as the result of international calculations and considerations, are consistently affected also—and often more so—by domestic

---

b. Robert Gilpin (1987, 140) asserts that this was the first trade deficit for the United States since 1893.

political concerns. In suspending the convertibility of dollars to gold, while also imposing a surcharge on imports into the United States, as well as wage-and-price controls, President Nixon was clearly intent on dealing with domestic economic problems that threatened his electoral prospects, and those of his party, in 1972.

C. Fred Bergsten (1972, 204) observed at the time that President Nixon's strategy was "a straightforward attempt to export U.S. unemployment to other countries." Even more to the point, David Calleo (1982, 3) explains that "rather than continue the recession to save the dollar, Nixon let the dollar depreciate to save his Administration." In short, this foreign policy decision, although certainly affected by calculations of competitive advantage within the global economic system, was probably influenced most heavily by the Nixon administration's concern about domestic political pressures and continuing economic problems; these might well have carried over into an election year unless something drastic was done to modify the situation.

Nixon's policy changes represented a startling deviation from the status quo, leading the major economic powers to meet at the Smithsonian Institution in Washington, D.C., to see whether some new, stable arrangements might be devised to deal with the shock. The result was the Smithsonian Agreement, which provided for a somewhat more flexible system of exchange rates. President Nixon proclaimed it "the greatest monetary agreement in the history of the world," but it lasted only a little over a year (Spero and Hart 1997, 21–22).

Nixon's decision to terminate the U.S. role as the linchpin of the Bretton Woods system for regulating exchange rates among the world's leading currencies looked like a retreat from a position of leadership. The president, in effect, was announcing that the United States henceforth would determine its economic policies by giving priority to domestic goals over the international responsibilities that it had assumed since the end of the Second World War.

THE IMPACT OF OPEC AND THE REACTION BY RONALD REAGAN

The decline of the United States from a position of economic leadership—if not downright predominance—was accentuated by another key event in the early 1970s. Partly in response to the Yom Kippur War between Israel and several of its Arab enemies (Egypt, Iraq, Syria, Jordan, and Saudi Arabia),[c] the Organization of Petroleum Exporting Countries (OPEC) managed to engineer a 400 percent increase in the price of a barrel of oil on the international market, raising it from about $3 a barrel to about $12 a barrel. As William Keylor (1996, 346) explains: "The oil embargo and the precipitous price increases exposed the industrial nations of the northern hemisphere (the United States, Canada, Western Europe and Japan) to an unprecedented type of economic warfare waged by a coalition of developing nations in the southern hemisphere."

---

c. This war, which began with an Egyptian attack on Israel, is usually perceived as predominantly a conflict between those two countries. However, while Egypt lost 5,000 soldiers in the conflict, Syria actually lost more—as many as 8,000 battle fatalities. See Small and Singer 1982, 95.

In the short run, this economic warfare was rather spectacularly successful. The increase in the price of oil threw the economies of all the major industrial powers into a kind of tailspin that lasted through most of the decade. The price of oil remained high, helping to fuel inflation. Because fuel prices play such a crucial role in the transportation industry, and because virtually all consumer goods need to be transported in order to make them available to consumers, the high price of oil and gasoline had wide reverberations throughout the international economic system. At the same time, although previous inflationary periods had been marked by relatively rapid rates of economic growth, the spiraling inflation of the 1970s was combined—unexpectedly, from a Keynesian point of view—with slow economic growth. So, as the 1970s came to an end, economists and policymakers, and even the general public, focused intense scrutiny on the phenomenon of **stagflation**, a theoretically anomalous combination of high inflation and slow economic growth.

And then, as the decade drew to a close, the situation became dramatically worse. The Iranian Revolution erupted, producing panic in the oil markets. The price of oil, having risen 400 percent in 1973, increased in 1979 by *another* 300 percent, from around $12 to $36 or more per barrel. In the United States, shortages produced by the oil embargo created long waiting lines at gas stations, the price of gasoline remained very high, interest rates soared, and inflation went even higher. This virtual epidemic of economic problems contributed significantly to the defeat of President Jimmy Carter in the election of 1980.

Ronald Reagan thus came into office amid considerable economic uncertainty. The Federal Reserve dealt with the high inflation rates in place at the beginning of the decade by repeatedly raising interest rates; this mechanism worked, and inflation was, in fact, reduced rather substantially in a reasonably short amount of time. But the American economy came to what could *not* be called a "soft landing" in 1982. It continued to suffer from a relatively high rate of unemployment and from growth so slow that the recession of that year was the worst seen in the United States since the end of World War II.

The Reagan administration, meanwhile, chose to lower taxes while raising defense expenditures dramatically. What followed were record-breaking federal budget deficits—in current dollars, Reagan's budget deficits equaled those of every previous administration in the country's history combined—and continuing high interest rates. Interest rates were kept high, in part, to attract investors to finance the huge federal budget deficits, but they also made the dollar attractive, and very strong—that is, increasingly more valuable vis-à-vis other national currencies.[d] On the surface, this effect might seem to be a good thing, but a strong currency makes a state's exports expensive, and its imports cheaper and more tempting to its own citizens. And so, during the Reagan years, the U.S. annual trade deficits also expanded rather dramatically. By the middle of the 1980s, the United States was experiencing unprecedented budget deficits, as well as trade deficits in the area of $150 billion.

Japan, in contrast, was enjoying a hugely positive balance of trade—that is, the Japanese exported much more on an annual basis than they imported, in their trade with the United States in particular. Some analysts traced this development to substantial improvements in the productivity of the Japanese economy, while productivity growth in the United States

---

d. "The dollar had appreciated approximately 60 percent between June 1980 and March 1985" (Gilpin 1987, 156).

remained lackluster. All in all, during the middle and late 1980s, the United States seemed to be losing out in international economic competition to Japan. Robert Gilpin (1987, 340), one of the most prominent academic analysts of international political economy in that era, certainly interpreted contemporary developments in that manner:

> American mismanagement of its own internal affairs and of the international financial system has caused the responsibilities of the financial hegemon to fall largely upon the Japanese.... Great Britain performed this role well in the nineteenth century and, for a time, so did the United States in the twentieth. Now it is Japan's turn at financial leadership.

THE END OF THE COLD WAR, AND AN AMERICAN REVIVAL?

Gilpin was not alone in seeing, during this period, a United States in precipitous decline. American foreign policy analyst Walter Mead (1990, 59) observed in 1990 that

> our oil production is no longer adequate for our own uses. World markets in minerals and food are glutted. Our industrial economy has lost its supremacy—it is at best, first among equals. We now owe foreigners more than Argentina, Brazil, and Mexico combined; Germany and Japan can set the value of the dollar. This is the road to Argentina.

Toward the end of the 1980s—and the timing here is especially significant in light of the events soon to unfold—such observations of American decline were not limited to the economic sphere. In a book that appeared on the *New York Times* best-seller list, offering the benefit of an exhaustive analysis of the historical background from 1500 to 2000, Paul Kennedy (1987, 515, 521) observed:

> [T]he United States now runs the risk, so familiar to historians of the rise and fall of previous Great Powers, of what might roughly be called "imperial overstretch": that is to say, decision-makers in Washington must face the awkward and enduring fact that the sum total of the United States' global interests and obligations is nowadays far larger than the country's power to defend them all simultaneously.[e]

Thus, as the 1990s approached, many observers of its politics and its economy saw the United States in deep trouble, about to relinquish the position of leadership and preeminence that it had held since the end of the Second World War. These gloomy feelings were reinforced by the advent of an economic recession in the United States in the early 1990s, which clearly played a role in bringing to power the new president, Bill Clinton. By the time Clinton assumed the presidency, of course, the Cold War had ended and the Soviet Union had fallen apart. Suddenly, the United States faced no important challenger in terms of military force. It

---

e. This pessimism was largely based on Kennedy's perception of the same economic problems that analysts such as Gilpin and Mead saw as so debilitating. In Kennedy's (1987, 529) view, "Given the worldwide array of military liabilities which the United States has assumed since 1945, its capacity to carry those burdens is obviously less than it was several decades ago, when its share of global manufacturing and GNP was much larger, its agriculture was not in crisis, its balance of payments was far healthier, the government budget was also in balance, and it was not so heavily in debt to the rest of the world."

had what was, by far, the largest, most sophisticated military force in the world, and its nation-al defense budget was considerably larger than those of all of the largest, most influential states in the world combined (see table 4.2). And most of those important states were allies, rather than even potential enemies, of the United States.

On the economic front, however, the state of affairs was not so happy. Unemployment in the United States stood at 7.6 percent. The federal budget deficit for fiscal 1992 was, in absolute terms, the largest in the nation's history, at $292 billion. Admittedly, this amount was "only" 4.7 percent of the gross national product, while the deficit resulting in part from the recession of 1982 had been closer to 6.5 percent of the GNP (DeLong 1997). Nevertheless, as the new administration took office, the American economy seemed burdened by serious problems, including a trade deficit, a recession, and a ballooning federal budget deficit, which was adding ever more to the mounting national debt.

Most of these problems were to melt away in a remarkably short period of time. Since the 1992 federal budget deficit was the largest in terms of current dollars in the nation's history, that problem was particularly worrisome. And yet, by 1997, the budget deficit was reduced to .3 percent of the GDP (see figure 4.1); it had been, in relation to the GDP, over *fifteen times* larger in 1992. And at least some of this reduction was attributable to concerted action on the part of the federal government. According to economist Brad DeLong (1997): "Of the improvement [in the federal budget deficit from 1992 to 1997], about half is due to policies enacted in the 1990 and 1993 agreements: increases in taxes, and reductions in spending—or, rather, reductions in spending growth below the growth rate of the economy." In addition, the unemployment rate in the United States had fallen from 7.6 percent in 1992 to around 5 per-cent in 1997.

In general, the U.S. economy performed very impressively in the 1990s. The GNP—albeit in current dollars, but inflation was relatively low during the 1990s—rose from $5.5 trillion to $9.3 trillion. (CIA 1992, 2000). The Dow Jones average rose from 3,301 in 1992 to 10,787 in the year 2000, while the federal budget went from a deficit of $290 billion to a surplus of $237 billion over the same period, and median family income rose from $42,428 to $48,950. Also, economic progress in the United States during this period was not confined to a narrow stratum at the higher levels of the socioeconomic system. Overall, the poverty rate in the United States decreased from 14.8 percent in 1992 to 11.3 percent in 2000; over roughly the same time period, the poverty rates for African Americans fell from 33.4 percent to 22.5 per-cent, and for Hispanics from 29.6 percent to 21.5 percent (U.S. Census Bureau 2004).

Thus, in a remarkably brief span of time, the American hegemon, or leader of the interna-tional economic system, went from a situation (around the beginning of the 1980s) in which it was seemingly under economic siege by OPEC and Japan—and also menaced on the mili-tary front by the burgeoning strength of a nuclear superpower, the Soviet Union—to a quite different situation (at the end of the twentieth century) in which oil was plentiful and very low in price (and OPEC seemingly impotent), Japan had been an economic basket case for almost a decade, and the Soviet Union had fallen apart altogether.

TABLE 4.2	Military Expenditures of the Major Powers, 1993

States	Expenditures (in $billions)
United States	297.6
China	41.7
France	37.2
Germany	36.7
United Kingdom	34.0
Russia	29.1
Japan	27.4

Sources: Singer, Bremer, and Stuckey, 1972; Bennett and Stam, 2000.

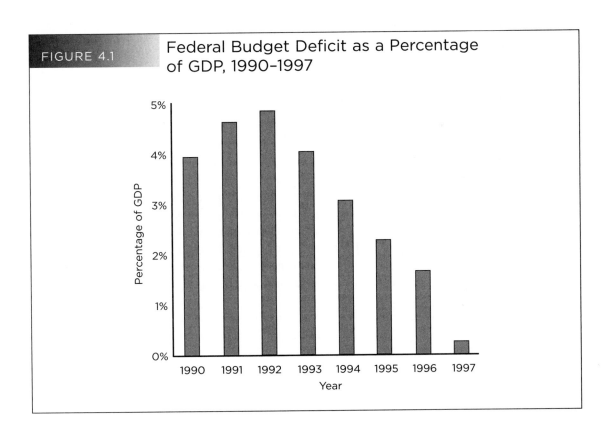

FIGURE 4.1   Federal Budget Deficit as a Percentage of GDP, 1990–1997

THE BEGINNING OF THE TWENTY-FIRST CENTURY: NEW CHALLENGES

The status of the United States as global economic hegemon at the start of the new century was nicely reflected in the debates that figured in the 2000 presidential campaign between George W. Bush and Al Gore. Both candidates offered detailed plans as to how their respective administrations would invest the trillions of dollars in federal budget surpluses that were then expected in the coming years. In fact, during the campaign, substantial budget surpluses were projected into the future "as far as the eye can see."

This optimism about the federal government's fiscal health continued after the election was over. In January 2001, the Congressional Budget Office, a nonpartisan agency, added $1 trillion to its projections, thus anticipating a surplus of $5.6 over the next ten years (Congressional Budget Office 2001). Nevertheless, in the first year of the new president's term, it was discovered that the economy was, after a record-breaking period of growth in the 1990s, in the process of slowing down. That realization, among other factors, allowed President George W. Bush to persuade Congress, in 2001, to pass a large tax cut.

And then came September 11, 2001.

It is difficult to gauge the economic effects of the terrorist attacks of that day, but, clearly, they were significant. One of the more serious involved the flow of foreign direct investment (FDI) into the United States. Prior to 2001, the United States had been for some time the world's leading recipient of foreign direct investment—a concrete indicator of the confidence that investors around the world had in the strength and stability of the American economy. The 9/11 attacks had a negative impact on outflows of foreign investment throughout most of the industrialized world; there was an overall decline of 20 percent from 2001 to 2002. But the falloff was especially dramatic in the United States, where inflows of FDI were $144 billion in 2001 but dwindled to $30.1 billion in 2002. Even these figures, which reflect a reduction of 79 percent, may well underestimate the full impact of the terrorist attacks. In the year 2000, foreign direct investment in the United States totaled $307.7 billion, so the decrease to $30.1 billion in 2002 represents a two-year decline of over *90 percent* (PPI 2003, 1).

This calculation may overstate the deleterious effects of international terrorism on confidence in the American economy; there was a broad economic slowdown in the global economy even before the attacks of 9/11, and so there would probably have been some decline in FDI into the United States between 2000 and 2002 in any case. Still, the perception that the attacks of 9/11 had something to do with the drastic decline in inflows of foreign investment into the United States seems beyond dispute. It may also be of some importance in the effort to gauge the economic standing of the United States in the world in the initial years of the new century to note that it was China that, by the year 2003, had replaced the United States as the world's largest recipient of FDI, "attracting an estimated $60 billion" (Forney 2003, 43–44). Also, in that same year, China surpassed Japan as the country with the largest trade surplus vis-à-vis the United States.

Financial and political developments also had a dramatic and damaging impact on the federal budget process in the United States. Having anticipated virtually unending budget surpluses at the beginning of the century, the Congressional Budget Office (CBO) saw those surpluses disappear a mere two or three years later. What had once seemed likely to be an endless stream of budgetary black ink came to an end in 2001, when the surplus was tagged at $127 billion. The following fiscal year showed a deficit of $158 billion, and in 2003 the shortfall reached almost $370 billion. In a breathtakingly short time (from 2001 to 2003), the CBO went from forecasting a federal budget surplus of close to $6 trillion over the next ten years to projecting a $6 trillion deficit over virtually the same ten-year period (Irons 2003).

At the same time, the global economic system's international trade regime seemed in some danger of falling apart. The Bush administration came into power at the onset of the World Trade Organization's Doha Round of trade negotiations (so named for the capital of Qatar, where the round of negotiations was initiated). This series of talks was aimed specifically at reforms that would be of particular benefit to the poor countries of the world; it was to be focused, for example, on tariffs in rich countries and on the subsidies granted to their agricultural sectors. However, at a meeting in Cancún, Mexico, in September of 2003, the WTO negotiations broke down, in large part because of disagreements about how to deal with protectionism on behalf of agricultural interests in rich countries as well as poor countries. (Poor countries, in a coalition that came to be known as the Group of 22—including Brazil, South Africa, India, and China—wanted rich countries such as the United States to reduce barriers against agricultural imports, while they retained their own barriers in order to shore up their fledgling economies.)

Another reason for the collapse of the WTO talks at Cancún had to do with the fact that the United States had in previous months deviated rather substantially from its stand in favor of the principle of free trade. In March 2002, the Bush administration imposed substantial tariffs on imports of steel—a step that fell classically in line with the idea that national leaders base foreign policy decisions primarily on the goal of preserving their own power. These tariffs were of particular importance in states where George W. Bush had won narrowly (such as Ohio) or lost narrowly (such as Pennsylvania) in the presidential election of 2000. The protectionist measures for the steel industry were quite transparently aimed at improving the president's electoral prospects in the 2004 electoral campaign. A couple of months later, the administration also increased subsidies to American farmers, under the influence of similar motives. As Jagdish Bhagwati (2004, 56), a knowledgeable observer, pointed out in reference to these measures, "the symbolism was bad: one cannot start negotiations to reduce protection and then follow immediately by raising subsidies and trade barriers."

The Bush administration's decisions to implement protectionist measures on behalf of the steel industry and agricultural interests were almost certainly not in the national interest. Instead, they benefited rather small sectors of the American economy, at substantial costs to its broader interests. Furthermore, they may have put at risk the entire global trading regime that had been built up over the decades since World War II. "The breakdown in Mexico," observed *The Economist* (2003a, 11) in the wake of the collapse of the WTO talks, "may have dealt a mortal blow to the multilateral trading system itself—a system that, for more than half a century, has underpinned global prosperity."

In short, the global trading system, post-Cancún, appears to be headed for trouble, in part because of the lack of leadership posited as necessary by hegemonic stability theory. Furthermore, it may well be difficult for the United States in upcoming years and decades to maintain its leadership role in the military sphere as well. As we have discussed, the annual budget of the U.S. government has in a shockingly short time gone from massive annual surpluses to worrisome annual deficits. This budgetary meltdown is one reason why the value of the dollar vis-à-vis other important national currencies, such as the yen and the euro, has dropped precipitously in the first years of the twenty-first century.[f]

Unfortunately, the U.S. federal budget deficits may also be headed, in a relatively short time, toward even greater and more debilitating depths. They are currently the result of slow growth and substantial military expenditures, as well as related outlays for "nation-building" in Afghanistan and Iraq. Tax cuts enacted over the first three years of the Bush administration also make some contribution to the federal government's declining revenues.

But perhaps all these sources of fiscal imbalance will ultimately be overshadowed by a looming intergenerational imbalance in the United States. (Many other industrialized countries face similar problems.) Within a few years, the first of the "baby boomers" who were born in the aftermath of World War II, will begin collecting Social Security benefits. By the year 2030, the proportion of the U.S. population in the over-65 age group will have doubled, while the proportion of the population working—and paying taxes to fund such programs benefiting primarily the elderly—will have increased by only 18 percent. The result of these demographic trends, according to a study commissioned by the U.S. Department of the Treasury, will be a $45 *trillion* deficit for the federal government in the coming decades (Gokhale and Smetters 2002).[g]

This domestic problem may well have a profound impact on the foreign policy of the United States in the not-too-distant future. "The decline and fall of America's undeclared empire," according to Niall Ferguson and Laurence J. Kotlikoff (2003, 31), "will be due not to terrorists at our gates nor to the rogue regimes that sponsor them, but to a fiscal crisis of the welfare state." In this view, the United States will soon need to withdraw from its ambitious political and military projects in such places as Bosnia, Afghanistan, and Iraq, not so much because of the "imperial overstretch" foreseen by Paul Kennedy (1987), but because of a domestic fiscal crisis. And it seems likely that if such a political retreat becomes necessary, the ability of the United States to play its current leadership role in the global economy would be called into serious question.

This potential impact of federal budget deficits on the role the United States can and will play in the world is an intriguing example in the context of rational political ambition theory. It appears that the political leaders of the United States, clearly motivated in important part by the incentive of staying in power, are currently allocating so many resources to the recipients of Social Security, Medicare, and Medicaid, that those programs will ultimately make it

---

f. For example, in late 2003, *The Economist* (2003c, 9) noted that "the total movement in the dollar-euro exchange rate has been far from tame: in July 2001 one euro bought just under 84 cents; this week it hit a new high of over $1.20. Depending on how you look at it, this is a 44 percent rise in the euro or a 31 percent fall in the dollar." In the same issue (2003e, 65), it was pointed out that the dollar that week had hit a three-year low against the yen and a five-year low against the British pound sterling; that this drop in the value of the dollar seemed likely to continue for some time; and, finally, that one major reason for this progressive decline was the escalating size of U.S. federal budget deficits.

g. Jagedeesh Gokhale is a senior economist at the Federal Reserve Bank of Cleveland; Kent Smetters is a former deputy assistant secretary of economic policy at the U.S. Treasury, and currently a professor of economics at the University of Pennsylvania.

necessary for the United States to draw back in several rather drastic ways from its position of leadership in the world. Are such decisions in the national interest, as realists would expect? Or, with respect to these particular programs, are U.S. political leaders giving priority to their own desire to stay in power over the preservation of an influential role for the United States in the international political and economic system?

It may, however, be a mistake to succumb too easily to pessimism about the ability of the United States to continue playing the role of leader in the global economic system. Although the Bush administration gave in to the temptation to implement rather severe protectionist measures at the behest of steel and agricultural interests early in 2002, once the adverse reactions to those steps had registered, "Washington turned its policy around in a remarkable fashion" (Bhagwati 2004, 56). The WTO declared in November of 2002 that U.S. tariffs on steel were illegal, and, after pondering its reaction to that ruling for some time, the Bush administration ultimately withdrew the tariffs. Perhaps the crucial factor in prompting this reversal was the fact that the WTO ruling had authorized the targets of those tariffs to retaliate. European steel exporters, in particular, demonstrated an astute awareness of the origins of the new American protectionism—they threatened tariffs on Florida oranges and on other exports from southern and western states that were vital to President Bush's electoral coalition (*The Economist* 2003d, 28).

This episode thus offers an important example of how the priority that leaders give to staying in power, especially in democratic states, can, in the end, serve the public interest. In 2002 President Bush, as we have seen, chose to sacrifice his country's broader interests by implementing tariffs that would garner him electoral support in steel-producing states such as Ohio and Pennsylvania, and by providing agricultural subsidies that would appeal to voters in farm states. But the reaction to those protectionist steps prompted loud complaints from steel-using states such as Michigan, as well as retaliation from steel producers in Europe, eventually making it clear to the Bush administration that its initial tactics on these issues would be likely to cost more than they would benefit the president's prospects in the coming election. So, primarily because of a reassessment of its self-interested concerns, the administration adopted policies that were arguably more in keeping with the national interest.

Furthermore, although the setback at Cancún in 2003 has the potential to derail the WTO and so create anarchy in the global trading system, past history indicates that such an unfortunate outcome is far from predetermined. Bhagwati (2004, 52) predicts that, on the contrary, "Cancún will serve as a stepping stone to a successful conclusion of the Doha Round of trade negotiations." As he points out, the Tokyo Round and the Uruguay Round of trade negotiations within GATT took five and seven years, respectively, to complete, while the Doha Round has been underway since 2001.

Another issue that may justify renewed optimism about the continuation of U.S. economic leadership involves the special trade negotiating authority that has intermittently been granted to the president by Congress in recent years. In response to a crisis that was perceived to have been precipitated in important part by the Smoot-Hawley Tariff Act of 1930, Congress passed in 1934 the Reciprocal Trade Agreements Act, which gave the president the power to reduce existing tariffs by 50 percent by executive agreement. This step away from protectionism was buttressed in the 1970s, when the president was given **fast track authority** to negotiate trade agreements—these agreements had to be voted up or down by Congress in a process that did not allow that body to amend such agreements. When a recalcitrant Congress refused to reauthorize this negotiating authority for President Bill Clinton, some analysts took it as another sign that the United States was succumbing to isolationism and moving toward abdication of its leadership role in the global economic system. However, the Bush administration successfully persuaded a more compliant Congress to renew the fast track authority in 2002—though under the more palatable rubric of "trade promotion."

In general, while it is easy to conjure up a plausible scenario that foresees the United States tumbling hard from its position of leadership in the global economy—to the detriment, possibly, of both the United States and the global economy as a whole—it is important to maintain a sense of perspective on that possibility. In the 1970s, when the United States was losing its war in Vietnam, was under siege from OPEC, and was being victimized by stagflation as well as by sky-high interest rates toward the end of the decade, it seemed logical to predict that the United States was losing its grip. And, as we have seen, such a scenario became even more plausible in the 1980s, when the United States experienced its worst recession in the post–World War II era, as well as skyrocketing trade deficits, spiraling federal budget deficits, and an apparently permanent loss of economic virtuosity to the rising state of Japan.

Yet the 1990s saw the United States enjoying what was, perhaps, the fastest, longest-lasting period of economic growth in its history. At the very least, the U.S. economy was again doing well enough that it no longer seemed likely to most observers that Japan was on the verge of becoming the leader of the global economy in the twenty-first century. The United States does not look nearly so economically impregnable in the first decade of the new century as it did during the last decade of the old one, but it may yet be too soon to conclude that it is destined for the "dust bin of history" in economic, political, or military terms.

CONCLUSION

Economic factors have profound impacts on political processes, but political processes likewise have important effects on economic developments. The United States has been the largest, most productive economy in the world since at least the beginning of the twentieth century, and, as such, it has long had vital impacts on the operation and fate of the global economic system. The U.S. stock market crash of 1929 reverberated around the world, arguably for the next ten years. The Great Depression was reinforced and prolonged in important part by the American reaction to the economic slowdown evoked by that financial crash. When U.S. leaders raised tariffs to record levels, abandoned the gold standard, and intentionally reduced the international exchange rate of the dollar, these strategies predictably provoked retaliation in-kind from the other major states in the system, to the detriment of them all.

In the period following World War II, the United States, like most other major states in the world, was determined to avoid the mistakes of the 1930s. It therefore led the way in the process that resulted in creation of the International Monetary Fund, the International Bank for Reconstruction and Development, and the General Agreement on Tariffs and Trade. And all of those institutions seemed to work pretty well, until the 1970s. Then, primarily, it seems, for domestic political reasons, but also because the United States then encountered its first balance-of-trade deficit in the twentieth century, the Nixon administration abruptly terminated the system of currency management based on the principle that $35 was redeemable for one ounce of gold. Since that time, the values of different national currencies have fluctuated mostly according to market processes (in which governments intervene, on occasion, but with less effect, probably, as time goes on, while the volume of currency trading in the international market increases dramatically every year).

The economic problems faced by the United States in the 1970s seemed to worsen in the early 1980s, as the nation suffered through successive, and massive, federal budget and trade deficits. By the end of that turbulent decade, knowledgeable observers predicted that Japan was destined to become the new economic leader of the global financial, trading, and investment system. But then the Cold War ended, Japan went into an economic tailspin, and oil once again became plentiful. The U.S. economy in the 1990s grew at a record pace, and for a record-setting period of time. Federal budget deficits disappeared, the Dow Jones average soared from 3,000 to 10,000 and upward, and the rate of poverty in the United States fell substantially.

But economic growth in the United States slowed in the first year of the new century, and then the terrorist attacks of September 2001 brought on more serious economic setbacks. The Bush administration's ambitious foreign policy, involving wars and nation-building in Afghanistan and Iraq, increased pressure on the federal budget, which began again to experience serious deficits in 2003 and beyond. Domestic political and economic commitments involving social welfare programs for the elderly now seem destined to put severe strain on the resources available to the federal government for decades to come. Both the capacity of the United States to deal with these domestic priorities and its ability to continue to fulfill the responsibilities of the leader of the global economic system are in doubt. But the United States has dealt with stiff challenges to its position of economic leadership in the recent past, so perhaps it is not inevitable that it will fail to cope with its current set of problems.

KEY CONCEPTS

beggar-thy-neighbor devaluations   65
Bretton Woods system   66
fast track authority   81
free trade   66
hegemon   68

hegemonic stability theory   68
most-favored-nation principle   67
stagflation   74
tariff wars   64

RATIONAL POLITICAL AMBITION AND . . .
The POLITICAL ECONOMY OF AMERICAN FOREIGN POLICY

☑ The United States became desperate in the 1930s to escape the deprivations of the Great Depression. It adopted policies, such as high tariffs and low official exchange rates, that were based in part on calculations about how best to deal with international competitors and pressures. But such strategies (adopted by all industrialized countries) also were driven by the desire of political leaders to stay in power. These competitive, counterproductive policies had a profound impact on interstate politics and economics in the 1930s.

☑ In the early 1970s, President Nixon felt that the United States needed more flexibility to deal with international economic challenges. He ended the convertibility of dollars to gold (at the rate of $35 an ounce) and imposed wage and price controls. Although aimed ostensibly at international economic pressures, these policies also were motivated by President Nixon's desire to win reelection in 1972.

☑ Federal programs, such as Social Security, Medicare, and Medicaid, are destined to accumulate massive deficits in the next few decades as the elderly portion of the population who collects benefits expands much more rapidly than the younger generation who pays taxes to support the federal programs. Vigorous responses are necessary to prevent disastrous federal budget deficits and a skyrocketing national debt. Political leaders in the United States are obviously reluctant to adopt such measures because they would pose an immediate threat to their continuation in power. Crushing deficits and national debt ultimately may require less ambitious and expensive American foreign policies and lead to reduced American power and influence in the international system.

CHAPTER **5**

THE IMPACT OF EXTRA-GOVERNMENTAL FACTORS ON AMERICAN FOREIGN POLICY

Public Opinion, the Mass Media, Interest Groups, and Political Parties

IN THIS CHAPTER AND THE NEXT, WE WILL FOCUS ON THE PROCESSES leading to the formation and the execution of American foreign policies. Here, we deal with inputs to these processes from the people at large and from various groups operating outside the government. After first exploring questions about the relevance and consistency of public opinion in general as an influence on American foreign policy, we will assess the impact of the mass media and the roles played by various interest groups and by the major political parties in shaping foreign policy processes. Having thus clarified the effects that actors outside the government can have on foreign policy decision making, we will move on, in the next chapter, to examine the roles played by actors inside the government, including governmental agencies, Congress, and the president.

PUBLIC OPINION: SHOULD IT HAVE AN IMPACT ON FOREIGN POLICY?

Before we consider the question of whether **public opinion** actually *does* have an impact on American foreign policy, we should ask what is in some ways a related and prior question: whether or not public opinion *should* have an impact on foreign policy. Certainly one of the alleged virtues of democracies is that governmental policies reflect the wishes and priorities of their constituents. At least as important, democratic governments are supposed to be particularly attentive to the needs and desires of the relatively large coalition from which they must retain support in order to stay in power. This concept of accountability to a broad swath of the citizenry is an important reason that democracies can be expected to deliver policy outputs that better serve the needs of the general population than do those of autocratic systems whose governments can focus instead on providing bribes and corrupt services for the relatively small

Congressional leaders as well as the president are influenced by public opinion as they deal with U.S. foreign policy issues, even as they also devote considerable effort to shaping public opinion on those issues. This is because it is through elections that the general public and specific interest groups can have an impact on the ability of political officials to stay in power. Here, House Speaker Nancy Pelosi, House Majority Whip James Clyburn, Senate Majority Leader Harry Reid, and Senate Majority Whip Richard Durbin speak to the press about a meeting they have just concluded with President George W. Bush in April 2007.

coalitions on which they depend to remain in power.[a] In short, if the foreign policies of the U.S. government fail to reflect the opinions of the American public, that would seem to be a violation of the democratic principles to which it is ostensibly devoted.

But should those policies reflect public opinion to a substantial extent if it turns out that the general public typically does not know, or care, very much about foreign policy issues or international politics? In fact, the evidence that the average U.S. citizen is typically uninformed about foreign policy issues is voluminous and basically undisputable. For example, one survey in 1998 found that while 50 percent of the general public felt that amounts allocated by the federal government to foreign aid ought to be cut back, in the sample of leaders from government, academic institutions, and the media, only 18 percent believed that such cutbacks would be wise. Gaps of that size were also found in similar surveys conducted in 1994, 1990, and 1974 (Page and Barabas 2000, 349).

In principle, it is, of course, possible that the opinions of the general public on this issue are well-founded, and perhaps even more prudent than those of the political experts surveyed. But that argument is difficult to sustain in light of the persistent evidence that most of the general public believe that the U.S. government spends huge proportions of the federal budget on foreign aid every year. As Martin Gilens (2001, 381–382) reports, in 1998 "foreign aid of all kinds amounted to eight-tenths of one percent of the federal budget," yet a survey of a representative sample of respondents in the United States found that only 17 percent of them guessed correctly that the proportion of the federal budget allocated that year to foreign aid was less than 5 percent.[b]

How much of the mammoth budget of the U.S. government is spent on foreign aid annually is, however, a relatively obscure issue, and so it is perhaps not surprising that most Americans are not well-informed about it. However, in advance of the U.S. invasion of Iraq in 2003, whether or not there was any connection between Iraq's Saddam Hussein and al-Qaeda in general, or between Saddam and the terrorist attacks of September 11, 2001, in particular, were hardly obscure issues. Nevertheless, surveys conducted in early 2003 found that the majority of American citizens believed that the Iraqi leader had played an important role in the attacks of 9/11, although it had been reported that "the U.S. intelligence community has said that there is no evidence to support the view that Iraq was directly involved in September 11" (Kull 2003). And, after the invasion, about half the respondents in one survey believed that the United States had found evidence that Iraq and al-Qaeda were working closely together.

Furthermore, surveys showed that substantial portions of Americans believed, even after the initial stage of the war was over, that U.S. forces had found "weapons of mass destruction" in Iraq, and even that Iraq had used such weapons during the war. Polls also found that many Americans believed that most citizens in most other countries supported the U.S. war against Iraq, when, in fact, "in polls conducted throughout the world before and during the war, a

---

a. "Because polities such as democracies rely on relatively large winning coalitions, they must provide more public goods than those that depend on small winning coalitions" (Bueno de Mesquita et al. 2003, 101). See also Lake and Baum 2001.

b. The source cited by Gilens is the U.S. Bureau of the Census 1998, 339, 796.

very clear majority of world public opinion opposed the U.S. going to war with Iraq without UN approval" (Kull 2003).

Evidence of this kind, as well as surveys throughout recent decades showing that most American citizens have difficulty finding various states on a map of the world, or determining whether the United States is supporting the government or the rebels in some Central American country; that many people believed during the Cold War that the Soviet Union was a member of NATO; and that most respondents did not know which ethnic groups the United States was supporting in Yugoslavia—all reinforce the "traditional scholarly consensus ... that the mass public is woefully ignorant about ... foreign affairs" (Baum 2002, 91; see also Delli Carpini and Keeter 1996). How should a proponent of democracy respond to such evidence?

One possible response to the average voter's apparent ignorance about foreign policy issues is to argue that even in a democracy elected leaders may legitimately disregard public opinion when making decisions on these issues. The eighteenth-century British political thinker and statesman Edmund Burke is perhaps most famously associated with this view of the duties of elected representatives in a democracy. Burke (1774) believed that public opinion deserved respect—the opinion of constituents, he declared, "is a weighty and respectable opinion, which a Representative ought always rejoice to hear." And yet, "if the local Constituent should have an Interest, or should form an hasty Opinion, evidently opposite to the real good for the rest of the Community, the Member from that place ought to be as far, as any other, from any endeavor to give it Effect." In other words, in Burke's view, what a democratically elected representative owes to his or her constituents is not voting in legislative assemblies to reflect their wishes and the opinions, but voting according to his or her own reasoning and good judgment about what is best for the nation as a whole. Thus, if representatives in a democracy typically pay little attention to the opinions of the majority of typically uninformed voters on foreign policy issues, that fact does not necessarily make the political system undemocratic.

However, it is not certain that public opinion on foreign policy issues is always uninformed and imprudent, nor is it clear that political leaders in Congress or in the executive branch always ignore public opinion. Just because individual citizens may not know or care very much about foreign policy issues does not necessarily mean that, in the aggregate, the public comes to the wrong conclusions about foreign policy matters. Mary and John Doe may not be knowledgeable about a given foreign policy issue, but their opinions may be affected by what they can learn from better informed friends, or from various experts they may read in the newspapers or see on television (Zaller 1992).

Since average citizens in massive numbers can come to reasonable conclusions based on cues from better informed public opinion leaders, it is possible, somewhat paradoxically, that the sum of the opinions of individual citizens, most of whom are not well versed on an issue, may nevertheless be prudent when they decide *in the aggregate* what positions to take on that issue. And, in fact, survey evidence about citizens' positions on foreign policy issues—as opposed to what they know about this issue or that historical event or the location of Zimbabwe on a map—suggests that the public on average responds to historical events and political issues in a manner that can plausibly be described as "rational." That, at least, is the conclusion reached by political scientists Benjamin Page and Robert Shapiro, in their book entitled *The Rational Public: Fifty Years of Trends in Americans' Policy Preferences* (1992).

WHAT DOES THE PUBLIC WANT?

If, then, public opinion does with some consistency respond in a reasoned and even apparently well-informed manner to foreign policy issues, a supporter of democracy is entitled to hope that it does, in fact, have an impact on foreign policy. In one sense, it is fairly obvious that public opinion influences policy on a consistent basis, in that the opinions of specific subsets of the population often shape American foreign policy on certain issues. There is little doubt, for example, that Jewish Americans, in lobbying groups such as the American Israel Public Affairs Committee (AIPAC), have an impact on U.S. foreign policy with respect to Israel, as is reflected in numerous votes in Congress over many years on issues important to Israel. Similarly, Cuban exiles living in Florida have brought pressure to bear on the policies that the United States adopts with respect to Fidel Castro's Cuba. We will discuss the influence of such special interest groups later in this chapter; here we are more interested in the potential impact of what might be termed "mass public opinion," or the preferences of the majority of Americans, on foreign policy decision makers.

One important difficulty in assessing the impact of mass public opinion has to do with the direction of the causal arrow, as it were. It is fairly easy to demonstrate that foreign policies and the shape and drift of majority opinion on foreign policy issues tend to mirror one another. But correlation does not prove causation, and in this case it may be that public opinion is, in fact, shaped less by the independent preferences of individual citizens than by the efforts of policymakers to educate them, so to speak, to support policies that these leaders want to put into effect regardless of the public's original opinions. There is, moreover, a related difficulty having to do with the fact that virtually every time a foreign policy decision appears to reflect the opinions of a majority of Americans, one or more influential special interest group will also have been urging the adoption of that same policy, rendering it perhaps impossible to say whether the majority opinion had any significant impact over and above that of the more deeply involved, better informed, and more narrowly focused interest group.

So, what does the American public generally want with respect to American foreign policy? In general, Americans expect their political leaders to deliver peace and prosperity. These are, of course, very general goals; even assuming that the leaders intend to be responsive to public opinion, these goals do not provide much by way of specific guidance as to which policies they ought to pursue. Some believe, for example, that peace is best achieved by being well prepared to fight a war, and that therefore the best policies for achieving peace emphasize military strength and large defense budgets. Others believe that conciliation, compromise, and confidence-building measures are the best road to peace, which can best be achieved by reductions in armaments as well as in defense budgets.

Furthermore, while peace is clearly a foreign policy issue, the strength of the economy and the rate of economic growth are only partially related to relationships between the United States and other countries. And, usually, voters are more concerned about such domestic issues than about foreign policy issues. One recent study shows that survey respondents who feel that the president is doing a good job in dealing with the economy are about thirteen times more likely to approve of the president's performance overall than are those who feel that the president is not dealing with the economy in a competent fashion, while respondents who feel that the president's foreign policies are admirable are only about three times more likely to approve of the president's performance overall than are those who disapprove of the president's foreign policies (Soroka 2003, 36). Thus, when the economy is doing well, presidents probably have more leeway in the extent to which they can ignore, or at least pay less deference to, public opinion on foreign policy issues. In other words, as long as the economy is growing, the president may feel more free to pursue foreign policy goals regarding which the majority of the public is dubious, because he can count on the performance of the economy to preserve his popularity with the electorate overall.

While it is safe to assume that the public in general will always prefer an economy that is growing to one that is stagnant or depressed, one classic study from decades ago found that, with respect to foreign policy issues, the American public is "moody." Indeed, Gabriel Almond (1960) argued that public opinion on foreign policy issues is quite volatile and lacking in coherence, and he went to conclude that, for these reasons, it rarely has any sustained impact on foreign policies.

More recent research typically suggests that the general public is more consistent (and influential) than Almond believed. One important study in the 1990s, for example, contends that the mass public tends to fall with impressive regularity into four main categories with respect to foreign policy beliefs. A basic division involves the difference between **isolationists**, who believe that the United States should avoid foreign involvements of almost every kind, and **internationalists**, who feel that it is important for the nation to regularly play an active role on the stage of world affairs. But the members of both these groups tend themselves to divide roughly into opposing camps comprised of **hawks**, or **hard-liners**, who support an aggressive, militant foreign policy, and **doves**, or **accommodationists**, who believe that the foreign policy of the United States should focus more consistently on cooperation, conciliation, and compromise. Internationalists consistently favor an active and assertive foreign policy, whether aggressive or conciliatory. In contrast, isolationists, be they hawks or doves, tend to oppose any foreign policy initiative that draws the United States more deeply into the world's problems.

Accommodationists tend to agree with internationalists on the importance of consistent U.S. involvement in foreign affairs, but they want its interventions and foreign involvements to emphasize cooperation over confrontation; they part company with the internationalists, in other words, if the United States is active but also aggressive, or resorts to military force. Finally, hard-liners tend to share the commitment of internationalists to an active, assertive American foreign policy, but they prefer that those actions emphasize military, or at least very forceful, alternatives; they part company with internationalists on foreign involvements that emphasize compromise and cooperation. Eugene Wittkopf (1990, 1994) reports that about 25 percent of American survey respondents fell into each of these categories on a consistent basis between 1974 and 1994.

PUBLIC OPINION ON U.S. MILITARY ACTIONS

It was the Vietnam War that provoked much of the research, including Wittkopf's, that disagrees with Almond's depiction of a diffuse, unstable quality in public opinion and a negligible impact on foreign policy (Holsti 1992). The rekindling of interest in the nexus between public opinion and foreign policy in the wake of that conflict in Southeast Asia was almost certainly a result, to some extent, of the general impression that public opinion had had an important impact on the U.S. government's conduct of the war. The American public in general was quite supportive of the war in its early stages, which may well account for the hugely increased resources that President Johnson committed to the conflict once he had won the 1964 election. By 1968, however, public opinion had turned so decisively against the war that he felt compelled, apparently, to relinquish the presidency without running for the second full term for which he was constitutionally eligible. (See figure 5.1 on the growing proportion of Gallup poll respondents who concluded, as the war evolved, that it was a mistake.)

But the conclusion that public opinion had a significant impact on U.S. policy with respect to the war in Vietnam may not be warranted, even though it did perhaps play a large role in driving from office the president who had been the main architect of that policy in its initial stages. In a careful study of the impact of public opinion on policy decisions during the Vietnam War, Richard Sobel (2001) assesses the role the American public played in determining the choices made not only by President Johnson, but also by Secretary of State Dean Rusk, Secretary of Defense Robert McNamara, and close presidential adviser and, later, Secretary of Defense Clark Clifford. Sobel's conclusion is that public opinion did not have much impact on the decisions made by any of these men, but for different reasons. In his view, Johnson and Rusk were both realists, who made decisions based on geopolitical *realpolitik* criteria.[c] McNamara and Clifford, in contrast, were not much affected by public opinion because they had been skeptical about the prudence of the war from the very beginning (Sobel 2001, 78–79).[d]

Still, is it not obvious that public opinion had a dramatic impact on U.S. policy in Vietnam, since it drove President Johnson from office? Not necessarily. While it probably played an important role in persuading Lyndon Johnson not to run for reelection, public opinion also—mobilized as it was for the election of 1968—brought Richard Nixon into office to replace him. And the new president certainly did not step in to quickly terminate the unpopular war. On the contrary, Nixon took longer (from January 1969 to January 1973, or forty-nine months) to terminate direct U.S. military involvement in Vietnam—a war that had already been under way for at least three years before he came into office—than it had taken for the United States to get into and out of World War II (wherein U.S. involvement began in December 1941 and was over by August 1945, a period of forty-five months.)

Furthermore, although President Nixon, possibly in response to public opinion, did take some steps toward ending U.S. involvement in Vietnam, such as withdrawing some American troops and turning over an ever-larger share of the fighting to Vietnamese soldiers—a process referred to at the time as "Vietnamization" of the war—he also escalated the fighting in important ways. In April of 1970, for example, he launched an attack on Cambodia. As a result of

---

c. To an important extent, I would disagree. In fact, as I argue later in this chapter, President Johnson's decisions were in fact based very much on public opinion—that is, on what he assumed public opinion would be in the wake of a lost war in Vietnam.

d. In a manner that is paradoxical if not downright contradictory, however, Sobel also argues (2001, 77) that "Clifford maintains that Johnson was very sensitive to public opinion. He attributes the change in Johnson's policy on the war to the change in the public's attitude on the war."

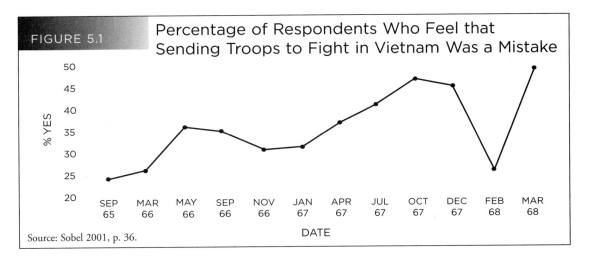

FIGURE 5.1 — Percentage of Respondents Who Feel that Sending Troops to Fight in Vietnam Was a Mistake

Source: Sobel 2001, p. 36.

Nixon's "second-phase" escalation from 1970 until 1973, in fact, "the number of casualties was higher on both sides, and the destruction of Vietnam and Cambodia by far exceeded anything under the former administration" (Sobel 2001, 97–98).

Finally, it must be noted that, having adopted this escalatory policy in apparent disregard of predominant public opinion—which signaled, by steadily increasing majorities starting in 1969, that the war in Vietnam was a mistake (see figure 5.1)—President Nixon went on to win reelection in a landslide victory over a vocal critic of the war, George McGovern, in 1972. Perhaps the public was not so enamored of peace after all?

The Rally Round the Flag Effect

That suspicion might well be heightened by what is known as the **rally round the flag effect**. President Kennedy noticed, for instance, that his public approval ratings increased substantially after the Bay of Pigs incident, even though that invasion of Cuba, organized by the Central Intelligence Agency and dependent on Cuban exiles as the invading force, turned into a complete debacle. In the wake of such events, analysts of public opinion on foreign policy have commented on the people's instinctive tendency to "rally round the flag," so that crises in general tend to increase support of the president and his foreign policy (Mueller 1973). The public, it seems, will support almost any forceful, even military, action that a president undertakes, at least in the immediate aftermath of the intervention.

But recent research suggests that there are limitations to the rally effect—that the president cannot expect to create a strong and lasting increase in his public opinion approval ratings by initiating a military conflict somewhere in the world. In fact, Bradley Lian and John R. Oneal (1993) analyzed 102 cases in which public opinion might have been expected to back up the president's action, and found that the rally effect in all of those cases averaged 0 percent. Bruce Jentleson (1992; also Jentleson and Britton 1998) has argued that since the end of the Vietnam War, whether or not public opinion will support a military intervention initiated by the president actually depends on the principal policy objective. If the intervention is aimed primarily at bringing about changes in the regime that is its target, the public's support is likely to be tenuous at best. Such support is much more likely, according to Jentleson, if the intervention is aimed at encouraging foreign policy restraint on the part of a regime that has engaged in aggressive, anti-American actions.

Thus, the American public is, in Jentleson's phrase, "pretty prudent" in its evaluations of presidential uses of military force, at least in the post–Vietnam era. Oneal, Lian, and James Joyner Jr. (1996), however, modify Jentleson's argument rather fundamentally by analyzing thirty-eight major uses of force by the United States in the period from 1950 to 1988. They, too, report that public opinion is much more likely to be supportive of military interventions aimed at curbing or restraining aggression than of those aimed at regime change. But they find that this tendency also existed before—not just after—the traumatic U.S. experience in Vietnam.

Whether or not U.S. presidents can count on a rally effect if they elect to initiate military force, one of the most venerable ideas in the literature on international politics is that leaders of states are likely to manufacture foreign policy crises, and even to initiate foreign military conflicts, in order to divert attention from domestic problems and bolster support for their regimes on the home front. T. Clifton Morgan and Christopher J. Anderson (1999, 800) suggest, in fact, that "nearly every war in the past two centuries has been attributed by some scholar to state leaders' desire to improve their domestic standing."[e] Some version of this idea becomes part of the popular discourse on American politics whenever the United States becomes involved in a foreign policy crisis, especially if a military intervention or military conflict is involved.

And, indeed, Bruce Russett (1990) reports that U.S. presidents are more likely to resort to military force during times of high unemployment. Benjamin Fordham (1998b), too, finds that high unemployment in the United States is likely to lead to a "motivated bias" in U.S. presidents, heightening their perceptions of threats abroad and making them more likely to resort to force. Morgan and Kenneth N. Bickers (1992) argue that presidents are more likely to fall prey to the temptation to use foreign conflict to bolster domestic support when they are threatened with a loss of support from their own political party or coalition.

But analysts such as James Meernik and Peter Waterman (1996, 573) contend that "few if any relationships are likely to be found between presidential popularity ... economic conditions ... and the use of force." They conclude that there is "little evidence of any kind of link between domestic political conditions in the United States and uses of force or international crises." Several others have offered reasons why this might be the case. Both Alistair Smith (1996, 1998) and David H. Clark (2003) argue that strategic interaction between the United States and its potential adversaries makes it very difficult to discern simple patterns such as a greater propensity for U.S. presidents to use force when unemployment is high. "The strategic approach," says Clark (1034) "claims that foreign states seek to avoid becoming scapegoats when, based on domestic conditions, they believe themselves to be vulnerable. As a result, opportunities should be most scarce when the need to use force is greatest, and opportunities should be most plentiful when they are needed least."

---

e. In support of this assertion, Morgan and Anderson cite Levy 1989.

In other words, U.S. presidents may be more inclined to use force abroad when unemployment is relatively high, in order to distract attention from their economic performance, but they are likely to find that those are the very times when opportunities to use force abroad are most difficult to come across, because potential foreign opponents will maintain low profiles when they suspect that a president is, in fact, "itching for a fight." What Clark and others find, in fact, is that different conditions are more likely to evoke aggressive military actions from presidents depending on whether they are members of the Democratic or the Republican Party. (We will discuss this potential impact of the political party later in this chapter.)

The Impact of *Anticipated* Public Reactions

Finally, public opinion may have its greatest impact on U.S. foreign policy because of the president's concern about how the populace will *probably* react to failed foreign policies, such as a loss in an interstate war. Public opinion in democracies, the United States included, is not predictably or dependably "dovish" or pacifistic in its preferences; in fact, as we have seen, at the initial stages of crises and even wars, it can be very supportive of military initiatives.

However, according to rational political ambition theory, political leaders' highest priority when making foreign policy decisions is to retain their hold on power. As discussed in chapter 3, the leaders of democracies cannot hope to distribute enough private goods, or bribes, corruption, and such, to buy off their large winning coalitions, as autocratic leaders can do with their relatively small winning coalitions. Therefore, leaders in democratic states necessarily concentrate on the provision of public goods, such as success in wars. Indeed, they are particularly likely to lose power when they lose wars (Bueno de Mesquita and Siverson 1995). Therefore, the president is typically quite cautious about initiating wars that the United States might lose. No political leader of any state wants to lose a war, but, as Bueno de Mesquita et al. (2003, 237) point out, the leaders of nondemocratic states face less risk in case of defeat on the battlefield: "Of course, autocrats prefer winning to losing, but their political (and personal) survival is primarily a function of satisfying their small band of supporters with private goods rather than providing their citizens with successful policies."

The role of public opinion in making democratic leaders such as the U.S. president particularly cautious when it comes to initiating military conflict is quite clear. A president may well be aware of the rally round the flag effect and so may reasonably expect that public opinion will rally to his support at the *initial* stages of a military conflict. But he will, quite likely, be equally able to calculate that the public will turn against him if he should start a war and lose it. In fact, he can expect the public to turn to opposition in the case of any lost war, whether initiated by the United States or not.

It is reasonable to argue that the war in Vietnam is the only interstate war that the United States has lost. And surely enough, one president (Lyndon Johnson) seems to have been driven from office when he failed to win it within a substantial period of time (1965–1968), while the Republican Party lost the White House, which it had held since 1968, in the wake of the American withdrawal from Vietnam in 1975. (Admittedly, the Republicans lost the 1976 election for lots of other reasons, chief among them, perhaps, the Watergate scandal that had forced President Nixon to resign well before his second term was completed.) Of course, U.S.

presidents do not have many examples of lost wars with which to gauge the impact of such defeats on the reelection prospects of the presidents who experience them. But the probability that a substantial proportion of the public will turn against an incumbent president who is apparently responsible for losing a war is so obvious that it does require copious empirical data to substantiate it. U.S. presidents and their close political supporters and advisers cannot fail to be cognizant of the probable impact of an unsuccessful war on their political fate.

For example, when Nixon won the presidential election of 1968, he had to be aware of how intensely unpopular the war in Vietnam had become. As we have seen in figure 5.1 (p. 93), by the time Nixon took office, over 50 percent of respondents in a survey said that the United States had made a mistake in sending troops to Vietnam. The new president might, understandably, have concluded that the way to ensure his hold on office was to remove the troops from Vietnam as soon as their transportation home could be arranged. Instead, as Sobel (2001, 96) reports: "Nixon calculated that the public would not tolerate a military defeat in Vietnam, and that his own reelection prospects depended in part on ending the war on honorable terms." Thus, although he started to bring American troops home from Vietnam soon after he took office, President Nixon simultaneously escalated the war by initiating an attack against Vietnamese military units in Cambodia and by stepping up bombing raids on North Vietnam. By the next election, in 1972, the war in Vietnam had not been won, but it hadn't been lost either, and so it was still possible to hope that it would be brought to a successful conclusion. Sobel comments (96): "By voting for Nixon in 1972 rather than the peace candidate George McGovern, the American public confirmed the Nixon administration's reading of its preferences." In other words, when President Nixon anticipated that, even as unpopular as the war in Vietnam had become, in the minds of most voters, prolonging the war would be preferable to losing it, he was apparently correct.

In chapter 9, we will discuss the difficulties that the United States and its European allies faced in dealing with the disintegration of Yugoslavia in the 1990s. At this point, however, let us note President Clinton's response when asked how he thought the U.S. intervention in Bosnia might affect the 1996 presidential election:

> If you look at recent American history, the evidence is that the success of the Bosnia operation may not have much to do with the election in 1996, but the failure of the Bosnia operation or the sustaining of significant casualties could have a great deal to do with it in a negative way.... The conventional political wisdom is " ... there's no upside and tons of downside." (Sobel 2001, 218)

This view of the impact of public opinion on foreign policy, especially on military interventions, is congruent with rational political ambition theory. Leaders in general—and presidents of the United States in particular—want to stay in power. Military interventions and wars are very risky for leaders of democratic states, who must recognize that, although public opinion can be swayed, often quite easily, to support a military intervention or even the initiation of a war, it will certainly turn against a president who becomes involved in an intervention or war that turns out badly. To repeat, it is the leader's *anticipation* of this reaction to failed or problematic military initiatives that gives public opinion its most profound, consistent impact on U.S. foreign policy, according to rational political ambition theory.

President George W. Bush's experience with the war in Iraq (which we will discuss in greater detail in chapter 13) serves to illustrate several points in this discussion. First, in the wake of the terrorist attacks of 9/11—and consistent with the rally effect that can be antici-pated in the aftermath of such disasters—Bush received the largest single boost in public approval ratings ever recorded for a U.S. president in such surveys. Whereas a Gallup poll con-ducted between September 7 and September 10, 2001, had shown that 51 percent of survey respondents approved of the way in which President Bush was handling his job, by September 15, that rating had skyrocketed to 86 percent. And, by September 22, it was 90 percent—the highest public approval rating recorded for any president in the history of the Gallup polling organization (PollingReport.com 2005b).

Second, Bush also received solid public support in the early stages of his war against Iraq, which began in March 2003. As figure 5.2 shows, fully 75 percent of respondents in an ABC/*Washington Post* poll in April 2003 approved of the manner in which the president was handling the "situation in Iraq" (PollingReport.com 2005a). But, as that same figure shows, by April of the following year, the proportion of survey respondents approving of Bush's han-dling of the conflict had fallen precipitously, to 45 percent.

Surveys taken during the course of the U.S. intervention in Iraq also show that while only 23 percent of Americans believed that it was a mistake for the United States to send troops into Iraq at the beginning of the war, that figure had more than doubled, to 52 percent, by early 2005. As reflected in figure 5.1 (p. 93), when President Johnson felt called upon to announce, in March of 1968, that he would not run for reelection, the proportion of Americans then convinced that sending troops to fight in Vietnam had been a mistake was 49 percent—several points lower than the percentage of Americans who felt in 2005 that it had been a mistake to invade Iraq.

Finally, public opinion polls taken in early 2005 indicated that President Bush's overall public approval rating was lower near the beginning of his second term than the early-second-term rating for any two-term president in the post–World War II era (NPR 2005).

Such poll results indicate, first, that Americans are likely to support the president initially during crises, military interventions, or wars, but that such support is almost certainly going to wane over time. They may also support the judgment of analysts who argue, as mentioned earlier, that the American public is "pretty prudent" when it comes to evaluating interventions abroad by U.S. military forces. Recall that authors such as Bruce Jentleson (1992), as well as John Oneal, Brad Lian, and James Joyner (1996), cite polling evidence to suggest that Americans are more likely to provide sustained support for American military interventions aimed at deterring or punishing aggressive anti-American behavior than they are to support the use of U.S. troops to bring about regime change in foreign countries.

At the beginning of the war in Iraq, the Bush administration's professed war aim was admit-tedly regime change, but it was justified as necessary because the regime of Saddam Hussein had allegedly developed weapons of mass destruction. Thus, the war could easily be construed, at least at first, as a necessary effort to punish and deter the aggressive behavior of developing nuclear weapons that might someday be utilized against the United States or its allies. But when it became obvious that Saddam was not in possession of nuclear weapons—or any other weapons of mass destruction, at least that anyone could find—the venture instead became focused, according to the Bush administration, on regime change for the sake of regime change, with the hope of evoking more widespread democratization around the Middle East. The deterioration in American public support for the war in Iraq between 2003 and 2005,

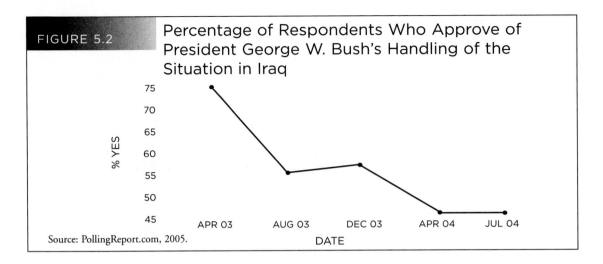

FIGURE 5.2 — Percentage of Respondents Who Approve of President George W. Bush's Handling of the Situation in Iraq

Source: PollingReport.com, 2005.

therefore, may be largely attributable to the shifting focus of official depictions of the main aims of the war.

The evolving American war in Iraq may also exemplify another important point about the impact of public opinion on foreign policy that is congruent with rational political ambition theory. Bueno de Mesquita et al. (2003, 242) argue that "leaders with large winning coalitions typically try hard during conflict, dedicating additional resources to the war effort...." By early 2005, the U.S. government had devoted well over $200 billion to the war in Iraq, whereas the GNP of the entire state of Iraq was only $60 billion in 2002, the year before the United States initiated its war against Saddam Hussein.[f] These figures indicate pretty clearly that the U.S. government—and, in particular, the administration of President George W. Bush—was "trying hard" to assure a successful outcome for its military intervention in Iraq. One important reason for that extraordinarily expensive effort surely had to do with the adverse public reaction, and likely political consequences for the Republican Party, that the Bush administration could anticipate in case the venture should end badly.

MASS COMMUNICATIONS MEDIA AND FOREIGN POLICY

Communications media have had a substantial impact on the American foreign-policy-making process ever since newspapers began to be published in significant numbers in the late nineteenth century. The media play at least three important roles in that process. First, they create, or mold, public opinion: "Without news media coverage, there is little chance that a given event will arouse public awareness or political action" (Powlick and Katz 1998, 39). Second, by selecting stories and events to cover, and by reporting polling results and providing outlets for citizens to express their viewpoints, they communicate to government officials what public opinion is on the various issues of the day, informing those officials about what the public wants and which issues it considers most important. Finally, the media serve as a

---

f. Iraq's military expenditures in 2002 were $1.3 billion; see Central Intelligence Agency 2003.

tool that the government can use to communicate to the public about foreign policy issues, to persuade the public and important, influential elements within it that its policy choices are prudent, and to argue that their impacts are beneficial. Let us discuss each of these roles in turn.

Creating Public Opinion

The American public becomes aware of important events in foreign countries and learns about foreign policy issues by hearing them discussed on television and radio or reading about them in newspapers and magazines. In the early years of the Republic, newspapers dominated the process; there were some two hundred newspapers in existence in the United States when Thomas Jefferson was president. Their ability to spread the news in a rapid and comprehensive fashion received a tremendous boost when Samuel Morse invented the telegraph in 1844. Newspapers became the most important customers for telegraph companies, and specialized wire services such as the Associated Press came into being in 1846 to facilitate the dissemination of news reports. American newspapers came of age during the Civil War, and the second half of the nineteenth century was a period of tremendous growth. Whereas, in 1860, there were 3,000 newspapers in the United States, by 1880, there were 7,000 (Stephens 1994).

As the twentieth century dawned, the battle for readership among such early newspaper moguls as Joseph Pulitzer and William Randolph Hearst became so vigorous that each cut the price of his paper to a penny. Hearst, in particular, because of a series of inflammatory stories published in his newspaper, was credited with having fomented the Spanish-American War in 1898. Newspapers remained the dominant source of news for Americans for the first half of the twentieth century, although the invention of radio in the 1920s gave them some competition.

However, in the age of television that dawned after World War II, newspapers have dramatically decreased in number, and their once-pervasive influence has waned. By the early 1990s, only thirty-seven cities in the United States still had separately owned, competing newspapers. Although, in the nineteenth century, the United States had more newspapers than any other country in the world, by the 1980s one study showed that it had fallen to nineteenth in per capita circulation of newspapers (Stephens 1994). Indeed, according to the World Association of Newspapers (2004a), "between 1940 and 1990, newspaper circulation in America dropped from one newspaper for every two adults to one for every three adults."

One of the main reasons for this decline—and almost certainly, the most important one—is the popularity of television. In fact, most Americans, at the end of the twentieth century, at any rate, depended on television as their main source of news. According to Philip Powlick and Andrew Katz (1998, 39): "In recent years, 69 percent of Americans have reported that they use television as a major source of news information, followed by 43 percent for newspapers, 15 percent for radio, and 4 percent for magazines. Moreover, Americans appear to trust television news far more than other sources of information; newspapers run a distant second."

There are, of course, hundreds of newspapers in the United States, and, now, hundreds of TV channels offering hundreds of programs every week. But it is clear that, especially with respect to news about foreign policy issues and events in foreign countries, a very few of these media outlets are able to serve as "gatekeepers." That is, these elite news organizations decide which events will be covered, because they are among the few that maintain the expensive networks of reporters and communications necessary to gather news in countries throughout the world. The *New York Times* is probably the most important source of such news in the United States—although both *USA Today* and the *Wall Street Journal* have larger daily circulations (see World Association of Newspapers 2004b)—along with the *Washington Post,* the *Chicago Tribune,* and the *Los Angeles Times,* and the predominance of these print media sources is matched on television by ABC News, CBS News, NBC News, and CNN, recently joined by the Fox News Network (Powlick and Katz 1998). [g]

In recent years, the extent to which these few outlets dominate discourse and discussion about foreign policy issues has been diluted. Matthew A. Baum (2002, 91) argues that "due to selective political coverage by entertainment-oriented, soft news media, many otherwise politically inattentive individuals are exposed to information about high-profile political issues, most prominently foreign policy crises, as an incidental by-product of seeking entertainment." He provides persuasive evidence, based on surveys, that a significant number of Americans now pick up what they know about foreign policy crises by watching such TV programs as *60 Minutes* and *20/20,* as well as those hosted by such luminaries as Jay Leno, David Letterman, and Oprah Winfrey. The Pew Research Center reported in 2004 that at least as many young people in the 19-to-26 age bracket learn what they know about news stories from Jon Stewart's *The Daily Show* as from the major networks' nightly news broadcasts (CNN.com 2004b). And, of course, opinions on foreign policy issues are often to be found on the Internet weblogs, or "blogs," that have cropped up in great numbers in recent years—such as those posted by a Tufts University political science professor, Daniel W. Drezner (www.danieldrezner.com/blog/), by Andrew Sullivan (www.andrewsullivan.com/), and by Glenn Reynolds (www.instapundit.com/).

So, what impact do these diverse forms of mass media have on public opinion about foreign affairs and foreign policy issues? Some observers claim that the media, overall, betray a distinct liberal bias, portraying liberal causes, candidates, and policies as enlightened and beneficial, while denigrating the conservative values and policies to which they are overwhelmingly opposed. Others argue that the mass media display a distinctly conservative bias, and that they strive to keep the masses in the dark about all the negative impacts of conservative policies and conservative lawmakers. Also, as Tim Groeling and Samuel Kernell (1998) point out, U.S. presidents almost invariably feel that the press is unfair to them. In fact, "nearly everyone agrees that the media is [*sic*] biased—they just disagree on the direction of this bias" (Dalton, Beck, and Huckfeldt 1998, 124).

Conservatives tend to believe that the *New York Times,* for example, is part of an East Coast media establishment whose news coverage has a distinctly liberal slant. Liberals, on the other hand, feel that its coverage, especially of economic policy issues, tends to be biased toward the concerns of the middle and upper classes. In fact, the *Times* has not supported a Republican Party candidate for president since the days of Dwight D. Eisenhower; in other words, it has endorsed John Kennedy, Lyndon Johnson, Hubert Humphrey, George McGovern, Jimmy Carter, Walter Mondale, Michael Dukakis, Bill Clinton, Al Gore, and John Kerry.

---

g. Fox News has a much smaller staff, especially in foreign countries, than does CNN; see Farhi 2003.

Moreover, as studies periodically report, "while most … journalists, like many Americans, describe themselves as 'moderate,' a far higher number are 'liberal' than in the general population" (E&P Staff 2004).[h] On the other hand, all the major media outlets are owned by large, wealthy corporations, and it is safe to bet that the heads of most of those corporations are not liberals (Winter 1997). It is also safe to bet that perceptions of bias by individual observers are predictably a function of the points of view and the ideologies of those observers. A survey of journalists in 2004, for example, found that "views of how the press treated President Bush break down along partisan lines. More than two out of three liberals feel the press has not been tough enough on Bush, while half the conservatives feel the media has been too tough" (E&P Staff 2004).

I, for one, will tell you, without fear of contradiction, that every last media outlet in the United States of America is biased. There is not a single newspaper, or TV station, or radio station (or Web site or blog) that is "totally objective," or even effectively neutral. How can I know that? Because in order for any news source or any human being to be totally objective, he, she, or it would have to have access to all of the information necessary to determine the "truth" about every issue. And yet every human being's—and every news organization's—access to the flood of information about every political issue is selective, and inescapably partial. The range of information that all political observers absorb, process, and utilize in order to arrive at political conclusions is affected by their environment, the households in which they grew up, the schools they attended, the part of the country in which they live, how old they are, how intelligent they are, and other factors that are too numerous to mention or even to be aware of. Having access to only a limited sample of the information available about political issues, no observers can avoid making decisions that are biased—that is, affected fundamentally by that slice of the available information upon which they choose to focus, and perhaps even more by the massive amounts of data and information that they choose to ignore. Only an omniscient God, in other words, can arrive at truly objective conclusions about political issues, and if such a one is editing a newspaper or owns a television network in the United States, he is well-disguised.

Nevertheless, is it not true that the dominant mass communications media—the *New York Times,* the major television networks, and CNN—are significantly biased in a liberal (or a conservative) direction? Who could answer such a question? Perceptions of bias are almost always a function of political biases and disagreements. It is a rare observer who detects bias in a source with which he or she agrees most of the time. Any observer capable of objectively determining whether the most important media outlets in the United States are biased would have to be, him- or herself, unbiased. To repeat, there are no such observers.

There is, of course, some consensus about which media sources are more liberal or conservative than others. Almost all observers would agree that the *New York Times* is more liberal than the *Chicago Tribune,* and that Fox News is more consistently conservative than CNN. So, why is it not possible to specify whether the major U.S. media outlets are predominantly liberal or conservative, or, in other words, whether they are biased in a liberal or a conservative

---

h. These results are based on a survey conducted by the Pew Research Center focused on 547 media professionals from newspapers, TV, and radio.

direction? One reason is that it is easier to discern where any two entities might be with respect to each other on the continuum from conservative to liberal than to specify where the center of ideological gravity is for the rather lengthy list of elite media outlets in the United States.

Another reason for the ambiguity of media bias is that it is not always the case that the truth lies in the middle of an ideological spectrum, or somehow midway between those taking extreme positions on political issues. If I could establish that the dominant mass media in the United States were in fact "middle of the road"—falling near the middle of an ideological spectrum encompassing the views of all American citizens—would that prove that they are unbiased? Allow me to answer that question with another, even more rhetorical one. If a historian wrote an account of the relationship between the Nazis and the Jews during World War II that was equally sympathetic to both parties, could one accurately describe that account as unbiased, or, in other words, "fair and balanced"? During the era when monarchs ruled by "divine right," advocates of democracy were considered extremists, just as, early in the nineteenth century in the United States, the abolitionists who wanted slavery to be terminated immediately were certainly outside the mainstream in the debate on that issue. Would it be accurate to conclude that these democrats and abolitionists were biased, unbalanced, or unfair? On similar grounds, I would ask, who is to say that Fox News—or, for that matter, National Public Radio, or Dan Rather, or Jon Stewart—is *not* fair and balanced?

The CNN Effect?

While it may not be clear that the mass media (at least try to) push public opinion in either a conservative or a liberal direction, journalists in print, on the air, or online are probably more effective in calling the attention of the public to some issues, while leaving it unaware of and uninvolved in others. Decades ago, in a classic study of the impact of print media on foreign policy, Bernard C. Cohen (1963, 14) argued that the press "may not be successful much of the time in telling people what to think, but it is stunningly successful in telling its readers what to think about." By the early 1990s, at least, some foreign policy analysts became convinced that the news media, especially television, had become so pervasive and persuasive that it had the ability to *create* crises by making decisions about what to cover (and what not to mention).

In perhaps the most prominent example cited in this debate, television newscasts in the early 1990s frequently featured pictures of starving people, especially children, in Somalia. According to some accounts, these nightly broadcasts moved the George H.W. Bush administration to undertake an American military mission to Somalia, mostly for humanitarian reasons, to ensure that international food aid would get to the people who needed it in that unfortunate country. In the end, however, the mission went badly, and President Bill Clinton was eventually forced to withdraw American forces under rather humiliating circumstances in 1994. (We will discuss these events in more detail in chapter 11.) In the aftermath of this failed intervention, critics charged that the videotaped images of starving masses in Somalia, especially those broadcast on CNN, had enticed the U.S. government into a foreign policy venture that it would have otherwise avoided. The alleged ability of the news media to motivate the U.S. government to engage in foreign policy initiatives of this kind came to be known as the **CNN effect**.

To be sure, not everyone felt that the CNN effect was (or is) a bad thing. As Piers Robinson (1999, 303) notes, some analysts, as well as advocates of humanitarian causes, "applauded the role played by non-state actors in expanding the policy debate beyond the narrow corridors of political power" and "praised the new activism and sought to harness the perceived potential of the media to encourage humanitarian intervention" (see, for example, Girardet 1995; Rotberg and Weiss 1996). In contrast, realists, who tended to regard the intervention in Somalia as an ill-advised venture, devoid of any important connection to the national interest, argued that elites should have more effective control of the foreign-policy-making process than any CNN effect would allow (Robinson 1999, 302).

Television, in particular, can have an important impact on foreign policy. Governments have long been obsessed with media coverage of wars, for example, probably for good reason. Televised coverage of the war in Vietnam almost certainly played a role, over time, in encouraging more Americans to question the justification for that war, and to press for withdrawal of American troops. Again, however, it is important to remember that public opinion may have driven Lyndon Johnson from office, but it then supported his successor, Richard Nixon, who continued the war and even expanded it for years afterward. Also, a case can be made that public opinion in the early 1970s was decisive in leading Congress to cut off funds from the effort to save South Vietnam, at a time when that effort was crucial to its survival.

It is also important to realize, however, that the government of the United States—like other states' governments—is not a helpless pawn at the mercy of the mass media. In fact, the U.S. government devotes a lot of time, money, and effort to "managing" the news, by generating media coverage that is favorable and designed to increase support for its actions in general, and for its foreign policies in particular. Having carefully analyzed the process leading to the 1990s news stories about Somalia, Steven Livingston and Todd Eachus (1995) conclude that media coverage of that situation actually was prompted by government officials who thus utilized the media to bring attention to an issue they wanted to raise to a higher priority in government circles. More generally, in a book suggestively entitled *Manufacturing Consent,* Noam Chomsky and Edward Hermann (1988) argue that, in general, the government and media elites work together to manipulate news coverage so as to produce the necessary public support for the foreign policy priorities upon which they have decided without any independent input from the public.

Chomsky and Hermann also exemplify a thread of media criticism that relies in large part on what the media do *not* talk about, in order to make the case that the media are actually tools used by the government to manipulate public opinion. On the one hand, it is certainly possible to argue on logical grounds that the media could have, and almost certainly do have on occasion, a profound impact on American foreign policies not because of what stories they broadcast or publish, but because of the potential issues that they ignore for one reason or another. On the other hand, it is also important to recognize that there is, quite naturally, a vast range of topics to which the media rarely pays any attention. And this tremendous wealth of material that is regularly ignored by the media makes it likely that some "evidence" can be found to support an equally wide array of allegations by those who suspect that the mass media exert an unfortunate or nefarious impact on American foreign policy.

So, which impression is more accurate? Are the communications media an environmental factor that lies outside government control, pushing and pulling policymakers willy-nilly in one direction and then another with regard to foreign policy priorities? Or do the media serve as a tool to be utilized by governmental (and/or economic) elites to prod and shape public opinion in ways that best suit their purposes? Paradoxically, these incompatible images may both have elements of truth, as Robinson (1999) points out. In his view, when the government has formulated definitive policies upon which there is a strong consensus within government circles (especially at the top of those circles), the president and officials at the State Department and the Pentagon, for example, are able to exert a lot of influence over the various media outlets and can often utilize them successfully to generate support for those policies. When, on the other hand, issues arise on which the government has no settled policy, lacks interest, or has been surprised by problems with no obvious solutions, the media can, more or less free of manipulation by the government, play a decisive role in influencing the American foreign-policy-making process.

INTEREST GROUPS AND FOREIGN POLICY

U.S. presidents and other politicians pay close attention to public opinion, because staying in power ultimately means winning elections, which requires attracting broad support from the U.S. public. Politicians are also concerned about the mass media, because it is from the media that citizens learn about their activities and pick up most of the information on which their votes are based. But politicians also must heed the concerns of specific sets of people within the general public, usually referred to as **interest groups**, or **special interests**. Running for office is massively expensive, and many of these interest groups provide significant amounts of the necessary funding in the form of campaign contributions. They also participate in elections in other ways—by promoting "get out the vote" campaigns among their members, or producing supportive advertisements to be published or broadcast to the wider public. Interest groups are also important sources of information for political leaders. They let politicians know about the priorities of the people they represent, and they provide data and other information that political leaders can utilize to defend their positions in public debates on political issues.

Interest groups and special interests often are deeply involved in the foreign-policy-making process, thus giving rise to a controversy that is analogous to the dispute about the role of public opinion in that process. From the optimistic point of view, interest groups provide valid inputs from legitimate sources that, in the aggregate, have a healthy impact on the democratic process. The various groups oppose or ally with one another, compromises are worked out, and, in the end, the interests of the nation as a whole are well-served. From a more pessimistic—or, perhaps, more realistic?—point of view, the idea that competition among the various special interest groups in society produces outcomes that are balanced, rational, and beneficial for the country seems naïve. For not all groups are represented by effective and efficient political organizations. A noted analyst of American politics described this problem decades ago:

> Broadly, the pressure system has an upper-class bias. There is overwhelming evidence that participation in voluntary organizations is related to upper social and economic status; the rate of participation is much higher in the upper strata than it is elsewhere. (Schattschneider 1960, 32)

Business Interests

The segment of the upper class that is widely assumed to be the most influential special interest consists of the capitalists involved in the corporate business world. Indeed, Karl Marx and Friedrich Engels (1848) recognized the political dominance of this emerging interest group in the middle of the nineteenth century:

> The bourgeoisie has at last, since the establishment of Modern Industry and of the world market, conquered for itself, in the modern representative state, exclusive political sway. The executive of the modern state is but a committee for managing the common affairs of the whole bourgeoisie.

Since the end of the Cold War dealt a devastating blow to world Communism, most of the classic Marxist ideas seem to be on a path to obscurity previously trod by such concepts as the divine right of kings. Still, many critics of U.S. foreign policy were convinced that the American war in Vietnam, for example, was motivated primarily by a desire to make the world safe for capitalism, while, even more recently, it is apparent that many observers, including some academic specialists, feel that both of the U.S. wars against Iraq in the past two decades are best explained by the need of its capitalist economy for oil.

Such **economistic explanations** of U.S. foreign policy remain popular, despite the end of the Cold War, and despite the sparsity in the United States of true adherents to Marxism in the general public, and even in academic circles. One reason is that the basic assumption that people in general are fundamentally motivated by their economic interests is as characteristic of the classical economic theories of Adam Smith as of the radical economics that traces it roots to Marx. Indeed, these two influential thinkers started out with at least some similar premises; they just came to very different conclusions. And the correspondence of their initial assumptions helps to explain why—even in an age in which Smith's market-oriented ideas generally seem to be in ascendance, while the socialist ideology of Marx is on the wane—the economic motives of important players in the foreign-policy-making establishment receive a lot of attention.

Then, too, important elements in the George W. Bush administration reinforce this tendency to attribute primacy to economic incentives and to suspect the influence of American business on U.S. foreign policy initiatives. Vice President Dick Cheney served as chief executive officer for the oil services and construction firm Halliburton from 1995 until 2000, when he decided to join the Bush ticket. During his service at Halliburton, that firm enjoyed a booming business in contracts with the U.S. government—a lucrative connection that was reinvigorated after the terrorist attacks of September 11, 2001.

Then, even before the United States invaded Iraq in 2003, the Army Corps of Engineers secretly awarded to Kellogg, Brown and Root (a Halliburton subsidiary) a no-bid contract to fight anticipated oil-well fires in Iraq and to make other repairs that might be required to revive Iraq's oil industry. Another contract awarded to KBR gave it a prominent role in running Iraq's oil-drilling facilities and in the distribution of its oil. According to Michael Renner (2003, 3), "the secret deal was apparently struck as early as November 2002—at a time when the administration insisted that no decision had yet been made to go to war." And, a memo issued by the Minority Staff of the Committee on Government Reform in the U.S. House of Representatives (2003, 2) hinted at the suspect nature of the transaction: " … normally, federal contracting rules require public notice and full and open competition. But the U.S. Army Corps of Engineers awarded the contract secretly and without any competition.... The fact that the Corps would issue such a large contract without competition is highly unusual."

It is true that by this time, Cheney was no longer an employee of the Halliburton Corporation. But he obviously retained close personal and professional ties with many of its highest officials, and he continued to receive annual deferred compensation from the company until 2005. Therefore, circumstantial evidence suggests that, in the case of Iraq in 2003, certain business interests had a powerful advocate close to the center of power when decisions were made about how to deal with Saddam Hussein, and that, in the end, those business interests benefited enormously from the decisions that were made. Coincidence? ("I think not," a radical or leftist analyst would surely conclude.)

Business interests also have an obvious impact on foreign policy with respect to more mundane matters than peace or war. By 1998, imports of steel had reached an all-time high, capturing over 30 percent of the U.S. market. Steel producers pressed President Clinton for relief in the form of tariff protection, but, as Robert A. Blecker (2005, 259) notes, "Clinton was a lame-duck president, so reelection did not concern him." Between 1999 and 2002, thirty-one steel companies went bankrupt, and employment in the U.S. steel industry declined from 168,000 to 124,000; by 2002, political pressure on the new president to provide relief to the steel industry was intense. Nevertheless, all of President Bush's primary economic and foreign policy advisers—the secretaries of state, commerce, and the Treasury, as well as the budget director and the chairman of the Council of Economic Advisers—all advised against raising tariffs on the import of foreign steel.

But the president's leading political adviser, Karl Rove, was in favor of the tariffs, and for a reason that was quite clear: the steel industry was extremely important in several states that would be crucial both to President Bush's chances for reelection and to the Republican Party's prospects for winning control of both houses of Congress in the midterm elections of 2002. So, although virtually all of the president's economic and foreign policy advisers warned that raising tariffs on imported steel was not in the national interest, Rove advised that doing so would be beneficial in such key states as Michigan, Ohio, and Pennsylvania. In March of 2002, therefore, President Bush took the action best designed to keep himself in power: he raised tariffs on steel (Blecker 2005, 251).

Countries affected by the tariffs objected to the World Trade Organization (WTO), and in July 2003, the WTO pronounced the tariffs illegal; the United States appealed that decision but lost. In the meantime, as many U.S. steel *consumers* were faced with the increased costs of foreign steel, they began to complain loudly. As Mike Allen and Jonathan Weisman (2003) reported: "A study backed by steel-using companies concluded that by the end of last year, higher steel prices had cost the country about 200,000 manufacturing jobs.... Small machine-tool and metal stamping shops say they have been decimated by steel costs that rose ... by as much as 30 percent." Moreover, the tariffs did not attract the support of the United Steelworkers of America (even though several labor unions had originally supported the tariffs), and "thousands of small businessmen who run steel-consuming industries were antagonized." In December 2003, the Bush administration terminated the tariffs—months ahead of schedule.

This steel tariffs episode is illustrative of several basic principles about "pressure groups." First, such groups are most likely to have an impact if they can credibly threaten the electoral prospects of the president and/or members of Congress. Second, it is not always the largest organizations, with the most members, that can most effectively pose such a threat. In fact, larger groups in pursuit of collective goals have a severe handicap: their large size means that one member's failure to contribute to the acquisition of the collective goal is unlikely to make a difference in the fate of the effort to attain that goal. Then, too, such groups are often not in a position to deny the benefits of attaining the goal to any members of the group who did not contribute to the group effort. In the case of the issue of steel tariffs, the group of people and organizations benefiting from cheap steel imports was much larger than the group who would profit from the cutoff of imports caused by the tariffs. However, the group favoring protection was not only smaller and better organized, but it had more to gain, or lose, than the typical steel consumer. And, as I have explained (Ray 1998, 94), "because the group is small, if one member of the group refuses to contribute to the group effort, he or she is easily identifiable and may be subject to penalties imposed by the rest of the group" (see also Olson 1968, 33–36).

Generally, in the case of tariffs, the benefits of **protectionism** are concentrated among a relatively small number of people, while the costs are spread out among groups that are so large and so diffuse that many of their members may not even be able to perceive them (Griswold 1999). It is this general structural fact that supports the current system of tariffs, which costs the average family in the United States some $1,600 a year. In the aggregate, American consumers pay higher costs totaling many billions of dollars annually because of tariffs imposed by their government, and they sustain the loss of additional billions because opportunities to export goods are eliminated by the tariffs that other countries adopt in retaliation (Office of U.S. Trade Representative 2002).

Thus, President Bush, when faced with urgent calls from relatively small numbers of people for tariffs on steel, might well have realized that the people benefiting from cheap imported steel were a lot more numerous than those who would benefit from steel tariffs. But those benefiting from cheaper steel imports, such as car buyers, for example, might pay $500 or even $1,000 more for a car after the imposition of tariffs, while, in the absence of tariffs, some steel companies might go out of business altogether, and many steelworkers would lose their jobs. The smaller number of people whose lives would be impacted so much more severely would be more likely to base their votes on the tariff issue than would the members of the larger, more diffuse group, who might not care enough to let the issue affect their decisions on Election Day. In this particular case, however, once the benefits of cheap steel imports were eliminated, and the higher costs of foreign steel began to be felt, the large group of tariff opponents became energized, and the looming threat of their disaffection apparently persuaded President Bush that the time had come to eliminate the tariffs he had so recently imposed.

As for business interests such as Halliburton, it would be naïve to conclude that they can have no impact at all on decisions such as the one leading to war with Iraq in 2003. But several factors should be kept in mind when gauging the magnitude of that impact. First, the U.S. government had had a close working relationship with the Halliburton Corporation long before Dick Cheney became vice-president. Halliburton had carried out several government-sponsored projects during World War II and during the first Persian Gulf War in the early 1990s. During the Clinton administration, the government had issued a no-bid contract to its subsidiary, Kellogg, Brown & Root, to continue work resulting from the wars in Yugoslavia.

Moreover, Halliburton's contracts with respect to the second Iraq war were not all the result of no-bid contracts. In 2001, in open competition, it secured an arrangement under what is known as the Logistics Civil Augmentation Program, or LOGCAP, which is a long-term, rather open-ended contract obligating the company in question to provide logistical services when and where they may be needed. LOGCAP had been awarded to a different corporation, DynCorp, in 1997 (Brooks 2003; Chatterjee 2003).

U.S. business is not a monolithic entity. Contracts awarded to one firm are necessarily denied to another. Contracts awarded by the U.S. government to Halliburton or to its subsidiary cannot be awarded to some other corporation, such as DynCorp. Perhaps Halliburton did exert some influence in favor of the U.S. war in Iraq, in part or wholly because it saw that it could profit enormously from such a conflict. But other business interests would have urged the Bush administration to pursue a militarily assertive policy elsewhere in the world, while still others would have preferred that war be avoided altogether.

Ethnic Groups, NGOs, and Intellectuals

Ethnic groups in the United States are often apparently successful in their attempts to influence American foreign policy both because they are small—and so have a low proportion of the **free riders** who are tempted to let somebody else do it—and because they care deeply about issues regarding which most other Americans are only tangentially interested at best. The classically effective group here is Jewish Americans, who are represented most prominently by the American Israel Public Affairs Committee (AIPAC). This organization has some 100,000 members throughout the fifty states, and its influence is legendary: *Fortune* magazine consistently ranks it as one of the most effective interest groups in the country, and it claims to play a crucial role in persuading Congress to pass more than one hundred pro-Israel legislative initiatives every year (AIPAC 2005).

AIPAC's influence is so legendary that it may, in fact, be exaggerated. It is, undoubtedly, effective, and there is a temptation in some circles to attribute its political leverage to the "fact" that Jews predominate in American banking and media circles—a perception that typically reflects some degree of anti-Jewish bias. But AIPAC is effective partly because it pushes in such a determined fashion for the defense of Israel, while the countervailing influence on behalf of that nation's enemies or critics in the Middle East is minimal by comparison. Arab Americans are becoming more numerous—there is a particularly large enclave in Detroit—but, for the most part, Americans in general are inclined to be more sympathetic to Israel than to the Palestinians, in particular, even in the absence of any efforts by AIPAC. Furthermore, the attacks of 9/11 have obviously had the impact of increasing suspicion and even hostility among many Americans toward Arab and Islamic countries, as well as toward the immigrants from those countries whose presence in the United States is growing.

Hispanics have become the largest ethnic minority in the country, but their political interests and agendas are rather diverse. The Cuban American National Foundation in Florida has ostensibly been quite effective in its attempts to influence American foreign policy toward Cuba (as we will discuss in chapter 10), and one well-known political scientist has become famously (or infamously) worried that increasingly numerous and politically active Hispanics—some of whom are undocumented—pose a danger to the economic and political integrity of the country. In defense of his warnings, Samuel P. Huntington (2004, 44) has noted that a former Mexican president, Ernesto Zedillo, asserted in the 1990s that "the Mexican nation extends beyond the territory enclosed by its borders," while another, Vicente Fox, once described himself as president of 123 million Mexicans, 23 million of whom live in the United States. There is no doubt that Hispanic Americans have a special interest in American policy on immigration into the United States, as well as on policies regarding the treatment of the immigrants already living there, whether documented or not.

African Americans have been less concerned—certainly less than Jewish Americans and probably even less than Hispanic Americans—about foreign policy issues. As we will discuss in more detail in chapter 11, they have occasionally had an apparent influence on American foreign policy with respect to South Africa, especially in the days of apartheid. But African Americans do not, on average, take an interest in Liberia, for example, that is anything like the passion that Jewish Americans typically exhibit regarding Israel. Greek Americans have taken a special interest in U.S. policies toward Greece, particularly as they may impinge on Greek relations with Turkey. The end of the Cold War brought into play more pressures from representatives of various ethnic groups from East-Central Europe, including Poles, Hungarians, and even the small numbers of immigrants from the Baltic states of Estonia, Latvia, and Lithuania.

Increasingly, transnational **nongovernmental organizations (NGOs)** play an important role in the American foreign-policy-making process. When environmental issues such as saving whales or global warming arise, the international activist group Greenpeace is likely to make some attempt to have an impact on American legislation or policy decisions. On international human rights issues, voices from Amnesty International and Human Rights Watch are likely to be part of the foreign policy debate. In 2005, for example, Amnesty International released a report that "branded the U.S. prison camp at Guantanamo Bay a human rights failure, calling it 'the gulag of our time'" (Dodds 2005).

One sure sign that such organizations are becoming more important in the foreign-policy-making process is the vehement antagonism they are generating among some foreign policy analysts. Lee A.Casey and David B. Rivkin Jr. (2005), for example, are highly critical of the International Committee of the Red Cross (ICRC) for its persistent condemnation of the U.S. treatment of detainees in the wars in Afghanistan and Iraq, as well as at the detention facility in Guantanamo Bay. The ICRC, which receives millions of U.S. tax dollars every year, has insisted in public and judgmental statements that these detainees deserve the traditional protections accorded to prisoners of war in treaties such as the Geneva convention. Another analyst, John Fonte (2004), argues that such organizations as Human Rights Watch, the National Council of Churches, the International Human Rights Law Group, and the American Friends Service Committee threaten to undermine democracy in the United States and, indeed, around the world in the name of "global governance."[i]

---

i. "Yet, the twenty-first century could well turn out to be, not the democratic century, but the 'post-democratic' century—the century in which liberal democracy as we know it is slowly, almost imperceptibly, replaced by a new form of global governance" (Fonte 2004, 117).

A final set of interest groups that play an important role in the foreign-policy-making process is made up of intellectuals and academics, referred to variously as **epistemic communities**, or **knowledge-based experts**. Certainly one of the most prominent of these groups is the Council on Foreign Relations, which was founded in 1921, in the wake of the 1919 Paris Peace Conference that ended World War I. Based in New York, the Council has a restricted membership of 4,200, by invitation only. Perhaps its most visible contribution to the foreign policy debate involves the publication of its journal, *Foreign Affairs,* the country's "preeminent journal covering international affairs and U.S. foreign policy" (Council on Foreign Relations 2004). That journal, for example, published an article entitled "Sources of Soviet Conduct," by an anonymous author, X—who turned out to be George F. Kennan—which became a kind of blueprint for the Cold War policy of "containment" over the next few decades. (The article is also given credit for some prescience concerning the eventual demise of the Soviet Union.) The Carnegie Endowment for International Peace also is well-known for its publication of *Foreign Policy,* a periodical that has, in recent years, turned to a more colorful slick magazine format.

In addition, a wide array of private foundations and **think tanks** produce papers, articles, books, and research projects aimed at influencing the American foreign-policy-making process. Perhaps the most well-known such think tank, and the one that is identified as most influential among leaders of the Democratic Party, is the Brookings Institution in Washington, D.C. More influential in conservative circles and within the Republican Party are organizations such as the Heritage Foundation and the American Enterprise Institute.

Political Parties

The two major political parties in the United States—the Democrats and the Republicans—rather straddle the line between the government and the civil society outside the government. They consist of citizens from all over the country who are devoted to influencing the elected members of their party, to orchestrating political campaigns that will keep those members in power, and to recruiting new entrants into the political process as elected officials. The party organizations consist of elected officials, not only in the federal government, but in state and local governments as well. What influence do they have on foreign policy?

Both the Democratic and Republican parties claim to have a beneficial impact on U.S. foreign policy, and each argues that the policies it advocates are consistently more effective and make a larger contribution to the welfare and the national interest of the United States. In the early 1950s, some Republicans made much of the fact that Democratic presidents had been in power at the beginning of each major war in which the United States became involved during the twentieth century. (The wars in question at that point were World Wars I and II and the Korean War.) The United States had been involved in the Boxer Rebellion when Republican William McKinley was president, but it suffered only twenty-one battle fatalities in the conflict (see Small and Singer 1982, 87). And, although Republican President Dwight D. Eisenhower made some initial decisions leading to U.S. involvement in the Vietnam War, that involvement began to escalate significantly under Democratic President Lyndon Johnson in 1965. Thus, the Republican claim that every U.S. wartime activity in the twentieth century had begun under a Democratic president had some apparent validity.

But Republican George H. W. Bush was in power to initiate the Persian Gulf War of 1990, and in the early years of the next century, his son, the equally Republican George W. Bush, occupied the White House when U.S. troops were sent to war against Afghanistan and Iraq. So, even though it might also be claimed that Democratic President Bill Clinton initiated the war against Serbia in 1999, it can no longer be argued that Republican presidents have a perfect record within living memory of keeping the United States out of interstate wars.

During the Cold War, Democratic presidents were apparently more vulnerable to the charge of being "soft on communism" (as we will discuss in more detail in chapter 8), and it would be reasonable to assume that this suspicion reflected a tendency of Democratic presidents to adhere to a less belligerent stand against the Soviet Union in the decades immediately after World War II. But, in fact, it was Democratic President Harry Truman who responded forcefully to the attack by North Korea on South Korea, thus leading to U.S. involvement in the ensuing Korean War, and, as we have noted, Democratic President Lyndon Johnson took steps that escalated the Vietnam War. In addition, Democratic President John Kennedy ordered the Bay of Pigs invasion in Cuba, while Johnson ordered an invasion of the Dominican Republic in 1965.

Republican presidents, meanwhile, may actually have pursued the more conciliatory policies in dealings with Communist powers. President Eisenhower accepted a truce and a tie to end the war against the Communist states of North Korea and the People's Republic of China, on terms that no Democratic president could probably have accepted—precisely because Democrats were vulnerable to the charge of being soft on Communism. Also, in spite of brave talk during the presidential campaign of 1952 about "rolling back" the iron curtain, when the Soviet Union invaded Hungary in 1956, Eisenhower and his secretary of state, John Foster Dulles, limited their reactions to denunciatory speeches in the United Nations. Not only did President Nixon in 1973 accept a peace treaty ending the war against North Vietnam that allowed the North to keep some of its troops stationed in South Vietnam, but he also took steps to modify fundamentally the U.S. policy of refusing to recognize the Communist regime in the People's Republic of China.

This is not to say that Republican presidents during the Cold War were consistently soft on Communism. In 1954, for example, President Eisenhower authorized the Central Intelligence Agency to launch a subversive war against a leftist regime in Guatemala. President Reagan, in his first term, adopted various aggressive policies aimed at the Soviet Union, including large defense budgets and a commitment to the Strategic Defense Initiative, and he launched an invasion to overthrow a leftist regime in Grenada in 1983. But, especially in light of the positive relationship that Reagan established with Soviet leader Mikhail Gorbachev during his second term, it is difficult to argue that administrations headed by Republican presidents during the Cold War consistently adopted more hard-line policies toward Communism in general and the Soviet Union in particular than did Democratic presidents. In fact, Democratic presidents, to protect themselves against the charge of being soft on Communism, may have felt compelled to be less conciliatory on Cold War foreign policy issues than Republican presidents could be (Ray 1998, 55–56)

Nevertheless, since Republican presidents put together winning coalitions that consist of substantially different elements of the population than do Democratic presidents, it would be surprising if it were impossible to discern any systematic differences between the two major political parties in the United States. Foreign policy analyst Benjamin Fordham (1998a) makes the interesting argument that Republican presidents, who are more attuned to economic elites, are more reluctant to adopt inflationary macroeconomic policies at times of high unemployment than are Democratic presidents. Business interests, and wealthy individuals in general, are particularly sensitive to inflation, because over time it erodes the value of their substantial financial assets; any debts owed to them, for example, can be paid off with dollars whose value sinks with every passing month farther below the value at which they were originally loaned. On the other hand, less affluent individuals, who may carry heavy debt burdens, will be less harmed by inflation; at the very least, they may find their debts easier to pay. In contrast, Democratic presidents faced with high inflation will be more reluctant to pursue macroeconomic policies, such as increasing interest rates or curbing federal government expenditures, that might prove especially painful to important groups within the Democratic Party coalition (such as labor unions) by increasing unemployment.

So, what are the possible foreign policy consequences of the differing constituencies in the major political parties on which presidents (and other elected officials) depend to stay in power? Fordham (1998a) speculates that, when political or economic problems accumulate, all presidents are tempted to divert attention from those issues, and to generate support for themselves, by becoming involved in foreign policy crises and/or interstate conflicts short of war. (Full-fledged war, he argues, is too risky and expensive to serve these purposes.) Examining all political uses of force by the United States from 1949 to 1994, he finds that Republican presidents are more likely than Democratic presidents to use military force when unemployment is high, while Democratic presidents are more likely than Republican presidents to use military force when facing high inflation. In other words, presidents from both parties turn to diversionary tactics when faced with the particular domestic problem—unemployment for Republicans and inflation for Democrats—that they find too difficult to deal with in some more direct fashion without alienating their core constituencies.

And, in this context, it is relevant to consider again the point made by David Clark (2003): that these patterns would be even clearer than they actually are were it not for the fact that leaders of foreign states with which the United States interacts are apparently sensitive to the domestic political needs of American presidents. These leaders—even potential antagonists—tend to adopt conciliatory policies and to avoid conflict with the United States when they suspect that because of problematic domestic issues, the American president might find the diversionary use of force a particularly attractive option.

Fordham (1998a, 421) is careful to point out, however, that if the patterns about which he hypothesizes actually exist, they are not necessarily produced by cynical presidents who go to bed at night thinking explicitly to themselves, "My public opinion ratings are really low right now because unemployment is so high. Tomorrow I have to find some issue with some state over which I can generate a foreign policy crisis to divert the attention of voters from the unemployment rate." Instead, Fordham argues, "when the use of force carries appreciable domestic benefits, as it does when unemployment is high, a national leader might simply be more likely to conclude that it is appropriate in a wider range of international circumstances."

CONCLUSION

It is not easy to discern any specific impact that the general public has on U.S. foreign policy, partly because most of the public does not know or care very much about foreign policy issues. Then, too, even when there is a rough correlation between what the public wants and the foreign policy decisions that are implemented, the coincidence may have been brought about by foreign policy makers' efforts to educate and influence public opinion, rather than by the spontaneous impact of citizens' preferences on policy decisions. Still, in the aggregate, the public tends to take reasonable positions on foreign policy issues, and its most important impact may result from anticipation by the president of the United States about how the public will react to important foreign policy ventures, including unsuccessful wars.

The mass media may not successfully tell people what to think, but they clearly do influence which foreign policy issues the public thinks about. The media are, also, often manipulated by government elites in order to create favorable impressions of foreign policy initiatives. Whether or not the American media are systematically biased in a liberal or a conservative direction could be truly divined only by a totally unbiased source with access to unlimited information—but there are no such sources.

Interest groups, such as those associated with business or with labor unions or with ethnic groups, undoubtedly have an impact on foreign policies, even if only within the somewhat narrow range of interests they typically focus on. It is not always the largest special interest groups that have the most influence; in fact, smaller groups have some advantages in their attempts to influence the policy process. Finally, the two major political parties in the United States clearly have the potential to significantly influence U.S. foreign policy, partly because the president, who plays such a central role in the foreign policy process, is so dependent on his party's support to keep him in power.

KEY CONCEPTS

CNN effect   102

doves, *or* accommodationists   91

economistic explanations   105

epistemic communities, *or* knowledge-based experts   110

free riders   108

hawks, *or* hard-liners   91

interest groups, *or* special interests   104

internationalists   91

isolationists   91

nongovernmental organizations (NGOs)   109

protectionism   107

public opinion   87

rally round the flag effect   93

think tanks   110

RATIONAL POLITICAL AMBITION AND . . .
EXTERNAL POLICY INPUTS

☑ The general public may not know or care much about foreign policy issues, but public opinion can have a powerful impact on foreign policies nevertheless. U.S. presidents such as Lyndon Johnson, Richard Nixon, and George W. Bush, for example, demonstrated a keen awareness of the extent to which pubic opinion, and votes in elections, would turn against lost interstate wars.

☑ Mass media can have an important impact on foreign policy by giving the president (and other elected leaders) an impression about which foreign policy issues matter most to the public and interest groups. They also can be a powerful tool used by political leaders to keep themselves in power.

☑ In general, interest groups can have an impact on foreign policy to the extent that they can credibly threaten the hold on power by the president, as well as members of Congress. Paradoxically, smaller groups often can be more effective, even though they directly control a smaller number of votes.

☑ U.S. presidents are dependent on their political parties to keep them in power. The winning coalitions they assemble have different economic interests. Republican presidents are more likely to use military force when unemployment is high, whereas Democratic presidents are more likely to use military force when inflation is high.

CHAPTER **6**

FOREIGN POLICY PROCESSES WITHIN THE GOVERNMENT

THE GENERAL PUBLIC, THE MEDIA, VARIOUS INTEREST GROUPS, AND political parties all have an influence on the American foreign policy process. Some analysts feel that the inputs from some of these extra-governmental sources are absolutely crucial to determining the outcomes of that process. Nevertheless, the foreign-policy-making process is formally centered in the federal government, and it occupies a significant portion of that huge enterprise. In this chapter, we will look first at the administrative organizations that play central roles in the process, and then we will conclude by analyzing the roles of Congress and the president, whose impact is particularly crucial from the viewpoint of rational political ambition theory.

THE DEPARTMENT OF STATE

At the apex (on paper, at least) of the federal government's foreign policy administrative structure is the **Department of State**. Originally the Department of Foreign Affairs, this entity's name was changed to the Department of State in 1789. The secretary of state is the highest-ranking cabinet member and, in principle, the most important foreign policy adviser to the president. George Washington appointed Thomas Jefferson to be the first secretary of state, and the fact that this post was truly the preeminent position within the president's cabinet is clearly suggested by the fact that "of the first nine presidents of the United States, six had previously served as secretary of state" (Mead 2001, 12).

Throughout most of the nineteenth century, the State Department had fewer than 1,000 employees; currently, it has about 30,000 employees, and a budget of almost $10 billion. These basic data suggest that, as an organization, it has become steadily larger and more influential within the foreign-policy-making process. But, while there is no doubt that it has

American foreign policy is to an important extent a function of interactions and bargaining between members of Congress and the president of the United States. In this photo, Republican congressional leaders, namely House Minority Leader John Boehner, Senate Minority Leader Mitch McConnell, Senate Minority Whip Trent Lott, and House Minority Whip Roy Blunt, are seen walking out of a May 2007 White House meeting with President George W. Bush devoted to a discussion of funding for the war in Iraq.

increased in size throughout its history, most observers, as we shall see, agree that it has not become steadily more influential.

That the State Department is, nevertheless, a large and complex organization is clearly indicated by the organization chart in figure 6.1. Although it may seem that it is unnecessarily large and complex, the State Department is responsible for a wide array of duties extending across the world. It must, first of all, coordinate the large number of agencies within the U.S. government that become involved in the development and implementation of U.S. foreign policy. It also manages the foreign affairs budget, and it is in charge of all the embassies and consulates that the United States maintains in almost every country in the world. It conducts international negotiations and concludes agreements and treaties on a range of issues, from international trade to nonproliferation of nuclear weapons (Bureau of Public Affairs 2001a).

The State Department is also responsible for providing a wide range of services to Americans, often outside the United States. It offers protection and assistance to U.S. nationals living or traveling abroad, and it helps American business interests to cope with the challenges of the international marketplace. The State Department organizes programs to inform the public about U.S. foreign policy, and it provides feedback from American citizens to public officials.

Generally speaking, the Department of State is an imposing and impressive organization. Still, there is nearly universal agreement that it has—since at least the end of World War II—failed to exercise the influence and control over American foreign policy that its formal place within the policymaking structure of the U.S. government would seem to warrant. One of the reasons for this alleged underachievement may have to do with its elite corps, the **Foreign Service**. Despite a common misperception that virtually all employees of the Department of State are members of the Foreign Service, the staff is, in fact, made up of both Foreign Service and Civil Service appointees, and the Foreign Service officers typically constitute less than 60 percent of the total (Bureau of Public Affairs, 2001b).

It may be, however, that this elite corps is too elite. A common impression is that Foreign Service officers are mostly white males with Ivy League degrees, usually the offspring of privileged, wealthy families. According to one analyst of the evolution of the State Department: "Throughout its history, the Foreign Service ... has been subjected to criticism.... Some of these have applied to the personnel" (Plischke 1999, 664). Nonetheless, to the extent that one can base such inferences on degrees earned from prestigious institutions of higher learning and on scores on demanding examinations focusing on history, politics, and economics, it is reasonable to infer that Foreign Services officers are, in the main, highly qualified professionals. Applicants for the service must first pass a demanding written test, and then the small percentage who are allowed to advance to the next stage are subjected to an oral examination that weeds out all but an equally small proportion for employment.

For decades, this process did produce a rather homogenous group of Foreign Service officers, but efforts to increase diversity among them have met with some success in recent years. Nevertheless, there is in the State Department an "up or out" personnel process, which requires that after a certain period of time, employees must be either promoted or terminated. This system, according to some observers, fosters excessive caution in Foreign Service officers, who strive above all to avoid mistakes.

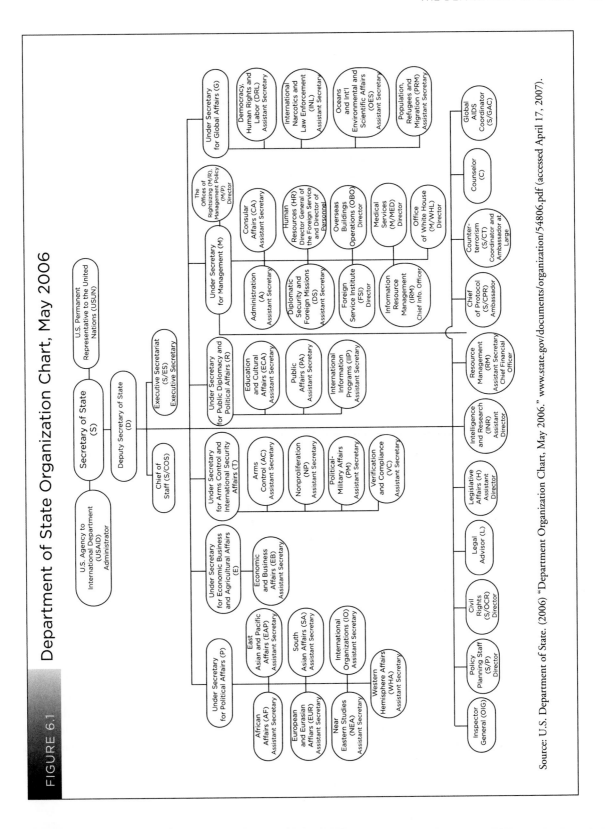

Source: U.S. Department of State. (2006) "Department Organization Chart, May 2006." www.state.gov/documents/organization/54806.pdf (accessed April 17, 2007).

Somewhat paradoxically, the State Department's reputation also suffers, to some extent, from excessive professionalism and from the existence of an exclusive subculture among its Foreign Service officers. However, its image is also damaged by the fact that many of its most important posts are filled not by "careerists," but by political appointees whose qualifications may be limited mostly to the donation of large contributions to successful presidential candidates. Elmer Plischke (1999, 659) notes that "the appointment of amateurs to provide them with diplomatic sinecures and lucrative consular positions for political or partisan purposes, which produced a deplorably low level of honesty and efficiency, was long condemned by objective analysis."[a] There have undoubtedly been improvements within the State Department on this issue in recent decades, but table 6.1 shows that, for example, the proportion of "noncareerists" appointed to top ambassadorial posts has remained quite consistent since the 1960s.

The influence of the State Department on the foreign policy process is also hindered by the fact that it lacks a domestic constituency. The departments of Commerce, Labor, Agriculture, and, especially, Defense all have important blocs of domestic constituents who support them and who lobby actively and often effectively on behalf of interests and programs vital to those departments. The "clients" of the State Department, in contrast, tend to be foreign countries and overseas organizations, which often have less clout and knowledge about the American political process.

Furthermore, Foreign Service officers and other employees of the State Department—especially if they live and work overseas for extended periods of time (as many must in order to do their jobs)—themselves become rather suspect. Officials in the executive and the legislative branches of the government often wonder if these State Department employees have "gone native," becoming so familiar with the people and governments in foreign countries that they have developed sympathies that may dilute their attachment to the United States and cloud their judgment when it comes to making decisions about issues vital to the U.S. national interest.

These suspicions reached a crescendo during the era of McCarthyism in the early 1950s. Indeed, Senator Joe McCarthy charged, early on in his xenophobic campaign, that the State Department in particular was riddled with officials having Communist ties and sympathies. Following the fall of China to Mao Zedong's Communist revolution, some Foreign Service officers were found to have predicted Mao's success, and their predictions were taken as evidence that they had not only forecast, but also had desired, his takeover. Whatever the merits of revisionist efforts to revive McCarthy's reputation since the end of the Cold War, there is no doubt that the experiences of those in the State Department who were the targets of his accusations had the effect of making some employees quite cautious about the kinds of reports and analyses they wrote, or that this wary attitude persisted for many decades after McCarthy himself was censured by the Senate in December of 1954. This episode, along with several other important forces inducing caution in the department's style, helps to create the impression—among American presidents and the executive branch, in particular—that the State Department is too conservative, unwilling to change its ways, and unlikely to develop bold new insights or to recommend innovative ways to deal with novel or truly unusual problems.

---

a. One example of such analysis is Macomber 1975.

TABLE 6.1	Career and Noncareer Ambassadorial Appointments, 1961–2000		
Administration	Term of Office	Percentage of Career Appointees	Percentage of Noncareer Appointees
Kennedy	1961–1963	68	32
Johnson	1963–1968	71	29
Nixon	1969–1974	70	30
Ford	1974–1976	71	29
Carter	1977–1980	76	24
Reagan	1981–1988	68	32
Bush	1989–1992	72	28
Clinton	1993–2000	70	30
40-year average		70	30

Source: American Foreign Service Association. 2002. "Historical Comparison: Ambassadorial (Chiefs of Mission) Appointments." www.afsa.org/ambassadorsgraph2.cfm (accessed May 1, 2007).

Modern communications and transportation technologies have also diminished the role of the State Department in the policymaking process. Decades ago, ambassadors in far-flung posts around the world were important sources of information—which might not have been available through any alternative means—about the countries in which they served. Now, in cases of emergency, the secretary of state can easily visit the sites of concern herself, rather than relying heavily on ambassadors or embassy staff to keep up with ongoing developments. This increased mobility of its head does not, in itself, reduce the department's role in the foreign-policy-making process. But the fact that officials throughout the executive branch can so easily access timely reporting about virtually any place in the world via CNN or the Internet certainly makes the State Department a less important source of information about international crises or long-term foreign policy issues.

All these points should not suggest that the Department of State no longer plays a role of any importance in the American foreign policy process. There is, in fact, a vast array of issues and problems involving U.S. relations with large numbers of countries to which only the State Department pays much attention on a daily basis, and the department's staff, both overseas and at home, certainly plays a vital role in dealing with these continuing issues. Also, on occasion, the secretary of state can be a major player in the foreign-policy-making process, depending primarily on her relationship with the president.

There is no doubt, for example, that President Eisenhower depended heavily on his secretary of state, John Foster Dulles, as a foreign policy adviser. At the other end of the spectrum in recent decades, Secretary of State William Rogers, who served under President Nixon, was seemingly excluded from almost all important foreign policy deliberations. During that administration, it was obvious that the president's main foreign policy adviser, instead, was Henry Kissinger, who served in the earlier years of Nixon's term as the national security adviser, at the head of the National Security Council. Indeed, Kissinger was one of the most important foreign policy advisers in any administration in the post–World War II era. When he also became secretary of state in September 1973, the appointment seemed likely to bring about a tremendous boost in the reputation and influence of the Department of State.

But Kissinger obviously felt that his personal relationship with the president was the most important source of his influence over foreign policy, and he never established a very close relationship with his colleagues in the Department of State. His description of the department's administrative structure (Kissinger 1982, 439) is instructive on several counts:

> Left to its own devices, the State Department machinery tends toward inertia rather than creativity; it is always on the verge of turning itself into an enormous cable machine. Too often policy filters up from the bottom in response to events, complaints, or pleas that originate abroad. Each significant country is assigned to an officer with the revealing title of "country director"; indeed some of these officials seem more interested in directing "their" country than in shaping the foreign policy of the United States.

Kissinger here summarizes many attitudes that typically surface in the executive branch, especially among advisers close to the president: the State Department is too large, too complicated, too much influenced by its foreign "clientele," and too status quo–oriented, bogged down by inertia, to provide much help with serious foreign policy issues and crises. Imbued with that attitude, Kissinger remained rather aloof from the department when he became secretary of state. His ascension to the post therefore did not boost the morale or the influence of the State Department within the foreign-policy-making establishment to any notable degree.

When President George W. Bush appointed Colin Powell as his first secretary of state, it was widely assumed that Powell would become a central player on the president's foreign policy team, and that he would help to restore the Department of State to a position of prominence in the foreign policy establishment. Powell brought to the position a stellar reputation—even as a possible presidential candidate himself in the not-too-distant future. And, in truth, Powell did achieve some successes in the area of reforming and revitalizing the State Department. In 2003, for example, the Foreign Affairs Council, an "umbrella group" of eleven organizations concerned about diplomacy, published an independent assessment of Secretary Powell's attempts to increase the allocation of resources to the department, to change its organizational culture, and to improve both its public diplomacy and its congressional relations efforts. In the opinion of the report's authors, Powell's efforts had achieved results that were "substantial, even historic" (Foreign Affairs Council 2003).[b]

As early as September of 2001, however, a *Time* magazine cover story about Secretary Powell proclaimed him the "odd man out" in the Bush administration. The article asserted that "it comes as one of the biggest surprises in the emerging Bush era that Colin Powell, the man many thought would walk into the presidency himself a few years ago, is leaving such shallow footprints.... Powell's megastar wattage looks curiously dimmed" (McGeary 2001).

---

b. "Powell has certainly had his successes. He brilliantly rallied the troops at State and rebuilt a demoralized institution" (McGeary 2001).

Ironically enough, this article was published on September 10, 2001, the day before the terrorist attacks on New York and Washington. In the wake of those attacks, Powell's star shone more brightly in most people's eyes, as he traveled widely and successfully assembled a broad international coalition that soon intervened in Afghanistan and rapidly deposed the Taliban government that had long offered a safe haven for al-Qaeda.

But Powell was not so enthusiastic about the war in Iraq, and so, soon after the successful intervention in Afghanistan, it became widely perceived that he was out of sync with the neoconservative ideological thrust within the Bush administration. In an article published shortly after Powell had stepped down as secretary of state at the beginning of President Bush's second term, the *Foreign Service Journal* expressed the apparently prevailing opinion: "History will judge Colin Powell's tenure as Secretary of State to have been somewhere between a failure and a fraud.... Historians ... will consider the record of the past four years and find it wanting" (Jett 2005, 22).[c]

Thus, Secretary Powell, in spite of—or, perhaps, in part because of—the high expectations created by his ascension to the post, was, when he left it, widely regarded as yet another secretary of state who had been rather consistently left on the outside looking in at most of the crucial foreign policy processes and decisions occurring during his tenure. Secretaries of state regularly suffer this problem not only because they lack a domestic constituency for whom they can speak in an influential manner in their discussions with the president, but also because they do have a large constituency consisting of all the employees of the State Department, who themselves tend to speak out in favor of the interests and priorities of the people in foreign countries with whom they work on a daily basis.

A secretary can mitigate this problem of outsider status by making it clear, in the manner of Henry Kissinger, to remain separate and independent from the State Department. As Bert Rockman (1981, 918) puts it: "Strong secretaries often have been strong precisely because they ignored the department." But this personal strategy only serves to diminish further the role of the State Department as a whole in the foreign policy process. President's Bush's second secretary of state, Condoleezza Rice, followed the path of Kissinger, moving from the position of national security adviser to that of secretary of state, and one might have suspected that she would similarly maintain a certain aloofness from the organizational structure of the department as a whole. And, indeed, she seems to have maintained much of the confidence the president had in her when she was national security adviser, without increasing in any obvious manner the prestige or clout of the Department of State.

In any case, presidents are likely to perceive secretaries of state as lacking clout in the domestic political arena because they speak for no important groups within the American electorate, and as being at least vaguely disloyal because they represent the staff of the State Department, which is filled with employees suspected of giving inappropriately high priority to the interests of the foreign countries with which the United States interacts.

Although the staff of the State Department seems large, for the purpose of influencing foreign policy it is, arguably, too small, at least in contrast to one of its main competitors for

---

c. Jett concludes his assessment (26) by asserting that "it would take a major literary miracle to find accomplishment in a record noteworthy mainly for subservience and devotion to self-interest."

influence in the foreign policy process, the Department of Defense. While the State Department's 30,000 employees operate on a budget that is currently about $10 billion a year, the Department of Defense commands a much larger portion of federal expenditures, annually spending *hundreds* of billions of dollars—at a time, of course, when it is fighting wars, or, at least, conducting dangerous, violence-plagued continuing attempts to keep the peace, in both Afghanistan and Iraq.[d] The roles of the military and the defense establishment in the American foreign policy process expanded significantly during the Second World War, and these enhanced positions were solidified during the prolonged war in Vietnam of the 1960s and 1970s.

It may well be a mistake, however, to attribute too much of the State Department's limited role in the foreign policy process to the fact that its staff and budget are so much smaller than those of the Department of Defense. For the State Department has also lost out in recent decades to a bureaucratic branch of the foreign-policy-making establishment that is even smaller than the State Department—namely, the National Security Council. We will discuss further the foreign policy roles of this entity and its head, the national security adviser, in short order. For the moment, let us note that although the Defense Department's staff numbers in the millions (including members of the armed forces), the staff of the National Security Council is around two or three hundred, and its budget is minuscule in comparison to that of the Defense Department. Yet it, too, has become an obvious and successful competitor to the State Department for influence over the foreign-policy-making process.

In its report on the tragic events of 9/11, the National Commission on Terrorist Attacks upon the United States (Kean and Hamilton 2004, 138) summarized the recent fate of the State Department in the following manner:

> The State Department retained primacy until the 1960s, when the Kennedy and Johnson administrations turned instead to [the] ... Defense Department.... President Nixon then concentrated policy planning and policy coordination in a powerful National Security Council staff, overseen by Henry Kissinger.... In later years, individual secretaries of state were important figures, but the department's role continued to erode. State came into the 1990s overmatched by the resources of other departments and with little support for its budget either in Congress or in the president's [o]ffice....

THE NATIONAL SECURITY COUNCIL: A PSEUDO-STATE DEPARTMENT?

On the path toward marginalization of the State Department within the American foreign policy establishment, an important legal and institutional milestone was the National Security Act of 1947, which Douglas T. Stuart (2003, 296) has called "the second most important piece of legislation in modern American history."[e] Instituting a major reorganization of the

---

d. In 2005 the Defense Department spent something on the order of $400 billion, or roughly forty times as much as the State Department.

e. According to Stuart, "Only the 1964 Civil Rights Act has had a greater impact on American society and government."

foreign-policy-making and national defense organs within the federal government, the act created the **National Security Council (NSC)**, merged the old War and Navy departments into the Department of Defense, and called for the fusion of the Office of Strategic Services (created during World War II to deal with intelligence-gathering activities as well as "special operations") with several smaller postwar intelligence organizations to create the Central Intelligence Agency (CIA). Before discussing the roles of the Defense Department and the CIA, as well as the broader, recently reformed intelligence community, we focus first on the crucial part played by the National Security Council in the American foreign policy process.

Formally speaking, the NSC is to serve as the principal forum for the consideration of national security and foreign policy matters. It is supposed to advise and assist the president in formulating policies to deal with those matters, and to coordinate the implementation of those policies by the multiple governmental agencies that become involved in the foreign policy process. The NSC is chaired by the president, and its meetings are regularly attended by the vice president, the secretaries of state, Treasury, and defense, and the assistant to the president for national security affairs (who has become known as the national security adviser, or NSA).

The NSC very early on established for itself a reputation as an important source of foreign policy ideas when, in 1950, it produced a report written by Paul Nitze—a document officially referred to as NSC-68. This report outlined a national security strategy focused on the U.S. rivalry with the Soviet Union in the emerging Cold War context. It called for a massive military buildup and for energetic measures to thwart the ambitions of the Soviet Union, whose main goal, it asserted, was worldwide domination. NSC-68 has become known, in short, as a kind of blueprint for the U.S. Cold War policy of "containment," and it served as a basis for that policy for at least the next twenty years.

But the NSC remained a relatively minor factor during the Eisenhower administration, and, although President Kennedy was well-known for being dissatisfied with the State Department, neither the NSC nor its head gained much importance under him or President Johnson.[f] The role of national security adviser became truly important, even preeminent (after the president), within the foreign policy establishment under Henry Kissinger. Kissinger and Nixon, in fact, were a close-knit team, in charge of virtually all foreign policy initiatives, which were often conducted or orchestrated through "back channels" that circumvented the State Department altogether. According to Kissinger himself (1979, 1049–1096), these back channels were particularly important in the process that led to President Nixon's surprise trip to Beijiing and to the resumption of diplomatic relations with the People's Republic of China.

President Carter solidified the importance of the position of national security adviser by appointing the well-known scholar Zbigniew Brzezinski to the post. While President Reagan did not rely heavily on any of the six men who held the position during his two terms, President George H. W. Bush worked very closely with his NSA, Brent Scowcroft. President Clinton's first NSA, Anthony Lake, had a difficult time establishing himself as an important

---

f. For example, Richard A. Johnson (1971, 186) reports that "President Kennedy not only convened the National Security Council less frequently than did President Eisenhower, but convened it only when he was on the brink of a decision. Kennedy saw no sense in placing unformulated problems before the miscellaneous body of men designated in the statute and preferred to set up task forces specifically qualified to deal with particular problems."

cog in the foreign policy machinery, but his successor, Sandy Berger, was obviously powerful and influential during Clinton's second term. Condoleezza Rice, who served as NSA during the first term of President George W. Bush, was clearly a crucial player on Bush's foreign policy team—as mentioned earlier, she exerted more influence on Bush's foreign policy than did Secretary of State Colin Powell. One key to the success of any NSA, it has become obvious, is his or her access to and relationship with the president. Even two decades ago, Rockman (1981, 914) concluded that "whatever clout the national security assistant has exists only at the sufferance of the president."

Contemporary presidents seem systematically more inclined to depend on the NSA than on the secretary of state as a foreign policy adviser. And this pattern is unlikely to be entirely the result of accidents of personality—that is, that most presidents and NSAs just happen to get along better on a personal level than do presidents and secretaries of state. In fact, the national security adviser and the NSC have several advantages over the secretary and the Department of State when it comes to exerting influence over the president in the foreign policy process. Many of these advantages have already been mentioned. The State Department is considerably larger and is staffed mostly by foreign policy professionals who devote most of their careers to the foreign policy establishment, perhaps mostly within the department. The National Security Council, in contrast, is staffed, to some extent, by "irregulars," or independent experts who have careers outside of government both before and after they serve their terms at NSC; other members may have long careers in government but are imported into the NSC for relatively brief periods of time. The president handpicks the national security adviser, who then fills staff positions in the NSC with members who are much more attuned to the foreign policy agenda of the president than are the "regulars" in the State Department. The Foreign Service officers and other staffers in the State Department tend to regard presidents as short-timers in an ongoing enterprise; the response of these career bureaucrats to attempted innovations tends to be, from the president's point of view, affected by attitudes such as "that's all been tried before," or "that's not the way we do things."

Thus, while presidents tend to see secretaries of state as representatives of a huge bureaucracy without any important domestic constituency, and most of the staff in the State Department as proxies for the foreign countries in which they specialize and/or live and work for extended periods of time, they tend, in contrast, to see the national security adviser and the NSC as more open to new ideas, less compromised by attachments overseas, and more attentive to their own foreign policy agenda. One of the signs of the NSC's closer relationship to the president is that the State Department is more systematically suspected of "leaks" to the media that may embarrass the administration or put pressure on it to engage in foreign policy initiatives that it would rather avoid. In sum, Rockman (1981, 919) says, "if presidents are served amorphous goo from the State Department bureaucracy (which they often see as representing other nations' interests to Washington), they may be provided with clear-headed principles from their in-house foreign policy advisers."

All these generalizations seem clearly exemplified by the presidential administration of George W. Bush. Near the beginning of President Bush's second term, David J. Rothkopf (2005, 31–32) pointed out that neither the national security adviser nor any other member of the NSC is confirmed by the U.S. Senate, and that the NSC is not subject to congressional oversight "even though it now performs many of the policymaking functions once reserved for the State Department." During Bush's first term, Condoleezza Rice was, reportedly, closer to the president than any of her predecessors in the position of NSA. In fact, she was so close, and spent so much time with the president, that some observers felt that she neglected her duty to supervise the National Security Council as an organization. In any case, there is little doubt that Rice, Secretary of Defense Donald Rumsfeld, and Vice President Dick Cheney constituted a powerful triumvirate within the administration and were key players in the design and execution of the so-called war on terror that was the central focus of Bush's foreign policy.

At the beginning of the second Bush term, when Rice moved from the National Security Council to become secretary of state, her replacement as national security adviser was her former assistant within the NSC, Stephen Hadley. What impact these changes might have on U.S. foreign policy during the second Bush term remained an open question, but after two years in their new positions, neither Rice nor Hadley seemed to have overcome President Bush's tendency to depend primarily on his secretary of defense—now Robert Gates, who replaced Donald Rumsfeld—or on military leaders for advice on what were clearly his most pressing foreign policy issues, the wars in Afghanistan and Iraq.

THE DEPARTMENT OF DEFENSE

The **Department of Defense** emerged out of the fusion of the War Department and the Navy Department in 1947. The intent was to give the military sector of the foreign policy and national security establishment a more unified voice, as well as a better organized administration overall. The new combined structure had been in existence for only a little over a decade, however, when an American president—and one with a lengthy and distinguished military record—was inclined to warn about the possibly dangerous influence that the Defense Department and its allies within the national security complex could have on American foreign policy. In his farewell address to the nation, Dwight Eisenhower (1961) asserted:

> We have been compelled to create a permanent armaments industry of vast proportions. Added to this, three and a half million men and women are directly engaged in the defense establishment. We annually spend on military security more than the net income of all United States corporations. This conjunction of an immense military establishment and a large arms industry is new in the American experience. *In the councils of government, we must guard against the acquisition of unwarranted influence ... by the military-industrial complex.* (Emphasis added.)

One useful indicator of the influence of the Defense Department and its allied interests within the American economy—such as large corporations with contracts from the Pentagon to produce military equipment ranging from rifles to airplanes to nuclear missiles—is the size of the defense budget in the United States, relative to the size of the entire economy. Variations in this proportion are traced over the years from 1939 to 2002 in figure 6.2. The data provided there show, unsurprisingly, that the budget, and the likely influence of the Defense Department, increases substantially when the United States is at war. The highest proportions occurred during the period of U.S. participation in World War II, and there was another

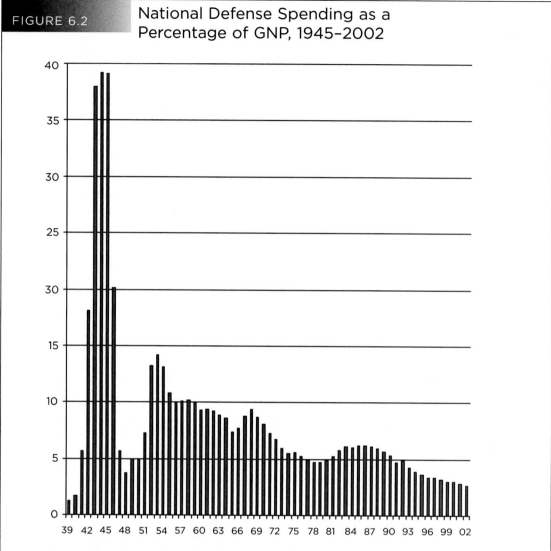

FIGURE 6.2

National Defense Spending as a Percentage of GNP, 1945–2002

Source: Figure is from Anthony H. Cordesman, "Trends in US Defense Spending, Procurement, and Readiness: The Growing Gap between Strategy, Force Plans, and Resources," April 1998. Report published by the Center for Strategic and International Studies, Washington, D.C. (this figure on is p. 5). www.csis.org/media/csis/pubs/usspend4-2-98[1].pdf.

substantial upswing during the Korean War in the early 1950s. Certainly one of the most controversial increases in U.S. defense spending as a proportion of GNP occurred during the 1960s, as the country became more deeply involved in the military conflict in Vietnam.

But the figure also shows that, as the Vietnam War wound down, the budget for the Defense Department decreased rather substantially. This pattern of flux suggests that there are, perhaps, limits on the influence of the Defense Department on U.S. foreign policy. When, from the point of view of a substantial portion of the American people, the Vietnam War went badly, the flow of funds to the Pentagon slowed considerably. It picked up again in the wake of the Soviet invasion of Afghanistan in 1979 and the subsequent (and possibly related) election of Ronald Reagan.

Perhaps the most important evidence of the limits on the Defense Department's influence on U.S. foreign policy involves the impact on defense spending of the end of the Cold War. If, in fact, defense spending were generated primarily by the political influence of the Pentagon, and of the large corporations to which it allocates huge sums of money every year, even the sudden collapse of the nation's sole major-power rival would not have hampered the ability of these domestic interests to evoke from Congress ever-increasing defense appropriations every year. But figure 6.3, focusing on the trend in the defense budget as a percentage of GNP in the years immediately after the end of the Cold War, shows that when the threat from the Soviet Union had undeniably receded, U.S. defense expenditures were cut back substantially.

That reduction, however, was not to be permanent. Figure 6.4 shows the trend in defense expenditures in the wake of the terrorist attacks of 9/11. As the United States became involved in wars in both Afghanistan and Iraq, U.S. defense spending rebounded accordingly. It is safe to infer that the Pentagon's influence over the general thrust of U.S. foreign policy is likely to increase as we move from the post–Cold War era to that of the war on terror. But there are limits to this increase also, as we will discuss when considering the roles of intelligence agencies and the new Department of Homeland Security in the foreign-policy-making process.

The organizational chart of the Department of Defense, presented in figure 6.5, shows that the separate services preserved at least some of their autonomy in the wake of the National Security Act of 1947. The system created by that act allocated substantial authority to the chiefs of staff of the army, navy, and air force, who made up the Joint Chiefs of Staff. The Joint Chiefs would then elect a chairman, who served as liaison to both the secretary of defense and the president—the latter being the commander in chief of the armed forces. As such, the president embodies the American commitment (at least on paper, skeptics would say) of civilian control over the military forces.

By the mid-1980s, widespread concerns about interservice rivalries led to the **Goldwater-Nichols Department of Defense Reorganization Act of 1986**, which passed both houses of Congress by huge margins. (The vote in the Senate was, in fact, unanimous: 95–0.) One of the main goals of this legislative initiative was to overcome what critics saw as the debilitating effects of competition for resources and influence among the several branches of the military. The act centered the duty to provide military advice to the president in the hands of the chairman of the Joint Chiefs of Staff. It also took some authority away from the separate services' departments and allocated it instead to regional commanders (known as commanders in chief, or CINCs), such as those in Europe or the Pacific, and to commanders responsible for different functions, such as transportation, space, or special operations. According to Stuart (2003, 299): "The Goldwater-Nichols Act . . . significantly enhanced the powers of the Commanders in Chief (CINCs) within the armed forces. . . . They have been able to exercise considerable direct control over the forces within their areas of regional and functional responsibility." In other words, the 1986 act had the effect of making all the branches of the military responsible to a single commander within specific regions, or when carrying out different functions,

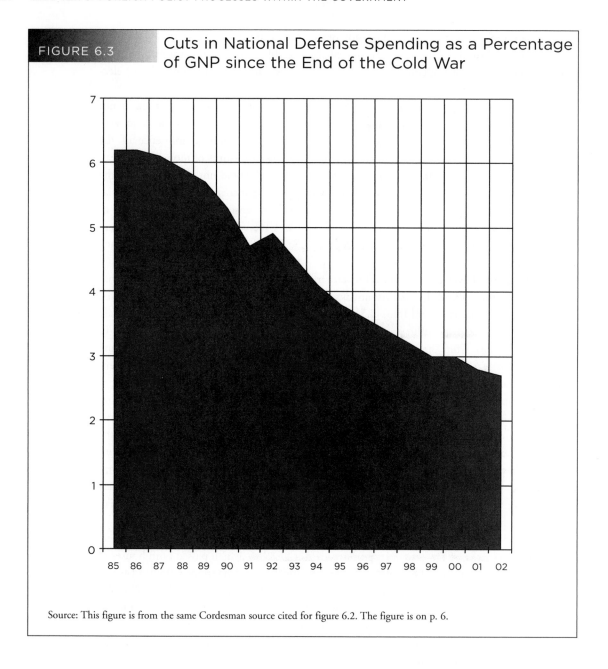

FIGURE 6.3   Cuts in National Defense Spending as a Percentage of GNP since the End of the Cold War

Source: This figure is from the same Cordesman source cited for figure 6.2. The figure is on p. 6.

and the commander had the responsibility to coordinate and integrate the forces from the different branches of the military.

One further impact of the Goldwater-Nichols Act was to increase the authority of the chairman of the Joint Chiefs of Staff. The mission of the Joint Chiefs is to assist the chairman in carrying out his responsibilities to provide unified strategic direction of U.S. military forces, the operations of those forces under a unified command, and to integrate the land, naval, and air forces of the United States into an efficient team. By the early 1990s, there was little doubt

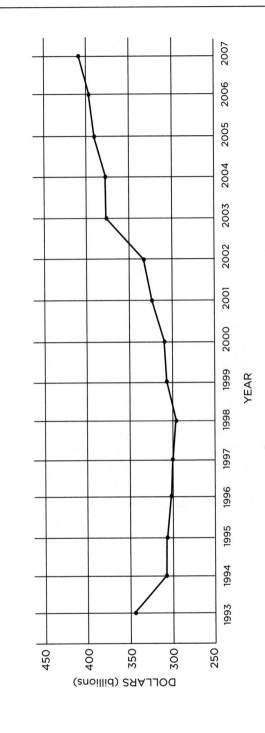

FIGURE 6.4

Department of Defense Expenditures, 1993–2007 (in constant dollars)

Source: Center for Strategic and Budgetary Assessments. 2006. "Department of Defense (051) Budget Authority by Title." www.csbaonline.org/2006-1/2.DefenseBudget/By_Title.shtml.

FIGURE 6.5

Department of Defense Organization Chart, 2007

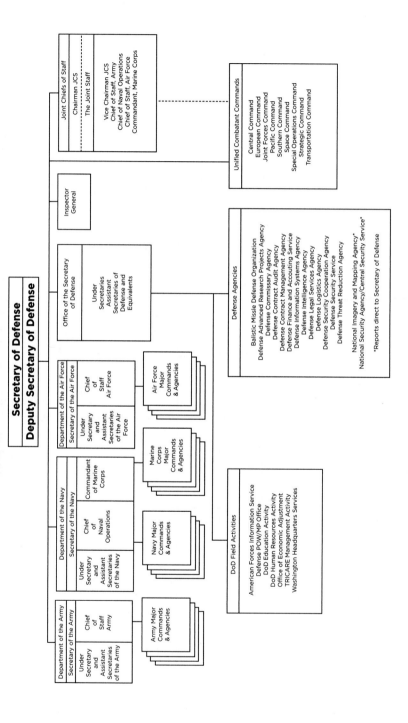

Department of Defense

Secretary of Defense
Deputy Secretary of Defense

Department of the Army
Secretary of the Army
Under Secretary and Assistant Secretaries of the Army
Chief of Staff Army
Army Major Commands & Agencies

Department of the Navy
Secretary of the Navy
Under Secretary and Assistant Secretaries of the Navy
Chief of Naval Operations
Commandant of Marine Corps
Navy Major Commands & Agencies
Marine Corps Major Commands & Agencies

Department of the Air Force
Secretary of the Air Force
Under Secretary and Assistant Secretaries of the Air Force
Chief of Staff Air Force
Air Force Major Commands & Agencies

Office of the Secretary of Defense
Under Secretaries Assistant Secretaries of Defense and Equivalents

Inspector General

Joint Chiefs of Staff
Chairman JCS
The Joint Staff
Vice Chairman JCS
Chief of Staff, Army
Chief of Naval Operations
Chief of Staff, Air Force
Commandant, Marine Corps

Unified Combatant Commands
Central Command
European Command
Joint Forces Command
Pacific Command
Southern Command
Space Command
Special Operations Command
Strategic Command
Transportation Command

DoD Field Activities
American Forces Information Service
Defense POW/MP Office
DoD Education Activity
DoD Human Resources Activity
Office of Economic Adjustment
TRICARE Management Activity
Washington Headquarters Services

Defense Agencies
Ballistic Missile Defense Organization
Defense Advanced Research Projects Agency
Defense Commissary Agency
Defense Contract Audit Agency
Defense Contract Management Agency
Defense Finance and Accounting Service
Defense Information Systems Agency
Defense Intelligence Agency
Defense Legal Services Agency
Defense Logistics Agency
Defense Security Cooperation Agency
Defense Security Service
Defense Threat Reduction Agency
National Imagery and Mapping Agency*
National Security Agency/Central Security Service*

*Reports direct to Secretary of Defense

Source: U.S. Department of Defense Organization Chart, 2007. www.defenselink.mil/odam/omp/pubs/GuideBook/Pdf/DoD.PDF

that the intention of the Goldwater-Nichols act to increase the authority of the chairman had met with success. General Colin Powell was appointed to the post in 1989, and, according to Stuart (2003, 298), within a few years, "the chairman of the Joint Chiefs had become an extremely powerful and relatively independent actor in the Washington policy community." Stuart quotes analyst Lawrence J. Korb (1997) to support his judgment:

> General Powell was to the chairmanship of the Joint Chiefs of Staff what Henry Kissinger was to the Assistant to the President for National Security Affairs. He defined the position in a way that nobody else has, and exercised the power inherent in that position to really dominate the process.

However, Powell's successors, John Shalikashvili (1993–1997), Henry Shelton (1997–2001), Richard Myers (2001–2005), and Peter Pace (2005–), have failed to achieve the prominence that Powell attained. Perhaps the potential is still there, but the new organizational structure created by the Goldwater-Nichols Act apparently does not guarantee that the chairman of the Joint Chiefs of Staff will play a truly formidable role in the making of foreign policy.

THE INTELLIGENCE COMMUNITY

The **Central Intelligence Agency (CIA)** is by far the best-known government bureau devoted to intelligence generation and interpretation, and many Americans believe that it is the only such agency. Actually, however, about 80 percent of what the U.S. government spends on intelligence annually goes to a wide variety of intelligence agencies within the Department of Defense. The army, the navy, the air force, the Marine Corps, and even the Coast Guard each have their own intelligence agencies. The Defense Department also includes such organizations as the National Security Agency, which intercepts and analyzes foreign communications; the National Reconnaissance Office, which is responsible for developing, launching, and maintaining information-gathering satellites; and the National Geospatial-Intelligence Agency (formerly known as the National Imagery and Mapping Agency), which focuses on interpreting the information provided by satellites and other sources. Within the Defense Department, there is also the Defense Intelligence Agency, which "provides timely and objective military intelligence to warfighters, policymakers, and force planners" (U.S. Intelligence Community 2005).g And, as the 9/11 Commission Report (Kean and Hamilton 2004, 128–129) observes:

> In addition to those from the Department of Defense, other elements in the intelligence community include the national security parts of the FBI; the Bureau of Intelligence and Research in the State Department; the intelligence component of the Treasury Department; the Energy Department's Office of Intelligence and Counterintelligence, the former of which, through leveraging the expertise of the national laboratory system, has special competence in nuclear weapons; the Office of Intelligence of the Coast Guard; and today, the Directorate of Intelligence Analysis and Infrastructure Protection in the Department of Homeland Security.

---

g. A naïve observer might wonder how this role differs from that of the defense organizations within the various military branches.

Thus, the intelligence function is spread throughout the federal government, operating in a complex array of diverse nooks and crannies, and, for the most part, unintegrated and uncoordinated. This lack of coordination is a feature of the **intelligence community** to which the government has responded in energetic ways since 9/11; we will discuss the most important measures taken in due course. But, historically, the CIA has been by far the most important intelligence organization in the government, exerting the most significant impact on U.S. foreign policy.

And that impact has often been controversial, if not downright counterproductive. One of the earliest and most notable CIA interventions in the Cold War era—certainly in terms of its long-term impact—occurred in Iran in 1953. Mohammed Reza Shah Pahlavi had been placed on the throne as shah of Iran in 1941, at a time when the British and the Soviets (who occupied the country) feared that his father was on the verge of aligning Iran with Germany. At the same time, Mohammed Mossadegh became a member of the Iranian parliament, making a name for himself by denouncing Britain's control of his nation's oil industry. In 1951 the Iranian parliament voted to nationalize its oil industry, and Mossadegh became prime minister. Though not a Communist himself, he was supported by Iran's Communist party. When the shah attempted to dismiss him, Mossadegh's supporters took to the streets, and the shah fled the country (Sciolino 2000). It was at that point, James Risen (2000) reports, that the "United States and British officials plotted the military coup that returned the shah of Iran to power and toppled Iran's elected prime minister."

For almost thirty years afterward, the shah was a dependable ally of the United States, and the CIA's role in bringing him to power seemed to bring credit to the agency, as well as benefits to the United States. He minimized the power of the Communists within Iran and, through his White Revolution, implemented modernization measures, such as extending suffrage to women, that also brought rapid economic growth during the 1960s and the 1970s. But he also built up a secret police force, the SAVAK, that became notorious for imprisoning and torturing political dissidents and opponents to the shah.

In 1979, seemingly without warning, the shah was overthrown in a revolution led by the Ayatollah Khomeini. That revolution was born in a spasm of anti-Americanism that focused on the holding of American hostages in the U.S. embassy for 444 days starting in 1979. The fundamentalist Islamic regime established by Khomeini remains in power today; now under the leadership of his successor, Ayatollah Khamenei, it is as fervently anti-American as ever. George W. Bush has categorized Iran as belonging to an "axis of evil," and it seems increasingly intent on developing nuclear weapons. It may also come to have what the United States would have to perceive as a pernicious influence on the government developing in strife-torn Iraq, as well as throughout much of the rest of the Middle East. In short, the CIA's initiative in overthrowing Mossadegh and installing the shah of Iran in the early 1950s may have had long-run consequences that, even today, continue to prove contrary to the interests of the United States.

At about the same time that the CIA was meddling in the domestic political processes of Iran, it also intervened in Guatemala against the elected government of Jacobo Arbenz, who was perceived to be allied to Communists and about to receive weapons from the Communist Bloc; he also had expropriated large amounts of land belonging to the United Fruit Company. The CIA organized Guatemalan exiles and, in 1954, rather easily engineered an attack that led to the overthrow of the Arbenz government, in a process to be discussed in more detail in chapter 10 (Immerman 1982).

As we will also discuss in chapter 10, that CIA operation had long-range impacts not only in Guatemala, but throughout Latin America. It set the stage for a series of governments that killed or brutally repressed many Guatemalans in political strife that continued for decades. The ease with which the Arbenz regime had been ousted soon led the CIA to believe that it could just as easily overthrow the government of Fidel Castro in Cuba, but that intervention, launched by CIA-organized Cuban exiles, foundered at the Bay of Pigs in 1961. This embarrassing failure helped to solidify, rather than overthrow, the Castro regime, which remains in power over forty-five years later.

The CIA was also very active in an attempt to destabilize the elected but left-leaning government of Salvador Allende in Chile in the early 1970s. Its efforts in that case provoked a U.S. Senate Committee, chaired by Frank Church, to investigate the CIA's covert activities. The Church Committee eventually produced an exhaustive critical review of the CIA's history of secret interventions into the political affairs of a multitude of states around the world. It enumerated, for example, 81 covert projects initiated under the Truman administration, 104 projects under the Eisenhower administration, 163 under the Kennedy administration, and 142 during the Johnson administration. It also suggested, however, that between 1961 and the 1976 publication of the committee's final report, there had been, in fact, "several thousand covert projects undertaken" (Assassination Archives and Research Center 1976).

The Church Committee also focused on the CIA's attempts to assassinate several foreign leaders, in addition to Allende. The committee found evidence that the CIA had also targeted Patrice Lumumba, prime minister of the Congo; Fidel Castro of Cuba; Rafael Trujillo, president of the Dominican Republic; Cuban revolutionary Che Guevara; and President Ngo Dinh Diem of South Vietnam. In the wake of these revelations, President Gerald Ford issued Executive Order 11905, declaring that "no employee of the United States Government shall engage in, or conspire to engage in, political assassination" (CNN.com 2002). That ban is still in effect, although in response to the events of 9/11, there were calls on the president and Congress to repeal it (Fanton and Roth 2001).

The effects of covert activities in Latin America since the 1950s can certainly be debated, but they do cast doubt on the sincerity of the U.S. commitment to democracy, since they have with some regularity been aimed at leaders elected in ostensibly democratic processes. They have also encouraged leaders who want to pursue policies that they know will be unwelcome to the U.S. government to feel that they must move in the direction of more autocratic processes in order to protect themselves from the subversive practices of the CIA. The CIA, in short, may well deserve some responsibility for the growing list of leftist governments in contemporary Latin America, reinforced in recent years by the successes of Hugo Chavez in the oil-rich state of Venezuela.

Nevertheless, having endured rather penetrating investigation and skeptical appraisals in the 1970s, the CIA was revived in the 1980s, when Ronald Reagan used it as a main tool for the implementation of the **Reagan Doctrine**. This doctrine called for active efforts to subvert Communist or leftist regimes, replacing the more passive policy of "containment" that had merely tried to combat its spread to new areas and countries. Perhaps the most important of the CIA's efforts in this regard were focused on overthrowing the leftist Sandinista government in Nicaragua, supporting the Islamic fundamentalist *mujahadeen* in their struggle against

Soviet occupying forces in Afghanistan, and aiding the rebel group UNITA, led by Jonas Savimbi, in its effort to take over power in Angola.

The effort in Nicaragua ultimately led to substantial embarrassment for the Reagan administration, after Congress passed legislation prohibiting the CIA or any other U.S. government organization from materially assisting the anti-Sandinista *contra* rebels. To circumvent these prohibitions, Marine Lt. Col. Oliver North, an aide to Reagan's national security adviser, Admiral John Poindexter, arranged to sell weapons to the government of Iran, and then directed the proceeds from the sale to the support of the *contras*. By 1986, most of the details of this clandestine arrangement became public, and the Reagan administration was profoundly shamed by its complicity in what became known as the "Iran-*contra* affair."

The CIA's role in Afghanistan may well have played a key role in the defeat of the Soviet troops there, leading to their departure in 1989. In the process, though, the CIA strengthened Islamic fundamentalist elements in Afghanistan, in whose midst eventually arose the Taliban regime that came to rule the country—and to create problems for the United States that are all too obvious today.

But the Soviet defeat in Afghanistan may also have been an important step toward the ultimate demise of the Soviet Union. Somewhat paradoxically, then, its success in bringing an end to the Cold War led to lean budgetary times for the CIA, especially for the covert activities carried out by its Clandestine Service. According to the 9/11 Commission Report (Kean and Hamilton 2004, 132): "The Clandestine Service felt the impact of the post–Cold War peace dividend, with cuts beginning in 1992. . . . The nadir for the Clandestine Service was in 1995, when only 25 trainees became new officers."

The CIA therefore entered the twenty-first century in a state of some disarray, partly because it had not really found a purpose to supplant its Cold War mission of combating the Soviet Union and a worldwide Communist movement. After September 11, 2001, however, there suddenly arose an obvious need for "intelligence"—that is, information about enemies of the United States generated by undercover activities—as well as analysis of "open sources." Some observers charged that the CIA was at least somewhat to blame for the terrorist attacks of 9/11, in that it should have been able to penetrate al-Qaeda and like-minded organizations so as to prevent those attacks from occurring. While the critics were still analyzing the mistakes that led to this catastrophe, the United States went to war against Iraq in 2003, partly on information from the CIA that that nation possessed weapons of mass destruction. In fact, it was revealed in 2004 that "about two weeks before deciding to invade Iraq, President Bush was told by CIA Director George Tenet there was a 'slam dunk case' that dictator Saddam Hussein had unconventional weapons" (CNN.com 2004a).[h]

In the wake of its alleged failures with respect to 9/11 and the misinformation it provided to President Bush in the run-up to the war against Iraq, the CIA came under siege, and there were calls for reorganization of the entire intelligence community. The 9/11 Commission Report noted that the CIA, at the beginning of the twenty-first century, was still structured in such a way as to deal with Cold War threats. It also asserted that twenty-four-hour,

---

h. CNN here is reporting on an account in Woodward 2004.

round-the-clock news had increased pressure on analysts in the CIA to come up with fresh reports at an ever-faster pace, and that this haste had consistently led to shallow and unhelpful analysis.

Then, too, in the 1990s, the CIA had been hugely embarrassed by the discovery of a Soviet "mole" within the agency: Aldrich Ames, who "had been protected and promoted by fellow officers while he paid his bills by selling to the Soviet Union the names of U.S. operatives and agents..." (Kean and Hamilton 2004, 134). The result was an agency in which information-sharing was tremendously compartmentalized, in an effort to protect both sources and intelligence from exposure to potential spies within the agency, and where there was a decided reluctance to share information with other agencies of the U.S. government.

Fear of penetration also made it difficult to recruit effective agents to deal with the threat of terrorism. Individuals who had traveled extensively outside the United States had to wait a long time for initial clearance, and it was almost certain that people born abroad or who had numerous relatives abroad would not be accepted. This personnel problem was compounded by the fact that there were, in the pre-2001 era, very few programs in the nation's universities and colleges focusing on Islam, the Middle East, or Arabic language studies. In fact, in 2002, only six undergraduate degrees in Arabic were awarded (Kean and Hamilton 2004, 135).

The combined impacts of 9/11 and the CIA's alleged failure to provide accurate intelligence about Iraq's weapons of mass destruction led Congress, by the end of 2004, to resolve to reform the intelligence community. Both houses passed, with few dissenting votes, the Intelligence Reform and Terrorism Prevention Act, and President Bush signed the bill into law in December 2004. One obvious intent of this legislation was to provide some coordinated, centralized direction of the intelligence activities taking place not only within the CIA, but also in the Defense Department and the FBI, and even in the State Department and the Department of the Treasury.

To accomplish this goal, the act created a position with the title Director of National Intelligence. John Negroponte served as the first director from April 2005 until February 2007, when he was succeeded by John Michael McConnell. Previously, the head of the CIA had held the title Director of Central Intelligence, and he had at least nominal authority over the entire intelligence community. Under the new regime, however, the director of national intelligence has replaced the CIA director as the administrative head of the intelligence community as a whole—thus becoming the new "intelligence czar"—as the intelligence representative at the meetings of the National Security Council, and as the top official in charge of providing daily intelligence briefings to the president.

The director of national intelligence faces a major bureaucratic challenge in the attempt to bring coordination and cooperation to so many separate agencies, all now confronted by rather unprecedented challenges from transnational terrorism. Richard Clarke (2005) feels that it is necessary to shake up the CIA fundamentally. Contrary to its popular image, the CIA is not made up almost entirely of secret undercover agents; at least half its employees are analysts, who may work mostly with open sources. These analysts might be separated entirely from the "spies," according to one idea about how the reform of the CIA should proceed. The director might also create a National Security Service within the FBI, the head of which could report directly to the president. Allegedly, 75 percent of a $40 billion annual budget for intelligence is devoted to Defense Department agencies that might be consolidated so as to save billions of dollars annually, and, in the process, all their operations might become better coordinated and effective.

One of the fifteen organizations under the authority of the director of national intelligence is the new **Department of Homeland Security (DHS)**. It was created by the Homeland Security Act of 2002, and its "primary mission … is to prevent terrorist attacks within the United States, reduce the vulnerability of the United States to terrorism; and minimize the damage, and assist in the recovery, from terrorist attacks that do occur within the United States" (Department of Homeland Security 2005). Consolidating into one organization what had previously been twenty-two different governmental agencies, the new department has about 190,000 employees and devotes itself on any given day to a host of activities that, according to Matthew Brzezinski (2004), includes

> screening 1.5 million airline passengers, inspecting 57,000 trucks and shipping containers, and making 266 arrests and 24 drug seizures. Each day, the department reviews 2,200 intelligence reports and cables, issues information bulletins to as many as 18,000 recipients, and trains 3,500 federal officers from 75 different agencies. It deploys 108 patrol aircraft, has a fleet of more than 350,000 vehicles, operates 238 remote video surveillance systems, and stands watch over 8,000 federal facilities, ports, power plants, tunnels, and bridges.

The Department of Homeland Security also has famously (or infamously) relied on a color-coded terrorism risk advisory scale (actually devised by a presidential adviser before the department was created), whose major impact so far seems to have been to provide useful material for late-night talk show hosts during their opening monologues. The scale runs from "low risk" (green), through intermediate levels (yellow and orange), to "severe risk" (red) of a terrorist attack. Mostly, these color-coded advisories have provoked questions about what information is relied on to determine how serious the risk of a terrorist event is on any given day, and exactly what individual citizens should do when they are warned that the risk is severe.

Other complaints about DHS are that the department devotes too high a proportion of its resources to airport security, and not enough to other forms of transportation, or to threats to power plants or water supplies, for example, and that its funding has suffered in part because of the tremendous budgetary demands of the war in Iraq. What funding it does have is often allocated according to idiosyncratic political priorities within Congress rather than by means of some logical assessment of threat. As Brzezinksi (2004) reports, "Alaska and North Dakota get twice as much federal antiterror funding per capita as New York. Wyoming gets four times more than California."

One thing that can be said in favor of the Department of Homeland Security is that several years after the horrendous attacks of 9/11, there had been no repetition of such terrorist aggression within the United States. And that had to be something of a surprise. Another thing that might be said is that the Department of Homeland Security faces what is ultimately an impossible task. Operatives of al-Qaeda and like-minded groups can strike anywhere, at any time, in whatever way is most convenient and likely to be most effective from their point of view. When security measures are stepped up at airports, terrorists can instead choose targets among railways, subways, buses, athletic events with massive crowds, concerts, political rallies, nuclear power plants, shopping centers, schools, or churches. When DHS succeeds, nothing happens, and it is difficult to know whether the department deserves any credit for that. If and when it fails—as someday, to some extent, it almost certainly will—everybody will know.

CONGRESS AND AMERICAN FOREIGN POLICY

The obvious place to begin an analysis of the role of the U.S. Congress in the country's foreign-policy-making process is the Constitution of the United States. Article I, Section 8 of that document bestows upon Congress the power to lay and collect duties, to provide for the common defense, to regulate commerce with foreign nations, to define and punish piracies, to declare war, to issue letters of marque and reprisal, to raise and support armies, and to maintain a navy. Article II, which deals with the executive branch, stipulates that the president "shall have the Power, by and with the Advice and Consent of the Senate, to make Treaties, provided two thirds of the Senators present concur." Article II, Section 2 also asserts that the president must obtain the advice and consent of the Senate for the appointment of ambassadors, as well as "other public Ministers and Consuls."

The legislative branch is thus given an impressive array of powers. But, much as the State Department seems, on paper, to stand at the apex of all the federal agencies involved in foreign policy making when, in fact, its impact is rather limited, the powers bestowed upon Congress in the area of foreign policy making often turn out to be less robust than they appear on a first reading of the Constitution. For example, the document's simple and straightforward assertion that Congress has the power to "declare war" may understandably lead to the assumption that the United States does not become involved in wars unless Congress authorizes the use of military force through formal declarations of war. That inference is, to say the least, misleading.

Perhaps the most important limitation on the powers of Congress in the area of peace and war stems originally from the constitutional provision, in Article II, Section 2, that the "President shall be Commander-in-Chief of the Army and Navy of the United States." Until the end of the Second World War, the president did, on rare occasions, request Congress to pass declarations of war. Specifically, this procedure was followed with respect to five interstate wars in American history: the War of 1812, the Mexican-American War (1846–1848), the Spanish-American War (1898), World War I, and World War II. (In World War I, official declarations of war were issued against both Germany and Austria, while in World War II, there were separate declarations of war aimed at Japan, Germany, Italy, Bulgaria, Rumania, and Hungary. All together, a total of eleven declarations of war have been passed by Congress.)

All eight declarations of war in the twentieth century were strikingly similar in one respect. As David Ackerman and Richard Grimmett (2003, 3) note: "In the twentieth century, without exception, presidential requests for formal declarations of war by Congress were based on findings by the President that U.S. territory or sovereign rights had been attacked or threatened by a foreign nation." But since World War II, the United States has fought wars in Korea, in Vietnam, against Iraq in 1991, against Serbia in 1999, against Afghanistan starting in 2001, and again against Iraq starting in 2003—all conflicts in which Congress has never officially declared war. (Also, the nation was never directly attacked by any of those countries.) In addition, the United States has deployed troops in situations where they have occasionally become involved in deadly combat, such as Lebanon in 1958 and again in 1983, Bosnia in 1995, Iraq in the 1990s after the end of the first Gulf War, Somalia in 1983, and Haiti in 1994. On none of these occasions did Congress officially declare war.

That Congress can, in the modern era, exercise control over U.S. policy regarding military conflicts abroad was demonstrated with some clarity during the war in Vietnam. One potential source of such control stems from its "power of the purse"—that is, if it disapproves of some U.S. military action abroad, it can cut off the funds necessary to support it. Implementation of that strategy was certainly approached in the case of the war in Vietnam, which was ostensibly brought to an end with a peace treaty in 1973. But, as Norman Friedman (2000, 394) reports:

> The North Vietnamese began to violate the 1973 peace treaty as soon as it was signed.... Treaty violations were so serious that in March 1973 Henry Kissinger recommended that Nixon order bombing of the Ho Chi Minh Trail or the DMZ or both. Nixon ordered some limited attacks in Laos and Cambodia. In June Congress cut off any funds for additional operations.

The situation deteriorated steadily for the regime of South Vietnam until, in March 1975, North Vietnam initiated a military attack intended to take over the South. The Nixon administration requested some $700 million in emergency aid, to help the South Vietnamese regime defend itself, but Congress refused to provide the funds. The South Vietnamese government was quickly defeated, and, in Friedman's words (2000, 397), "for the first time, the United States had lost a war."

Under most circumstances, however, Congress is reluctant to cut off funds, especially if U.S. military forces are still engaged in combat with enemy troops. After the United States had experienced tens of thousands of battle fatalities in extended military combat in Korea in the 1950s and then again in Vietnam in the 1960s and the 1970s, even though war had never been formally declared in either case, Congress moved to try to increase its influence over decisions to involve the U.S. military in combat operations. In November 1973, it passed—and then overrode President Nixon's veto of—the **War Powers Resolution** (or Public Law 93-148). This resolution declared that the president is authorized to deploy U.S. military forces into hostilities, or imminent hostilities if (1) there has been a formal declaration of war, (2) the deployment has been authorized by a specific statute, or (3) the United States or its military forces have been attacked.

The War Powers Resolution also requires the president to consult with Congress before introducing American armed forces into hostilities, and to report to Congress if armed forces are ordered into hostilities or imminent hostilities. Once that report has been submitted (or if it should have been submitted), the War Powers Resolution stipulates that Congress must authorize the use of American military forces in question within sixty or ninety days; if it fails to do so, those forces must be withdrawn.

How well has the War Powers Resolution worked? According to Richard Grimmett (2004): "Some observers contend that the War Powers Resolution has not significantly increased congressional participation, while others emphasize that it has promoted consultation and served as leverage." Since the passage of the resolution, presidents have submitted 115 reports to Congress about various military operations, but it has not, as a result of that resolution, been consulted ahead of time about most such presidential decisions. Grimmett concludes (12): "A review of instances involving the use of armed forces since passage of the Resolution . . . indicates there has been very little consultation with Congress under the Resolution. . . ."

For example, President Clinton ordered U.S. military forces to join NATO allies in an attack on Serbian forces in Kosovo, which began on March 24, 1999; Clinton notified Congress about these operations two days later. In April a resolution was introduced in the House of Representatives that would have directed the president, under the War Powers Resolution, to remove U.S. forces from Serbia, but it was defeated. A formal call for a declaration of war against Serbia was then also rejected in the House by a vote of 427–2. But, on the same day, in a tie vote, the House also defeated a resolution that would have provided (nonbinding) support for President Clinton's decision to employ U.S. military forces against Serbia because of its allegedly genocidal policies in the province of Kosovo.

Eighteen House members filed suit in federal district court, trying to force the president to secure authorization from Congress to continue the war against Serbia. Meanwhile, the sixty-day limit on military operations unauthorized by Congress passed, but President Clinton simply asserted—as have all presidents—that the War Powers Resolution is constitutionally defective, and he continued the military involvement. The lawsuit was pursued all the way to the Supreme Court, which finally refused to hear an appeal to overturn lower courts' rulings that Congress lacked legal standing to sue the president under these circumstances.

In the aftermath of the attacks of 9/11, Congress almost immediately passed a joint resolution authorizing the president to use all necessary and appropriate force against nations, organizations, or persons that he had determined were either involved in those attacks or harbored such organizations or persons. According to a report written for the Congressional Research Service (Ackerman and Grimmett 2003, 17): "This authorization of military action against organizations and persons is unprecedented in American history. . . ." However, as this same report points out, President Thomas Jefferson was authorized by Congress to take military action against "private vessels" engaged in piracy in the Mediterranean in 1802, and, in general, Congress authorized the use of military force against the Barbary Pirates in that part of the world during that era (see Leiby 2001).

In October 2002, Congress passed a joint resolution authorizing President Bush to use military force against Iraq. The resolution stipulated that the president might use force to defend the national security of the United States against the threat posed by Iraq, and to enforce all relevant UN Security Council resolutions regarding Iraq. It also stated that this authorization of force is "intended to constitute specific statutory authorization within the meaning of section 5(b) of the War Powers Resolution." Arguably, the War Powers Resolution specifies that the president is required to provide "clear" evidence of an "imminent" threat by an adversary in order to take military action against it. Arguably, too, President Bush failed to provide such evidence of an imminent threat in advance of his attack on Iraq in March of 2003. In fact, says D. Lindley Young (2005), "since the war in Iraq started, there have been repeated admissions by members of the Bush administration and by Bush supporters that there was no 'imminent' threat to the U.S. and that Bush never said there was one. This is tantamount to an admission that the [War Powers Resolution] was violated and that the war in Iraq was illegal."

That is a debatable claim. More defensible, perhaps, is the assertion that Congress has failed to carry out its constitutionally mandated function of declaring war in cases where the

United States finds itself confronted with choices about embarking on military operations. This is not a new phenomenon, for Congress started "authorizing the use of force" rather than "declaring war" in the earliest days of the Republic. For example, it authorized President Adams to use force against French naval vessels in 1898, President Jefferson to use force against the Bey of Tripoli in the Mediterranean Sea in 1802, and President Madison to use force against Algiers and the Barbary Pirates in 1815 (Ackerman and Grimmett 2003, 7–8). Thus, although Congress is not totally impotent when confronted with a president determined to take advantage of her role as commander in chief of the armed forces, it is quite clear that foreign policy processes in the United States have developed in such a way that the ability of Congress to exert control over the commander in chief is not as extensive as it appears in the Constitution.

Another important foreign policy function for Congress, on paper, involves the role of the Senate in the approval of treaties made by the president. The Constitution specifies that **treaty ratification** requires a supporting vote of two-thirds of the Senate. This role became highly visible in the aftermath of World War I, when the Senate refused to ratify the Treaty of Versailles in 1920, thus keeping the United States out of the League of Nations. Ironically, the prime mover behind the creation of the League had been U.S. President Woodrow Wilson.

The Senate's refusal to ratify the Versailles Treaty was unusual, however. In fact, it has since 1789 considered hundreds of treaties and has failed to ratify only twenty-one of them. Since the end of the Second World War, the Senate has rejected only three treaties: the Law of the Sea Treaty in 1960, the Montreal Aviation Protocols in 1983, and the Comprehensive Nuclear Test Ban Treaty of 1999.

It may be, however, that the distinct tendency of the Senate to ratify treaties submitted to it by the president understates the legislators' influence on the treaty-making process (and therefore on foreign policy making in general). Although the Senate has rejected relatively few treaties, "many others ... have died in committee or been withdrawn by the president rather than face defeat" (Senate Historical Office, n.d.). And the requirement that treaties must be ratified by a two-thirds vote may also have had an important impact on U.S. foreign policy on several occasions. As the Senate's official Web page on the topic explains: "The effect of this requirement is that successful treatymaking can never be a partisan affair, since only under the rarest circumstances has a party ever enjoyed a two-thirds majority in the Senate."

On the other hand, the requirement of two-thirds majority for ratification has encouraged presidents to search for ways to circumvent the Senate and its constitutionally specified role of providing advice and consent. And in this quest, presidents have been quite successful. They may come to an agreement with the government of a foreign country and commit to abide by it without submitting the document for Senate approval. Such international compacts, although sometimes referred to as treaties, are, in the U.S. case, better known as **executive agreements**, and they have become especially popular among U.S. presidents in the post–World War II era. In 1952 the U.S. government entered into 291 executive agreements—a larger number in that one year than had been concluded in the entire century from 1789 to 1889. Not surprisingly, then, "the United States is currently a party to nearly nine hundred treaties and more than five thousand executive agreements" (Senate Historical Office, n.d.).

These data would seem to support the suggestion by James A. Nathan and James K. Oliver (1994, 99) that presidents "have developed and employed the executive agreement to circumvent Senate involvement in international agreements almost altogether." Political analyst Lisa Martin (2003), however, makes the interesting counterargument that treaties, since they require the president to go to the Senate to get that two-thirds vote, are "costly signals" that serve the useful purpose of indicating to other states—both those who sign the treaties and third-party observers—a greater commitment to abide by the terms of the agreement. In other words, states that interact with the United States may conclude or suspect that executive agreements devised by presidents without the advice and consent of the Senate are not as credible as treaties. This possibility, as well as the fact that presidents may modify treaties in anticipation of Senate preferences in order to win the necessary two-thirds vote, should be kept in mind in evaluating the roles of Congress in general and of the Senate in particular in the foreign-policy-making process. Nevertheless, as is the case with its constitutionally mandated right to formally declare war, the Senate's treaty-making role as specified in the Constitution has apparently been rather successfully abridged by presidents as they struggle to increase their power over the foreign-policy-making process.

Another foreign policy issue area for which the Constitution delegates clear and important authority to Congress is international trade. Article I stipulates that Congress shall "regulate commerce with foreign nations" and also gives it the power to "lay and collect taxes, duties, imposts, and excises." Until the 1930s, Congress exercised this authority over trade, and especially over tariffs, in a rather untrammeled fashion. As Stephen D. Cohen (2000, 17) explains: "From the earliest years of its existence, the Congress listened to the demands of domestic interest groups and unilaterally established the U.S. tariff schedule to protect key constituents. U.S. tariffs were relatively high and inflexible."

The congressional tendency to keep U.S. tariffs high and inflexible reached an important crescendo in 1930. In the wake of the stock market crash of 1929 and the onset of the Great Depression, Congress passed the **Smoot-Hawley Tariff Act**, which Joan Spero and Jeffrey Hart (2003, 66) label "the most protectionist law of the century." To say that the Smoot-Hawley tariffs did not work well would be a spectacular understatement. In fact, as we noted in chapter 4, there is widespread (though not, of course, universal) agreement that, as Spero and Hart (67) put it, "protectionism in the interwar period led not only to economic disaster but also to international war." Among many members of Congress, as well as many outside analysts, it has become an accepted "fact" that the Smoot-Hawley tariffs provoked retaliatory tariffs from many of the most important trading partners of the United States. And, it is widely believed, these beggar-thy-neighbor tariffs, in turn, deepened and prolonged the depression, made it especially severe in Germany—creating devastating conditions there that brought Adolf Hitler to power—and so played a key role in the path leading to World War II.

This is, to be sure, a rather complex and elongated causal chain whose validity will never be verifiable to any degree of certainty. But many congressional leaders consistently accept the standard indictment of the Smoot-Hawley tariffs, and they react accordingly. Within three years after the passage of the tariff act, Congress took an important step toward controlling what its members themselves apparently saw as self-destructive tendencies. In 1934 it passed the Reciprocal Trade Agreements Act, which gave the president the power to negotiate reductions in tariffs without getting the approval of Congress.

The president is less accountable than are members of Congress to local interests. Indeed, his dependence on a national constituency makes him more sensitive to the welfare of the economy as a whole, and so apparently more inclined to keep tariffs relatively low. For several decades after the passage of the Reciprocal Trade Agreements Act, says Lenore Sek (2001), "Congress extended the President's tariff-cutting authority several times. Under this authority, the President negotiated reductions in tariff levels multilaterally in five rounds [of international bargaining]" that have taken place since World War II.

In 1974 Richard Nixon sought to extend even further his presidential authority over the regulation of trade between the United States and its trading partners. By the early 1970s, tariffs had been substantially reduced, and nontariff barriers—such as quotas or restrictions on trade based on environmental or safety issues—had become more important. President Nixon proposed that he be allowed to reduce these conditional restrictions, and the Trade Act of 1974 granted him temporary fast track authority (discussed in chapter 4) to negotiate trade agreements, including issues focusing on nontariff barriers. Once having negotiated such agreements, the president was required to submit implementing legislation to Congress. This provision gave Congress important input into the process of regulating trade, but only under restrictive conditions, including mandatory deadlines, limited debate, and, most importantly, a prohibition from amending the implementing legislation.

The congressional grant of fast track authority to the president lasted from 1974 until 1994. Various presidents used that authority—to implement the Tokyo Round and the Uruguay Round of tariff reductions under the authority of the General Agreement on Tariffs and Trade (GATT), to establish free trade agreements with Israel and with Canada, and finally, to negotiate the North American Free Trade Agreement (NAFTA). In 1995, however, Congress refused to extend fast track authority for President Clinton. His administration made several attempts to get the authority renewed, but they all failed.

In 2002 President Bush finally persuaded Congress to renew the fast track authority—which his administration referred to as *trade promotion authority*—and he used that authority to push through Congress implementing legislation creating the Central American Free Trade Area (CAFTA). So, once again, as in the cases of the congressional powers to declare war and to ratify treaties, the president has found ways to curb and circumvent the influence of Congress in the foreign-policy-making issue area of trade and tariffs.

Nevertheless, special interests groups, utilizing members of Congress as important partners, do still have considerable influence over trade policies and tariffs. It was estimated in 1988 that restrictions on the import of sugar added $3 billion to American citizens' grocery bills every year. In 2002 the U.S. International Trade Commission estimated that if all trade barriers had been eliminated in 1999, 175,000 jobs would have been lost, 90 percent of them in the textile industry. But it also estimated that 192,400 jobs would have been created by the elimination of tariff barriers, and that the GNP of the United States would have been augmented by $59 billion. Furthermore, import barriers do harm to the trading partners of the United States, many of them poor developing countries. If the United States and the rest of the world were to remove such tariff barriers, the resulting economic growth would add between $250 billion and $650 billion to the world's economic output, while the elimination of agricultural supports alone would create benefits valued at $30 billion for poor, developing countries (Manzella 2004).

THE PRESIDENT AND AMERICAN FOREIGN POLICY

Logically, on paper (that is, the Constitution), and according to rational political ambition theory, the president plays an absolutely crucial role in the American foreign policy process. As the head of the executive branch of the government, she would be expected, independent of any other powers, to have an important impact on foreign policy. But the Constitution also makes the president the commander in chief of the armed forces and bestows upon her the responsibility for making treaties, as well as the duty to appoint and receive ambassadors.

On paper, too, as we have seen, Congress is also given many important responsibilities that sharply circumscribe what a president can do in the area of foreign policy. In one of the best-known academic analyses of the relationship between the president and Congress over the making of foreign policy, Edward S. Corwin (1957) suggests that the Constitution actually offers to the two institutions an "invitation to struggle" over the direction of American foreign policy. (Only Congress can officially declare war, for example, even though the president is the commander in chief of the armed forces.) But, as we have also seen, presidents have, since the nation's founding, come up with effective ways to circumvent Congress in virtually every important issue area. And, according to rational political ambition theory, the driving force behind most major foreign policy decisions is the president's wish to retain office and the attendant political power.

Thus, the proposition that the president is powerful and crucially important to the foreign-policy-making process in the United States is beyond doubt. Nevertheless, there is widespread agreement that the president's power has changed over time. Franklin Roosevelt responded to the Great Depression with a series of energetic federal programs that vastly expanded the scope and the strength of the presidency. World War II magnified and reinforced that increase in power, and then the onset of the Cold War invested in the president control over an incredible range of military force, as well as increasing superiority over Congress in the area of foreign policy. As we mentioned earlier, Presidents Truman and Johnson took the country into wars costing tens of thousands of soldiers' lives, without bothering to ask Congress to declare war.

Those events led many political observers to worry about the rise of an "imperial presidency"—a phrase that served as the title of a widely noted book on the problem by historian Arthur Schlesinger Jr. (1973).[i] That concern about the rising power of the presidency had much to do with the passing of the War Powers Act, which we discussed earlier. Ironically, however, at just about the time that Schlesinger's book was published, President Nixon was in the process of being overwhelmed by the Watergate scandal, which led to impeachment proceedings in the House and to his resignation in advance of a probable conviction by the Senate.

Nixon's disgrace was followed by the presidency of Gerald Ford, who had not even been elected vice president—the elected vice president, Spiro Agnew, having departed his office in disgrace in advance of Nixon's resignation—and then by that of Jimmy Carter, who appeared

---

i. Schlesinger's book received particular attention because he had written several prominent books on former presidents, as well as having served as a high-ranking special assistant and speechwriter for President Kennedy from 1961 until 1963.

to some observers unable to cope with the combined challenges of an energy crisis, galloping inflation, and a hostage crisis in Iran. So, only a few short years after the publication of *The Imperial Presidency*, some analysts began to wonder instead if the office had not been weakened to the point that the president had too *little* power to cope with crucial challenges, especially in the area of foreign policy.

Ever since Ronald Reagan managed to win reelection and serve two full terms, however, little has been heard about concerns that the presidency has been unduly weakened. The tragedy of 9/11 almost certainly served to centralize power more markedly in the hands of the president. In any case, there has long been a respected argument among students of the presidency that that there are actually "two presidents": a domestic policy president and a foreign policy president. U.S. presidents are much more likely to receive support from Congress when they undertake major foreign policy initiatives than when they address essentially domestic issues. Aaron Wildavsky (1966) noted this tendency decades ago, in an article focusing on the years 1948–1964; during that era, presidential initiatives having to do with defense and foreign policy issues were supported by Congress 70 percent of the time, while policy proposals dealing with domestic matters evoked support from Congress only about 40 percent of the time. James M. McCormick (2005, 277) provides specific data to support his observation that this tendency for Congress to support the president on foreign policy matters has continued up to the current day.[j]

In one potentially vital way, however, the U.S. presidency has been the target of a constitutional limitation since World War II. The Twenty-second Amendment to the Constitution stipulates that "No person shall be elected to the office of the President more than twice...." This amendment, passed by Congress in 1947 and ratified by the requisite number of states by 1951, was quite clearly a reaction to Franklin Roosevelt's election to four straight terms as president. No earlier president had served more than two terms, although Ulysses S. Grant had sought a third term in 1888, and in 1912 Theodore Roosevelt made a bid for another term as president after he had succeeded the assassinated President McKinley in 1901 and then won election himself in 1904.[k]

The Twenty-second Amendment was adopted out of concern that, without term limits, a president with enough popular support might become, in effect, chief executive for life, assuming over time near-dictatorial powers. But it is clear that the amendment does severely weaken a second-term president, who becomes a "lame duck" from the moment he or she is reelected. Everyone knows exactly when his or her time in office will be over, and so can weigh the benefits of simply awaiting the turnover of power to a successor. On the other hand, the effect of the Twenty-second Amendment may be liberating, in both a negative and a positive sense. Second-term presidents are no longer accountable to the voters; their time in office can-

---

j. "In our calculation of the degree of presidential success from Harry S Truman to George W. Bush on foreign policy voting in Congress, we also found that the recent presidents have been enormously successful in getting votes for issues on which they took a position" (McCormick 2005, 277).

k. President Bill Clinton has argued that the Twenty-second Amendment should be modified to prevent only more than two *consecutive* terms as president, so that former presidents such as himself could run again after a period of time away from the office. See Gardinier 2003.

not be extended no matter how well, or how badly, they do. Bueno de Mesquita et al. (2003, 314) draw the logical conclusion: "As the end of their legal term approaches, leaders know they will be removed whatever their policy performance. This undermines their incentive to generate effective policy."

Since a central assumption of rational political ambition theory is that leaders want to stay in power, one might infer that term limits could have a dramatic impact on the foreign policies of the United States. Second-term presidents could be expected to adopt and support foreign policies very different from the policies of first-term presidents.[1] If presidents facing constitutionally limited terms are concerned about the success of their political parties after they have left office, or the fate of their potential successors, or if they want to maximize their influence on the choice of their successors, they may respond to such incentives in a manner similar to the way that they would react to their own desire to stay in power. On the other hand, if they are concerned about their place in history, or how they will be remembered by future generations, they may adopt policies with an eye much more focused on long-term implications than on their short-term political impacts. Presidents focusing on their "historical legacy," in other words, may respond to incentives quite different in their impact on policymaking than those who are primarily intent on winning reelection. In short, rational political ambition theory does not, so far, provide a complete answer to what, for it, is clearly a crucial question: What are the impacts of term limits on U.S. presidents when they make foreign policy choices?

While rational political ambition theory does clearly place great emphasis on the role of the president in the foreign-policy-making process, it also recognizes limitations on that role. The president cannot, for example, focus continually on the entire range of foreign policy issues facing the United States; especially on a day-by-day basis, the huge foreign policy bureaucracy under her supervision deals with those issues in ways that best serve its own interests and perspectives more than by any direction or guidance from the president. One well-known analysis of the impact of "bureaucratic politics" on foreign policies holds that such policy is often, perhaps usually, not the outcome of some unitary actor such as the president providing consistent, logical input that primarily serves her interest in retaining power. Instead, according to Graham Allison and Philip Zelikow (1999, 255):

> Outcomes are formed, and deformed, by the interaction of competing preferences.... Many actors as players ... focus not on a single strategic issue but on many diverse intranational problems as well; players who act in terms of no consistent set of strategic objectives but rather according to various conceptions of national, organizational, and personal goals; players who make government decisions not by a single, rational choice but by the pulling and hauling that is politics.

This perspective on the impact of foreign policy bureaucracies on policy choices is often summarized by the aphorism "where you stand depends on where you sit." In other words, each sector of the foreign-policy-making establishment—be it the military forces and the Defense Department, the State Department, the CIA, or the Department of Homeland Security—will

---

1. Bueno de Mesquita et al. (2003, 313–319) speculate at some length about the possible impacts of term limits, but they tend to focus almost exclusively on examples from ancient Greece and Rome, and on the extent to which officeholders faced with term limits develop kleptocratic tendencies.

have its own interests at stake, which will affect its perceptions of developing foreign policy issues and tend to shape its responses to those issues.

In a way, the president is no different. She stands at the head of the executive branch of government, and how she perceives foreign policy problems and responds to them will obviously be affected by her institutional place in the government and especially, according to rational political ambition theory, by her desire to stay in power. This basic assumption, however, is not intended to suggest that the key to perceptive foreign policy analysis is rampant skepticism or even cynicism about the president's motives, or those of the people around her in the foreign-policy-making establishment. Admittedly, the president does want to stay in power, and this desire is likely to have a continuing, important impact on the foreign policy decisions that she makes.

But this is not to say that the most important source of foreign policy decisions coming out of the White House is the president's ego, her love of the pomp and circumstance surrounding the office, or the pride she feels every time "Hail to the Chief" rings out when she enters the room. The assumption, instead, is that the president feels that she and her allies in the government know what is best for the country and are better able than their political opponents to formulate and execute effective foreign policies in particular, and to govern the country in general. In other words, rational political ambition theory does not assume that all presidents (or the leaders of other countries, for that matter) are involved in a single-minded, totally cynical pursuit of power. Instead, presidents, as well as the political officeholders and appointees around them, are assumed to have genuine, sincere, and perhaps even prudent, policy goals to which they are dedicated. They are simply very sensitive, according to rational political ambition theory, to the fact that they will not be able to pursue those goals effectively if they are replaced in office by their political opponents, whose ideas about foreign policy choices are misguided (in their view), and who also are not as well-placed or as able to effectively carry out whatever policy goals they may have.

Rational political ambition theory is compatible with the assumption, in other words, that the president of the United States (like the leaders of other countries) sincerely believes that what is good for her—most especially, staying in power—is good for the country. Admittedly, this is a simplifying assumption, and there are surely many exceptions to this "rule." But rational political ambition theory does not boil down to a suspicion that every president's foreign policy agenda is a function primarily of a megalomaniacal campaign of self-aggrandizement.

CONCLUSION

The Department of State stands at the apex of the structure beneath the president in the U.S. government's foreign policy establishment. Although it still serves many important functions, the State Department has tended to lose clout, comparatively speaking, to such agencies as the Department of Defense and the National Security Council, and to intelligence organizations such as the Central Intelligence Agency. This loss of influence derives partly from the tendency of presidents to view State Department personnel as representatives of the foreign governments and interests with which they interact on a continuing basis. The Department of

Defense, which expanded its power greatly during World War II, typically enjoys annual budgets that dwarf those of the Department of State. The National Security Council is smaller, more flexible, and usually perceived by the president to be more loyal to her agenda. The Central Intelligence Agency has, over the years, carried out a series of covert actions whose value seems doubtful in retrospect. Its role has been subsumed recently under the umbrella of the director of national intelligence.

The constitutionally endowed power of Congress to declare war has fallen into a limbo status and may never be used again, as presidents consistently feel entitled to deploy U.S. military forces without congressional approval. Still, as the end of the Vietnam War demonstrates, Congress's power of the purse remains a credible check on the president's ability to utilize American military force. The Constitution also gives the Senate the power of advice and consent regarding any international treaties entered into by the United States. Presidents have routinely circumvented this provision as well, by entering into executive agreements with governments in other states without seeking Senate approval, and, anyway, the Senate almost always approves treaties submitted to it by presidents. But treaties may be better than executive agreements at signaling commitment to other states, and presidents may respond to anticipated objections in the Senate by modifying treaties before they are submitted.

Finally, Congress is empowered by the Constitution to deal with international trade and tariffs, but here, too, it has relinquished much of that power to the president. But Congress can withdraw fast track authority from the president—as it did in the case of President Clinton—and the high levels of some tariffs in the United States certainly suggest that Congress has not forfeited all its influence over international trade. If we also take into account the individual initiatives undertaken by members of Congress—by taking trips, for example, to the sites of crises overseas, by holding public hearings on foreign policy crises, and by exercising their collective right to approve appointments to ambassadorial posts, as well as to many other positions in the foreign policy establishment (including the secretary of state)—we must conclude that Congress plays a vital role in the foreign-policy-making process, even though it is not as important a role as was, perhaps, envisioned by the writers of the Constitution.

Obviously, American presidents have a very powerful foreign policy role. Congress made an attempt to bring that power more under its control in the wake of the Vietnam War, but subsequent experiences limited concern about an "imperial" presidency. Such concerns may, perhaps, be revived as a result of the Bush administration's obvious desire to expand presidential powers in various ways, and by a feeling (reminiscent of that produced by the Vietnam War) that assertive, uncontrolled presidents can lead the country into serious problems. According to rational political ambition theory, second-term presidents should be relatively free of concerns about retaining power, since they are constitutionally ineligible for reelection. If they want to influence the choice of their successor, however, they may feel similar pressures not to antagonize too many groups or interests who will be involved in the selection of the next president.

KEY CONCEPTS

RATIONAL POLITICAL AMBITION AND... LESSONS
FOREIGN POLICY PROCESSES WITHIN THE GOVERNMENT LEARNED

☑ The State Department plays a leading role in foreign policy formation, on paper. The fact that it has little direct contact with the electorate may be one factor that has limited its influence on foreign policy in recent decades.

☑ The Defense Department and the National Security Administration (along with the National Security Advisor), along with other intelligence agencies, have domestic constituencies, or are better attuned to the President's aims abroad, as well as his domestic concerns; this augments their influence on foreign policy processes.

☑ The Constitution presents to the President and the Congress an "invitation to struggle" over American foreign policy. The President and members of Congress both fashion foreign policies in a manner that they hope will keep them in power.

☑ The President is obviously a key figure, according to rational political ambition theory. Rational political ambition theory does not suggest that he or she cynically manipulates foreign policy solely for the purpose of holding onto power. The President's hold on power is likely to be solidified by policies that appear to make the country more secure. The influence of people and organizations outside the Executive Branch will be magnified to the extent that they can reinforce or threaten the President's hold on power. Second-term presidents cannot maintain themselves in power when their term is over, but they do hope to be able to influence the selection of their successor.

PART 3

THE CONTEST WITH COMMUNISM

THE OVERRIDING ISSUE FOR AMERICAN FOREIGN POLICY THROUGHOUT most of the post–World War II era was the so-called Cold War against Communism—or, more precisely, against the Soviet Union. (The Soviet Union and China were important allies only through the first half of this period.) In chapter 7 we will analyze various notions about the origins of the Cold War, focusing in turn on arguments that it was primarily the fault of the United States or of the Soviet Union, and then concluding with analyses that highlight some structural factors that may well have made the superpower standoff either inevitable or, at least, very likely.

The most obvious and most bitterly prolonged contest between the United States and the Soviet Union during the Cold War era was centered in Vietnam, even though there were no direct confrontations between American and Russian military forces in that Asian country. Because of its traumatic effect on the American political system, as well as its lasting impact on American foreign policies in its wake, Vietnam rates a chapter all its own—that is, chapter 8. (The Korean War was also an important episode in the history of this period, but it came very early on in the Cold War; it focused on the relationship with China rather than on the more central Cold War foe, the Soviet Union; and it ended, if not in a win for the United States, at least without a defeat like that suffered in Vietnam. We will deal with the Korean War in chapter 12 on U.S. policies with respect to Asia.)

7

THE BEGINNING OF THE COLD WAR

WHEN DID THE **COLD WAR** BETWEEN THE UNITED STATES AND THE SOVIET Union begin? Actually, since this standoff between the two major powers was not an official war, there was no official beginning date. Nevertheless, the answer to that question has a clear bearing on the question of why the Cold War occurred, which is the focus of this chapter.

One answer to the prior question suggests that the Cold War began during the Russian Revolution, soon after the Bolsheviks took control of that upheaval in October 1917. The German government had played a role of some significance in bringing about the original rebellion against the tsarist autocracy by supporting Russian revolutionary groups that were in exile. It had also allowed Vladimir Lenin to travel by railway from Switzerland across German territory into Russia, where he played an indispensable role in bringing the Bolsheviks to power. According to William Keylor (1996, 61): "This event was widely viewed in Allied countries as the first successful application of the German policy of instigating insurrection behind the lines of the Entente."

Apparently, Lenin immediately repaid this German assistance by signing the Treaty of Brest Litovsk, which effectively ceded control of Finland, Poland, the Baltic provinces, Ukraine, and Transcaucasia to Germany and Austria-Hungary. The territory thus given up constituted about one-third of the Russian empire's population, along with one-third of its agricultural land and three-quarters of its industrial capacity (Smele 2004). This is a classic case of a foreign policy decision that was motivated in part by the desire of the leader to stay in power: Lenin felt that he had to have peace with the Germans in order to consolidate his hold on power at home.

From the point of view of Germany's opponents, this treaty between the Russians and the Germans was troublesome mostly because it took Russia out of the coalition trying to defeat the Central powers of Germany and Austria-Hungary. One reaction by the anti-German coalition was to send troops to the Russian territory of Murmansk and Archangel in northern Russia. The main, or at least ostensible, purpose of this expedition was to prevent military supplies that had been sent to the Russians from falling into the hands of the Germans.

U.S. President Woodrow Wilson's original reaction to the Russian Revolution had been supportive. Historian Richard Pipes (1991, 600) comments: "Woodrow Wilson seems to have

The Cold War had no official beginning, but it had clearly started by the time President Truman announced plans for the United States to aid free peoples resisting Communist aggression. On March 12, 1947, Truman addressed Congress about plans to provide aid to Greece and Turkey, a step toward the implementation of what was to become known as the Truman Doctrine.

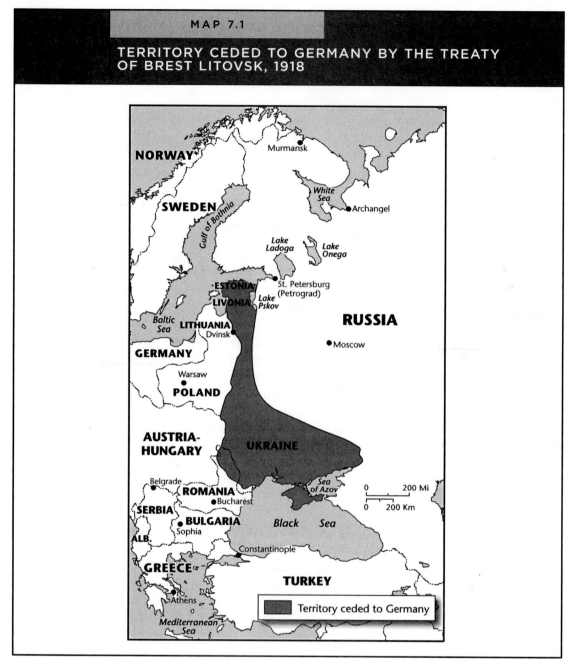

MAP 7.1

TERRITORY CEDED TO GERMANY BY THE TREATY OF BREST LITOVSK, 1918

In order to consolidate its tenuous hold on power, in 1918 the revolutionary Soviet regime ceded in the Treaty of Brest Litovsk vast territories shown here to Germany. The Soviets also gave up claims to additional territory in Finland and Poland, which became "sovereign" states under German protection.

believed that the Bolsheviks truly spoke for the Russian people...." Indeed, Wilson had sent a message to a Congress of Soviets that was meeting in March of 1918, declaring that "the whole heart of the people of the United States is with the people of Russia in the attempt to free themselves forever from autocratic government and become masters of their own life" (602).

Nevertheless, President Wilson ordered American troops into northern Russia in 1918. As Leonard Coombs (1988) reports, "when the American troops reached their destination in early September, they joined an international force commanded by the British that ... was fighting the Bolsheviks." Lenin then became convinced, apparently, that at the conclusion of World War I, all of the major capitalist states would launch a military attack against the new Bolshevik regime in the emerging Soviet Union. In analyzing the revolution, Pipes (1991, 607) argues that, in fact, "only the British intervened actively." And yet, although the ostensible purpose of the U.S. intervention in northern Russia related to the battle against the Germans in World War I, the American troops continued military operations there until well after the larger conflict had ended in November of 1918. Indeed, two companies of U.S. Army soldiers did not even arrive in Murmansk until April 1919. Coombs (1988) remarks: "A winter of fighting Bolsheviks and wondering why they were still in combat when the war with Germany had ended led to severe morale problems among the American troops, including an alleged mutiny in March of 1919." The troops finally did leave by June of that year, but it certainly seems plausible that these prolonged military operations in northern Russia confirmed in the minds of Bolshevik leaders the idea that capitalist states would be quite determined to undermine the revolutionary Bolshevik regime.

On the other hand, for their part, the Bolsheviks early on issued a so-called Peace Decree, exhorting workers around the world to rise up against capitalist regimes in their countries. Pipes (1991, 608) comments: "This was a declaration of war on all the existing governments, and intervention in the internal affairs of sovereign countries that would be often repeated...." And, in the view of this prominent analyst of the Russian Revolution, "such incitement of their citizens to rebellion and civil war by a foreign government gave the 'imperialist plunderers' every right to retaliate in kind." From this perspective, the Cold War was well under way as early as the 1920s.

Even though President Wilson had reacted initially with sympathy for the Bolshevik cause, the United States withheld diplomatic recognition from the Soviet Union for some time. Presidents Harding, Coolidge, and Hoover all declined to recognize the new revolutionary state, but Franklin Roosevelt finally decided to move in that direction in 1933. At that point, there was some hope that trade with the Soviet Union might help to ease the effects of the Great Depression in the United States, but the more important motives were international and diplomatic: as he grew more concerned about the increasingly assertive foreign policies of Germany in Europe and Japan in Asia, President Roosevelt came to realize that the Soviets might serve as a useful counterweight in both places.

In return for U.S. recognition, then, the Soviets promised to respect the religious rights of Americans living in the Soviet Union, to refrain from propaganda and subversive activity against the United States, and to negotiate about the international debts that the Bolsheviks had repudiated when they came to power. However, the United States was soon disappointed by the results of its decision to extend formal diplomatic recognition. Alexander DeConde

FDR 1st to recognize communist Russia

(1963, 532) explains: "Trade with the Soviets never reached the expectations of those who desired it; Russia made no settlement of the debts question; Communist propaganda continued; and the Soviet Union did not cooperate in any policy of opposition to Japan."

Nevertheless, it is important, for a sense of historical perspective, to understand that during the 1930s, there was in the United States a certain amount of sympathy for the Russian Revolution, and even for Communism—and not just among a narrow band of extremists. The head of the Communist Party in the United States, Earl Browder, authored an unemployment insurance bill that was introduced for congressional consideration by Representative Ernest Lundeen of Minnesota. In the late 1930s, Browder was even invited to sit on a platform in Cleveland with Ohio Senator Robert A. Taft (a very conservative Republican), who "wanted all the votes from the left he could get" (Manchester 1974, 97).

Soviet leader Joseph Stalin had disappointed even many dyed-in-the-wool communists around the world when he signed the Nazi-Soviet Pact in 1939, but the basis for a cooperative relationship between the Soviet Union and the United States was created shortly thereafter, when Adolf Hitler's forces invaded the Soviet Union on June 22, 1941. Even so, the United States did not come into the war on the anti-German (and therefore pro-Soviet) side until it had been attacked by Japan, another of the Axis powers, at Pearl Harbor in December of that year.

Still, their recognition of common enemies, especially Germany, brought about a period of substantial cooperation between the United States and the Soviet Union. In November of 1941—even before Pearl Harbor—the Roosevelt administration had authorized a $1 billion lend-lease credit to the Soviets (Keylor 1996, 184), and by 1942, the United States had replaced Great Britain as their major supplier of military aid. "From the beginning of the war Soviet lend-lease shipments had enjoyed a unique status. At Roosevelt's insistence, American authorities accepted Russian aid requests at face value, without the close scrutiny given applications from other allies" (Gaddis 1972/2000, 178). Originally, the agreement with the Soviet Union had called for repayment of lend-lease materials, without interest, starting five years after the end of the war, but in June of 1942, the formal requirement for repayment was eliminated.

STRAINS IN THE WORLD WAR II COALITION

The United States and the Soviet Union—as well as, some of the most powerful countries of the world, Britain, France, and China—thus agreed that both Germany and Japan should be defeated. And the leaders of the United States and the Soviet Union worked together efficiently to overpower the Germans.

But strains and stresses on this alliance began to develop even during the war. Almost as soon as Germany attacked the Soviet Union, in June of 1941, Stalin began to urge his new allies in the West to relieve the pressure on his beleaguered military forces by attacking Germany across the English Channel. The United States first considered such an attack soon after Germany declared war on the United States within a matter of days after Pearl Harbor. But the Western Allies decided to first create an anti-Axis front in Northern Africa, working toward Italy, before attempting an attack across the English Channel. And so, that cross-channel attack did not occur in 1942, or even in 1943. Through those two long years, and halfway through 1944, the Soviets were required to deal with the German military juggernaut without the relief that might have been brought by an attack on Germany's western front. This long delay created suspicion in the minds of many Soviet citizens, as well as in the Communist leadership, that the United States, in particular, was content to let Nazis and Communists go on killing each other in great numbers as long as possible.[a]

Once Germany was defeated, the Allies turned their attention to Japan. Expecting a long and bloody campaign in the Pacific, the United States was, at first, anxious to get the Soviet Union involved in that battle, in order to spread out the anticipated burdens of defeating Japan. But then, on July 16, 1945, American scientists successfully tested an atomic weapon in the New Mexico desert. According to some analysts, the U.S. government at that point became more interested in keeping the Soviet Union out of the military conflict aimed at bringing down the Japanese regime. In fact, according to Alperovitz (1965), the United States bombed Hiroshima and Nagasaki in 1945 not so much to ensure that the Japanese would surrender quickly, as to impress the Soviet Union with the power of the new technology that it had developed. These devastating attacks would also serve the purpose of keeping the Soviet Union out of the process of dismantling the wartime Japanese regime. In other words, the dropping of the atomic bombs were, in this view, among the first "shots" fired during the Cold War.[b]

Another important indicator of stresses in the U.S.-Soviet coalition that surfaced as World War II came to a close concerned the future of Iran. In 1942 Great Britain and the Soviet Union had occupied southern and northern Iran, respectively, in order to keep that oil-rich country from being taken over by the Germans. The Allies reached an understanding that the occupying troops would respect the sovereignty of Iran, and that they would remove their troops within six months after the termination of the conflict against the Axis powers.

However, by the end of the 1945, U.S. officials came to suspect that the Soviets were planning to annex the Iranian province of Azerbaijan, as a step toward incorporating the whole state of Iran within its sphere of influence. By January of 1946, concern about this issue increased to the point that the Iranian government submitted it to the Security Council of the United Nations. Still, when a deadline for the withdrawal of foreign troops from Iran passed on March 2, the Soviets showed no signs of moving in that direction. Cold War historian John Lewis Gaddis (1972/2000, 310) reports: "The week which followed was an extremely tense one—*Newsweek* found the atmosphere reminiscent of the fall of 1938, when the Munich crisis was at its height."

The tension increased even more as the Soviets engaged in substantial troop movements—not on the way out of Iran, but in a way that made it appear that they might intend to invade Turkey, Iraq, and/or Tehran, Iran's capital. Meanwhile, in accordance with a UN Security

---

a. This suspicion would seem to be supported by Sen. Harry Truman's assertion (which we noted in chapter 2) that "if we see that Germany is winning we ought to help Russia and if Russia is winning we ought to help Germany and that way let them kill as many as possible...." In a similar vein, Sen. Bennett C. Clark of Missouri argued that "Stalin is as bloody-handed as Hitler. I don't think we should help either one" (Catledge 1941). (Truman, however, did go on to say, "I don't want to see Hitler victorious under any circumstances.")

b. Of course, not all historians agree. See, for example, Rappaport 1967; Alperovitz 2005.

Council resolution, representatives from the Soviet Union and Iran were engaged in negotiations with each other. On the day that the Security Council was to deal with the crisis created by the Soviet troop movements, the Soviets announced that they intended to withdraw all of the troops from Azerbaijan within five or six weeks. In light of that announcement, the Soviet representative to the United Nations, Andrei Gromyko, suggested that the issue of Soviet troop movements be withdrawn from the agenda of the Security Council. When the United States refused to do so, Gromyko walked out of the UN in a dramatic display of Soviet displeasure. Nevertheless, in the end, the Soviets conceded the point. Within a week, "the Soviet and Iranian governments announced a formal agreement calling for the withdrawal of Soviet troops by early May" (Gaddis 1972/2000, 311–312).

Interestingly, Gaddis goes on to point out that the U.S. decision to insist on Security Council deliberations over the Soviet troop movements even after the Soviets had announced their intention to remove the troops from Iran "stemmed chiefly from domestic considerations: the Secretary of State wanted to make clear to his critics at home that the United States had abandoned the politics of appeasement once and for all." Tensions between the United States and the Soviets over international issues were real enough, as the Cold War emerged and developed. But, as rational political ambition theory would suggest, the temptation to utilize vigorous anti-Soviet policies to shore up political support at home was always an exacerbating factor.

Disagreements between the United States and the Soviet Union over the future of Eastern Europe were not so readily resolved. One of the important bases for this conflict was created at a meeting between leaders of the anti-Axis coalition at Yalta in February of 1945. At the time, Roosevelt and his advisers were so anxious to get the Soviet Union involved in the war against Japan that they agreed that if the Soviets would enter that war three months after the surrender by Germany, the Soviet Union would be granted Japan's Kurile Islands, as well as control of Outer Mongolia and recovery of territory lost in the Russo-Japanese war near the beginning of the twentieth century (DeConde 1963, 629).

Despite the very different interpretations that arose in later decades, it could be argued that, at Yalta, President Roosevelt drove a rather hard bargain over the future fate of Eastern Europe. He did agree to allow Poland to take over territory that was then part of Germany, but he also persuaded Stalin to agree to add to the existing Polish government some leaders from democratic elements in exile outside of Poland (mostly in London). In addition, Stalin agreed to hold postwar elections in Poland. Moreover, as Steven Hurst (2005, 14) explains, "this agreement on Poland was accompanied by a 'Declaration on a Liberated Europe,' prepared by the U.S. State Department, in which the three powers [i.e., the United States, the Soviet Union, and Great Britain] called for free elections throughout the countries of Europe that had been, or were being, freed from the Nazi yoke."

In retrospect, it is clear that the democratic governments that Roosevelt hoped to encourage in Eastern Europe in the wake of World War II never came to pass. The states in that region became, instead, subservient "satellites" of the Soviet Union, headed by Communist governments that never allowed democratic elections, in the sense that they were never open to competition between independent political parties. But, Keylor (1996, 194) says, President Roosevelt "went to his grave apparently convinced that the 'spheres of influence' formula adopted by Stalin and Churchill in Moscow four months earlier had been superseded by a

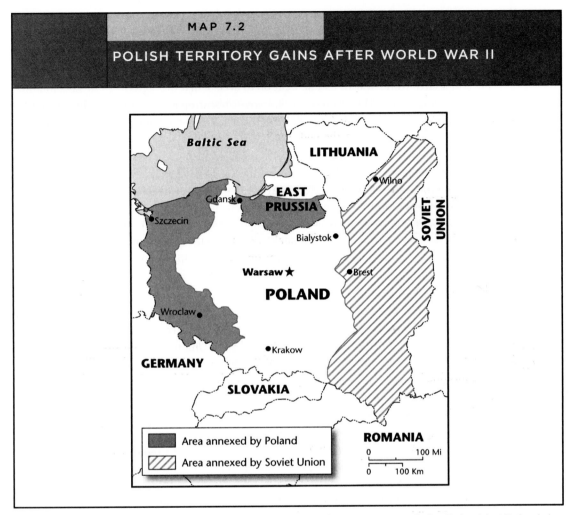

MAP 7.2

POLISH TERRITORY GAINS AFTER WORLD WAR II

As a result of post–World War II settlements, Germany lost territory that was ceded to Poland, but Poland also lost territory that was ceded to the Soviet Union.

neo-Wilsonian principle of national self-determination that revived the spirit of the Atlantic Charter." In other words, Roosevelt believed that at Yalta he had extracted from Stalin a promise to allow democratic governments to arise in Eastern Europe in the wake of the defeat of the Nazis.

Was President Roosevelt just incredibly naïve to accept such a promise from a leader like Joseph Stalin? Was he manipulated by advisers (including Alger Hiss) so as to be an unwitting dupe for those who preferred to see Eastern Europe become firmly ensconced within a Soviet sphere of influence? There is very little doubt, in any case, that the issue that did more than any other to spark the Cold War confrontation centered on the future of Eastern Europe after the defeat of Nazi Germany. Also, there is no doubt that the agreement at Yalta serves as the basis for one of the more enduring controversies regarding U.S. foreign policy in the postwar era. As recently as May 2005, for example, President George W. Bush asserted in a speech in Latvia that the United States bore some of the blame for the division of Europe into opposing camps after World War II, and he went on to declare that the "agreement in Yalta followed the unjust tradition of Munich and the Molotov-Ribbentrop pact.... Once again, when powerful governments negotiated, the freedom of small nations was somehow expendable" (Baker 2005).

Nevertheless, the specific dispute in which the Cold War might be said to have had a quasi-official start did not concern Eastern Europe directly. Instead, it focused, mostly, on the postwar future of Greece. Amaury de Riencourt (1968, 82) provides the background: "As in so many other areas under German ... occupation, some of the most effective underground and guerilla movements were organized and led by local Communists." After—and even somewhat before—the Germans were defeated, the Communists in Greece made a bid to take over control of the country, and political strife raged between them and the royalist government backed by the British.

Britain's prime minister, Winston Churchill, it turns out, had discussed the future of Greece, and other states in the area, with Stalin in a meeting in Moscow in October of 1944. There, Churchill proposed a sphere-of-influence agreement between the United Kingdom and the United States, on the one hand, and the Soviet Union, on the other. In the case of Romania, for example, he suggested that the Russians would have 90 percent control, and the two other nations would have 10 percent; in Yugoslavia, the proposed division would be 50–50. And with respect to Greece, the suggestion was that Britain and the United States would have 90 percent control, while the Russian influence would be limited to 10 percent (Smith, n.d.).

Although Churchill insisted later that these were meant to be temporary, wartime arrangements only, Stalin apparently took the agreement quite seriously. When German troops pulled out of Greece in October of 1944 and British troops moved in, Norman Friedman (2000, 46) reports, "Stalin ordered the Greek Communists to cooperate with the Government of National Unity the British were forming." However, the Communists in Greece were supported mainly by Yugoslavia's Marshal Tito, who disagreed with Stalin's order to cooperate with the British. Tito continued supporting the Greek Communists, and they engaged in a prolonged civil war. Friedman comments: "Stalin's men, ironically, without Stalin's blessing, were now at war with a major Western power, Britain."

This war continued into 1947. At that point, Great Britain was in dire straits economically, and its leaders decided that they could no longer bear the burden of defending the Greek government from its internal opponents. At the same time, the Soviets were also putting pressure on Turkey to cede territory that would allow them joint control over the Turkish Straits of the Dardenelles, leading from the Black Sea to the Aegean and Mediterranean seas. On February 21, 1947, "the British Foreign Office officially informed the American State Department of its intention to terminate all financial assistance to Greece and Turkey and to remove the 40,000 British troops from Greece"(Keylor 1996, 260).

The reaction of the Truman administration to the British government's act of deferral was dramatic, and of lasting significance. Addressing Congress on March 12, 1947, President

Truman declared that "it must be the policy of the United States to support free people who are resisting attempted subjugation by armed minorities or by outside pressures." He was calling for aid to Greece and Turkey specifically, but this so-called **Truman Doctrine** more generally "implied American commitment to assist victims of aggression and intimidation throughout the world" (Gaddis 2005, 95).

Admittedly, this U.S. response to the unfolding situations in Greece (and Turkey) was largely provoked by previous actions by the Soviet Union that had clearly been aimed at establishing control of Eastern Europe. Gaddis (1972/2000, 350–351) also makes clear, however, the extent to which the Truman administration was reacting to public opinion—and, by implication, acting on its own desire to stay in power:

> The Truman speech was, in fact, aimed more toward the American public than toward the world. … The Truman Doctrine constituted a … last-ditch effort by the Administration to prod Congress and the American people into accepting the responsibilities of world leadership which one year earlier, largely in response to public opinion, Washington officials had assumed by deciding to "get tough with Russia."

Ironically, however, the crisis in Greece that played a key role in evoking this quasi-formal declaration marking the beginning of the Cold War was, in fact, a situation in which Stalin, as we have seen, had specifically attempted to play a pacifying and cooperative role.

Thus, by proclaiming the Truman Doctrine in 1947, the United States became quite visibly embroiled in the Cold War confrontation with the Soviet Union that would continue at least until November of 1989, when the Berlin Wall collapsed. In those forty-two years, the two "superpowers" engaged in important proxy wars, such as those in Korea and Vietnam; became enmeshed in a tense crisis over missiles in Cuba that came close to precipitating a nuclear war; and spent billions of dollars on military hardware and technology, including missiles and nuclear weapons that had the potential to destroy modern civilization. Was this hugely expensive, incredibly dangerous, and criminally wasteful confrontation primarily the fault of one side or the other, or was it the more or less inevitable product of structural features of the international system as it emerged from World War II?

WAS THE COLD WAR THE RESPONSIBILITY OF THE UNITED STATES? *misperception*

One important argument to the effect that the Cold War's onset was primarily the fault of the United States focuses on the relative power, or military-industrial capabilities, of the two superpowers as World War II came to a close. It is true that the Soviet Union had a formidable military force, especially on land, and so the U.S. government might reasonably have been concerned that the Soviet Army could overrun Western Europe, should it choose to do so, without great difficulty.

However, the United States—as it demonstrated dramatically at Hiroshima and Nagasaki—maintained a monopoly in nuclear weapons. It also had by far the largest economy in the world. American forces emerged relatively unscathed from World War II, especially compared to their counterparts in the Soviet Union. By the war's end in 1945, the United States had lost some 408,000 military personnel, while the Soviet Union had lost 7.5 million (Small and

Singer 1982, 91). In addition, Soviet civilian losses numbered in the tens of millions; no military conflict at all had taken place in the United States. (Pearl Harbor, though located in territory belonging to the United States, was not at that point a part of the country.) In short, in terms of raw military power, political influence, and economic clout, the Soviet Union suffered from a disparity in power and influence vis-à-vis the United States that surely should be kept in mind when assessing the relative culpability of each side for the onset of the Cold War.

Especially in light of this power disparity, U.S. hopes for the emergence of democratic governments in Eastern Europe after World War II were not realistic. A sense of historical perspective, for example, should have led American foreign policy makers to realize that the United States itself had, at least since the beginning of the twentieth century, insisted on friendly governments in states in the Western Hemisphere, especially those near its border—but also, on occasion, in more distant states, such as Chile. There was, indeed, at least one American government leader during the immediate postwar years who did display this sense of historical perspective. He was Henry L. Stimson, a distinguished member of the Republican Party who had been appointed secretary of war by President William Howard Taft in 1911, then secretary of state by President Herbert Hoover in 1929, and, finally, secretary of war by Democratic President Franklin Delano Roosevelt, who chose him in an attempt to encourage bipartisan unity in the wake of Germany's attack on Poland in 1939.

Stimson still held that last position in 1945, when the controversy over Soviet actions in Eastern Europe began to emerge. Judging the Russian desire for a preferred position in Eastern Europe to be reasonable, he told President Truman specifically that "the Russians perhaps were being more realistic than we were in regard to their own security." He even perceived the similarities between the Russian attitude about Eastern Europe and the historical position of the United States in regard to Latin America. Arthur Schlesinger (1967, 28) comments: "Stimson was therefore skeptical of what he regarded as the prevailing tendency 'to hang on to exaggerated views of the Monroe Doctrine and at the same time butt into every question that comes up in Central Europe.'"[c] In short, Stimson felt that the United States should accept the establishment by the Russians of a sphere of influence in Central Europe that he perceived as analogous to that established by the United States in Latin America.

If a lifelong Republican such as Henry Stimson could see the symmetry between the superpowers' interests in securing their respective neighborhoods, surely the American government as a whole might have been more sensitive than it was to Russian concerns about the governments that might come to power in Eastern Europe after World War II. "Free" elections there and then might well have resulted in the installation of factions sympathetic to the defunct Nazi regime in Germany, and it would have been unreasonable for the United States to expect the Russians to accept such political developments in countries adjacent to their western border. Moreover, this anxiety would only have been heightened by the steps that the Americans (and the British) took to ensure that unfriendly, or Communist, elements would not assume

---

c. Schlesinger (29) also points out that George Kennan, the U.S. ambassador in Moscow at the time, and one of the principal architects of the U.S. foreign policy at the onset of the Cold War, argued that "nothing that we could do would possibly alter the course of events in Eastern Europe; that we were deceiving ourselves by supposing that these countries had any future but Russian domination; that we should therefore relinquish Eastern Europe to the Soviet Union...."

too much power (from their point of view) in Italy and France, for example. Nevertheless, the United States apparently did expect the Soviets to allow elections in Eastern Europe that might bring to power vigorously anti-Soviet elements. That inconsistent position, and the policies resulting from it, arguably played a crucial role in precipitating what was to become, in the ensuing decades, the Cold War struggle between the superpowers.

OR, WAS IT PRIMARILY THE FAULT OF THE SOVIET UNION?

provocative

One obvious argument that the onset of the Cold War was primarily the fault of the Soviet Union focuses on its leader for some two decades beforehand, Joseph Stalin, who was certainly one of the most—perhaps *the* most—bloodthirsty, violent, and powerful dictators in history. Estimates of how many deaths he brought about among the citizens of his own land range from 30 million (Conquest 1968, 1986) to 42.7 million (Rummel 1990), and even higher. American leaders in the immediate post–World War II era may not have been aware of the extent of Stalin's campaigns to imprison, torture, execute, starve, and slaughter his internal enemies (real and imagined), but there was plenty of evidence available to convince them that they faced a ruthless and corrupt dictator. In addition, he had signed a pact with Adolf Hitler in 1939, and proceeded to take advantage of that opportunity to attack and annex territory belonging to several states bordering the Soviet Union to the west. There was, in short, in the revealed character of the dictatorial leader of the Soviet Union a solid basis for American concern, and for the conviction that the United States faced a dangerous regime that might well be intent upon extending its power significantly beyond its current borders in the immediate postwar years.

misperception on the part of U.S.

Furthermore, Stalin stood at the center of a totalitarian regime with many similarities to the Nazi regime that the United States had just, with great difficulty, helped to defeat. It would have been easy to conclude that Stalin's Soviet government was as inherently and determinedly expansionist as that of Hitler and the Nazis. As Paul Johnson (1983, 296) puts it: "Hitler learnt from Lenin and Stalin how to set up a large-scale terror regime. But he had much to teach too." It had been fairly obvious that Hitler's regime needed foreign enemies in order to survive, and Stalin's regime had a similar look about it. Many American leaders concluded, understandably, that totalitarianism in the Soviet Union, in Schlesinger's words (1967, 50), "created a structure of thought and behavior which made postwar collaboration between Russia and America . . . inherently impossible."

Then, too, the Marxist-Leninist ideology on which the Soviet regime was based would reasonably have created suspicions and antagonism among political leaders in the United States. Again, Schlesinger (1967, 47) offers the relevant perspective: "Marxism-Leninism gave the Russian leaders a view of the world according to which all societies were inexorably destined to proceed along appointed roads by appointed stages until they achieved the classless nirvana." The Soviet Union, from the American point of view, was committed to assisting this historical process whenever and wherever it could, and so it behooved the United States to resist, with similar determination, such Soviet attempts to spread the worldwide communist revolution. The Cold War, from this perspective, was quite simply the result of an understandable attempt by the United States to protect itself from the expansionism inherent in the Marxist-Leninist ideology of its main competitor.

Moreover, Schlesinger (1967, 47) says,

> Stalin and his associates, whatever Roosevelt and Truman did or failed to do, were bound to regard the United States as an enemy, not because of this deed or that, but because of the primordial fact that America was the leading capitalist power and thus, by Leninist syllogism, unappeasably hostile, driven by the logic of its system to oppose, encircle, and destroy the Soviet Union.

Faced with such an antagonist, neither the United States nor anybody within its foreign policy establishment could reasonably be blamed for precipitating the onset of the Cold War.

Also, American leaders' resistance to the Soviet plans to subordinate Eastern Europe was especially logical, given that World War II had been sparked, in the first place, by the Western powers' attempt to preserve the independence of Poland against German aggression. And so, it is certainly understandable, in light of the vast costs in lives and treasure they had devoted to preventing Germany from taking Poland, that the United States (and other Western powers) would be reluctant to see the Soviet Union subdue that same country (as well as the rest of Eastern Europe) in the years immediately after the war.

Finally, the Cold War was ignited, in important part, by suspicions among the United States and its allies that the Soviet Union would, ultimately, not be satisfied with establishing a buffer zone to its west. American leaders, in particular, feared that the Soviets intended to expand their sphere of influence to include the whole of Europe, including the western part of the continent. Whether or not this was a reasonable fear will never be established for certain. But one of the leading analysts of the history of the Cold War, writing well after its end permitted access to much valuable information in Russian archives and elsewhere, asserts that "Stalin's goal … was not to restore a balance of power in Europe, but rather to dominate that continent as thoroughly as Hitler had sought to do." In other words, Gaddis (2005, 14) continues, "Stalin's was, therefore, a grand vision: the peacefully accomplished but historically determined domination of Europe." Clearly, then, the actions taken by the United States in opposition to the Soviet Union after World War II can be seen as largely defensive in character, and it can be argued that the Cold War ensued mostly because of the aggressive intentions and actions of the Soviet Union.

OR, WAS THE STRUCTURE OF THE POSTWAR INTERNATIONAL SYSTEM TO BLAME?

Perhaps the quest to determine which of the rival superpowers was mostly at fault for the onset of the Cold War is misguided. It is possible that they were equally at fault. Or that neither the United States nor the Soviet Union could realistically have avoided the confrontation after the close of World War II.

From this point of view, following the defeat of their common enemy, the United States and the Soviet Union were, in the words of J. Robert Oppenheimer (1953, 529), like two "scorpions in a bottle, each capable of killing each other, but only at the risk of his own life." Adversaries in such a situation do not need any additional reasons beyond the structure of the situation in which they find themselves to become very suspicious and antagonistic toward one another. Like those scorpions, the United States and the Soviet Union, after World War II, found themselves bottled up in a global competition in which each could see that the other was the only state in the world with the potential either to immediately threaten its existence or to effectively resist its pursuit of almost any conceivable foreign policy goal. Under such circumstances—the dramatic and substantive peril of which was soon spectacularly reinforced by the acquisition of atomic weapons on both sides—was there any realistic chance that the United States and the Soviet Union would *not* become suspicious of and antagonistic toward each other?

As early as 1953, Oppenheimer (a physicist who had played a key role in the American project to develop atomic weapons during World War II) analyzed the accelerating arms race between the United States and the Soviet Union, and foresaw that conflict between the two was so likely as to be inevitable: "There are some peculiarities of this arms race, marked by a very great rigidity of policy, and a terrifyingly rapid accumulation, probably on both sides of a deadly munition.... Thus the prevailing view is that we are probably faced with a long period of cold war...."

Another assessment of the impact of system structure on the onset of the Cold War originates in game theory; it is based on what is known as the **size principle**.[d] Developed by William Riker (1962, 32–33), this principle asserts that, in a variety of social and political settings, "participants create coalitions that are just as large as they believe will ensure winning and no larger." The logic behind this principle is straightforward. In any setting where political coalitions can be formed, potential members of such coalitions have two fundamental aims that are in part contradictory: they want to become part of a coalition that is able to win, but they also want to win as much as possible. All else being equal, the larger a coalition is, the more likely it is to win. But the more members there are in a winning coalition,[e] the more claims will be made on the fruits of victory, and the smaller the shares that can be allocated to each coalition member. The best, most logical way to deal with these inescapable trade-offs is to create a **minimum winning coalition**—one that is just large enough to win but entirely free of members who are unnecessary to bring about the victory, so that the spoils of victory can be shared among the smallest possible number of coalition members.

coalition just large enough to win.

The size principle is unlikely to describe accurately the process of alliance formation in the international system. One reason involves the risks and costs associated with forming international alliances that are just large enough to win any military conflict that might develop, but no larger. Interstate wars are extremely complicated, and it is difficult to predict their outcomes. It is, accordingly, very difficult to calculate just how much by way of military-industrial capabilities may be necessary to achieve victory against any given opponent and any allies that might come to its defense. In addition, there are obvious advantages to assembling a coalition that has at its disposal a lot more than just enough power to emerge victorious. An alliance fighting a war against an opponent over which it enjoys only a slim margin of

---

d. The following discussion of the size principle as a potential explanation for the onset of the Cold War relies substantially on a similar discussion in Ray (1998, 353–356).

e. This notion about winning coalitions in international politics is similar and related to the emphasis on the importance of the size of winning coalitions in domestic political contexts emphasized by rational political ambition theory, an emphasis with roots obviously traceable to the "selectorate theory" of Bueno de Mesquita et al. (2003, 10), who cite Riker 1962.

superiority may well have to fight long and hard to achieve victory. In short, in the international political system, a minimum winning coalition suffers from two crucial disadvantages: it may turn out *not* be to quite large enough to win, and even if it does win, its members will probably face an extremely costly military conflict in order to achieve that victory.

Nevertheless, the size principle may provide some insight into important international political processes. Its logic implies that **grand coalitions**—that is, those consisting of almost all states against no really formidable opponents—are bound to fall apart in short order. Such coalitions have nobody left to win *from*, and they can therefore be expected to break up so that the members of the erstwhile grand coalition can engage in political and military contests against each other. Such a conclusion can be supported by a brief analysis of international politics over the past two centuries.

Grand coalitions do not emerge very often in international politics. At the beginning of the nineteenth century, however, Great Britain, Austria, Prussia, and Russia emerged as a grand coalition, in the wake of the defeat of Napoleonic France. This coalition began to disintegrate in 1815 at the Congress of Vienna, which was devoted to postwar issues. Austria and Britain conspired against their former allies in Prussia and Russia. Riker (1962, 69) explains what happened next: "Hence followed this astonishing result: Austria and England, both of whom had been fighting France for nearly a generation, brought a reconstituted French government back into world politics and allied with it against their own former allies in the very moment of victory."

A similar process unfolded in the wake of World War I. Germany and Austria-Hungary had been defeated by 1918, and Russia had been severely weakened by the Russian Revolution. The United States, Great Britain, and France therefore became a grand coalition of almost everybody against almost nobody. And it began to break up almost immediately after it became victorious. The United States, for example, refused to sign the Versailles Peace Treaty, and therefore also failed to join the League of Nations. Great Britain and France fell into serious disagreements about how the defeated Germany should be treated. In general, France favored more draconian retaliatory measures against Germany than did the British. When the Germans were slow (from the French point of view) in paying war reparations, the French decided in January of 1923 to occupy Germany's Ruhr Valley in order to compel the Germans to deliver on their obligations. The British objected to this "invasion" quite strenuously (Fischer 2003).

The Japanese and the Italians, too, were dissatisfied with the grand coalition that had emerged victorious from World War I—the Japanese because the League of Nations created by the Versailles Treaty had refused to adopt a principle of racial equality, and the Italians because their territorial demands had not been met. In short, the winning coalition that emerged from World War I fell apart quite quickly, just as the size principle would predict.

In light of the size principle—and of the history of grand coalitions in international politics—the Cold War was a predictable result of the structure of the international system after the defeat of the Axis powers. The United States and the Soviet Union, along with Great Britain, constituted a grand coalition. As Riker, who devised the size principle, asserts (1962, 7): "Having defeated the Axis, the winners had nothing to win from unless they split up and tried to win from each other."

Furthermore, as another game theorist points out, Riker's argument about grand coalitions has the virtue of being based on an analysis of "all instances of relevant cases within the spatially and temporally defined limits he set" (Brams 1975, 244). In other words, Riker did not ransack history looking for cases that confirm his argument but, instead, reviewed all the grand coalitions that had emerged in the modern international political system up to 1962, when he published *The Theory of Political Coalitions*.

Since that time, of course, the Cold War has ended, arguably creating another grand coalition in the form of the group of states that opposed the Soviet Union before its demise. Has this successor coalition fallen apart, as the size principle would predict? The United States and some of its most important European allies have been at odds over several issues, most notably the second Bush administration's war in Iraq. However, the United States and Japan are certainly not overtly antagonistic toward each other, partly because of common concerns about the emergence of China. In short, nothing like Cold War tensions have arisen so far among the winning coalition that emerged from that postwar confrontation. This relative stability may have something to do with the extent to which the current coalition has been less than "grand." It has never involved China, the most populous state in the world, and its members have faced a formidable common opponent in the form of loosely allied nonstate actors, al Qaeda and like-minded militant groups.

Much of the same, basic empirical evidence can be viewed from a different theoretical standpoint that leads to the same conclusion. This alternative argument holds that the onset of the Cold War was yet another in a long line of historical examples of countervailing coalitions forming more or less automatically to preserve a balance of power in the international system, especially on what has long been the central stage of international politics, the continent of Europe. From this point of view, as World War II came to a close, the Soviet Union and Stalin posed a threat to the balance of power in Europe that was reminiscent of those posed, in their respective eras, by Philip II of Spain, by Louis XIV and then Napoleon Bonaparte of France, and by Kaiser Wilhelm II and then Adolf Hitler of Germany. On all these occasions in the past, when an expansionist leader had marshaled the military capabilities of his country in such a way as to threaten to dominate the entire European continent, Great Britain had intervened, along with whatever allies it could muster, to preserve the balance of power. That is, the British aimed to prevent any one of the powers on the European continent from dominating the others in such a way as to enable it to add all the resources of the continent to its own power base, and thus threaten to dominate the entire global political system.

In the aftermath of World War II, however, Great Britain was unable to play its typical, historical role in this balance-of-power process, which had by that time been in operation for several hundred years. As we saw earlier in this chapter, by February of 1947, the British government was ready to acknowledge its inability to cope any longer with the demands of that role. When the first secretary at the British embassy in Washington visited the U.S. State Department to warn that his government would no longer be able to deal with what were perceived as Communist threats to Turkey and Greece, the meaning of his message was clear: "A Soviet breakthrough could be prevented only by an American commitment to stopping it" (Hook and Spanier 2004, 43).

Again, the American reaction to these developments was contained formally in the Truman Doctrine. From the theoretical point of view of this particular discussion, however, the fact that the confrontation between Stalin's Soviet Union and Truman's United States had moved to the forefront of the world stage had little to do, in its fundamentals, with the ideology of the Soviet Union, its dictatorial political regime, the character flaws of Stalin, or any particular behavior or policy of the Soviet Union in the aftermath of World War II. Nor did it result from the ideology of the United States, its democratic political regime, the personality traits of Truman, or any particular policy move by the United States after Germany and Japan were defeated. A similar dynamic—involving different leaders and states and ideologies and policies in every case—had produced resistance to any state threatening to dominate the European landmass for hundreds of years.

Fundamentally, then, the United States was simply responding to the Soviet threat as part of a process that had been in place long before the Soviet Union and the United States had emerged as the two states playing the leading roles in the balance-of-power system. And recognition of this historical dynamic is yet another argument that it was the structure of the international system after World War II that had made the onset of the Cold War, if not inevitable, at least highly probable.

CONCLUSION

It is possible to make a persuasive case that most of the blame for the onset of the Cold War should fall on the United States. One of the most important points of that case is the fact that the United States was considerably more powerful than the Soviet Union at the close of World War II, and it therefore had more leeway for being conciliatory and compromising—which it arguably failed to be. Instead, it sought to deny the Soviet Union the opportunity to set up a sphere of influence in Eastern Europe, based on governments whose favorable and supportive attitude it could count on.

Nevertheless, it is not difficult to understand why the United States felt called upon to defend itself from what it saw as threats from the Soviet Union's expansionist ideology. Furthermore, the political structure of the Soviet Union was in fundamental ways similar to the totalitarian system of the Nazis, and the Americans had just lived through an era that amply demonstrated the potential dangers inherent in such political systems. The dictator Stalin, an erstwhile ally of Hitler, and a leader who was similarly capable of brutal and aggressive behavior, also provided American policymakers with reason to be concerned, as well as defensive. (And, sometimes at least, the best defense is a good offense.)

On the other hand, even if it is true that both American and Soviet policymakers could have adopted wiser, more temperate policies that might have forestalled—perhaps even permanently—the Cold War confrontation, it is also true that the structure of the international system after World War II made it probable that the United States and the Soviet Union would, instead, fall into active antagonism. They were like two "scorpions in a bottle," whose capability to harm each other was so obvious as to create inevitable suspicion and hostility. Grand coalitions in world politics (as in other political contexts) tend to fall apart, since they have nobody left to win from. Balance-of-power calculations led first Great Britain, and then the United States, to respond actively whenever it appeared that one state might come to dominate the entire European continent, as it seemed that the Soviet Union aimed to do in the years immediately after World War II.

One of the more intriguing bits of evidence that the structure of the international system made a Cold War confrontation likely can be found in a classic study of the United States by Alexis de Tocqueville, *Democracy in America,* the first volume of which was published in 1835. In the concluding paragraphs of that volume, Tocqueville offers some fascinating speculation. He asserts first that "there are at the present time two great nations in the world, which started from different points, but seem to tend towards the same end. I allude to the Russians and the Americans." That common end is simply preeminence among the nations of the world. All the other nations, Tocqueville believes, have "reached their natural limits." But he claims to see no apparent limits to the extent to which the United States and Russia can expand and grow more powerful.

Ultimately, Tocqueville points out, the archetypal American "relies upon personal interest to accomplish his ends and gives free scope to the unguided strength and common sense of the people." The Russian, in contrast, "centers all the authority of society in a single arm." He concludes that "the principal instrument of the former is freedom; of the latter servitude," and finally, that "their starting-point is different and their courses are not the same; yet each of them seems marked by the will of Heaven to sway the destinies of half the globe."

Thus, early in the nineteenth century, Tocqueville recognizes that the United States and Russia were likely to become the two most powerful states in the world, and that they adhere to very different systems of governance. Perhaps it is these two defining characteristics of the future superpowers—discernible to at least this one perceptive observer 110 years before it occurred—that were most responsible for the onset of the Cold War. Indeed, such a conclusion would be compatible with the emphasis placed by rational political ambition theory on the impact of domestic political structures on interactions between states.

KEY CONCEPTS

Cold War   153

grand coalition   166

minimum winning coalition   165

size principle   165

Truman Doctrine   161

monroe Doctrine: sphere of influence in central and south America

RATIONAL POLITICAL AMBITION AND . . .
THE BEGINNING OF THE COLD WAR

☑ Among the many factors exacerbating relations between the United States and the Soviet Union in the period after World War II was the temptation faced by American decision makers to rely on vigorous anti-Soviet policies to help keep themselves in power. One early example of this pattern occurred during the confrontation between the United States and the Soviet Union over the future of Iran, in 1945.

☑ The 1947 speech in which President Truman outlined the Truman Doctrine, pledging the United States to resist Soviet expansionism, was delivered in part to affect public opinion in the United States. President Truman and other governmental leaders felt that in order to resist that expansionism effectively, they had to convince the American public of the threat posed by the Soviet Union. In other words, in order to generate and preserve public support for anti-Soviet policies, as well as support for their continuation in power, U.S. government leaders felt that they needed to evoke a fear of the Soviet Union in the general public.

☑ The idea that interactions between states will be affected fundamentally by differences in domestic political structures is compatible with rational political ambition theory, which would explain the onset and continuation of the Cold War, for example, by stressing the impact of the differences in the domestic political regimes of the United States and the Soviet Union. Early in the nineteenth century, Alexis de Tocqueville predicted that the United States and the Soviet Union would eventually emerge as the two most powerful states in the world, and he hinted at the profound impact the contrasts in their political regimes might have on their relationship with each other.

CHAPTER 8

VIETNAM

The Unnecessary War?

THE WAR BETWEEN THE UNITED STATES AND NORTH VIETNAM (AND ITS Vietcong allies in South Vietnam) was one of the most significant conflicts of the Cold War era. It might reasonably be classified as the first international war that the United States lost.[a] In fact, the conflict between the two Vietnamese states was, to an important extent, a **proxy war** between the Soviet Union and the People's Republic of China, which were supporting North Vietnam, and the United States, which was fighting to preserve the state of South Vietnam. The war imposed serious economic and political strains on the United States, although those strains were actually quite limited in comparison to the massive death and suffering inflicted on the people of Vietnam. (Estimates of civilian deaths in Vietnam during the 1965–1975 period range from 500,000 to 3 million.) The Vietnam War was largely a result of "lessons learned" by U.S. policymakers from events in its recent past, but that war, in turn, taught its own lessons—which U.S. policymakers continue to grapple with today.

This chapter will be devoted to an analysis of the origins of the war in Vietnam, then to various explanations for its outcome, and, finally, to a discussion of its impact on the evolution of the Cold War and on U.S. foreign policy. Although generalizing from single cases is difficult, the special case of the war in Vietnam is of such importance to American history that any serious theory of U.S. foreign policy, or of foreign policies and international politics in general, should be of significant assistance to those who seek to understand it. Our discussion of the Vietnam War will focus consistently on the theoretical implications of its most important features.

President Lyndon B. Johnson made a determined effort to avoid losing the war in Vietnam partly because (as rational political ambition theory would suggest) he felt that a defeat there would lead to his loss of power in the next election. Ironically, the war became so unpopular that he came to believe he had no chance to win that election. Johnson is shown here addressing the nation on March 31, 1968, to announce that he would not be running for reelection.

---

a. Alternatively, it might be argued that the United States withdrew from the fighting for something over a year before the war resulted in a victory by North Vietnam over the regime in South Vietnam.

[handwritten: originally supported nationalist movement vs. France]

THE ORIGINS OF THE WAR

[handwritten: anti-colonialism]

The war in Vietnam may be said to have begun when France took over the country, in stages, between 1867 and 1883. France then ruled Vietnam as a colony until World War II, when Japanese military expansion succeeded in terminating French control. As the Japanese were repulsed toward the war's end, France was allowed to retake the southern part of Vietnam, while China controlled the northern half of the country, which lies adjacent to its own border. Eventually, the situation evolved in such a way that the French warred against the forces of the revolutionary leader Ho Chi Minh from 1945 to 1954 in order to retain control of their colony in Vietnam.

The American attitude toward this conflict between France and Ho's rebel forces in Vietnam changed markedly over the years. Originally, the U.S. government viewed the war as a battle by nationalists trying to free their country from colonial control. President Truman, for example, was so opposed to the French effort to hold onto Vietnam that in 1947 he went so far as to insist that the British remove American-made propellers from aircraft they were providing to the French for use in their war against Ho Chi Minh (Stoessinger 2001, 82).

But the regional situation shifted radically in 1949, when the rebel movement of Mao Zedong succeeded in taking control of China. The United States had made a determined effort to keep the Nationalist government of Chiang Kai-shek in power against the Communist opposition led by Mao (Tuchman 1966). The failure of that effort was a traumatic experience for many U.S. policymakers, and even for ordinary citizens in the United States who paid attention to foreign affairs. Having sacrificed over 400,000 American soldiers—as well as countless more wounded or scarred psychologically—in the struggle against dictatorial governments during World War II, many in the United States began to feel that that exhausting, heroic effort had been rewarded, so to speak, by the emergence of an even more daunting political, military, and ideological enemy in the form of Communist aggression led by the Soviet Union.

In August of 1949, the Soviets exploded an atomic weapon, making them seem an even more ominous threat. And this disturbing development had been only half-absorbed, at best, when Mao's Communists took over in China in October of that year. Now, the country with the largest landmass in the world, the Soviet Union, was joined in the Communist orbit by the state with what had, at the time, by far the largest population of any state in the world, and this combination gave Communism the look of the "wave of the future." And certainly, to many Americans in the aftermath of World War II, it seemed that things could not go so terribly wrong, so breathtakingly fast, just by accident.

In short, by 1950, many Americans were looking for some kind of explanation for these troubling international events, and a U.S. senator from Wisconsin, Joseph McCarthy, provided one that seemed plausible to great numbers of them at the time. In a speech in February 1950 in Wheeling, West Virginia, McCarthy asserted that he had evidence that over two hundred Communists were employed in the U.S. State Department. According to Norman Friedman (2000, 87): "McCarthy's charges seemed to explain why the United States had just 'lost' China, and the outbreak of the Korean War in June 1950 seemed to make subversives in government a more urgent issue."

His Wheeling speech having attracted an enormous amount of attention, McCarthy sensed that he was onto something; by 1951, he was accusing Secretary of State George C. Marshall of being a Communist. In 1952 Dwight Eisenhower won the presidential election, and the Republicans took control of both houses of Congress in a contest in which it is fair to say that they took advantage of the Democratic Party's vulnerability to the charge of being "soft on communism." (In the meantime, in the last months of his presidency, Harry Truman had made substantial financial commitments to the French in their efforts to hold onto Vietnam.)

Intriguingly enough, President Eisenhower soon demonstrated that he was not invariably a hard-liner against Communism himself. In 1953, for example, he accepted an armistice bringing to a halt the fighting in the Korean War, on terms that no Democratic president could likely have accepted. Then, in the following year, he faced a crisis in Vietnam, where the French found themselves on the brink of a disastrous defeat at the village of Dien Bien Phu. The idea that Vietnam might be lost to the Communist forces was sufficiently unwelcome to American policymakers that the use of nuclear weapons there to fend off the defeat of the French was seriously considered; in the end, however, President Eisenhower decided against it (Gaddis 1986, 137). The French were defeated, and a 1954 peace conference in Geneva divided the country into northern and southern portions (see map 8.1). This division and the border it created were intended to be temporary, as the agreement called for elections two years later, which were meant to unify the country under a single government.

Even before President Truman left office, the United States had become heavily involved in the effort to stave off the defeat of the French—paying, by varying estimates, 50 to 80 percent of the war's costs by 1952. When the French withdrew after their defeat at Dien Bien Phu, the United States immediately became involved in a serious attempt to prevent Ho Chi Minh and his Communist forces, the Viet Minh, from taking over the entire country. That is exactly what would have happened, according to many observers, if the 1956 elections called for in the Geneva Accords had been allowed to take place. Among the many interested parties who felt that way was President Eisenhower.[b]

In the end, the elections did not take place, and the Eisenhower administration embarked instead on an effort to preserve the independence and the national integrity of the South Vietnamese state, which it had done so much to bring into existence in the first place. By the time he left office, Eisenhower had committed some 1,000 American military advisers to the effort to preserve the regime of Ngo Dinh Diem. Key figures in his administration were committed to this policy because they saw Vietnam as a key battleground in the fight to stem the Communist tide. Most important, they feared that a victory by the forces of Ho Chi Minh would represent a victory by the People's Republic of China.

KENNEDY'S FATEFUL DECISIONS

The administration of John F. Kennedy came into power with a similar view of the struggle in Vietnam. Kennedy himself was more skeptical about the war than many important players

---

b. Citing a statement by Eisenhower himself (1963, 372), John Stoessinger (2001, 88) reports: "President Eisenhower thought that elections, if held on the basis of the Geneva Accords, would lead to a communist victory." Norman Friedman (2000, 184) holds a dissenting view: "Ho feared the wrath of his own peasants, should they be permitted to vote freely. When the South Vietnamese said they wanted to defer an election, the North Vietnamese assented."

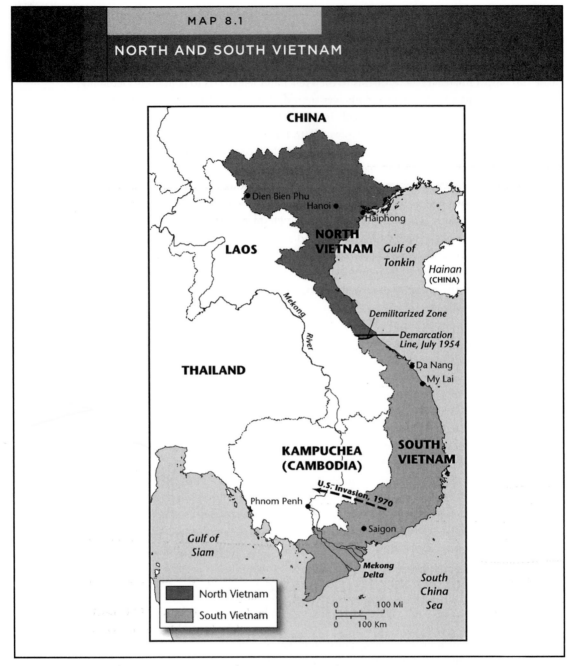

MAP 8.1

NORTH AND SOUTH VIETNAM

Vietnam was divided into two parts along the 17th parallel by the Geneva Accords drafted in 1954. The division was supposed to be temporary, until scheduled elections took place, but the elections never occurred.

in his administration, and after his death rumors surfaced that he had intended to withdraw from the struggle after he won reelection in 1964. But during his time in the White House, Kennedy instead expanded the U.S. role in Vietnam. As John Stoessinger (2001, 90) explains, his reasons for doing so are not difficult to fathom: "Kennedy felt compelled to demonstrate his toughness in the international arena, after the disaster at the Bay of Pigs." This compulsion stemmed in part from his concern that he would be at a disadvantage in future conflicts and disputes in the international arena if a widespread impression that he was "soft" or easily intimidated were to be reinforced by another policy failure.

But perhaps the more important reason that Kennedy felt that he could not back down in the confrontation in Vietnam had to do with domestic, rather than international, politics. One of the most intensive studies of key decision makers during the Vietnam War is David Halberstam's *The Best and the Brightest* (1972). Halberstam points out that, even as early as the campaign of 1960, "Kennedy moved toward the right to reassure America that he was just as tough as Nixon, that he wanted a firm foreign policy" (20). Obviously, he took this turn on the campaign trail because he felt it was the best way to win votes and gain power, and after he was in office, he felt similar pressures to maintain his reputation as being tough on Communism. In the words of Halberstam (120):

> The confluence and the mixing of these three events, the fall of China, the rise of McCarthy, and the outbreak of the Korean War, would have a profound effect on American domestic politics, and consequently an equally significant effect on foreign policy. The Democratic Administration was on the defensive; a country could not be lost without serious political consequences.

Thus, in spite of his skepticism, President Kennedy stepped up the level of American involvement in the war in Vietnam. He increased the deployment levels of the U.S. Army's Special Forces (the Green Berets) who were specialists in antiguerrilla warfare, to assist in training the South Vietnamese army. He resisted pressure to deploy actual combat troops, but by the time he was assassinated, he had raised the number of American military advisers in Vietnam to 17,000. Meanwhile, Kennedy became increasingly concerned about the unpopularity of Vietnamese President Ngo Dinh Diem, whom the United States had backed quite strongly in earlier years. Diem was assassinated in November of 1963, in a plot which, if it was not inspired or planned by the United States, also did not provoke any opposition from U.S. agents on the ground in Vietnam. Three weeks after Diem's death, John F. Kennedy himself was assassinated.

President Kennedy thus played a vital role in upgrading the American commitment to the war in defense of South Vietnam. He might, or might not have withdrawn from the war had he not been assassinated and had he also won reelection. But an evaluation of his partial responsibility for the developing tragedy in Vietnam should reflect the fact that, by the end of 1963, only about seventy American soldiers had died in Vietnam.

THE DEFINITIVE DECISION TO ESCALATE

The most important decisions about the Vietnam War were made during the administration of Lyndon Johnson. Inheriting the unstable situation created by the two assassinations, President Johnson himself, however, felt trapped, recognizing that he had a very limited array of options for dealing with the situation in Vietnam. The contours of this trap were revealed starkly when he ran for election to a term in his own right in 1964. His opponent was Senator Barry Goldwater, who accepted his party's nomination at the Republican Convention in San Francisco by accusing the Johnson administration of "timidity before Communism" and "cringing" before the "bullying of Communism." Goldwater concluded his harangue with the charge that the stench of "failures" in the life and death struggles with Communism ranged widely over the globe, but particularly in the "jungles of Vietnam" (Manchester 1974, 1018).

During the ensuing electoral campaign, President Johnson was motivated, in part, to take advantage of events in the Tonkin Gulf in Vietnam as a way to deal with the "soft on communism" issue raised by Goldwater. When two American ships, the *Turner Joy* and the *Maddox,* were allegedly attacked by North Vietnam in the waters off its coastline, President Johnson accused the North Vietnamese of "open aggression." The **Gulf of Tonkin Resolution** of 1964, in effect, authorized Johnson to wage war in Vietnam; there were only two votes against it in the U.S. Senate, and it passed in the House of Representatives by a 414–0 margin.

The overwhelming votes in Congress in favor of the Gulf of Tonkin Resolution should be kept in mind in interpreting what was to follow. First, they offer substantial evidence that no matter how unpopular the war in Vietnam ultimately became, its initial stages were very widely supported in the United States. The virtually unanimous congressional support for the resolution also helps to explain why the United States became involved in the war. The emphasis here will be on the domestic political pressures that pushed President Johnson in the direction of escalation, but that factor alone would probably not have sufficed to produce the ultimate result. In the beginning, huge proportions of the American public, as well as elite decision-making groups, felt that the war in Vietnam was necessary and just, partly because the Cold War contest with the Soviet Union was so intense at that time.

In addition, the determination not to lose in Vietnam was, in important part, a result of a lesson of history that was accepted with very little dissent in the United States in the 1960s. The results of the British and French agreement with Hitler at Munich in 1938 had shown, according to the most widely credited interpretation of this lesson, that appeasement of totalitarian dictatorships is almost always a terrible mistake. Given an inch, anywhere in the world, dictators will utilize their powers and the attractions of their ideology to carry out an endless series of aggressions until they are confronted by an effective countervailing force. And it is easier to organize and utilize this countervailing force early on, before the enemy reaches the pinnacle of its power and influence. American foreign policy makers, along with the rest of the world, had drawn this lesson from subsequent events in the conflict between Hitler and his major European opponents in 1938 and 1939. The United States was not about to repeat such errors in Southeast Asia in the early 1960s.

So, there were lots of reasons that President Johnson, along with his key foreign policy advisers and the leadership of the military, decided to augment dramatically the commitment of the United States to defend the regime in South Vietnam. And, when the Vietcong (rebels against the government in South Vietnam) attacked barracks housing American advisers early in 1965, Johnson responded with the beginnings of what became a massive campaign of aerial bombardment against North Vietnam. Unfortunately, as Stoessinger (2001, 97) reports: "The bombing campaign, or 'Operation Rolling Thunder,' . . . did not produce the desired effect. Ho Chi Minh . . . matched the American air escalation with his own escalation, through infiltration on the ground." In fact, says Peter Calvocoressi (1991, 448–449), "the government of North Vietnam ... began to send regular divisions.... The war became, with scant disguise, a war between the United States and North Vietnam."

At the end of 1964, the United States had only 23,000 troops in Vietnam, but, by the end of 1966, that number had reached 390,000, and by 1968, it was 550,000. The costs escalated accordingly: in fiscal year 1965, the war cost only $100 million; by 1966, the annual cost was $14 *billion*. It is possible to find widely ranging estimates of just how extensive the bombing campaign against North Vietnam was. Stoessinger (2001, 106) declares that it was eighty times more intense than what Britain had suffered during World War II, while Stephen Ambrose and Douglas Brinkley (1997, 204) assert that, by the end of 1970, "more bombs had been dropped on Vietnam than on all targets in human history."[c] What is not in doubt is that the American bombing campaign against North Vietnam was massive, and that it did not work. The North Vietnamese did not surrender, and they did not stop sending troops into South Vietnam.

President Johnson refused to accept defeat in the face of this situation largely because he felt that a loss of the war in Vietnam would result in a loss of power for him in the United States. The president had what many observers saw as pressing reasons in the realm of foreign policy for remaining firm in his confrontation with North Vietnam, but as Steven Hook and John Spanier (2004, 121) explain,

> perhaps even more important than foreign policy considerations in this escalation was American domestic politics.... [O]nce an administration had justified its policy in terms of an anticommunist crusade and had aroused the public by promising to stop communism, it opened itself up to attacks by the opposition party if setbacks were encountered.... The ousted party could then exploit such foreign policy issues by accusing the party in power of appeasement, of having "lost" this or that country, and of being "soft on communism."[d]

This lesson about the importance of adhering to a tough line against Communist threats for domestic political reasons had been reinforced at a critical time in Lyndon Johnson's experience by a crisis in the Dominican Republic in 1965. As Halberstam (1972, 573) points out about that crisis, "when leftist rebels began to make a challenge, Johnson moved quickly to stop another Cuba. Presidents in the past had been soft on Cuba, and had paid for it." President Johnson, both initially and ultimately, was determined that he would not pay the domestic political price for being soft on Communism in Vietnam.

As Alan Brinkley (2006, 11) notes in reviewing a recent biography of this president (Woods 2006), Johnson was never enthusiastic about the war: "What drove his commitment was a justified fear of a powerful conservative reaction to any retreat—his conviction that a failure in Vietnam would subject him, and the nation, to a new age of McCarthyism." In other words, President Johnson decided to escalate the war in Vietnam more out of fear of what his

---

c. Actually, to be fair, what Ambrose and Brinkley may be reporting here is not their best estimate, or the most authoritative estimate they could find, but what "the headlines proclaimed" about the magnitude of the bombing campaign in Vietnam as it unfolded.

d. This interpretation is particularly interesting in that it is offered by "realist" analysts of American foreign policy who, by theoretical inclination, would not normally be inclined to give such weight to considerations of domestic politics.

Republican opponents would do to him at home in the domestic political arena than out of a conviction regarding the adverse international consequences of a Communist victory in that war. In short, the U.S. war in Vietnam was fought with such determination in important part because the key Democratic administrations in power at the crucial stages of the war felt that they had to hold the line in Vietnam in order to hold onto power in the United States.

Of course, the ironic fact is that President Johnson's attempt to retain power by means of a hard-line policy in Vietnam ultimately made him very unpopular. As can be seen in figure 8.1, Johnson enjoyed public approval ratings above 70 percent in 1965, but three years later, his approval ratings had fallen by half, down to about 35 percent. One study of public opinion during the Vietnam War found, in a statistical analysis of the relationship between American battle casualties in Vietnam and public opinion about the war, that "every time American casualties increased by a factor of 10, support for the war dropped by about 15 percentage points" (Mueller 1973, 60). Ultimately, President Johnson became so unpopular that he withdrew from the presidential election of 1968. So, his policies in Vietnam were arguably responsible for his losing office.

Does this self-destructive course of action not cast some doubt on the validity of rational political ambition theory, which asserts that foreign policy choices will be made with a view, primarily, to staying *in* power? The answer to that question is no. Rational political ambition theory does not suggest that leaders of states are necessarily wise, prudent, intelligent, or incapable of error. It only suggests that they will base decisions on their *desire* or preference to stay in power. They will, all else being equal, select policy options that they *believe* will maximize their chances of staying in power. Sometimes, as appears to be the case with respect to Lyndon Johnson and the Vietnam War, they will, instead, pursue policies that lead to loss of the official position they hope to maintain.

THE DENOUEMENT: CHOICES BY NIXON AND KISSINGER

In the election campaign of 1968, Richard Nixon suggested that he had a secret plan to end the war in Vietnam. To the extent that he had such a plan—it is not clear that he did—it involved what was known as Vietnamization, or turning over ever-larger shares of the responsibility for defending the South Vietnamese regime to the South Vietnamese military. In June of 1969, the withdrawal of American troops began, reducing their number by 25,000 from its peak of 541,500. However, by 1970, in a paradoxical if not flatly contradictory way, the United States announced an "incursion" into Cambodia and attacks on Vietnamese "sanctuaries" and supply depots. (See map 8.2.) This step evoked antiwar demonstrations at many American college campuses, including Kent State University in Ohio, where four students were killed in May of that year, and it was an important factor in the U.S. Senate's decision to repeal the Gulf of Tonkin resolution, in June.

In the early 1970s, the Nixon administration's strategy was to appeal to the Soviet Union and the People's Republic of China to stop their aid to the North Vietnamese. Henry Kissinger found the Chinese especially receptive in these discussions. According to Kissinger's memoir (1979, 704–705): "The war in Vietnam might impede domestic tranquility in America; it was no obstacle to reconciliation with the People's Republic of China.... China desperately

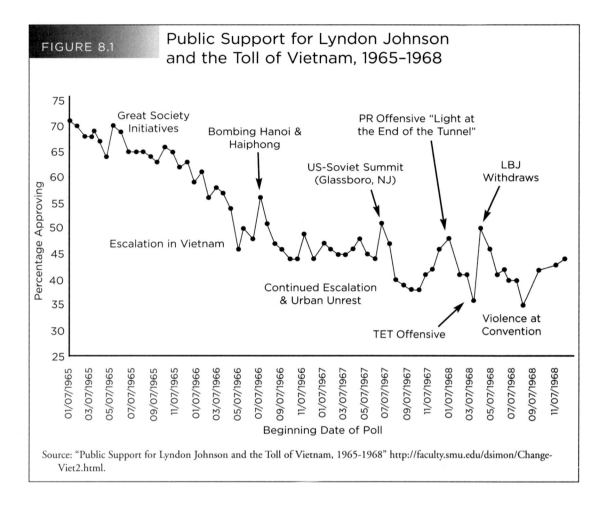

FIGURE 8.1 Public Support for Lyndon Johnson and the Toll of Vietnam, 1965–1968

Source: "Public Support for Lyndon Johnson and the Toll of Vietnam, 1965-1968" http://faculty.smu.edu/dsimon/Change-Viet2.html.

wanted us *in* Asia as a counterweight to the Soviet Union." In fact, the U.S. efforts to isolate North Vietnam ultimately met with some success with respect to both of its major power allies. By 1972, Kissinger says (1087), "Peking's priority was not the war on its southern border but its relationship with us. Three months later Moscow revealed the same priorities.... Against all odds, our diplomacy was on the verge of isolating Hanoi."

Perhaps partly for that reason, the North Vietnamese launched a major offensive early in 1972. In response, President Nixon increased the bombing of the North Vietnamese cities of Hanoi and Haiphong to a higher level even than that ever ordered by President Johnson. In addition, he ordered the mining of the harbors in Vietnam in order to cut off its supplies of weapons, especially from its Soviet ally. By October of 1972 (shortly before the presidential election of that year), Secretary of State Henry Kissinger announced that "peace is at hand" in Vietnam.

In the event, negotiations broke down by December, and President Nixon ordered "one more" round of U.S. bombings of Hanoi and Haiphong—although he could not have known for sure that this would be the last round. These bombing attacks were terminated before the end of the year, and by January of 1973, at last, a ceasefire was arranged.

Unfortunately, the Paris Accords that confirmed this peace left the deck stacked in some ways against the regime in South Vietnam. By that time, only 25,000 American troops were left in Vietnam, and it was agreed that they would leave; on the other hand, the North Vietnamese were allowed to keep their troops in South Vietnam. Then, in June of 1973, the U.S. Congress voted to deny any funds to finance combat activities anywhere in Vietnam or Cambodia. Derek Leebaert (2002, 419) explains the gravity of this action: "Never before had money for an ongoing military action been denied a president."

In 1975 North Vietnam moved in force into South Vietnam, and the American-supported regime fell in April of that year. Saigon, South Vietnam's capital, was renamed Ho Chi Minh City. The war had cost the United States something on the order of $150 billion, and the lives of over 58,000 soldiers. The South Vietnamese had incurred over 254,000 battle deaths, while North Vietnam had lost around 700,000 (Sarkees 2000). Civilian deaths in both Vietnams, and in Cambodia and Laos, probably numbered in the millions.

HOW COULD THE UNITED STATES LOSE THIS WAR?

As I have written elsewhere (Ray and Kaarbo 2005, 99–11) in discussing such contests between states that are widely disparate in military-industrial capabilities, or "power," three or four explanations are commonly offered to account for the kind of upset that occurred in the Vietnam War. Certainly, in terms of raw firepower, technological sophistication, and economic resources, the U.S. military in the mid-1960s to the mid-1970s was *much* more powerful than that of North Vietnam. And that vast disparity makes it difficult to understand how the United States could be defeated by North Vietnam.

One of the most intuitively appealing explanations for upsets in military conflicts of this type points to differing levels of desire, or resolve, between the contestants. From this perspective, if the state that is weaker militarily wins the war, it must have been more committed to the struggle. And in the case of the United States versus North Vietnam, the stakes for the latter were obviously higher. The North Vietnamese people and their government, as well as those sympathetic to the cause in the South, were, from their point of view, fighting for national independence and liberation after a prolonged period of domination by foreigners. In contrast, neither the American people nor their government had very pressing reasons, relatively speaking, for fighting this war. North Vietnam certainly did not, by itself, pose any direct threat to the national security of the United States. And, even if we assume that its Soviet and Chinese allies were threatening to the United States, it is not entirely clear how a victory for the communists in Vietnam would have dramatically impacted the global struggle between these major-power communists and their capitalist, democratic foes. In short, the United States had nothing at stake in Vietnam that was nearly as compelling as national liberation and independence.

Still, there is at least one good reason not to put too much emphasis on the argument that the apparently weaker side in a military conflict must have won because it simply tried harder. The problem is that this kind of argument can be impossible to disprove. Initially, theories that are impossible to disprove may seem to be the best kind of theories, but, in fact, they cannot help us to understand political events; by explaining everything, as the saying goes, they explain nothing. In other words, a theory of war asserting that the state with the larger, more powerful military force almost always wins, unless the weaker state tries harder, will apply with apparent validity to any military conflict. Since no conceivable evidence could invalidate it, this assertion will continue to appear meaningful although, in fact, it is virtually tautological, or true by definition.

Nevertheless, such a theory need not be tautological if agreement can be reached on some operational, concrete indicator of "trying harder." If it is agreed, for example, that resolve is reflected in the willingness to suffer larger numbers of battle fatalities, then obviously the North Vietnamese and their Vietcong allies in South Vietnam demonstrated greater resolve than did the United States. They had, in other words, the greater "willingness to suffer" (Rosen 1972; Mack 1975).

The difference in this level of resolve between the United States and North Vietnam may have been revealed most dramatically in the wake of the **Tet Offensive** by the Viet Cong in January of 1968. "Tet was a military disaster for Hanoi, which incurred around forty-five thousand dead and disabled," according to Leebaert (2002, 351). In contrast, the U.S. military suffered some 4,000 battle fatalities. Nevertheless, the Tet Offensive was reported and perceived as a defeat for the United States and South Vietnam.

In concrete, or arithmetic terms, this interpretation makes little sense. Yet many observers either intuited or concluded that the Tet Offensive did, in fact, represent a defeat for the United States and South Vietnam, even though their opponents suffered much higher casualties, because it was by that time obvious to all that the North Vietnamese and the Vietcong were willing to tolerate much higher losses and yet continue the fight, while there was relatively limited "willingness to suffer" on the American–South Vietnamese side. In short, the Tet Offensive may have been a tactical defeat for North Vietnam and the Vietcong, but the war up to that point had made it obvious that the leadership in Hanoi was willing to incur a string of setbacks, because it believed that the sum total of such tactical defeats would be a strategic success.

From the perspective of a related theory, we might be tempted to say that North Vietnam won this war because of its autocratic political system, as compared to the more democratic system in the United States. The dictatorial North Vietnamese regime, in other words, was able to impose iron discipline on its people, perhaps explaining, in part, why they persisted in the fight even in the face of huge casualties among both the military and civilian populations.

However, it would probably be a mistake to conclude that North Vietnam's autocratic political system gave it a decisive edge in its war against the United States. In fact, as a variety of analysts have argued (see Lake 1992; Reiter and Stam 2002; Bueno de Mesquita et al. 2003), democratic states have a tendency to win the wars that they fight.[e] This tendency may actually reflect, at least in part, the fact that democratic leaders are more likely to lose power in the wake of an unsuccessful war, and so they must be more careful in the selection of opponents. It is also possible, of course, that democratic states fight the wars in which they become involved with more skill and determination. In any case, given the general evidence from all

---

e. Michael C. Desch (2002) lodges a spirited counterargument to this idea.

interstate wars over the past two centuries, it may be more logical to conclude that North Vietnam won the war in spite of, rather than because of, its autocratic regime.

Another, possibly more important, reason that the United States lost this war against a much weaker enemy has to do with the fact that the "power" of states is not a simple, unidimensional concept. There are many different sources of power, not all of them equally effective in different contexts, or for various purposes. Much of the military power in the hands of the United States was, frankly, not relevant to the conflict in Vietnam. Perhaps the most striking example was its nuclear capability. The United States possessed a huge force potential in the form of its many nuclear weapons, which could, in principle, have been used with devastating effectiveness, in a manner that North Vietnam itself could have done nothing to prevent.

However, the North Vietnamese had two powerful allies that were equipped with nuclear weapons: the Soviet Union and the People's Republic of China. The Soviets, in fact, had the ability to launch a nuclear attack on just about any point in the world. The fear of escalation, then, made the vast nuclear arsenal possessed by the United States more or less irrelevant to its struggle against North Vietnam. And much of its conventional military power was, likewise, not well-suited to countering the guerrilla warfare relied on by the Vietcong, in particular. Thus, to some extent, the United States lost this war because much of its margin of military superiority over North Vietnam consisted of military resources that were not effective in the context of that war.

But perhaps the two most important reasons that the United States lost the war in Vietnam lie in relatively simple factors that deserve priority and emphasis mainly because they are so simple and straightforward. All else being equal, simple, straightforward explanations are preferable to more complex ones that may be based on a number of variable factors. This does not mean that simple theories should be preferred even if they are inadequate to deal with the explanatory task at hand; it does mean that explanations should be shorn of *unnecessary* complexity. And any theory or explanation of the outcome of a military contest between two states that are widely disparate in aggregate military capability needs to take into account in a fundamental way the potential effects of (1) the location of the fighting, and (2) the contributions of friends or allies of the weaker state.

In general, states confront several obstacles in any effort to project power over long distances. There are simple logistical difficulties in transporting personnel and materiel for hundreds or thousands of miles. Then, too, soldiers are likely to feel greater urgency in fighting to protect or hold onto turf that is close to home, and to be less invested or engaged in contests over territory that is far-removed from their homeland. This combination of physical and psychological factors is summarized in the **loss-of-strength gradient**, which formalizes the idea that the power of a state decreases as the locus of any military contest moves farther from its home base (Boulding 1963, 231).[f]

This is not a complicated idea, but again, simple, straightforward factors should not be overlooked in attempts to understand complex phenomena such as the war between the United States and Vietnam in the 1960s and 1970s. Clearly, one reason for its outcome had

---

f. This concept was reintroduced into more recent analyses of interstate conflict in Bueno de Mesquita 1981.

to do with the locus of the conflict, so far from the United States, and on the home turf of the Vietnamese government. If North Vietnam had tried to establish a friendly Communist regime, say, in the state of Florida, it would have faced analogous difficulties, and they would certainly have been overwhelming.

The other primary factor that is typically overlooked in assessments of American difficulties in the war in Vietnam is the help that North Vietnam received from powerful friends. In fact, when weaker states prevail in military conflicts with apparently more powerful states, analysts are generally well advised to consider the possibility that the contest was not as one-sided as it might have appeared on the surface, because of contributions made by allies or by less formal supporters of the apparently less powerful state.

Ultimately, the most important ally of the North Vietnamese regime was the Soviet Union. The support provided by the People's Republic of China was probably not as important as it was perceived to be by Americans in the 1950s, and, as we have seen, by the 1970s, Chinese leaders' concern about the antagonism of the Soviet Union had severely dampened their enthusiasm for the North Vietnamese cause (just because that regime was, by that time, more closely allied with the Soviet Union).

However, among the revelations that have surfaced since the end of the Cold War is evidence that the role of the Chinese in the Vietnam War during the 1960s was more critical than was widely known during the war. It was quite clear at the time—and perhaps even more so in the aftermath—that one of the key restraints on U.S. policymakers was the fear that vigorous military action by the American military against the North Vietnamese, especially in the form of troops on the ground invading North Vietnam, might provoke intervention by the Chinese in a manner reminiscent of their intervention in the Korean War. The difficulties that the Americans had faced in dealing with the Chinese in that earlier war—which we discuss in chapter 12—made them quite cautious about this danger.

Indeed, the danger, or the possibility, was even more explicit than was generally known at the time. According to Norman Friedman (2000, 314): "In December 1964 the Chinese agreed to move *three hundred thousand troops* ... into northern Vietnam to free North Vietnamese troops to go into South Vietnam" (emphasis added).[g] Furthermore, by 1965, American decision makers were aware of the presence of those Chinese troops in North Vietnam, and, Friedman says (320), they had reached a secret agreement with the Chinese that China would not intervene in South Vietnam as long as the United States (and South Vietnam) refrained from sending ground troops into North Vietnam.

Critics of American strategy in Vietnam sometimes focus on the fact that the United States failed to do what was necessary to win the war. What was necessary, probably—short of the use of nuclear weapons—was troops on the ground in North Vietnam. But both Presidents Johnson and Nixon, who might have made the decision to send American ground troops into the North, faced not the mere possibility that this strategy would provoke a confrontation with China, but, since they apparently knew that Chinese troops were already there, the near-certainty that such an invasion of the North would involve clashes with those troops.

---

g. In defense of this assertion, Friedman cites Gaiduk 1996.

In short, if the fighting had involved only the U.S. and North Vietnamese militaries—if North Vietnam had not had ample assistance from two quite powerful and important allies—chances are that the Americans would have won the war, in spite of its geographic location so far from the United States, and in spite of the fact that the stakes were much higher for the North Vietnamese. But the Soviet Union provided substantial assistance in materiel to North Vietnam, and its extensive nuclear capabilities created the possibility that any U.S. use of nuclear weapons in North Vietnam would evoke a nuclear response from the Russians.

Likewise, on the conventional front, an invasion of the North by U.S. ground troops might have allowed the United States to prevail against North Vietnam in isolation. But the Chinese threat to retaliate—made concrete by the presence of hundreds of thousands of Chinese troops in North Vietnam—eliminated perhaps the only conventional strategy that offered the United States a reasonable chance of success. In other words, the assistance that the weaker North Vietnam received from its powerful friends was, perhaps, the crucial factor for the success of the North Vietnamese in their struggle to overthrow the U.S.-backed South Vietnamese regime, and so unify their country.

WHAT LESSONS SHOULD HAVE BEEN (AND WERE) LEARNED?

There is little doubt that the lesson learned from the Vietnam War by many in the American foreign-policy-making establishment was that the United States should be very cautious about getting involved in foreign military interventions. This lesson might be dubbed the "anti-Munich" principle, in reference to the compromise agreed to at Munich in 1938, which ceded the Sudetenland portion of Czechoslovakia to Hitler in the hope of appeasing him in such a way that he would terminate his expansionist foreign policy. It failed to do so; in fact, the Munich agreement instead seemed to encourage Hitler to believe that additional expansionist moves would be met with feeble resistance. The lesson from that experience for many analysts and policymakers was that it is better to take active, vigorous steps early in the game to ward off expansionist policies by dissatisfied states or regimes.

In the years after the Vietnam War, the debate in the United States about how to deal with political unrest in Central America pitted traditional, usually more senior, observers who found the lessons of Munich compelling, against more cautious, typically younger, strategists for whom the lessons of Vietnam appeared to be more germane. This disagreement between relative hard-liners, who were sensitive to the dangers of inaction in the face of expansionism by dissatisfied regimes, and more dovish elements, who were fearful of "another Vietnam," was most obvious in the case of the Sandinista regime in Nicaragua. Basically, the Reagan administration saw the rise to power of the leftist Sandinistas as foreign aggression supported by the Soviet Union, which should be resisted vigorously lest the Soviet leadership draw the same conclusion from a successful venture in Nicaragua that Hitler apparently drew from the conference at Munich, where he gained control of the Sudetenland without firing a shot.

The Reagan administration aimed to dislodge the Sandinista regime by supporting Nicaraguan rebels and exiles—known as *contras*—who were trying to overthrow it, and by mining the harbors of Nicaragua. Opponents of this U.S. policy cited Vietnam as a precedent, suggesting that the United States might be getting involved in another prolonged, unsuccessful, and ultimately very unpopular war there. A similar situation was developing in El

Salvador, where the United States once again found itself supporting a besieged government against left-wing forces that were resorting to guerrilla tactics and were (perhaps) receiving support from Communist allies such as Cuba, and even the Soviet Union.

The caution engendered in the U.S. military by its experience in Vietnam seemed to surface explicitly in two quasi-official declarations by leading U.S. policymakers in the 1980s and the 1990s, respectively. In the first, Secretary of Defense Caspar Weinberger, speaking at the National Press Club in November 1984, was responding, ostensibly, to the deployment of U.S. troops to Beirut, Lebanon—which ultimately resulted in the deaths of 241 marines at the hands of a suicide bomber. But there is not much doubt that he was also responding to the Vietnam debacle.[h] In his remarks, Weinberger (1984) stipulated six basic criteria that, in his opinion, needed to be met before the United States should deploy and utilize its combat forces in foreign countries. The terms of what came to be known as the **Weinberger Doctrine** were as follows:

1. The engagement must be deemed vital to the national interest of the United States or its allies.

2. Troops must be deployed only if there is a clear intention of winning.

3. The military intervention in question must have clear political and military objectives.

4. The size, composition and disposition of the armed forces deployed must fit the goals to be achieved.

5. There must be some "reasonable assurance" that the American people and their representatives in Congress will support the military action in question.

6. The commitment of U.S. forces should be a last resort; in other words, all other options must have been exhausted.

In the aftermath of the first Persian Gulf War, then Chairman of the Joint Chiefs of Staff (and, later, Secretary of State under President George W. Bush) Colin Powell promulgated, in another quasi-official statement reflecting a post-Vietnam sense of caution, what would be known as the **Powell Doctrine**. Like Weinberger, Powell (1992) emphasized that U.S. troops should not be deployed in foreign conflict situations unless a clear national interest was involved, unless support from the government and the public was assured, and unless military force was the last remaining option. And, even then, according to Powell, the size of the force in question should be decisive, even "overwhelming."

Both the utility and the impact of the Weinberger and Powell Doctrines are questionable. It is all well and good to insist that a venture have public support, for example. But the public may support a venture initially—as it did in the case of the Vietnam War—and then turn against it in the long run, at a time when it is most vital to the success of the mission. It is, moreover, understandable that military leaders want to apply overwhelming force whenever possible. But sometimes assembling massive military resources for one venture may create dangerous vulnerabilities in another part of the world. Then, too, as in Vietnam, the application

---

h. "The Weinberger Doctrine reflects the collective lessons of the Vietnam War learned by the U.S. military with its resolution to avoid such quagmires in the future" (Handel 1996).

of overwhelming force risks evoking a countervailing reaction that may escalate a confrontation with a minor power into a major-power war.

Finally, it sounds good—and, in fact, the phrase is apparently irresistible to foreign policy makers and politicians—to say that before the United States commits its military forces, it must have ascertained to a certainty that the venture in question is in "the national interest." But, as Jeffrey Record (2000) remarks, "beyond the defense of U.S. territory and citizens, there is no consensus on what constitutes vital interests."

There is, also, some doubt as to whether the preferences of the military establishment for great caution in the initiation of military interventions abroad, and for the use of overwhelming force when such interventions are deemed necessary, are, in fact, dispositions resulting from the U.S. experience in Vietnam. In an intriguing study of the impact on U.S. foreign policy of the presence of military veterans in positions of political leadership, Peter Feaver and Christopher Gelpi (2004, 185) report that "as the percentage of veterans serving in the executive branch and the legislature increases … the probability that the United States will initiate militarized disputes declines substantially. At the same time, however, as the percentage of veterans increases, so too does the likelihood that any use of force will be at a higher level of escalation." This pattern, pertaining to the United States since 1816, is reinforced by analyses performed by Feaver and Gelpi that focus on the post–World War II period. Thus it may be that the military elites in the government learned from the experience in Vietnam to be cautious about military interventions abroad and, when such interventions are deemed necessary, to insist that overwhelming force be deployed. But military veterans in elite governmental positions have historically and consistently been cautious about the use of force, and in favor of overwhelming application of force if it is used, since the nation's founding.

In any case, the United States did manage to put together an overwhelmingly powerful coalition in the first Persian Gulf war against Saddam Hussein in 1990–1991. It also managed to put together a kind of technological colossus, based mainly on air power, that pushed Slobodan Milosevic and his Serbian troops out of Kosovo in 1999 without incurring a single American fatality by hostile fire. The policies implemented in both of those cases were apparently impacted by lessons learned in Vietnam.

Current U.S. policies, adopted in response to the terrorist attacks of September 11, 2001, are less clearly affected by lessons from the Vietnam War. Confidence in military technology, based on so-called smart bombs and other precision-guided munitions, may have replaced, at least among elite decision makers in the Bush administration, the caution induced by the Vietnam experience, including the belief that it is necessary to assemble military forces that are overwhelming in conventional terms. The intervention in Afghanistan, led by a sophisticated aerial bombing campaign, was sufficient to dislodge the Taliban in short order in late 2001. And the heavily mechanized "shock and awe" tactics displayed in the early stages of the 2003 invasion of Iraq also sufficed to bring down Saddam Hussein's regime in a relatively short time.

But the American-installed government in Afghanistan continues to struggle to establish its authority outside the capital city of Kabul, while in Iraq, unrest, rebellion, suicide attacks, and other forms of terrorism have outlasted even the capture and eventual execution of Saddam Hussein himself. Furthermore, in both cases, increasing numbers of critics charge that the problems stem in part from the failure of the U.S. government to deploy sufficient numbers of troops on the ground (*International Herald Tribune* 2004). Obviously, even if American military leaders did, in fact, learn from the experience of Vietnam that military interventions should be supported by overwhelming force, their civilian superiors have apparently not been convinced.

Another lesson that Americans might have learned from the Vietnam War involves what was known as the **domino theory**. Very early on in the war, President Eisenhower expressed the opinion that the loss of Vietnam would "open the door" to Communism in Burma and Thailand, and even India (Leebaert 2002, 161). And, by the 1960s, as William Manchester (1974, 918) reports, *Time* magazine was openly asserting that "South Vietnam must be defended at all costs.... If the U.S. cannot or will not save South Viet Nam from the Communist assault, no Asian nation can ever again feel safe putting its faith in the U.S.—and the fall of all of Southeast Asia would only be a matter of time."

President Lyndon Johnson was perhaps one of the most enthusiastic purveyors of the domino theory with respect to the war in Vietnam, arguing on occasion that unless the Communists were stopped there, they would in due course appear on the beaches of California. And yet, although North Vietnam did take over South Vietnam in 1975, California was never seriously threatened by a Communist takeover. In that respect, the domino theory—on which the U.S. policy in Vietnam was largely based—was discredited by events subsequent to the unification of Vietnam under Ho Chi Minh.

However, to the extent that the domino theory drew on the simple idea that, in politics, precedents matter, and on the observation that, under many circumstances, precedents may set in motion a **bandwagon effect** that can be difficult to resist, other events subsequent to the end of the war in Vietnam served, instead, to validate the domino theory. The Nixon administration—and Henry Kissinger, in particular—felt that it was important that the United States not suffer a humiliating defeat in Vietnam, warning that such a defeat would produce severe consequences for the United States and its allies elsewhere in the world. Indeed, Kissinger remained convinced long afterward that the consequences of the American loss in Vietnam were, in fact, severe. In his memoirs (1982, 83), he notes that "the global turmoil that followed the final collapse of the non-Communist governments in Indochina owed not a little to the loss of confidence in the stabilizing role of America; Soviet adventurism accelerated with American weakness...."

Just what was the "global turmoil" and "Soviet adventurism" that Kissinger refers to here? The notion that a victory for Communism in Vietnam would soon pose a serious threat in California was always rather far-fetched, but the idea that a North Vietnamese victory over the United States and its puppet regime in the South would be a precedent of some importance in the global political system was always quite reasonable by comparison. Three Southeast Asian countries—South Vietnam, Laos, and Cambodia—fell into the Communist camp almost immediately as the result of North Vietnam's victory. And, as had been feared by proponents of the domino theory, many leftist and guerrilla movements in far-flung parts of the world apparently took heart from the success of the national liberation movement in Vietnam, and proceeded to take over in states such as Angola in 1976, Mozambique and Ethiopia in 1977, South Yemen and Afghanistan in 1978, and Grenada and Nicaragua in 1979.

Ironically, however, it is possible to see, in retrospect, that each of these acquisitions by the Communist movement—or, more specifically, by the Soviet Union—represented Pyrrhic victories. According to John Mueller (1995, 81): "All of the new acquisitions soon became economic and political basket cases, fraught with dissension, financial mismanagement, and civil warfare." Many of these sites also created opportunities for mischief-making by the United States, as in Nicaragua, and especially in Afghanistan, where, Mueller reports, American subversion helped to escalate the Soviet Union's expenditures on its newly acquired empire from 2 percent to 7 percent of its GNP between 1971 and 1980. Since these expenditures surely contributed to the economic hardships that brought the Soviet empire tumbling down by 1991, perhaps, from this perspective, losing the Vietnam War was one of the smartest moves the United States ever made in its confrontation with the Soviets.

There may also have been benefits for the United States, in its conflict with the forces of Communism, from propping up the regime in South Vietnam as long as it did. One example involves the fate of Indonesia, which, in the mid-1960s, was the fifth most populous state in the world (after China, India, the Soviet Union, and the United States). It also had the largest Communist party outside the Communist Bloc—the PKI, which had been "embraced" by Sukarno, the leader of Indonesia at the time. By 1965, however, Sukarno was ill, and the stage was set for a battle between the Indonesian army and the PKI, for control of the country in the wake of Sukarno's expected demise. In the ensuing bloodbath, the PKI was virtually destroyed by the Indonesian military. Friedman (2000, 316) comments: "Indonesia was an illustration of a domino effect, in this case only narrowly averted.... To jittery Indonesian generals, the massive U.S. commitment to Vietnam begun in 1965 helped prevent any PKI resurgence."

Some analysts view the stabilizing impact in Asia of the prolonged, thirteen-year American effort in Vietnam as even more widespread. Philip Bobbitt (2002, 59) explains: "During those thirteen years, pro-Western governments consolidated their power in Indonesia, Malaysia, and Singapore, while economic growth ignited in the region's key Western states, South Korea, Japan, Thailand, and Taiwan. By 1975 ..., the threats to all these states and territories, from within and from a hostile China, had far receded."

But in the end, surely one lesson from the Vietnam War for U.S. policymakers is that it is difficult, at best, to create a new, stable government in a foreign country by means, primarily, of military force. In spite of the fact that North Vietnam may well have tried harder, the United States did make quite a determined effort to protect and build up a stable political regime in South Vietnam, devoting to the task billions of dollars and nearly half a million troops—some 58,000 of whom were killed—for a period of time lasting more than a decade. What the United States achieved in the end, however, was a peace agreement, signed in Paris, that was quite similar to the one set up by the Geneva Accords of 1954.[i] And even that 1973 peace agreement fell apart a little less than two years later, when North Vietnam eliminated the regime in South Vietnam.

It is possible that the delay in the fall of South Vietnam, resulting from the determined U.S. opposition to the North, was a crucial step toward bringing about the end of the Cold War—in that a quicker victory by the Communists might have had such a devastating impact as to fundamentally alter the course of the larger conflict. But it seems more likely that if Ho Chi

---

i. "Essentially what was achieved in Paris in 1973 was Vietnam's reversion to its status at the time of the Geneva Accords" (Stoessinger 2001, 105).

Minh had been allowed to take over the whole of Vietnam in the 1950s, his regime might well have emerged as relatively independent of both the Soviet Union and China, somewhat in the manner of Yugoslavia in East Europe. (Ho's regime, like Tito's, was "homegrown," established without benefit of a massive intervention by an outside military force, as had been the case in other Eastern European states after World War II.) If such a relatively benign transition was indeed possible in Vietnam in those years, then it may well be, as Stoessinger (2001, 107) puts it, that "the awesome truth about Vietnam is clear: It was in vain that combatants and civilians had suffered, the land had been devastated, and the dead had died."

CONCLUSION

The war in Vietnam was one of the key events of the Cold War struggle between the United States and the Soviet Union. It was also a devastating blow to the Vietnamese people. The United States became involved in conflict in Vietnam shortly after the successful Communist revolution in the People's Republic of China. There is little doubt that one of the original factors accounting for U.S. policy there was the perception by American policymakers that a victory for Ho Chi Minh would be, essentially, a victory for Chinese Communism and, ultimately, for the worldwide Communist movement.

President Eisenhower made important initial commitments to defend South Vietnam, after playing, perhaps, the most fundamental role in creating that country in the first place by encouraging the South Vietnamese government not to participate in scheduled 1956 elections that might have united South and North Vietnam under Ho's leadership. President Kennedy stepped up U.S. involvement by sending thousands of American military advisers in an attempt to shore up the increasingly unpopular South Vietnamese regime. And President Johnson then started the process of escalation that led to the sending of over 500,000 American troops to that Southeast Asian nation.

Clearly, important geopolitical calculations helped to bring about this massive commitment by the United States to the protection of a relatively small country in a remote sector of the globe—a country that would not even have come into existence without determined input from the United States. But it also seems clear that Lyndon Johnson's primary motivation for prosecuting this war involved domestic political pressure from his Republican opponents in the United States. He felt that if he "lost" Vietnam, he would lose power and, therefore, the opportunity to push his ambitious domestic goals. Ironically, his commitment to the struggle in Vietnam ended up costing him his job—exactly what he (and every other political leader of every other state in most circumstances) feared most, and what he was striving most assiduously to avoid.

American foreign policy makers learned from Vietnam to be cautious about committing American troops to violent political struggles in remote parts of the globe. This standard of caution was rather precisely the opposite of what their predecessors had learned from the Munich experience during the Second World War. Thus, to an important extent, ever since the fall of South Vietnam in 1975, American foreign policy has been created in a struggle between those implementing lessons learned from Munich and others who feel that the lessons of Vietnam are more fundamental.

Although the domino theory, predicting that the defeat of South Vietnam by the Communist North would lead to Communists on the beaches of California, was not borne out, several "dominos" in Asia, Africa, and Latin America did, in fact, fall to Communism subsequent to Ho's victory in South Vietnam. Ironically, several of these Communist successes ended up imposing on the Soviet Union very expensive, troublesome clients that may have played an important role in hastening its demise in 1991. Then, too, U.S. persistence in Vietnam, even though it did not succeed in preserving South Vietnam for long, may have provided needed encouragement to anti-Communist forces in Indonesia, as well as an important breathing space for resistance forces in several other important countries in Asia that might have otherwise succumbed to the influence of Communism.

Nevertheless, it is reasonable to speculate that, had the United States not become so deeply involved in the fate of Vietnam in the 1950s, that fate might have been resolved early on in a way that would have been no more harmful to U.S. interests than the emergence of the Communist regime in Yugoslavia after World War II. In other words, Ho Chi Minh's regime might well have remained relatively independent of both China and, especially, the Soviet Union, and therefore might have become a quasi-ally of the United States in the manner of Tito's Yugoslavia during the Cold War.

KEY CONCEPTS

bandwagon effect   189
domino theory   189
Gulf of Tonkin Resolution   178
loss-of-strength gradient   184

Powell Doctrine   187
proxy war   173
Tet Offensive   183
Weinberger Doctrine   187

RATIONAL POLITICAL AMBITION AND . . .
THE VIETNAM WAR

LESSONS LEARNED

☑ President Lyndon Johnson was not unconcerned about the Communist threat to South Vietnam in the 1960s, but various sources indicate that he was even more concerned about what would happen to his chances of retaining power—and enacting his domestic political agenda—were South Vietnam to fall to the Communists during his term in office.

☑ Ironically, Lyndon Johnson's determined effort to defend the regime in South Vietnam made him so unpopular that he decided not to run for a second term in 1968. This example does not undermine the argument of rational political ambition theory that foreign policies will be fashioned with a view toward keeping leaders in power. What the theory asserts, in fact, is that leaders will adopt policies that they *believe* will keep them in power. On occasion, they miscalculate.

☑ One might plausibly argue that North Vietnam defeated the United States in the Vietnam War because its autocratic regime was able to extract greater effort from and impose more stringent discipline on its population than the democratic government of the United States was able to evoke from or impose upon the American population. However, rational political ambition theory suggests that democratic states are more likely than autocratic states to win the wars they fight, and empirical evidence supports this claim. So, the theory and related evidence imply that the most credible explanation of the U.S. defeat in Vietnam is that North Vietnam won in spite of, rather than because of, its autocratic political regime.

U.S. FOREIGN POLICY IN REGIONAL CONTEXTS

THE UNITED STATES HAS DEALT WITH CRUCIAL FOREIGN POLICY ISSUES and opportunities in every corner of the world, and Part 4 focuses on its policies in the various geographical regions. Throughout its history, the U.S. government has consistently given the highest priority in its foreign-policy-making ventures to the continent of Europe and to its relationships with the major powers—which have, until recently, mostly been European states. Europe is still a very important area of concern, even after the end of the Cold War, and even though the leading states on that continent seem on the verge of being overshadowed by such states as China, Japan, and even India. The European Union, however, may emerge as a roughly state-like entity, and chapter 9, dealing with U.S.-European relationships, emphasizes the role of the EU in the evolving cross-Atlantic relationship.

Since Latin America is on the southern border of the United States, its geography alone gives it special importance to U.S. foreign policy makers. The United States has, in fact, consistently treated the Latin American region as one in which it feels entitled to exert hegemonic aspirations. Surely, as we will discuss in chapter 10, that presumption is one reason why a great wave of anti-American, radical, or leftist regimes seems currently to be coming to power south of the U.S. border. (Mexico has recently bucked this trend, just barely.)

Although the United States has tended to relegate the continent of Africa to a relatively low priority, its foreign policies have, nonetheless, had profound impacts on sub-Saharan African states. Chapter 11 analyzes the reasons for this chronic lack of attention, and explains why that tendency may be about to change somewhat in the age of worldwide terrorist threats. Before the end of the twenty-first century, China, and the whole continent of Asia, may well surpass the United States in terms of geopolitical clout. As we see in chapter 12, both theory and some history suggest that this transition in the relationship between China and the United States may be particularly fraught with significance, and even danger.

Finally, as the Bush administration's war on terror focuses on Afghanistan and especially on Iraq, the Middle East is currently accorded the highest priority of all the regions of the world by U.S. foreign policy makers. Chapter 13 deals both with the war on terror, and with the much more protracted role of the United States in the seemingly never-ending struggle between Israel and its Arab neighbors.

HAVING EMERGED INTO INDEPENDENT, UNIFIED STATEHOOD FROM THE status of a collection British colonies, the United States has always had close ties to Europe. In fighting for liberation from the British in the eighteenth century, the American revolutionaries sought and received substantial help from the French. The new Republic fought its first interstate war against Great Britain in 1812, and then it maintained a rather stormy relationship with the British throughout the remainder of the century, facing several more crises that somehow always stopped short of actual warfare.

As we discussed in chapter 2, the United States interacted, throughout the nineteenth century, with several important European states—including the French, the Spanish and, to some extent, the Russians—each of whom had colonial holdings in North America. In addition, throughout much of the nineteenth and twentieth centuries, European immigrants entered the United States in large numbers. The British had been predominant among the earliest colonialists, and between 1820 and 1920, some 2.5 million more British subjects immigrated to the United States. The Irish Famine in the mid-nineteenth century provoked a wave of emigration from that country that resulted in a quarter of its population (about 2 million people) coming to the United States by 1854; by 1920, the total number of Irish immigrants had reached 4.4 million. In that same period, 1820–1920, 5.5 million immigrants arrived from Germany, 4.1 million from Italy, 3.7 million from Austria-Hungary, 3.2 million from Russia, and 1 million from Sweden (as well as smaller numbers from such states as France, Greece, Switzerland, Holland, and Spain). Statistics on total European immigration to the United States up to 1978 show that 14.3 percent of the newcomers were of German origin, while 10.9 percent came from Italy, 10 percent from Britain, 9.7 percent from Ireland, and 8.9 percent from Austria-Hungary (Simpkins 2001).

After the dissolution of the Soviet Union, the purpose of NATO's continued existence was called into question. At this NATO summit in Riga, Latvia, the representatives of member states discuss combat operations undertaken by NATO against Taliban insurgents in Afghanistan.

By its victory in the Spanish-American War in 1898, the United States made it clear that it was ready to play a role in international politics outside the Western Hemisphere. As we have discussed in previous chapters, the United States played a key role in both world wars, and by the end of World War II, it had established an important political, economic, and military presence in Europe. At a conference in Potsdam, Germany, the victorious powers divided Germany into portions to be occupied by the Americans, the Russians, the British, and the French. When the British decided in 1946 that they were no longer able to help Greece and Turkey resist pressure from Communist elements, President Truman reacted by announcing, in the following year, that the United States would step into the breach with $400 million in aid for the two beleaguered nations; U.S. policy on this issue became known as the Truman Doctrine. Also in 1947, the United States launched the **Marshall Plan**, formally known as the European Recovery Program, which extended significant U.S. foreign aid to Europe.

THE EARLY COLD WAR YEARS

Nineteen forty-eight was a pivotal year in U.S.-European relations. The Soviet Union consolidated its control in Eastern Europe, as a particularly dramatic step in that direction took place in Czechoslovakia, the site of a pro-Communist coup. Also in that year, the Soviets tried to cut off the German capital of Berlin from the Western world, but the city was kept supplied with food and medical supplies for many months by means of a massive airlift by the Western powers, most importantly, the United States.

By 1949, the division of Europe between the Soviet Union and the West was solidified, and ten West European countries, plus the United States and Canada, signed the treaty creating the **North Atlantic Treaty Organization (NATO)**. The operative **Article 5 of the NATO treaty** stipulates that "an armed attack against one or more of them in Europe or North America shall be considered an attack against them all." In 1950 the United States had about 121,000 troops stationed in Europe, the bulk of them in West Germany. That number increased throughout most of the decade; by 1960, it had reached almost 341,000, of whom, again, the majority were stationed in West Germany (Kane 2004).

In the early years of the Cold War, the United States focused at least as much energy on the economic problems of Europe as on its purely military confrontation with the Soviet Union. Under the Marshall Plan, about $13 billion of U.S. aid—approximately $100 billion in current dollars—was funneled to Western Europe from 1948 to 1952. Originally, the Soviet Union was invited to participate in this program, but the Soviets refused, partly because the plan called for extensive American access to internal economic data from the recipient states, and partly because of the requirement that the funds be spent on American exports. Furthermore, the United States insisted that, in order to be able to receive the aid, the European states organize themselves in a cooperative, integrated fashion. As William Keylor (1996, 262–263) reports, the institutional manifestation of this effort to deal with U.S. foreign aid in a collaborative and rational fashion was the Organization for European Economic Cooperation (OEEC).

Why the United States was apparently so generous to European states in the wake of World War II is an interesting theoretical question. Liberals are inclined to believe that some genuine altruism was involved, although they would certainly admit—and realists would agree—that the United States also feared that continued economic deprivation in Europe would discredit capitalism there and eventually redound to the benefit of Communism. Liberals also believe—and on this point, realists are more skeptical—that a certain amount of cooperation is natural among democratic states.

Radicals and leftists, in contrast, tend to see no altruism in the U.S. effort to foster economic recovery in Europe. In eyes of radical analysts both then and now, the Marshall Plan instead tended to "confirm the Leninist prediction of the impending collapse of capitalism and the capitalists' frantic efforts to prevent it: American corporate monopolies, squeezed by the drastic decline in domestic demand for their products as war-related orders dried up, now strove to save themselves by obtaining markets in Europe ..." (Keylor 1996, 263).

But this radical argument that the Marshall Plan was entirely self-interested, rather than altruistic, actually has intriguing implications for capitalism, and for the operation of market forces as they apply to interactions among states. What it suggests is that the situation, as well as the structure of capitalism and the market forces on which it relies, created powerful incentives in the United States to "do well by doing good." In other words, the economic interdependence between Europe and the United States meant that Americans would be doing themselves a favor by engaging in energetic efforts to assist the Europeans in recovering economically. In this particular case at least—and, of course, liberals would argue that this case is more characteristic than unusual—capitalism created powerful incentives for economic cooperation between the United States and Europe, stimulating a "win-win" process that benefited all concerned. This happy model of give-and-take definitely does not conform to the cutthroat competitive image that capitalism and market forces tend to have.

THE BEGINNINGS OF EUROPEAN INTEGRATION: THE FAILURE OF THE EUROPEAN DEFENSE FORCE

Having been the main battleground for two wars of global dimensions in the twentieth century, Europe was, by the 1950s, viewed by many of its citizens and leaders as being in dire need of fundamental economic and political reforms. The U.S. government agreed, and the onset of the Korean War significantly increased its desire to get Europe better organized so that it could deal more effectively with what was perceived as a growing threat from the Soviet Union.

In spite of Europe's horrific experiences with German military might in the first half of the twentieth century, the United States was particularly anxious to see Germany rearmed and capable of making an important contribution to the defense of Europe. The U.S. government's preference was to add German divisions to NATO, but, in October of 1950, the Europeans responded with a counterproposal that would allay their own fears regarding the rearming of Germany. The idea was to create an integrated European military force, to be known as the **European Defense Force (EDF)**, that would consist of personnel and resources contributed by the Benelux states (Belgium, Netherlands, and Luxembourg), as well as by France, Germany, and Italy. The original proposal, offered by the French, was to accept these contributions in the form of very small military units, so that the German units could be spread throughout the integrated force in such a way as to prevent a unified German army from emerging out of this new European military organization.

The treaty to form the EDF, signed in May of 1952, was, ultimately, doomed to fail. One of the reasons was that the treaty, as it emerged from negotiations, differed from the French proposal in that, allegedly for reasons of efficiency, the national contributions were to be of divisional strength, rather than the smaller contributions originally envisioned. This arrangement would allow the rebuilding of the German military in an integrated fashion, which the original proposal had been designed to prevent. Then, too, the British refused to join the EDF, and the French found it necessary to send some of their forces to deal with an anticolonial rebellion in Vietnam. Both of these developments increased French fears that the Germans would come to dominate the new European military force. Finally, Joseph Stalin died in 1953, thus somewhat decreasing Cold War pressures to form the EDF and, in fact, creating French hopes that some kind of détente with the new Soviet government might be possible. So, in 1954, even though its own government had originally proposed the idea, the French National Assembly refused to ratify the treaty that would have created the EDF (Parsons 2002, 62).

The United States considered the defeat of the EDF a substantial setback in its efforts to deal with the Soviet threat. In anticipation of the vote in the French National Assembly, U.S. Secretary of State John Foster Dulles, while actually in Paris in December of 1953, remarked that were the Assembly to vote against ratification of the treaty, the United States would be forced to undergo an "agonizing reappraisal" of its most basic foreign policy premises. The implication of this thinly veiled threat was that unless France voted to approve the EDF, the United States might reconsider its commitment to the defense of Europe or, at least, of France. Did Dulles's statement mean, *Time* magazine (1953) wondered at the time, "that the U.S. would withdraw its troops from Europe...?"

This threat did not work; in fact, some observers felt that it might have backfired. In any case, the French National Assembly's vote against the EDF brought an end to what some analysts refer to as the "federalist" approach to integration in Europe, which sought to go right to the heart of the sovereignty of the member states by subsuming their separate military forces under a supranational authority. The logic of this approach rests on the idea that "it is difficult to cross a chasm in little steps," and so the best way to overcome the obstacles to integrating independent, sovereign states is to leap all the way to the culminating point of the process by creating a federal unit in one giant step.

ANOTHER ATTEMPT: LAUNCHING EUROPEAN ECONOMIC INTEGRATION

Another approach to uniting or integrating the separate states of Europe was also a French idea in the beginning. In 1950 Jean Monnet, ultimately to become known as the founder of the European Union, persuaded French Foreign Minister Robert Schuman to propose the creation of a **European Coal and Steel Community (ECSC)**, which would combine the separate coal and steel markets of France and Germany—and those of other nations if they wished to join—under a political authority that would monitor and supervise the market once tariffs and quotas had been eliminated. The hope was that Germany's coal and steel industries could be revived after the devastation of World War II without giving Germany itself access to its reinvigorated industrial might. These German industries, in other words, would become so intertwined with those of France and other possible members, that the German government would never be able to devote its resources to expansionist military projects as it had done in the all-too-recent past.

After an initial hesitation, the United States supported this proposal, and not only France and Germany, but Italy and the Benelux countries as well, launched the ECSC in 1951. The ECSC Treaty created for this supranational authority a rather elaborate governmental structure, consisting of an executive branch, a parliament, and a court of justice. Part of the reason for making the structure so elaborate was that the ECSC was intended to serve as a stepping-stone to launch the independent states of Western Europe toward a more ambitious project of economic integration.

And that plan worked out well. The ECSC was sufficiently successful that the member states started to make plans to establish a more general and ambitious integrative organization. The **European Economic Community (EEC)** came into being in 1957. It, too, had executive, legislative, and judicial branches, and it attracted the same membership as the ECSC. The Treaty of Rome, its founding document, called for the creation not only of the EEC, but also of an European Atomic Energy Community.

The initial successes of the ECSC had something to do with this advance in European integration, but a more profound reason for it was the determination of the Europeans to avoid the internecine warfare that had been so prominent in their history in the first half of the twentieth century. The United States was sympathetic to the creation of the EEC in part because binding the Europeans together in such an organization seemed likely to make relationships among them more peaceful, and also because it served to solidify their unity against the threat from the Soviet Union.

Early Tensions between France and the United States

From the point of view of the French, who were then the driving force behind the integration movement in Europe, formation of the EEC was, to some extent, an attempt to counter, or at least dilute, U.S. influence in Europe and throughout the world. When Charles de Gaulle became president of France in 1958, under a new constitution giving him broad powers, one of his most pressing priorities was resolving an uprising in the French colony of Algeria. Many of the French thought of Algeria as part of France proper, and the notion of letting it become an independent state was so objectionable to so many influential French interests that civil war threatened to break out over the issue. De Gaulle, however, opted to arrange for Algerian independence by 1962.

We can surmise, especially in keeping with rational political ambition theory, that de Gaulle, who had accepted a certain amount of humiliation for France in letting Algeria win its independence, felt that he needed to restore his nation's *grandeur* on a wider stage if he was to retain the support of a winning coalition at home.[a] Thus it is understandable that, as Craig Parsons (2002, 73) puts it, "de Gaulle's main reasons for accepting the EEC in 1958 ...

---

a. "De Gaulle's Cold War policy was largely dictated by his need to unite France in the aftermath of the Algerian defeat" (Friedman 2000, 296).

focused on leading Europe in a 'third way' between superpowers." The French president was particularly concerned at this stage to exclude the British from the European integration process, and the EEC, as it was originally structured, allowed him achieve that goal.

France detonated a nuclear weapon in 1960, and then devoted considerable resources to the development of its nuclear forces in the ensuing years. These efforts reflected de Gaulle's belief that France needed to attain some important measure of independence from NATO, and from the United States. Disagreements between France and the United States accumulated until March of 1966, when de Gaulle made a dramatic announcement: France would withdraw from NATO's military structures. (It did not withdraw from NATO altogether.) Furthermore, he insisted that American troops be withdrawn from France, and that the headquarters for NATO be moved out of Paris. (It was relocated to Brussels, Belgium.)

At about the same time, the French (among others) were also concerned about American economic domination of Europe and the extent to which the United States was benefiting from economic integration processes within the EEC. These concerns were expressed eloquently, and to enthusiastic reception in France, in *The American Challenge,* by French author Jean-Jacques Servan-Schreiber (1968). The thesis of the book, as summarized by *Time* magazine (1967), was that the economy of Western Europe was being taken over by American industry, "which is better organized, more computerized and far more imaginative than anything the Europeans, including France, can produce." It pointed out that Americans controlled, at that time, 50 percent of the Western European production of transistors, as well as 80 percent of computer production.

One might reasonably assume that Servan-Schreiber and de Gaulle, sharing such a high degree of anxiety about the role of the United States in Europe, would also share common views on how to solve the problem. But, in fact, Servan-Schreiber considered de Gaulle to be a reactionary obstacle to the very economic and political reforms that France needed to deal with the challenge from the United States. De Gaulle, for example, resisted vigorously any expansion of supranational powers within the political structures of the EEC during the 1960s, twice vetoing Great Britain's application to enter the organization. Servan-Schreiber, in contrast, was convinced that the EEC "must be expanded to include Britain and allowed to operate by majority decision rather than being restricted by the veto power that de Gaulle insists is the right of all member states" (*Time* 1967).

De Gaulle was attempting to place Europe, under French leadership, somewhere in between the United States and the Soviet Union within the global political system. His aspirations were damaged considerably by the Soviet invasion of Czechoslovakia in 1968. The reaction of most Western European governments, including that of France, was tepid. Nevertheless, the invasion demonstrated that the Soviet Union could not confidently be considered a benign and peaceful neighbor, and that American defensive power might still be needed to keep it at bay.

De Gaulle made one last anti-American move of significance in 1968. In order to protest U.S. policy in Vietnam, he insisted on turning in French-held dollars to be exchanged for gold by the U.S. Treasury. Since the Treasury was short on gold—certainly in comparison to the stock of American currency in the hands of foreigners, who were entitled to gold in exchange for it under international rules in effect at the time—de Gaulle apparently hoped that this maneuver would put pressure on the Americans to end their expensive war in Vietnam

(Friedman 2000, 339). That strategy did not work, as the United States continued to fight in Vietnam for five more years, and de Gaulle was soon required to turn his attention toward dealing with considerable internal unrest in Paris and elsewhere in France. He retired from the presidency in 1969 and died in 1970.

The 1970s: A Time of Troubles for the European Community?

In 1967 European integration took an important step forward when the three separate supranational organizations—the ECSC, the EEC, and the European Atomic Energy Community—adopted a single, integrated set of governing institutions, so that from that point on there was only one Commission, one Council of Ministers, and one European Parliament for all three organizations. Subsequently, the disappearance of de Gaulle from the scene removed an important obstacle to the entry of Great Britain into the **European Community (EC)**, a step that was accomplished in 1973. Denmark and Ireland were added to the organization at the same time.

In general, though, the 1970s and the 1980s were widely perceived as a time of troubles for European integration. Such perceptions were not without basis. The first effective international action by the Organization of Petroleum Exporting Countries (OPEC) to raise the price of oil involved a boycott against the United States and the Netherlands in 1973. The European Community did very little, at least in a visible way, to help the Netherlands deal with the difficulties created by that boycott. Then, too, while trade among the members of the EEC had increased rapidly during the 1960s, the subsequent decade brought economic stagnation and an end to rapid increases in intra-European trade.

Nevertheless, in the late 1970s, the Europeans did take the first step toward developing a common currency when they created the European Monetary System. Also, the European Parliament, hitherto selected by parliaments in the separate member states, was directly elected by voters for the first time in 1979 (Smith and Ray 1993).

Both NATO and the European Community took on lower priority from the viewpoint of U.S. policymakers in the 1970s (and possibly from the perspective of many Europeans as well) because that was the decade of détente between the United States and the Soviet Union. Neither military nor economic unity seemed so pressing in the context of apparently improving and normalizing relations between the superpowers. Attention focused instead on the energy crisis, featuring high-priced oil, and the resulting high inflation combined with slow growth, or "stagflation," that bedeviled most industrialized economies during this decade.

THE REBIRTH OF THE COLD WAR, AND U.S.-EUROPEAN RELATIONS

The Soviet invasion of Afghanistan in 1979 radically changed a lot of things. (It did not bring an end to the energy crisis in the United States, however, because in that year OPEC engineered its second major increase in the price of oil.) Alarmed by the Soviet invasion, President Jimmy Carter took several steps in retaliation, including boycotting the 1980 Olympic Games, which happened to be scheduled for Moscow. He also increased spending levels in what would be his final defense budget, and it was Carter (not Reagan) who initially sent covert aid to the anti-Soviet resistance forces in Afghanistan.

But one of the last key confrontations of the Cold War focused on intermediate-range missiles in Europe. In 1977 (well before its invasion of Afghanistan), the Soviet Union had begun to deploy new SS-20 mobile missiles, which had a range of over 3,000 miles, carried three warheads each, and possessed a degree of mobility that would make them very difficult to locate or counteract. These missiles could have destroyed NATO's nuclear-armed aircraft, as well as NATO's command system. President Carter responded to the deployment of the SS-20s with a plan to position 572 new intermediate-range missiles in Western Europe—namely, in Great Britain, Belgium, Germany, Italy, and the Netherlands. The U.S. weapons chosen for deployment were extremely accurate, and they were capable of reaching "Soviet command centers after a flight so short that the Soviets might not be able to launch any of their own weapons before [they] arrived" (Friedman 2000, 429–430).

The Cold War was over by the end of the 1980s (or at least by the beginning of the 1990s), but it is important to remember that as late as the early 1980s, the Soviet Union and the United States were engaged in a tense standoff on European soil regarding these intermediate-range missiles. Soon after it came into office, the Reagan administration offered to refrain from deploying the 572 missiles called for in the plan suggested by the Carter administration and approved by NATO, but the Soviet Union was—understandably, according to many critics of the Reagan administration's proposal—unwilling to give up missiles it already had in place in exchange for a mere promise by its antagonists in NATO not to deploy their own missiles in the future. One reason the Soviets refused to accept such a deal, perhaps, is that they expected that public opposition in Western Europe, and even in the United States, to the deployment of new nuclear-tipped missiles in such close proximity to Moscow would, in the end, make it impossible for NATO to carry out its decision. And, indeed, shortly before their deployment, Friedman (2000, 465) reports, West Germany "saw the largest street protest in its history." In addition, polls showed, the majority of West Germans opposed deployment of such missiles on their land and in other Western European states.

The offsetting deployments proceeded, nonetheless, provoking several serious war scares, especially in the Soviet Union and in Western Europe. The immediate reaction by the Soviets to the installation of NATO's new nuclear missiles was to walk out of arms control talks. But, ultimately (in 1988), this nerve-racking confrontation led to (or, at least, preceded) the **Intermediate-Range Nuclear Forces (INF) Treaty**, the first agreement between the Cold War superpowers to actually reduce the number of nuclear weapons on both sides, rather than simply slowing down their rate of increase (Shulman 1987–1988).

THE END OF THE COLD WAR IN EUROPE

From 1945 until at least 1985, the international politics of Europe was dominated by the Cold War confrontation between the United States and the Soviet Union. In the last five years of the 1980s, however, that relationship underwent a transformation as dramatic as that of any interstate relationship in history. And many of the most historic, as well as the most spectacular, ramifications of this transformation occurred in Europe. The Soviet grip on what had been commonly referred to as Soviet "satellites" in Eastern Europe was first relaxed, and then obliterated. These events are symbolized most famously by the collapse of the barrier that had separated Communist East Berlin, on the one hand, and West Berlin, on the other, since it had been built in 1961. The fall of the Berlin Wall in November of 1989 is commonly thought of as the point at which the Cold War ended.

But, in fact, the wall's collapse created a situation that was fraught with serious tensions, as well as potential conflict, between the Soviet Union and the United States, and even within Europe. Friedman (2000, 479) explains: "The Soviets expected that ultimately a liberalized East German regime might join West Germany in a confederation...." In other words, while they might have wished that the two Germanys would remain forever separated, the Soviets at this stage were willing to see them join together in some ideally (from their point of view) loose confederation. That the two states might be merged instead into a single, unitary state was something they probably hoped could be avoided. That a united Germany might become a full-fledged member of NATO, according to Gorbachev in early 1990, was "absolutely out of the question" (Hook and Spanier 2004, 223). And, although the Soviet Union was clearly in a weakened state by this time, it still had some 380,000 troops stationed in East Germany, and was therefore clearly in a position to put substantial barriers in the way of any process aimed at not only reuniting Germany, but integrating it into NATO.

However, in no small part because of firm support for the process by the administration of George H.W. Bush in the United States, the transformation of a divided Germany into a united Germany fully integrated into NATO took place with breathtaking speed (Beschloss and Talbott 1993).[b] Erich Honecker, the last head of the (Communist) German Democratic Republic (GDR), resigned in October 1989. On March 13, 1990, the first (and last) free elections were held in the GDR, bringing to power a government that negotiated the reunification of Germany in a process involving West Germany, Great Britain, France, the United States, and the Soviet Union. That treaty was signed by representatives of both East and West Germany in August; Germany was reunified officially on October 3, 1990—and as a member of NATO.

Following the end of the Cold War, and the end of Soviet domination of Eastern Europe—which now, in the post–Cold War period, is more commonly referred to as East-Central Europe—the issue of the relationship between Western Europe and the former Soviet satellites moved to the forefront for Europe as a whole, and it became a pressing concern for U.S. foreign policy as well.

Simultaneously, and somewhat independently, the European Community was going through an important period of deepening and strengthening its interstate ties. Partly because of sluggish economic growth, the members of the Community had passed the **Single European Act** in 1986, committing themselves to implement some three hundred measures by 1992. The basic aim was to create a better-integrated market by abolishing many of the obstacles to the freer movement of capital and labor within and among the member states. But the Single European Act also had significant political objectives, as described by Alberta Sbragia (1993, 92–93):

---

b. "While for many persons the chief American figure in the collapse of the Soviet Union was Ronald Reagan, a better case can be made for the team of George Bush and James Baker, who in 1990 faced a delicate and dangerous set of issues they managed to resolve with consummate skill.... Nothing could be more misleading than the cliché that the Bush administration 'presided' over the demise of the Soviet Union" (Bobbitt 2002, 626–627).

Not since the American single market was painstakingly stitched together in the nineteenth century has an economic effort of this magnitude and complexity been seen. Furthermore, the timetable established by its protagonists is so compressed that the creation of the single integrated market within the European Community may rank as a unique effort in economic history.... The far-reaching political significance of ... the Single European Act, has received less attention.... The Single European Act (SEA) in fact establishes the institutional conditions necessary to begin thinking of closer political union in a serious way.

Thus, as the Cold War ended, the Soviet empire in Eastern Europe fell apart, and with it the military alliance (the Warsaw Pact) and the economic integration organization (COMECON, or the Council for Mutual Economic Assistance) that had united the Soviet Union and its neighbors in Eastern Europe. Meanwhile, the Western European states were headed toward significantly closer economic and political integration. The Treaty of Maastricht put into effect the Single European Act as of the end of 1992, and the European Community became known thereafter as the **European Union (EU)**.

DEALING WITH THE POST–COLD WAR ERA

The European Community, on its way toward becoming the European Union, had added three new members in the 1980s. Shedding their military dictatorships, Greece (in 1981) and then Spain and Portugal (in 1986) became members of the EC. As soon as it became the EU, the members of the defunct Warsaw Pact and COMECON made known their desire to become members of the Western European integration organization. In the early 1990s, however, the EU was willing to expand only in a limited way as an immediate response to the end of the Cold War. Three states had found it preferable to stay more neutral during that confrontation than was compatible with membership in the European Community. When the Cold War's end meant that this choice was no longer required, Austria, Finland, and Sweden chose to join the EU, and all three were admitted in 1995.

But at that point the EU was not willing to admit such Eastern European applicants as Poland, Czechoslovakia, or Hungary, and there were some indications that Europe as a whole, East and West, was headed for dark and dangerous times in the post–Cold War era. Kenneth Waltz (1979) had argued that the bipolar international system, marked largely by the nuclear confrontation between the United States and the Soviet Union, was actually quite a stable system. Naturally enough, the end of the Cold War and the demise of the nuclear confrontation were greeted with skepticism by Waltz and other neorealists who shared that theoretical premise.

Most prominently, perhaps, John Mearsheimer (1990, 7) argued that "the departure of the superpowers [from Europe] would ... remove the large nuclear arsenals they now maintain in Central Europe. This would remove the pacifying effect that these weapons have had on European politics." Thus, in the wake of the end of the Cold War, from Mearsheimer's neorealist point of view, the entire continent of Europe—from Russia in the east to France on the west, from the Arctic Circle down to the Mediterranean Sea—would become "safe" for conventional war (36), which would therefore become much more likely to occur than had been the case during the superpowers' nuclear confrontation that had focused so prominently on Europe.

The future of Europe was likely to be war-torn, in Mearsheimer's view, as a result both of the absence of the pacifying power of nuclear weapons and from a rebirth, in their absence, of nationalistic and hypernationalistic passions and antagonisms. As Stephen Van Evera (1990–1991, 48) pointed out, "a tour of the map of Eastern Europe reveals at least nine potential border disputes, and at least thirteen significant ethnic pockets that may either seek independence or be claimed by other countries."[c]

Yugoslavia in World War II and Its Aftermath

Such pessimistic prognostications seemed well on their way to being validated, in the mid-1990s, by the demise of the state of Yugoslavia, which had arisen out of the ashes of the Austro-Hungarian Empire at the end of World War I. Originally referred to as the Kingdom of Serbs, Croats and Slovenes when it was created in December of 1918, its name was changed to Yugoslavia in 1929. The relatively new state found itself deeply torn by the international political currents swirling around it during World War II. By 1941, it had been reduced to the status of a satellite of Hitler's Germany, when it was taken over by a coup led by military officers. According to William L. Shirer (1990, 924): "The coup in Belgrade threw Adolf Hitler into one of the wildest rages of his entire life. He took it as a personal affront...."[d] Hitler proceeded to attack, conquer, and occupy Yugoslavia.

Once the Germans were in control, they established the quasi-independent state in the Yugoslavian province of Croatia, and put in charge a group known as the Ustashes. Many Serbian resistance fighters joined together in a group that became known as the Chetniks, who received support throughout the war from such states on the Allied side as Britain and France. Another group of resistance fighters, the Communists, emerged under the leadership of Joseph Broz, a half-Serb and half-Croatian who became known as Tito. Paul Garde (1996) describes this group as "the communist partisans, under the leadership of Tito who officially was pluri-ethnic, was supposed to gather all the peoples, and this is possibly the main reason for his victory."

Thus, Yugoslavia came out of World War II as a federation, in which each of the republics—Slovenia, Croatia, Bosnia-Herzegovina, Montenegro, Macedonia, and Serbia—were granted a certain amount of autonomy under Tito's dictatorial leadership (see map 9.1). The different republics were of diverse ethnic and religious heritages: Slovenia and Croatia predominantly Catholic; Bosnia multi-ethnic with a Muslim plurality; and Serbia, Montenegro, and Macedonia dominated by Orthodox Christians.

---

c. Possibly disputed frontiers pointed out by Van Evera included the Romanian-Soviet, Romanian-Hungarian, Polish-Soviet, Polish-German, Polish-Czechoslovakian, Hungarian-Czechoslovakian, Yugoslav-Albanian, Greek-Albanian, Greek-Turkish, and the Greek-Yugoslavian-Bulgarian borders, while potentially troublesome pockets of ethnic groups included the Romanians in the Soviet Union; Hungarians in Romania, Czechoslovakia, and the Soviet Union; Poles in the Soviet Union and Czechoslovakia; Germans in Poland, Czechoslovakia, and Romania; Macedonians in Bulgaria and Greece; Turks in Bulgaria; Greeks in Albania; and Albanians in Yugoslavia. Van Evera (1990–1991), however, was not so pessimistically inclined as Mearsheimer to believe that one or more of these disputes or pockets of ethnic groups would be likely to lead to interstate war in Europe during the post–Cold War period.

d. Shirer (824) also points out that "the postponement of the attack on Russia in order that the Nazi warlord might vent his personal spite against a small Balkan country which had dared to defy him was probably the most catastrophic single decision in Hitler's career." It was catastrophic, in Shirer's view at least, because the delay in the attack on Russia ultimately got Hitler's army caught in the brutal Russian winter of 1941–1942, and led to a disastrous defeat at the hands of the Russians.

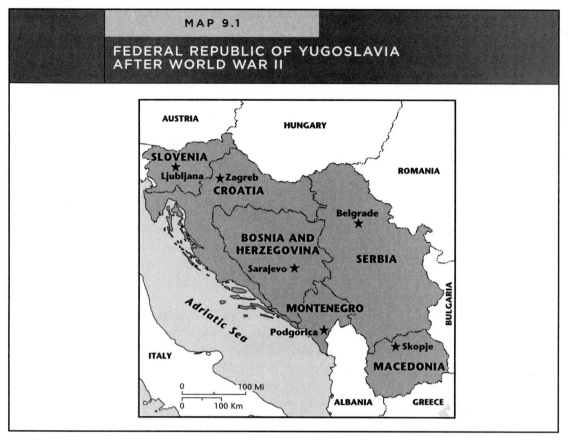

MAP 9.1

FEDERAL REPUBLIC OF YUGOSLAVIA AFTER WORLD WAR II

The former Yugoslavia consisted of the separate provinces shown here, each with some measure of autonomy. Today, all of the separate provinces are independent states.

Yugoslavia took on an unusual, but not entirely unique role during the Cold War. Although indubitably Communist, it received substantial military as well as economic aid from the United States during most of Tito's years in power. Given the apparent anti-Communist thrust of American foreign policy during the Cold War years, this support would certainly appear to be anomalous. However, Tito's regime was quite unlike those of the other Eastern European states in its relationship with the Soviet Union. Those other Communist regimes had all been installed with important, probably indispensable, help from the Soviet Red Army, whereas Tito's regime was home-grown, having been established independently of Soviet military force (except, of course, to the extent that Soviet military might contributed to the defeat of Nazi Germany, and therefore to the end of German occupation of Yugoslavia). Indeed, the military and economic aid that Yugoslavia received from the United States constitutes important evidence that anti-Communism was not, in fact, the central thrust of American foreign policy during the Cold War. Instead, U.S. foreign policy during this period was more consistently focused on opposition to the Soviet Union, and it was perfectly capable of establishing supportive relationships with other Communist states, such as the People's Republic of China during the 1970s and the 1980s, as long as those states demonstrated independence from, or even antagonism toward, the Soviets.

Dissolution after Tito

With the help of the United States, then, Tito held Yugoslavia together and stayed in power until 1980. Ominous signs emerged soon after his death, however. One of the first signs of trouble occurred in Kosovo, a region of Serbia that enjoyed some autonomy and contained a population whose ethnicity was mostly Muslim and Albanian. Kosovo is territory of major iconic significance to Serbs, because it was the site in 1389 of a battle against the Ottoman Turks at a crucial juncture in history; the Serbs' loss there inaugurated five hundred years of domination by the Ottomans.

In 1981, soon after the death of Tito, Albanian Muslim students demonstrated in favor of more power for their ethnic compatriots in the autonomous region of Kosovo. In an attempt to deal with the situation, the government of Yugoslavia sent to Kosovo a functionary of the Communist regime named Slobodan Milosevic. Having witnessed, from the balcony of a government building, Albanians throwing rocks at Serbs, Milosevic made a defiant speech urging the Serbs to maintain their presence in Kosovo. John Stoessinger (2001, 219) reports: "Milosevic returned to Belgrade a changed man. The Yugoslav Communist had become a Serb nationalist." Within six months, in 1987, he became president of the disintegrating state of Yugoslavia.

By the late 1980s, parties in opposition to the Communists had sprung up in the republics of Slovenia and Croatia; the Slovenians were especially obvious in their support of the Kosovars. Then, in 1989, Communism fell in virtually all of Yugoslavia's Eastern European neighbors. Early in the following year, at a meeting of Yugoslavia's Communist party, Garde (1996) says, "there was the dissolution: Slovenia left the congress followed by the Croats. That was it. That was the end of the Yugoslav communist party." Elections in Croatia and Slovenia soon brought to power parties opposed to Communism, and both republics had declared their independence by June of 1991.

At this point, the outside world began to play a possibly crucial role in the evolving situation in Yugoslavia. Ostensibly, it was the Europeans who would have the greatest, most immediate impact. The United States had just completed military operations in the first Gulf War against Saddam Hussein's Iraq, and its leading policymakers were in no mood to take on new responsibilities in the obviously volatile situation in Yugoslavia. But the Europeans were not of one mind about what path Yugoslavia should take into the new, post–Cold War world. David Halberstam (2001, 88) reports: "The British and the French were pro-Serb and pro-Belgrade, with a desire to sustain ... the existing Yugoslav union.... The Germans, who were now emerging as an important force, united for the first time since 1945, sympathized with the Croats and the Slovenes, their old allies from World War II, and favored their independence."[e]

Still, passive though the United States was at this crucial early stage of the disintegration of Yugoslavia, it arguably also had an impact of some importance on developments in the Balkans. At the end of the first Gulf War, the Kurds in the northern part of Iraq had been

---

e. Halberstam (90) goes on to explain that "to understand where the most important European powers stood in relation to the Balkans in 1992, it was only necessary to see where they had been in 1914 and 1940," for the attitudes of the most important European states about the unfolding situation in Yugoslavia were, in large part, reflections of historic ties to the area that had been developed during both world wars.

encouraged by U.S. military successes to take over some villages. But, when the United States implemented a ceasefire, the Iraqi army struck against the Kurds. Halberstam (321–322) recounts what happened next: "Suddenly a major tragedy loomed. The Kurds had fled into the mountains, perhaps as many as six or seven hundred thousand of them, it was believed, and their condition was desperate." The U.S. military came to their rescue, moving the Kurds into temporary camps and providing food and water; by some estimates, the U.S. military operation "Provide Comfort" saved the lives of 600,000 Kurds.

Since it was U.S. military action against Iraq that had led the Kurds to engage in the activities that provoked such savage retaliation from Saddam Hussein's government in the first place, it is understandable, and even commendable, that the United States took this action in defense of its former supporters. But this humanitarian intervention was arguably a violation of Iraq's sovereignty, and it was also bound to be seen by some observers as setting a precedent. Not too far from the northern border of Iraq, for example, in Croatia, rebels pondering an attempt to liberate themselves from the dictatorial yoke of Slobodan Milosevic might reasonably have assumed that the U.S. military would be inclined to come to their rescue should they need help in that struggle.[f] From the point of view of the Croatians, Milosevic was as tyrannical as Saddam Hussein, and the U.S. had plenty of military assets already available in that part of the world. (In chapter 11, we will discuss in more detail such "moral hazards" as may be created by interventions such as that by the United States in defense of the Iraqi Kurds in 1991.)

In any case, the severing of Croatia and Slovenia from the former Yugoslavia was relatively quick and painless compared to what was to follow in the province of Bosnia-Herzegovina. Although Muslims were the largest ethnic group in Bosnia, about one-third of the population was Serbian. In January of 1992, the European Community, after some hesitation, recognized the independence of Croatia and Slovenia, but the Europeans hesitated even longer in the case of Bosnia. In February Bosnia held a referendum on independence, in which the Serbs refused to vote, but those who did cast ballots were 99 percent in favor of independence. On April 6, the EC recognized the independence of Bosnia; the United States did so one day later.

From the Serbian point of view, the world had ganged up on it, providing important reinforcement for centrifugal forces that were tearing the Yugoslavian federal state to pieces. The Serbs had proved unable to resist those forces with respect to Slovenia and Croatia, but they put up a much more serious fight in the case of Bosnia. When the United Nations extended membership to Bosnia in May of 1992, Milosevic announced that all Yugoslavian troops had been withdrawn from the newly admitted state. But, although something like 80,000 Serbian troops stationed inside Bosnia had been "officially" released from the Yugoslavian National Army, in fact, they remained loyal to Milosevic. And they were to play a key role in the events to follow.

Already by 1992, according to Philip Bobbitt (2002, 423), "the Bosnian Serbs [had] set up a gulag of prison camps and detention facilities holding tens of thousands of Muslims and Croats. International investigators were denied access...." The Bosnian city of Sarajevo was shelled by Serbian military units throughout most of 1992, while "ethnic cleansing" on a mas-

---

f. This speculation is based in part on broadcasts by the shortwave broadcasting service Radio Croatia, heard by the
    author as the conflict between Croatia and Serbia began to escalate in 1991.

sive scale was carried out in small towns and villages throughout the country. The United Nations sent 7,000 troops into Bosnia at that point, and the United States, together with the EC, proposed what came to be known as the Vance-Owen Plan (named for Cyrus Vance from the United States, representing the UN, and David Owen representing the EC). The plan divided up Bosnia into a patchwork of separate enclaves for different ethnic groups.

But the implementation of the plan really settled nothing, and the atrocities continued. Halberstam (2001, 197) comments: "Slowly dawning on Western consciences was that the Serbs in Bosnia were committing the worst crimes in Europe since the era of the Nazis." Through it all, the Western powers imposed an arms embargo, which rather effectively made it difficult for the Muslims in Bosnia to arm themselves but did very little, if anything, to deny weapons to the Serbs. The Europeans felt that the United States possessed such overwhelming military capabilities that it really should be the one to sort out the vexing problems in Bosnia. American foreign policy makers felt, in turn, that Bosnia was a European problem that Europeans should solve.

Even more discouraging to prospects that the world would act to end the bloodshed in Bosnia, the new Clinton administration came into office with domestic priorities in mind. At one point, when a young aide in Policy Planning at the State Department agitated for effective action to deal with the violent mess in Bosnia, his superior reminded him that "the foreign policy president now lives in Houston" (Halberstam 2001, 229). He was referring to the first President Bush, who, in this view, had lost the presidency by giving foreign policy issues, in the eyes of the voters at least, too high a priority. Bill Clinton and his major foreign policy advisers were not about to make the same mistake. In other words, as we assume here is usually the case with all leaders of states, President Clinton's priority was to stay in office. And, for many long months, he perceived the troubles in Bosnia as a terribly complex mess that threatened his grasp on power and, therefore, the domestic priorities that he felt were more important.

But the 1994 midterm elections were something of a disaster for the Democratic Party, and the continuing bloodshed in Bosnia, along with the impotent response by the United States, may have played some role in the outcome of those elections. Thereafter, the situation in Bosnia worsened, becoming so much more dramatic and horrifying that it began to look like a potential threat to Clinton's reelection in 1996. His most likely opponent, Senator Bob Dole, who had become an activist on behalf of the Bosnians, was calling openly for a resolution to end the arms embargo, which was still having a one-sided impact on the conflict. The United Nations tried to set up "safe areas" for Bosnian Muslims, sometimes to be protected by NATO air power, but the Serbs would attack those areas and kill the Muslims, allegedly under the protection of the international community.

Then, in July of 1995, the Bosnian city of Srebrenica was subjected to a particularly devastating attack by Serbs. Srebrenica was one of those allegedly safe areas—in this case "protected" by about 400 Dutch peacekeepers, who could only stand by and watch helplessly as the Serbs rounded up some 8,200 Muslim men and women, trucked them out of sight, and murdered them. When this atrocity was followed up by yet another shelling of Sarajevo, NATO and the United States, at long last, intervened forcefully with air power.[g]

---

g. "The murder of Muslim civilians with [Serbian] heavy weapons ... had been stopped by air and artillery strikes that took only about fourteen days and incurred not a single American casualty" (Bobbitt 2002, 427).

The most active phase of the fighting in Bosnia was brought to an end by negotiations in Dayton, Ohio, producing the **Dayton Peace Accords**, which were finalized near the end of 1995. The agreement put into place a complex system of quasi-boundaries between separate areas for the different ethnic groups that would clearly call for supervision and enforcement by outside military forces for many years to come. For this purpose, the Clinton White House agreed to the stationing of some American troops in Bosnia, but it put a limit of twelve months on their stay. According to Halberstam (2001, 359), this was "a completely unrealistic deadline that had nothing to do with the problems ... on the ground. But it would cover the period of the 1996 election. It was a waffle of the first order, done strictly for domestic political considerations."

EXPANDING NATO, OR EXPANDING THE EU?

President Clinton's foreign policy focused largely on Europe during his second term in office. One of the major issues to which he committed substantial time and energy was the future of NATO—which, one idea of striking simplicity and plausibility suggested, ought to be disbanded. The Western powers' military alliance had been created in the first place to deal with the threat of the Soviet Union, which, by the mid-1990s, had been dead for half a decade. Therefore, what point was it to serve?

President Clinton did not accept this argument but pushed instead for expansion of NATO. As analyst Stephen M. Walt (1998, 30) observed at the time, "the debate over NATO expansion looks different depending on which theory one employs." Realists, he continued, opposed the expansion of NATO at that juncture because such a move would probably be perceived by Russia as taking undue advantage of its time of troubles, and so was "likely to provoke a harsh response from Moscow." Liberals, on the other hand, at least according to this particular analyst, were likely to favor the expansion of NATO on the grounds that it would strengthen and reinforce the nascent democracies in important Central European countries such as Poland, Hungary, and the Czech Republic.

The Clinton administration did tend to defend the expansion of NATO with a "democratic peace" rationale. As Jon C. Pevehouse (2005, 1) puts it, "the idea of regional institutions promoting and protecting democracy became a major justification for NATO expansion."[h] However, even though the administration argued that expanding NATO to Central Europe would solidify the new democratic regimes in the area, which would then have a pacifying impact on the region, at least some prominent proponents of the democratic peace idea opposed the expansion of NATO. Bruce Russett and Allan C. Stam (1998, 362), for example, argued that an expansion of NATO would be unwise because it would, predictably, antagonize Russia: "Over time, likely results include intransigence on arms control issues, an increase in the resources Russia devotes to rebuilding military capabilities, and a turn of its diplomatic orientation in a hostile direction." A particular concern involved its probable impact on domestic politics in Russia—NATO's expansion would mean, in the words of Michael E.

---

h. An important source cited by Pevehouse in support of this assertion is an editorial by then–Secretary of State Madeleine Albright (1997).

Brown (1999, 207–208), that "Russian nationalists and political opportunists have another weapon to use against pro-Western factions in Russia's domestic political arena.... The worst-case scenario is that embittered nationalists and opportunists will come to power and adopt much more aggressive policies toward Europe and the United States."

The Clinton administration moved ahead with the expansion of NATO, in spite of the relatively clear danger that such a move would have a negative impact on U.S.-Russian relations and possibly on domestic politics within Russia. One reason for this decision had to do with domestic politics in the United States: the administration was moved by the possibility that NATO expansion would endear it to some 9 million voters of Polish ethnic background, and to a lesser extent (because their numbers are smaller), to voters of Hungarian and Czech extraction. (U.S. Census Bureau data suggest that there are 1.6 million Hungarian Americans and 1.3 Czech Americans.)

However, it should be pointed out, in defense of the Clinton administration's policy on this issue, that it was sensitive to the danger that expanding NATO might antagonize Russia. At the same time it was pushing for the inclusion of Poland, Hungary, and the Czech Republic, it created the **Partnership for Peace (PFP)**, which was seen as a kind of substitute for membership in NATO. This initiative was designed to help aspiring members of NATO—Central European states rather than Russia—to improve their military forces so as to make them more eligible to join eventually. But it was also designed to reassure states such as Russia that they could maintain friendly relations with NATO, even though they might not be members of the organization. Russia was not at first impressed by the potential of the PFP, but it did ultimately join in 1995, whereupon the United States arranged for 1,500 Russian soldiers to be made part of a NATO-led force to implement the provisions of the Dayton Accords in Bosnia.

This conciliatory gesture was followed up in 1997 by the **Founding Act**, which established a NATO-Russian Permanent Joint Council. This agreement protected the right of NATO to make decisions about adding new members without interference from the Russians, but it also promised consultation, cooperation, and possibly even joint action between NATO and Russia in the future. As Robert Hunter (1999, 194) put it, "Thus the alliance sought to 'bracket' Russia's future: to hold out the chance of becoming a full participant in European security, if internal reform progresses well, but at the same time to preserve an alliance able to defend itself if reform fails and Russia again threatens the West."

Amid these provisions designed to mitigate the possibility that NATO expansion might solidify democracy in East-Central Europe at the cost of imperiling democratic reform in Russia—not a rational tradeoff in light of Russia's greater importance in the global political system—the expansion of NATO took place in early 1999, with the addition of Poland, Hungary, and the Czech Republic to the alliance. This expansion was quite rapidly ratified in all the member countries—even in the United States, where the Senate had in recent times rather consistently opposed President Clinton's foreign policy initiatives. This one, however, passed in the Senate by a vote of 80–19.

Arguably, however, the EU, not NATO, was the organization that should have been expanded at this point. Indeed, most Eastern European states would probably have preferred inclusion in the EU over NATO membership. As Brown (1999, 214) comments: "They recognize[d] that EU membership is the ticket to becoming prosperous and rejoining the West." And becoming prosperous would probably have been a lot more relevant to stabilizing democracy in the region than expanding NATO, which might not have done much, if anything, in that regard.[i] So, why (I ask, somewhat rhetorically) was the EU not expanded, rather than NATO?

One reason is that some of the poorer EU states were reluctant to see additional poor states added to the organization, because they would increase the competition for the various redistributive funds set up by the organization for the benefit of its less economically successful members. Also, at least some of the wealthier members were wary of huge waves of immigrants from new Eastern European members coming into their states; and they were concerned about the impact of cheap imports arriving in their home states from the lower-wage Eastern European countries.

In fact, the reluctance of the existing EU countries to add new members in the late 1990s is, possibly, an intriguing example in support of rational political ambition theory. It is quite clear that many European government leaders supported the expansion of NATO as a kind of consolation prize for East-Central European states. These leaders realized that those states were keenly disappointed at being denied entry to the EU, for the time being anyway. But at least some of them feared that waves of immigrants and cheap imports from Eastern Europe might have such deleterious impacts on their own economies that their personal fate in upcoming elections would have been affected. In short, they were primarily concerned about staying in power, and, from that point of view, expanding NATO seemed a lot safer than expanding the EU in the late 1990s. These leaders, then, were quite willing to accept the risk that expanding NATO might provoke Russia in a manner that could have threatened the national security interests of each of their countries, in order to avoid the risk that the expansion of the EU might result in electoral defeats leading to their own loss of power.

This argument can easily be pushed too hard or too far. The fact is that, some five years later, as we shall see, the EU did expand significantly into East-Central Europe. In addition, the United States may well have been pushing, behind the scenes, rather hard for the expansion of NATO rather than of the EU. There is a very simple yet plausible explanation for such a possibility: the United States is a member—more than that, it is the undisputed leader—of NATO, but it is not, obviously, a member of the EU. So, NATO expansion would augment the influence of the United States in the geographic area targeted for expansion, while EU expansion would increase the prestige and influence of the United States only in relatively indirect and, in fact, questionable ways. Accordingly, it is reasonable to conclude that the United States played an important behind-the-scenes role in bringing about the earliest post–Cold War expansion of NATO, and that it tried to discourage equally rapid expansion of the EU.

THE WAR AGAINST SERBIA OVER KOSOVO

Just about the time that NATO was concluding its expansion into former Warsaw Pact territory, things got messy again in the former Yugoslavia. Stoessinger (2001, 236) sets the scene: "When Slobodan Milosevic was chased out of Croatia and Bosnia and then lost an election in Belgrade in 1996, he decided to shore up his own power in Serbia by expelling over 1 million

---

i. See Przeworski and Limongi 1997 on how economic development does stabilize already existing democracies, even if their evidence suggests that it does not make transitions from autocracy to democracy more likely. Also, Dan Reiter (2001) provides a skeptical evaluation of the alleged democracy-solidifying impact of NATO membership.

Albanians from Kosovo." Kosovo had already, at Milosevic's doing, lost its former autonomous status within the Yugoslav federation. Now, as the twentieth century neared its end, Milosevic seemed determined to engage in a policy of ethnic cleansing, forcing some 80–90 percent of the Albanian Muslims among the population of that province to move elsewhere.

In 1998 the United Nations passed two resolutions condemning the violence in Kosovo, as the Serbian campaign against the Muslim residents there escalated. As Michael Hogan (2002) reports, on January 15, 1999, "about 45 ethnic Albanians, mostly men, several elderly, were killed in an act of unnecessary and deliberate slaughter in the course of the capture of a town by security forces of the Federal Republic of Yugoslavia."[j] The name of the town was Racak. "The massacre at Racak," according to Halberstam (2001, 410), "became the critical lever for those in the American government and in allied Western governments to move for military action against the Serbs...." As we shall see, however, there is a vigorous controversy among foreign policy analysts about exactly what was the true impetus for the ensuing military campaign against Serbia. For instance, Stoessinger (2001, 239) argues that, at about this time, Western allies came across evidence of "Operation Horseshoe, a plan by Milosevic and his government that called for Serbian military operations to round up the Kosovars, seize their identity papers, and force them out of the Kosovo, permanently."

Madeleine Albright, the U.S. secretary of state, organized a conference that began in February 1999 at Rambouillet, a chateau outside Paris, in an attempt to resolve the conflict between the Kosovars and the Serbs without military intervention by outside forces. There, the representatives of the Kosovo Liberation Army (KLA) were cajoled and threatened into signing an accord aimed at that peaceful resolution by March 18, but the Milosevic regime refused to sign.[k]

And so NATO—about 85 percent of whose firepower was supplied by the United States—launched a bombing campaign against Serbia on March 24, 1999, for the express purpose of pressuring the Serbs to end their campaign of ethnic cleansing in Kosovo. The resulting war was unprecedented in a number of ways. It was, for example, the first sustained use of military force by NATO in the fifty years of its existence, as well as the first time that armed force had ever been employed for the purpose of carrying out UN resolutions, although there was no approval by the UN Security Council for such operations. The war over Kosovo also involved the first-ever military action based entirely on aerial bombardment intended to halt crimes against humanity being committed by a state entirely within its own borders. (There was, and is, no doubt that Kosovo is a province of Serbia.) Finally, it was the first bombing campaign that can plausibly be claimed to have brought about a distinct change in the policy of the target government without the support of extensive operations by troops on the ground (Roberts 1999, 102).

NATO's war against Serbia took longer than anticipated—ultimately, it was an eleven-week bombing campaign. Milosevic finally capitulated on June 3, 1999, and he lost the presidency

---

j. This description of events is not uncontested. Hogan discusses in some detail several sources who alleged, shortly after the events in Racak, that this massacre was to some extent a "hoax." Halberstam (409), however, provides an account of the event that agrees entirely with that of Hogan, but without alluding to any controversy about its authenticity.

k. In January of 1999, Milosevic had explained to U.S. envoy Richard Holbrooke that if he lost Kosovo, he would lose his head (Halberstam 2001, 420).

shortly thereafter. Arrested and imprisoned by the new Serbian government in April 2001, he was soon turned over to a tribunal in The Hague. His trial went on for five years, finally coming to an end when Milosevic died in prison before the trial could be completed.

The U.S.-led NATO war against Serbia brings to mind at least three important questions. First, why did the United States and its NATO allies attack Serbia over the issue of Kosovo in 1999? Second, was this attack in violation of international law? And, finally, what was the impact of this war—in short, was the war justified, and why?

President Clinton made a special effort to portray the war in Kosovo as motivated primarily by ethical concerns, saying that it was intended to save the lives of Kosovars who were threatened by the genocidal policies of Slobodan Milosevic. Most of the allies seemed to have agreed that the human rights issues at stake in Kosovo were quite pressing. According to Michael Mandelbaum (1999, 3): "NATO waged the war not for its interests but on behalf of its values." But it would be a mistake to think that the United States and its NATO allies were entirely motivated by altruistic concerns. In fact, according to the realist approach to international politics, the policymakers of states always portray their foreign policies as motivated solely by the highest ethical standards and pressing moral concerns. There were, in fact, potentially explosive geopolitical issues at stake in Kosovo.

It did not take much imagination to foresee—and it is relatively clear that policymakers in both the Pentagon and the State Department did foresee—the possibility that continued genocidal violence and determined rebellion in Kosovo could lead to a spreading conflict in the Balkans. Members of the KLA, for example, might start escaping into neighboring Albania, and Serbian troops might pursue them there, eventually coming into conflict with the Albanian military. Or, a continually mounting death toll in Kosovo might have ultimately tempted Albanian military leaders to intervene in Kosovo to save their ethnic compatriots there. And if Albanian troops were to come into conflict with Serbian troops, there would have been bloodshed between Muslims on one side and Orthodox Christians on the other. Turkey might have been tempted, in sufficiently dire circumstances, to come to the defense of fellow Muslims in Albania or in Kosovo, should they suffer spectacularly at the hands of Serbs engaged in ethnic cleansing. And if Turkey were to intervene on behalf of Muslims, surely the Greeks might then have rushed to the defense of their fellow Orthodox Christians in Serbia. A war between NATO allies would have been a terribly messy conflict for the United States to contemplate or deal with, especially if even Russia were ultimately drawn into a sufficiently bloody or lengthy conflict of this kind.

In light of these scenarios, President Clinton and Britain's Prime Minister Tony Blair were both justified in arguing that "a large new wave of refugees from Kosovo could destabilize neighboring countries and lead to an expansion of the war" (Roberts 1999, 107). After the war, in fact, a spokesman for the Clinton administration denied that U.S. policy in response to the Kosovo crisis had been based entirely on altruistic or ethical concerns. As Deputy Assistant to the President for National Security Affairs James Steinberg (1999, 131) explained, "If NATO had not acted, Kosovo's neighbors might have felt compelled to respond to the threat themselves, and a wider war might have begun."

There is also little doubt that the United States and its allies resolved to intervene in Kosovo partly out of some embarrassment over how long it had taken them to respond to the unfolding situation in Bosnia earlier in the 1990s. President Clinton had received much criticism for that delay from members of his own party, as well as from Republicans. As Halberstam (2001, 421) notes, Bob Dole, Clinton's Republican opponent in 1996, "was considered a hero by most Kosovars because of his support."

It is not possible to argue convincingly that President Clinton intervened in Kosovo in an attempt to secure his own hold on power. He was, in fact, nearing the end of his term, and constitutionally ineligible to run again. But an extension of rational political ambition theory to cover situations such as this would posit that leaders prohibited from reelection for constitutional or other reasons will still seek to hold onto power indirectly by seeing to it that their favored candidates and/or supporters succeed them in office. President Clinton clearly wanted his vice president, Al Gore, to become the next president, and he may have felt that inaction by his administration in the case of Kosovo could have been used effectively as a campaign issue by Gore's Republican opponent in the 2000 election.[l]

The legality of NATO's military intervention in Kosovo in 1999 was questionable at best. The United States and NATO could claim that they were enforcing UN resolutions calling for the Serbian government to terminate its policy of ethnic cleansing in Kosovo, but the UN Security Council did not approve NATO's attack on Serbia. Indeed, it was not even asked to do so, because it was clear that China and/or Russia would have vetoed any resolution calling for a military intervention in Kosovo. And according to a common and straightforward interpretation of international law: "In the absence of Security Council authorization, no Member of the United Nations or regional arrangement is allowed to use force unless required for self-defense" (Alexander 2000, 411).

International legal issues, however, are rarely straightforward and simple, and a case can be made that NATO's intervention in Kosovo actually was in accordance with international law. State practice in recent decades suggests that interventions to protect human rights can be justified legally, even in the absence of Security Council authorization. The Indian intervention in Bangladesh in 1971, the Vietnamese invasion of Cambodia in 1978, and Tanzania's invasion and overthrow of Uganda's leader, Idi Amin, in 1979, to cite a few examples, have all set precedents for such unilateral interventions (Alexander 2000). In addition, two days after NATO's bombing of Serbia began, Russia introduced a resolution in the Security Council calling for it to cease immediately. The resolution was defeated by a vote of 12–3. This failure by the Security Council to condemn the bombing or even take an official stance against it gives NATO's action in Kosovo at least a patina of legality.[m]

One obvious problem with such arguments is that they leave up to each state decisions about the use of military force against its counterparts. And President Clinton's decision to circumvent the Security Council in the case of Kosovo provided yet another precedent in support of such unilateral military actions. As a result, Democratic opponents of the decision by

---

l. Admittedly, it is not clear that these fears were justified. George W. Bush hinted instead during the campaign that he disapproved of the use of American troops in such cases, and that he would be inclined to pull American troops out of the former Yugoslavia as soon as possible.

m. Still, as Roberts (1999, 105) acknowledges, "a failed resolution is not a strong basis for arguing the legality of a military action."

President George W. Bush to attack Iraq in 2003 without approval from the Security Council were left in a weaker position to criticize that decision. In general, one possible long-term cost of NATO's operation against Serbia in 1999 was to weaken international legal constraints against unilateral or, at least, unsanctioned military attacks.

Was it a cost worth paying? The alleged purpose of the intervention was to save the lives of Kosovars. But only about 2,500 people had died in the military strife before NATO's attack. Yet, as Mandelbaum (1999, 3) reports: "During the 11 weeks of bombardment, an estimated 10,000 people died violently in the province, most of them Albanian civilians murdered by Serbs." Another humanitarian purpose was to avoid displacement of Kosovars by Serbian military forces. But in advance of NATO's military campaign, only about 230,000 Kosovars had been displaced; by the time NATO's bombing ceased, 1.4 million Kosovars had been displaced, with most of them herded into camps in Albania and Macedonia.

Defenders of the Clinton administration respond to such criticisms by arguing that Milosevic was on the verge of murdering or displacing hundreds of thousands of Kosovars in any case, and that these atrocities would have taken place even in the absence of NATO's intervention. Admittedly, the record of Serbian atrocities in Bosnia in the mid-1990s lends credibility to these charges. And it is also true that NATO managed to force Milosevic to capitulate and relinquish control of Kosovo (even if not permanently) while not suffering the death of even one soldier. Eventual expansion of the war in Kosovo to include several of its neighbors was not difficult to foresee. Thus, it is possible that, as Steinberg (1999) argues, this more limited military action in 1999 did preclude a larger, much more difficult, multilateral military conflict in later months and years.

U.S.-EUROPEAN RELATIONS DURING THE BUSH ADMINISTRATION

The apparent isolationist tendencies of George W. Bush gave some European observers cause for concern when he was elected president in 2000. Bush had suggested, for example, that U.S. interventions in Yugoslavia during the Clinton administration had been ill-advised, and he had hinted that he might, if elected, pull American troops out of the former Yugoslav republics rather rapidly. This position led not only to concerns about stability in such places as Bosnia and Kosovo, but also to worries that a new Bush administration might have a disturbing tendency to let Europeans fend for themselves in a manner unprecedented since World War II at least.

The attacks by Islamic fundamentalist militants on the World Trade Center and the Pentagon on September 11, 2001, changed a lot of things, among them U.S.-European relationships, in ways that are still being worked out years later. The initial European reaction was one of substantial sympathy for the United States in its role as victim of a spectacular terrorist strike, and the Europeans reacted with more than kind words and symbolic gestures. On September 12, NATO met in an emergency session and, for the first time in its history, formally invoked Article 5 of the NATO treaty, which stipulates that an attack on one member of the organization will be treated as an attack against all. Fourteen of the nineteen members of NATO sent forces to the ensuing war in Afghanistan, where troops from nine of those countries actually participated in combat operations (Bureau of European and Eurasian Affairs 2002).

It is instructive to recall that, at the beginning of NATO's war against the Taliban in Afghanistan, some analysts were inclined to point out that, historically, the British and the Russians had both found it very difficult to subdue antagonistic elements in that rugged, mountainous, geographically distant and isolated country. In fact, only a couple of decades earlier, the Russians had found it impossible to stabilize the political situation there in their favor, and had retreated in the late 1980s after a thorough and humiliating defeat. Thus, it was not a foregone conclusion that the Taliban would be driven from power by December of 2001, and an interim government installed in Afghanistan shortly thereafter. Unfortunately, even several years later, the situation in Afghanistan has not yet become either tranquil or stable, despite the installation of an elected government and the establishment, by NATO, of an International Security Assistance Force, aimed at helping the government of Afghanistan to preserve security and reconstruct the country (North Atlantic Treaty Organization 2005a).

So, in the initial response to the 9/11 terrorist attacks, the United States and its European allies were mutually supportive, cooperative, and effective. One step in a possibly different direction occurred in September 2002, when the Bush administration issued a new National Security Strategy that called for "pre-emptive" attacks on states suspected of supporting or harboring terrorists, or of developing weapons of mass destruction (Bush 2002b). At about the same time, President Bush also spoke to the UN General Assembly, where he urged the Security Council to enforce a number of resolutions regarding the regime of Saddam Hussein that it had passed in the wake of the Persian Gulf War in 1990–1991 (Bush 2002c). The most important of these resolutions called for the Iraqi government to cooperate with UN efforts to assure that it had not developed and did not possess any weapons of mass destruction (WMDs), whether biological, chemical, or nuclear.

In October of 2002, both houses of Congress passed resolutions approving military action against Iraq, whether or not the UN Security Council voted in favor of it. In midterm elections in November 2002, the Republican Party gained control of both the House of Representatives and the Senate. Then, in December, the UN Security Council took a step closer to authorizing military action against Iraq, passing Resolution 1441, which declared Iraq to have violated past resolutions and called upon the Iraqi government to provide access to a wide variety of sites in Iraq where WMDs, or the technologies necessary to produce them, might be hidden. The resolution concluded that if Iraq refused to cooperate with UN inspectors, who wanted access to all these sites, it would face "serious consequences."

A series of UN inspections at the beginning of 2003 produced no definitive results, as well as some lack of cooperation from the Iraqi authorities. Even so, the Security Council refused to approve military action against Iraq. France was perhaps the most vocal opponent, but Russia and China, among the permanent members of the Security Council, also opposed a military strike against Saddam's regime. Germany's delegate was chair of the Security Council, and Germany took advantage of that position to express its disapproval of the Americans' apparent plans to attack Iraq. In short, the NATO allies were split on the matter. Germany and France were clearly opposed, while Great Britain, Denmark, Italy, Portugal, and Spain supported Bush's plans for dealing with the perceived threat in Iraq.

On March 19, 2003, the United States, along with a "coalition of the willing" that included only Great Britain among the permanent members of the Security Council, launched its Operation Iraqi Freedom. The legality of this military action was at least debatable. UN Secretary-General Kofi Annan declared forthrightly in the war's aftermath that the U.S.-led war against Iraq "was not in conformity with the UN charter. From our point of view and from the charter point of view it was illegal" (MacAskill and Borger 2004). According to this view, the use of military force by one state against another is justified legally under only two circumstances: states can use force in self-defense (after they have been attacked, or are about to be attacked), or if the use of force has been approved by the Security Council. Defenders of the Bush administration, on the other hand, argue that states have used force with great consistency ever since the UN Charter was approved, without sanctions from the Security Council, and that it is, therefore, erroneous to conclude that "mere inaction" by the Security Council precludes the option of military force for its members. In other words, "because states that signed and ratified the UN Charter, particularly those substantially capable of using military force, have continued to consider themselves free to defend their interests by force of arms with or without Security Council approval, the Charter must be interpreted as consistent with that right" (Rivkin and Casey 2003, 6).

We will discuss the evolution and the outcomes of the wars in Afghanistan and Iraq further in chapter 13. Suffice it to say here that the war in Iraq seriously divided the United States from some of its important allies in NATO. Even before the war, a report in the *New York Times* observed that "Europe's unconditional solidarity with the Bush administration, declared so quickly in the shock after the Sept. 11 attacks on New York and Washington, has faded almost as suddenly" (Erlanger 2002, A8). The reaction of many Europeans to President Bush's January 2002 State of the Union address (Bush 2002a)—in which he branded Iraq, Iran, and North Korea an "axis of evil"—foreshadowed their response to his decision to act on those words and initiate the war against the Iraqi portion of that axis. Meanwhile, Bush's refusal either to cooperate with or to seek ratification of the Kyoto Protocol on global warming, or to support the new International Criminal Court, only solidified the impression of important sectors of public and official opinion in Europe, which had come to see the foreign policy of the United States as marked by "unilateralism, arrogance, bad manners, and oversimplification."

In spite of the disarray in NATO that resulted largely from disagreements within the alliance about how to deal with Saddam Hussein, the organization expanded its membership significantly in 2004. Table 9.1 shows the original membership of NATO, along with the additions made in 1999 and 2004. As the table shows, NATO has expanded from an original membership of twelve states to its current total of twenty-six members. The addition of the Czech Republic, Hungary, and Poland extended the organization into former Warsaw Pact territory, and, as we have already discussed, that expansion may well have been considered an unwelcome encroachment by the Russian government, and perhaps by many Russian citizens as well. Thus, we can easily imagine that the second post–Cold War NATO enlargement, involving not only former members of the Warsaw Pact such as Bulgaria and Romania, but also some states that were once formally integral parts of the Soviet Union, such as Estonia, Latvia, and Lithuania, may have even greater potential for evoking distrust, antagonism, and perhaps even fear, in Russia.

TABLE 9.1	NATO Membership (with dates of enlargement)

Original Members	Enlargement during the Cold War
Belgium	Greece (1952)
Canada	Turkey (1952)
Denmark	West Germany (1955)
France	Spain (1982)
Iceland	
Italy	
Luxembourg	
Netherlands	
Norway	
Portugal	
United Kingdom	
United States	

Enlargements since the End of the Cold War

In 1999	In 2004
Czech Republic	Bulgaria
Hungary	Estonia
Poland	Latvia
	Lithuania
	Romania
	Slovakia
	Slovenia

At virtually the same time as NATO was instituting this second post–Cold War enlargement, the European Union, having hesitated and dragged its feet for about fifteen years since the end of the Cold War regarding the addition of post-Communist states, finally took the plunge and added ten new members from the East-Central European (and Mediterranean) region. The expansion of the EU from its inception (involving only six original members) in 1957 is traced in table 9.2. With its 2004 enlargement, the EU, like NATO, moved to incorporate not only some former members of the Warsaw Pact, but also some former Soviet republics, including Estonia, Latvia, and Lithuania. Bulgaria and Romania were also added to its membership at the beginning of 2007.

Even as the EU was engaged in this rather dramatic broadening of the integration process, it was also in the middle of a substantial strengthening of the ties among its member states. In 2004 the EU heads of state agreed on the text of the Treaty Establishing a Constitution for

TABLE 9.2	EU Membership (with dates of enlargement)				
Original Members	**First Enlargement (1973)**	**Enlargement in the 1980s**	**Enlargement in 1995**	**Enlargement in 2004**	**Enlargement in 2007**
Belgium	Denmark	Greece, 1981	Austria	Cyrus	Bulgaria
France	Great Britain	Portugal, 1986	Finland	Czech Republic	Romania
Italy	Ireland	Spain, 1986	Sweden	Estonia	
Netherlands				Hungary	
Luxembourg				Latvia	
West Germany (Germany)				Lithuania	
				Malta	
				Poland	
				Slovakia	
				Slovenia	

Europe. As one (sympathetic) observer put it, "Europeans, like their American cousins two centuries ago, are on the verge of treating themselves to a full-blown constitution" (Nicolaïdis 2004, 97).

However, in 2005, voters in France and the Netherlands rejected the proposed constitution, and it was suggested that this rejection might actually be beneficial to U.S.-European relations. At least one analyst had argued that "by structure and inclination, the new Europe would focus on aggrandizing EU power at the expense of NATO, the foundation of the transatlantic security relationship for more than half a century. In other words, it would seek to balance rather than complement U.S. power ..." (Cimbalo 2004, 111). A truly federal EU might have created, in other words, conflicting loyalties for those states that were members of both NATO and the EU, and most of those conflicts might likely have been resolved in favor of the EU. Additional complications might have been created because not all members of the EU are members of NATO—this group includes Ireland, Austria, Finland, and Sweden—and vice versa—in addition to the United States, Canada, Iceland, Norway, Bulgaria, Romania, and Turkey are members of NATO, but not of the EU.

Nevertheless, there are several reasons to anticipate that the close relationship developed between the United States and Europe in the twentieth century may become less close as the twenty-first century proceeds. Stephen Walt (1998–1999) argues that U.S.-European ties are likely to weaken in the future because America's economic stake in Asia is becoming relatively more important to it, and because the percentage of U.S. citizens who are of European origin is rapidly declining. In addition, the binding force of the Soviet threat has disappeared.

Related to that receding threat, a simple balance-of-power approach to world politics would suggest that since the United States is—as is repeated continually these days—the lone remaining superpower, one might expect the other major powers to coalesce against it, at least to some degree. And some such counterbalancing, coalescing movement by Europe may well be inferred from the EU's decision in 2005 to put an end to the arms embargo against China that was put in place after the Communist regime's violent suppression of pro-democracy demonstrators in Tiananmen Square in 1989. For some time, the United States complained rather vigorously about European plans to sell sophisticated military equipment and technology to China, but the Europeans turned an apparently deaf ear to such complaints until the Chinese National People's Congress passed (by a vote of 2,896–0, with 2 abstentions) an anti-secession law that was obviously aimed at Taiwan. At about the same time, "India and China agreed … to form a 'strategic partnership,' creating a diplomatic bond between Asia's two emerging powers that would tie together nearly one-third of the world's population" (McDonald 2005). These apparently emerging and evolving relationships between the EU and China, and between India and China, are not imbued with distinctly anti-American sentiments at this early stage in their development. But a balance-of-power theorist would expect these coalitions to progress and to counter the influence of the United States in the near future.

CONCLUSION

Since its inception, the United States has had a close relationship with Europe. It allied with France to gain freedom from Britain in the eighteenth century, and during the nineteenth century it engaged in maneuvers and even some wars to wrest control of what it saw as its share of North America from such European powers as Spain, France, and Russia. During much of the nineteenth and twentieth centuries, most U.S. citizens were European immigrants. The United States became involved in, and had a decisive influence on, World Wars I and II, which can reasonably be viewed as "Europe's Civil War."

The United States helped to create the North Atlantic Treaty Organization in order to deal with what it saw as the threat from the Soviet Union after World War II. Partly for the same reason, the United States has always been supportive of economic integration in Europe, a process that got underway with the creation of the European Coal and Steel Community in 1951. The European Economic Community was launched in 1957, and during the 1960s it considered accepting Great Britain as a member. President Charles de Gaulle of France successfully excluded Great Britain from the EEC—he feared that it would be a "Trojan horse" for increasing the influence of the United States in Europe—and he also pulled France out of its full-fledged military relationship with NATO. De Gaulle did not pull out of NATO altogether, but he did have its headquarters moved out of France, he asked American troops to leave France, and he developed France's own nuclear weapons.

Economic problems dominated Europe's attention in the 1970s, while the 1980s saw the rebirth of the Cold War. The Soviet Union and the United States became engaged in a confrontation over the installation of intermediate-range missiles on the European continent, which was resolved in 1988 by the first treaty between the two superpowers to actually reduce the number of nuclear weapons on both sides. Soon thereafter, the Cold War melted away, ending the division of the state of Germany, which not only unified but became a member of NATO.

The post–Cold War years saw the United States and Europe deal in sometimes awkward ways with the breakup of the federal republic of Yugoslavia. Those years have also been marked by the expansion of both NATO and the EU into what was once a part of the Soviet Empire in East-Central Europe. Three former Soviet republics—Latvia, Lithuania, and Estonia—have even become members of both organizations. The expansion of NATO, in particular, may set the stage for problematic confrontations with Russia in the future. Forty percent of Latvia's population is Russian-speaking, but the government has declared that only people in residence in Latvia before 1940, and their descendants, can be citizens; some 740,000 Russians were categorized as "aliens" by this measure. As the *Wall Street Journal* noted recently, "The Kremlin's willingness to defend Russian speakers' rights across former Soviet lands is putting it at odds with the West.... Latvia is a nation the U.S. has a legal obligation to defend, militarily if needed, because it is a NATO member" (Trofimov 2005, A9). The expansion of NATO right up to, and past, what were the borders of the former Soviet Union certainly has the potential to involve that organization in serious conflicts with Russia.

KEY CONCEPTS

Article 5 of the NATO Treaty   196

Dayton Peace Accords   210

European Coal and Steel Community
   (ECSC)   198

European Community (EC)   201

European Defense Force (EDF)   197

European Economic Community
   (EEC)   199

European Union (EU)   204

Founding Act   211

Intermediate-Range Nuclear Forces
   (INF) Treaty   202

Marshall Plan   196

North Atlantic Treaty Organization
   (NATO)   196

Partnership for Peace (PFP)   211

Single European Act   203

RATIONAL POLITICAL AMBITION AND...
THE RELATIONSHIP WITH EUROPE

☑ European leaders, in the years immediately after the Cold War ended, preferred to jeopardize national security by extending NATO membership in a way that antagonized Russia, rather than adding new members to the EU, which might have endangered their hold on domestic power by diverting EU funds to the new, poorer members and bringing in cheap exports from these new members that would be an economic threat to producers and workers at home.

☑ Following President George H.W. Bush, who may have lost the 1992 election by giving foreign policy issues a high priority, President Clinton was reluctant to make the same mistake by taking an activist stance in the unfolding crisis in Bosnia in the mid-1990s.

☑ Having helped to arrange peace in Bosnia through the Dayton Peace Accords, President Clinton put unrealistic limits on the commitment to station American troops there for domestic political reasons.

☑ Even though he was prohibited from running for president again, President Clinton felt pressured to "do something" about the unfolding crisis in Kosovo in 1999 so as to enhance the electoral prospects of his chosen successor, Al Gore.

☑ President Clinton favored the expansion of NATO to include Poland, for example, in an attempt to strengthen his support among some 9 million Polish-American citizens.

THE STATES OF THE WESTERN HEMISPHERE ARE TIED TOGETHER BY geographic proximity (see map 10.1) and by some concurrent historical developments. Both North America and South America were colonized by Europeans—predominantly the Spanish and the Portuguese in the south, and the English in the north. The United States was the first important territory in the hemisphere to win its independence from a colonial power, and the states of South America followed suit soon thereafter, with the last states winning independence by 1825.

Almost at the same moment that most of the states of Latin America had achieved their independence, the United States declared its intention to prevent extra-regional powers from exerting significant degrees of influence in "its" hemisphere. John Mearsheimer (2001a, 168–169) observes that "powerful states should seek regional hegemony whenever the possibility arises." Once the United States had defeated its British colonizers, and the South American states had liberated themselves from their Spanish and Portuguese colonial masters, the possibility of regional hegemony for the United States became readily apparent. In light of Mearsheimer's theoretical approach, at any rate, the Monroe Doctrine (discussed in chapter 2) constituted an American announcement to all major powers of the world that they should stay out of the Western Hemisphere, because, to put it in a politically incorrect way, the United States intended to run the place.

EARLY U.S. INTERVENTIONS IN SOUTH AMERICA

The aspiring regional hegemon was not capable of running the place for most of the nineteenth century (as we observed in chapter 2), but its pretensions in that direction became ever

In recent years, there has been a "pink tide" in Latin America, as leftist regimes have come into power in several countries. Most of these regimes have considerable antagonism toward the United States. This trend has led to important financial and political support from Venezuela's Hugo Chavez, shown here raising his fist at a rally in Buenos Aires, Argentina, on March 9, 2007. Chavez was speaking out against a tour President George W. Bush was taking of several Latin American countries.

more obvious as the twentieth century approached. When a dispute broke out in 1895 between Venezuela and Great Britain over the boundary between British Guiana (now Guyana) and Venezuela, the United States insisted, over the initial objection of the British, that the dispute be settled by arbitration. In his message calling on the British to submit to this demand, Secretary of State Richard Olney observed:

> Today the United States is practically sovereign on this continent, and its fiat is law upon the subjects to which it confines its interposition. Why? It is not simply by reason of its high character as a civilized state.... It is because, in addition to all other grounds, its infinite resources combined with its isolated position render it master of the situation and practically invulnerable as against any and all other powers.

This statement, which became known as the **Olney Corollary** of the Monroe Doctrine (Atkins 1977, 95), came close to asserting that "might makes right" in the Western Hemisphere—and that the United States had the might. Olney's claim of primacy was soon supplemented by the Roosevelt Corollary of 1904 (discussed in chapter 2). These two rather aggressive statements are indicative of an attitude by U.S. foreign policy makers that the United States was entitled to establish the regional hegemony that Mearsheimer suggests should be a goal for all major powers.

In the Spanish-American War in 1898, the United States took a significant step toward achieving major-power status and toward establishing its regional hegemony. A detailed analysis of the causes of that war can be found in chapter 2; here it is enough to say that it fits very well with this book's emphasis on the impact of domestic political considerations on foreign policy. In short, President McKinley pursued the war largely because of pressures from domestic public opinion, which seemed to warn that a lack of vigor in his handling of the dispute with Spain over the future of Cuba might result in his defeat in the upcoming presidential election (Offner 1992; Ray 1995). In the process of defeating the Spanish, the United States came into the possession of not only Cuba, but also Puerto Rico and the Philippines.

A few days before the war began in April of 1898, Congress had passed a resolution recognizing Cuba's independence, and in the **Teller Amendment** to that resolution had pledged that the United States would not annex Cuba. In the event, however, this pledge was superseded in short order by the **Platt Amendment**, which was first offered as a "rider" to an Army appropriation bill in 1901 and then incorporated into a treaty with Cuba in 1903, making that island territory a virtual protectorate. It gave the United States, for example, a legal right to intervene in Cuban affairs. At about the same time, the United States helped to arrange Panamanian independence from Colombia, and then proceeded to sign a treaty with Panama granting itself the right to intervene in that country's internal affairs.[a] It further obtained from Panama the right to use, occupy, and control "in perpetuity" the **Panama Canal Zone**.

These arrangements involving Cuba and Panama initiated a period during which the United States was very active in its dealings with smaller, weaker states in proximity to its southern border (Atkins 1977, 222). U.S. troops remained stationed in Panama from 1903 to

---

a. The Panamanian Constitution of 1904 contained a clause granting legal permission to the United States to intervene militarily in Panama should that republic be unable, "in the judgment of the United States," to maintain order (Atkins 1977, 215).

MAP 10.1

CENTRAL AND SOUTH AMERICA

Mexico lies along the southern border of the United States, Cuba is only 90 miles from Florida, and the rest of Latin America is sufficiently close to the United States that interactions between the United States and Latin America typically have been relatively intense and important. In particular, states in Central America and the Caribbean have been the sites of numerous military interventions by the United States.

1914 (during the construction of the Panama Canal), and they intervened in Cuba from 1906 to 1909, again in 1912, and yet again in 1916, after which some troops remained there until 1922. American soldiers occupied Nicaragua from 1912 to 1925, and then again from 1926 to 1933; Haiti from 1914 to 1934; and the Dominican Republic from 1916 to 1924. U.S. Marines were sent into Mexico in 1913, and other American troops captured and held the Mexican port of Veracruz for seven months in 1914. General Pershing also led an expedition into Mexico in 1916. Finally, U.S. troops intervened briefly in Guatemala in 1920.

Why did the U.S. government find it prudent, necessary, or tempting to intervene militarily in so many Latin American states in the first two or three decades of the twentieth century? Radical theorists argue that the primary motivation behind all these interventions and occupations was economic. And, in truth, in virtually every case it is possible to find an economic purpose or interest that was served in some way by the insertion of U.S. military forces. (Of course, it is possible to find *some* economic purpose or interest that is served by almost any foreign policy move that the United States might make—or not make, for that matter.)

But realists would insist that the primary purpose served by most of these early twentieth-century interventions was national security. In virtually every case, the American president decided to send troops to protect the lives of American citizens in countries that were experiencing political unrest, and/or U.S. decision makers felt that the unrest might serve as a rationale for some other major power to intervene. In 1904, for example, after Germany, Great Britain, and Italy had blockaded Venezuela in an attempt to collect on debts, the United States insisted on arbitration, and the dispute was submitted to the Court of Arbitration in The Hague. The Court, intriguingly enough, not only ruled in favor of the European powers but also implied in its ruling that the states that had resorted to force deserved priority when Venezuela's debts were to be repaid.

President Theodore Roosevelt issued the statement containing the Roosevelt Corollary when European creditor states next threatened to use force to collect debts owed by the Dominican Republic. Partly to prevent this intervention by the European powers, the United States coerced the Dominican government into signing an agreement giving it control of Dominican customs. By 1905, in other words, the United States had imposed a kind of protectorate on the Dominicans, which the U.S. government utilized in order to generate revenues to pay off Dominican debts.

In other cases—such as Nicaragua in 1912 and Haiti in 1914—there were fears that the Japanese, or the Germans, would use political unrest as an excuse to intervene in Central America or in the Caribbean. Again, in every case of a potential threat of intervention by some other major power, it is also possible to perceive threats to economic interests of the United States and/or economic benefits to Americans resulting from the U.S. military intervention.

In sum, in virtually every case of U.S. intervention, radicals are able to point out economic interests that were served by U.S. policies, while realists are able to point out threats of intervention by other major powers. Liberals can almost always argue that the United States made apparently sincere but uniformly unsuccessful efforts to instill democracy in the targets of the intervention. In light of these conflicting views of the causes of U.S. interventions in Latin America, is it possible to come to any conclusion about which theoretical approach provides the most valid interpretation of American imperialism in the Western Hemisphere in the early twentieth century? One path to a tentative conclusion along these lines involves an American intervention in Mexico in 1913.

The Mexican Revolution in 1911 brought to power one Francisco Madero, who replaced longtime dictator Porfirio Díaz. Madero's leading general, Victoriano Huerta, staged a coup d'état against him, to the satisfaction of many conservative elements in Mexico, as well as that of the U.S. ambassador to Mexico, Henry Lane Wilson. Ambassador Wilson, together with important American financial and business interests, urged President Woodrow Wilson to recognize the government of Huerta. A radical approach to American foreign policy might anticipate that the president would have bowed to pressure from American economic interests and accepted his ambassador's suggestion. However, President Wilson, apparently motivated by a desire to bring democracy to Mexico and, possibly, concerned about Huerta's attempt to acquire weapons that were to be delivered to him on a German ship, took energetic steps—including seizure of the Mexican port of Veracruz—to depose the Huerta government.

In short, in most cases of American military intervention in Latin American states in the early decades of the twentieth century, economic interests and national security concerns were complementary and consistent. Both influences, in other words, created incentives for American presidents to intervene on behalf of the same local, typically rather conservative, political leaders. In the case of Mexico in 1913, however, at least some important American business interests clearly wanted the Huerta government to be recognized, but Huerta's attempt to acquire weapons from the Germans created a potential threat to the national security of the United States. President Wilson resolved this dilemma by acting to curb the German threat—and, to be fair to a liberal interpretation of his foreign policy, to help more democratic forces in Mexico take over the government—rather than responding favorably to pressure from American business interests. This decision does not prove that realist concerns about national security issues are always more important than the economic incentives emphasized by radicals, but it does provide at least some interesting evidence regarding the relative potency of those factors in American foreign policy in this region of the world in the early twentieth century.

We may also note that, virtually without exception, when the United States sent troops into a Latin American state in this era, their destination was in close proximity to the United States—in Central America or the Caribbean—and not in states on the South American continent. This pattern undoubtedly reflected, in part, the fact that those Central American and Caribbean states were smaller and weaker, and therefore made more inviting targets for intervention than the more distant, larger, and less manageable states in South America. But it is also clear that the United States typically had greater economic interests at stake in the much larger economies of South America than in the smaller states near its border. So, if economic incentives were the driving force behind these American interventions, it would be reasonable to expect that those incentives would have led more often to American military interventions in South America. Instead, American troops were virtually always sent to areas close to the U.S. border, within a geographic range in which national security concerns were, all else being equal, more likely to be concentrated.

THE GOOD NEIGHBOR POLICY

By the time Herbert Hoover became president, U.S. foreign policy makers were inclined to modify the nation's relationship with neighboring states in fundamental ways. Franklin Roosevelt is typically given credit for establishing the **Good Neighbor Policy**, but, in fact, says one analyst, "President Hoover repudiated the Roosevelt Corollary to the Monroe Doctrine and significantly reduced Caribbean intervention" (Atkins 1977, 97). Intriguingly, explanations for this change of heart by U.S. foreign policy makers tend to emphasize either that it came about because of a significant increase in the power of the United States in the Western Hemisphere, or, conversely, that it reflected a condition of weakness and increased vulnerability of the United States in the Western Hemisphere. The venerable analyst of inter-national politics Hans Morgenthau (1967, 78) asserts, for example, that "during the era of the Good Neighbor policy ... the superiority of the United States in the Western Hemisphere was so obvious and overwhelming that prestige alone was sufficient to assure the United States the position among the American republics commensurate with its power." In other words, the United States was so overwhelmingly powerful in this era that it did not need to exercise its power in any manner so blunt and crude as it had done in the earlier era of repeated military interventions.[b]

But during the 1930s, the United States certainly did not feel particularly strong or invul-nerable. It was in the throes of the Great Depression—not a phenomenon designed to enhance prestige or self-confidence. Most of the European powers were also negatively affect-ed by the depression, although one of them recovered more quickly and made successful attempts to cultivate its influence in the Western Hemisphere. "The Nazis," says Peter H. Smith (1996, 66), "... made vigorous efforts to establish footholds in Latin America."

Thus, perhaps the Good Neighbor Policy did not reflect the onset of a period of over-whelming superiority of U.S. power in the Western Hemisphere, but was instead caused by the obvious costs of the previous policy of intervention and by the vulnerability of the United States created by the rise of the Axis powers in Europe and Asia. Smith puts it succinctly (67): "As often occurs, the inception of a new U.S. policy emerged from the self-evident failure of a prior policy." Previous interventions had provoked substantial hostility in Latin America, and it was fairly obvious that the United States was entering an era when it needed to avoid, if possible, further offending its neighbors to the south. According to Hubert Herring (1972, 914): "The stage had been set for a more generous United States attitude toward Latin America ... set ... by the United States' need for allies against the looming danger from Europe."

In any case, there is little doubt that near the end of the Hoover administration and in the early years of the Roosevelt administration, the United States chose to refrain from pursuing previous policies that had led to so many military interventions in Latin American countries. In the 1930s, Franklin Roosevelt faced at least two important opportunities to revert to those interventionist policies, in Cuba and in Mexico, but he resisted temptation in both instances.

EXIT THE GOOD NEIGHBOR POLICY, ENTER THE COLD WAR

If the Good Neighbor Policy was an attempt by the United States to cultivate supportive rela-tionships with its neighbors in the Western Hemisphere while it braced for serious problems elsewhere in the globe, it worked fairly well. U.S.-Latin American relations were, for the most part, not problematic during World War II, nor in its immediate aftermath. Peru and Ecuador did fall into a relatively serious border dispute in 1941 and 1942, just as the United States was

---

b. In a similar vein, Atkins (1977, 98) explains that "the reasons for the change in tactics to achieve traditional goals seem to lie in U.S. calculations of a changing strategic situation. After World War I, European threats to hemi-spheric security were virtually nonexistent...." In short, the U.S. refrained from intervening militarily in Latin America during this period because its superiority in the region was so overwhelming that no actual military inter-ventions were necessary to preserve its security interests and influence.

entering World War II in the wake of Pearl Harbor. But, according to G. Pope Atkins (1977, 206): "The United States … was unwilling to allow the destabilizing influences of fighting in South America; it forced a settlement of the dispute." Both the Brazilians and the Mexicans actually committed troops to the anti-Axis cause during the 1940s. The Brazilian troops participated in the attack on Italy, while Mexican pilots fought in the Philippines and in Formosa (now Taiwan). After Pearl Harbor, all Latin American states except Chile and Argentina broke off relations with the Axis powers. Chile followed suit by 1943; Argentina held out until 1944.

As relations between the United States and the Soviet Union became increasingly tense in the aftermath of World War II, the United States proceeded to organize the most extensive series of international alliances in the history of the world, and Latin America was, of course, included in this U.S. campaign. By 1947, the nations of the Western Hemisphere had formalized the Rio Pact, a collective defense organization binding each member state to come to the defense of any other member victimized by military aggression. At about the same time, a more general hemispheric alliance, the **Organization of American States (OAS)**, was also launched.

The OAS is arguably the world's first and oldest regional international organization. Its charter was adopted at the Ninth International Conference of American States, held in Bogotá, Colombia, in 1948. The charter reflects the determination of the Latin American states to restrain the United States from taking advantage of its superior military (as well as economic) power in its relations with the neighbors to the south. Article 19, for example, asserts:

> No State or group of States has the right to intervene, directly or indirectly, for any reason whatever, in the internal or external affairs of any other State. The forgoing principle prohibits not only armed force but also any other form of interference or attempted threat against the personality of the State or against its political, economic, and cultural elements.[c]

In other words, in the charter, the Latin American states continued their attempt—originating at least as far back as the beginning of the twentieth century—to use international law to restrain the hegemonic ambitions of the United States in the Western Hemisphere. In all fairness, it must be observed that this attempt met with repeated failure throughout most of the twentieth century, as the era of the Good Neighbor Policy proved more an exception than the rule. The sincerity of the U.S. pledge to adhere to the legal principle of nonintervention, expressed so fervently in the charter of the OAS, met an important test in the form of internal political developments in Guatemala in the early 1950s. Its reaction to those events demonstrated quite clearly that the United States had, at that time, more urgent priorities than abiding by the international legal principle of nonintervention, or by the principles of international law in general.

During the first forty years of the twentieth century, Guatemala was governed by a series of conservative, repressive dictatorships that protected the rights and privileges of a small minority of landowners and developed an economy based on coffee as its principal export. In reaction to the economic difficulties created by the Great Depression, Jorge Ubico Castaneda

---

c. This was Article 15 in the original charter of the OAS.

came to power to preserve the traditional economic and political structure of Guatemala. Ubico was a firm ally of the United States; subsequent to the attack on Pearl Harbor, for example, his government immediately declared war on Japan, Italy, and Germany. He also maintained a good relationship with the **United Fruit Company (UF)**, owner of vast stretches of Guatemalan territory.

After Ubico was overthrown in a coup in 1944, subsequent elections led to the presidency of Juan José Arevalo, who implemented what he described as "spiritual socialism." One of the constitutional reforms of this period provided a legal basis for ambitious land reform. Although Arevalo's progressive attitudes and policies evoked a lot of suspicion—especially in U.S. government circles (and among the elite in Guatemala)—it is interesting to note that he did manage to complete his term in office.

The Guatemalan election of 1950 was won by Jacobo Arbenz Guzman, who would not be so lucky. He faced daunting economic problems, resulting largely from a drastically unequal distribution of economic resources. Even the U.S. State Department's Office of the Historian (2004)—hardly a radical or leftist source—notes that when Arbenz came into power: "A mere 2 percent of the population controlled more than 72 percent of Guatemala's arable land. Of all privately held land, less than 12 percent was being cultivated. In a country dedicated primarily to agriculture, this translated into sweeping poverty and malnutrition."

Arbenz chose to address these problems by taking on the United Fruit Company, which owned thousands of acres, about 85 percent of which were uncultivated at any given time—a necessary strategy, according to the company, for dealing with the threat of disease to its banana trees. The Guatemalan government expropriated much of United Fruit's land, for which the company was offered some $628,000 in compensation, although, according to the U.S. government, the land in question was actually worth almost $16 million (P. H. Smith 1996, 135).

Complicating this issue enormously, from the point of view of the U.S. government and its defenders, was the support of the Arbenz regime by members of the Communist Party in Guatemala. Herring (1972, 476) reports: "Competent observers set the Communist party membership somewhere between 500 and 2000 in 1954...." Whether Arbenz himself was a Communist is an issue not entirely resolved to this day. Conservative sources such as the *Wall Street Journal,* for example, attribute substantial significance to the fact that Arbenz spent much of his subsequent period of exile in Fidel Castro's Cuba (see Falcoff 1999, A18).

The Arbenz regime attracted the attention of the U.S. government even during the Truman administration. According to Kate Doyle and Peter Kornbluh (2004, 1): "The first CIA effort to overthrow the Guatemalan president—a CIA collaboration with Nicaraguan dictator Anastasio Somoza to support a disgruntled general named Carlos Castilla Armas and code-named Operation PBFORTUNE—was authorized by President Truman in 1952." This effort was superseded by another operation, authorized by President Eisenhower in August of 1953, which organized a group of Guatemalan exiles under Castilla Armas that ultimately overthrew the Arbenz regime in June of 1954. Depending on your ideological and/or theoretical point of view, it may or may not be significant that this operation was actually approved before the discovery and announcement by the U.S. State Department in May of that year that the Arbenz regime had received a shipment of weapons from Czechoslovakia, whose government, it was safe to presume, was operating with the permission of, or perhaps even under orders from, the Soviet Union.[d]

Possibly even more important—certainly from the point of view of radical analysts—than the presence of Communist Party members in Guatemala and support from Communists internationally for the Arbenz regime, were the close ties of key figures in the Eisenhower administration to the United Fruit Company. Some of them were only mid-level officers, such as John Moors Cabot (a UF stockholder), who was assistant secretary of state for inter-American affairs. But such high-ranking officials as Henry Cabot Lodge, the U.S. ambassador to the United Nations, and Allen Dulles, the head of the Central Intelligence Agency, were former members of the UF board of directors, while John Foster Dulles, the secretary of state, was a former employee of the law firm that had drawn up contracts between UF and the Guatemalan government. The presence of so many major figures in the administration who had such important connections to the company bolstered suspicions that U.S. policy toward Guatemala in the early 1950s had its origins in concerns about the financial interests of the United Fruit Company (Connell-Smith 1974; Immerman 1982; P. H. Smith 1996; W. S. Smith 1998.)

The intervention by the CIA and the United States against a Guatemalan government that was arguably elected in a reasonably democratic way reflects the typical combination of security concerns and economic interests that marked most U.S. interventions in Latin America in the twentieth century. Nevertheless, in *this* case, the economic interests concerned were *markedly* well represented at a very high level in foreign-policy-making circles of the U.S. administration. The radical explanation of this particular intervention is, accordingly, unusually persuasive.

Most accounts of the events in Guatemala in the early 1950s do not dwell much on domestic political concerns, except those of the United Fruit Company. But one can certainly surmise that both the Truman administration and the Eisenhower administration were motivated in part by a desire to avoid "losing" Guatemala to Communism because of the anticipated adverse electoral consequences of such a loss. By this time, Truman had already lost China, and it would certainly have had an inkling that there would be a political price to pay for another such ideological setback. Eisenhower came to power partly on promises to "roll back" the Iron Curtain in Eastern Europe, and it would certainly have been contrary to any hopes that might have been raised by such promises to stand by while a Communist regime took over a country so close to the United States (and to the Panama Canal) as Guatemala.

Although the Communist threat, such as it was, did certainly disappear from Guatemala under the CIA-supported regime that took over after Arbenz fled the country, there was a heavy price to pay for this intervention. The Castillo Armas government, put into power with substantial assistance from the United States, was "awkward, incompetent, and unpopular" (Herring 1972, 477). It returned almost all of the expropriated land to the United Fruit

---

d. It is possible that the CIA's operation was a contingency plan that was actually launched only after it was discovered that the Arbenz regime was receiving military support from the Communist Bloc. In his defense, however, it should be noted that Arbenz was obviously fully aware of the danger to his regime from U.S. opposition, and that, in securing weapons from Czechoslovakia, he was merely seeking military support from the only source available to him in anticipation of some aggressive action supported by the United States.

Company, and it became the first in a series of brutal, repressive regimes that killed numbers of Guatemalans ranging from 100,000 (Doyle and Kornbluh 2004, 2) to 200,000 or more (Falcoff 1999, 1), depending on which source one believes. The U.S. intervention in Guatemala also evoked protests and complaints from Latin American states and others around the world about U.S. policies that ignored international law and the proper role of organizations such as the OAS and the United Nations.

The policies of the administrations of FDR and even Herbert Hoover suggested that U.S. leaders had learned useful lessons from the costs of the heavy-handed, interventionist policies of the first twenty or thirty years of the twentieth century. But, according to Bryce Wood (1985, xiv), "the noninterference aspect of the Good Neighbor policy … was finally and fatally attacked … beginning with the intervention and interference in Guatemala in 1954." The U.S. intervention in Guatemala in 1954, in short, set a precedent with far-reaching implications for U.S. policy in Latin America in the following decades.

NIXON'S TRIP TO VENEZUELA

When Vice President Richard Nixon contemplated a goodwill tour of South America in 1958, his attitude, as reflected in his book *Six Crises* (1962, 183), was this: "Of all the trips I made abroad as Vice President the one I least wanted to take was my visit to South America in 1958—not because I thought it would be difficult but because I thought it would be relatively unimportant and uninteresting." Unimportant and uninteresting—that sums up rather neatly what Americans in general and policymakers in particular thought about Latin America in the mid-1950s. But such attitudes would soon change, for Latin America was, from the U.S. point of view, about to become a key site of conflict with the forces of Communism over the next two decades or so.

That Latin America had the potential to become such a battlefield was made obvious by Nixon's trips to eight South American countries in 1958. Most of these visits proceeded without serious incident. In Peru, however, Nixon encountered violent demonstrators at San Marcos University in Lima. Then, when he rode in a motorcade through the streets of Caracas, Venezuela, the U.S. vice president ran into crowds determined on mayhem:

> Out of the alleys and the side streets poured a screaming mob of two to three hundred, throwing rocks, brandishing sticks and pieces of steel pipe. They swarmed around our car. A large rock smashed against the shatterproof window.… They hit the windows and doors of our car with pipes and sticks and those who had no weapons used their feet and bare fists to beat upon the car. The spit was flying so fast that the driver turned on his windshield wipers.… This crowd was out for blood. (Nixon 1962, 218)

Nixon and his wife escaped the scene without injury, but the attack of the Venezuelan mob screamed out for an explanation. Most American policymakers—certainly those at the higher reaches of the Eisenhower administration—seemed to have had no idea that so many Latin Americans harbored such zealous anti-American sentiments. Nixon himself believed that the violence in Venezuela (and in Peru) was "Communist led," but his view on the issue was certainly more nuanced than a simple belief that the whole episode should be written off as a Communist plot. Shortly before Nixon's trip, Venezuela had rid itself of Marcos Perez

Jimenez, who was, in Nixon's opinion (211), "the most hated dictator in all of Latin America." Perez Jimenez had gone into exile, in the safe haven of the United States. But that was not the only aspect of the situation that evoked such fury from significant numbers of Venezuelans in Caracas. This was not some dictator that the U.S. government merely tolerated; in admiration of his vigorous anti-Communist policies, the Eisenhower administration had awarded Perez Jimenez the prestigious Legion of Merit.

In the aftermath of his harrowing experience in Venezuela, Nixon was inclined to defend the policies of the Eisenhower administration with respect to the deposed regime in Venezuela. But he did not conclude that those policies were beyond improvement. In a report written subsequent to his trip to South America, he included among his recommendations the suggestion that the United States "should not appear to give dictators, of either the right or the left, the same moral approval that we gave to leaders who were trying to build free and democratic institutions" (229).

CONFRONTING CUBA: THE BAY OF PIGS AND THE CUBAN MISSILE CRISIS

After Nixon's 1958 trip, the president of Brazil suggested that the United States react to the problems exemplified by the serious antagonism Nixon had encountered in Peru and Venezuela by implementing **Operation Pan America**, which was meant to inaugurate a new era of political and economic cooperation between the United States and its Latin American neighbors. President Eisenhower's reaction to this proposal was cautious but not entirely uncooperative. Within a few weeks, for example, he agreed to the establishment of a new regional economic organization that eventually became known as the **Inter-American Development Bank**. In short, in the words of Gordon Connell-Smith (1974, 232), President Eisenhower's initiatives in the later years of his administration "paved the way for Kennedy's Alliance for Progress much as President Hoover's initiation of the policy of non-intervention had done for Franklin Roosevelt's Good Neighbor policy."

President Eisenhower, however, would bequeath to his successor a much different legacy with respect to relations between the United States and Cuba. In the second term of Eisenhower's presidency, Fidel Castro launched a rebellion against the regime of Fulgencio Batista in Cuba. In the early years of this rebellion, the Eisenhower administration's attitude toward Castro was ambivalent. In fact, "the United States continued to supply the Batista regime with weapons to fight the rebels, while on the other hand it secretly channeled funds to the 26th of July Movement [i.e., Castro's movement] through the Central Intelligence Agency" (Szulc 1986, 469).[e]

Castro marched into Havana on January 1, 1959, and shortly thereafter traveled to Washington, D.C. At that time, he was still talking a good democratic "game." (That it was

---

e. Szulc goes on to point out, however, that "it is unclear whether this operation was formally authorized by the Eisenhower administration or undertaken by the Agency entirely on its own." He speculates that perhaps the Agency simply wanted to hedge its bets in Cuba, cultivating goodwill among Castro and his supporters in case his rebellion was successful.

merely a game is a possibility to which we shall return.) President Eisenhower chose, some-what ostentatiously, to be out of town playing golf when Castro came to town, so it was arranged for him to have a rather lengthy conversation with Vice President Nixon instead. As a result of this conversation, Nixon wrote a memorandum for the benefit of President Eisenhower and the State Department—and, perhaps most crucially, for the CIA. Having decided that Castro was either a Communist or under the influence of Communists, Nixon recommended in his memo that the United States should train Cuban exiles to overthrow the Castro regime (Bender 1975, 16–17).

In his suggestion to depose Castro, Nixon was obviously responding to the international context of the Cold War. He and other policymakers who signed onto the project, so to speak, were also reacting to the CIA's earlier experience with organizing exiles to overthrow what the U.S. government had viewed as an undesirable regime in Guatemala in 1954. The fact that the Guatemalan venture had met with such success (from the point of view of the U.S. government, in the short run, at least) and at so little cost, clearly made the proposed **Bay of Pigs** invasion in Cuba more attractive to almost all involved among high-level policymakers.[f]

But the intense and profoundly significant set of interactions between Cuba and the United States (as well as the Soviet Union) in the early 1960s was also influenced fundamentally by domestic political considerations in the United States (and in Cuba). John Kennedy chose to make the rise of Castro in Cuba a campaign issue in the presidential election of 1960. Although he had earlier complained about the unsympathetic treatment that the Eisenhower administration had given to Castro, now he even called for vigorous action to overthrow that regime. He used this issue, in other words, in his attempt to achieve power. And then, having done so, he regarded U.S. relations with Cuba as a key issue to be dealt with forcefully as part of his ongoing attempts to hold onto power.

Castro's actions and policies were also influenced dramatically by his desire to acquire and then hold onto power. And the events in Guatemala in the early 1950s also affected his thinking on these issues. Intriguingly, one witness to those events was none other than Che Guevara, who had escaped from Guatemala when the U.S.-organized forces deposed Arbenz in 1954, fleeing to Mexico. There he met Fidel Castro, who was planning his return to Cuba to stage his rebellion, and it takes little imagination to suspect that Che must have discussed his experiences in Guatemala with Castro. Even at that early stage, Castro had to be thinking about how he might hold onto power in Cuba, once he had acquired it.

Castro did not announce to the world that he was a Communist until after the U.S.-organized invasion at the Bay of Pigs. This is one reason for the common speculation that it was U.S. opposition and hostility that drove Fidel Castro into the arms of the Soviet Union and a Communist ideology, only after he came to power. But Tad Szulc, in his biography of Castro (1986), argues quite conclusively that Castro was a committed Marxist, and attracted to the idea of receiving protection for his regime from the Soviet Union, at a very early stage in the planning of his rebellion. According to Szulc (38), "the historical decision that the [Castro] revolution should lead to the establishment of socialism and communism in Cuba was reached

---

f. "The CIA-planned invasion of Cuba was in essence an attempt to repeat the successful subversion of the Guatemalan government seven years earlier" (Connell-Smith 1974, 231).

by Castro alone with utter finality in the late spring of 1958...." So, it may have been U.S. opposition, in a sense, that led Castro to this decision, but not antagonistic actions after he came to power. Rather it was the U.S. actions toward the Arbenz regime in Guatemala in 1954—and, one can speculate, Che Guevara's firsthand accounts of those actions—that led Castro to conclude early on that if he were to maintain himself in power, once having achieved it, he would need the firm support of the Soviet Union.

And, of course, John Kennedy had his own concerns about staying in power. Having made such a campaign issue of the Eisenhower administration's weak and ineffectual response to the Castro regime, Kennedy almost certainly felt that he could not scuttle the plans already in place when he came into office to assist Cuban exiles in overthrowing the Castro regime. The fruit of those plans resulted in an invasion by some 1,300 CIA-trained exiles on the beaches of the Bay of Pigs early in the morning of April 17, 1963. The invasion planners were counting on a popular uprising against Castro once word of the invasion had spread. There might well not have been such an uprising in any case, but the fact that the Castro regime, fully anticipating an attack, had in the days immediately before the invasion arrested some 100,000 "suspects" (including 2,500 CIA agents and 20,000 sympathizers), certainly reduced the prospects for a successful invasion and rebellion (P. H. Smith 1996, 166).

In any case, the Bay of Pigs invasion failed miserably. After President Kennedy decided against providing much-needed air support to the invading forces, all but about 100 of the invaders were taken prisoner by the Cuban military and imprisoned for a year and a half. (A couple of the leaders were imprisoned for twenty-five years.) Kennedy accepted responsibility for the failure during the subsequent furor, but soon thereafter, he fired CIA Director Allen Dulles (who, we should recall, had played a crucial role in the intervention against Guatemala in 1954), as well as those of his deputies most deeply involved in the planning of the mission. (Fidel Castro, meanwhile, remains in power almost half a century after the invasion at the Bay of Pigs.)

It is quite clear—based on some decades of historical perspective—that the Bay of Pigs disaster played a key role in the process leading to what is generally considered to have been the single most dangerous Cold War confrontation between the United States and the Soviet Union. That failed attempt served to confirm Castro's fear that he was in danger of overt military invasion from the United States. So, in order to stay in power, he cooperated with, and may have even helped to inspire, Soviet plans to put nuclear missiles on the Cuban mainland.

But why would the Soviets come up with, or go along with, such an obviously risky plan? In the aftermath of the crisis, Premier Nikita Khrushchev explained that he had done it to forestall a possible U.S. attack on Cuba by the Kennedy administration. And although, at the time, most knowledgeable observers did not take this assertion seriously, it has become considerably more credible with the passing of time.

In fact, Pierre Salinger (1989, 25), at one time President Kennedy's press secretary, has asserted quite plainly about the **Cuban Missile Crisis**: "It seems clear ... that the Kennedy Administration, *under heavy political pressures,* was indeed planning to invade Cuba in the fall of 1962, and that the Kremlin sent the missiles to Cuba to forestall an attack" (emphasis added). There is no question that, as Graham Allison and Philip Zelikow (1999, 84) report, the "U.S. military developed contingency plans for such an invasion." There is, however, a dispute about whether or not President Kennedy had committed himself irrevocably to carrying out this attack. Kennedy's secretary of defense, Robert McNamara, for example, insists that there was no final commitment to an attack by U.S. forces on Cuba, aimed at removing Castro. But, according to Salinger, he admits that had he been among the Soviet observers of the unfolding crisis, knowing what they knew, he would have concluded that the United States was on the verge of attacking Cuba.

There was in place an elaborate CIA plot, with the name of Operation Mongoose, aimed at assassinating or otherwise deposing Castro. Declassified documents reveal that the commander in chief of the U.S. Armed Forces in the Atlantic received a memorandum dated October 6 ordering him to put into motion contingency plans for invading Cuba (Salinger 1989, 25). In short, even if there was some doubt as to whether or not, in the absence of the missile crisis, the United States would have invaded Cuba, there is little doubt that the Soviets thought that an invasion was imminent. Even though such authoritative sources as Allison and Zelikow insist (1999, 86) that "attempts to explain Soviet nuclear missiles in Cuba with the Cuban defense hypothesis will not withstand careful examination," Salinger (1995, 120) points out that the Soviet KGB had penetrated Operation Mongoose and had secured documents stating that if Castro could not be deposed otherwise, the United States would take direct action against him by October 1962. And, says Salinger: "That information was the basis for Khruschchev's belief—no, his *conviction*—that the United States was going to invade Cuba in October 1962."[g]

So, Kennedy had used the Cuba-Castro issue as leverage to obtain power, and then, apparently, key figures in his administration—not only the president, but also his brother Robert—came to feel that doing something about Castro's regime was a key to holding onto power. Whether or not, in their own minds, they ever became irrevocably committed to an invasion of Cuba, the Kennedy brain trust almost certainly managed to persuade the Soviet Union that an invasion was imminent. The Soviet commitment to the defense of Cuba was intense and, in retrospect, rather scary (because of its implication that full-scale military combat, perhaps complete with nuclear exchanges, might well have taken place). The Soviets shipped about two-thirds of their missile power to Cuba in 1962, and while the United States believed that only 10,000 Soviet troops were in Cuba, evidence subsequently uncovered suggests that the actual number was closer to 40,000 (Salinger 1989, 25).

In traditional realpolitik terms, the Cuban Missile Crisis was provoked by a desperate gamble on the part of the Soviet Union to close a power gap between itself and the United States in the nuclear confrontation—to which the United States responded in a typical, balance-of-power, determined fashion. From a rational political ambition theory perspective, however, the obsession with Castro displayed by the Kennedy administration had much to do with its overarching determination to stay in power; like other Democratic officeholders before and after them, key figures in the Kennedy administration felt vulnerable to the charge of being "soft on communism," and they concluded, especially after the Bay of Pigs fiasco, that they had to take some decisive action against Castro's regime in order to be able to counter such

---

g. Referring to Allison and Zelikow's new edition of their well-known book about the Cuban Missile Crisis, one convincing (to this author, at least) analyst observes, "The revised *Essence* [*of Decision*] dismisses the 'Cuban defense' motive on various unconvincing grounds" (Bernstein 2000, 150).

charges effectively. In short, Barton J. Bernstein (2000, 152) explains, "President Kennedy could not tolerate Soviet missiles and he had to act to get them out or face political reprisals at home. As Robert Kennedy soon privately told his brother, the president, 'there isn't any choice . . . you would have been [otherwise] impeached.'"

For his part, Castro, recalling Che Guevara's reports about CIA activities in Guatemala in 1954, felt that to remain in power, once having seized it, he would need the protection of the Soviet Union. He cultivated that support, with a commitment to Communism, in part, from the first days of his regime. And he accepted Russian missiles on his soil in a desperate attempt to preserve his regime. Finally, the Soviets—or, more precisely, Nikita Khrushchev—were motivated to engage in this affair by their own domestic concerns.[h] In fact, the whole episode is best understood, perhaps, as a set of interactions among three regimes doing what each thought necessary to stay in power under the circumstances facing them in the early 1960s.

THE FORMATION AND THE FAILURE OF THE ALLIANCE FOR PROGRESS

President Kennedy went along with the plans for a Bay of Pigs invasion that were in place when he assumed office, and he may well have renewed his determination to bring about the downfall of the Castro regime by force in a way that precipitated the missile crisis. But his approach to Latin America was not entirely militaristic or subversive. In fact, it is probably fair to say, as Szulc (1986, 597) does, that "Kennedy approached the Alliance for Progress with much greater enthusiasm than the supposedly secret plans for the Bay of Pigs."[i]

Kennedy announced the launching of the **Alliance for Progress** in March of 1961, and an international meeting in Punta del Este, Uruguay, in August of that year represented the initial step toward implementing his idea of what amounted to a Marshall Plan for Latin America. The heart of the program was a substantial increase in foreign aid for Latin American states, along with support for the Food for Peace program, support for economic integration, and efforts to stabilize the prices of Latin American exports. Basically, the Alliance called for a "decade of maximum effort" by the United States to help Latin America resolve its most serious economic problems, as a step toward dealing with political instability.

In between Kennedy's speech in March and the meeting in Uruguay in August, came the Bay of Pigs invasion in April 1961. This sequence of events made it even clearer that the Alliance for Progress was, in essence, an effort to deal with the threat of Communism in Latin America, symbolized and manifested most importantly by Castro's revolution: "Cuba's growing allegiance to the Communist bloc helped to accelerate and shape the creation of the Alliance as a democratic alternative to Cuba's revolutionary socialist formula for development in Latin America" (Levinson and de Onís 1970, 7).

---

h. "Khrushchev's domestic position set the stage for his foreign policy behavior. He needed a foreign policy success more than ever. . . . The Cuban missile venture offered him the prospect, however slim, that he could emerge from this situation and salvage his already declining authority" (Richter 1994, 150, cited in Allison and Zelikow 1999; see also Lebow and Stein 1994, 58–60).

i. Szulc (1986, 597) asserts that "both enterprises, however, had their roots in the Castro revolution," a sentiment certainly in line with an important theme of this chapter.

What the Kennedy administration hoped to accomplish with the Alliance for Progress was to encourage progressive elements in Latin America who would be devoted to democratic political principles, and to foster at least a tolerance for the United States. But that basically political goal was frustrated from the very beginning. In the first year of the Alliance, the president of Brazil resigned (initiating a series of events that led to a military coup in 1964), and military coups overthrew constitutional governments in Argentina and Peru. President Kennedy's initial inclination was to resist such antidemocratic, unconstitutional political developments. But he got no support for this stance from Latin American governments, who considered such resistance to be unacceptable meddling in their domestic affairs—a kind of pretentious, arrogant "Wilsonianism." To some extent, it seems that Kennedy's support for more progressive political elements in Latin America frightened its more conservative, even reactionary forces into action, for there were, in all, sixteen military coups in the first eight years of the Alliance for Progress (Levinson and de Onís 1970, 77). In short, the Alliance, ostensibly designed as a healthy antidote to past U.S. support for right-wing, reactionary, anti-democratic military governments in Latin America, seemed instead to have the perverse effect of bringing just such governments to power throughout South and Central America.

Why did the Alliance fail (as most observers agree that it did)? Kennedy's assassination removed a vital force behind it at the highest level of the government, but the Alliance was foundering well before that tragic loss. Business interests had managed to make its foreign aid programs a kind of Christmas tree for themselves, arranging to have aid disbursements "tied" in such a way that the Latin American recipients had to purchase goods and services from American corporations. As one prominent academic observer of Latin America (Lowenthal 1973) has pointed out, liberals tend to believe that the Alliance failed because of mistakes by policymakers who had unfortunate priorities; radicals believe that it turned out just as it was supposed to, resulting in more reactionary governments in Latin America and big profits for American capitalists; and advocates of a "bureaucratic politics" approach argue that the top leaders launched the Alliance in good faith, but then left the day-to-day policymaking to lower-level bureaucrats who proved susceptible to pressure from well-organized groups such as those in the business community.

From the point of view of the rational political ambition approach, however, the Kennedy administration formulated the Alliance for Progress as a way of reducing the prospects for future "Cubas" in Latin America, as it was mindful of their great potential for negative domestic electoral consequences. Also, the point made by the bureaucratic politics approach, emphasizing the impact on policy of political maneuverings and machinations by lower-level officials defending the interests of their particular sector of the policymaking bureaucracy, is a nice complementary idea to the perspective of the rational political ambition approach, which places emphasis on policymakers at lower levels acting in defense of their own power positions.

PRESIDENT JOHNSON AND THE DOMINICAN REPUBLIC

Preoccupied by Vietnam as a foreign policy issue throughout his term of office, Lyndon Johnson did not have much time or energy left over for Latin America. Nevertheless, he was among the Democratic Party figures most sensitive to the danger of being called "soft on communism." As vice president, he had watched the Kennedy administration struggle unsuccessfully to depose Castro, and then, as president in his own right, he faced what he thought was the threat of another Cuba, in the Dominican Republic.

Juan Bosch had been overthrown in a coup there in 1963. Two years later, various elements were in revolt against the coup plotters in an attempt to restore him to power. Although Bosch himself was not a Communist, he was considered by many in the U.S. government to be too weak to deal with Communists, and it was suspected that there were Communist elements among his supporters. Friedman (2000, 279) reports: "The CIA identified efforts by three left-wing groups in [the Dominican Republic] to bring in a Castroite government."

President Johnson was determined not to let this happen, in part because of international competition between Soviet Communism, on the one hand, and the United States, on the other. But Johnson's determination not to lose the Dominican Republic to Communism probably stemmed at least as much from his fear that his domestic political opponents would use it against him if another state in the Western Hemisphere went Communist on his watch. The evidence of an impending Communist takeover in the Dominican Republic was not very good. As the crisis unfolded, the State Department released a list of fifty-eight Communists who, it asserted, were active there in the spring of 1965, but U.S. news sources soon established that most of those named were either in jail, out of the country, sick, or dead (P. H. Smith 1996, 170).

Nevertheless, President Johnson ordered 23,000 troops onto the island—about half the number of American troops that were in Vietnam at the time—without consulting with the Organization of American States (or the United Nations). When asked about this "oversight," the president reportedly explained that "the OAS couldn't pour piss out of a boot if the instructions were written on the heel" (Ambrose and Brinkley 1997, 208). He did eventually cooperate with the OAS, which organized and supervised elections in the Dominican Republic. The man elected, however, was soon superseded by Joaquin Balaguer, an old comrade of the longtime Dominican dictator, Rafael Trujillo. This perverse outcome was one reason that "the intervention was a profoundly humiliating experience for Latin Americans, recalling the worst humiliations of the past" (Connell-Smith 1974, 245).

Again, the U.S. action was, to some extent, international politics as usual—a result of the competition between the United States and the Soviet Union. But there is little doubt that domestic political considerations, centered on President Johnson's desire to remain in office, played an important role in leading him to deal with the 1965 crisis in the Dominican Republic in the largely unilateral (and rather heavy-handed) manner that he displayed (Slater 1970; Lowenthal 1972).

THE RISE AND FALL OF SALVADOR ALLENDE

The next flash point in relations between the United States and Latin America occurred at the far end of the South American continent, in Chile, a country with an unusually democratic history for a Latin American state. Salvador Allende, an avowed Socialist (albeit of the democratic variety), first attracted international attention in the 1958 presidential election there, in which he came in second. Partly to thwart Allende's future prospects, the U.S. government then became rather deeply involved in Chilean internal politics, playing an important role in bringing to power Christian Democrat Eduardo Frei, whose regime received substantial amounts of foreign aid from the United States through the 1960s.

Nevertheless, in the presidential election of 1970, Allende won a plurality of the vote, and historical precedents suggested that the Chilean parliament would elect him president of the country. In reaction, the International Telephone and Telegraph Company (ITT), which had important investments in Chile, offered to fund a CIA campaign to prevent Allende from coming to power. According to Paul E. Sigmund (1974), the CIA ultimately refused to accept that funding, but the United States still made a concerted (subversive) effort, through the CIA, to block Allende's becoming the Chilean president. Henry Kissinger (1982, 376) explains: "Nixon and his principal advisers were convinced that Allende represented a challenge to the United States and to the stability of the Western Hemisphere." This assessment, of course, comes from one of the most important of those "principal advisers," who is also famously on the record for asserting at one point during the Allende saga that he did not "see why we need to stand by and watch a country go Communist due to the irresponsibility of its own people" (Horne 1990, 26).

The CIA's effort to prevent Allende's accession to power failed. In the succeeding years, the United States did manage to deny the Allende regime full access to foreign aid from Western sources, and private foreign investment also dried up, for the most part. On the other hand, during the Allende years Chile picked up support—financial as well as military to some extent—from the Soviet Union, Cuba, and several Eastern European states.

Whether or not the United States or the CIA was directly involved in the military coup that ultimately ousted Allende from power on September 11, 1973, is not entirely clear. It is clear, however, that the United States and the CIA and American multinational corporations conspired against Allende at various crucial points during his time in power. And in Latin America, certainly, there is a widespread impression that the United States showed its "true colors," by acting so antagonistically toward Allende, even though he had been elected democratically, and by taking actions that made it much easier for the right-wing, oppressive military regime of Augusto Pinochet to eventually replace him.

Why were American foreign policy makers so opposed to Salvador Allende? The United States did have a considerable economic stake in Chile, through corporations such as ITT and Kennecott Copper, which held important investments there. American officials were also concerned that the precedent of an elected Socialist government might lead to the establishment of additional Socialist and anti-American regimes in Latin America. Also, it is easy to forget that, at the time, the Communist Party was large and influential in France as well as in Italy, and there was some fear that the successful seizure of power through electoral means by a Socialist party in Chile might have encouraged Italians and French citizens to entrust power, or at least more power, to the Communist parties in those countries.[j]

In the aftermath of Allende's fall, Kissinger (1982, 411) complained that, in the debate about the U.S. role in that leader's demise, "there was recurring reference to Allende as

---

j. "The political lessons taught by the Allende victory in Chile were thought to be most dangerous to an increasingly fragile Western Europe, particularly Italy and France .... [I]f the Chileans can do it, so the argument goes, then certainly Italian and French socialists will have new life breathed into their vision—as will the Soviets" (Fagen 1975).

a 'democratically elected leader,' with nary a mention that he never had a majority mandate to impose the transformation he was attempting; that his antidemocratic policies, had they succeeded, would have meant the end of Chile's constitutional system; and that he was viciously hostile to the United States." But it is not uncommon for leaders and parties in multiparty systems to assume power without winning a majority of votes cast in any election. And while Allende may have had long-range plans to curb democracy, he had been elected democratically, and he abided by the democratic rules of the game for as long as he was in power. The U.S. role in his downfall reinforced suspicions throughout Latin America (and elsewhere) that the U.S. government's foreign policy was primarily focused on protecting the interests of large multinational corporations, and that it would not tolerate anticapitalist or anti-U.S. policies—in states within the Western Hemisphere, at least—even if those policies were the product of legitimate, democratic political processes.

BRINGING THE COLD WAR TO AN END IN LATIN AMERICA

By the mid-1970s, the United States had clearly lost the war in Vietnam, and that setback, combined with revelations about the activities of the CIA in Chile (and elsewhere), led to a widespread feeling in the United States that subversive military interventions in other countries were of dubious utility—not to mention morality. Such reactions helped bring to power Jimmy Carter, who promised a more ethical approach to interstate (as well as domestic) politics, as a kind of antidote to the disaster in Vietnam, revelations about Chile, and the turmoil of the Watergate scandal.

In foreign affairs, President Carter emphasized respect for, and even activism on behalf of, human rights, and his administration directed much of its energy on that issue toward eradicating human rights abuses in Latin America, especially targeting the regimes of Pinochet in Chile and Anastasio Somoza in Nicaragua. Carter did not actively seek the downfall of Somoza's regime, but neither did he give it the kind of support that many reactionary autocratic regimes had formerly received from the American government, in gratitude for their staunch anti-Communism.

To this extent, perhaps, the Carter administration did play a role in undermining the Somoza government in its battle against the Sandinista rebellion, and in so doing was partly responsible for the Sandinistas' coming to power in Nicaragua in 1979.[k] At the same time, President Carter's lukewarm support of the shah of Iran in his efforts to resist the fundamentalist Islamic revolution in that country also contributed, conceivably, to the demise of the shah's government. These events inspired Jeane Kirkpatrick (1979, 34) to write an essay entitled "Dictatorships and Double Standards," in which she argued that with respect to Nicaragua and Iran in the 1970s, "the Carter Administration not only failed to prevent the undesired outcome, it actively collaborated in the replacement of moderate autocrats friendly to American interests with less friendly autocrats of extremist persuasion." She went on to observe (37) that "although there is no instance of a revolutionary 'socialist' or Communist

k. "U.S. intelligence had predicted in May [1979] that Anastasio Somoza's National Guard would crush his opponents. Cutting off aid, because of theft as well as brutality, proved to be a mortal blow" (Leebaert 2002, 551).).

society being democratized, right-wing autocracies do sometimes evolve into democracies," thus providing one more reason, according this analyst who eventually became President Reagan's UN ambassador, that the United States should stand by its allies in spite of their flaws—as long as they are right-wing, rather than left-wing, autocrats.

So the Reagan administration came to power determined to rectify Carter's errors in foreign policy, particularly in Latin America. In some respects, it was true to its word. The Carter administration had avoided both overt military interventions in Latin America, such as the U.S. invasion of the Dominican Republic in 1965, and covert actions, such as the CIA-led operations in Guatemala in 1954 and the Bay of Pigs invasion of Cuba in 1961. The Reagan administration, however, did mount one overt military invasion, on the small Caribbean island of Grenada, where a rather leftist-oriented government had been ousted by even more radically oriented elements, who executed the former leader (Maurice Bishop). There were several hundred American students at St. George's University in Grenada, whose safety might have been endangered by any ensuing violence. Another potentially ominous development was the ongoing construction of an airstrip that, the Reagan administration suspected, might be used for Soviet military operations. So, on October 25, 1983, some 6,000 American troops joined military units from six surrounding Caribbean states to invade Grenada. The new government was quickly deposed, and the Americans "booted out thirty Soviet military advisers and several hundred Cuban combat engineers..." (Leebaert 2002, 543).

According to analyst Peter Schweizer (2003, 209): "In the United States, the military victory [in Grenada] was greeted with an outpouring of patriotism." However, Madeleine Albright—then a professor of government at Georgetown University, and destined to become President Clinton's secretary of state—denounced the invasion of Grenada as bullying (Leebaert 2002, 544). The UN Security Council "deplored" the invasion in a resolution favored by eleven of its fifteen members (but, of course, vetoed by the United States), and the same resolution passed in the General Assembly by a vote of 108–9. Even Margaret Thatcher, Reagan's like-minded ally on many issues over the years, was quite critical of the U.S. invasion of Grenada in 1993 (P. H. Smith 1996, 180).

But the Reagan administration's intervention in Grenada pales in significance compared to its energetic involvement in the internal political processes of Central American countries during the 1980s. The Sandinista revolution in Nicaragua, for example, incurred the serious wrath of the Reagan foreign policy making team. Actually, even Jimmy Carter had, in his last days in office, authorized some CIA covert action to destabilize the revolutionary government there. But the Reagan administration devoted $4 billion to support the government's security forces in El Salvador, where rebel forces, post–Cold War evidence suggests, were receiving important assistance from the Sandinistas in Nicaragua, as well as from Cuba.[1]

Reagan also allocated $3 billion to supporting the *contras,* Nicaraguan exiles who were devoted to the overthrow of the Sandinista regime in their country. When this support and the U.S. action of mining Nicaraguan harbors were declared violations of international law by the International Court of Justice in 1986, the Reagan administration's response was simply

---

1. Such assistance also was provided to rebel forces in Guatemala, Colombia, Honduras, and Costa Rica; see Leebaert 2002, 552.

to reject the idea that the Court had any jurisdiction over such disputes. Ultimately, however, Congress also objected to the funding of the *contras* by the U.S. government, and this legislative prohibition led some members of the administration to get involved in an extra-legal—possibly even illegal—scheme involving an arms-for-hostages deal with Iran, from which some of the proceeds were funneled to the *contras*. The resulting "Iran-*contra*" scandal led some in Washington to call for the impeachment of President Reagan.

In the end, the Sandinista revolution in Nicaragua was vanquished at the ballot box in an election in 1990. That election was one of many to bring about a change in political power through procedures that were arguably democratic in Latin America in the 1980s and early 1990s. Ironically, when Kennedy had come to power in 1960, vowing as part of his Alliance for Progress initiative to support democratic governance in the Western Hemisphere, what followed instead, as discussed earlier, was a rash of military coups against democratic governments. These military coups, as well as conservative governments with programs aimed at economic modernization (but definitely not political democratization), became so common by the early 1970s that a prominent academic work, *Modernization and Bureaucratic Authoritarianism* by Guillermo O'Donnell (1973) argued that, contrary to previous expectations, economic modernization in Latin America was apparently destined to go hand-in-hand, not with democracy, but with autocratic political systems. On top of that trend, Ronald Reagan came to power in 1980 vowing to provide more vigorous support to conservative, authoritarian regimes in Latin America (and the rest of the world) than had the Carter administration or previous administrations with an unfortunate—from the point of view of President Reagan and his UN ambassador, Jeane Kirkpatrick—lack of sympathy for authoritarian regimes that support U.S. political interests.

But what happened in the late 1970s, the 1980s, and the early 1990s was that, in the words of Karen Remmer (1990, 315), "the politics of Latin America [were] transformed by the longest and deepest wave of democratization in the region's history." Specific data on these developments are provided in table 10.1. Freedom House in New York generates annual scores on political rights and civil liberties for virtually every country in the world; the most democratic states receive scores of 1 on these two scales, while the most undemocratic states receive scores of 7. What is shown in table 10.1 are the sums of these two scores. Thus, Costa Rica, the most democratic state in South America, according to Freedom House, received scores of 2 and 3 in 1974 and 1994 respectively, while Cuba received scores of 14 in both years. The average score for these Latin American states in 1974 was 8.6; by 1994, that average score was 6.75. Perhaps more important, as we can see in table 10.1, countries are also categorized as Free (F), Partly Free (PF), and Not Free (NF). In 1974 six states were categorized as Not Free but, by 1994, only one state (Cuba) was categorized as Not Free.

The validity of these Freedom House scores is, of course, not beyond reproach. But there is not much doubt that from about the mid-1970s until the mid-1990s, there was a significant trend toward more democratic governance in Latin America. Analyst Derek Leebaert (2002, 557) summarizes that trend this way: "At the start of the 1980s, only about 10 percent of the nearly half billion people in those ... countries south of the border lived in anything that could be called democracies. Eight years later, around 90 percent did."

How did it happen that in the years following 1960, when the U.S. government was, ostensibly at least, committed to encouraging democratic governance in Latin America, autocratic

| TABLE 10.1 | Freedom House Democracy Scores for Latin American States, 1974, 1994 |

Country	1974		1994	
Argentina	6	PF	5	F
Bolivia	11	NF	5	F
Brazil	8	PF	6	PF
Chile	12	NF	4	F
Colombia	4	F	7	PF
Costa Rica	2	F	3	F
Cuba	14	NF	14	NF
Dominican Republic	6	PF	7	PF
Ecuador	11	PF	5	F
El Salvador	5	F	6	PF
Guatemala	7	PF	9	PF
Haiti	12	NF	10	PF
Honduras	9	PF	6	PF
Mexico	7	PF	8	PF
Nicaragua	9	PF	9	PF
Panama	13	NF	5	F
Paraguay	10	PF	7	PF
Peru	12	NF	9	PF
Uruguay	10	PF	4	F
Venezuela	4	F	6	PF

Note: F = Free; PF = Partially Free; NF = Not Free

Source: "FH Country Ratings," *Freedom House,* 2004. http://freedomhouse.org/ratings/index.htm (accessed July 1, 2004).

regimes came into being in great profusion, while in the period after the Reagan administration came into power vowing to support conservative, autocratic regimes if they were friendly to the United States, democratic governments replaced autocratic governments time after time? One possible answer, offered by Samuel P. Huntington (1991), is that, in both cases, Latin America got caught up in broader global trends having to do with "waves" of political transitions—toward autocracy in the earlier period, and toward democracy in the later period. But these apparently contrarian trends may also have been a useful indicator of the limits on U.S. ability to affect internal political developments in foreign countries, even those located in the Western Hemisphere. In any case, in a final irony, the Reagan administration's attitude evolved on such issues to the point that it played a role in undermining several autocratic regimes, in spite of their generally pro-American stands, much in the manner of the Carter administration. It helped ease out of power the Duvalier regime in Haiti, for example, as well as the Marcos regime in the Philippines.

Paradoxically, and somewhat unaccountably, the United States engaged in one more forceful military intervention to overthrow a Latin American government just as the Cold War came to an end. Tensions had grown between the government of Manuel Noriega in Panama and the administration of George H.W. Bush in the United States, throughout 1989. Noriega was said to be profiting from trafficking in illegal drugs, most of which ended up in the United States. There were some clashes between American troops stationed at the Canal Zone and the citizens of Panama. At one point, Noriega asserted, in an obviously metaphorical fashion, that Panama was "at war" with the United States. For reasons that, to this day, are not entirely clear, President Bush decided to send American troops into Panama to depose Manuel Noriega.

Historically, such interventions have been apparently motivated by a combination of economic and political or national security interests. In this case, however, there were no obviously important economic interests at stake. There was the Panama Canal, of course, and the U.S. government had hinted on occasion that it had concerns about the future of the canal. But Panama is so dependent on income from the canal that it is difficult to believe that any Panamanian government there would ever do anything to compromise U.S. access to it. Absent any knowledge of the specifics of the situation, and basing our opinion only on a general familiarity with Cold War–era interventions in Latin America by the United States, we might infer that Noriega was suspected by the Bush administration of Communist sympathies, or insufficient anti-Communist zeal, at least. But in past years, Noriega had actually been on the payroll of the CIA. Also, the Cold War was essentially over by the time this intervention took place—the Berlin Wall had come down in November of 1989, one month before President Bush sent American troops into Panama. Thus, this invasion could not, in any plausible way, be interpreted as a move against a Communist threat.

In accord with the theoretical basis of this book, it is tempting to conclude that Bush's main motive in this affair involved domestic politics: perhaps he hoped that this invasion would be seen back home as a strong step against international drug traffickers, at a time when drug addiction and the crimes associated with it were high-priority domestic political issues. On the international level, this particular intervention seemed peculiarly unrelated to the typical economic or national security concerns often associated with U.S. moves against unwanted regimes in the Western Hemisphere. Also, the U.S. invasion of Panama was—as has historically been the case—on shaky ground, so to speak, in terms of international law. As Charles

Maechling (1990, 113, 125), a professor of international law (and a former senior State Department official), observed shortly after the invasion:

> Just when the confrontation between power blocs is withering away and global interdependence is becoming a reality, the rule of law has received another body-blow.... In light of the insufficiency of provocation, the disproportionate response to a minimal threat, and the inability or refusal of the United States to obtain prior or subsequent authorization from an appropriate international body, the invasion of Panama violated in both letter and spirit the U.N. Charter and the inter-American treaties.

INTER-AMERICAN RELATIONS AFTER THE END OF THE COLD WAR

One might have expected the end of the Cold War to create conditions conducive to unusually stable and amicable relationships between the United States and its Latin American neighbors. Certainly, many of the most contentious issues of the previous forty to forty-five years—in Guatemala, Cuba, the Dominican Republic, Chile, Grenada, and in much of Central America, for example—had involved disagreements about how to deal with alleged threats from Communism. After the end of the Cold War and the demise of the Soviet Union, it would have been reasonable to assume that such issues would no longer arise.

To some extent, such expectations were fulfilled. For example, the United States and the states of Latin America took a cooperative approach to a 1991 coup in Haiti that ousted the elected, and at least tenuously democratic, government of Jean-Bertrand Aristide. Three months earlier, the OAS had adopted the Santiago Commitment to Democracy, a resolution that committed the organization to stand behind the region's democratic regimes. Latin American states have traditionally been suspicious that U.S. attempts to promote democracy have served primarily to disguise interventions against governments of which it disapproves. But, as the Santiago Commitment indicated, by that time most Latin American states had become at least somewhat less suspicious on this issue. The OAS did promptly condemn the coup that overthrew Aristide, and it enacted economic sanctions against Haiti. In 1993 the United Nations stepped in, authorizing a peacekeeping force of 1,300, whose purpose was to allow the return of Aristide. But this UN contingent was, in effect, scared off by a small mob of protestors awaiting it on the docks at Port-au-Prince.

In July of 1994, the United Nations authorized the United States to use whatever means necessary to restore the Aristide regime to power. In the end, the intervention proceeded without much resistance from the anti-Aristide forces. Thus, this particular intervention conformed, to an extent quite unusual in such matters, to the principles of international law. Unfortunately, in the longer run, U.S. and international efforts to create and sustain democracy in Haiti have not been notably successful. In 2004 the U.S. government cooperated with an international effort to persuade Aristide to leave the country, and once again U.S. troops were sent into Haiti. Who will rule in Haiti, and by what methods, are questions that are still unresolved.

Another major initiative of the Clinton administration involving Latin America was the **North American Free Trade Agreement (NAFTA)**, which brought about a significant increase in the level of economic integration between the United States and Mexico, as well as Canada. By the beginning of 1994, President Clinton had invested considerable political capital in putting NAFTA in place, against the opposition of labor unions, environmental activists, and antiglobalization interests of various kinds. In Mexico, the launching of NAFTA coincided with the beginning of a kind of antiglobalization rebellion in the province of Chiapas, and an economic crisis that led to huge outflows of foreign capital from Mexico and a loss of confidence in the Mexican peso, which rather quickly dropped over half its value. This crisis led to deterioration in the economic status of Mexican workers, and its impact lingered for many years.

In spite of the fact that, by the first decade of the twenty-first century, NAFTA has become quite unpopular in all three of its member-states, it would be simplistic to conclude that it is a failure. In the United States, NAFTA was associated with the loss of some 100,000 manufacturing jobs annually from 1994 until the year 2000, but during that same period, the U.S. economy produced over 2 million new jobs (mostly in areas other than manufacturing), and surely some of those jobs were indirectly encouraged by the fact that trade with Mexico and Canada had increased substantially in the early years of the agreement. When NAFTA was launched, about one-quarter of U.S. trade was with Canada and Mexico; by 2004, that share had increased to about one-third of its overall annual trade (*Economist* 2004a).

In Mexico, farmers were hurt in many areas by the import of corn from the United States. However, this corn was subsidized by the U.S. government, and so whatever deleterious impact those U.S. exports may have had in Mexico cannot logically be attributed to free trade or globalization. On the other hand, Mexico has, as a result of NAFTA, attracted significant sums of foreign investment, and its trade with the United States has surged, converting trade deficits with the United States into substantial trade surpluses.

In short, drawing conclusions about the overall economic impact of NAFTA is not an easy task. It is, however, easy to conclude that NAFTA represents a kind of economic and political experiment with potentially profound impacts. The gap in the annual per capita GNP between the United States and Mexico is quite unusual for countries that border one another; the only larger gap between neighboring countries in the contemporary international system may be that between North and South Korea. By joining NAFTA, Mexico has chosen to develop economically by integrating itself more tightly with the largest, wealthiest economy in the world. If that strategy works, it will be an object lesson for many other poor, developing states around the world. However, if it becomes clear at some point that Mexico's choice to tie itself so tightly to its wealthy neighbor to the north was a mistake, developing countries around the world will have a substantial reason, and an important supporting example, to doubt that the economic future of poorer, developing countries can best be secured by closer integration with the industrialized, wealthier countries.

One problem that NAFTA clearly has not resolved is the flood of immigrants, many of them undocumented, crossing into the United States at its southern border. The most widely accepted current estimate is that there are some 11 million illegal immigrants in the United States (Beveridge 2006). Whether they "steal" jobs from Americans or take jobs that no Americans would want, and whether they make a net positive contribution to the American economy or impose a large burden on it, are among the notable controversies regarding these immigrants. Huntington (2004) argues that because these immigrants come from a neighboring country, because there are so many of them, because so many are illegal, because they are concentrated so heavily in the Southwest, and because they have a historical claim on U.S. territory—in Texas, New Mexico, Arizona, California, Nevada, and Utah, which were all once part of Mexico—they pose a serious threat to the future integrity of the United States. Immigration, especially of the illegal variety, therefore seems likely to remain a major issue in American elections for the foreseeable future.

The Clinton administration clearly broke new ground in its policy toward Mexico, successfully bringing about a transformation in that nation's traditional economic policies. In addition, whether coincidentally or not, in the wake of NAFTA, came the first election in Mexico's postrevolutionary history in which executive power was transferred from the Institutional Revolutionary Party (PRI) to another political party, in the year 2000. But with respect to U.S. relations with Cuba, the policy of the Clinton administration remained rather strangely unchanged from the days of the Cold War.

In fact, in some ways, it became even more antagonistic. In 1996 the Cuban air force shot down two planes flown by members of a group of Cuban exiles residing in South Florida. Partly in retaliation, the U.S. Congress passed, and the Clinton administration signed into law, the **Helms-Burton Act**, which gave "U.S. citizens the right to sue in U.S. courts foreign companies that 'traffic' in stolen property in Cuba" (Vanderbush and Haney 1999, 402). In other words, the intent of this legislation was extraterritorial—attempting to coerce citizens in other countries to reduce trade and investment in Cuba. "It represents nothing less," according to analyst Wayne S. Smith (1998, 292), "than an effort on the part of the United States unilaterally to dictate to the rest of the world without regard to the rules of the international system." This initiative received scant support, to put it mildly, from the international community. In November of 1996, the UN General Assembly condemned the U.S. embargo of Cuba by a vote of 138–3; the only two states voting with the United States to defeat the resolution were Israel and Uzbekistan, both of which were, at the time, involved in trade with Cuba.

Why, one might wonder, would the United States persist in such antagonistic policies toward a small, weak country, regardless of how repulsive that country's politics might be to some in the United States? The answer seems obvious to many informed observers of the situation. At one time, Castro's revolutionary government did pose a credible national security threat, as it had a powerful Soviet ally, which had tried to place missiles in Cuba in 1962. In subsequent years, Castro sent support, often in the form of troops as well as other types of foreign aid, to rebellions in Central and South America, and to revolutionary governments in Africa, such as Angola and Ethiopia.

By the 1990s, however, the Soviet Union, which had once provided aid to the tune of $3 or $4 billion a year to Cuba, had fallen apart. Between 1988 and 1993, in the wake of this loss of its main support, the Cuban economy contracted by some 35–50 percent. William M. LeoGrande (1998, 73) describes the wider effects: "Troops came home from Africa, Cuban advisers no longer instructed Latin American revolutionaries, and military ties to Russia shrank to almost nothing. By 1993, all the principal security issues that had prevented a normalization of relations with Washington had disappeared."

But the result of the vanishing of national security issues posed by Castro's revolution was not *rapprochement* between Cuba and the United States, because U.S. policy with respect to

Cuba—and with respect to every other foreign policy matter—is what Robert Putnam (1988) describes as a **two-level game**. At level 1, leaders seek agreements with other international actors; at level 2, they must seek to put together domestic coalitions to support whatever agreements or policies might be agreed upon at the international level. As LeoGrande (1998, 81–82) points out, "the theory of two-level games applies well to the three-and-a half decades of U.S. Cuban relations since the 1959 revolution"; by the 1990s, "the level 2 game on Cuba had wholly eclipsed the level 1 game." In short, domestic political considerations—mostly having to do with electoral politics in Florida and the powerful lobbying group made up largely of Cuban-American exiles, the **Cuban American National Foundation**—perpetuated antagonism in U.S. policy toward Cuba at a time when international considerations, in isolation, might well have led to a significant reduction in tensions. The fact that Florida proved to be pivotal in the presidential election of 2000 suggests that these domestic political considerations are likely to continue to have a vital impact on U.S.-Cuban relations for some time to come.

President George W. Bush has faced priorities in the area of foreign policy that have pushed Latin America rather far into the background. Colombia, however, has been something of a front in Bush's war on terrorism. The government there has for decades battled a guerrilla group known as the **Colombian Revolutionary Armed Forces (FARC)**. In earlier decades, concerns about that group focused on its Marxist ideology and its connections to traffic in illegal drugs, but in the twenty-first century, its alleged ties to al-Qaeda have received more attention. In any case, the U.S. government has, for some time, allocated considerable aid of various kinds to the Colombian government in the hope that it will eventually win its confrontation with FARC. Toward the end of Bush's first term in office, a new, rather hard-line approach taken by Colombia's new president, Alvaro Uribe, was, at least according to some sources, achieving some success.

The Bush administration has not attempted to intervene militarily, or (as far as is known) covertly, in the affairs of any Latin American state, at least not in such a way as to bring about the removal of the government in power. It did intervene in more subtle ways in the affairs of Venezuela, in a manner that did nothing to convince Latin American observers of the sincerity of its support for democracy. The populist, leftist leader of Venezuela, Hugo Chavez, was the victim of a coup attempt in April of 2002, leaving Venezuela with another president for about a day. Neither President Bush nor any other U.S. foreign policy spokesperson expressed concern about this deviation from democratic procedures in Venezuela; on the contrary, the American government had no success at all in hiding its satisfaction that Chavez had been removed from power. According to Michael Shifter (2004, 64–65): "The Bush Administration's ... mishandled response to the April 2002 military coup—failing to show any concern and instead expressing undisguised glee—eroded the administration's credibility on the democracy question."

Venezuela was not the only state in Latin America to exhibit signs of a growing anti-U.S. sentiment, as well as a possible loss of faith or commitment to free markets and democracy, during the first years of the twenty-first century. Argentina, for example, had in 1991 adopted a neoliberal economic approach based on the so-called **Washington Consensus** and featuring policies advocated by the United States. By 1995, Argentina had an unemployment rate of 18.6 percent (Levitsky and Murillo 2003, 13), and by 2001–2002, it was suffering depression-like conditions, including 22 percent unemployment, a drastically reduced GNP, and a rapidly increasing poverty rate (Peruzzotti 2004, 86). In 2003, all these problems brought to power a Peronist president, Néstor Kirchner, who was notably suspicious of advice from the United States and of the virtues of globalization.

In Bolivia, a longtime supporter of neoliberal, pro-U.S. policies, Gonzalo Sánchez de Lozada, was driven from office in 2003 by street protests against the economic policies of his administration. His replacement, Carlos Mesa, complained bitterly about U.S.-sponsored economic policies and called for a return to more "statist" economic tactics. Then, in 2006, Evo Morales, a leftist who would become closely allied with Hugo Chávez, came to power in Bolivia; he promptly moved toward nationalization of Bolivia's large reserves of natural gas. Finally, in the largest state in South America, economic pressures were apparently responsible for bringing to power Luiz Inácio Lula da Silva, a member of Brazil's Worker's Party and, in general, a leftist leader whose election would have caused panic in Washington during the days of the Cold War. In fact, the widespread political trends toward leftist positions throughout most of Latin America during the Bush administration would have been a cause of great concern during the days of the Cold War. It remains to be seen whether, at some point, Bush, or some successor, will be held responsible for "losing" Latin America.[m] For the time being, there is little doubt that, as Shifter (2004, 64–65) points out, "the common language of open democracies and free markets used in the past decade by reform-minded opinion leaders throughout the hemisphere has less and less resonance."

CONCLUSION

Starting with the Monroe Doctrine in 1823, the United States has attempted to eliminate influences of other major powers in the Western Hemisphere, and to solidify its control over political and economic processes in its close geographic proximity. Its policies along those lines were particularly heavy-handed in the first decades of the twentieth century, during which it repeatedly sent troops into states in Central America and the Caribbean, and occupied a number of states, such as the Dominican Republic, Haiti, and Nicaragua, for many years.

As the threat of World War II approached, the United States adopted a so-called Good Neighbor Policy of refraining from antagonistic actions, either overt or covert, toward Latin American governments, while working to garner support from them for its efforts against enemies in Europe and Asia. That period came to an end after the war, as the United States attempted to manipulate internal political developments in Guatemala in 1954. This effort was the first of a series of overt and covert battles against Communist influence in the Western Hemisphere during the Cold War. Many such battles involved the regime of Fidel Castro in Cuba. A particularly dramatic episode was the Cuban Missile Crisis of 1962, during which the

m. That the loss of Latin America will become a concern in the future can be inferred from China's activities in South America, especially in Venezuela. "China is devoting considerable diplomatic and economic resources to strengthen its strategic energy alliance with Venezuela—a country that at present provides 20 percent of U.S. oil imports. To the apparent ignorance of Washington, a great game, set in this century and continent, is currently underway" (Collins and Ramos-Mrosovsky 2006, 88).

United States planned to invade Cuba, while the Cubans and their Soviet patrons prepared to resist that invasion—each side motivated by the desire to remain in power.

In the post–Cold War era, President Clinton pushed for closer economic integration between the United States and Mexico through the North American Free Trade Agreement, but he maintained an antagonistic policy toward Cuba even after the Cold War, mostly for reasons having to do with domestic politics. President George W. Bush seemed too preoccupied with his war on terrorism and his invasion of Iraq to devote much attention to Latin America. Somewhat paradoxically, after the Cold War, leftist or at least antiglobalization political elements are gaining increasing influence in such Latin American states as Bolivia, Mexico, Venezuela, Argentina, and Brazil. If current trends continue, unfortunately, anti-U.S. sentiments in Latin America may reach crisis proportions in the not-too-distant future.

KEY CONCEPTS

Alliance for Progress   239

Bay of Pigs   236

Colombian Revolutionary Armed
    Forces (FARC)   251

Cuban American National
    Foundation   251

Cuban Missile Crisis   237

Good Neighbor Policy   229

Helms-Burton Act   250

Inter-American Development Bank   235

North American Free Trade
    Agreement (NAFTA)   248

Olney Corollary   226

Operation Pan America   235

Organization of American States
    (OAS)   231

Panama Canal Zone   226

Platt Amendment   226

Teller Amendment   226

two-level game   251

United Fruit Company (UF)   232

Washington Consensus   251

RATIONAL POLITICAL AMBITION AND...
THE RELATIONSHIP WITH LATIN AMERICA

LESSONS LEARNED

☑ In 1898 President William McKinley came to believe that he had to adopt an assertive policy in the U.S. dispute with Spain over Cuba in order to retain power in the upcoming presidential election.

☑ The Eisenhower administration felt compelled to adopt an aggressive policy against the Guatemalan regime in 1954, in part because of strong anti-Communist rhetoric it had used to acquire power in the 1952 election.

☑ President Johnson's military intervention into the Dominican Republic in 1965 was apparently motivated in large part by fear of the likely impact a leftist success there would have on his domestic political fortunes.

☑ The priority placed on staying in power played a crucial role in the policies and tactics adopted by the United States and Cuba, as well as by the Soviet Union, in the Cuban Missile Crisis.

☑ The persistence of vigorously anti-Castro policies by the U.S. government despite the end of the Cold War—and in spite of a lack of support from virtually every other country in the world—is obviously related to Florida's potentially decisive role in presidential elections. The ability of presidential candidates to obtain and hold onto political power is heavily affected by anti-Castro lobbying groups and Cuban exiles in southern Florida.

CHAPTER **11**

THE UNITED STATES AND SUB-SAHARAN AFRICA

EVEN BEFORE THEY UNITED TO BECOME AN INDEPENDENT COUNTRY, THE thirteen colonies that would become the United States developed an important relationship with Africa, from which all of them "imported" slaves. Slavery then became a divisive issue in domestic politics from the beginning of the new Republic, and it played a crucial role in the Civil War, which came quite close to dissolving it. In the early twentieth century, relations between the United States and sub-Saharan Africa were minimal, because most of that portion of Africa had been colonized by Europeans, who limited its peoples' contact and interactions with anybody else.

, as new states were created in sub-Saharan Africa in great profusion, the interact with them. In truth, however, Africa has almost always been y level among U.S. foreign policy priorities, for reasons that we will But the continent did become the site of some significant proxy bat- States and Communist forces during the Cold War. And since the end ited States has faced complex challenges, involving political as well as places as Somalia, Rwanda, the Democratic Republic of the Congo,

FORGING THE LINK: THE SLAVE TRADE

The first slaves among the European settlers along the east coast of North America were apparently brought on a Dutch vessel into Jamestown, Virginia, in 1619. Originally, they worked primarily on tobacco farms in that colony. According to Monica Barba et al. (1999): "Not

U.S. support for anticommunist leaders in Africa during the Cold War left several African states burdened with "kleptocratic" regimes that proved disastrous for their countries in the long run. One of the most spectacularly corrupt was the president of Zaire, Mobutu Sese Seko, shown here in a photo from July 27, 1961.

until 1660 did the institution of slavery appear in the statute books of Jamestown, which has led most historians to think that until this time, a slave or a Negro was seen in a social point of view, no less than a white indentured servant."

Although slaves were brought into every colony, most were located in the southern part of the United States. By the time the separate colonies had united and established themselves as an independent country, there were about half a million slaves within its borders. They actually constituted a majority of the population in some southern states, creating a serious issue that could have prevented the formation of the Union. In fact, the emergence of the Union was made possible only by a rather unseemly bargain that appears in Article 1, Section 2, of the U.S. Constitution. Stipulating that members of the House of Representatives shall be allocated among the different states according to population, that section suggests that "other Persons"—meaning slaves—are to be counted as three-fifths of a person.

Despite a perfectly understandable misinterpretation of this passage, the assignment of only 60 percent personhood to slaves was not an indication of discrimination against them, or reflective of an attitude that they were considered subhuman. On the contrary, the three-fifths compromise was largely an effort by non-slaveholding states to curtail or reduce the influence of slaveholding states in the newly emerging United States. If slaves were not to be counted at all, the southern, slaveholding states would have refused to enter the Union. Those states would have preferred to be able to count all slaves as complete persons (even though they would not be allowed to vote), for the purpose of calculating the number of representatives they would be allocated in the House, but the non-slaveholding states refused to accept that idea. Instead, the southern states were allocated a number of congressional representatives reflecting in part the number of slaves residing in them, but only up to 60 percent of that number.

The Constitution also contains a provision that might be said to be the new nation's first effort to control immigration. "Migration" and "importation" of persons into any state existing at the time was to be allowed up to the year 1808. The persons being "imported," of course, were slaves.

Although the majority of the founding fathers professed opposition to slavery,[a] many of them were, in fact, slaveholders; George Washington, Thomas Jefferson, and James Madison were perhaps the most well-known. Slavery was dealt with in the Constitution, and as an issue it was intimately intertwined with the country's foreign policy from the beginning. Again, the Constitution explicitly protected the importation of slaves until 1808, but when that deadline arrived, the still relatively new nation legally banned the practice. In the **Treaty of Ghent**, which brought the War of 1812 to an end, the United States pledged to cooperate with Great Britain in the suppression of the trans-Atlantic slave trade. As early as 1820, U.S. naval units began to suppress slave traffic off the coast of Africa, and from 1830 to 1850, they cooperated with Great Britain in efforts to suppress the slave trade to the United States and elsewhere. Nevertheless, even as the importing of slaves became illegal, it may, in fact, have increased. At

---

a. Thomas Jefferson, for example, proposed a law in 1779 to abolish slavery in Virginia, offered another law in Congress in 1784 to ban slavery in the entire Western territory of the United States, wrote an eloquent denunciation of slavery in his *Notes on the State of Virginia*, and in 1807 publicly supported the abolition of the slave trade. In addition, he expressed his opposition to slavery in a lengthy list of private letters (West 1997, 2).

the very least, the practice continued. Estimates of the number of slaves imported into the United States after the slave trade was legally abolished range from 250,000 to 1 million (Becker 1999).

As an issue, slavery became inextricably intertwined with the expansion of the United States in the decades before the Civil War almost divided the country permanently into anti- and pro-slavery sectors. In the first decades of the nineteenth century, for example, slaves often escaped and fled into Florida, which at the time was officially owned by Spain and populated by Seminole Indians. Tiring of occasional cross-border raids by the Seminoles and by the use of Florida as a safe haven for fugitive slaves, the U.S. government authorized General Andrew Jackson to launch retaliatory raids into this Spanish territory. Jackson rather clearly over- stepped his authorization, proceeding to take control of most of eastern Florida. Years of diplomatic wrangling with Spain ensued—resulting, ultimately, in Spain's ceding the territo- ry to the United States in the Adams-Onìs Treaty of 1821.

The slaves imported from Africa into the United States also played an important role in the expansionist dynamic that led the original thirteen colonies to take over all of the territory west to the Pacific Ocean. The Constitution contained several compromises between the non- slaveholding and the slaveholding states, and, in later years, almost every step of expansion related somehow to the issue of slavery. In general, each expansion that added slaveholding ter- ritory needed to be countered, in the view of anti-slavery elements, by a countervailing expan- sion that added territory that would be free of slaves. Such compromises were rather formally institutionalized in 1820. The admission of Alabama as a slave state in 1819 had created a bal- ance between slave states and free states. A bill to add Maine as a non-slaveholding state passed the House in the following year, made possible only by a compromise provision that called for adding Missouri as a state with no restrictions on slavery at the same time. What thus became known as the **Missouri Compromise** also established the precedent stipulating that slavery would be prohibited in the remainder of the Louisiana Purchase north of 36°30′ latitude.

THE CREATION OF LIBERIA

Most of the relationship between the United States and Africa in the nineteenth century was bound up with the importing of slaves. But the United States did also become involved in a project to establish a new state in sub-Saharan Africa. (Admittedly, the inspiration for this project was also related to the slave trade.) Probably, the idea for **Liberia** originated in an organization known as the **American Colonization Society**, founded in 1816 by Bushrod Washington, who was a nephew of George Washington (Beyan 1991). Including such influ- ential leaders as James Monroe and Henry Clay, the organization's members were the classic "strange bedfellows" that politics produces with regularity. Some of its members wanted to encourage free blacks to emigrate to Africa because they felt that these people threatened the institution of slavery. Others were motivated instead by moral objections to slavery; many in this latter group were also hopeful that emigrating blacks might help to spread Christianity to Africa (Lowenkopf 1976, 14).

With the support of the U.S. government, the American Colonization Society sent the ship *Elizabeth* to Africa with the first group of eighty-six colonists in 1820. The first settlement was established at Cape Montserado, which was sold to the settlers in 1821 by the African King

Peter, who reportedly agreed to the sale only with "a pistol at his head" (Library of Congress 2004). Over the remainder of the nineteenth century, about 22,000 black Americans then emigrated to Liberia (Lowenkopf 1976, 14–15).

Liberia declared its independence in 1847, but the United States did not recognize it for some time. According to Katherine Harris (1985, 69): "Throughout the 1850s, Presidents Millard Fillmore (Whig), Franklin Pierce (Democrat), and James Buchanan (Democrat) ... withheld recognition from Liberia ... because recognition of a republic of free blacks, many of them former slaves, could worsen the slavery-emancipation controversy." Finally, President Abraham Lincoln engineered a change in the U.S.-Liberian relationship, moving in 1862 to conclude a treaty of commerce and navigation with Liberia, which in 1860 exported more to the United States than any other state. Harris (71) notes: "Ratification of the U.S.-Liberia treaty marked the completion of Liberia's evolution as a sovereign state, and the end of the kind of informal colonial control that had begun in 1819."

In the years immediately after declaring its sovereignty, Liberia itself, as well as U.S.-Liberian relations, were caught up in Europe's **new imperialism** in Africa. In 1880 only about 10 percent of Africa was controlled, at least formally, by Europeans, but four years later, the great powers met at a conference in Berlin and, in effect, partitioned Africa amongst themselves. A vast tract in the heart of Africa was ceded to King Leopold of Belgium, becoming known as the Belgian Congo. Great Britain and France led the way in claiming territory for themselves, while Germany came in third in this "scramble for Africa" (Pakenham 1991). By 1900, the whole of Africa, allocated as shown on map 11.1, was entirely under European control, with the exceptions of Liberia and Ethiopia.

If they had had their way, the European imperial powers would have swallowed up Liberia, too, says Harris (1985, 73): "The French and the British seized territory from Liberia and threatened to absorb it into their respective colonial empires." When Liberia appealed for help against the European imperialists, the United States did attempt to provide some political protection for its erstwhile "colony." These efforts were later solidified during the administration of Republican President William H. Taft, who paid off Liberian debts and reestablished some formal contracts between the United States and Liberia.

U.S.-AFRICAN RELATIONS IN THE EARLY TWENTIETH CENTURY

Thus, by 1900, European domination of Africa was so complete that U.S.-African relations hardly existed. This domination was symbolized neatly by the way foreign policy decisions regarding Africa were handled by the U.S. government: until World War II, reports David A. Dickson (1985, 3), "most governmental decisions dealing with Africa were made in the State Department Division of European Affairs."

Up to a point, this situation seems to support the theory of **offensive realism** originally propounded by John Mearsheimer (2001a) in *The Tragedy of Great Power Politics* (discussed in context of the Monroe Doctrine in chapter 2). In a more recent exposition of this theory (while discussing the future of U.S.-China relations, which we will examine in chapter 12), Mearsheimer (2005, 48) explains that "the best outcome that a [major power] can hope for is to dominate its own backyard." And, indeed, in the early part of the twentieth

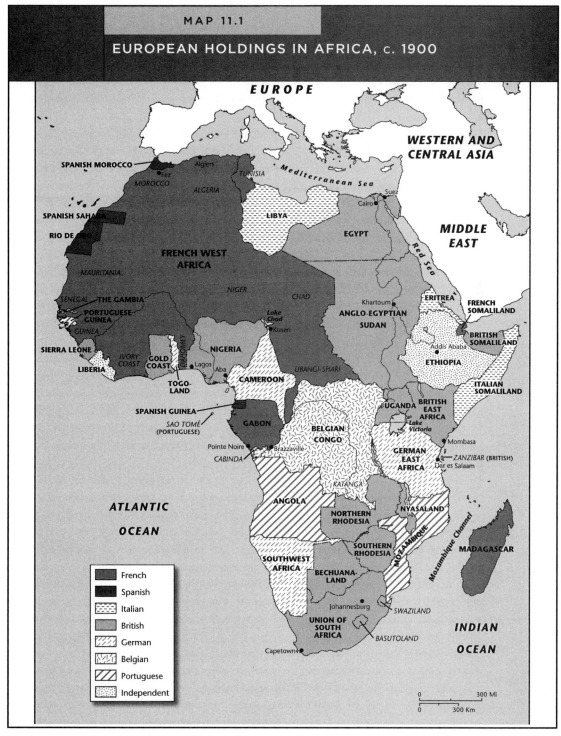

MAP 11.1

EUROPEAN HOLDINGS IN AFRICA, c. 1900

Legend:
- French
- Spanish
- Italian
- British
- German
- Belgian
- Portuguese
- Independent

As a result of the "New Imperialism" in the latter part of the nineteenth century, most of Africa came under European control. Shown here are the parts of Africa controlled by the several European colonial powers; European control was formalized during an 1884 international conference held in Berlin.

century, the United States apparently was so preoccupied with establishing its hegemony in the Western Hemisphere that it was content to allow European states to dominate in Africa. But Mearsheimer also argues that "states that gain regional hegemony have a further aim: to prevent other geographical areas from being dominated by other great powers." This aim the United States did not pursue—perhaps because *several* great powers were vying for hegemony in Africa after the turn of the century, which decreased its concern about these developments.

Liberia was one exception to the rule that the United States did not much concern itself with events in sub-Saharan Africa in the decades before World War II. In 1912 the Liberians received a large loan with the help of some U.S. and international banks; in return, the Liberian government agreed to be placed under a Customs Receivership administered by an appointee of the American president. (Similar arrangements, which typically involve the administration, collection, and, often, the allocation of receipts from tariffs on imports were made by the U. S. government with several Central American and Caribbean states during this era.)

These economic ties between the United States and Liberia paved the way for the Firestone Rubber Company to offer Liberia a $5 million loan in 1925, for which Firestone received access to one million acres of land, on which it created one of the largest rubber plantations in the world (Shick 1980). Added to the investments by Bethlehem Steel, and the establishment of bank affiliates in Liberia by Chase Manhattan and Citibank, the role of Firestone in Liberia became so predominant by the end of the 1920s that Liberia's political independence was compromised (Harris 1985, 74). Eventually, accusations of slavery, in part on Firestone's rubber plantations, led the League of Nations to investigate, and to create a committee to assist Liberians in regaining self-rule (Duignan and Gann 1984, 203–204). Sadly, this substantial American economic involvement in Liberia in the early part of the twentieth century did not lay the foundation for a prosperous and stable Liberia—a fact that was to become quite obvious by the end of the century.

The other issue regarding sub-Saharan Africa that did attract some sustained attention by the United States before World War II involved Italy's attack on Ethiopia in 1935. This act of aggression constituted one of the most important challenges to the principle of collective security to which the League of Nations was devoted. In accordance with this principle, Britain and France imposed economic sanctions against Italy in the wake of its attack on Ethiopia, but this action was arguably hypocritical, given that those two states had divided up between them most of the continent of Africa in the decades before World War I. In addition to being hypocritical, the reaction of Britain and France was only half-hearted, as the sanctions did not include oil, a commodity on which Italy depended for its mechanized assault on Ethiopia (Keylor 1996, 150–151).

Black Americans, in contrast, displayed considerable sympathy for their ethnic compatriots in Ethiopia, engaging in various activities to shape the reaction by the United States (as well as the rest of the world) to Italian aggression. In fact, "Italy's invasion of Ethiopia," according to one analyst of the role of black Americans in American foreign policy processes, "provoked the strongest Afro-American reaction ever demonstrated over an African question" (Challenor 1977, 151). The Council of Friends of Ethiopia appealed to the League of Nations, while the Nationalist Negro Movement petitioned the League, the government of Great Britain, and the U.S. State Department to come to the assistance of the Ethiopia. There were rallies in Harlem to recruit volunteers to fight in the war. After the Italians used poison gas against the Ethiopians, the Ethiopian Pacific Movement held a "huge rally" in Harlem, and the organizers sent cables to Australia, African nations, Asian states, and Latin American countries imploring one and all to come to the defense of Ethiopia. The National Association for the Advancement of Colored People (NAACP) lobbied U.S. Secretary of State Cordell Hull to support Ethiopia, and, when it came to light that Britain and France, in the Hoare/Laval accord, had agreed to support Italy's attempt to control most of Ethiopia, the NAACP sent a "vociferous" cable to the League of Nations in objection.

Still, according to Hershelle S. Challenor (1977, 153): "These protests and demonstrations of concern did not alter fundamentally the U.S. policy of neutrality throughout the Abyssinian affair." In fact, when Italy became especially desperate for oil to support its Ethiopian venture, instead of using whatever leverage its oil exports might have given it to modify Italy's policy, the United States doubled its shipments to Italy (Keylor 1996, 151). Did African American voters hold these developments against the administration of Franklin Delano Roosevelt? Apparently not. The majority of black voters had cast their ballots in support of Herbert Hoover in 1932, but the election of 1936 was to be a turning point for the black vote in the United States. In spite of Roosevelt's failure to do anything effective in support of Ethiopia against the blatant Italian aggression, most blacks in that election voted for the Democratic candidate for president.

This episode is just one early example of a pattern that would become established in attempts by African Americans to influence U.S. policy toward Africa—a pattern that is of particular interest to those inclined to interpret foreign policy decisions through the lens of rational political ambition theory. In general, African American voters have tended to give priority to domestic issues over whatever concerns they have had about U.S. foreign policy in Africa. So American presidents, as well as legislators, have typically not felt it necessary to pay much attention to African Americans' preferences on foreign policy issues regarding Africa or elsewhere. This pattern has been reinforced in recent decades by the tendency of African Americans to vote for Democratic candidates, especially at the presidential level. Democratic presidents feel little pressure to respond to African Americans' preferences with respect to foreign policy issues, since they can be confident that African Americans will vote for them in any case. Conversely, Republican presidents have little incentive to fashion foreign policies in response to the preferences of African Americans, since they apparently have little hope of garnering very many votes from that ethnic group under any circumstances.

WORLD WAR II AND ITS AFTERMATH

To some extent, World War II served to increase American appreciation of the geopolitical importance of Africa. When the United States and its allies chose to take the initiative first against the Italians and the Germans in North Africa, the United States established a sizable military presence in Liberia. During the war, there was also some concern about the possibility of an attack on the Western Hemisphere that could be launched from West Africa.

Meanwhile, "Jim Crowed" African American soldiers—that is, soldiers segregated into all African American units—had the opportunity to interact with citizens of Liberia, or encountered Francophone African troops in Europe or Asia (Challenor 1977, 153).

It was also during World War II that the United States began calling for the liberation of colonies. Roosevelt's secretary of state, Cordell Hull, spoke out in favor of the liberation of colonies in 1942 and again in 1944 (Dickson 1985, 4). At the Fifth Pan-African Congress in 1945—the first such meeting initiated by Africans—leaders of the African American community such as W. E. B. DuBois met future leaders of African states, including Kwame Nkrumah (an independence leader and the first president of Ghana) and Jomo Kenyatta (the first prime minister of the new state of Kenya). Still, at that point, there were only three "independent" African states not under white rule—Egypt, Ethiopia, and Liberia—and a fourth independent state ruled by whites—South Africa. By 1980, with the exception of small Spanish holdings in Morocco, all of the European possessions in Africa were to achieve independence from their colonial masters (Hargreaves 1988, 1).

Even though the United States did urge the Europeans to liberate their colonies during World War II, decolonization was not an important political issue on the domestic front after the war. In fact, during the presidential campaign of 1948, the Republican candidate for president, Thomas Dewey, offered his opinion that Italy should be allowed to continue control over its former African colonies because, "after all, no other ethnic group in the United States had any real interest in Africa." However insensitive it may seem today, this comment was not necessarily inaccurate. Challenor (1977, 155), an analyst who is clearly sympathetic to the concerns of African Americans, and to their potential impact on American foreign policy, acknowledges that "it was not until Ghana's independence in 1957 ... that blacks expressed widespread interest in Africa."

U.S.-AFRICAN RELATIONS DURING THE COLD WAR

Two basic factors had the greatest impact on U.S. foreign policy toward Africa during the Cold War era. First, although African Americans went from lingering disenfranchisement, especially in southern states, in the 1950s, to a sizable migration out of the South and a civil rights revolution in the 1960s, they (understandably) continued to accord domestic concerns a higher priority than policies toward Africa. Partly for that reason, and partly because the rivalry with the Soviet Union was so pervasive, U.S. foreign policy makers were more influenced by that competition than by input from African American constituents when they made policy decisions regarding Africa.

Supporting a Dictator: The Democratic Republic of the Congo (Zaire)

Improbably, at least, one of the early "hot spots" in the Cold War confrontation between the United States and the Soviet Union was in the heart of sub-Saharan Africa (see map 11.2). The former Belgian Congo assumed its independence with the name of Zaire on July 1, 1960. Within five days, there was a significant mutiny among Zairean soldiers against their Belgian commanders. Even more momentous was the action of Katanga, the wealthiest province in the country, which declared its own independence on July 11.

At the time, Zaire's president was Joseph Kasavubu, and its prime minister was Patrice Lumumba. The government officially broke off diplomatic relations with its former colonial master, Belgium, on July 14, 1960, and announced its intention to invite Soviet intervention if the impending arrival of UN troops did not soon lead to the expulsion of Belgian troops. By August, Lumumba became impatient with the lack of UN action against the insurgents in Katanga, demanded the removal of all white UN troops from Zaire, and welcomed to the country 100 Soviet technicians, who arrived simultaneously with a substantial shipment of military matériel from the Soviets.

At this point, the CIA apparently became the major player in the decision-making "game" in Washington, D.C. Until then, the State Department had been inclined to argue that Patrice Lumumba was the type of nationalist leader with whom the United States might work. But, as Peter J. Schraeder (1994, 58) reports: "The more hard-line position of the CIA prevailed ... when Lumumba was killed on January 17, 1961, just three days prior to Kennedy's assumption of the presidency." Kennedy was, according to most reports, inclined to be sympathetic to nationalist or neutral leaders who might serve as a barrier to Communist expansion in developing countries in general, and in African states in particular.

However, Zaire fell into civil war, and the breakaway province of Katanga was not subdued, even with the intervention of troops under the auspices of the United Nations. President Kennedy did come under domestic pressure regarding events in Zaire, not from African Americans in particular, but from conservatives and Republicans who felt that he was insufficiently zealous in pursuit of anti-Communism in Zaire, and who were sympathetic to the rebels in Katanga under Moise Tshombe. That pressure, and the perceived competition with the Soviets throughout the world, ultimately led Kennedy to opt for stability under a dictator, rather than nationalism, democracy, neutralist factions, or protection of human rights in Zaire.

The dictator upon whom the Kennedy administration ultimately settled was Mobutu Sese Seko (with whom the CIA had cooperated, apparently, in the assassination of Lumumba in 1961). Meeting personally with the Zairean strongman in May of 1963, "Kennedy extolled Mobutu's crucial behind-the-scenes role in the Cold War struggle against communism in Zaire" and expressed his gratitude for Mobutu's actions by declaring, "General, if it hadn't been for you, the whole thing would have collapsed and the communists would have taken over" (Schraeder 1994, 67, 280).[b]

In taking such an attitude, President Kennedy was not apparently influenced by the opinions of African Americans, who would have been a "natural constituency" for a more liberal approach to Africa, with increased emphasis on self-determination and racial justice. In fact, says Dickson (1985, 31–32), "it is difficult to find any major correlation between concrete administration African policies and black input." At least one important reason for this lack

---

b. The source of this quote is a memorandum regarding the conversation between President Kennedy and General Mobutu that Schraeder obtained from the John F. Kennedy Library.

of impact is not difficult to discern. According to Dixon (1985): "The chief concern" [of black leaders] and the black populace at large, continued to be the yet unfinished business of securing civil rights within the United States." In short, the Kennedy administration, and the administrations to follow, did not respond significantly to lobbying efforts by black Americans in shaping their African policies, in part because black Americans had higher priorities, mostly on the domestic front.

By 1965 (during the Johnson administration), Mobutu seized power more formally and proceeded to establish a regime based on providing graft, corruption, and payoffs to a small winning coalition, which, in a setting like Zaire, was sufficient to keep him in power for thirty-two years. The *World News Digest* (1997) succinctly—and, one suspects, quite accurately—describes the Mobutu regime in the following manner:

> Mobutu generally relied on a system of government ... described as "kleptocracy." Reportedly stealing billions of dollars from export earnings and Western aid, he amassed a vast personal fortune. He stayed in power by sharing the wealth with his political allies and controlling access to sources of government revenue.

This description, from an independent source, constitutes validating evidence in support of rational political ambition theory. In short, "leaders in systems with small winning coalitions and large selectorates (e.g., autocracies) find it easier to survive in office" (Bueno de Mesquita et al. 2003, 100). This is so not really *in spite of the fact* that they are corrupt and tend to impoverish the countries they rule by **kleptocracy**—or, as Bueno de Mesquita et al. (131) put it, "outright theft of a nation's income by its leaders"—but *because* they impoverish those countries. It is through kleptocracy, in other words, that autocrats maintain themselves in power, using its proceeds to solidify the support of their relatively small winning coalitions.[c]

Even though the rest of the country suffered grievously as a result of this greed and corruption, the U.S. government was quite consistently a solid supporter of the Mobutu regime. As we noted in chapter 1, Mobutu received $1.5 billion in U.S. foreign aid from 1960 to 1976, for example. By the time of Jimmy Carter's presidency, there arose a tendency in the U.S. government to question the support of authoritarian but anti-Communist dictators of the Mobutu variety, but, even so, the Carter administration could not bring itself to cut off support from the Mobutu regime. As Schraeder (1994, 89) reports, there remained a concern that the collapse of the Mobutu regime might be followed by the "disintegration of Zaire." Whether or not such fears were justified is a question to which we shall return later in this chapter. What is clear at this point is that the Carter administration, when given a choice between pressing for a less corrupt government in Zaire and protecting itself against whatever domestic political disadvantage might ensue should Zaire fall into Communist hands on its watch, opted for the strategy that best protected its priority of staying in power.

Dealing with Soviet Success: Angola, Ethiopia, and Mozambique

Whatever else might be said with respect to U.S. policies regarding Zaire during the Cold War, it must be acknowledged that they were successful in one respect: no radical government

---

c. Bueno de Mesquita et al. (167) point out that Mobutu managed to accumulate, during his thirty-two-year reign, a personal fortune of more than $4 billion.

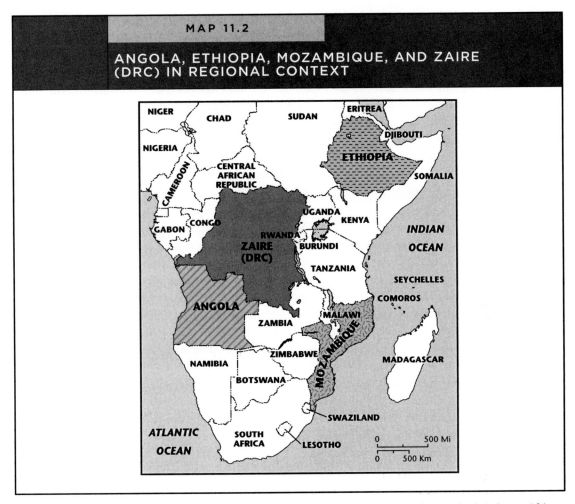

MAP 11.2

ANGOLA, ETHIOPIA, MOZAMBIQUE, AND ZAIRE (DRC) IN REGIONAL CONTEXT

A "hot spot" in the earlier days of the Cold War involved Zaire, shown here in the heart of sub-Saharan Africa. In more recent times, Zaire has become known as the Democratic Republic of the Congo.

sympathetic to or having important ties to the Soviet Union came to power in the state of Zaire during those years. To the extent that American policymakers paid attention to Africa at all during the Cold War, minimizing Soviet influence there was certainly a high, perhaps the highest, priority they had with respect to that region. They were not uniformly successful in achieving that goal, especially during the 1970s, when radical governments with substantial ties to the Soviet Union came into power in at least three sub-Saharan states—Angola, Ethiopia, and Mozambique.

Angola

Until 1975, Angola was a Portuguese colony. In 1974, when a new government came to power in Lisbon and proceeded to dismantle Portugal's colonial empire, Angola confronted it with a problem: there was no existing government to which the new Portuguese government wished to cede power. So, instead, it transferred power to the "people of Angola."

At the time, a series of rebel groups were contending for control of the country. The most powerful and important was the Popular Movement for the Liberation of Angola (MPLA), which had been founded in the 1950s. By the 1960s, Agostino Neto had emerged as its leader, and it was receiving support from the Soviet Union even before it became the predominant political force within the newly liberated Angola.

The rebel organization that came to be the principal rival of the MPLA was the National Union for the Total Independence of Angola (UNITA), whose leader was Jonas Savimbi. In 1965 Savimbi traveled to China, where he received four months of military training; he also became a disciple of Maoism (Library of Congress 1989). So, for a while, political strife within Angola reflected tensions between the Soviet Union and the People's Republic of China. Also, in spite of its ties to China, UNITA received substantial support from South Africa.

In addition, the emerging political situation after the sudden departure of Portugal from Angola attracted the attention of the United States. In 1975, from the point of view of the Ford administration, this situation "constituted a major crisis for the White House and eventually led President Ford and Secretary of State Kissinger to ... embark upon a major covert action program in Angola" (Schraeder 1994, 211). Actually, U.S. aid was focused on a third rebel group in Angola, the National Front for the Liberation of Angola (FNLA), which was loosely allied to UNITA. Therefore, the U.S. covert program helped UNITA to stay in the field, so to speak, at least indirectly.

However, the MPLA gained control of most of the country soon after the departure of the Portuguese. It continued to receive substantial aid from the Soviet Union, and it established ties with Castro's regime in Cuba as early as the 1960s. In the 1970s, the Cubans even sent troops to Angola to defend the MPLA regime. Eventually, in fact, Castro sent 50,000 Cuban troops "to serve as the power behind the throne of Angola's new regime" (Leebaert 2002, 467).

Meanwhile, on the other side of the coin, the U.S. Congress effectively curtailed support for the enemies of the MPLA. While Ford and Kissinger were in the process of mounting their covert operation against the MPLA, the war in Vietnam came to its sad (at least for the United States and the South Vietnamese regime) conclusion. In that atmosphere, Congress became concerned that the Ford administration's covert program in Angola, by involving the country in another far-off civil war, might be laying the basis for "another Vietnam." When the Senate voted in December 1975 to cut off all aid to any faction in Angola as part of the 1976 Foreign Assistance Act, President Ford vetoed that bill. The Senate then responded by passing the 1976 Defense Appropriations bill, with a provision that cut off all covert aid to Angola (Schraeder 1994, 47–48). These steps thus helped to clear the way for the MPLA, with Soviet and Cuban support, to take control of the central government of Angola.

However, Savimbi and the UNITA movement had, in some ways, just begun to fight. Savimbi had as an important base the Ovimbundu, Angola's largest ethnic group, consisting of some 30 percent of the population. Partly for this reason, it was estimated at the time of Angola's becoming independent that UNITA was supported by 40–65 percent of Angolans, while only about 33 percent supported the MPLA (Rodman 1994; cited in Friedman 2000). South African troops entered Angola in 1975, intent on supporting Savimbi's cause, but they were countered by Cuban troops, and the South Africans began withdrawing by early 1976.

Savimbi's UNITA still maintained itself in the field, since it represented the ethnic major-ity in the country and was more sympathetic to peasants than the more urban-based MPLA. Then, in 1985, the U.S. Congress repealed the law restricting assistance to rebel groups in Angola, and by 1986, as part of President Reagan's vigorous efforts to undermine and subvert Soviet influence in many parts of the world, UNITA was equipped with the same Stinger mis-siles that were being provided to the rebels in Afghanistan. And, to some extent, U.S. aid in Angola had a similar effect to that in Afghanistan—stimulating the Soviet Union, in spite of what we now know was its imminent demise, to supply to the MPLA $1 billion in new weapons in 1986, and another $1.5 billion between 1988 and 1990. Analyzing the early twen-ty-first-century situation in Angola, Derek Leebaert (2002, 545) concludes that "U.S. back-ing of Savimbi helped drain the Soviet Union, but it also perpetuated a pointless civil war that is still going on today."

The CIA's even more recent assessment of the situation today in Angola (Central Intelligence Agency 2004) offers the following summary: "Up to 1.5 million lives may have been lost in fighting over the past quarter century. The death of insurgent leader Jonas Savimbi in 2002 and a subsequent cease-fire with UNITA may bode well for the country." This tragedy may be cited as yet another example of a small country caught up to its terrible detriment in the superpowers' Cold War confrontation, but it should be noted, as well, that the civil war in Angola persisted for more than a decade after the demise of the Soviet Union and the Cold War.

Ethiopia

Another sub-Saharan country in which the Soviet Union and its Cuban allies made serious inroads during the 1970s was Ethiopia. Things began to fall apart in Ethiopia, from the point of view of the United States, when longtime leader Haile Selassie was overthrown in a mili-tary coup in 1974. The government that emerged in the immediate wake of the coup was pro-Western and friendly toward the United States, but, by the end of the year, Colonel Mengistu Haile Mariam came to power and, in the ensuing months, proceeded to create a one-party socialist state and to initiate a full-scale offensive against a rebellion in the Ethiopian province of Eritrea.

In part because the Soviet Union was at the time providing support to Ethiopia's antago-nistic neighbor, Somalia, the U.S. government was at first inclined to provide military support to the Mengistu regime. However, at the end of 1976, Mengistu signed a $100 million mili-tary aid agreement with the Soviet Union, posing a problem for the new U.S. administration. Jimmy Carter came into office intending to alter the Ford administration's policy of automat-ically rejecting any regime that was radical or nationalistic. But Carter was also committed to supporting human rights, and it was clear that the Mengistu regime violated human rights in a particularly gross and outrageous manner. In the end, the Carter administration decided to prioritize its human rights commitment, and it terminated all support of the Ethiopian regime in 1977 (Schraeder 1994, 136–140).

On the other hand, the Carter administration also created an extensive relationship with Ethiopa's neighbor, Somalia. But just two days after President Carter officially approved send-ing military aid to Somalia, its military forces initiated an attack on the region of Ogaden, the focus of a long-standing dispute between Ethiopia and Somalia. Within a few months of the Somalian attack, Ethiopia received $2 billion worth of military hardware from the Soviet Union and about 15,000 Cuban troops (some of them shifted from Angola to the Horn of Africa). Thus, the conflict between Somalia and Ethiopia was imbued with significance for the Cold War confrontation between the United States and the Soviet Union.

When the Reagan administration came to power in 1981, it did not immediately extend enthusiastic support to Somalia's attempt to undermine the radical, Marxist regime of Mengistu in Ethiopia, although such a policy would have been congruent with Reagan administration initiatives in other parts of the globe. It apparently had higher priorities that left it with little attention (or resources) remaining for conflicts in that region of Africa in it earliest years. U.S. aid to Somalia, however, was increased in the wake of renewed border disputes between Somalia and Ethiopia in 1982. Then, a well-publicized famine hit Ethiopia in 1984. Pressure to offer humanitarian assistance to victims of the famine, built up by televised newscasts of starving Ethiopian children, pushed the Reagan administration to dramatically step up its provision of food aid to that country. Schraeder (1994, 157) notes: "In one of the greatest ironies of U.S. Africa policies during the Reagan administration, popular pressures to 'do something' clearly forced the staunchest anti-communist administration during the post–World War II period to become the largest official donor to the most doctrinaire Marxist country on the African continent."

In the end, the regime of that Marxist outpost proved unable to withstand the stresses created by a civil conflict with the Ethiopian region of Eritrea in the early 1990s, and perhaps even more importantly, by the demise of the Soviet Union. The Mengistu regime was toppled in 1991, a new constitution adopted in 1994, and multiparty elections held for the first time in 1995. Freedom House (2005), which releases data annually on the status of democracy in every country of the world, categorizes Ethiopia as "partly free," giving it scores of 5 in both political rights and civil liberties (on a scale from 1 to 7, where 1 is the "most democratic" category). In short, although it has escaped the brutality of the Mengistu regime, it is hardly a model of democracy.

Mozambique

A third country wherein the Soviet Union achieved considerable influence during the 1970s (in the wake of the Vietnam War) was Mozambique. Yet another Portuguese colony, it, like Angola, achieved its independence in 1975. A rebel group known as the Mozambique Liberation Front (FRELIMO) had been engaged since 1964 in guerrilla warfare against Portuguese colonial control. By the early 1970s, the rebel group's estimated 7,000 troops were engaged in continual bloody battles with Portuguese military forces of around 60,000. Then, with the acquiescence of the same new, rather radical Portuguese government that brought about the liberation of Angola, FRELIMO took over control in Mozambique. It proceeded to establish a one-party, Marxist state that nationalized all industries, abolished private ownership of land, and established vigorous reforms of health and education (Infoplease 2004).

Mozambique was also caught up in international currents of conflict. To its west and south, it shared borders with what was then Rhodesia (later to become Zimbabwe) and South Africa.

At the time of Mozambique's independence, both of these neighboring states had white regimes ruling overwhelmingly black populations. Both were suspicious of the committed Marxist, FRELIMO-based government of Mozambique, and both supported a rebel group devoted to the overthrow of that government—namely, the Mozambique National Resistance Movement, or RENAMO. The U.S. government, on the other hand, focused its activities on the anti-Marxist rebels in Angola, and on trying to foster peace between Mozambique and its meddling neighbors. After Jimmy Carter was elected, he sent his UN ambassador, Andrew Young (an African American), to a 1977 UN conference on African liberation, held in Mozambique, where Young "equated the legitimacy of the liberation struggle in southern Africa with the U.S. civil rights movement of the 1960s" (Schraeder 1994, 216).

In 1979 Rhodesia, in a desperate attempt to shore up its white regime, attacked Mozambique, which it considered an important base for rebels against its government. That antagonism to FRELIMO ceased in 1980, when a majority-rule regime came to power in Rhodesia, which then renamed itself Zimbabwe. But no sooner had peace been established with Zimbabwe than hostility stepped up on the South African front, which became RENAMO's main source of support. Having been initially hostile, the Reagan administration moved, toward the end of its first term, to restore diplomatic relations with the government of Mozambique. The apparent aim of this policy was to relieve the pressure against the government of South Africa that might originate in Mozambique. In fact, in 1984 the United States played an important role in bringing about a peace agreement between these two countries. The agreement called for the government of South Africa to cease its support of RENAMO; in return, the government of Mozambique agreed to halt its support of what was then a rebel group in South Africa—the African National Congress.

That peace agreement soon fell apart, but Mozambique had, meanwhile, ceased to be a foreign policy concern for the United States, as the Soviet Union first altered its own policies in the region and then, shortly thereafter, fell apart itself. These developments were rapidly and dramatically reflected within Mozambique. By 1989, FRELIMO formally abandoned Marxism, and, by 1992, a peace agreement was negotiated between FRELIMO and RENAMO. In 1994 multiparty elections were held, and won by FRELIMO. Since then, Mozambique has suffered natural disasters, such as a cyclone in 2000, but it has been generally stable politically. Freedom House (2005), rates it "partly free," with scores of 3 on political rights, and 4 on civil liberties (on a scale from 1 to 7, where 1 equates to "most democratic").

Confronting Apartheid: South Africa

During the Cold War, much of the attention of U.S. foreign policy makers—as well as a relatively substantial amount of public attention—was focused on South Africa. There, the policy of racial segregation known as **apartheid** intermingled with what the United States, and especially the CIA, saw as a threat of Communist subversion, in a way that made U.S. policy toward South Africa a continual bone of contention and a source of multiple contradictions.

The first white settlers from the Netherlands arrived at the southern tip of Africa in 1652, becoming known as **Afrikaners**. By the beginning of the nineteenth century, however, British colonialists had seized the area around the Cape of Good Hope, sending the Afrikaners farther inland, where they eventually formed the states of Transvaal and the Orange Free State. The discovery of diamonds in 1867, and of gold in 1886, increased the interest and the immigration of the British, leading them to ruthlessly subjugate the black Africans in the area. The predominance of the British was further confirmed by their victory over the Afrikaners in the Boer War, which lasted from 1899 to 1902. South Africa then became a British-controlled colony, whose independent status within the British Commonwealth was recognized in 1931.

From that point on, South Africa developed as a reasonably respectable member of the international community that was, it was widely assumed, evolving in the direction of a pluralist political system, within which all ethnic groups, blacks as well as Indians, would ultimately be included. But in 1948 the Afrikaners won unexpectedly in a parliamentary election, and they proceeded to lay the legal basis for the apartheid system of separation of the races. Nevertheless, the United States, and the CIA, in particular, continued to believe that South Africa was such a valuable asset in the Cold War contest with the Soviet Union that close ties between the United States and the pro-apartheid government should be maintained. (The CIA's opinion was based in part on deposits of uranium and other important minerals in South Africa.)

When South Africa withdrew from the British Commonwealth in 1961, the CIA's impression was that the black political group pushing for majority rule in South Africa—the African National Congress (ANC)—was, in Schraeder's words (1994, 202), "heavily 'infiltrated' or completely 'dominated' by South African communists," and so it continued to cooperate with the South African regime. The CIA even helped the security services of South Africa to apprehend the ANC leader, Nelson Mandela, who, Schraeder remarks, "remained in jail for nearly twenty-eight years and came to personify the international struggle against apartheid."

In March of 1960, black Africans gathered for a demonstration outside a police station in Sharpeville, South Africa. After a gun was fired, the police began shooting at the demonstrators, killing dozens of them. Over time, it became increasingly difficult for the South African government to maintain apartheid. Peter Calvocoressi (1991, 579) describes the deteriorating situation: "Prisons filled, floggings became an habitual process of government, executions took place at the rate of one a day, the mail ceased to be private, spies and informers multiplied, an inevitably brutalized police became a law of assault unto itself, and the regime itself felt obliged to build up a white citizen army with a potential strength of 250,000."

As early as 1957, Martin Luther King Jr. had led a demonstration in the United States to call attention to, and to denounce, the apartheid system in South Africa. As the apartheid system became ever more odious, it attracted increased attention from the outside world. Eventually, starting in the 1960s, the governments of various nations responded with economic sanctions against the regime in South Africa. After its withdrawal from the British Commonwealth, African states called for economic and political sanctions against South Africa. In 1962 the UN General Assembly passed a nonbinding resolution, suggesting that member states terminate diplomatic relations with South Africa and adopt economic sanctions. By the end of the 1960s, the UN had recommended an arms embargo, the U.S. had prohibited loans to South Africa to facilitate trade, and India had put in place a complete embargo on trade with South Africa.

In the early 1970s, however, the Nixon administration decided that the best way to induce reforms in South Africa was to avoid confrontation with the regime, which continued adhering to its apartheid policy. The coup in Portugal mentioned earlier, which permitted the establishment of Marxist governments in Angola and Mozambique, led the Nixon and then the Ford administration to place a higher priority on the southern African region. The U.S. government became more protective of the South African regime, valuing it even more in the context of the emergence of Marxist governments on the continent, as an ally in the Cold War struggle with the Soviet Union. In 1974, the United States vetoed a resolution in the Security Council that would have expelled South Africa from the United Nations, and in 1976, it voted against a UN resolution that categorized South Africa as a threat to international security and called for comprehensive economic sanctions against the apartheid regime (Dickson 1985, 73–90).

During the Republican administrations of this era, liberal and black groups had limited influence on American policy toward Africa in general or South Africa in particular. Challenor (1977, 167) explained, at the time, that "the competition between an African interest and black domestic concerns ... is still unresolved. Some blacks question funds for an African lobby ... while many blacks here live below the poverty line."

The Carter administration came into office in 1976 intent on emphasizing the defense of human rights as an important feature of its foreign policy. Stephen Ambrose and Douglas Brinkley (1997, 283) comment: "Carter felt the issue deeply himself, and, in addition, it provided an opportunity for him to distinguish his foreign policy from that of Nixon and Kissinger." One might expect such an emphasis to result in rather intense pressure from the United States on the South African regime to dismantle its apartheid system, and such an impression would have been reinforced by Carter's appointment of African American activist Andrew Young as the U.S. ambassador to the United Nations.

And, indeed, in its early days the Carter administration did take some steps to increase the pressure for reform on the South African regime, strengthening, for example, an embargo on arms to that nation. It also, in 1978, "reprimanded South Africa for a possible explosion of a nuclear device" (Dickson 1985, 107). In the end, however, the Carter administration refused to take any actions that would differentiate its policy toward South Africa substantially from that of its Republican predecessors. According to the Digital National Security Archive (2004): "Like its predecessor, the Carter Administration ... actively discouraged revolutionary change in South Africa and advocated moderate reforms." The inclination to press hard on human rights issues in South Africa was muted toward the end of the Carter years by increasing tensions with the Soviet Union, especially after the Soviet invasion of Afghanistan in 1979. And once again, there was a lack of effective lobbying on the domestic front for a strong policy on apartheid in South Africa. Active engagement by African Americans on such issues was still precluded by "a preoccupation with domestic concerns" (Dickson 1985, 123).

And if the Carter administration was reluctant, because of Cold War pressures, to push the South African regime too hard for a change in its policy of apartheid, the Reagan administration was even more likely to give priority to its struggle against the Soviet Union over any effort to bring about rapid political reform in South Africa. It called, instead, for a policy of **constructive engagement** with the South African regime, which basically meant that the

United States would try to remain on good terms with it, reasoning that friendly interactions would provide more leverage than hostile pronouncements or actions aimed at pressuring the government to modify its apartheid policy.

But South Africa's militancy in its own defense played a role in undermining the Reagan administration's policy of constructive engagement. It launched aggressive military actions against Angola and Mozambique, considering both to be dangerous sources of instability inspired by Marxism. Schraeder (1994, 225–226) describes the reaction in the United States: "Dissatisfaction within Congress over the escalation of military conflict in southern Africa and the failure of constructive engagement to achieve any of its major goals led to renewed attempts at legislating economic sanctions against South Africa."

Those efforts did not meet with immediate success, especially when the Reagan administration managed to arrange the Lusaka Accord and the Nkomati Accord—both agreements aimed at de-escalation of the conflicts between South Africa, on the one hand, and Angola and Mozambique, on the other. These agreements did not resolve the conflicts in the long run, but they did manage to make it appear that constructive engagement was making some progress.

Beginning in 1984, however, political strife in South Africa once again undermined the support in Congress and the United States for constructive engagement. Protests by black South Africans in 1984, for example, led to the deaths of over 2,000 of them, while another 30,000 were detained as political prisoners. In response to these events, black activist groups in the United States began to engage in more focused efforts at political action than they had attempted on previous occasions when reacting to issues that were less clear-cut than the literally black vs. white confrontation in South Africa.

In May of 1986, the South African government launched military raids against the headquarters of the African National Congress in Botswana, Zambia, and Zimbabwe. Motivated by this aggression and by effective lobbying and public demonstrations by prominent African American individuals and groups, the U.S. Congress then passed the **Comprehensive Anti-Apartheid Act** of 1986, which severely limited trade with and foreign investment in South Africa. President Reagan vetoed the bill and then embarked on an extensive public relations campaign to defend his policy, but the House voted 317–83, and the Senate voted 78–21 to pass the anti-apartheid act over his veto. Schraeder (1994, 230) comments: "Marking one of the greatest foreign policy defeats of the Reagan administration, these two votes constituted the official death of the policy of constructive engagement."

In the ensuing years, the proponents and opponents of sanctions against South Africa continued to struggle, fighting mostly to a standstill. For example, in 1987, in an annual report required by the Comprehensive Anti-Apartheid Act, President Reagan argued that the sanctions were not working and that he would not recommend any more of them. In 1988 the House passed legislation that would have ended almost all trade with South Africa, but the measure never came to a vote in the Senate (Institute for International Economics 1999).

Both U.S. President George H. W. Bush and South African President F. W. de Klerk came to power in 1989. Like his predecessor, President Bush then issued an annual report to Congress in which he concluded that the sanctions were not working. In general, though, he was more conciliatory toward black leaders in South Africa—meeting, for example, with Archbishop Desmond Tutu. Meanwhile, de Klerk instituted a policy of reform that brought the system of apartheid to an end. He ended the ban on the ANC and released Nelson

Mandela from jail. In July of 1991, President Bush lifted U.S. sanctions on South Africa, a step that was criticized by Mandela as well as by the Congressional Black Caucus and the NAACP. Nevertheless, in 1993, President de Klerk and Nelson Mandela were jointly awarded the Nobel Peace Prize, and by 1994, Mandela had been elected president of South Africa. The apartheid system had been totally demolished, at least on the governmental level.

Whether South Africa's apartheid system was dismantled mainly because of sanctions applied by states in cooperation with the United Nations or by the United States specifically, or because of sanctions imposed by private actors such as multinational corporations, is a matter of debate to this day. There are alternative explanations for the demise of apartheid that do not credit any of these sanctions with a very important role in the process. One such argument points out that the apartheid system was very inefficient economically, as it called for strict restrictions on where blacks could travel and on which jobs they could hold. By the 1970s at the latest, as the South African economy grew, it came to need the contributions of black citizens, who made up, after all, the large majority of its population.

Then, too, at a critical point in the process, the Cold War came to an end, and the Soviet Union fell apart. For decades, white citizens of South Africa had been especially fearful of the African National Congress because they saw it as dominated by Communists with strong attachments to the Soviet Union. And potential sympathizers of the ANC in the United States had hesitated to make that sympathy public because it might make them look soft on Communism. When the Cold War ended and the Soviet Union ceased to be, white opposition to the ANC grew somewhat less zealous, and support for the ANC in the United States and elsewhere became less restrained (Levy 1999).

Nevertheless, it is quite clear that African Americans made more determined, better organized efforts to affect U.S. foreign policy on South Africa than they had done in the case of any other issue regarding U.S. relations with sub-Saharan Africa since World War II. "Their mobilization against apartheid ... demonstrated the powerful force of a diaspora in altering U.S. foreign policy...," according to political scientist Yossi Shain (1994–1995, 813). Since sanctions were imposed, and the apartheid system was then dismantled, it is impossible to deny that the sanctions may have played a role of some importance in the process. And even if sanctions had, in fact, only a limited impact, the activities of African Americans during the 1980s and the early 1990s on U.S.–South African relations clearly demonstrate the substantial influence of African Americans on the U.S. foreign policy process. When African Americans place a high priority on foreign policy issues, rather than giving consistent priority to domestic issues, they effectively negotiate the channels of U.S. foreign policy.

U.S.-AFRICAN RELATIONS AFTER THE END OF THE COLD WAR

It is probably fair to say that during the Cold War, sub-Saharan Africa received less attention from U.S. foreign policy makers and their constituents than did any other region in the world. And, since the end of the Cold War, such attention may have decreased even further. Perhaps what is most notable about U.S. foreign policy in Africa in the post–Cold War era involves what has *not* been done—that is, conspicuous examples of inaction.

Somalia

One partial and incomplete exception to that rule occurred in Somalia, just as the Cold War was coming to an end. This African state was falling further into chaos, starvation, and political strife as the U.S. presidential election of 1992 unfolded. In December—following the first President Bush's loss to Bill Clinton in that election—the UN Security Council passed a resolution calling for UN forces to "use all necessary means" to establish security for the humanitarian missions underway in Somalia. The next day, Bush decided to send U.S. Marines to Mogadishu, the capital city, and within a week they were arriving onshore in Somalia. Jeffrey A. Lefebvre (1993, 44) comments: "By agreeing to provide the bulk of troops for the [UN mission in Somalia]..., the Bush Administration ... had taken an unprecedented action. For the first time American military forces were deployed by the commander-in-chief for humanitarian reasons, rather than for securing vital strategic, political or economic interests."

Once he had lost the presidential election, and his political career was basically over, President Bush finally made the decision to send troops to Somalia in order to facilitate the delivery of food. It is, therefore, reasonable to suppose that this decision was unusually independent of short-run domestic or international political motives. Nevertheless, it is widely believed that Bush was, in fact, responding to pressure generated by the images of starving Somalian men, women, and children featured on nightly news broadcasts. No less an authority on foreign policy than George Kennan argued shortly after American troops arrived in Somalia that media coverage of the suffering thousands there had overwhelmed traditional foreign-policy-making processes, and was ultimately responsible for an ill-conceived intervention (Kennan 1993; cited in Robinson 1999, 302).[d]

But there was more to this departing president's decision than just an emotional reaction to CNN news broadcasts or inexplicable altruistic impulses. The Bush administration had recently completed its victorious assault on Saddam Hussein's Iraq (in defense of the Islamic state of Kuwait). That intervention had provoked considerable cynicism from some observers who had described that war as "all about oil." And, shortly thereafter, Yugoslavia began to fall apart, leading to gruesome stories and some photos of "ethnic cleansing," especially in Bosnia, which was populated by a considerable proportion of Muslims. The Bush administration had refrained from offering any support for the Bosnians against the Serbs.

This lack of action had provoked considerable criticism of George H. W. Bush, in part from Islamic states, but also from domestic opponents. "The Bush Administration," observed David Halberstam (2001, 250–251), "had taken a 'pounding' from the Democrats, particularly candidate Clinton, about places like Bosnia ... as well as Somalia." President Bush was particularly sensitive to the criticism that he had been willing to use military force to protect U.S. access to oil, as in the Persian Gulf War, but when it was "merely" human lives at stake, especially Muslim lives, he had been indifferent. Sending U.S. troops to Somalia—where there was no oil, nor any other obvious or pressing U.S. economic interests—provided a neat response to all these criticisms. There was, in short, a lot of "pressure to do something *somewhere*," and—compared to Bosnia—"Somalia was a better choice."

---

d. As Joseph Nye (2002, 149) has observed, "Few Americans can look at television pictures of starving people ... on the evening news just before dinner and not feel that we should do something about it if we can."

Or, so it appeared initially. Estimates of the number of lives that were saved by the U.S.-led intervention in Somalia, because of the deliveries of emergency aid of various kinds that it facilitated, tend to range from 100,000 to at least 300,000, and beyond. Thus it would clearly be capricious to categorize that intervention as simply a waste of time and a foolish mistake. Nevertheless, the mission led to a significant trauma for U.S. forces, and for the administration of President Clinton, who inherited the situation in flux upon taking office in January of 1993.

By May of that year, the United Nations had launched a **nation-building** project known as the UN Operation in Somalia II, or UNISOM II. Depending on your point of view, this was either an unavoidable response to a chaotic situation on the ground, or a foolish expansion of a project that had started out as a "neutral" attempt to safeguard the delivery of emergency and relief supplies. But it is difficult to escape the conclusion that it would be impossible to intervene in such anarchic circumstances as had evolved in Somalia by 1992 and yet remain neutral. One explanation of how the goal of neutrality escaped U.S. troops in Somalia in 1992 is as follows:

> The United States ... sought to stay neutral.... Instead of remaining neutral, however, the United States ... ended up enhancing the roles and status of the warlords. U.S. rules of engagement in Somalia forbade any interference in Somali-on-Somali violence. Most important, the failure to disarm the major combatants meant that the United States ... in effect sided with those who had the most weapons. (Clarke and Herbst 1996, 79)

By August of 1993, the U.S. government had decided that one of the warlords was a source of instability that needed to be dealt with. All pretense of neutrality was dropped, and U.S. troops set out in pursuit of General Mohamed Farah Aideed. The ensuing conflict between Aideed's supporters and the U.S. military led to a firefight in the streets of Mogadishu in October of 1993, in which eighteen U.S. Army Rangers were killed. Halberstam (2001, 262) reports: "Clinton was furious.... He was appalled that the United States was being pushed around by what he called 'two-bit pricks'." Still, appalled though he may have been, he did not respond forcefully—or effectively, for that matter. He did send more military equipment (which had been requested before the disastrous firefight), but, under heavy congressional pressure, he instructed the U.S. military in Somalia to assume an entirely defensive posture, which they did until they were withdrawn entirely in 1994. UN forces were withdrawn in 1995.

The CIA's description of the situation in Somalia as of 2004 states that "numerous warlords and factions are still fighting for control of Mogadishu and the other southern regions. Suspicion of Somali links with global terrorism further complicates the picture." Indeed, Somalia has apparently had links to global terrorism for some time. In fact, the U.S. government indicted Osama bin Laden in 1998 for al-Qaeda's contribution to the attack suffered by the U.S. Army Rangers in Mogadishu in 1993 (PBS *Online* and WGBH/*Frontline* 1998). Since al-Qaeda claims "credit" for being there, one can be reasonably confident that Mogadishu in 1993 was the site of an early confrontation between al-Qaeda and the United States.

Rwanda

The debacle in Somalia had fairly obvious effects on the administration and the foreign policy of President Clinton. Primarily, it made that administration much more cautious about **humanitarian intervention**. By 1994, ethnic conflict between the Hutus and Tutsis in the Central African state of Rwanda had reached a fever pitch. Still, in spite of some dire warnings about what was to unfold, neither the United States nor any other international actor took any effective action to stop the **genocide**, in which Hutus killed mostly Tutsis by the hundreds of thousands—800,000 is a common estimate. Explanations for this lack of action are not difficult to find. Halberstam (2002, 276), for example, asserts in a totally straightforward manner that "Washington wanted no part of Rwanda. The political fallout from Somalia had caused enough damage." Other analysts argue that in April 1994, the "world" was "paralyzed by the Somalia debacle," and so "did nothing as the Hutu government slaughtered upward of a half a million Tutsis" (Clark and Herbst 1996, 82).

In 1998 President Clinton made a trip to Rwanda to apologize for his lack of action in reaction to the genocidal violence that had taken place there in 1994 (Amanpour 2004).[e] And it would certainly appear, on the surface, that the lack of action on the part of the United States and the entire international community in the face of this massive tragedy was inexcusable. But appearances, as compelling as they are in this case, are arguably misleading. In the first place, analyst Alan J. Kuperman (2004), who has studied this and other humanitarian crises in recent times, argues that the genocide in Rwanda occurred so quickly that it is not realistic to believe that the United States, or anybody else, could have mobilized sufficient force in a sufficiently short time to have done much good. According to Kuperman, it would have taken the United States six weeks to mobilize and deploy a mission of 15,000 personnel; the genocidal violence had in Rwanda had killed some 400,000 in the first three weeks.

Then, too, humanitarian interventions in general have created what Kuperman (2001, 2004) refers to as a **moral hazard**. This unintended effect is created by attempts to alleviate the impact of harmful events. Consider the potential psychological impact of having automobile insurance: it is at least logically possible that people with auto insurance will drive less carefully, because they are aware that the costs of any accident they may cause will not be charged to them—their insurance company will cover some large portion of the damage. So, to some extent, auto insurance may well have the effect of increasing the amount of reckless driving and the number of accidents.

Similarly, humanitarian interventions in the face of gross human rights violations may, conceivably, increase the number of incidents in which such violations occur. "Each instance of humanitarian intervention," Kuperman (2004, 68) argues, "raises expectations of further interventions and thus encourages additional armed challenges that may provoke still more genocidal retaliation—further overwhelming the international capacity for intervention." Kuperman acknowledges that such a process applies only to a limited extent to the horrible

---

e. In this same story, Lord David Hannay, the former U.K. ambassador to the United Nations, is quoted as explaining: "No one will ever understand Rwanda properly if they don't read it through the prism of Somalia.... Why did the international community not do something? Because they were traumatized by the collapse of the mission in Somalia."

events of 1994 in Rwanda, but he also insists (2001, 118) that the deployment of a small number of UN peacekeepers to Rwanda in advance of the genocide, in fact, increased the uncompromising attitude of the Tutsis in their interactions with the Hutu government, thus making a contribution to the outbreak and the overwhelming scope of the violence.

Admittedly, it was almost certainly not concerns about the moral hazards created by intervening in Rwanda that determined the outcome of decision-making processes in the Clinton administration in 1994. Samantha Power, a journalist and lawyer, and the founder of the Carr Center for Human Rights Policy in the Kennedy School of Government Harvard University, has studied intensively the unfolding genocide in Rwanda, as well as roughly analogous human rights tragedies in Cambodia, Iraq, and Bosnia. A common thread running through all these massive human rights violations was inaction by the U.S. government. Power (2002, xxi) clearly thinks that she has figured out why the United States has refrained from effective action in all of these cases: "No U.S. president has ever made genocide prevention a priority, and no U.S. president has ever suffered politically for his indifference to its occurrence." About U.S. inaction in the case of the unfolding violence in Rwanda in 1994, Power (335) observes: "Remembering Somalia and hearing no American demands for intervention, President Clinton and his advisers knew that the military and political risks of involving the United States in a bloody conflict in central Africa were great, yet there were no costs to avoiding Rwanda altogether."

In short, Power's explanation for the inaction in the face of genocide in Rwanda (and elsewhere) is quite congruent with the basic tenets of rational political ambition theory. Such an interpretation is made even more plausible by the fact that African Americans have typically not been deeply interested in foreign policy issues, even those involving Africa. In addition, unlike the case of South African apartheid, in which African American lobbying efforts were arguably successful, the conflict in Rwanda was black-on-black, not whites against blacks.

Furthermore, as mentioned earlier, African Americans have dependably voted for the Democratic Party's candidate for president in every election in recent decades. Bill Clinton received around 85 percent of the African American vote in the elections of the 1990s, while Al Gore in 2000 and John Kerry in 2004 captured 90 percent and 88 percent of black votes, respectively. Democratic presidents, in short, apparently have nothing to fear if they ignore the preferences of African American voters when they formulate foreign policies in general, or even with respect to African issues, while Republican presidents may understandably feel that there is little prospect for gain by paying any attention to the wishes of those same voters. Finally, in addition to all these domestic political considerations regarding the genocide in Rwanda, the absence of national security risks—to which realists might have been inclined to respond—makes it quite unsurprising that the United States did not take forceful action to prevent the tragedy there in 1994.

And when the international community finally did intervene in the wake of the genocide, its impact proved to be of questionable utility—and even of dubious morality. Again, it is not possible for such interventions to be neutral. When the French sent in troops after the genocidal violence had been ongoing for six weeks, Gerald Caplan (2004) reports: "The French forces created a safe haven in the south-west of the country which provided sanctuary ... for the very *Hutu Power militants* who had organized and carried out the genocide." Many of these militants then escaped into Zaire and began launching murderous excursions back into Rwanda.

Subsequently, the international donor community provided $1.4 billion in aid to the camps for the Hutu refugees. Caplan comments: "Since, as was universally known, the 'genocidaires' had taken over the camps, a good part of these funds went to feed and shelter them and to fund their re-training and re-arming as they planned cross-border raids back into Rwanda."

So, arguably, the small intervention the UN provided, and the anticipation of greater interventionist activity by the international community (including the United States), actually had the unintended consequence of bringing about the genocidal violence, and perhaps speeding it up and increasing its scope. Then, the significant intervention that took place in the aftermath of the genocidal violence provided aid and comfort primarily to the killers, who set up operations primarily in neighboring Zaire, with consequences to which we shall soon turn our attention.

The Rwandan genocide, thus, was a hugely significant event in Africa toward which the United States exhibited the indifference that is characteristic of its foreign policy toward African states, perhaps especially in the post–Cold War period. Was this indifference indubitably shameful, egregious, unethical, totally regrettable? Would it have been ethical for the U.S. government to send American troops to Rwanda, risking and, in many cases, surely losing their lives, to support a mission of little relevance to the physical security or other national interests of the United States? Again, superficial appearances to the contrary, these are not easy questions to answer.

Zaire

In any case, there is little doubt that the events that unfolded in Rwanda in 1994 led to a crisis of even greater proportions (in terms of the number of human lives lost) in neighboring Zaire, to which the United States, as well as the international community, has paid relatively little attention. The collapse of the Mobutu regime, whose autocratic rule through kleptocracy we discussed earlier, finally occurred in 1997. Mobutu was replaced by Laurent Kabila, who came into power talking about establishing a new, democratic regime, in the country that he then renamed the Democratic Republic of the Congo (DRC). Kabila was helped into power by the governments of the neighboring states of Rwanda and Uganda. Rwanda's motives clearly stemmed from the genocidal violence in 1994, which ended—only after approximately 800,000 Tutsis had been slaughtered by the Hutus—with the Tutsis in control of the Rwandan government. Tens of thousands of Hutus, among them many perpetrators of the genocide against the Tutsis, then escaped into Zaire. From the point of view of Rwanda, the Mobutu government had offered a haven of protection for their Hutu enemies. Kabila, on the other hand, had cooperated with military actions during the rebellion against the Mobutu regime that resulted in the deaths of thousands of Hutus in Rwanda (Kumar 2001).

When Kabila came into control of the government of the Democratic Republic of the Congo, he brought with him many advisers from the government of Rwanda, which had been instrumental in bringing him to power. Kabila's movement had carried out rebellious activities against the Mobutu regime for decades, before he obtained crucial assistance from Rwandan sources. But the presence of Rwandan advisers in Kabila's new government angered many Congolese, apparently threatening Kabila's hold on power, so he cut his ties to the Rwandans. In response, in August of 1998 Rwandan forces, soon followed by forces from

Uganda, invaded the DRC, and a new war—this one with even more international overtones than the previous struggle against the Mobutu regime—was on (Fisher and Onishi 2000).

Very early on in this war, Kabila attracted the support of Angola and Zimbabwe, both of which sent troops. In fact, these allies' troops came to dominate many parts of the DRC that were nominally under the control of Kabila's central government. Other parts of the country were held by at least three rebel groups that managed to cooperate to some extent to achieve their joint aim of overthrowing the Kabila regime. The government of Burundi—where the Hutus and the Tutsis have a bloody history much like that in Rwanda—also sent troops into the DRC, not in support of or against the Kabila government, but in pursuit of Hutu rebels. Sudan, motivated partly out of antagonism toward its neighbor Uganda, also reportedly provided modest amounts of military support to the Kabila government in the 1990s. Angola and Zimbabwe also played a role in persuading Namibia to send troops into the Congo in support of Kabila. All in all, by 2000, at least six outside states had some 35,000 troops involved in the military action within the DRC, engaged in what became known as **"Africa's First World War"** (Fisher and Onishi 2000). Laurent Kabila was assassinated in 2001; power was assumed by his son, Joseph Kabila, who, after a transitional period, won a presidential election in 2006.

There have been several efforts to bring peace to the DRC, including a rather substantial peacekeeping force sent there by the United Nations. In fact, in 2004 it could be said that the UN peacekeeping force of around 10,000 troops in the DRC (MONUC) was the world's largest. However, Rwanda—whose invasion in 1998 provoked years of conflict that has never really ceased, and which has been responsible for an estimated 3 million deaths—has announced its intention to invade the DRC yet again, while the UN forces have already declared that they have no intention of attempting to resist another such invasion. Some analysts estimate that a UN peacekeeping force large enough to make a credible, possibly effective effort to create some semblance of stability in the DRC would require about 50,000 troops (*Economist* 2004b, 45). There is no prospect of such a force being created.

So, who or what is responsible for this immense disaster in the DRC, which has largely been ignored by the outside world? One analysis holds that the chaos and the violence over the past seven or eight years in the DRC are largely the product of the thirty-two years of rapacious, corrupt rule by the Mobutu regime. The implication of this conclusion is that the blame for the ongoing tragedy in the DRC should be placed on the shoulders of that regime, and on those outsiders who supported it—most importantly, the United States. But, as we have seen, one of the reasons that U.S. decision makers supported the Mobutu regime, whose shortcomings were obvious to any informed observer, was that they felt that Mobutu was the only ruler who could prevent the country from falling into bloody chaos—which has, in fact, ensued in the wake of his departure from the scene.

So, is Africa's First World War the result mainly of what Mobutu (and his supporters) did over those thirty-two years he was in power? Or is it, more precisely, a product of his removal from power? Perhaps only a stable democratic government could have provided a transfer of power within the DRC, or Zaire, that would *not* have led to a bloody and prolonged disaster of some sort. And it is not clear that anyone had the power or the knowledge required to bring such a government into being in Zaire, or the Democratic Republic of the Congo, during the time that Mobutu was in power, or in the years immediately after his removal, although there has been some movement in the direction of democracy in the country in recent years.

THE ERA OF THE GLOBAL WAR ON TERRORISM

One place to begin to examine the foreign policy of the George W. Bush administration with respect to Africa would be the bombings of a pair of embassies in Africa in 1998. Those bombings, occurring almost simultaneously, killed mostly Africans (over two hundred of them), but also twelve Americans. Subsequent legal proceedings have traced them to al-Qaeda operatives, who have been tried and convicted in trials in the United States (BBC News Online 2001).

The Bush administration came to power in 2001 without any high-priority goals with respect to Africa. By 2003, however, the epidemic of HIV/AIDs had caught its attention, and President Bush pledged in that year's State of the Union address to devote $15 billion to an "Emergency Relief Plan for AIDS," most of which was slated to be spent in sub-Saharan Africa. Just how deadly AIDS is in this part of the world is difficult to evaluate. Journalist Rian Malan (2003), for example, notes data indicating that some 30 million Africans have HIV/AIDS, but finds also that the figures are computer-generated estimates that appear to be exaggerated when compared to population statistics. Nevertheless, a UN report (UNAIDS, 2006) asserts that "Africa remains the global epicenter of the AIDS pandemic," and that in 2005 an estimated 930,000 adults and children in sub-Saharan Africa died from AIDS-related illness.

Even so, the pledge by the Bush administration to devote $15 billion dollars to this issue is apparently not being fulfilled, at least not in its entirety, despite the continuing enormity of the problem. In 2005 the administration claimed to have tripled foreign aid to sub-Saharan Africa, but the estimate provided in a report by the Brookings Institution (which is generally perceived to be a relatively liberal think tank) suggests that, by that time, the aid levels had only increased in real terms by 56 percent (Rice 2005).

Still, it is interesting, from the point of view of an analyst of American foreign policy, that the Bush administration would have made a pledge of such significant proportions to alleviate the AIDS problem in Africa in the first place. Only about 10 percent of African Americans voted for Bush in the elections of 2000 and 2004, so it seems unlikely that he made such a pledge, even in part, because he believed that it would evoke substantial support from African Americans in the voting booth. Perhaps—and this is admittedly speculation on the basis of very little evidence—the thinking of the Bush administration was that the campaign against AIDS in Africa is an important part of the global war on terrorism. African states ravaged by AIDS are more likely to become **failed states**, areas of anarchy and political disorder where al-Qaeda could set up training camps for new recruits. There are also signs that some religious conservatives, who are an important part of President Bush's winning coalition, are enthusiastic supporters of AIDS prevention efforts, especially those that encourage abstinence (instead of condoms) as a solution.

But, on another front, the Bush administration is exhibiting what has been the more typical American foreign policy response to Africa, especially since the end of the Cold War. The Darfur region of Sudan has in recent years suffered what was, until the devastation wrought by the tsunami in Asia at the end of 2004, the world's most serious humanitarian crisis. In 2003 non-Arab African groups started to rebel against the Arab central government of Sudan. In response, the government mobilized Arab militia—now commonly referred to as "Janjaweed"—that have allegedly committed large numbers of atrocities against black Africans living in the Darfur region. An estimate made at the beginning of 2005 by a U.S. commission survey suggests that the Sudanese military and the Janjaweed together have killed up to 200,000 in Darfur, while over a million people have been "internally displaced" and/or have escaped into neighboring Chad. In 2004 then–Secretary of State Colin Powell declared what is occurring in Darfur to be "genocide" (Knickmeyer 2005).

One might expect, in light of the consequences of their inaction in the face of the Rwandan genocide in 1994, that the major powers (including the United States) and international institutions would take quick action in Sudan. One would be wrong. One reason for the U.S. inaction in the current case is that the Sudanese regime has cultivated a positive relationship with the United States in the wake of the 9/11 attacks by cutting off support to various radical Islamic groups in the area and inviting the United States to play a leading role in mediating the ongoing civil war between the northern and southern regions of Sudan itself.

Another reason for U.S. inaction is, perhaps, that intervention in Darfur may be yet another case wherein the moral hazard of such interventions comes into play. A *New York Times* story in 2004 reported a Sudanese government official as saying that the rebels in the Darfur region have been encouraged to believe that ultimately "the U.S. and England will come here and occupy this country and they will give you everything and take off the Arabs from Sudan" (Anderson 2004, 61).

Of course, the U.S. military at present obviously has all the international commitments it can handle, and then some. It is no wonder that the Bush administration is not eager to take on another burdensome task of peacekeeping, or nation-building, in the vast stretches of Sudan, on top of those with which it is already struggling in Afghanistan and Iraq. Nevertheless, by 2007, as China modified somewhat its support of the Sudanese regime when it began to appear that such support might result in protests aimed at the 2008 Olympic Games (scheduled for Beijing), the Bush administration, too, finally made some tentative moves toward applying increased pressure on the Sudanese government to curb the genocidal activities of its supporters in the region.

CONCLUSION

That Africa does not typically occupy a place of high priority on the list of concerns for American foreign policy makers is certainly not a mystery from the point of view of rational political ambition theory. It was seen as a place worth competing for during the Cold War, but especially in the wake of the Vietnam War, Congress put severe limitations on how much effort and resources the United States could expend in pursuing anti-Soviet policies in such places as Angola, Mozambique, or Ethiopia. The one exception to this rule, during the Cold War, was South Africa. Continuation in power for Republican administrations is not likely to be threatened by African American voters, because so few of them vote for Republican presidential candidates in any case. The debilitating impact of this highly skewed distribution of presidential votes on the African American community's leverage on foreign policy is reinforced by the fact that, typically during the post–World War II era, that community has given a much higher priority to pressing domestic issues (such as civil rights) than to any foreign policy issues, regarding Africa or otherwise.

The African American scholar Ali Mazrui (2004, 59–61) has asked an interesting question: why does U.S. support for Liberia not approach its contributions to the defense of Israel? Racism in the United States may have something to do with it,[f] but there are other important factors that also help to account for the consistent patterns in U.S. foreign policy toward Africa. Among the more important of these factors is that African-American voters are not nearly so well-organized or fervent in their support for Liberia as Jewish Americans are on behalf of Israel. American presidents know that missteps—from the point of view of Jewish voters—on policies toward the Middle East can seriously endanger their hold on power. But U.S. policies with respect to Liberia are much less likely to have either negative or positive impacts on the political fortunes of the president, or on members of Congress.

Nevertheless, the case of South Africa did apparently energize significant numbers of energetic and influential African Americans, who succeeded in mobilizing significant support in Congress (over the firm objections of the Reagan administration) for the Comprehensive Anti-Apartheid Act of 1986. Absent this domestic pressure from African Americans and many of their supporters on the issue, the Reagan and first Bush administrations had, for the most part, let their policy with respect to South Africa be determined mostly by international pressures and by influence from domestic interest groups more concerned with combating Communism than in opposing apartheid in South Africa.

The end of the Cold War did, probably, make it significantly easier to end apartheid in South Africa. But it has also robbed Africa, as well as American domestic interest groups, of significant potential to arouse the concern of U.S. foreign policy makers on African problems. The United States (and virtually the entire international community) has stood by aimlessly and impotently as one disaster after another has unfolded in Africa in the past ten to fifteen years, in such places as Somalia, Ethiopia, Rwanda, and now Sudan. The second Bush administration has pledged $15 billion to deal with the ongoing AIDS crisis in southern Africa. But this initiative is more idiosyncratic and anomalous than characteristic of U.S. foreign policy in Africa, and it remains unclear at this point how much of the $15 billion will actually be delivered to those struggling to provide assistance to the hundreds of thousands in sub-Saharan Africa who are afflicted with HIV/AIDS.

---

f. For an analysis of racism's effects on this issue, as well as on several other aspects of U.S. foreign policy, see, for example, Hunt 1987, especially 46–91.

KEY CONCEPTS

RATIONAL POLITICAL AMBITION AND...
THE RELATIONSHIP WITH SUB-SAHARAN AFRICA

LESSONS LEARNED

☑ Africa has typically been a low priority for American foreign policy makers because the issues it presents generally have little impact on American elections. U.S. presidents are unlikely to suffer electoral consequences, for example, for bad policy choices on issues regarding Africa, because African American voters have typically been more focused on domestic issues. U.S. policy choices regarding Africa therefore tend to respond primarily to international constraints and incentives.

☑ The tendency for presidents to pay little attention to Africa—or to African American voters—is reinforced by those voters' tendency in recent decades to vote, by huge majorities, for Democratic presidential candidates. Neither Democratic nor Republican presidents can gain electoral benefits by making policy choices with respect to Africa in response to the preferences of African American voters, because they will apparently vote for the Democratic candidate for president in any case.

☑ U.S. presidents have been reluctant to take vigorous action in response to crises in Africa—such as the mass murder of Tutsis by Hutus in Rwanda, or the genocidal violence in the Darfur region of Sudan—because the electoral benefits to be gained from doing so are virtually nonexistent, while the domestic political costs of ostensibly humanitarian interventions—such as the action by U.S. forces in Somalia in the early 1990s—can be substantial.

☑ One African issue in which domestic political input in the United States played an apparently critical role in the foreign policy process was South Africa's apartheid system. African Americans were energized to demand action on this issue partly because it involved black-on-white as opposed to black-on-black conflict, and their impact was augmented by the fact that the vast majority of Americans shared their distaste for the apartheid system.

CHAPTER **12**

THE UNITED STATES IN ASIA

The Coming Clash with China?

ASIA IS THE MOST POPULOUS CONTINENT; NEARLY THREE-FIFTHS OF THE world's people live on its landmass. The two most populous countries, China and India, are located there, and when Indonesia (which ranks fourth, behind the United States) is added to those two, Asia can lay claim to three of the four largest states in the world (Central Intelligence Agency 2004; Eberstadt 2004).

Asia is also increasingly important economically. In 1990 Japan was the only Asian state ranked among the world's ten largest economies, coming in third behind the United States and the Soviet Union. By 2004, three of the four largest economies in the world were Asian: China, Japan, and India (in that order) follow the United States in this ranking (see Coutsoukis 2003; Central Intelligence Agency 2004).

Currently, the major focus of U.S. foreign policy is on the Middle East, and on the global war on terrorism. In the long run, however, U.S. foreign policy concerns may shift toward Asia, and, more specifically, to issues that are likely to arise between China and the United States. But there are other reasons for the increasing attention that Asia is likely to attract from U.S. foreign policy makers in the next decade or two. One of them is that Asia currently looks rather similar to Europe in the late nineteenth and early twentieth centuries.

IS EUROPE'S PAST ASIA'S FUTURE?

Until the current era, Asia was typically dominated by imperial powers. Only in recent decades are most Asian nations coming into their own as independent states and beginning to interact more intensively with each other. This increased political and economic interaction may

The future of international politics in the twenty-first century will depend a great deal on the evolution of the relationship between the United States and China, two of the world's most powerful states. On October 20, 2006, U.S. Secretary of State Condoleezza Rice spoke with Chinese president Hu Jintao during a meeting in the Great Hall of the People in Beijing.

prove beneficial. Increased economic integration, for example, can be advantageous for most of the economies of the region, but increased intensity of interaction has its dangers, too.

Many of these dangers are highlighted in a comparison of Asia's current status with that of Europe at the beginning of the twentieth century. There was, at that time, quite a bit of optimism that increased trade and interactions of other types, too, would lead to peaceful, dynamic relationships among the most important states on the European continent (see, for example, Angell 1913). Instead, political and economic tensions in 1914 led to (or at least preceded) what was the bloodiest interstate war in history. And in spite of the best efforts of statesmen from all the most powerful states in the world to do what was necessary afterward to avoid any more such tragedies, Europe was at the heart of World War II, as well.

Is it likely that modern Asia will repeat that history? One of the apparent sources of tension in twentieth-century Europe involved changes in the distribution of power among the most significant states in the region. Similarly, Asia now has many states going through dramatic changes in terms of population and economic growth. For example, in 1975, Japan's population was three times that of South Korea, but current projections suggest that, by 2025, South Korea's population will be about 40 percent as large as Japan's. If South Korea should in the meantime reunite with North Korea, the new Korea's population would be 60 percent that of Japan's. In 1975 Vietnam's population was larger than that of Thailand by 7 million people (48 million vs. 41 million); by 2025, since Vietnam's population is growing more rapidly, its advantage over Thailand will expand to over 25 million. Finally—and most important—between 1975 and 2025 China's population is expected to grow by nearly 50 percent (from 930 million to 1.4 billion), while India's population will more than double, from 620 million to 1.3 billion (see Eberstadt 2004, 9).

Such changes will not necessarily lead to tensions and war. But Japan attacked China twice in the twentieth century, and Koreans also have bitter memories of military occupation by the Japanese. India and China have already fought one war (in 1962), and it is clear that one reason India has acquired nuclear weapons is to protect itself from future aggression from that regional rival. China is sufficiently powerful that it may, in fact, come to dominate the continent in a peaceful process, but, according to Aaron Friedberg (2000a, 152), "Indonesia and Vietnam have repeatedly demonstrated an inclination to balance and contain China. . . ." And, again, China's advantage over India is probably dwindling.

On the other hand, as Friedberg points out, Asia's future may not resemble Europe's war-torn past, because Asia is different from Europe in many ways. While most of Europe's larger states are closely packed together, and not separated by natural barriers, many of the most important Asian states are entirely surrounded by water (Japan and Indonesia), or separated by forbidding mountain ranges (China and India). In Asia, as one analyst puts it, "distances between the major capitals are far greater than in Europe, and the powers do not jostle against one another in the same way" (Richardson 1994–95; cited in Friedberg 2000a).

Then, too, it seems possible that the "liberal trinity" of democracy, trade, and international organizations (identified in Russett and Oneal 2001) will work its pacifying wonders in Asia, where several states have become or are becoming more democratic and more engaged in trade with each other, and where international organizations such as **Asia-Pacific Economic Cooperation (APEC)** and the **Association of South-East Asian Nations**

(ASEAN) seem to be becoming more institutionalized and influential. Finally, Asian states may not fight each other in future wars because they will have learned from Europe's sad history in the twentieth century.

But there is no guarantee that any of these factors will produce a peaceful future for Asia. Developments in military technology, such as ballistic missiles, are diluting the impact of geographic barriers to conflict. Democracy, trade, and international organizations may be important pacifying factors, but their effects are not certain for a number of reasons: it may be a long time before Asia is uniformly democratic; very high levels of intra-European trade (even by current standards) in 1914 did not prevent World War I; and international organizations did not become well-established and influential in Europe until after the two world wars had been fought. And, while Asians have the potential benefit of learning from Europe's historical mistakes, Friedberg reminds us (157), "there are also reasons to be wary of placing too much faith in the collective human capacity for learning." At the beginning of the twentieth century, many Europeans were convinced that "war was idiotic, outmoded, even obsolete," but this belief did not prevent them from falling into World War I. And, having experienced that catastrophe, they embarked upon yet another massive conflict only a little more than twenty years later.

Meanwhile, perhaps the greatest potential for serious interstate conflict in Asia in the coming decades will arise in its relationships with states outside the region, rather than from interactions among them. John Mearsheimer's argument (2001a, 168) that "especially powerful states usually pursue regional hegemony" is clearly relevant here, for China surely seems to be in the process of becoming an especially powerful state. Should it choose to enlarge the scope and strength of its influence within Asia in the coming decades, this general aim could easily bring it into conflict with the United States. Specifically, China may be tempted at some point to rein in what it sees as its "renegade province" in Taiwan, and any attempt to do so by military force is likely to provoke a serious response from Taiwan's main protector, the United States (Carpenter 2006). Thus, this chapter will focus on one factor that appears crucial to an understanding of the future of Asia: the relationship between China and the United States.

THE UNITED STATES ENTERS ASIA

As we discussed in chapter 2, U.S. military units were engaged in rather substantial conflicts in China as early as the 1840s, and they continued to be deployed there in virtually every decade after that. Then, too, Commodore Matthew C. Perry sailed into Japanese waters with small naval forces in 1853 and 1854, signed a treaty of friendship with the shogun, and began the process of opening up Japan to trade with the United States, as well as such other Western powers as Britain, Russia, and Holland. But the first continuing and sustained U.S. presence in Asia came about as a result of a much less pleasant experience, the Spanish-American War, at the end of which the United States took possession of the Philippines from the Spanish.

The United States had declared war against Spain, ostensibly over a rebellion in Cuba, in 1898. Originally, Filipino forces were organized under Emilio Aguinaldo to rebel, as allies of the United States, against the Spanish colonialists in their island territory. In May of 1896, the United States made a significant contribution to ending the Spanish colonial control of the

Philippines when Commodore George Dewey steamed into Manila Bay and sank all of Spain's fleet. In this "battle," 380 Spanish sailors lost their lives, while the U.S. Navy suffered only one fatality (Library of Congress 1991a).

After the Spanish had been defeated, the Filipinos declared their independence on June 12, 1898, with a declaration modeled on that of the United States. By September, a constitution for the newly independent country had been approved, but the Treaty of Paris, which ended the Spanish-American War, ceded control of the Philippines to the United States. President McKinley reportedly prayed for divine guidance on how to deal with this situation and then decided that it was the duty of the United States to "educate the Filipinos, and uplift and Christianize them." Additionally, "expansionists" in the United States had mounted a campaign to keep control of the Philippines, apparently inspired by the idea that they "could serve as a portal to the rich trade of the Orient" (De Conde 1963, 351).

The movement to establish a free and independent Philippines was obviously on a collision course with the U.S. intention to educate, uplift, and Christianize the Filipinos, and war broke out between the advocates of these opposing causes in February of 1899. The war lasted two years, although insurgents continued to fight in various parts of the far-flung country well into 1903. The United States sent 126,000 troops to subdue this war of independence. Over 4,000 of them died in combat, while 16,000 Filipino solders lost their lives, and some 200,000 civilians died from famine and disease during the war. The Muslim portion of the Philippines, Mindanao, was not brought under control for some time, and U.S. military rule was maintained there until 1914 (Library of Congress 1991b).

Having secured a stepping-stone into the Orient, the United States soon became involved in a war in China, where it was something of a latecomer. Foreign powers had been establishing spheres of influence in China for some decades during the nineteenth century, in a process that was accelerated by China's loss in a war with Japan in 1895. By the turn of the new century, Austria, France, Great Britain, Italy, Japan, and Russia had all claimed exclusive trading rights with respect to "their" particular portions of China. But, newly interested in trade with China in the wake of its acquisition of the Philippines, and taking advantage of what it hoped would be increased influence resulting from the potential of the Philippines as a base for its military forces, the United States in 1899 declared an **Open Door Policy** with respect to China. Secretary of State John Hay sent diplomatic notes to all the powers with exclusive spheres of influence in China, suggesting that all states should have equal trading rights everywhere in China. Ostensibly, the other powers accepted the idea of an Open Door, but their agreement was more formal than real.

Meanwhile, in China itself there was increasing anger against the domination by foreigners. One manifestation of this anger was the rise of a secret society called "Righteous Harmonious Fists," who became known as "Boxers" because of their emphasis on the martial arts. Mounting what became known as the **Boxer Rebellion**, they adopted the aim of expelling the foreigners. In 1900 the Boxers surrounded a number of foreign legations in Beijing and remained there for two months. The situation began to look desperate, even catastrophic, until eight states with trading interests in China, including the United States, finally managed to send a rescue force, which not only freed the legations from the surrounding Boxers, but "looted the capital and even ransacked the Forbidden City"

(Buschini, 2000).[a] President Theodore Roosevelt defended U.S. participation in the suppression of this nativist rebellion by invoking the need "to secure for our merchants, farmers and wage-workers the benefits of the open market" (De Conde 1963, 364).

The humiliation involved in the suppression of the Boxer Rebellion, added to decades of foreign domination, proved to be a crucial step toward the end of 2,000 years of imperial rule in China. The Ching Dynasty never recovered from it; by 1911, Sun Yat-sen was leading a Republican Revolution. In 1912 Sun was inaugurated as the new provisional president of China, but he was not able to consolidate his rule, so power passed almost immediately to a military leader, Yuan Shikai. Yuan's opponents, including Sun, then unified under the banner of a new political party, the **Kuomintang** (the National People's Party), and won a majority of seats in the Chinese parliament in 1913. Even so, Yuan intimidated that party into electing him president.

But Yuan, too, failed in the effort to unify the country behind his leadership, even though he did successfully outlaw the Kuomintang, disband the parliament, and promulgate a new constitution that, in effect, made him president for life. In fact, he had himself declared king in 1915, but this move just provoked even more rebellion, increasing the power of various warlords. Yuan Shikai died in 1916.

This internal disunity invited continued domination by foreigners, and Japan increasingly took advantage of the situation. In the 1920s, in fact, Japan developed a relationship with China that was reminiscent of that between the United States and Latin America. Sun Yat-sen became so disillusioned in his attempts to gain Chinese independence from the Japanese and other foreign powers that in the mid-1920s he turned to the revolutionary government of the Soviet Union for assistance. William Keylor (1996, 229) reports what happened next:

> In 1924 Russian representatives of the Communist International (Comintern) were dispatched to Canton [where Sun Yat-sen had established a government] to reorganize Sun's political movement, the Kuomintang, into a disciplined revolutionary organization capable of leading a mass movement in alliance with the small Chinese Communist party that had been founded three years earlier.

But Sun Yat-sen died in 1925, and it was at this point that the United States became more deeply involved in Chinese domestic and foreign politics, in a manner whose ramifications continue to reverberate into the twenty-first century. Sun's successor was Chiang Kai-shek, who proclaimed the Kuomintang—with him at its head—as a national government on July 4, 1926. He turned to the United States to help consolidate his rule in 1927, and, also in that year, he married a daughter of a wealthy Christian businessman from Shanghai, who had been educated in the United States, at Wellesley College. Madame Chiang converted her husband to Christianity, and helped to solidify ties between him and the loyal, fervent supporters in the United States who were to play a key role in determining his fate over the next two or three decades. At the same time, Chiang broke his ties with the Communist Party in China,

---

a. An historical analysis published by the U.S. Navy concludes: "The United States was able to play a significant role in suppressing the Boxer Rebellion because of the large number of American ships and troops deployed in the Philippines as a result of the U.S. conquest of the islands during the Spanish American War (1898) and subsequent insurgent activity" (Department of the Navy 2000).

ruthlessly suppressing it. He also achieved some success against the foreign domination of Japan, by reuniting Manchuria with China, for example, in 1928. In that year, the United States granted China most-favored-nation status, and by the early 1930s, it had surpassed Japan as China's leading supplier of imports (Keylor 1996, 229–230).

However, Chiang Kai-shek's apparent attempt to develop ties to the United States in order to escape domination by the Japanese backfired, at least in the short run. In response, the Japanese blew up part of a Japanese-owned railroad in Manchuria, blamed Chinese terrorists, and used the incident as an excuse for invading and occupying the entire province of Manchuria. The Japanese then proceeded to put the last Chinese emperor of the Ching Dynasty, Pu Yi, at the head of a new state they named Manchukuo. Only Germany and Italy recognized this new state, while the League of Nations censured Japan for its actions. But Japan just withdrew from the League, and solidified its hold on the former Chinese province.

Japan's effort to dominate China escalated when its forces attacked Beijing in 1937, precipitating, to their surprise, a full-fledged war. In other words, the Japanese had not expected the Kuomintang regime to put up much of a fight. But fight it did, even though the Japanese ultimately captured Shanghai, as well as Nanjing. The attack and occupation of the latter city— typically referred to as the **Rape of Nanjing**—was particularly brutal. Historian Michael P. Riccards (2000, 93–94) provides this graphic account:

> The Japanese used Chinese prisoners for bayonet practice, raped thousands of women (often in schools and nunneries), and created their first wartime "facility for sexual comfort," forcing innocent Chinese women into prostitution, referred to in Japanese as "public toilets." Japanese soldiers disemboweled women, cut off their breasts, and nailed them to walls. Fathers were forced to rape their daughters and sons their mothers as other family members looked on. Chinese were hung by their tongues on iron hooks, roasted alive, and ripped apart by German shepherds. It was said that even Nazis in the city were shocked by what they saw—an extraordinary commentary indeed.

In spite of this unspeakable brutality, the Japanese had a difficult time subduing the whole of China. Edwin Reischauer (1964, 188) explains: "[T]he war reached a stalemate because the Chinese, although pushed more into the more remote and backward parts of the country and cut off from foreign aid and the industrial production of their own cities, simply refused to surrender."

According to an authoritative, widely recognized source of data on interstate wars since 1816 (Small and Singer 1982, 90), the **Sino-Japanese War**, which began on July 7, 1937, resulted in the deaths of 1 million military personnel (250,000 Japanese and 750,000 Chinese) and ended on December 7, 1941. It is quite apparent, however, that this massive military conflict between Japan and China did not come to an end on that day, which also figures in Small and Singer's data set as the date on which China entered World War II.[b] On the ground, the Sino-Japanese War that began in 1937 thus formed a seamless web with China's conflict with Japan during World War II. In light of these data, it can be argued that the notion that World War II began with Germany's invasion of Poland in 1939 is a Eurocentric

---

b. China lost 1.35 million more soldiers during World War II (Small and Singer 1982, 91). It is safe to assume that many of them were lost in conflict with the Japanese, while millions more Chinese civilians died under the brutal occupation of the Japanese.

and arguably illogical view. In fact, that global conflict can more objectively be said to have started with Japan's invasion of China in 1937.

Japan's military actions and its occupation of China during World War II brought the Kuomintang into a closer relationship with the United States. That wartime connection tended to focus on Chiang Kai-shek, the head of the Kuomintang, and "Vinegar" Joe Stillwell, the U.S. commander of what became known as the "China-India-Burma" theatre, whose interactions are famously recounted by the historian Barbara Tuchman in *Stillwell and the American Experience in China* (1970). Although the United States devoted millions of dollars to the effort to support Chiang in his war against the Japanese, most of those resources were allocated instead to the struggle against a threat that Chiang apparently saw as more dangerous to his hold on power. Part of the problem was personal antagonism (discussed in detail by Tuchman) between Stillwell and Chiang, but a more fundamental cause of friction was the fact that Chiang did not regard the Japanese as his most important enemy. He apparently calculated that the Japanese would, ultimately, be defeated for him by the United States. Meanwhile, the enemy he most feared—and the conflict toward which he directed most of his energy and resources (even those provided to him by the United States for the battle against the Japanese)—was the Communists under Mao Zedong.[c]

In 1944 a Japanese offensive in China brought the army of the Kuomintang close to defeat. At that point, Chiang effectively lobbied for the removal of Joe Stillwell, who was replaced. The situation then stabilized, but what ultimately saved Chiang Kai-shek and the Chinese Nationalist government from annihilation by the Japanese was the U.S. nuclear bombing of Hiroshima and Nagasaki in 1945. After that, the Japanese troops in China surrendered.

THE CHINESE CIVIL WAR AND THE ROLE OF THE UNITED STATES

By the end of World War II, China had experienced decades of violent political strife and instability. But the war's end brought it no peace, even though both the Soviets and the United States tried, initially, to bring about cooperation and reconciliation between the Communists and the Nationalists. In fact, Chiang Kai-shek got along surprisingly well with Communists— outside of China. In 1945, for example, he sent 180,000 troops into the northern part of Vietnam to support Ho Chi Minh's regime. The Soviet Union rather openly called for the Nationalists to take over in Manchuria, and in 1946 Chiang wrote to an American envoy in China that "Stalin says the so-called Chinese Communists are nothing but bandits and he has nothing whatever to do with them." Also, Stalin invited both Chiang and his eldest son to visit him in Moscow, where Stalin pressed his case for a peaceful coexistence between the Nationalists and the Communists in China (Riccards 2000, 109–112).

The United States agreed to sell $1 billion of surplus war supplies to Chiang Kai-shek in 1946 (Riccards 2000, 109), and President Truman asked Congress for $570 million more to

---

c. "Throughout the war, however, the generalissimo had seemed more concerned with the Chinese Communists than with the marauding Japanese army. Indeed, in the end, that neglect cost him significant support among many patriotic and nationalist Chinese" (Riccards 2000, 109).

support the Chinese government in 1948 (Purifoy 1976, 27). Still, the U.S. government was never very enthusiastic in its support for Chiang (even though he did have very loyal supporters in Congress), in spite of its doubts and fears about the Communists under Mao Zedong. In fact, the Communists were better organized, more popular, and less corrupt than Chiang's Kuomintang, and they had come out of World War II with a reputation as better patriots in the struggle against the Japanese. The United States, therefore, was willing to provide military equipment and economic support to Chiang, but no active military support. In early 1949, the Communists gained control of Beijing, and, by that year's end, Chiang Kai-shek and hundreds of thousands of Nationalist troops had left the mainland. Chiang named Taipei, Taiwan, an island off the shore of mainland China, as the temporary capital of the Republic of China.

Republicans in Congress were soon asking "Who lost China?" They argued that President Truman and the State Department were to blame. Riccards (2000, 121) explains: "Added to Truman's problems was a well organized 'China Lobby,' funded in part in the United States by Chiang and his American-educated wife, which embraced missionaries, businessmen, and others with interests in China." In short, Chiang's dramatic defeat, the efforts by his friends in the United States to help him recover from that defeat, and the tendency of members of Congress to exploit Chiang's defeat for their own domestic political purposes laid the groundwork for an important relationship between Taiwan and the United States that continues, somewhat anomalously, into the twenty-first century.

THE KOREAN WAR AND THE U.S.-CHINESE RELATIONSHIP

During World War II, the Soviet Union and the United States decided to place Korea under an international trusteeship, in which the Soviets took responsibility for the portion north of the 38th Parallel, and the Americans were in charge south of that parallel. Tension between the two halves of Korea soon followed, as each half threatened to seize the other and so reunify the country. In June of 1950, in an apparent attempt to carry out its particular unification plan, North Korea attacked South Korea. Who made the decision to launch this attack and why are controversial questions.

At the time, it was commonly assumed that the attack was Joseph Stalin's idea, although some analysts believed that Mao Zedong, the newly installed leader of China, was the main inspiration for the attack. Perhaps the preponderance of evidence discovered in recent decades suggests that Kim Il Sung, the leader of North Korea, effectively maneuvered in such a way as to attract the support of both the Soviet Union and China for what was essentially his original idea. Historian James Matray (quoted in Steele 2000) concludes, for example, that "Kim Il Sung displayed remarkable political talent, as he manipulated his patrons into supporting his plan for invasion. He was able to persuade Stalin and Mao that his forces would achieve victory before the United States could intervene...."

In a speech to the National Press Club in Washington, D.C., in January 1950, Secretary of State Dean Acheson (1969, 357) asserted that the "defense perimeter" of the United States "runs along the Aleutians to Japan and then goes to the Ryukus." (The Aleutians are a string of islands that extend south from Alaska, while the Ryuku Islands extend south from mainland Japan toward Taiwan, see map 12.1.) During the presidential election campaign of 1952, Republican candidate Dwight Eisenhower charged that Acheson's speech had "invited" the

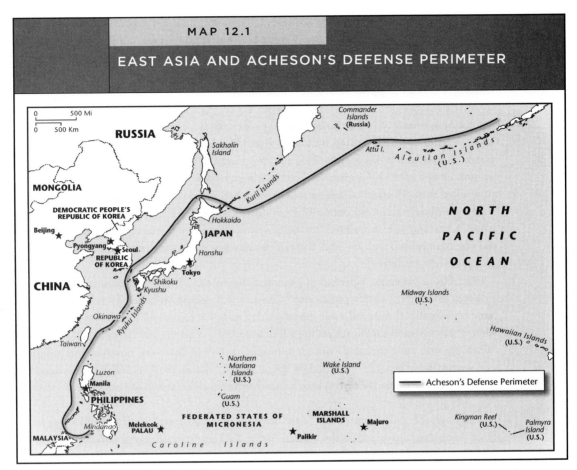

MAP 12.1

EAST ASIA AND ACHESON'S DEFENSE PERIMETER

In a January 1950 speech, Secretary of State Dean Acheson referred to a U.S. "defense perimeter" that apparently left South Korea in an area of lesser concern for the United States. (North Korea attacked South Korea in June 1950.) The defense perimeter, as defined by Dean Acheson, is shown on this map.

attack by the North Koreans on the South, presumably because South Korea lies beyond the designated perimeter of U.S. protection. Acheson vigorously denied that the speech had any such effect, pointing out (691) that his comment also "excluded" such states as Thailand, India, and Pakistan, and that he never specifically designated Korea as of no interest to the United States.[d]

In any case, the North Korean attack was initially successful, and, as it soon became clear that South Korea might fall, the United States decided to come to its defense. Fortuitously, the Soviet Union was boycotting the UN Security Council at the time (in protest against the exclusion of the new Communist regime in China from the Security Council), and the Soviets' absence allowed the United States to win a Security Council vote to respond to North

---

d. Historian James Matray also asserts that declassified Soviet and Chinese documents available before 1989 contain no indication that Acheson's comments played any role in the deliberations about Korea; see Steele 2000.

Korea's move against South Korea. Officially, therefore, the response came from the United Nations, even though the United States contributed by far the largest number of troops to the multinational force.[e] Also, this military intervention was described as a "police action," not as a war, because Truman chose not to seek a declaration of war from Congress in advance of sending American troops to the Korean theatre.

After a struggle, the American troops began to take the initiative, advancing to a point near the northern border of North Korea, where the Yalu River separated that country from China. There, despite several warnings by China that it would not stand "idly by" while American troops approached its border, the U.S. military forces were surprised by a determined intervention by two to three hundred thousand Chinese troops. Partly because the element of surprise aided their efforts, the Chinese military forces enjoyed spectacular early successes, which the U.S. military countered only with great difficulty. By 1952, a prolonged stalemate was in place. According to History Net (2004): "With victory no longer in sight, public support for the war plummeted, and in 1952 Truman decided not to run for reelection rather than risk an almost certain defeat."

Republican candidate Eisenhower promised during the 1952 presidential campaign to go to Korea to bring the conflict to an end.[f] Once he was elected, however, Eisenhower's administration allegedly threatened, near the beginning of 1953, to expand the war into China, and even to use nuclear weapons unless the Chinese agreed to end the war (Hinton 1966, 26–27). When the war was concluded with an armistice, in July of that year, however, the promised end seemed anticlimactic: "Dwarfed by the total U.S. victory in World War II, the negotiated settlement in Korea seemed to many observers to be a defeat and at best a draw" (History Net 2004).

Although the United States lost 54,000 soldiers in the Korean War, the conflict was largely an Asian tragedy, in which the United States, by comparison, played an almost marginal role. The South Koreans suffered 415,000 battle deaths, and the North Koreans 520,000, while around 900,000 Chinese soldiers were killed. (North Korea's losses amounted to 536 per 10,000 of its total population, while the ratio for the United States was 3.6 per 10,000; see Singer and Small 1982, 93).

Why did the United States devote so many resources to the defense of South Korea against the forces of the North, who were ultimately joined by the Chinese?[g] It is quite possible that international strategic and political considerations were primary to any explanation of the Truman administration's decision to resist the North Korean invasion, for the World War II

---

e. At its peak strength, the UN force consisted of 302,483 troops from the United States, and only a little over 39,000 from such nations as the United Kingdom, Canada, and Turkey; see History Net 2004.

f. In his October 1952 speech, Eisenhower specifically said: "Where will a new administration begin? It will begin with its President taking a simple, firm resolution. That resolution will be: to forego the diversions of politics and to concentrate on the job of ending the Korean War—until that job is honorably done. That job requires a personal trip to Korea. I shall make that trip. Only in that way could I learn how best to serve the American People in the cause of peace. I shall go to Korea!" (Wyszynski 2002).

g. The Soviet military may also have been deeply and directly involved in the Korean War. Historian Stanley Sandler asserts that 67,000 Soviet air and ground personnel fought in North Korea, most wearing Chinese uniforms; see Steele 2000.

lesson that dictators who experience success in one aggressive move will soon follow with others was fresh in the minds of many American decision makers in June of 1950.

But domestic political considerations were almost certainly influential as well—at least in the back of the mind of Harry Truman, who was perfectly aware that he and his Democratic Party were vulnerable to criticism regarding the recent "loss" of China to the global forces of Communism. A failure by the Democratic administration to resist quite blatant aggression by the Communist regime of North Korea against the non-Communist South Koreans would have provided a very tempting target for the Republicans in the 1952 election. In the event, however, the war had become so unpopular by 1952 that it may be persuasively argued that Truman's decision to intervene in Korea cost him his office, rather than prolonging his time in power. But, as we established in discussing Lyndon Johnson's losing strategy regarding the Vietnam War, rational political ambition theory does not assert that leaders of states consistently make decisions that will preserve their hold on power, but that they consistently base their decisions, in important part, on their desire to stay in power, consistently selecting policy options that they *believe* will keep them in power.

Furthermore, in this case, in spite of the fact that the unpopularity of the Korean War may have been an important factor in Truman's loss of power, it is not clear that, had he instead accepted North Korea's annexation of South Korea, that course of action (or inaction) would have made it possible for Truman to win a second full term in 1952. For all we know, Congress might, in the wake of a North Korean takeover of South Korea, have impeached the president. Or, public opinion might have reacted so negatively to such a turn of events that Truman would have had even less chance of winning the 1952 election in a time of peace, than he did while the unpopular war continued.

THE EVOLVING COLD WAR RELATIONSHIP BETWEEN THE UNITED STATES, CHINA, AND THE SOVIET UNION

The U.S.-China relationship during the Cold War responded in important ways to both parties' relationships to the Soviet Union. At the beginning, shortly after Mao's Communists came to power in China, the relationship between the United States and China appeared to be hopelessly hostile and conflict-ridden. The United States had political, military, and emotional ties to the Nationalist regime that was now ensconced on the island of Taiwan, and it loathed the ideology of the mainland regime in "Red China." Even worse, the fact that the most populous state in the world had changed from a U.S. ally to an implacable enemy that was closely allied with the state that appeared most dangerous and inimical to U.S. interests, the Soviet Union, made Red China appear just that much more despicable.

The relationship between the Soviet Union and Red China at the beginning of the Cold War, on the other hand, appeared to be solidly based on ideological compatibility, as well as a common opposition to the United States and the rest of the bourgeois capitalist, democratic world. Having come into power in October of 1949, Mao traveled to Moscow to meet with Stalin in December, and he stayed there—at what had to be a crucial time for his newly successful Communist revolution—for two whole months. The main product of the visit and his discussions with Stalin was a **Treaty of Friendship, Alliance and Mutual Assistance**. The bottom line of this treaty was a $300 million loan from the Soviets to the revolutionary regime in China. Apparently, however, Mao considered this a rather paltry sum; he had asked for ten times that amount. According to David Floyd (1963, 12–13): "There can be no doubt but that he was disappointed and it seems probable that this first and only meeting between Mao and Stalin was not the happiest.... Mao left Moscow a wiser and probably a sadder man."

None of this interplay was visible to U.S. policymakers, whose relations with both the Soviet Union and China were still antagonistic. The U.S.-Chinese opposition remained focused on the status of Chiang Kai-shek's regime on the island of Taiwan. In the waning months of the Korean War, President Eisenhower had "unleashed" Chiang—by removing any restrictions on offensive operations the Nationalist Chinese might contemplate against the mainland—in order to increase the pressure on the Communists to agree to an armistice. In 1954 the United States increased military aid to Chiang, and encouraged him to occupy the offshore islands of Quemoy and Matsu; by July of that same year, Mao was talking about liberating Taiwan, and the Communist regime began shelling Quemoy. In retaliation, the United States signed a treaty of alliance with Taiwan, and Congress passed a resolution authorizing the president to use American military force to defend the islands. In March of 1955, the ill will generated by this and other issues reached the point that Secretary of State John Foster Dulles threatened to retaliate with nuclear weapons if the Chinese Communists were to engage in armed aggression against the Nationalist Chinese regime (Hinton 1966, 28–29).

As the 1950s progressed, the tension over Quemoy and Matsu refused to die. By 1957, the Americans were supplying to the Nationalists missiles armed with nuclear weapons capable of reaching the mainland. Chiang increased to 100,000 the number of Nationalist troops stationed on the coastal islands, and by 1958, Communist China resumed heavy shelling of Quemoy in an apparent attempt to dislodge those troops. The escalation continued, as the United States then sent American planes to airlift supplies to the Nationalist troops on the offshore islands, while the American Seventh Fleet provided cover and protection to a Nationalist convoy carrying reinforcements to the islands. At a particularly tense point in this crisis, the U.S. State Department saw fit to warn Communist China that the United States would intervene militarily should Mao's regime make an attempt to recover Quemoy and Matsu (Keylor 1996, 362). All in all, it is reasonable to conclude, with Strobe Talbott (2003, 3), that "after the birth of the People's Republic of China (PRC), that country's relationship with the United States was one of the most antagonistic on the face of the earth, and one of the most antagonistic in history."

Meanwhile, although the escalating tensions between the United States and Communist China might logically have encouraged increasing cooperation between the Communist regimes in China and the Soviet Union, the relationship between Khrushchev and Mao, instead, deteriorated. There was a brief honeymoon period after the death of Stalin in March of 1953; since Stalin had never been very supportive of the Communists in China—and, in fact, had on numerous occasions shown a clear preference for Chiang Kai-shek—the Chinese hoped that Stalin's death might lead to an improvement in their ties to the Soviets. And, in the mid-1950s, Nikita Khrushchev indeed proved to be more forthcoming in the provision of economic aid to China than Stalin had been. Floyd (1963, 31) sums up these early signs:

"In short, at the beginning of 1956, it was reasonable to regard the Moscow-Peking axis as a powerful factor in world politics, which was likely to grow stronger rather than break up."

But in spite of these appearances to the contrary, the relationship between the Soviet Union and the PRC became increasingly antagonistic during the 1950s and on into the 1960s. The beginnings of serious difficulties between the two may be traced to the 20th Congress of the Communist Party in the Soviet Union in 1956. At that meeting, Khrushchev denounced the violent and oppressive excesses of Stalin and moved toward a policy of **peaceful coexistence** with the West and the United States. Up to that point, the official stance of the predominant form of Marxist ideology had been that armed conflict between the Communist world and the capitalist world was inevitable. The Chinese government's initial reactions to the denunciation of Stalin were positive, but in the end, the Chinese could not accept the policy of peaceful coexistence, which Khrushchev regarded as a necessary accommodation of Marxist ideology to the age of nuclear weapons, in which a war between the capitalist and Communist worlds would mean the end of both.

In 1957, when Mao issued his "let a hundred flowers bloom" statement, inviting some movement toward freedom of expression in the People's Republic, the result was such an outpouring of harsh criticism of the Chinese Communist Party that serious conflict emerged between the right and left wings of the party. Mao took the leadership of the left wing, which emerged victorious. That left-wing faction was much encouraged by the Soviets' progress in military technology, especially their ballistic missiles and nuclear weapons. Mao expressed this confidence in a speech at the end of 1957, in which he declared that these technological developments signaled an era in which the "East Wind" (the Communist movement) was destined to prevail over the "West Wind" (the capitalists), and that the Communist camp should take advantage of its strength by seizing the offshore islands of Quemoy and Matsu. When China began to bombard Quemoy in August of 1958, however, the Soviets did not offer support at the height of the ensuing crisis. In fact, says Floyd (1963, 71), the crisis "drew attention to the Russians' reluctance to commit themselves in a military sense to support for the Chinese Communists' aspirations. It made clear that the Chinese Communists had not received nuclear weapons from the Russians...."

In the following year, the Chinese Communist regime ruthlessly suppressed a rebellion in the province of Tibet (which had been forcibly annexed by Beijing in 1950), a move that ultimately led to border clashes with India. Keylor (1996, 363) describes what happened next: "Suddenly in September 1959..., Moscow infuriated Beijing by declaring its neutrality in the Sino-Indian dispute, and then announcing its intention to grant New Delhi a loan much larger than any that had ever been furnished to" China. This betrayal added fuel to an ideological battle that had broken out between the Soviets and the Chinese over a domestic economic reform campaign launched by Mao, based on agricultural communes and backyard iron-smelting operations, that became known as the **Great Leap Forward**. Khrushchev ultimately denounced the Great Leap as ill-advised, and he was clearly justified in this opinion: Mao's campaign created such economic chaos that perhaps the most massive famine in the history of the world resulted; as many as 30 million died.

In the wake of the disagreement over this ideological issue, Khrushchev rescinded his pledge to aid the Chinese Communists' efforts to develop nuclear weapons. He had obviously become convinced that Mao's regime could not be trusted with such powerful weapons. Nevertheless, the Chinese managed to develop nuclear weapons by 1964.

In the early 1960s, the Soviets terminated military aid to China altogether. When war broke out between China and India in 1962, the Soviet Union declared its neutrality. Then, the interactions between the United States, China, and the Soviet Union during the war in Vietnam (discussed in chapter 8) tended to increase the tension between the two Communist powers, while decreasing hostilities between the United States and China. Relations between the Communist powers deteriorated further when the Soviet Union invaded Czechoslovakia in 1968 and announced the **Brezhnev Doctrine**, which justified such interventions by Communist Bloc countries in any of their number that might be threatened by subversion.

The momentum toward the breaking apart of the Communist powers and *rapprochement* between the United States and China continued as serious border clashes broke out between the Soviet Union and China in 1969,[h] and the U.S. secretary of state, Henry Kissinger, made a series of secret visits to Beijing in the early 1970s. Just how antagonistic the relationship between the Soviet Union and China had become was dramatically illustrated at about this time when, as Talbot (2003, 4) reports, "the Brezhnev regime actually sent a signal to the Nixon administration asking if the United States would tolerate—and perhaps even welcome—a Soviet preemptive strike against the Chinese nuclear facilities." There are even rumors that the Soviet Union was considering a nuclear strike on those Chinese nuclear facilities.

These escalating tensions between the Soviet Union and China were clearly the most important factor pushing the United States and China to improve their relations with each other. As Kissinger himself has pointed out (1979, 693, 746): "China's cautious overtures to us were caused by the rapid and relentless Soviet military buildup in the Far East.... That China and the United States would seek rapprochement in the early 1970s was inherent in the world environment." In addition, although no prior U.S. president could have risked the domestic political consequences of conciliatory moves toward the regime in Red China, President Nixon was a conservative Republican who had been prominently anti-Communist throughout his political career; he was quite safe against accusations of being "soft on communism." In other words, Nixon could move toward a dramatic breakthrough in U.S.-Chinese relations without endangering his hold on power in the United States.

So, President Nixon made his famous trip to China in 1972, beginning a period of relatively friendly relations between the United States and the People's Republic of China, based more on common suspicions of the Soviet Union, perhaps, than anything else. Meanwhile—and rather unexpectedly to some—the Nixon administration was also able to establish détente with the Soviet Union, sign an arms control agreement with the Soviets (the **Strategic Arms Limitation Treaty**, or **SALT I**), and move the relationship with the Soviet Union to a less sus-

---

h. These incidents came on top of frontier clashes that had occurred earlier in the 1960s, sparked in part by Chinese territorial claims to about a million square miles that had formerly been part of imperial China, but were taken over by tsarist Russia in the nineteenth century. Keylor (1996, 364) explains: "As the problem of overpopulation began to be recognized as a serious impediment to China's hopes for rapid industrialization in the course of the 1960s, the sparsely inhabited spaces of the former Chinese domains in the Soviet Far East exerted an understandable attraction on the economic modernizers in Beijing."

picious, more normal footing at the same time that the U.S.-Chinese relationship was being refashioned.

The improvement in U.S.-China relations occurred in the midst of domestic political turmoil in China, which became known as the **Great Proletarian Cultural Revolution**. In the wake of the disastrous failures of the Great Leap Forward, Mao retreated into the background for about three years starting in 1963. By 1966, however, he was ready to reassert himself, and the vehicle he chose for reestablishing his influence was the Cultural Revolution. Apparently, he decided that the Communist Party of China had become infiltrated and subverted by elements that were too conservative, or rightist. In order to bring leftists to the fore instead, he mobilized students, who became known as Red Guards, and he became increasingly reliant on the People's Liberation Army (the PLA) as a basis of power. The Red Guards' main source of inspiration was Mao's ideas as popularized in *Quotations from Chairman Mao* (the "little red book"); the result was political strife and chaos, which reached particularly high levels in 1966 and on into 1967.

By 1968 and 1969, perhaps partly because of the increasingly serious strains in China's relationship with the Soviet Union (highlighted by the Soviet invasion of Czechoslovakia in 1968 and the border clashes between the Soviets and the Chinese in 1969), Mao began to put more emphasis on stability and order than on revolutionary fervor and political ferment. Then President Nixon visited Beijing in 1972, and the Maoist regime, rather ironically, became dependent on the United States as an ally against its fellow Communist regime in the Soviet Union. At about the same time, Mao's health began to decline, and there ensued a leadership struggle in China. Mao's close confidant, Zhou Enlai, was one of the main contenders for power, against a more radical faction headed by Mao's wife, Jiang Qing. When Mao died in 1976, the faction headed by Jiang Qing was predominant, but by the end of the year, a more conservative coalition of military and political leaders joined together to arrest and imprison Jiang Qing and her associates, who were labeled the "Gang of Four." In short, the rightists began to emerge as the victors from the Great Proletarian Cultural Revolution, whose end point is commonly designated as 1976 (Library of Congress 1987; Train, n.d.; Watkins, n.d.).

Shortly after Mao's death, Deng Xiaoping emerged as the new leader of China. At the Third Plenum of the Eleventh National Party Congress Central Committee in December 1978, Deng was apparently mainly responsible for launching a kind of economic revolution in China, the reverberations of which promise to be felt well into the twenty-first century. From that point forward, the emphasis of the Communist Party in China shifted from revolutionary class struggle to an initiative that became known as the **Four Modernizations**, focused on agriculture, industry, science and technology, and national defense. One of the first important areas of reform was the agricultural system, where communes were deemphasized and peasants were encouraged to devote time and energy to their own small plots. Considerable capital was also invested in the mechanization of agriculture and in improved irrigation systems.

Agricultural reform substantially boosted food production and helped to free up labor in the countryside for migration to the cities, where industrialization was emphasized. This migration was concentrated in **special economic zones**, created very early during Deng's reform movement, along the southern coast of China. The movement toward industrialization was fueled, to an important extent, by massive amounts of foreign investment, which had been frowned upon in the era of Mao. In the twenty-first century, in contrast, China has become the leading recipient of foreign investment in the developing world—and, perhaps, in the entire world in some years. Overall, since the reforms started in the late 1970s, China has attracted some $500 billion in foreign investment (Gilboy 2004, 36).

China's startling economic reform has created some serious problems. One is a substantial disparity in economic progress between urban coastal areas and the rural areas farther inland. According to David Hale and Lyric Hughes Hale (2003, 41): "China now produces 57 percent of its GDP in its east, 26 percent in the central region, and only 17 percent in the west. Foreign investors have reinforced this division by placing 86.4 percent of their capital in the east, 9 percent in the central region, and only 4.6 percent in the west."

Early on in the period of economic reform, Deng Xiaoping reinforced fundamental changes in China's foreign policy. In 1979, for example, there was a formal exchange of diplomatic recognition between the People's Republic of China and the United States. Then, too, Deng decided not to extend the thirty-year-old Treaty of Friendship, Alliance and Mutual Assistance with the Soviet Union, the signing of which had been one of the more significant steps taken by the new revolution in China at its onset in 1950.

On the other hand, both China's relationship with the United States and its image in the rest of the world suffered a serious setback from events in 1989. Political developments in the Soviet Union and Eastern Europe had created unrest and impatience in Beijing, where students were among the leaders of demonstrations calling for political reforms to accompany the dramatic economic reforms that had, by then, been in place in China for ten years. Student demonstrators in Tiananmen Square carried a huge replica of the Statue of Liberty, as well as banners asking "Where is our Gorbachev?" Talbot (2003, 6) explains: "The answer was that he was not around. The Chinese had Deng Ziaoping ... who sent tanks into Tiananmen, resulting in televised slaughter, martyrs, outrage, and disillusionment in the United States and around the world."

But China has recovered well from that dramatic episode of political instability and violence; at the beginning of twenty-first century, its economy is in its third decade of economic growth, which has put it near or at the top of the world's fastest-growing economies throughout that time period. In spite of the fact that the benefits of this economic growth are not evenly distributed, two prominent analysts (Oksenberg and Economy 1999, 6) report: "China's gross national product has more than quadrupled in the past 25 years. Never in history has the economy of so many people grown as rapidly, as extensively, and for as sustained a time as has the economy of China's now 1.3 billion people."

POWER TRANSITION THEORY AND THE FUTURE OF U.S.-CHINESE RELATIONS

Approximately forty years ago, foreign policy analyst A.F.K. Organski (1968, 486–487) evaluated power trends in the largest, most important states in the international system at that time, and came to the following conclusion:

> The question is not whether China will become the most powerful nation on earth, but rather how long it will take her to achieve this status.... [T]he United States will retain world leadership for at

least the remainder of the twentieth century, perhaps for even a longer time, but that position will eventually pass to China.[i]

Organski further speculated that once China does catch up with the United States in terms of power, there is likely to be conflict—and possibly a war—between them.[j]

From that kernel has sprung **power transition theory**, which suggests that when the most powerful state in the system is challenged by some ascending second-ranked state, conflict and even war are likely. Organski and Jacek Kugler elaborated and formalized the theory in *The War Ledger* (1980), a work that has since inspired extensive systematic empirical investigations that have suggested, for example, that power transitions made war more likely between major powers in the years between the 1648 Peace of Westphalia and the 1815 defeat of Napoleon at Waterloo (Kim 1992), and that power transitions can account for wars in a subsystem of minor powers on the continent of South America in the nineteenth and twentieth centuries (Lemke 1993). Furthermore, there are by now a significant number of important theorists of international politics who argue that challenges to the most powerful state in the international system by some up-and-coming state are likely to destabilize the system and lead to significant, system-altering wars (see, for example, Gilpin 1981; Keohane 1984; Modelski and Thompson 1987; Wallerstein 1983; and Goldstein 1988). Conversely, most of these theorists feel that an international system in which a predominating state is free of significant competition is likely to be more stable and peaceful.

To be frank, the empirical evidence regarding this basic notion that a predominant leading state stabilizes the international system, while challenges to that leader often precede and/or lead to substantial conflict and wars, is mixed and difficult to interpret.[k] Nevertheless, some important systematic analyses of the available evidence do support the power transition theory. Organski and Kugler (1980) themselves provide some of that evidence, while Kim (1989) makes a persuasive argument that power transitions have been regularly associated with major wars in the international system since 1816. Pollins (1996) and Pollins and Murrin (1999) provide important evidence that the amount of militarized conflict in the international system is particularly impacted by combinations of cycles in economic and political leadership in the international system. Many analyses over the past twenty-five years suggest that, in general, pairs of states relatively equal in power are more likely to become involved in war with each other than are states separated by a significant gap in power (see, especially, Bremer 1992; Russett and Oneal 2001). And, from a power transition perspective, both world wars can be seen as the results of Germany's challenges to the systemic leadership of Great Britain.

---

i. Actually, Organski made almost exactly the same prediction even ten years earlier in the first edition of *World Politics*; see Organski 1958, 446.

j. "If [China] demands too much too soon, if she arouses fears by absorbing her Asian neighbors, if she wounds America's pride by seizing her outposts of power, or if, worst of all, she attacks America's friends, the United States will fight" (Organski 1968, 489).

k. A useful review of much of the evidence related to power transition theory can be found in Lemke and Kugler 1996.

The Strong Points of Power Transition Theory's Analysis

For power transition theorists Organski and Kugler, in particular, the best measure of a state's power is its gross domestic product (GDP) or gross national product (GNP)—either of which reflects the value of the sum total of goods and services produced by a state's economy. If we look at the relationship between the GDPs of the United States and China from 1980 to 2005 (covering a period of time during which the economic reforms in China produced a sustained period of rapid economic growth), we can see that China has moved closer to power parity with the United States. As figure 12.1 shows, China's GDP was only about 15 percent that of the United States in 1980, but it had risen to almost 70 percent of the U.S. figure by 2005. Projecting into the future, if we assume that China's GDP will grow at a rate of 8 percent, while that of the United States will expand at the rate of 3 percent, we can estimate that China will surpass the United States in terms of GDP within something like ten years.[l] This is, of course, a rough estimate, but it does suggest that, given plausible assumptions about future economic growth rates in China and the United States, China will, at some point soon, become more "powerful" than the United States, according to the index of power most favored by the leading power transition theorists.

Thus, the evidence that a power transition involving China and the United States—as rather precisely defined by power transition theorists—will take place in the near future is both straightforward and persuasive. How convinced should we be that this transition will, in fact, lead to war between the two great powers?

One reason to take seriously the power transition theorists' prediction of a future war between the United States and China is that the theory has to its credit an impressive prediction about the dynamics of a crucial great power relationship in the contemporary, post–World War II international system. Specifically, by applying his theory's logic, Organski anticipated, years before its eventual realization, the peaceful demise of the Cold War between the Soviet Union and the United States. In the 1960s, when tensions between the superpowers were high, war between them was widely anticipated, especially since the Soviet Union still appeared capable of mounting a serious challenge to the economic as well as the military superiority of the United States. Nevertheless, Organski (1968, 360) asserted that "both economic growth and population increase are slackening off in the Soviet Union, and ... the United States already has a sufficient power advantage so that the Soviets will not be able to close the gap separating them from the United States."[m] Taking that fact, as well as China's greater potential into account, he concluded (488) that "the challenger America will face will be China and not the USSR."

As Lemke (1997, 27) points out, "a good theory of the causes of war must simultaneously be a theory of the causes of peace." And he goes on to emphasize that during the Cold War,

---

l. Joseph Nye (2002, 19) estimates that "if the American economy grows at a 2 percent rate and China's grows at 6 percent, the two economies would be equal in size sometime around 2020."

m. In his earlier edition, Organski (1958, 321–322) had also expressed doubts that the Soviets would be able to surpass the United States, and confidence that China certainly would outgrow both the United States and the Soviet Union.

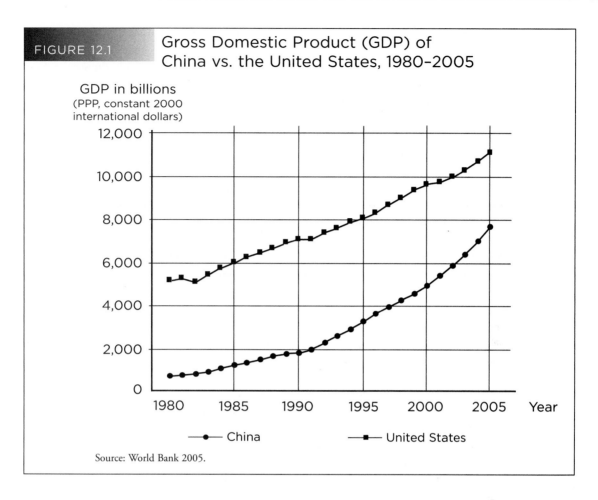

FIGURE 12.1 Gross Domestic Product (GDP) of China vs. the United States, 1980–2005

GDP in billions (PPP, constant 2000 international dollars)

Source: World Bank 2005.

the Soviet Union never achieved parity with the United States, and that therefore, in the view of power transition theory, "war was not expected."[n]

Much of the plausibility of power transition theory's scenario suggesting that China will ultimately become involved in a war with the United States derives from an analogy between Germany in the late nineteenth and early twentieth centuries, and contemporary China. As Zbigniew Brzezinski (2000, 11) notes: "Though all analogies, by definition, are partially misleading, there are some important parallels between China's current situation and imperial Germany's circa 1890." From the point of view of power transition theory, Germany twice figured during the twentieth century as the up-and-coming challenger, intent on changing the international status quo, which was the driving force behind processes leading to both world

---

n. It might also be pointed out that during the Cold War a power transition did occur, or was at least approached, by China's relationship with the Soviet Union, and that the tension—if not the full-fledged war—that power transition theorists would expect this transition to produce, certainly did appear. That tension was also anticipated by Organski (1968).

wars. Like the Germany of that era, today's China is arguably "dissatisfied" with its status in the international system, whose current institutional arrangements were established before it became a great power. According to the size of its GDP, China is currently the second most powerful state in the world. This is a newly acquired status; like that of Germany in the early twentieth century (and in the 1930s under Hitler), China's power is increasing dramatically. Yet, in several ways, China is not accorded as much influence or prestige as its rapidly advancing power ranking might justify.

Then, too, Germany gained status within the European subsystem relatively late in the game; it was not until the aftermath of the Franco-Prussian War in 1870 that it even became unified into the state that exists today. China, on the other hand, is an ancient society, one that has been unified in some form or other for centuries. Nevertheless, as we saw earlier in this chapter, China was dominated by foreigners for most of the nineteenth century, and even after it emerged from rule by an emperor, it continued to be dominated or ravaged by foreign forces well into the twentieth century. Before and during World War II, for example, it was fighting against Japan, to which it lost control of much of its territory. So, in some ways, China did not emerge as a modern state, with territorial integrity and an independent government, until its Communist revolution in 1949. And, just as being a new kid on the block, so to speak, may have had something to do with Germany's propensity, during the early decades of the twentieth century, to throw its weight around, hoping to impress upon the outside world that it was a power to be reckoned with, many of the same pressures and incentives may be operative in present-day China.

In addition, like twentieth-century Germany, twenty-first-century China may well feel itself to be surrounded by enemies. The German foreign policy elite became embroiled in World War I in part because of its leaders' fears of **encirclement**—in other words, that, with Russia to the east, and the powerful French and British to the west, they needed to "defend" themselves before their enemies in all directions became too powerful to be dealt with successfully. When today's China looks to its west and south, it sees India and Vietnam; it has, in recent decades, fought wars with both of those states. To its east lies South Korea, with which it fought a bloody war in the 1950s, resulting in the retention of tens of thousands of U.S. military forces on the Korean peninsula. To China's east also is Japan, with which it has had such a long and sometimes bloody involvement. And, of course, to its north lies Russia. Currently, the relationship between Russia and China is relatively stable, even friendly, but those two states share the longest international boundary in the world, as well as a long history of periodic tension and antagonism. Finally, there is the "state" of Taiwan, which China considers a province but which has a virtual military alliance with the United States. Given this list of contentious neighbors, it would hardly be surprising if China were to react to fears of such encirclement by striking out against one or more of its numerous enemies, actual or potential, just as Germany did at least twice in the twentieth century.

Reasons to Doubt the Prediction of a Future War

In spite of the general credibility of power transition theory, and the plausibility of several aspects of the analogy between twentieth-century Germany and twenty-first-century China, there are reasons to be dubious about a prediction that China is destined soon to fight a war against the United States. One is the possession of nuclear weapons by both sides; no two major powers with nuclear weapons have ever fought a war against each other.

Power transition theorists tend to be skeptical about the stabilizing impact of nuclear weapons (see Kugler and Zagare 1990; Kugler 1996).[o] And, admittedly, since the current U.S. nuclear arsenal is considerably larger than that of China, it will be a long time before China will have achieved anything resembling nuclear parity with the United States—or before both will have sufficiently large numbers of nuclear weapons as to be assured that they would have secure second-strike capabilities. That is, even more specifically, it will be a long time before China has a nuclear force that is large and diverse enough to make it confident that it can withstand a surprise attack by the United States and still have enough nuclear weapons remaining to deliver a devastating counterattack. Such confrontations between states going through the transition from great disparity to apparent parity in nuclear arsenals can be dangerous, according to both power transition theory and other formal, mathematical analyses of nuclear confrontations (Intriligator and Brito 1984). Nevertheless, while we know, or at least have evidence to suggest, that power transitions make wars more likely between states possessing conventional military weapons, we have no evidence, yet, that major powers with nuclear weapons experiencing a power transition are likely to fight wars against each other.

Another reason to doubt power transition theory's prediction of a future war between China and the United States is that at least one fundamental transition has occurred in relatively recent history that did not lead to war. At some point around the beginning of the twentieth century, the United States replaced Great Britain as the world's most powerful state, and yet the two did not fight a war against each other. (There was a rather tense confrontation between the two because of a boundary dispute between Great Britain and Venezuela in 1895, but the dispute was, in the end, resolved peacefully.) Organksi (1968) and other power transition theorists are aware of this apparent anomaly, and they do offer explanations for it. Some argue that, at the time the transition occurred, the United States was too remote geographically for its transition to power superiority to seem threatening to the declining power. Others point out that the United States, in spite of its power, was isolationist and did not seek world leadership until much later. Therefore, the transition occurred peacefully.

Power transition theorists also argue that, in addition to a change in power relationships, the challenging state must be dissatisfied with the existing international order, if conflict is to occur. In the case of the early-twentieth-century power transition, the United States was content with the rules of the international system as established by Great Britain, so when it came to be as powerful, or more so, than its predecessor as the world leader, there was no basis for conflict. All of these explanations are plausible, but they do not change the fact that there is an important precedent for one state replacing another as the preeminent state in the system without serious conflict breaking out. And this precedent surely increases the credibility of a prediction that even if China does surpass the United States in GNP and/or in military

---

o. "The stability of deterrence is threatened, however, when nuclear parity is approached, maintained, or breached over time, and the leading contenders have fundamental and persistent differences in their world view" (Kugler and Zagare 1990, 273).

capabilities in the near future, it is not necessary to assume that the transition will result in serious military conflict between them.

Confidence that a future power transition between China and the United States need not lead to serious, militarized conflict might be increased if China were to move in the direction of becoming a democratic state, for democratic states rarely, if ever, fight interstate wars against each other (see Rummel 1979; Russett 1993; Ray 1995; Russett and Oneal 2001). Indeed, another possible explanation for the peaceful transition that occurred when Great Britain was surpassed by the United States early in the twentieth century is that both states were democratic. There is, in addition, some evidence that, although power transitions in general are likely to generate conflict between states, that conflict will be muted and probably nonviolent if the states involved are democratic (Schweller 1992, 268). As John Oneal, Bruce Russett, and Michael Berbaum (2003, 388) observe about the U.S.-China relationship specifically:

> Rapid economic growth in China has eroded the U.S. advantage in recent years. [However], increased trade, greater contact in international organizations, and some moderation in the authoritarian character of the Chinese government have reduced the probability of a fatal dispute between these major powers 58 percent.... Eventually China may become democratic, further increasing the prospects for peace.

Whether or not China is evolving in a democratic direction is an issue about which there is considerable disagreement among knowledgeable observers.[p] There is less disagreement that China is experiencing rapid economic growth, and there is something of a consensus—the strength of which we will analyze shortly—that states with large middle classes are more likely to evolve in the direction of and/or sustain democratic political systems. (This is the hope, as we shall see, on which the U.S. foreign policy toward China has been based in at least the past two presidential administrations.)

A final reason, perhaps, to doubt that the United States and China are on the verge of serious military conflict within the next two or three decades has to do with the measure of power preferred by power transition theorists, and the results obtained by applying that measure to comparisons of the United States and China. That measure—the gross domestic or gross national product—may well be the best single number by which to measure a state's power. One of the primary reasons that Organski correctly predicted the Cold War's peaceful end is that he focused on the GNP of the Soviet Union as the indicator of its power. Other indicators, focusing instead on the size of Soviet military budgets or the manpower dedicated to Soviet military forces, might well have suggested that the Soviet Union was on the brink of catching up with or even surpassing the United States, and that war would result. But the Soviet Union's GNP never did approximate that of the United States, and except, perhaps, for a brief period in the late 1950s and early 1960s, it never looked as though it would. So, relying on GNP as an indicator of power when making estimates about the U.S.-Soviet relationship worked out well for Organski and other power transition theorists.

However, it is not clear that GNP or GDP is, in fact, a good measure of the power of China. It may well overstate China's power, basically because its population is so large. A state's

---

p. Minxin Pei (2003) nicely summarizes a range of contending and competing views on the future of the Chinese regime.

total population is, of course, another important indicator of power, and, to the extent that a state's GNP is large because its population is large, this factor is not by itself a serious problem. But surely there must be rapidly diminishing benefits to a state's power aggregate from additional millions of people after some threshold well below that of China's population of 1.3 billion people. In other words, the first half-billion people probably add a lot more to China's power potential than do the second half-billion. In fact, the second half-billion may even be somewhat detrimental, partly because so many of that second half-billion are still very poor and, in spite of China's economic growth, will remain so for some time to come. In short, as Zbigniew Brzezinski (2000, 8) comments, "[China's] backward and debilitated social infrastructure, combined with the per capita poverty of its enormous population, represents a staggering liability" for China. That liability shows up partly in the technological backwardness of its admittedly large military force, as Brzezinski (7) also notes: "The Chinese military build-up has been steady but neither massive nor rapid, nor technologically very impressive."

Thus, China's GDP may well catch up with and even surpass that of the United States within the next decade or two. But while a state's GDP is generally a valid indicator of its power, that measure may overstate it considerably in the case of China. In reality, therefore, it is likely that China will not in fact become as powerful or more powerful than the United States in the next few decades. And so, to the extent that power transition theory is valid, the persistence of a significant gap between the power of the United States and the power of China suggests that the two will not be so liable to engage in conflict with each other as the theory's narrow focus on their respective GDPs would suggest.q

U.S. FOREIGN POLICY ALTERNATIVES FOR DEALING WITH CHINA

Since the end of the Cold War, or at least since the demise of the Soviet Union, the People's Republic of China has posed the most credible threat to the preeminence of the United States in the global political system. Interestingly, the administration of Bill Clinton and the second Bush administration have chosen to deal with China in a similar fashion—although both came into office with the declared intention of adopting policies quite different from those they ultimately fashioned.

As a Democratic presidential candidate, Bill Clinton was (as might be expected) quite critical of his Republican predecessor's policy toward China. Before he was elected, Clinton felt that the United States should be more critical of China's record on human rights, and he criticized then–President George H. W. Bush for apparently judging the profits to be made from trade with China to be more important than the need to push harder for an end to its most widespread human rights abuses. After Clinton was elected president, however, it was widely perceived that he decided to soft-pedal U.S. denunciations of China's human rights abuses— or at least, that he decided against cutting off trade, or using trade sanctions as a tool to

---

q. Brzezinski (2000, 7) makes another point, much less focused on concrete factors, that is worth considering: "Unlike the former Soviet Union, the People's Republic of China (PRC) is not capable of posing a universal ideological challenge to the United States." Similarly, Nye (2002, 19) argues that China's "official communist ideology holds little appeal."

encourage China to respect human rights. In short, although candidate Bill Clinton felt that trading with China while it abused human rights was a shameful compromise of principles, President Bill Clinton favored a policy of "constructive engagement," which called for strengthening both economic and political ties to China, and, at the same time, discreetly attempting to influence its leaders to move toward democracy, open markets, and greater respect for human rights. "Isolation of China," President Clinton explained in 1997, "is unworkable, counter-productive, and potentially dangerous" (Blitzer 1997).

When George W. Bush was a candidate, he, in turn, was critical of the Clinton administration's policy toward China. In candidate Bush's view, President Clinton had been too ready to treat China as a "strategic partner," and he promised that, if elected president, he would consider China to be, instead, a "strategic competitor" (Foster 2003). In short, as a candidate, George W. Bush, like presidential candidate Bill Clinton, felt that the current administration had been lamentably uncritical of the regime in the People's Republic of China. But, like President Clinton, President George W. Bush established a closer relationship with China than he had expected, or at least, hinted at as a candidate. Trade with China became ever more important to his administration, and especially after the terrorist attacks of September 11, 2001, President Bush mainly stressed the common interests of the United States and China in the global war on terrorism.

The policies of these two presidents toward China have been similar in another way. Both have been based on a hypothesized sequence of developments that is presented in figure 12.2. In other words, although they arrived at this conclusion in the circuitous ways we have described, both Presidents Clinton and Bush ultimately favored increased trade ties and investment in China. Ostensibly, at least, neither favored this policy simply for the economic gains to be produced by such a policy. Both expressed confidence that increasing China's economic integration into the world's economic processes would help its economy to grow rapidly, and that such economic growth would result in the expansion of a middle class in China, which would, in turn, reinforce whatever forces there were in China moving toward democratization. The assumption by both presidents that such democratization would have beneficial, pacifying effects on U.S.-Chinese relations is an idea that would be supported both by liberals and by advocates of rational political ambition theory.

That economic growth and development are ultimately beneficial for the chances of democratic transitions is an idea that has substantial support among analysts of democratization (see Lipset 1959). Some contemporary research has tended to support this "modernization" thesis, suggesting that economic development makes democratic transitions more likely (Burkhart and Lewis-Beck 1994), or at least, that higher levels of economic development encourage newly democratic states to remain democratic—even if they do not make the transition to democracy more likely in the first place (Przeworski and Limongi 1997). But will economic growth, spurred in part by the willingness of the United States to trade with and encourage investment in China, lead to a democratic transition in the People's Republic? Naturally, one can find a range of opinions on this issue. Mary Gallagher (2002), for example, argues that China has grown rapidly ever since Deng Xiaoping's economic revolution in 1978 without any significant political liberalization, and that, in fact, the Chinese Communist Party is utilizing foreign investment to postpone liberalization indefinitely, and to hold on to its power. (This argument certainly conforms to the basic tenets of rational political ambition

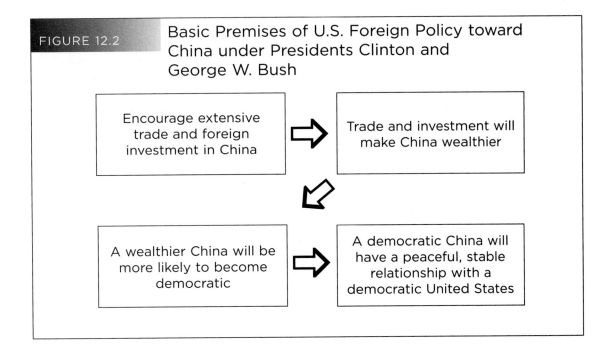

FIGURE 12.2 Basic Premises of U.S. Foreign Policy toward China under Presidents Clinton and George W. Bush

theory.) On the other hand, Sinologist Bruce Gilley (2004) feels that China's transition to democracy is nearly certain to occur, and no later than 2020.

Still, even if the future does bring democracy to China, there is no guarantee that the current U.S. policy aimed at encouraging democratization in the People's Republic is prudent. It may be true that democratic states rarely, if ever, fight wars against each other. But some analysts warn that the democratization process—that is, getting from an authoritarian regime to a fully democratic one—may not only be fraught with perils that can derail progress toward democracy, but may also create conflict-prone, and possibly assertive or aggressive, foreign policies in the democratizing state, even if that process is ultimately successful (Mansfield and Snyder 2002).

In addition, realists are skeptical that democracy actually has the pacifying impact that liberals (and the advocates of rational political ambition theory) attribute to it. Realists, therefore, tend to be dubious about U.S. policy toward China that aims at promoting economic growth in the hope that it will encourage the emergence of democracy. John Mearsheimer (2001b), for example, argues forcefully that the United States should be seeking to slow down economic growth in China, because that state threatens to become more dangerous to U.S. interests with every passing year. He understands that U.S. policy toward China in the post–Cold War era has in fact been aimed at encouraging China to become prosperous, in the belief that a prosperous China will become democratic, and so will adopt foreign policies compatible with the interests of the United States. In Mearsheimer's view (58), "this approach is misguided, however, because a wealthy China would not be a status quo power; it would be an aggressive one determined to achieve regional hegemony."

Clearly, Mearsheimer has pointed out a risk that is inherent in the current U.S. policy toward the People's Republic. That state does have the potential to become sufficiently powerful to threaten vital interests of the United States. Within a few decades, it may even have the potential to become more powerful in general than the United States. And, if in the process of becoming so powerful, it also adopts policies that are antagonistic to the United States, there is clearly a danger that the United States will have been foolish in adhering, for so many years, to policies designed to foster economic growth in China, and so allow it, even help it, to develop into such a powerful enemy.

On the other hand, if the United States were to adopt a policy based on purposeful measures to slow down China's economic progress, it would surely incur a vigorous antagonism from the People's Republic that might lead to dangerous confrontations sooner rather than later. In addition, the ethical basis of such a policy might be questionable—in other words, ought the United States to be hampering efforts to lift China's impoverished millions out of the destitution they now face? Clearly, the two most recent presidents' preference for developing stronger economic ties with China and thereby assisting rather than resisting economic growth there is not without its risks. But no risk-free policy option is available. Mearsheimer's realist policy option would also be risky, and it would almost certainly create crises in U.S.-Chinese relations more quickly than the current U.S. policy has done.[r]

THE TAIWAN ISSUE

From the point of view of the Communist regime in China, Taiwan is a renegade Chinese province that is destined, at some point, to be returned to the fold, or, in other words, to become fully integrated with the Chinese state on the mainland. The future status of Taiwan has been a thorny issue in U.S.-Chinese relations ever since 1949, when the Chinese Communists ascended to power just as the remnants of the Nationalist regime of Chiang Kai-shek were escaping to Taiwan. In order to establish a working relationship with the PRC, President Nixon and Secretary of State Henry Kissinger negotiated the Shanghai Communiqué of 1972, which asserted that "all Chinese on either side of the Taiwan Strait maintain that there is but one China and that Taiwan is part of China." At the time, this was seen as a clever way of cutting the Gordian knot of the Taiwan issue, which might otherwise have prevented normalization of relations following the twenty-year period after World War II during which the United States refused to recognize the Communist government in China.

U.S.-Chinese relations were upgraded in 1978, when President Carter agreed to extend full diplomatic recognition to the PRC, but the other side of this coin involved the termination of the American defense treaty with Taiwan, the withdrawal of U.S. military personnel, and the severing of all formal diplomatic ties with the island state. At that point, the U.S. Congress took the initiative, passing, by veto-proof majorities, the **Taiwan Relations Act of 1979**, by

---

r. Admittedly, a realist would probably respond that it would better to face such crises earlier rather than later, after China has become much more powerful than it is now.

which the United States pledged to consider any effort to determine the future of Taiwan by force to be a threat to the peace, and to provide to Taiwan sufficient military equipment to sustain its self-defense. In continuing to honor this pledge, the United States has piled ambiguity upon contradiction in its dealings with the issue of Taiwan and with U.S.–PRC relations. It has agreed with both sides that there is only "one China," while papering over the fact that each of those sides considers itself the true heart of that unique entity. And, in the Taiwan Relations Act, the United States is "committed by law to provide Taiwan with the arms it needs to defend its autonomy," even though, as Aaron Friedberg points out (2000b, 27), "the United States does not acknowledge Taiwan's existence as an autonomous political entity."

Democracy may, in general, be a pacifying force in interstate relations, but it is not at all clear that steps toward democracy in Taiwan, or even in the PRC itself, will necessarily help to resolve the conflict between those two feuding parties. In 1996 Taiwan held its first contested, democratic election, in which the Kuomintang candidate, Lee Teng Hui, was elected president. Lee was obviously opposed to the unification of the PRC and Taiwan as long as the Communist Party retained power in Beijing. In fact, from the PRC's point of view, "Lee was a 'chief behind the scenes backer' of Taiwan's independence movement" (Ross 2000, 93). Lee had been the focus of the U.S.-PRC-Taiwanese trilateral relationship in 1995, when he received an invitation to speak at Cornell University in New York State. President Clinton hesitated to issue him a visa, but after the U.S. Senate voted 97–1 and the House of Representatives voted 360–0 in support of the visa, the president acquiesced. When Lee then emerged as a leading presidential candidate, the Chinese government was sufficiently concerned that it conducted missile tests as well as naval and air military exercises in waters near Taiwan as the election approached; the United States responded by sending two carrier battle groups closer to Taiwan. The clear intent of the Chinese government was to scare Taiwanese voters away from Lee, but he was, nevertheless, elected by a substantial margin.

In its election of 2000, Taiwan reached another important milestone in its apparent transition to democracy: the first peaceful transition of power from one independent political party to another. Chen Shui-bian, the candidate of the Democratic Progressive Party, defeated the candidate of the Kuomintang. Chen was reelected in 2004, and he has periodically pushed in the direction of declaring Taiwan's independence. Meanwhile, China and the United States continue to clash, verbally, over the fate of Taiwan. In 2004, for example, the United States announced plans to sell $18 billion worth of military hardware to Taiwan, to which the Chinese Foreign Minister Li Zhaoxing responded that "we are firmly opposed to the sales of weapons by any foreign country to Taiwan, which is part of China…" (Kralev 2004, 1). Then, in 2005, when Japan and the United States announced that they shared a "common strategic direction" on policies toward Taiwan, the Chinese Foreign Ministry responded with a statement to the effect that "the United States has severely interfered with Chinese internal affairs and sent a false signal to the advocates of Taiwan independence" (Brinkley 2005, A6).

A RAND corporation study (Khalilzad et al. 1999) argues that the main goals of China's foreign policy are these: (1) modernization, (2) protecting its sovereignty, and (3) regime maintenance. These goals are not entirely complementary. The study's authors regard modernization as equivalent to "comprehensive power development," which realists would consider to be the overriding goal of Chinese foreign policy makers. Rational political ambition theorists, in contrast, would expect that regime maintenance would be the highest priority for the Chinese, as it would be for any other government.

In order to modernize, China probably needs to stay on good terms with the United States, and with other states having large export markets. China is very dependent on its exports to the United States, as well as on foreign investments by American corporations in China. At the same time, in order to protect and maintain its sovereignty, the regime in the People's Republic feels that it must not allow Taiwan to successfully declare its independence. It is widely observed that China's government has lost the ability to shore up support by making appeals in terms of Communist rhetoric and ideology, and so it has tried—and will continue to try—to replace Communist ideology with appeals to nationalism, in which context, maintaining control over Taiwan is an important source of pride.

However, if it pushes too hard or retaliates too vigorously against any Taiwanese movement toward independence, the PRC is likely to antagonize the United States and, possibly, other important Western countries. If that antagonism should reach a level inspiring the United States to cut off its market from Chinese exports or to prevent American firms from investing in the PRC, then the Communist regime will have significantly imperiled its plans for economic modernization. On the other hand, should it fail to vigorously defend its "rights" in Taiwan, that failure might also endanger the regime's hold on power. The Communist Party's legitimacy in the eyes of the Chinese people, in other words, is probably based in important part on the perception that the regime will deal effectively with the threat to China's territorial integrity posed by any movement by Taiwan toward independence.

How should the United States handle this ticklish situation? In fact, it is easier to deal with than it might otherwise be, if Taiwan were entirely dependent on the United States for its survival. As unlikely as it seems when one compares the "power" of Taiwan to that of China in terms of GNP—since China's GNP is currently about 12 times larger than that of Taiwan—it is not even clear that China could launch a successful amphibian invasion of its "renegade province." And, although it might be able to obliterate large portions of the Taiwanese population with aerial and even nuclear bombardment, that would be an odd way (to put it mildly) to treat people whom the PRC considers to be its own citizens.

Nevertheless, China is continuing to build up its military might, and the Taiwanese government periodically moves in the direction of independence in ways that provoke fears among Chinese foreign policy makers.[s] For the sake of deterring a Chinese attack on Taiwan, it behooves the United States to state as clearly as possible that it will respond to any such attack by coming to the defense of Taiwan. But if the United States promises to defend Taiwan regardless of what it does to provoke an attack by China, it is likely to increase the risk that Taiwan's government will engage in provocative behavior, and thus help to bring about the very attack that the United States would like to prevent.

The Taiwanese people as a whole do not appear to be hell-bent on independence from the mainland. Knowledgeable observers insist, as David Shambaugh (2004, 137) puts it, that

---

s. "Beijing seems convinced that Taiwan President Chen Shui-bian is bent on pursuing de jure independence for the island, and Chinese officials argue that Chen has essentially announced a timetable for independence by completing constitutional revision during the 2006–2008 period" (Shambaugh 2004, 137).

"Taiwan is now a robust democracy, and the majority of its people seek self-determination." Yet legislative elections in late 2004 left control of the parliament in the hands of parties that are critical of Chen Shui-bian's proposals to modify Taiwan's constitution in ways that the Chinese government sees as part of a "plot" to move Taiwan toward formal independence (Dean 2005).

Thus, although it is not a comfortable position to be in, perhaps the best way for the United States to deal with this delicate situation involves some intentional ambiguity. U.S. leaders need to let the Chinese government know that they are *unlikely* to stand idly by while the Chinese government engages in military action to forcibly annex Taiwan. But, at the same time, they need to make it clear to the Taiwanese that the United States will not stand by them and help to defend them against China *regardless* of any provocative action the Taiwanese government might take (Benson and Niou 2002). In short, the Americans should strive to create enough uncertainty in the minds of both Chinese and Taiwanese policymakers that both will be cautious in their behavior toward each other. Especially if the PRC does evolve in the direction of genuine democracy, it may well be possible, ultimately, to resolve the conflict between China and Taiwan in a clear, unambiguous, and permanent fashion. In the meantime, the best that can be hoped for is an unclear, ambiguous, and tentative but peaceful relationship between the People's Republic and what it will always see as its province in Taiwan.

CONCLUSION

The United States moved into Asia in an important way during the Spanish-American War in 1898, acquiring the Philippines from Spain in the process. Its motive for doing that was to gain a foothold and a stepping-stone to Asia, particularly China. The United States soon proclaimed an Open Door Policy with respect to China, calling for all great trading states to have equal access to the most populous nation in the world.

China began to escape from foreign domination near the beginning of the twentieth century. Chiang Kai-shek and his Nationalist movement had enjoyed some success by the late 1920s, but in the 1930s, much of China was taken over by Japan. That problem was resolved by Japan's defeat in World War II, but the war, in turn, created conditions favorable to the Communist takeover of China, and for the escape of Chiang Kai-shek to Taiwan.

Soon after its Communist revolution, China signed a treaty of friendship with the Soviet Union, but twenty years later, that relationship had deteriorated to the point that Mao Zedong chose to ally himself more closely with the United States. When Deng Xiaoping took over from the Maoists in 1979, he laid the groundwork for startling economic growth that makes it likely that China's GNP will surpass that of the United States in the next ten-to-twenty years. Power transition theory suggests that if China does become more powerful than the United States in the near future, war between those two states will be likely. On balance, this prediction is not entirely persuasive, partly because using the GNP as an indicator of power may be particularly misleading in the case of China.

Still, war could certainly break out between the United States and China, over the future of Taiwan, if for no other reason. An ambiguous U.S. policy that neither offers too much encouragement to Taiwan to move toward independence, nor leaves China confident that it can take over Taiwan militarily without significant U.S. resistance is probably the best way for the United States to deal with this delicate situation. More fundamentally, the United States should probably continue its policy of constructive engagement with China—even though it is to that state's great economic benefit—in the hope that such economic progress will lead to a democratic China in the not-too-distant future.

In the meantime, the United States should also explore possible common interests that the United States and China have in Asia. One of the most important of them, currently, is to encourage North Korea to give up its nuclear weapons program. Analyst Ted Galen Carpenter (2003/2004) argues that continued North Korean recalcitrance on this issue should lead the United States to announce that it believes South Korea and Japan should both develop their own nuclear weapons, although, of course, the United States should not actually encourage those countries to do so. Instead, the idea is that, merely by dropping its objections to South Korean or Japanese plans to acquire nuclear weapons, the United States would energize the Chinese government to become involved in managing the situation. In Carpenter's words (96): "The prospect of a nuclear-armed Japan is the one factor that could galvanize Beijing to put serious diplomatic and economic pressure on Pyongyang [the North Korean capital] to relinquish its nuclear ambitions."

Such a strategy would highlight the common interests that China and the United States have with respect to North Korea's nuclear ambitions. It would be, obviously, a risky strategy that might end up encouraging nuclear proliferation in Asia, but the nuclear threat from North Korea, arguably, calls for drastic action of some kind. As Stephen J. Morris (2003/2004, 102) explains: "The most chilling threat posed by North Korea gone nuclear is its ability to provide nuclear weapons material to terrorists, in particular Al-Qaeda." And this sticky issue is just one of what promises to be a series of challenging foreign policy choices in Asia in the coming decades.

KEY CONCEPTS

Asia-Pacific Economic Cooperation
    (APEC)   286
Association of South-East Asian Nations
    (ASEAN)   286
Boxer Rebellion   288
Brezhnev Doctrine   298
encirclement   304
Four Modernizations   299
Great Leap Forward   297
Great Proletarian Cultural
    Revolution   299
Kuomintang   289

Open Door Policy   288
peaceful coexistence   297
power transition theory   301
Rape of Nanjing   290
Sino-Japanese War   290
special economic zones   299
Strategic Arms Limitation
    Treaty, or SALT I   298
Taiwan Relations Act of 1979   310
Treaty of Friendship, Alliance and
    Mutual Assistance   295

RATIONAL POLITICAL AMBITION AND...
THE RELATIONSHIP WITH ASIA

☑ Because he was already being criticized for "losing" China during his administration, President Harry Truman felt—for domestic as well as international political reasons—that he could not tolerate North Korea's attempt to take over South Korea in June 1950.

☑ One reason that President Richard Nixon was able to establish contact with the People's Republic of China in 1972 was that his reputation as a staunch anti-Communist allowed him the flexibility to do so without fearing that the move would threaten his hold on power.

☑ Both Presidents Bill Clinton and George W. Bush based their policies with respect to China on the assumption that the United States would be able to maintain a peaceful relationship with a democratic China—an assumption that is supported by both liberalism and by rational political ambition theory.

☑ The current regime in the People's Republic of China faces a particularly thorny issue in its relationship with Taiwan. If it should allow Taiwan to achieve even the appearance of independence, it might lose legitimacy and, eventually, its hold on power. But, should the Communist regime antagonize the United States with really vigorous steps to curb Taiwan's independence, it might damage its relationship with the United States, which could in turn endanger its hold on power by dramatically slowing the economic growth in China that is an important basis of its domestic political support.

CHAPTER 13

THE UNITED STATES AND THE MIDDLE EAST

Israel, Oil, and Terrorists

THE CONTRADICTIONS WITH WHICH THE UNITED STATES NOW STRUGGLES on a daily basis in the Middle East stem originally from the desperate straits in which the United Kingdom found itself during World War I. As their fate in that war hung in the balance, the British flailed about in various directions in frantic attempts to line up support against their mortal enemies in Germany. In so doing, they made a number of contradictory promises and agreements whose ramifications continue to reverberate in the twenty-first century.

The first of these agreements was concluded with important Arabs in the Middle East. Admittedly, it was a rather informal understanding that arose out of correspondence between the British representative in Cairo, Henry MacMahon, and Sharif Hussein, who was the "sharif of Mecca," and therefore responsible for some of Islam's most important shrines. Hussein was also the leader of the emerging Arab nationalist movement, whose main purpose was to liberate Arab peoples from the Ottoman Empire, centered in Turkey. In 1915 Hussein sent a letter to MacMahon, stating his terms for joining the British in the military conflict with Turkey, which by that time was allied with the Germans. MacMahon responded with a letter that committed the British to "recognize and uphold the independence of the Arabs in all the regions laying within the frontiers proposed by the Sharif of Mecca" (Khouri 1968, 7). Reassured by this **Hussein-MacMahon Correspondence**, the Arabs, led by Hussein, began a revolt against the Ottoman Empire in 1916. It was supported by the British with supplies, money, and advisers—the best-known being T. E. Lawrence (Lawrence of Arabia).

At the same time that it was thus evoking Arab support against the Turks, the British government became concerned also about solidifying its ties to France. Helen Chapin Metz (1991) explains: "Following the British military defeat at the Dardanelles in 1915, the Foreign

The U.S. war in Iraq has distracted American attention from the longstanding conflict between Israel and the Palestinians, which shows no signs of abating. The Israeli soldier in this photo confronts a Palestinian man during a random search at a checkpoint in the West Bank city of Hebron in September 2006.

Office sought a new offensive in the Middle East, which it thought could only be carried out by reassuring the French of Britain's intentions in the region." The British attempt to reassure the French along these lines produced the **Sykes-Picot Agreement,** also signed by the Russians (who revealed this secret treaty after the Russian Revolution). As Michael Hudson (1998) reports, "the agreement suggested the establishment of colonies, mandates, and spheres of influence in all of the former Turkish territories...."

And, in yet another attempt to garner support against its wartime enemies, the British government came into contact with the World Zionist Organization, which had been formed in the 1890s in order to bring about the creation of a homeland for Jews. One of its leaders, Chaim Weizman, was a scientist who had been helpful to the Allied cause, and the British government was inclined to listen sympathetically to his appeals on behalf of **Zionism** for a number of reasons having to do with the ongoing conflict with Germany. The German government was, at the time, bidding for support from Jews in Germany as well as the rest of the world. The new Kerensky government in Russia had new Jewish appointees, who, the British felt, might be vital in the effort to keep Russia in the war. In addition, says Fred J. Khouri (1968, 5): "After the United States entered the conflict [i.e., World War I], Britain was concerned about the continued apathy toward the war of a major section of American Jewry."

For all these reasons—as well as the thought that encouraging Jews to immigrate to Palestine might strengthen the influence of the British in an area close to the vital Suez Canal—Foreign Secretary Arthur Balfour wrote an official letter to a leading Jewish citizen of Great Britain, Lord Lionel Walter Rothschild, in November of 1917. This letter, which came to be known as the **Balfour Declaration,** said in part: "His Majesty's government view with favor the establishment in Palestine of a national home for the Jewish people, and will use their best endeavors to facilitate the achievement of this objective."

Obviously, it was not possible for the British to keep, at one and the same time, their promise to the Arabs to give them independence, their promise to the French to divide the Middle East into spheres of influence, and their promise to the Zionists to support the creation of a Jewish homeland in Palestine. As Alawi D. Kayal (2002, 65), an observer who is apparently sympathetic to the Arabs involved in this process, puts it: "The British promised them their independence and unification in compensation for their support of the Allies' cause. They then divided their country, mandated their territories, and promised part of their land to other people." [a]

THE EMERGENCE OF ISRAEL

In choosing to uphold their agreement with the French to divide significant parts of the Middle East into separate spheres of influence, the British rather clearly violated their promise to grant national independence to the Arabs in exchange for their support in the war against Turkey. Whether or not the Hussein-MacMahon Correspondence applied to Palestine

---

a. Kayal details the agreement with the French about their respective spheres of influence in the following manner: "Under this agreement Mesopotamia [roughly, current day Iraq], Palestine, and Jordan were mandated to Britain. Syria, including Lebanon, was mandated to France."

is more controversial. MacMahon himself, in later years, insisted that Palestine was never mentioned in the correspondence, and that the British had never promised that the Arabs in that part of the world would be granted autonomy and independence (Bard 2005a). It is clear that the Balfour Declaration did recognize the right of Jews to establish a national home in Palestine, and that the Mandate for Palestine, created by the League of Nations to legitimate British control of the area after World War I, did include within it the Balfour Declaration (see map 13.1). However, it is also clear that the Balfour Declaration called for the preservation of the rights of existing non-Jewish communities in Palestine, as well as for the establishment of a national home for the Jews. Metz (1991) comments: "The incompatibility of these two goals sharpened over the succeeding years and became irreconcilable."

When the Mandate was set up, there were about 55,000 Jews in Palestine, which was ruled by a British commissioner. Jewish immigration to Palestine was not substantial before the Nazi persecution of the Jews began around 1933; by 1939, around 450,000 Jews lived there. In addition, Jewish organizations energetically bought land in Palestine, tripling the amount in the hands of Jewish immigrants between 1922 and 1939 (Khouri 1968, 18).

Continued, and then dramatically increased, Jewish immigration into Palestine provoked periodic resistance from Arabs living inside as well as outside the territory. The British made several attempts during the Mandate period to set up government structures based on cooperation between Jewish and Arab residents of Palestine, but these attempts never succeeded. By 1938, the British had become sufficiently concerned about the rise of Hitler's Germany that they grew increasingly sympathetic to Arab aspirations regarding Palestine. Richard Allen (1974, 319) explains the British thinking:

> They had at all costs to gather strength for the decisive challenge to Hitler in World War II.... This was to mean yet another change in Britain's position in the direction of concessions to the Arabs as she perceived the full risk, not just to imperial position but to the future of the whole free world, should the Arab countries, exasperated by London's Zionist commitments, align themselves with her Axis foes.

Mostly, this apprehension drove the British toward policies designed to limit Jewish immigration into Palestine, so that the Jewish residents there would remain a permanent minority of about one-third of the population. These steps embittered relations between the British government and the Zionist organizations in such a way that only the onset of World War II led to temporary improvement. Allen explains (330): "The Jews in Palestine and elsewhere had no choice but to fight with Britain against the greatest enemy their race ... had ever known."

So, during the war, tens of thousands of Palestinian Jews volunteered to serve with the British military in the effort against Nazi Germany. Meanwhile, however, illegal immigration by Jews into Palestine was stepped up, and Jewish settlers established communities in new areas of Palestine in anticipation of the struggle that seemed likely to ensue after the war was over. Some Arabs also volunteered to serve with the British military, although, at the same time, as William R. Polk (1975, 198) records, "both Jews and Arabs [in Palestine] did maintain their opposition to the local government, and demonstrations and terrorist attacks never ceased throughout the war."

Thus, by the end of World War II, the British had a serious problem on their hands in Palestine. The Arabs in general and the Palestinians in particular felt that "Palestine should

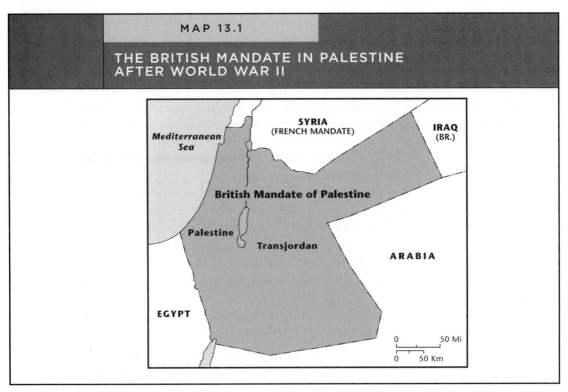

MAP 13.1

THE BRITISH MANDATE IN PALESTINE AFTER WORLD WAR II

After World War I, the British were given control of Palestine in a mandate by the League of Nations. During the war, the British had asserted in the Balfour Declaration their support for a national home for the Jewish people in Palestine.

become an independent state ruled by its native majority…" (Polk 1975, 200). In contrast, the position of the Zionists—who had become much better organized, and more numerous, during the war—was that Palestine should become a Jewish state, open to Jewish immigration, and controlled by Jews.

Immediately after the war, the British government turned to the United States for help. President Harry Truman urged them to allow 100,000 Jewish immigrants to enter Palestine without delay. But when the British requested that the United States provide economic and military support necessary to facilitate this large-scale migration, President Truman refused to provide any help. World War II was over, and the American public, which was demanding a rapid demobilization of its armed forces, would not have supported any deployment in support of a new commitment.

So, President Truman urged upon the British a pro-Zionist policy but refused to provide substantial U.S. support to carry it out. Meanwhile, Khouri (1968, 33) notes,

officials in the State and War Departments who were aware of the strategic and economic importance of the Middle East expressed … concern about Arab feelings towards the United States. They warned that the Soviet Union was already trying to extend her influence into the Middle East and that the long-range interests of the United States in that area depended upon the pursuit of friendly relations with the Arabs.

Not for the last time, President Truman was seemingly oblivious to such advice from the main cabinet-level departments in his government devoted to foreign policy—not to mention all the oil reserves in Arab hands in the Middle East.

Ultimately, the British government decided that it had no authority to give Palestine either to the Jews or to the Arabs, or to partition the land between them, and that it would turn the matter over to the United Nations. In May of 1947, that organization created the **United Nations Special Committee on Palestine (UNSCOP)**, and, by September, UNSCOP recommended partition of Palestine between Jews and Arabs, giving the Jews about 56 percent of the land, although they constituted only about a third of the population. The Arabs refused to accept the plan, but the Zionists devoted their efforts to getting it approved by the UN General Assembly. By November of 1947, the General Assembly passed it by the necessary two-thirds vote, drawing support from both the United States and the Soviet Union, while the British abstained. When the **Arab League** announced in December of 1947 that it would resist the partition plan by force, and the British announced their intention to evacuate Palestine by the following year, the stage was set for a series of clashes between Jewish settlers in Palestine and their Arab neighbors that continues to this day.

From Independence to War

As the May 15, 1948, deadline for the British evacuation approached, neither Britain, the United States, nor the United Nations could devise any solution to avoid the conflict and bloodshed that would surely occur subsequent to the departure of the British troops. Just one hour before the British Mandate was officially scheduled to end, the UN General Assembly held a meeting, during which it was announced that President Truman had given full diplomatic recognition to the new state of Israel, which had come into existence on May 14th, at 10 AM Eastern Standard Time. Truman made this decision in spite of the fact that, as Allen (1974, 386) reports, "the departments of State and Defense gave high priority to America's oil and strategic interests in the Middle East and saw clearly the dangers of arousing Arab countries against the United States by being too pro-Zionist." According to Norman Podhoretz (1998, 30): "Had it been up to George Marshall, then Secretary of State, Israel would never have been born, and when in 1948 and in spite of his wishes and those of his colleagues and subordinates (and their counterparts in the Pentagon), the new Jewish state officially came into existence, Washington would not even have extended diplomatic recognition to it if Marshall had had his way."[b]

Thus, both because the Middle East promised to be a crucial arena in the emerging Cold War with the Soviet Union, and because several Islamic states (including Saudi Arabia, Kuwait, Iraq, and Iran) possessed huge reserves of oil, the United States might have been expected—certainly by realists—to give a high priority to maintaining friendly, supportive ties with those Middle Eastern states. Instead, President Truman antagonized Muslims, and the

---

b. Somewhat surprisingly, Podhoretz goes on to assert that "President Harry Truman … recognized the new Jewish state … only after Stalin … had already beaten him to the punch." President Truman extended de facto recognition to Israel minutes after it came into existence; perhaps Podhoretz refers to de jure recognition.

governments of virtually all Middle Eastern states, by recognizing Israel minutes after it came into existence. It is alleged that when Truman was asked about this decision, which was seemingly questionable in light of the strategic and economic interests of the United States, he asked in turn, "How many Arabs are there in my constituency?" This anecdote may be apocryphal, but if so, it is one of those myths that *should* be true, because it conveys what is probably an accurate impression. That is, in spite of considerable pressure in the form of crucial international strategic and economic incentives to avoid antagonizing Arab and Islamic states—but in accordance with rational political ambition theory—President Truman decided to recognize Israel primarily because of the benefit of doing so within the *domestic* political arena.

This assertion is, to be sure, open to dispute. Michael Benson (1997), for example, argues that Truman's policy with respect to the newly emerging Israel was primarily a product of his personal humanitarian and moral standards. But John Snetsinger (1974, 140) asserts that "Truman's Palestine-Israel policy offers an extraordinary example of foreign policy conducted in line with short-range political expediency rather than long-range goals." This is not to say that Truman was not affected by ethical concerns when he made policy choices regarding the new state of Israel, nor that he was somehow oblivious to the strategic and economic interests of the United States. Nevertheless, absent some kind of privileged access to the workings of Truman's mind in the spring of 1948, our rational political ambition approach to American foreign policy (and international politics in general) would certainly not find it surprising if the president had his own political survival in mind as he mulled over the advice from practically all his main foreign policy advisers with respect to the emergence of Israel in 1948, and decided not to heed it. Indeed, this explanation certainly seems more congruent with the events in question than are standard realist accounts, and its plausibility is reinforced by the fact that it was apparent to everybody at the time that Truman was going to need all the help he could get to survive the election in the fall of 1948.

In any case, Israel needed more than just formal recognition from the United States in order to ensure its survival. Five Arab states—Egypt, Iraq, Jordan, Syria, and Lebanon—sent significant numbers of troops into Palestine, while Saudi Arabia and Yemen made nominal contributions. The five most important Arab enemies of the new state of Israel had combined populations of about 32 million, while Israel contained roughly 1 million people, some significant portion of whom were Arabs. This imbalance created the impression of a tiny Israel surrounded by a huge sea of Arabs, thus giving it very little chance to survive. But, in fact, according to Khouri (1968, 71), the Israeli army, the Haganah, was "made up of 60,000 to 70,000 trained members," of whom "some 20,000 to 25,000 had served in various Western military forces during World War II." The Arab armies, though almost equally numerous, were poorly organized, poorly equipped, poorly led, and, it is safe to surmise, not as dedicated to their cause as the Israelis, who were obviously fighting for the very survival of their new state.[c] By 1949, the Israeli army had succeeded in warding off the attacks by all the Arab armies, and a bitter armistice was arranged.

---

c. In a controversial analysis to be discussed later in this chapter, John Mearsheimer and Stephen Walt (2006b) assert that "Israel is often portrayed as David confronted by Goliath, but the converse is closer to the truth. Contrary to popular belief, the Zionists had larger, better equipped and better led forces during the 1947–1949 War of Independence."

The Suez Crisis (1956)

The Arab armies' defeat by the new, very small state of Israel had at least two main long-range effects on Arab-Israeli relations. First, about 1 million Arab residents of Palestine were uprooted; they moved into Syria, Jordan, and the Gaza Strip. And, according to John Stoessinger (2005, 197): "From their midst would rise the fedayeen and the Palestinian resistance fighters who would hold Israel responsible for depriving them of their homeland." Second, Arabs throughout the Middle East were humiliated by the defeat of the collective Arab armies by the military force of the tiny, nascent state of Israel. And one of those most bitterly humiliated was Gamal Abdul Nasser, who had risen from modest origins to become part of the officer corps in the Egyptian army. Nasser and his compatriots in the military felt that the old, corrupt government of Egypt had given them weapons that were "faulty, old and useless," and that the government-appointed leadership of the military was mostly incompetent. Nasser led a revolt against the old regime in Egypt in 1952, and he came to power himself by 1954.[d]

Dreaming of uniting Arab states behind him in a pan-Arabic federation, Nasser was determined to establish his independence from Great Britain, a former colonial master, as well as from the United States. In 1955 he concluded a major arms deal with the Soviet Union and other Warsaw Pact nations. Then, in May of 1956, he recognized Communist China—a step that was bound to antagonize the United States. In retaliation for that and other uncooperative policies, the United States announced in July of 1956 that it was withdrawing its financial support for Nasser's project to build the Aswan Dam on the Nile River, which was projected to augment Egypt's allotment of arable land by 30 percent and to generate huge amounts of hydroelectric power (Allen 1974, 451). In retaliation, Nasser announced the nationalization of the Suez Canal.

This step was of special concern to Great Britain and France, both of whom had special historical, political, and economic ties to the Suez Canal. At the same time, Israel was becoming increasingly concerned about Nasser, who was procuring ever-increasing amounts of weaponry from the Soviet bloc and implementing anti-Israeli policies, such as preventing Israeli ships, and even ships with goods bound for Israel, from using the Suez Canal; also, the Gaza Strip, under Egyptian control, served as a base for raids on Israeli territory by displaced Palestinians. So, Britain, France, and Israel jointly planned an attack on Egypt, the ultimate goal of which was deposing Gamal Abdul Nasser.

When the French and the British conferred about this plan with the United States in advance, they received the impression from Secretary of State John Foster Dulles that the United States would, at worst, "remain benevolently neutral" (Stoessinger 2005, 200). Confidence that the United States would play at least a tacitly supportive role in the joint British-French-Israeli effort to dislodge Nasser was reinforced by the fact that the attack was planned for late October 1956, only about a week before an American presidential election. None of those countries' leaders believed that an American president running for reelection

---

d. Egypt always plays a crucial role in Middle Eastern political processes because it is the most populous Arab state. In 1974, for example, it had a population of 36 million, while the next most populous states were Iraq, with a population of 10 million, and Syria, with 7 million. (Iran had a population of about 34 million, but while it is Islamic, it is not Arabic; see Sivard 1977, 22.)

would do anything to seriously antagonize Jewish voters—and millions of non-Jewish supporters of Israel, in particular—right before they were due to go to the polls.

But the British, French, and Israeli leaders were all wrong. As Stoessinger (2005, 202) reports: "On November 2, in an emergency session of the General Assembly, the United States took a leading role in calling for a cessation of the fighting and the immediate withdrawal of the Anglo-French-Israeli forces from Egypt." The United States was joined by the Soviet Union in this initiative—another feature of the situation that would have been inconceivable in advance of the unfolding events. The resolute action by the U.S. government against its oldest allies in Britain and France, and against Israel, and in cooperation with its bitter Cold War enemies in the Soviet Union, may seem difficult to understand even now, and, perhaps, not congruent with expectations, based on rational political ambition theory, about the paramount influence of domestic political considerations in foreign policy decisions.

However, rational political ambition theory posits that leaders of states, in general, and U.S. presidents, in particular, must deal with internal *and* external threats to their power. And the anti-Nasser steps taken by the Anglo-French-Israeli coalition posed what was perceived as a very serious threat to the future security of the United States. By that time, Nikita Khrushchev had come to power in the Soviet Union, adopting a policy in support of **wars of national liberation** around the globe. The Eisenhower administration, meanwhile, had come to view the Cold War as a titanic struggle, the outcome of which might be determined in the so-called Third World, made up of newly emerging, mostly poor and developing states in Asia, Africa, and Latin America. Almost none of these Third World states were sympathetic to Israel (and all of those in the Middle East were bitterly antagonistic). All of them were passionately opposed to colonialism, and to colonialist powers—and Britain and France were historically the most energetic and important of the European colonial powers. Supporting those former imperialists in an initiative with so distinctly a colonial flavor as deposing Nasser in Egypt would probably have cost the United States dearly in terms of public opinion in developing states around the world.[e]

In contrast, such a scenario would have been a public relations bonanza for the Soviet Union—a tremendous opportunity for it to burnish its anticolonial credentials. Under such pressures, and in spite of the upcoming presidential election, President Eisenhower sided with the Soviets. His decision was no doubt made easier by the fact that though the Jewish vote was important, "the vast majority of Jews were Democrats..." (Podhoretz 1998, 31). In other words, Eisenhower did not stand to lose a lot of Jewish votes by opposing Israel's military initiative in 1956, because he could not expect to receive many Jewish votes under any circumstances.

In a way, Eisenhower's decision in 1956 conformed to a pattern in U.S.-Israeli relations, as Podhoretz (1998) points out. In the 1950s and the 1960s, the main source of military support for Israel was France, not the United States. France, in the early postwar period, was rather embittered by the insistence of Arab states such as Lebanon and Syria on liberation from French colonial ties. (Lebanon achieved independence in 1943, while Syria became inde-

---

e. "In a move that reflected preoccupation with maintaining a strategic balance against the USSR, the United States applied heavy economic and diplomatic pressure to force the withdrawal of British, French, and Israeli troops from Egypt..." (Rajaee 2004, 85).

pendent in 1946.) It was only after the 1967 war between Israel and its Arab neighbors that the United States stepped into the role of the leading supplier of military aid to Israel.

The Six-Day War (1967)

Gamal Abdul Nasser had emerged from the 1956 war as a pan-Arab hero, having successfully resisted attacks from Israel and two major (and former colonial) powers, Britain and France. But, by 1967, his intention to lead a united Arab world into a glorious future had suffered important setbacks. At what might have been the height of his popularity and influence in the Arab world, Nasser had successfully engineered in 1958 the creation of the **United Arab Republic**, unifying Egypt, Syria, and North Yemen into one republic; in 1962, however, Syria seceded. Then, too, Egypt came out of the 1956 Suez crisis behind the shield of a United Nations Emergency Force (UNEF), a peacekeeping unit. Although it may well have served an important purpose in preserving peaceful relations between Egypt and Israel, this UN involvement also made it difficult for Egypt to offer meaningful support to Arab states in their confrontations with Israel.

As the 1960s unfolded, Syria became the Arab state most active in its antagonism and bellicosity toward Israel. In the late 1950s, Palestinians had formed **al-Fatah**, an organization dedicated to the liberation of Palestine, relying on paramilitary raids against Israeli territory by "commando units." By 1966, Polk (1975, 247) reports, "the Syrian government had for two years, sponsored, equipped, and paid the paramilitary force of al-Fattah [*sic*] to raid northern Israel." By May of the following year, Israel began to issue explicit warnings that it would take retaliatory action if Syria did not bring an end to these al-Fatah raids. Egypt's Nasser then came under increasing pressure to live up to his reputation as the leader of the Arab world, by doing something effective to support Syria in its escalating conflict with Israel. He did manage to put together a treaty promising to come to Syria's defense in case it was attacked, but the Syrian leadership reacted to this feeble gesture, in part, by "accusing him of 'hiding behind the sheltering skirts of the United Nations Emergency force'" (Stoessinger 2005, 205).

Nasser responded to that taunt with the fateful step of asking for the removal of the UN troops that had been stationed between Egypt and Israel ever since the end of the 1956 war. UN Secretary-General U Thant decided to abide by Nasser's request—a move for which he was widely criticized. But Egypt had agreed to the stationing of UN troops on Egyptian soil only with the formal understanding that they would leave if requested to do so. In addition, Egyptian soldiers had already begun to take over some UNEF posts, and two important contributors to the UN force, India and Yugoslavia, announced that they would agree to Nasser's request for removal of the UN troops, whatever U Thant decided. Finally, the secretary-general suggested that if the UNEF forces had to be moved from Egyptian territory, they might serve their purpose just as well if they were stationed on Israeli land. But Israel rejected this option (Khoury 1968, 247).

Next, Nasser's troops took up positions in Sharm el Sheik, from which they could exert control over the Gulf of Aqaba, leading to the Israeli port of Eilat (see map 13.2). Caught up in the emotions spreading throughout the Arab world, which had been fostered in part by Nasser's success in getting the UNEF troops removed, John Stoessinger (2005, 207) relates,

"President Nasser ... announced the decision that was to become the direct cause of the Six-Day War: closure of the Straits of Tiran at the entrance of the Gulf of Aqaba to Israeli shipping."

According to Stoessinger, this step amounted to a blockade—usually an act of war—of the port of Eilat. But this "blockade" applied to only one port, and only to ships flying the Israeli flag. At the time, Israel was receiving only about 10 percent of its annual exports through the Gulf of Aqaba and the port of Eilat, and only one Israeli vessel had passed through the Straits of Tiran in the previous two years (Khoury 1968, 248, 401). Thus, the blockade did not pose a dire economic threat to Israel.

Nevertheless, Israel had been promised, when it withdrew its troops from the Straits of Tiran at the end of the 1956 war, that the international community would guarantee access by its ships to the Gulf of Aqaba through the Straits. And the Israelis had stated, on several occasions in previous years, that the closing of the Straits of Tiran would be considered an "act of war." The U.S. government found the situation alarming; in fact, says Khouri (1968, 253), "American officials were seriously concerned that a major Arab-Israeli conflict might escalate into a world war." This conjecture was based largely on the fact that throughout this crisis, the Soviet Union took a position in steadfast support of Arab states against Israel, warning, in Khoury's words (252), that "should anyone try to unleash aggression in the Near East, he should be met not only with the united strength of the Arab countries but also with strong opposition from the Soviet Union...."

As concerned as the United States was about the mounting conflict between Israel and its Arab neighbors, it was also preoccupied at the time with its war in Vietnam. The UN Security Council met on May 24, 1967, but, partly because of the lack of strong leadership from the United States on this issue, it took no action to lift Egypt's blockade of the Gulf of Aqaba, nor did it do anything else to defuse the situation. Arab spokesmen took increasingly belligerent stances on the issue. President Nasser made a speech in which he declared that Israel committed aggression against Arab peoples simply by existing. And Ahmed Shukairy, the leader of the **Palestine Liberation Organization (PLO)**, made a speech on June 2, in which he called for a holy war to liberate Jerusalem (Stoessinger 2005, 207–208).

Arab hostility to Israel was not limited to bombastic speeches. Before this crisis, relations between Egypt and Jordan had grown quite hostile as well, because of Nasser's protection of the PLO, which was then calling for the overthrow of Jordan's King Hussein. But on May 30, 1967, the king flew to Cairo to sign a defense pact between the two countries; also, an Egyptian general took over the leadership of the Jordanian army. By June 4, Iraq had joined the defense pact, and Libya announced that, in the event of hostilities, it too would join forces with the pact's members in military action against Israel. Eventually, according to Richard Allen (1974, 488), "the number of Arab countries promising to help each other against Israel rose to eleven. By the start of the war it was to reach thirteen."

It was under these circumstances that, on the morning of June 5, 1967, the Israeli air force struck a first blow against Egyptian airfields. A little later, similar strikes were launched against Syria, Jordan, and Iraq. Asserting that a **preemptive war** breaks out primarily because a state feels that it will be attacked in the very near future, Dan Reiter (1995, 6) declares that "preemptive wars almost never happen." In fact, having carefully reviewed the record of interstate

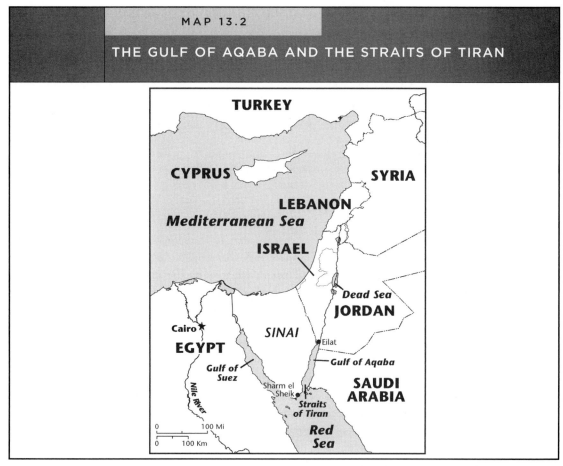

MAP 13.2

THE GULF OF AQABA AND THE STRAITS OF TIRAN

In 1967, having asked the United Nations to remove its peacekeeping forces, Egypt's Gamal Abdul Nasser sent troops to Sharm el Sheik and closed the Straits of Tiran to Israeli shipping. The June 1967 war between Israel and its Arab neighbors soon followed.

wars over the years from 1816 to 1980, Reiter (15) concludes that "the correct count would be one case of preemption"—the Israeli attack on Egypt in 1967.[f]

Most of the air force planes of all of Israel's Arab neighbors were destroyed while they were still on the ground. This successful surprise attack created the basis for a stunningly successful war (lasting only six days), during which Israel took control of the Sinai Peninsula, the Gaza Strip, the entire West Bank, the city of Jerusalem, and the Golan Heights—acquisitions that rather neatly set the agenda for political conflict between Israel and her Arab neighbors over

---

f. Reiter also mentions the German military initiative against Russia at the beginning of World War I, and the Chinese intervention in the Korean War in 1950. But both of those cases, he notes, involved third parties intervening in ongoing wars. Reiter also reviews five cases since 1980—the end date of the Correlates of War data set (see Small and Singer 1982) he analyzed—and concludes that none of them qualify as cases of preemption. Since the publication of Reiter's 1995 article, that Correlates of War data set has been updated through 1997 (see Sarkees 2000), but no war appears on that list that would apparently qualify as preemptive. It is also clear that the U.S. military initiatives against Afghanistan and Iraq in the wake of the attacks of 9/11 were not preemptive.

the ensuing forty years (see map 13.3). It is an agenda that has yet to be dealt with in a way that satisfies any of the disputing parties.

The Yom Kippur War (1973)

In the aftermath of the 1967 war, Nasser accused both the U.S. and the British air forces of aiding Israel during the conflict. Khouri (1968, 267) details the lasting impressions of the defeated peoples:

> Although, in time, many Arabs began to concede that the British and American planes had probably not helped Israel during the war, nearly all Arabs nevertheless continued to believe that the United States had at least indirectly encouraged Israel to attack, delayed Security Council action until Israel had made substantial territorial gains—especially at the expense of Syria, and helped to defeat all efforts to obtain an Israeli withdrawal.

One of the many disastrous impacts on the neighboring Arab states involved the Palestinians, some 200,000 of whom, having fled what had become Israel proper to the West Bank, now fled the West Bank into Jordan. Until this war, the assumption of many Palestinians had been that conventional military efforts, supported by Arab states in the area, would ultimately destroy Israel and restore them to what they saw as their rightful place before Israel had come into existence. The 1967 war, however, suggested that such dreams were unrealistic. The Palestine Liberation Organization took this lesson to heart. According to Allen (1974, 520): "At a meeting in Cairo in February [1969] of most of the Arab guerrilla organizations, Al Fatah gained control of the PLO, and Yasir Arafat its leader was elected chairman of the Organization's new executive committee."

The next Arab-Israeli war was initiated by Egypt (along with Syria) in 1973. By that time, Anwar Sadat had become the head of the Egyptian government. On October 6, 1973, which was Yom Kippur (the Jewish Day of Atonement), Egyptian and Syrian forces launched a well-coordinated surprise attack whose apparent aim was to recapture territories lost in the 1967 war. That attack enjoyed early and surprising successes, partly because Israeli forces were caught somewhat off guard, but perhaps more so because they assumed that they possessed a degree of military superiority that did not exist. "Before October 1973," according to Henry Kissinger (1982, 459), most analysts "agreed that Egypt and Syria lacked the military capability to regain their territory by force of arms; hence there would be no war. The Arab armies must lose; hence they would not attack. The premises were correct. The conclusions were not."

The Egyptian army managed to cross the Suez Canal in large numbers, and to overrun the Israeli Bar-Lev line, consisting of fortifications set up by Israel along the Suez Canal after it captured the Sinai Peninsula in 1967. The Syrians sent 800 tanks across the cease-fire line in the Golan Heights and managed to seize major Israeli positions there. "By the end of the first week of the war," Stoessinger (2005, 213) comments, "Israel had stemmed the Arab onslaught, but the myth of its invincibility had nevertheless been shattered."

Israel might have lost its myth of invincibility, but it was soon Egypt's Third Army that was in deep trouble. In his memoirs, Kissinger (1982, 571) points out that "the plight of the Egyptian Third Army was far more serious than our own intelligence had yet discovered."

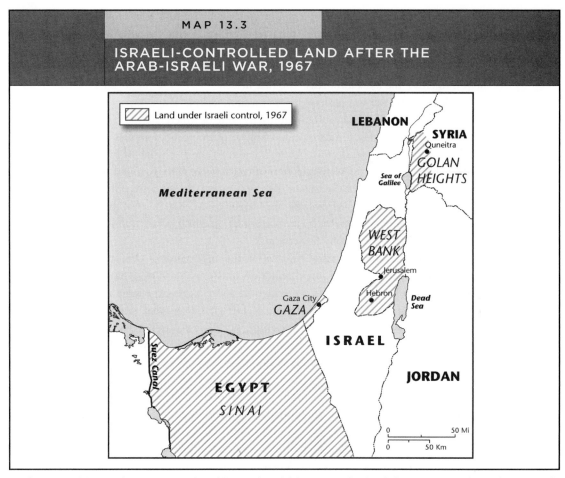

MAP 13.3

ISRAELI-CONTROLLED LAND AFTER THE ARAB-ISRAELI WAR, 1967

Land under Israeli control, 1967

LEBANON

SYRIA
Quneitra
GOLAN HEIGHTS

Sea of Galilee

Mediterranean Sea

WEST BANK
Jerusalem
Hebron
Dead Sea

Gaza City
GAZA

ISRAEL

JORDAN

Suez Canal

EGYPT
SINAI

0   50 Mi
0   50 Km

In the June 1967 war between Israel and its Arab neighbors, Israel seized the territories shown here, which previously belonged to Egypt, Jordan, and Syria.

Surrounded by Israeli military forces, it would soon have to fight to break out of that encirclement, or capitulate and surrender. Both Egypt and the Soviets began to talk about the possibility that Soviet troops would be sent to the area to rescue the Third Army, if necessary. "It was clear that if we let this go on," Kissinger (576) observes, "a confrontation with the Soviets was inevitable."[g] In response to the escalating crisis, Nixon and Kissinger decided to put American military forces worldwide into an advanced stage of readiness, a "world-wide red alert." Nixon in later years would refer to this confrontation as "my Cuban Missile Crisis," which perhaps exaggerated the danger of the situation. Nevertheless, the advanced state of readiness became front-page news in the United States almost immediately, thus creating a very public confrontation with the Soviets from which it would be difficult for either side to back down.

---

g. Kissinger also notes that "we were determined to resist by force if necessary the introduction of Soviet troops into the Middle East" (580), and that "we were heading into what could have become the gravest foreign policy crisis of the Nixon Presidency" (582).

At this tense stage of the crisis, a compromise was worked out in the Security Council of the United Nations. It called for sending a UN peacekeeping force to the area, from which troops from either superpower would be excluded. The peacekeepers soon arrived in the area where the Egyptian Third Army was surrounded by Israeli military forces, and those forces helped to create the basis for a cease-fire that held.

While the 1967 war was perhaps more crucial in its long-range impact on Arab-Israeli relations, the 1973 war also had profound impacts—one of which had to do with the price of oil. Israel had, at last, prevailed in the war, but only after emergency supplies of military hardware had been flown into Israel from the United States. At the beginning of the war, the U.S. government had been anxious to refrain from direct involvement, to avoid becoming too obviously engaged in support of the Israelis. But by October 11, 1973, according to Daniel Yergin (1992, 604), "the Americans realized that Israel could lose the war without resupply. In Kissinger's and even more so in Nixon's formulation, the United States could not allow an American ally to be defeated by Soviet arms."

Coincident with this very visible increase in the importance of U.S. support for Israel was increased dependency by the United States on oil from the Middle East. In April of 1973, President Nixon had made the first presidential address ever on energy issues; on that occasion, he abolished quotas on the import of foreign oil. At that point, Saudi Arabia had emerged as the "swing producer" for the entire world—a position held until that time by the state of Texas. Yergin (1992, 594) explains: "The United States would no longer be able to increase production to supply its allies in the event of a crisis, and the United States itself was now, finally, vulnerable."

That vulnerability became painfully obvious over the next seven or eight years. On October 19, 1973, President Nixon proposed a $2.2 billion military aid package for Israel. In retaliation, Saudi Arabia and other oil-exporting Arab states cut off shipments of oil to the United States. In addition, the Arab oil-exporting states began to roll back production of oil on a monthly basis, usually by about 5 percent. Yergin (615–616) comments: "The embargo and its consequences sent shock radiating through the social fabric of the industrial nations.... In the United States, the shortfall struck at fundamental beliefs in the endless abundance of resources ... American motorists saw retail gasoline prices climb by 40 percent—and for reasons that they did not understand."

The other important long-term impact of the 1973 Arab-Israeli war had to do with its impact on U.S.-Egyptian relations. In the wake of the war, Kissinger focused on arranging a lasting peace between Israel and Egypt, managing by 1975 to produce a peace agreement that called for Israel to return to Egypt two mountain passes, plus an oil field. In exchange, Egypt promised to refrain from using force, or even threats to use force, against Israel. Perhaps at least as important, Anwar Sadat promised to continue to negotiate the establishment of a more permanent peace between the two states.

In 1977 Sadat traveled to Israel and spoke to the Israeli parliament. This courageous action initiated a process, led by President Jimmy Carter, that, in the end, produced a peace agreement calling for Israel to withdraw from the Sinai desert, and for the Palestinian issue to be resolved over the next five years. Ultimately, in March of 1979, Stoessinger (2005, 221) reports, Egypt and Israel "signed a separate peace treaty. The president's tenacity and faith had finally borne fruit. After thirty years of war the Middle East had taken a large step toward peace."

This peace did come at a price, however. The U.S. strategy of pushing for a separate peace between Israel and Egypt inevitably appeared to the rest of the Arab world to be a rather imperial strategy of "divide and rule." Unity among Arab states was, in other words, subverted by the Camp David process. This continued for decades thereafter, during which Egypt, in payment for its complicity, became the second largest recipient (after Israel) of U.S. foreign aid on an annual basis. In addition, U.S. support of Egyptian dictator Hosni Mubarak, who came to power in the wake of Sadat's assassination in 1981, also made the U.S. commitment to democracy, in the Middle East and in general, look calculated, conditional, and even hypocritical.

Lebanon (1982)

Israel next came into sustained military conflict with its Arab neighbors in 1982. After the Arab-Israeli war of 1967, and again after Jordan's King Hussein cracked down on the PLO in his nation in 1970, Palestinians had moved into Lebanon in great numbers, probably in the hundreds of thousands. Yasir Arafat also moved his headquarters from Jordan to Lebanon. This migration set the stage for continual conflict between the Palestinians in general, and the PLO in particular, and the Israelis.

After Lebanon erupted into civil war in 1975, Syria ultimately intervened, occupying central Lebanon. In response to that intervention, and to a March 1978 terrorist attack by the PLO that originated in Israel and led to the deaths of thirty-four hostages, the Israeli Defense Forces moved into Lebanon and pushed the PLO militants away from the Israeli border. After a two-month occupation of this "security strip," Israeli forces withdrew and allowed UN forces to take their place (Bard 2005b).

But the UN forces in southern Lebanon were unable to prevent the PLO and its allies from assembling a formidable arsenal in the area, which Israel perceived to be quite threatening. The United States managed to arrange a cease-fire for the area in July 1981, although, according to the Israeli government, in the ensuing eleven months, the PLO staged 270 terrorist actions within Israel, in the West Bank and the Gaza Strip, as well as along the Lebanese and Jordanian borders. Ultimately, in June of 1982, Palestinian militants under the direction of terrorist leader Abu Nidal attempted to assassinate Israel's ambassador to Great Britain, and Israel responded by moving into southern Lebanon in force. The initial operations there were so successful that Israel decided to try to push the PLO out of Lebanon entirely, and to induce Lebanon to sign a peace treaty with Israel. Such a peace treaty was negotiated and signed, but a year later Syria forced the Lebanese government to renege on the agreement (Bard 2005b).

In September of 1982, the United States sent military forces into Lebanon as part of a peacekeeping force that also included British, French, and Italian soldiers. This multinational force was "intended to mediate the conflict, help to re-establish the authority of the Lebanese government, and to protect Palestinian refugees" (Rajaee 2004, 95). After the PLO departed Lebanon as part of a cease-fire agreement put together with the aid of the states involved in the multinational military force, these forces were withdrawn in early September—two weeks earlier than had originally been scheduled.

A few days later, however, Lebanon's president-elect (Bashir Gemayal) was assassinated. In response, Israeli forces invaded West Beirut. One source of Israeli concern was the internment camps for Palestinian refugees in Sabra and Shatila, where, the Israelis estimated, some 2,000–3,000 PLO fighters had been left behind, in spite of the agreed-upon evacuation of PLO troops. Rather than entering those camps, however, the Israeli forces surrounded them and decided to let their Lebanese allies deal with the insurgents. Lebanese Christian militiamen then entered the camps, intent, as it turned out, on revenge for the assassination of the Lebanese president-elect. Journalist Thomas Friedman (1995, 161) describes what happened next: "From Thursday, September 16, until Saturday morning, September 18, Phalangist squads [i.e., Lebanese Christian militias] combed through the Sabra and Shatila neighborhoods, liquidating whatever humanity came in their path." Exactly how many Palestinians were killed is unclear; some may have been carted off and killed elsewhere. In the aftermath, Red Cross officials estimated that the death toll was 800 to 1,000.

In response to this situation, the Reagan administration decided to send U.S. marines back into Lebanon. It was an ill-fated decision. On October 23, 1983, a suicide bomber drove a truck with 12,000 pounds of dynamite into a Marine Corps headquarters in Beirut, killing 241 American soldiers. Friedman (1995, 203) comments: "Having come to Beirut to protect the Lebanese, the Marines now seemed the ones needing protection."

On the following day, President Reagan (1983b) held a news conference in Washington, D.C., proclaiming that "we have vital interests in Lebanon" and that it was crucial for the marines to stay in place to protect those vital interests. In fact, he asserted, the marines in Lebanon were vital to protecting "peace throughout the Middle East." And then he went even further—much further—insisting that keeping the marines in Lebanon was "central to our credibility on a global scale."

Unfortunately for that credibility, Reagan soon began to plan for the evacuation of those same U.S. marines from Beirut. As late as December of 1983, he had insisted that the marines and the accompanying naval vessels would stay put until the Lebanese government had stabilized the situation in the war-torn country. But on February 7, 1984, he announced that he was "redeploying" the marines to ships off the coast of Beirut. By February 26, all of them were gone, as were the ships. Historians Stephen Ambrose and Douglas Brinkley (1997, 313) draw the painful conclusion: "Civil war [in Lebanon] still raged ... there was, in brief, nothing good to say about the Reagan administration's policies in Lebanon, and much to denounce."

THE OSLO ACCORDS, AND THE ROAD TO PEACE?

In the wake of the debacle in Lebanon, the United States assumed a lower profile in the Middle East, especially with respect to the Arab-Israeli conflict. Then, in 1991, U.S. Secretary of State James Baker managed to persuade Israelis, Arabs, and Palestinians to attend a conference in Madrid. Nothing of lasting importance was accomplished at this conference, but it did seem to serve as a catalyst for secret talks between Palestinian and Israeli delegates in Oslo, Norway, in 1992 and 1993. These talks produced a Declaration of Principles—the **Oslo Accords**—which were signed on the White House lawn in September of 1993. On this momentous occasion, Israeli Prime Minister Yizhak Rabin shook hands with PLO Chairman Yasir Arafat. The Accords called for Israel to relinquish control, ultimately, of the Gaza Strip and the West Bank, in exchange for PLO recognition of Israel's right to exist.

But the road to peace through the Oslo Accords has been exceedingly rocky. In 1995 the process did lead to a meeting between King Hussein of Jordan and Israel's Rabin, another handshake, and establishment of official peace between those two states. But in 1996, Rabin was assassinated by an Israeli extremist who objected to the prime minister's plans to (eventually) cede control of the Occupied Territories to the PLO. When Rabin was succeeded by Benjamin Netanyahu, who was less inclined to accept the proposed settlement with the Palestinians, the peace process slowed to a crawl.

Nevertheless, an Israeli election in 1999 resulted in victory for Ehud Barak, whose role model was Yitzhak Rabin. The new Israeli prime minister made a move toward reviving the peace process at a conference with Yasir Arafat at Camp David in the United States, presided over by President Clinton. Barak even went so far as to offer to give up part of East Jerusalem and to permit the Palestinians to designate it their capital. But, when Arafat insisted that, in addition, all Palestinians be granted the "right of return" to Israel—which could potentially reduce Jews to minority status in Israel—the proposed agreement was stalled. As Stoessinger (2005, 230) reports, after the collapse of those Camp David talks, "Bill Clinton made one last Herculean effort to break the deadlock in December 2000 at Taba, Egypt, but to no avail."

The twenty-first century brought hard-liner Ariel Sharon to power as prime minister of Israel, and the Palestinians shortly thereafter adopted tactics relying on suicide bombers inside Israel. The violence escalated, as suicide bombing missions by the Palestinians evoked military attacks by the Israelis; on occasion, Israeli tanks would reduce entire neighborhoods in Gaza to piles of rubble. By 2003, the aging and ailing Arafat had ceded most of his power to a new prime minister, Mahmoud Abbas, and the second Bush administration had come up with a "road map" to peace. One notable aspect of this directional initiative was that the United States became officially committed to a two-state solution to the conflict—one state for Israelis and one for the Palestinians.

By 2005, however, Sharon decided to order the unilateral withdrawal of Israeli troops from Gaza, and to establish a "security line" between Israel and Palestine, relying largely on a physical barrier—a wall designed to keep suicide bombers out of Israel. This plan evoked plenty of opposition in Israel, but Sharon seemed well on the way toward implementing its provisions when he suffered a debilitating stroke in January of 2006. There were some signs, by the time of Sharon's demise, that his controversial strategy for dealing with the Israeli-Palestinian conflict was working. As columnist Charles Krauthammer (2006) noted in the wake of Sharon's stroke:

> The success of this fence-plus-unilateral withdrawal strategy is easily seen in the collapse of the intifada. Palestinian terrorist attacks are down 90 percent. Israel's economy has revived. In 2005, it grew at the fastest rate of the developed countries. Tourists are back, and the country has regained its confidence.

But soon after Sharon's stroke, an election among the Palestinians resulted in a stunning defeat for al-Fatah, their ruling party for decades, and a victory for the fundamentalist Islamic group **Hamas**, whose platform calls for the destruction of Israel. According to Josef Federman

(2006): "Hamas' rise to power has damaged chances of renewing long-stalled peace negotiations. Israel refuses to deal with the group, which is responsible for dozens of suicide bombings in Israel, until it renounces violence and recognizes the Jewish state." The election results in Palestine also called into question the strategy of the Bush administration for dealing with terrorism by encouraging the spread of democracy in the Middle East. Is democracy a viable solution under current conditions in the Middle East, a skeptic might understandably wonder, if it results in electoral victories, and the ascent to political power, of terrorist groups such as Hamas?

Peace between Israel and its Arab neighbors seemed even more remote when war broke out in 2006 between Israel and troops loyal to a group known as **Hezbollah** in southern Lebanon. Israel had relinquished control of that territory several years earlier, with the understanding that it would be kept free of organizations such as Hezbollah, which is bitterly opposed to Israel's existence. Israeli plans to relinquish control of the West Bank were promptly shelved, and the question remained: when, again, might Israel be inclined to trade land for peace?

U.S. POLICIES IN THE REST OF THE MIDDLE EAST

All political interactions in the Middle East are fundamentally affected by the Arab-Israeli conflict, and it is possible that U.S. relationships with the Islamic states of that region would be profoundly altered if only some lasting solution to that conflict could be found. In other words, normalization of the relationship between Israel and the Palestinians would make U.S. relations with Islamic states, especially those in the Middle East, much less difficult and contentious than they now are. But those relations would still be complex, important, and almost certainly problematic on numerous occasions.

Iran

One of the most important policy decisions made by the United States in the immediate post–World War II period involved the state of Iran. In April of 1951, the Majlis (the Iranian parliament) elected Mohammad Mossadegh premier of the country, and then, a couple of days later, it passed legislation calling for the nationalization of British oil holdings in the country. Originally, the "United States was in complete support of the nationalization cause," according to Kayal (2002, 102). In the ensuing months and years, however, as Mossadegh became more influential, he grew increasingly friendly toward Moscow and increasingly antagonistic toward the shah of Iran. By 1953, at a meeting of the National Security Council in Washington, D.C., Secretary of State John Foster Dulles predicted that if the current drift of events in Iran were to continue, Mossadegh would take over as dictator, and then the Communists would take over the country. Moreover, says Daniel Yergin (1992, 468), "if Iran succumbed to the Communists," in Dulles's view, "there was little doubt that in short order the other areas of the Middle East, with some 60 percent of the world's oil reserves, would fall into Communist control."

The U.S. government, in short, became sufficiently concerned about the future of Iran that it deployed CIA agents, in cooperation with agents of the British M16 secret service, to intervene in Iranian politics. As a result of the activities of these foreign agents, the shah was encouraged to dismiss Mossadegh. Somewhat to his surprise, the dismissal stuck, and there were large demonstrations in the streets of Tehran in support of the shah.

Just how influential the actions of the CIA and M16 were in Iran in 1953 is still in dispute today (Yergin 1992, 469–470). But there is little doubt that, in the minds of most Iranians, the CIA, in particular, was indispensable in the effort to restore the shah to his throne. Moreover, in the decades that followed, the U.S. government played a key role in keeping him there until the Iranian Revolution in 1979. The shah, meanwhile, maintained his hold on power by means of a brutal secret police force, the SAVAK, which became known throughout the world for its gruesome torture of his political opponents.

The shah's corrupt tactics, and the very visible support he received from the United States, were certainly key factors in fostering the Islamic fundamentalist revolution in 1979. They also fueled the crisis involving the detention of American diplomats at the American embassy in Tehran, a hostage crisis that dragged on for 444 days, finally ending on the day of Ronald Reagan's swearing-in as president in January 1980.

The new Iranian regime under Ayatollah Khomeini was of sufficient concern as a threat to neighboring Iraq, that Saddam Hussein decided to initiate military action against it later in 1980. Iraq's attack was initially successful, in part because of the upheaval in the Iranian military after the ouster of the shah, but by 1982, a bloody stalemate was in place. The United States and the Soviet Union supplied weapons to both sides at various points during the seemingly never-ending war. And, in 1985–1986, President Reagan's administration started secret negotiations with the Iranian government, offering U.S. weapons in return for the Iranians' help in securing the release of hostages then being held in Lebanon. When the media uncovered this scheme—which also involved the use of proceeds from these arms sales to purchase weapons for Nicaraguan rebels against the Sandinista regime—what became known as the **Iran-*contra* project** came unglued (Rajaee 2004, 95–97; see also chapter 10).

The Iranian regime survived the bloody war with Iraq, which finally came to an end in 1988. More recently, Iran's new president, Mahmoud Ahmadinejad, has publicly denied that the Holocaust occurred, has called for Israel to be wiped off the map, and appears determined to develop the capability for Iran to produce its own nuclear weapons. Furthermore, the Iranian regime has close ties to the Shi'ite community in Iraq, and it promises to exert substantial influence on any government that comes to power in Iraq in the wake of the chaos reigning there as a consequence of the U.S. invasion and overthrow of Saddam Hussein. That Iranian influence will clearly not be considered beneficial by the U.S. government. In short, it is not unreasonable to conclude that the United States has paid a heavy price indeed, over several decades, for its decision to become so visibly (albeit covertly) involved in the overthrow of Mohammed Mossadeq in 1953.[h]

---

h. "Except for Ayatollah Ruhollah Khomeini, father of its revolution, no leader has left a deeper mark on Iran's 20th century history than Mohammed Mossadegh. And no 20th century event has fueled Iran's suspicion of the United States as his overthrow has" (Sciolino 2000).

The Iran-Iraq War

Egypt's Gamal Abdul Nasser came out of the 1956 Arab-Israeli war a hero in much of the Arab world. He was receiving arms from the Soviet Union, which also had stepped in with substitute funding after the U.S. government halted its financial support for the Aswan Dam. Energized by adulation from Arab populations, Nasser apparently saw himself as the leader of a pan-Arabic movement that could result in the unification of much of Arabia. As mentioned earlier in this chapter, concrete steps were taken toward creating such a union under his leadership in February of 1958, when Egypt and Syria proclaimed the formation of the United Arab Republic (UAR)—whose name was fashioned in such a way that it could have served for the unification of an unlimited number of Arab states. Yemen initated what seemed likely to become a bandwagon effect by joining the UAR in March of 1958.

Given what were widely perceived to be increasingly close ties between Nasser and the Soviet Union, this movement toward pan-Arabism evoked some concern in Washington, D.C. That concern escalated as demonstrations broke out in 1958 in Beirut in favor of having Lebanon join the UAR, and it reached something of a fever pitch when a revolution occurred in July of that year in Iraq, replacing a pro-Western government with a more radical one, headed by Karim Kassem, that showed some signs that it, too, was considering a move toward becoming a member of the Arab union. When the instability in Lebanon seemed on the verge of sweeping up that country in the rising tide of pan-Arabism, and into the United Arab Republic, the Eisenhower administration decided to send U.S. marines into Lebanon to "stabilize" the situation.

While the move was widely regarded at the time as anti-Soviet as well as anti-Nasser, some analysts now view this U.S. military action as at least as much intended to protect Lebanon against political currents emanating from Iraq. Friedman (2000, 226) comments: "That Lebanon was being protected against Iraq's Kassem rather than against Nasser showed that the U.S. focus was shifting to favor Nasser, as a nationalist rather than a Communist.... Kassem used the Iraqi Communist Party to destroy an Iraqi movement for union with Nasser's UAR." In any case, if the U.S. move into Lebanon in 1958 was intended at least in part to stem the tide of pan-Arabism under Nasser, it seems in retrospect to have worked. Neither Iraq, nor Lebanon (nor Jordan) joined the UAR, and, in fact, Syria itself withdrew from the union in 1961.

In Iraq, the Kassem regime, which was sympathetic to Soviet interests, soon lost out to a regime with more nationalistic sentiments, under the leadership of the Ba'athist Party. A minor member of that party, Saddam Hussein, took part in an attempt to assassinate the leader of the 1958 revolution. When that attempt failed, Saddam found himself sentenced to die for his part in the plot, and he fled to Egypt. By 1968, however, he was back in Iraq—now the second most powerful official within the Ba'athist regime. By 1979, Saddam took over as the unrivaled dictator of the state of Iraq.

Shortly thereafter, he was confronted with the danger and the opportunity created by the Islamic fundamentalist revolution in Iran. Saddam Hussein and the Iranian Ayatollah Khomeini were personal enemies. Yergin (1992, 709) explains: "Khomeini and his circle saw the secular, socialist Ba'athists as implacable enemies of their own creed and attacked Ba'athism as 'the racist ideology of Arabism.'" Saddam, for his own part, had plenty to fear from the revolution next door. Himself a Sunni, in a country that was at least half Shia, he could not but fear that the Shia in his own country might be more sympathetic to the Shia regime in Iran than to his own secular, Sunni-based rule.

In addition, it certainly appeared that in the wake of the fundamentalist revolution in Iran, the Iranian military was in disarray. As Yergin tells it (710), Saddam had multiple incentives to launch an attack on his closest and bitterest enemy: "Iraq could strike hard at Iran, topple Khomeini, put an end to the Shiite revolutionary threat to Iraq, and assert sovereignty over the Shatt-al-Arab waterway, protecting Iraq's oil position." In short, Saddam's strike against Iran in 1980 was motivated largely by fears that the revolutionary regime in the neighboring state posed a serious threat to his own hold on power, as well as by eagerness to seize what he saw as an opportunity to improve Iraq's situation externally.

So, when Saddam Hussein's military struck Iran hard in September of 1980, Friedman (2000, 432) notes, the United States was "placed in the ironic position of supporting a Soviet client state, Iraq, against a former U.S. client, Iran." Even though the Reagan administration later got caught up in the Iran-*contra* project in such a way that it ended up providing military weapons to the Iranian regime during that war, the United States, for the most part, "tilted" rather definitively in the direction of Saddam Hussein during his bloody, almost decade-long struggle against the Iranians.

The George H. W. Bush administration ended up providing $5.5 billion in loans to the Iraqi regime—funds that Saddam utilized, in part, to support Iraq's attempts to develop nuclear weapons. As Ambrose and Brinkley (1997, 382) report: "So close were Iraq and the United States in July 1990 that joint military maneuvers were being planned for later in the year." But this close relationship came to an abrupt end when, not long after Saddam Hussein had finally brought to a close his bloody conflict with Iran, he turned his aggressive instincts in the direction of another neighbor, Kuwait.

The Persian Gulf War

It would be reasonable to suppose that Iraq, having just completed a prolonged and disastrous war against Iran, would be exhausted and anxious to avoid military conflict with any of its neighbors for some time to come. Instead, in retrospect, the long war with Iran seemed to create conditions and incentives that soon led Saddam Hussein to seek another target for attack.

For one thing, the war against Iran had driven Iraq deep into debt—to the tune of $70 billion. A considerable portion of that amount was owed to Kuwait, which, ironically, had provided financial support to Iraq in its struggle with Iran in the hopes of maintaining a civil, if not actually friendly, relationship with Saddam. But, as the Kuwaiti regime found after the war, its good deed was not to go unpunished. In the run-up to his next military adventure, one of Saddam's complaints was that Kuwait would not forgive the $10 billion debt that Iraq owed it.

What had increased Saddam's antagonism toward Kuwait even more was that small nation's "over-production" of oil in 1989 and 1990, which drove down the price, costing Iraq billions that it would otherwise have earned from its oil exports. From the viewpoint of Saddam Hussein, this was not simply a case of Kuwait's selfishly attempting to generate more revenue for itself by increasing the volume of its oil exports—it was, instead, part of a plot to undermine his regime. In the mid-1980s, in fact, Saddam had seen how Saudi Arabia cooperated with the Reagan administration (as we will discuss in more detail in chapter 14) by pumping oil into the world market in such a way as to rapidly depress its price, thus depriving the Soviet Union of billions of dollars in hard currency that it might have otherwise earned from its exports of oil (Schweizer 2002, 238–239). Whether Saddam imagined, by August of 1990, that this price-fixing tactic had ultimately contributed to the collapse of the Soviet Union is impossible to say. But he could certainly have seen that it had preceded, and might well have been a key factor in, the sequence of events leading to the demise of the Soviet empire in Eastern Europe.

And so, in the summer of 1990, Saddam apparently perceived that the U.S. government was conniving with the emirate of Kuwait in a similar plot, relying on expedited exports of oil to deflate its price, and thus undermine, perhaps fatally, his hold on power. In a speech in July, he pointed explicitly to a conspiracy that was stabbing Iraq in the back by overproducing oil. This conspiracy, in his view, was led by the United States, and Kuwait was, in his words (cited in Stein 1992), part of a "'Zionist plot aided by imperialists against the Arab nation.'"

In short, Saddam Hussein decided to attack Kuwait in 1990 in part because he wanted to augment Iraq's holdings of oil. But he also thought that the option of inaction in that summer was unacceptable, because of a real danger that his regime might be fatally subverted by a scheme masterminded by the United States, which had so recently utilized the "oil weapon" successfully against its rapidly deteriorating Cold War antagonist. Then, too, when Saddam met with the U.S. ambassador to Iraq, April Glaspie, about the escalating crisis between Iraq and Kuwait, Glaspie assured him, according to Janice Gross Stein (1992, 152), that "we have no opinion on the Arab-Arab conflicts, like your border disagreement with Kuwait."

Invading and annexing Kuwait was quite easy for Iraq. The United States, supported by the United Nations and a large coalition, then announced that the Iraqi troops must withdraw immediately. This resistance to Iraq's move into Kuwait had something to do with a determination not to allow such bald-faced aggression to stand as a precedent, possibly encouraging to other potential aggressors. It also had a lot to do with the fear that Saddam Hussein would move from his base in Kuwait to take over oil wells in Saudi Arabia, thus giving him control of an enormous proportion of the world's reserves of oil.

Thus, it would have been easy to infer that the coalition opposing Saddam Hussein in the wake of Iraq's annexation of Kuwait was quite determined. It would have been equally easy to estimate the potency of the anti-Iraqi coalition's military forces. One simple but widely utilized indicator of a state's military-industrial capabilities, for example, is its GNP. At the time of this confrontation, Iraq's GNP was about .5 percent that of the GNP of the United States. Also, the United States had many powerful allies, while Iraq had none. Why, then, did Saddam Hussein decide *not* to relinquish control of Kuwait?[i]

---

i. One analysis of Saddam's options (based on a computer simulation of various possible outcomes) in advance of the military counterattack by the United States concludes that Iraq "missed an opportunity for peace. Had Mr. Hussein chosen to act, he could have unilaterally diffused the Gulf conflict. Our analysis discloses that a peaceful solution required Iraq to withdraw from Kuwait while retaining claims to the disputed oil fields and island" (Kugler, Snider, and Longwell 1994, 143).

One reason is that Iraq did, at the time, have an apparently formidable military force, relying on 1 million soldiers, plus hundreds of aircraft, 6,000 tanks, and 5,000 artillery pieces (IISS 1990). Another was that Saddam doubted that the U.S. military forces would fight with determination. He believed that the war in Vietnam, for example, had proved that the American government could not withstand public opposition to any military conflict that produced a substantial number of casualties. Also, President Reagan's sudden withdrawal of U.S. military forces from Lebanon, in the wake of a suicide bomber's attack, was apparently on Saddam Hussein's mind as he contemplated his options in advance of the promised assault by the United States and its formidable coalition. In other words, says Stein (1992, 175), "Saddam was persuaded that the United States would not have staying power, as it had demonstrated when it withdrew its marines from Beirut after an attack on the marine compound in October 1983." But, almost certainly, the most important reason that Iraq did not withdraw from Kuwait in advance of the war was that Saddam Hussein was convinced that the United States was determined to remove him from power, and that if he did withdraw, this conspiracy against him would be strengthened.

So, Iraqi troops did not withdraw from Kuwait when the U.S.-led coalition began its air assault on January 15, 1991. Saddam hoped that when that assault began, the governments in one or two key Arab states might fall, bringing to power regimes that would withdraw from the anti-Iraqi coalition, and perhaps even offer Iraq some military support. No such uprisings occurred, however, and by February 23, Saddam faced an ultimatum to withdraw from Kuwait or face military invasion by ground forces. Still, he refused to budge. Stoessinger (2005, 264) comments: "Saddam responded once again by inviting the coalition to drown in its own blood in the 'mother of all battles.' This was yet another costly error. By stalling and haggling, the Iraqi dictator doomed his army to a terrible defeat."

Nevertheless, Saddam did manage to hold on to power. In fact, soon after the aerial bombardment began, Saddam ordered his elite Republican Guard troops to retreat, in order to protect Baghdad, and himself. Then, when the fighting stopped, and the United States decided not to enter Baghdad to depose him, Saddam used his army, in Stoessinger's words (267), to "crush a rebellion in Basra, and then vent its full fury on the rebellious Kurds in the north and an unruly Shi'ite minority in the south." Despite this vengeful aftermath to their Kuwait incursion, the ensuing decade was a very difficult one for Iraqis. The economic sanctions imposed on Saddam's regime by the United Nations inflicted their harshest damage on Iraqi citizens outside the government. Also, the world community—and, especially, the United States—were not done with Saddam Hussein.

The 9/11 Attacks

The U.S. focus on the Middle East shifted away from the Arab-Israeli conflict and (at least briefly) from Saddam Hussein, toward remote Afghanistan, on September 11, 2001. Nineteen operatives mobilized by Osama bin Laden's transnational terrorist group, **al-Qaeda**, hijacked four American airliners, flying two into the World Trade Center towers in New York City and a third into the Pentagon, outside Washington, D.C. A fourth plane, possibly bound for the White House, apparently fell out of the control of the hijackers and crashed in rural Pennsylvania. Nearly 3,000 people lost their lives as a result of these al-Qaeda suicide missions.

The coordinated attack was reminiscent of Japan's bombing of Pearl Harbor in December of 1941. Although roughly the same number of people died in that surprise attack, the 9/11 attacks were, in some ways, more traumatic. Pearl Harbor, after all, is situated in territory that belonged to the United States at the time of the Japanese attack, but it was not then part of the United States proper. In contrast, New York City is the nation's largest urban center, a media and economic hub, and Washington, D.C., is the nation's capital. Also, quite unlike the events of 1941, which were described on radio some hours after the bombing raids had ended, the results of the hijackers' efforts in 2001 were televised nationwide, almost instantaneously.

On the other hand, Japan was a formidable military power, a major nation-state, while al-Qaeda is a shadowy transnational organization that, at the time of the terrorist attacks, was based thousands of miles away in the mostly rural, nearly medieval state of Afghanistan and possessed no conventional military force that would be capable of inflicting any large-scale damage on the United States. From that perspective, therefore, the attacks of 9/11 posed challenges that were substantially less daunting than those represented by powerful Japan (not to mention its allies, Germany and Italy) in 1941.

What, then, were the hijackers, and the al-Qaeda organization that supported and sponsored them, hoping to accomplish by their attacks? In a statement issued in 1998, Osama bin Laden (2002, 149) had explained his motives as follows:

> In compliance with God's order, we issue the following fatwa [religious injunction] to all Muslims: The ruling to kill the Americans and their allies—civilians and military—is an individual duty for every Muslim who can do it in any country in which it is possible to do it, in order to liberate the al-Aqsa mosque and the holy mosque [in Mecca] from their grip, and in order for their armies to move out of all the lands of Islam, defeated and unable to threaten any Muslim.

So, according to their instigator, the point of the 9/11 attacks was to convince the United States to remove itself and its military forces from the Middle East—especially from Saudi Arabia.

In other communications, bin Laden also expressed his hope to "liberate" other states in the Middle East, including the large and influential state of Egypt, and, in the wake of 9/11, he began to talk more consistently about his concern for the fate of the Palestinians. Indeed, the ultimate aim of al-Qaeda may be to reestablish the Caliphate, a religious institution (roughly equivalent to the Roman Catholic papacy) that existed from the death of Mohammed in AD 632 until the demise of the Ottoman Empire in the 1920s. According to analyst Daniel Pipes (2005): "The jihadi terrorists have a patently self-evident ambition: to establish a world dominated by Muslims, Islam, and Islamic law, the Shari'a.... Their 'real project is the extension of Islamic territory across the globe and the establishment of a world-wide "caliphate" founded on Shari'a law.'" [j]

It is reasonable to surmise that Osama bin Laden and other leaders of al-Qaeda hoped that the United States would respond to 9/11 with an attack on its bases in Afghanistan, and that the ensuing war would ultimately turn out to be as disastrous for the invaders as the Soviet war against the *mujahadeen* during the 1980s had been. Any such initial hopes along those

---

j. In the second statement, Pipes is quoting the *Daily Telegraph*. On the goal of restoring the Caliphate, see also Gunaratna (2002).

lines were fulfilled, when the United States launched military operations both against al-Qaeda and against the governing coalition in Afghanistan known as the Taliban, in October of 2001, only a matter of weeks after the terrorist attacks in the United States.

Unlike the Soviet invasion, however, that American counterattack enjoyed quick and stunning success, which may well have been a very unpleasant surprise for al-Qaeda, as well as for the Taliban. The U.S. air strikes began on October 7, 2001; by November 9, the Taliban regime had apparently collapsed. According to a team of military analysts (Andres, Wills, and Griffith 2005, 124): "A small group of Afghan rebels working with U.S. special forces and U.S. airpower defeated the Taliban's conventional army and overthrew the regime.... The speed with which these tactics worked in Afghanistan surprised everyone, from National Security Council (NSC) planners to the combatants participating in operations."

But the U.S. military forces in Afghanistan failed to capture Osama bin Laden, who would remain at large years after his spectacular assault on the United States. Furthermore, continuing reports indicated that, partly fueled by thriving exports of illegal drugs, the Taliban was soon making a comeback in Afghanistan, and that increasingly large areas of the country were not under the control of the frail central government in Kabul. The administration of George W. Bush never put very many troops into Afghanistan, and after the fall of the Taliban, it almost immediately turned its attention to Saddam Hussein and Iraq. In 2004 Richard A. Clarke, a specialist on terrorism formerly at the National Security Council, told journalist Seymour Hersh (2005, 146) that the Bush administration had "viewed Afghanistan as a military and political backwater—a detour along the road to Iraq, the war that mattered most to the President." Hersh also reported the words of another military consultant, who told him that in Afghanistan, "from January 2002 on, we were in the process of snatching defeat from the jaws of victory."

U.S. military fatalities in Afghanistan numbered a little over fifty in 2004, and almost twice that number in 2005 (Operation Enduring Freedom 2006). Keeping in mind that between December 1979 and February 1989 the Soviet Union sent some 620,000 troops to Afghanistan, almost 15,000 of whom were killed, it is clear that the U.S.-led occupation of Afghanistan has been nowhere near as disastrous as the Soviet intervention (Grau and Jorengsen 1998; Sarkees 2000). Still, the evolution of the political and military situation there is also a long way from being a lasting success, from the American point of view.

The Turn to Iraq

According to the author of a serious candidate (at an admittedly very early stage) for the definitive volume on the U.S. war against Iraq that began in March of 2003, it is difficult to answer the question, "Why did the United States invade Iraq?" Eventually, George Packer (2005, 46) concludes, "It still isn't possible to be sure—and this remains the most remarkable thing about the Iraq war."

Packer also argues that, judging from a January 2000 article in *Foreign Affairs* by Condoleezza Rice (who would later serve as President Bush's national security adviser and then as his secretary of state), the Bush administration seemed unlikely to become involved in "crusades to transform the world." Instead, in Packer's view (37), in that paper Rice "called for a return to the great power realism of Nixon, Kissinger, and Bush's father."

And, in fact, in that article, which is entitled "Promoting the National Interest" (2000, 62), Rice declares that foreign policy in a Republican administration, in which she would clearly play a prominent role, "will ... proceed from the firm ground of the national interest, not from the interests of an illusory international community." However, in a statement that is particularly intriguing with the benefit of hindsight, she also asserts (60) that the regime of Saddam Hussein "has no useful place in international politics," and that "nothing will change until Saddam is gone, so the United States must mobilize whatever resources it can, including support from his opposition, to remove him."

In the run-up to the war, the assurance that Saddam Hussein had, or at least was actively in pursuit of, nuclear weapons was presented by the Bush administration as the most pressing reason for taking military action against Iraq. There were also hints, sometimes rather explicit, that Saddam had connections to al-Qaeda, and even that he had played a role in the 9/11 attacks. One possibility that certainly seemed of great concern to many in the American foreign policy establishment was that the Iraqi leader would acquire nuclear weapons and then offer one to al-Qaeda, which would sneak that weapon into a major American city (probably New York) and detonate it, killing some horrifically large number of people in the process.

But, subsequent to the invasion of Iraq, the U.S. forces and operatives found no nuclear weapons, nor even any convincing evidence that Saddam's regime had possessed any actual, active program to develop nuclear weapons—or, indeed, any other weapons of mass destruction. When this lack of substantiating evidence became obvious, the major public rationale for the war was changed to deposing the dictatorial regime of Saddam Hussein and replacing it, ultimately, with a democratic regime that not only would assure peaceful, even cooperative, relations between Iraq and the United States in the future, but also would serve as a model and an inspiration for the spread of democracy throughout the Middle East. Democratic regimes in the Middle East would, in turn, deprive terrorist groups of the political support they need to survive and grow. As a former undersecretary of defense for policy in the Bush administration, Douglas Feith (2006, 235), has explained: "Extremism of the type that fuels terrorism is a political phenomenon. It's driven by ideology, and ideologies we know can be defeated."

According to this argument, the war in Iraq was driven, in the beginning, by the neoconservative vision of overturning dictatorships by military force if necessary, while relying on the pacifying force of democracy. Stoessinger (2005, 279), for example, believes that George W. Bush decided to launch the military initiative against Iraq because "he became increasingly attracted to a small but highly intelligent group of neoconservative intellectuals who believed that containment was no longer the answer in a post 9/11 world." He refers to Deputy Undersecretary of Defense Paul Wolfowitz; Richard Perle of the American Enterprise Institute; and Michael Ledeen, a former U.S. National Security official, who together persuaded President Bush to adopt a policy of "making the world safe for democracy through the full use of America's status as the world's sole remaining superpower."

One popular explanation regarding the motives for the U.S. war against Iraq is that it was all about oil. In May 2005, for example, a British Member of Parliament, Michael Meacher, declared that the reason that the United States attacked Iraq had "nothing to do with weapons of mass destruction, it was nothing to do with democracy in Iraq, it was nothing to do with the human rights abuses of Saddam Hussein." When asked at a press conference whether the war had something to do with oil, Meacher's response was that "the connection is 100 percent. It is absolutely overwhelming" (Porter 2005). Moreover, Michael T. Klare (2005) quotes an assertion by Vice President Dick Cheney himself in advance of the war:

> Should all [of Hussein's WMD] ambitions be realized, the implications would be enormous.... Armed with an arsenal of these weapons of terror and set atop 10 percent of the world's oil reserves, Saddam Hussein could then be expected to seek domination of the entire Middle East, take control of a great portion of the world's energy supplies ... and subject the United States or any other nation to nuclear blackmail.

According to Klare himself, the Bush administration, "having decided to eliminate Hussein,... set out to ensure that any successor regime would be predisposed to satisfy U.S. energy objectives."[k]

An analysis of the U.S. invasion of Iraq based on rational political ambition theory would focus, instead, on the potential impact of such a decision on the prospects for George W. Bush to stay in power. Surely, in the wake of the 9/11 attacks, key figures in the Bush administration had to be concerned about the potential impact of another major terrorist attack in advance of the presidential election in 2004. One can surmise, in fact, that key people in the administration must have been quite convinced of the likelihood of such an event. If one assumes that such an event is likely, then, from the point of view of rational political ambition theory, a key question is, "What would be the likely impact of another significant terrorist attack on the United States on the presidential election of 2004?" In order to preserve his hold on power in the wake of such a second attack, President Bush needed to be in position to say, credibly, to the electorate: It is true that in spite of our best efforts, we have not been able to deter or prevent yet another terrible attack by determined Islamofascists on the United States. But our efforts, nevertheless, have been vigorous and admirable.

If the Bush administration, having proclaimed a "war on terror," had then confined its most visible efforts to the conflict with the Taliban and al-Qaeda in Afghanistan, would it have been able to persuade voters that its antiterrorist campaign had been, in fact, vigorous and admirable? There is clearly room for doubt on that score. The likelihood is that the war in Afghanistan—especially in the absence of a simultaneous war in Iraq—would have been a relatively low-key affair, with few significant, identifiable accomplishments after the fall of the Taliban (which happened early and easily). In addition, a single-minded focus on the war in Afghanistan would have unavoidably featured as its central theme the search for Osama bin Laden—which was not, perhaps, likely to succeed. In fact, the likelihood was that if the Bush administration were to emphasize the search for bin Laden as the central feature of the war on terror, that war would, by 2004, appear rather inept and ineffectual. And if a failure to cap-

---

k. George Wright (2003), writing for the *Guardian/UK*, reported, on June 4, 2003, that "oil was the main reason for military action against Iraq, a leading White House hawk has claimed." The story quoted Paul Wolfowitz as replying to a question about the differences in the manner that the United States had chosen to deal with nuclear proliferation issues with respect to Iraq on the one hand and North Korea on the other by saying: "Let's look at it simply. The most important difference between North Korea and Iraq is that economically, we just had no choice in Iraq. The country swims on a sea of oil." However, shortly thereafter, the *Guardian* withdrew this story, acknowledging that Wolfowitz had *not* declared that the economic value of Iraq's oil had motivated the war. See also Pelleteire 2004.

ture bin Laden were then combined with an inability to prevent another successful al-Qaeda attack on the United States in advance of the 2004 election, might it not have been likely that a majority of the American electorate would then decide that it was time for a change in the national political leadership?

One key figure in the Bush administration who may have had thoughts along these lines—even in advance of the 2002 midterm elections—was the president's primary political adviser, Karl Rove. According to *New York Times* columnist Frank Rich (2005), even as early as January 2002, Rove became concerned that "Afghanistan was slipping off the radar screen of American voters, and the president's most grandiose objective, to capture Osama bin Laden 'dead or alive,' had not been achieved." Rich suggests that this realization led Rove to conclude that the war in Afghanistan was a weak base of achievements on which to rely in upcoming elections: "Mr. Rove could see that an untelevised and largely underground war against terrorists might not nail election victories…." This conclusion, in turn, led Rove to resolve that, in order for President Bush to appear to be a vigorous, effective protagonist against terrorism, he needed to move beyond the war in Afghanistan. Rich remarks: "The path was clear for a war in Iraq to serve as the political Viagra Mr. Rove needed for the election year."

Rich here imparts a flavor of tawdry, underhanded political conspiracy that neither rational political ambition theory nor I would necessarily endorse. All political leaders want to maintain power, and many may well have admirable motives beyond self-aggrandizement for putting such a priority on that goal. I have little doubt that President Bush and his key advisers felt that they were likely to be far superior leaders of the American war against terrorism than the alternative candidates in the Democratic Party, and that taking the war to Iraq was a good strategy against international terrorism, as well as a more effective domestic political strategy. In fact, I am fairly confident that most influential advisers in the Bush administration sincerely believed that if it were true that initiating the war in Iraq would secure more support from the American electorate than a single-minded pursuit of the war in Afghanistan, that would be because the American people in significant numbers would agree that the war in Iraq was an important supplement to the war in Afghanistan in an effective grand strategy against terrorism.

CONCLUSION

On March 19, 2003, the American war against Iraq was launched. By April 9, 2003, the statue of Saddam Hussein was toppled. On May 1, 2003, George W. Bush, standing under a banner proclaiming "Mission Accomplished," announced that major combat operations in Iraq had ended. And on December 14, 2003, Saddam Hussein was captured. This outline describes a brief and successful war.

In fact, the war per se was short, and it achieved its major goal of deposing Saddam Hussein. But the occupation of Iraq—the peace-building, so to speak—and the attempt to bring political and economic stability to post-Saddam Iraq have been anything but short and successful. Many critics, including George Packer (2005), argue that there were never enough American troops in Iraq to ensure stability in the wake of the downfall of the Iraqi regime. This problem was compounded by the early decision, once the Americans were in control, to disband the Iraqi military and police forces, helping to create a power vacuum that could not be filled for years.

Then, in April of 2004, it was revealed that American military personnel had been abusing and torturing prisoners at the Abu Ghraib facility in Baghdad. Horrifying photographs of happenings there were followed by all-too-credible rumors about mistreatment of detainees at the military base in Guantanamo Bay, Cuba, and also in "black prisons" set up by the CIA in various parts of the world (such as East-Central Europe). And the deadly violence continued, on a daily basis, week after week, and month after month, throughout Iraq. American soldiers, as well as Iraqis, continued to die; by mid-2007, the number of American soldiers killed was about 3,500. The clear majority of them had been killed since President Bush declared that major combat operations in Iraq were over.

The continuing problems the United States faces in Iraq have reminded some observers of the American war in Vietnam during the 1960s and the 1970s, but it is not clear that this is an apt analogy. The American military's difficulties in South Vietnam stemmed from opposition by the government of North Vietnam, which was assisted by two major powers, China and, especially, the Soviet Union. There is, however, no significant major-power opposition to the United States in Iraq; the external opposition comes from terrorist groups such as al-Qaeda. And probably the most important opposition comes from inside Iraq.

Although winning an interstate war was the crux of the problem in Vietnam, the issue in Iraq is not so much a struggle against an opposing military force as it is establishing a political regime that can govern the country, while not posing a greater danger to the United States than did that of Saddam Hussein. And the precedents for this attempt are not, perhaps, in Vietnam, or in Korea, but in all of those places where the United States has intervened to various degrees in order to depose political regimes its government has considered unacceptable and to establish stable, preferably democratic, political systems. Analyst Francis Fukuyama (2004, 61) observes that the United States "has been involved in approximately 18 nation-building projects between its conquest of the Philippines in 1899 and the current occupations of Afghanistan and Iraq, and the overall record is not a pretty one." He points out that the only cases of success, in fact, have been in Germany and Japan, where it was necessary only to re-legitimize societies in what had been very powerful states, and where U.S. forces intervened and stayed indefinitely.

Historian Stephen Kinzer (2006) analyzes fourteen cases during a 110-year period during which Americans overthrew governments that displeased them, starting with the case of Hawaii in 1893. He concludes that the current operation in Iraq "has had terrible unintended consequences"—as have "most of the other coups, revolutions, and invasions that the United States has mounted to depose governments it feared or mistrusted" (Goodman 2006). Cuba, Haiti, Nicaragua, Guatemala, Chile, Iran, and Iraq comprise a partial list of countries in which the United States has intervened over the past one hundred years in order to remove what it considered unacceptable governments, only to leave in its wake political instability and, quite often, bitter and long-lasting anti-Americanism.

Furthermore, the U.S. invasion of Iraq, though billed as a strategic move in the war on terrorism, brought obvious advantages to al-Qaeda. Osama bin Laden has long been dedicated to the overthrow of secular leaders in the Middle East, and the United States did him a favor by overthrowing Saddam Hussein and thus opening up Iraq as a base of operations for al-Qaeda.

Also, the photos from Abu Ghraib, the news stories about mistreatment of Muslims in the detention camp at Guantanamo, and the rumors of "black prisons" in undisclosed locations have clearly created a recruiting bonanza for Osama bin Laden's organization. The war in Iraq has diverted time, energy, resources, and military forces from the conflict in Afghanistan, where al-Qaeda and its Taliban hosts show more signs of making a comeback with every passing day.

Also, the war in Iraq has created serious divisions between the United States and its European allies and has damaged its reputation throughout much of the world—most grievously in the Muslim world (Odom 2004). Finally, Iran poses a clear threat to acquire nuclear weapons, as well as missiles to deliver them; North Korea already has them. But the war in Iraq has depleted the resources—military, political, and moral—available to the United States to deal with these threats. It is not even clear at this point that the United States can credibly threaten either of these hostile states with military action, much less actually carry out effective military operations against them, given the extent to which its resources are stretched thin in Afghanistan and Iraq.

An important theme of this chapter is the extent to which American foreign policy in the Middle East has responded to domestic political incentives, as opposed to strictly strategic, international considerations. Two prominent analysts of American foreign policy, and of international politics in general—John Mearsheimer and Stephen Walt (2006b)—have lately created a firestorm by developing a thesis that apparently resonates with this aspect of rational political ambition theory, in an article entitled "The Israeli Lobby."[1] They point out that Jewish voters make large campaign donations to presidential candidates in both parties, although it is Democratic presidential candidates who may depend on Jewish supporters for as much as 60 percent of their money. And Jewish voters, Mearsheimer and Walt also point out, are concentrated in states such as California, Florida, Illinois, New York, and Pennsylvania, which are very important in terms of the number of Electoral College votes they produce.

What has most evoked the wrath of many observers and analysts are the claims by Mearsheimer and Walt that "the thrust of U.S. policy in the region [i.e., the Middle East] derives almost entirely from domestic politics, and especially the activities of the Israel Lobby," and that "no lobby has managed to divert [American foreign policy] as far from what the national interest would suggest.…"

This argument departs rather strikingly from the general neorealist approach to international politics that is espoused by Mearsheimer and Walt in other contexts. Neorealists, in general, downplay the impact of domestic political considerations on foreign policy decisions. But these analysts also provide evidence that serves to differentiate their argument from the approach of rational political ambition theory, when they point out that, although neoconservatives in the Bush administration (some of whom were Jewish) and the important members of the Israel Lobby were eager for the United States to invade Iraq, the broader Jewish-American community was not in favor of that invasion. Shortly after the war started, national public opinion polls showed that Jews were less supportive of the Iraq War than was the

---

1. A somewhat lengthier version is available as a working paper—Mearsheimer and Walt 2006a.

population at large, by about 20 percentage points. Thus, Mearsheimer and Walt (2006b) conclude, "it would be wrong to blame the Iraq war on 'Jewish influence.' Rather, it was due in large part to the Lobby's influence, especially that of the neo-conservatives within it."

In other words, while rational political ambition theory would expect the president to be responsive to Jewish voters and the threat they might pose to his hold on power, Mearsheimer and Walt emphasize instead the influence of a more limited sector of the population (and Jews in total represent only about 3 percent of the U.S. population). And since Mearsheimer and Walt themselves point out that it is Democratic Party candidates who are most dependent on Jewish supporters for campaign contributions, the ability of the Jewish community in general, or even the pro-Israeli lobby to sway the Republican George W. Bush might be more limited than Mearsheimer and Walt suggest.

Nevertheless, it should also be pointed out, in defense of Mearsheimer and Walt, that they specifically assert, in a response to their critics, that "there is a powerful moral case for Israel's existence, and we firmly believe that the United States should take action to ensure its survival..." (Mearsheimer and Waltz 2006c). I am also inclined to agree with their observations there that "although many claim that the Iraq war was all about oil, there is hardly any evidence to support that supposition," and that "if the oil companies or the oil-producing countries were driving policy, Washington would be tempted to favour the Palestinians instead of Israel. Moreover, the United States would almost certainly not have gone to war against Iraq in March 2003."

But the Bush administration did decide to go to war against Iraq in 2003, and it seems likely that the United States will be living with the consequences of that decision for years—even decades—to come. It is also possible that, in future decades, the invasion of Iraq will be seen as a wise move bringing desirable consequences to the Iraqis, the Israelis, and the entire Middle Eastern region.

In the long run, the American foreign policy issue that is likely to be of greatest significance in the twenty-first century will be the relationship between the United States and China. In the immediate future, however, the headlines promise to focus more intensely on Israel, oil, and terrorists whose home base is in the Middle East.

KEY CONCEPTS

al-Fatah   325
al-Qaeda   339
Arab League   321
Balfour Declaration   318
Hamas   333
Hezbollah   334
Hussein-MacMahon
    Correspondence   317
Iran-*contra* project   335
Oslo Accords   332

Palestine Liberation Organization
    (PLO)   326
preemptive war   326
Sykes-Picot Agreement   318
United Arab Republic   325
United Nations Special Committee on
    Palestine (UNSCOP)   321
wars of national liberation   324
Zionism   318

RATIONAL POLITICAL AMBITION AND . . .
THE RELATIONSHIP WITH THE MIDDLE EAST

LESSONS
LEARNED

☑ Against advice from nearly all of his foreign policy advisers, President Harry Truman in 1948 recognized the new state of Israel almost certainly for domestic political reasons, rather than because of calculations of "national interest" in the Middle East. Continued support of Israel by American presidents and the government in general responds more to domestic political considerations than to calculations regarding international strategic advantage.

☑ In the first Persian Gulf War, Saddam Hussein devoted Iraq's most potent military forces to protecting his regime from domestic sources of opposition rather than to defeating invading military forces belonging to the U.S.-led international coalition. And he felt it necessary to attack Kuwait in the first place because he believed it was playing a major role in a U.S.-led plot to depose him.

☑ President George W. Bush may have deemphasized the conflict in Afghanistan and ordered the invasion of Iraq in 2003, in part, because of a calculation that focusing solely on the conflict in Afghanistan and pursuit of Osama bin Laden would not be an effective strategy for winning the next election, especially if, as was expected, the United States were to be hit by another major terrorist attack before 2004.

ENDING THE COLD WAR AS A TEMPLATE FOR THE WAR ON TERROR, AND OTHER PRIORITIES

AS ONE OF THE SIGNAL EVENTS IN THE HISTORY OF U.S. FOREIGN POLICY, the end of the Cold War is fraught with policy, as well as theoretical, significance. There are many explanations for the demise of that superpower confrontation, some of them diametrically opposed to each other. In chapter 14, we discuss some of the most prominent ideas about how the Cold War was brought to its successful (from the U.S. point of view) conclusion, and ask what lessons the George W. Bush administration may have drawn from that experience when formulating its policies for dealing with the threat of Islamic fundamentalism.

Finally, we will point out that there are other important problems and priorities, such as global climate change, that clearly warrant a sizable share of the time and energies of American foreign policy makers—and of the citizens of the country in whose name they formulate the policies that have served as the focus of this book.

CHAPTER 14

U.S. FOREIGN POLICY IN THE TWENTY-FIRST CENTURY

AS THE FIRST DECADE OF THE TWENTY-FIRST CENTURY NEARS AN END, THE United States is clearly the most powerful and influential country in the world, according to a wide variety of indicators. Yet it faces serious problems. Less than a decade ago, amid the millennial celebrations that greeted the new century, the nation was enjoying federal budget surpluses that seemed destined to continue into the foreseeable future. (One of the major points of discussion in the presidential election of 2000 focused on what the major-party candidates proposed to do with the $10 trillion in budget surpluses that were projected over the coming decade.) In recent years, however, the United States has once again posted massive annual deficits in its federal budget and its balance of trade. In order to finance those federal budget deficits every year, it has depended on the purchase of U.S. Treasury bonds by foreigners; currently, the second most important foreign holder of those bonds (after Japan) is the People's Republic of China (see Department of Treasury/Federal Reserve Board 2006). Also, as we saw in chapter 4, the obligations of the federal government implied by such social welfare programs as Social Security, Medicare, and Medicaid are so overwhelming that it is difficult to see how they can be met in future decades without devastating impacts on the American economy as a whole.

And yet the economic problems now facing the United States may not be as serious as its political and military problems. In response to the terrorist attacks of 9/11, the United States invaded Afghanistan and managed, as discussed in the previous chapter, to depose the Taliban government in short order, and to defeat al-Qaeda forces as well. But, some five years later, Afghanistan is far from a stable place, while both the Taliban and al-Qaeda seem to be making a comeback there. This apparent regression may reflect, in part, the competing commitment of resources by the United States to the conflict in Iraq. U.S. forces invaded Iraq

George W. Bush's administration appears to be attempting to emulate in the war on terror the successes attributed to President Ronald Reagan's vigorous anti-Soviet policies during the culminating decade of the Cold War in the 1980s. Here, President Bush stands before Reagan's casket after speaking during funeral services at the National Cathedral in Washington, D.C., in June 2004.

in March of 2003 and, in a manner reminiscent of the attack on Afghanistan, managed to quickly depose the target regime of Saddam Hussein. In addition, Saddam himself was captured shortly thereafter, brought to trial, and rather brutally executed by the new Iraqi government in 2006. Nonetheless, insurgents continue to launch daily attacks, by means of suicide bombers and improvised explosive devices (IEDs), on Iraqi citizens and on the American soldiers who continue to occupy the country. More than four years after the initial attack, it is difficult to foresee anything like a happy outcome to the struggle in Iraq.

In the meantime, the regimes of North Korea and Iran seem to pose increasingly dangerous threats; a nuclear test detected by seismic monitors in 2006 suggests that North Korea already possesses nuclear weapons (and missiles to deliver them),[a] while Iran shows every sign of being determined to acquire them. The struggles in Afghanistan and Iraq, however, leave the United States short of resources—diplomatic, political, and military—to deal with these threats. Indeed, the declining influence of the United States is reflected in public opinion polls in countries around the world. Brian Knowlton (2006) reports: "As the war in Iraq continues for a fourth year, the global image of America has slipped further, even among people in some countries closely allied with the United States...." One recent poll, for example, shows that by 41 percent to 34 percent, British respondents feel that the U.S. military presence in Iraq is a greater danger to world peace than is the government of Iran (Rieff 2006).

Meanwhile, according to an increasingly broad consensus, the global environment is threatened by accelerated climate change, and the United States is almost universally perceived as part of the problem, rather than a leader helping the international community to deal with the issue.

So how will the United States cope with the foreign policy challenges of the twenty-first century? Will it be forced to accept, as best it can, its own decline into irrelevance, becoming a mere shadow of its twentieth-century self? Or are there feasible, effective ways for U.S. policymakers to deal with the issues and challenges that appear to be so overwhelming?

LESSONS FROM THE END OF THE COLD WAR?

It is possible that the United States will not be able to effectively confront the challenges it currently faces, and that ten or twenty years from now it will have clearly entered a period of decline and deterioration. But an assessment of that possibility should be tempered with a sense of historical context. The United States, though powerful and influential today, has faced daunting challenges in almost every recent decade, many of which have created widespread impressions that it was in steep and probably permanent decline.

For example, the United States was on the winning side in World War I, and it enjoyed a prosperous 1920s, but then the stock market crashed in 1929, and the United States, along with the rest of the world, went into the Great Depression of the 1930s. During the 1940s, in the wake of the Japanese attack on Pearl Harbor, the entire U.S. economy and population

a. In the summer of 2006, "North Korea ratcheted up the rhetoric in its war of words with Washington by promising an 'annihilating strike' with its nuclear deterrent should the United States launch an attack.... 'The army and the people of the DPRK are now in full preparedness to answer a pre-emptive attack with a relentless annihilating strike and a nuclear war with a mighty nuclear deterrent'" (Reuters 2006).

were mobilized to combat Nazism and Fascism in a second global conflict. It emerged victorious from that war, too, but already by the 1950s it faced what seemed a possibly even more ominous threat to its national security from the aggressive Communist ideology of the Soviet Union and its allies in the most populous country in the world, the People's Republic of China. Its indirect confrontation with those Cold War foes in Korea resulted in what was commonly regarded as the first interstate war in its history that the United States did not win (although it did not actually lose that war). When the Soviet Union launched its Sputniks in the late 1950s, it was easy to conclude that Soviet Communism represented the wave of the future, against which the United States, with its old-fashioned notions about the virtues of the free market and bourgeois democracy, would be helpless.

Next, the nation became mired in the Vietnam War, dedicating billions of dollars and the lives of over 55,000 military personnel over a period of eight years in an effort to preserve the independence of South Vietnam, which finally fell to the Communist forces of North Vietnam in 1975. Shortly before that ignominious defeat, President Richard Nixon resigned rather than face impeachment and likely conviction for his actions in the Watergate cover-up. OPEC raised the price of oil at the beginning of the 1970s, and the U.S. economy ended that decade with a very high "misery index"—that is, high inflation and high unemployment, as well as slow growth and very high interest rates.

President Ronald Reagan brought optimism into the White House at the beginning of the 1980s, but, soon thereafter, he presided over the worst economic recession the country had experienced since World War II. Rapidly increasing defense expenditures helped to create massive federal budget deficits, while high interest rates strengthened the dollar, which, in turn, made U.S. exports expensive (and imports relatively cheap); the U.S. balance of trade turned distressingly negative. Relations with the Soviet Union in the early 1980s were quite tense, focusing in part on the deployment by the Soviets of SS-20 missiles, each containing three independently targeted thermonuclear weapons, within range of targets in Western Europe. The response by NATO, spearheaded at an important point by the Reagan administration, then placed intermediate-range missiles in Western Europe, within easy range of Moscow and other Russian cities. Massive numbers of demonstrators in Europe and the United States called for a nuclear freeze, and many feared that these off-setting missile deployments represented an escalation on the way toward a nuclear war.

At the same time, Japan seemed to be a paragon of economic virtue in many ways—especially when compared to the United States, with its massive budget and balance-of-trade deficits. According to Robert Gilpin (1987, 349): "The United States in the 1980s is exhibiting ... the classic manifestations of a declining economic and political power." Also, this noted analyst of international political economy thought (345) it was clear that "the policies of the Reagan Administration accelerated the deteriorating long-term economic position of the United States." As we noted in chapter 4, Gilpin concluded (340):

> American mismanagement of its own internal affairs and of the international financial system has caused the responsibilities of the financial hegemon to fall largely upon the Japanese.... Now it is Japan's turn at financial leadership.

However, as William Niskanen (1993, 2002) reports, "at the end of the Reagan administration, the U.S. economy had experienced the longest peacetime expansion ever." And, ten years after the anointing of Japan as the new financial hegemon, that nation's economy was enmeshed in a prolonged series of economic troubles that left it no longer able to claim that title. Also, by the mid-1990s, the U.S. budget and trade deficits that had seemed to be indicators of permanent decline were once again pretty much under control.

But, most significant from the point of view of this discussion, even before the 1990s began, the Cold War had come to an end, and the Soviet empire in Eastern Europe had fallen apart. And, a couple of years after the fall of the Berlin Wall, the Soviet Union itself fell apart. These events represented the culmination of a process that may offer important lessons for the future of U.S. foreign policy. A primary focus of this final chapter, therefore, is analysis of actions taken by the Reagan administration (and others) during the Cold War, for the purpose of drawing conclusions that may be applicable to the second Bush administration's handling of the current global conflict.

Why the Cold War ended is, of course, a question that has attracted a lot of attention from scholars of international politics and of U.S. foreign policy. One answer is that the end of the superpowers' standoff was brought about more or less independently of international politics and of U.S. foreign policy. According to this notion, what happened was that the Soviet Union ultimately dissolved because of flaws in its internal political and economic systems; these flaws weakened it irretrievably, and once the Soviet Union had fallen apart, the Cold War was over (Garthoff 1994).

So, in this view, the Cold War ended because the Soviet Union fell apart and died. There is probably some measure of validity to this argument. But also worthy of consideration is a contrasting point of view, suggesting that the Soviet Union fell apart and died because the Cold War had ended.

A problem with the argument that the Cold War ended primarily because of the dissolution of the Soviet Union is that the sequence of events does not clearly support it. The Soviet Union staggered to its end only in the final days of 1991, whereas the Cold War was over by November of 1989, when the Berlin Wall fell. In fact, the tension between the United States and the Soviet Union had almost entirely dissipated months—if not years—before the collapse of that symbolic barrier.

For example, as early as 1987, the United States and the Soviet Union had signed the Intermediate-Range Nuclear Forces Treaty (INF), which eliminated all nuclear-armed, ground-launched ballistic and cruise missiles with ranges between 300 and 3,400 miles. It was the first nuclear arms treaty between the United States and the Soviet Union that actually resulted in the elimination of nuclear weapons—846 U.S. missiles, and 1,846 Soviet missiles—instead of just slowing down, or putting an upper limit on, the growth and expansion of nuclear weapons systems on both sides.

One reason that this treaty was possible was that Soviet premier Mikhail Gorbachev had, for some time before 1987, discounted the threat from the United States and other capitalist states. In fact, by espousing economic and political reforms—referred to respectively as **perestroika** and **glasnost**—that moved the Soviet Union in the direction of becoming more like the United States (and other market-oriented, democratic states), Gorbachev removed almost entirely the ideological bases for the tension between the United States and the Soviet Union that had permeated the global political system ever since the end of World War II.

As George Kennan (1947, 570) had noted in his famous analysis of "The Sources of Soviet Conduct" at the onset of the Cold War, "Since capitalism no longer existed in Russia,... it became necessary to justify the retention of the dictatorship by stressing the menace of capitalism abroad." Kennan concluded that "there is ample evidence that the stress laid in Moscow on the menace confronting Soviet society from the world outside its borders is founded not in the realities of foreign antagonism but in the necessity of explaining away the maintenance of dictatorial authority at home."

What Gorbachev and the Soviet elites who supported him apparently did not anticipate was that once it was conceded that the Soviet Union did *not* face mortal danger in the form of threats from the United States and its capitalist allies, a principal rationale for its existence had been undermined. If, in fact, the Soviet Union was under constant, even if implicit or covert, attack by capitalist powers, then an autocratic firm hand was apparently needed to hold it together and to protect it. But if that danger no longer existed, then the centralized, autocratic system had lost one of its fundamental reasons for being. Nationalist, separatist, ethnic aspirations for independence that had long been suppressed in the name of self-defense by the Soviet empire were given relatively free rein in the Gorbachev era, and, with a speed that surprised most observers, they ultimately led to the dissolution of the Soviet Union. So, arguably, the Cold War did not end because the Soviet Union fell apart and died; instead, the Soviet Union fell apart and died because the Cold War had ended.

To the extent that this view has validity, it leaves open the question of why the Cold War ended. If it did not end entirely because of flaws in the economic and political systems of the Soviet Union—if, in fact, those flaws became apparent and deadly only because the Cold War had ended—then, perhaps, external factors, such as foreign policies adopted by the United States during the Cold War, had something to do with bringing about its demise.

Did Containment End the Cold War?

One perspective on this issue is that American foreign policy throughout most of the Cold War was effective, and was vindicated by its ultimate result, the demise of the Soviet Union. One of the architects of the policy of **containment**—to which, in this view, the United States adhered consistently during the Cold War—was George Kennan, a State Department expert on the Soviet Union who was based in Moscow after World War II. In the article mentioned earlier (Kennan 1947, 575), he offered the following advice on how to deal with the Soviets in the aftermath of that war: "The main element of any United States policy toward the Soviet Union must be that of a long-term, patient but firm and vigilant containment of Russian expansive tendencies." He then reiterated (576):

> The Soviet pressure against the free institutions of the western world is something that can be contained by the adroit and vigilant application of counter-force at a series of constantly shifting geographical and political points, corresponding to the shifts and maneuvers of Soviet policy....

Kennan concluded (582) that such a policy had the potential to "increase enormously the strains under which Soviet policy must operate," and to "promote tendencies which must eventually find their outlet in either the break-up or the gradual mellowing of Soviet power."

In the aftermath of the Cold War, statements such as these have been interpreted as accurate predictions regarding the ultimate fate of the Soviet Union, as well as arguments that a policy of containment had been a crucial part of the process of bringing about its demise.[b] In the view of one authoritative historical account of recent U.S. foreign policy, the end of the Cold War "vindicated four decades of American policy.... Credit for the victory went to all the Cold War presidents, who had maintained Truman's containment policy with the expectation that sooner or later the Soviet Empire would collapse because of its own internal contradictions" (Ambrose and Brinkley 1997, 371).

Did Reagan's Rollback Policies End the Cold War?

A very different view of the process leading to the demise of the Soviet Union, and to the end of the Cold War, holds that the policy of containment was seriously flawed and counterproductive. This perspective came to the surface in the early years of the Cold War, when President Eisenhower's secretary of state, John Foster Dulles, became identified with the view that the strategy of containment was too passive. Instead, Dulles advocated "rolling back" the Iron Curtain, and the Republican Party adopted this **rollback strategy** in its platform of 1952. Calling for the repudiation of the agreements with the Soviet Union signed at Yalta—which, it charged, "aid Soviet enslavements"—the platform looked forward to the "genuine independence of those captive peoples." It promised that a new Republican administration would "mark the end of the negative, futile, and immoral policy of 'containment' which abandons countless human beings to a despotism and godless terrorism" (Republican Party Platform 1952).

Kennan's policy of containment called, as we have seen, for the constant application of counterforce at "constantly shifting geographical and political points, corresponding to the shifts and maneuvers of Soviet policy." The problem with this type of policy, according to the early critics of containment, was that it ceded the initiative to the enemy. The Communists, under the policy of containment, had the advantage of picking the times and the places where confrontations would take place, and, naturally, they selected times and places that were most advantageous to them.

---

b. Actually, however, casting Kennan in the role of apostle and prophet for the policy of containment (see, for example, Gaddis 1992, 131–132) is something of a stretch. In the first place, Kennan very soon became disenchanted with the manner in which the policy of containment was implemented: "Mr. Kennan was deeply dismayed when the policy [of containment] was associated with the immense buildup in conventional arms and nuclear weapons that characterized the cold war from the 1950s onward.... He came to deplore the growing belligerence toward Moscow that gripped Washington by the early 1950s" (Weiner and Crossette 2005). And while Gaddis (1992) categorizes Reagan as the president who implemented the decisive stage of containment, Kennan himself at the time characterized Reagan and his foreign policy team as "dangerous," "stupid," and "childish" (Leebaert 2002, 499). Finally, when the Soviet Union was on the verge of collapse (but at a time when its demise was far from widely anticipated), Kennan "recommended in 1990 that Washington agree to a 'binding moratorium of at least three years duration' that would freeze Europe's post–World War II arrangements in place. There should be no changes in the Warsaw Pact, no 'alterations' of states" (Leebaert 2002, 592).

Actually, even during the Truman administration, a report from the National Security Council, known as NSC-68, had called for policies bringing about "the gradual retraction of undue Russian power and influence," and for the "emergence of the satellite countries as entities independent of the USSR" (National Security Council 1950). And the initial strategy in response to North Korea's attack on South Korea called for a rollback tactic, aiming for the liberation of North Korea. However, in the wake of the counterattack in Korea by the People's Republic of China, that goal was abandoned.

Similarly, although the Eisenhower administration came into office with brave talk about rolling back the Iron Curtain, and "administration spokesmen publicly encouraged the enslaved nations of Eastern and Central Europe to rise up against their Soviet masters," such statements proved to be empty talk, according to Francis Sempa (2004). When anti-Soviet uprisings actually occurred in East Germany in 1953, and in both Poland and Hungary in 1956, "the United States did nothing to aid the resistance forces."

President John F. Kennedy came into office with inspiring rhetoric about "bearing any burden" and "paying any price," thus suggesting a vigorous anti-Communist foreign policy. Instead, he backed away, at a crucial moment, from the Bay of Pigs invasion that was intended to overthrow Fidel Castro in Cuba; failed to respond effectively to the construction of the Berlin Wall by the East German government; and contributed to the undermining of the anti-Communist government of Ngo Dinh Diem in Vietnam. The Cuban Missile Crisis was resolved without catastrophe, but at the price of promising never to invade Cuba and agreeing to relinquish U.S. missiles in Turkey (Sempa 2004).

Lyndon Johnson did make a determined effort to protect the South Vietnamese regime from the aggression of its northern neighbor, but his administration conducted the war in a defensive manner that never effectively moved toward the liberation of North Vietnam from its Communist rulers. He did nothing to aid the popular uprising against the Communist government in Czechoslovakia in 1968, after which the Soviet Union proclaimed the Brezhnev Doctrine—asserting, in effect, that whatever territory came into Soviet control would always remain in Soviet control (Sempa 2004).

And President Richard Nixon, along with his secretary of state, Henry Kissinger, formulated what might be called the first end of the Cold War, by instituting a policy of "détente." According to Sempa: "Détente's consequences included U.S. acquiescence to the loss of strategic nuclear superiority, a willingness to overlook Soviet cheating on arms control agreements, the U.S. abandonment of longtime allies in Southeast Asia, and formal recognition—in the Helsinki Accords—of a Soviet sphere of influence in Central and Eastern Europe." Subsequently, President Jimmy Carter came into office promising to overcome what he labeled an "inordinate fear of communism," and then proceeded to undermine such anti-Communist allies as the shah of Iran and the Somoza regime in Nicaragua. Sempa concludes: "Under Carter, containment, while still surviving as an overall policy, reached its nadir."

So, in this view, containment was *not* a policy that effectively caused the demise of the Soviet Union and the end of the Cold War but an excessively passive strategy that ceded the initiative to the Soviet Union and its Communist allies, and led to one defeat after another for the United States and its allies. At the beginning of the Cold War, the United States had enjoyed clear military superiority, but, by the end of the Carter administration, the Soviet

Union had, at the very least, achieved military parity; Vietnam as well as South Vietnam, Cambodia, and Laos had come under Communist rule; and leftist guerrilla campaigns had successfully brought to power socialist regimes in such far-flung places as Mozambique, Angola, Ethiopia, Nicaragua, and South Yemen. Then, in 1979, the Soviet Union invaded Afghanistan.

That invasion may have been one reason for the election of Ronald Reagan in 1980. According to the anti-containment perspective, Reagan refused to join in the long line of American presidents to adhere to this essentially passive strategy. Instead, shortly after assuming power in 1981, he asserted that the United States would not "contain communism, it will transcend communism" (Sempa 2004). As early as 1963, Reagan had expressed the idea of putting pressure on the Soviets by engaging them in an arms race with which they could not cope economically, and, once elected, he proceeded to launch the largest peacetime military buildup in the country's history. Peter Schweizer (2002, 142) comments: "The defense buildup was as much about economic warfare against the Soviets as it was about restoring American military power."

Self-perceptions, and the intentions of the Reagan administration with regard to the Soviet Union are also revealed in a series of executive orders signed by Reagan during his first term in office. For example, in *National Security Decision Directive #32,* signed in May of 1982, one main objective of the Reagan administration was said to be "to contain and reverse the expansion of Soviet control and military presence throughout the world, and to increase the costs of Soviet support and use of proxy, terrorist, and subversive forces" (Reagan 1982). And *National Security Decision Directive #75* on "U.S. Relations with the USSR," from January of 1983 (Reagan 1983a), asserted that U.S. foreign policy would attempt to "contain and over time to reverse Soviet expansionism by competing effectively on a sustained basis with the Soviet Union in all international arenas," and "to promote ... the process of change in the Soviet Union toward a more pluralistic political and economic system in which the power of the privileged ruling elite is gradually reduced."

In pursuit of such goals, the Reagan administration adopted several tactics. Its commitment to substantial increases in the defense budget, and to the Strategic Defense Initiative (SDI) to develop technologies for a defense against attack by nuclear missiles, were public and well-known. It acted with equal energy on several more covert projects. For example, the CIA organized an effort—involving Saudi Arabia, Egypt, China, and Pakistan—to provide military aid to the Afghan resistance. Drawing contributions of $500 million in military aid just from the Saudis (Schweizer 2002, 203), U.S. efforts to support the *mujahadeen* in Afghanistan amounted, overall, says Derek Leebaert (2002, 484), to "the largest U.S. covert operation ever, into which secretly flowed somewhere around $5 billion before the last Soviet forces formally withdrew in February 1989." In 1985 the CIA delivered to the Afghan resistance some 10,000 rocket-propelled grenades and 200,000 rockets. Perhaps the most effective technological assistance came in the form of Stinger missile launchers; in 1985 anti-Soviet Afghan forces fired some 200 Stinger missiles, 75 percent of which hit their targets, which were typically Soviet HIND helicopters (Schweizer 2002, 255–256).

There is not much question that these energetic U.S. efforts in Afghanistan made an important contribution to what Schweizer (278) describes as "the first complete military defeat in Soviet history." Furthermore, the searing experience in Afghanistan was crucial to the process of bringing an end to the Soviet Union. The war had several critical impacts on Soviet politics. First, it created doubts within the Soviet leadership about the ability of military force to hold the Soviet empire together. The defeat in Afghanistan also ruined the reputation of the Soviets' Red Army, created a rift between the army and the Communist Party, and encouraged the non-Russian republics to push for independence. Finally, it inspired new forms of political participation in Russia, helped to bring about reforms in the Soviet press and other media even before Gorbachev launched his policy of glasnost, and yielded a significant number of war veterans, who moved effectively to end the political hegemony of the Communist Party in the Soviet Union (Reuveny and Prakash 1999).

Another strategy adopted by the Reagan administration in its apparent attempt to subvert the Soviet Union involved offering substantial support for the Solidarity movement in Poland. In that project, President Reagan apparently had the assistance of Pope John Paul II, who was born in Poland. When the two met at the Vatican in June of 1982, Carl Bernstein (1992) reported, "Reagan and the Pope agreed to undertake a clandestine campaign to hasten the dissolution of the communist empire." The campaign focused on Poland, where martial law had been proclaimed in 1981—and where, it appeared at the time, Soviet troops were apparently on the verge of an invasion. From that point until 1989, when Solidarity's legal status was restored, it was "supplied, nurtured, and advised" by a network (created and organized by Reagan and the pope) that provided printing presses, transmitters, telephones, shortwave radios, video cameras, photocopiers, telex machines, computers, and financial support.

Was this support effective? Lech Walesa, the leader of Solidarity during those years—and winner of the Nobel Peace Prize in 1983, as well as president of Poland from 1990 to 1995—later explained (Walesa 2004) that "when talking about Ronald Reagan, I have to be personal. Why? Because we owe him our liberty." Indeed, as one historical and political analysis of the history of the Cold War argues: "That Reagan did not regard even Europe's division as immutable was a crucial new fact. Practically no one else in Washington agreed" (Leebaert 2002, 542).[c]

In addition to his administration's focus on military tactics in Afghanistan and political maneuverings in Poland, President Reagan's anti-Soviet policies included a kind of economic warfare. Schweizer (2002, 238) comments: "Perhaps the most stunning economic weapon Reagan sought to wield against Moscow came not from Washington but from Saudi Arabia." At the time, in the mid-1980s, there were 1,500 Soviet military advisers in South Yemen, 500 in North Yemen, an additional 2,500 Soviet advisers in Syria, 1,000 in Ethiopia, and 1,000 in Iraq, not to mention the 10,000 Soviet troops in Afghanistan. In 1981 the Reagan administration had steered through Congress a bill providing the Saudis aircraft with Airborne Warning and Control System (AWACS) capabilities—allowing detection of potentially hostile aircraft up to 250 miles away—and several other fighter aircraft as well.

---

c. In light of the focal question here, whether Reagan's foreign policies represented a continuation of containment, or a break with the past, it might be useful to point out here that according to George Kennan, a principal architect of containment, "demands for freedom in Poland were 'inevitably self-defeating,' and Reagan was undermining détente" (Schweizer 2002, 169).

The Saudis were cultivated, in part, because they were an important swing producer of oil at the time—they could single-handedly have an important impact on the international price of oil. Reductions in the price of oil would be good for the U.S. economy, but they would impose serious costs on the Soviet Union, which was heavily dependent on oil exports to earn hard currency.[d] Thus, Schweizer (1994, 242) comments, in "August 1985, a stake was driven silently through the heart of the Soviet economy ... the Saudis opened the spigot and flooded the world market with oil." Within a matter of months, the international price of oil fell from $30 to $12 per barrel, which cost the Soviet economy an estimated $13 billion a year. At the same time, the United States had devalued its currency, costing the Soviets another $2 billion. And, finally, the steep decline in the price of oil had an important deleterious impact on the market for the next most important Soviet export at the time, military weapons. The primary customers for Soviet weapons in the 1980s were oil exporters such as Iran, Iraq, and Libya, who saw their earnings decline by 46 percent in the first half of 1986. Soviet arms sales then dropped by 20 percent in that year, costing the Soviets another $2 billion in hard currency (Schweizer 1994, 261–262).

A Critique of Reagan's Rollback Policies

That the Reagan administration intended to defeat, rather than merely contain, the Soviet Union, seems relatively clear.[e] Although this vision was greeted with widespread doubt and skepticism,[f] the Reagan administration did adopt a wide range of policies that were quite clearly intended to bring about the demise of the Soviet Union.

However, some well-informed observers are not persuaded by the juxtaposition of the Reagan administration's campaign to subvert the Soviet Union and the subsequent demise of that state. For example, Charles Kegley Jr. (1994, 28) insists that "co-variation of two phenomena, such as the Reagan military buildup and the reversal of the Soviet Union's policies, does not permit us to conclude that the former was the determinant of the latter.... Coincidence is not causation." Kegley also insists that Reagan's policies actually stiffened the resolve of hard-liners in the Kremlin, made life more difficult for reform elements, and prolonged the Cold War. In defense of this argument, he cites (14) Georgi Arbatov, the director of the Institute for the USA and Canada in Moscow, who in 1991 charged:

---

d. "CIA analysts had concluded that for every one-dollar drop in the price of a barrel of oil, Moscow would lose between $500 million and $1 billion per year in critical hard currency" (Schweizer 2002, 239).

e. Not all observers agree. "While it is tempting to link the observed changes in Moscow to the preferences of Washington policymakers..., such an inference would presume that the Reagan administration had from the start a deliberate strategy in mind for ending the Cold War. But we cannot document the existence of such a strategy" (Kegley 1994, 30).

f. In 1982 Arthur Schlesinger asserted that "those in the U.S. who think the Soviet Union is on the verge of economic and social collapse ... are ... only kidding themselves." In 1984 John Kenneth Galbraith agreed: "The Russian system succeeds because, in contrast to the Western industrial economies, it makes full use of its manpower." In 1982 Soviet expert Seweryn Bialer argued, "The Soviet Union is not now nor will it be during the next decade in the throes of a true systemic crisis, for it boasts enormous unused reserves of political and social stability that suffice to endure the deepest difficulties." See Schweizer 1994, xiv.

The version about President Reagan's "tough" policy and intensified arms race being the most important source of perestroika—that it persuaded communists to "give up"—is sheer nonsense. Quite to the contrary, this policy made the life for reformers, for all who yearned for democratic changes in their life, much more difficult....

Another, complementary argument by Reagan's critics—again offered by Kegley (1994, 30)—is that "we should note that [Yuri] Andropov and Gorbachev began to shift their country's course not when Reagan's unrestrained hostility toward the Russians was being most energetically practiced ... but only *after* Reagan himself shifted to a more accommodative course as reflected in his radical anti-nuclear turnaround."[g] In this view of the Cold War's denouement, neither Reagan's SDI program, nor the aid to the anti-Soviet militants in Afghanistan, nor the support of Solidarity in Poland (in cooperation with Pope John Paul II), nor the conspiracy with the Saudis to lower the international price of oil, brought about the demise of the Soviet Union. Instead, Reagan's proposal to scrap large numbers of nuclear weapons at a summit meeting in Reykjavik in 1986, the INF treaty in 1987, and four summit meetings with Gorbachev, as well as the toning down of Reagan's rhetoric regarding the "evil empire," made more important contributions to the momentum in favor of reform in the Soviet Union, which ultimately spun out of control and caused its demise.

THE RELATIONSHIP BETWEEN REAGAN'S FOREIGN POLICIES AND THE BUSH DOCTRINE

Whatever the actual connection between the policies of the Reagan administration and the end of the Cold War, there is little doubt that the foreign policies of the George W. Bush administration have been inspired largely by the belief that Reagan deserves substantial credit for bringing about the demise of the Soviet Union. Bush formulated what became the major principles of his foreign policy in the wake of the 9/11 attacks and then articulated them clearly in his *National Security Strategy* released in 2002 (Bush 2002b). That statement stressed unilateralism, the necessity of preemptive war to combat modern threats to security, and the spread of democracy—all themes that were emphasized and advocated by the neoconservatives in the Bush administration, as we discussed in chapter 4.[h] Paul Wolfowitz was perhaps the most influential of this group, along with Douglas Feith, Stephen Hadley, John Bolton, and Richard Perle. Their important patrons were Vice President Dick Cheney and Secretary of Defense Donald Rumsfeld.

As we discussed in chapter 4, perhaps the central inspiration of the Bush administration's foreign policy has been that it could accomplish in the Middle East and against Islamic fundamentalism what its main foreign policy architects perceive the Reagan administration to have achieved against Communism in the Soviet Union and Eastern Europe.[i] Furthermore,

---

g. Kegley cites Leng (1984) in support of this assertion.

h. "When the younger Bush's national security team began to take shape, one found sprinkled throughout the government the names of neoconservatives..." (Packer 2005, 37).

i. "Many of these officials had served at the middle levels under Reagan, embracing his hawkish idealism. The fall of communism and the emergence of the United States as the world's only superpower had given them a sense of historical victory" (Packer 2005, 38).

Bush and his advisers saw themselves as pursuing these goals by means of many of the same assertive and often unilateral tactics—based on a thorough optimism about what can be accomplished by American power, on the idea that democracy is cherished in all parts of the world, and on the assumption that, happily, its spread around the world is in the national interest of the United States.

David C. Hendrickson and Robert W. Tucker (2005, 16) comment: "A direct line can be traced from Reagan to Bush in their common rejection of the traditional bases of international order"—referring, in this last phrase, to international law, international organizations such as the United Nations, and multilateral cooperative ventures among states of various sorts. In addition, one of the important connections between the foreign policy of the Reagan and Bush administrations involves skepticism in both about a policy of containment. As another analyst of Bush's foreign policy has put it: "A notable feature of the *National Security Strategy 2002* is its repudiation of . . . containment" (Nuruzzaman 2006, 245).

It was not unreasonable for the Bush administration's foreign policy team to conclude that the history of the Reagan years contained lessons that might prove valuable in the confrontation with Islamic fundamentalism and terrorism that it faced in the wake of 9/11. Reagan's rhetoric, his commitment to huge defense expenditures and to the Strategic Defense Initiative, and his general approach to foreign policy problems had been greeted with skepticism not only by his political opponents, but also by large swaths of public opinion—and probably by a majority of academic specialists in foreign policy and international politics as well. In June of 1982, for example, as part of the nuclear freeze movement, a demonstration against Reagan's foreign policies attracted as many as a million people in New York City; it is still commemorated as probably the largest demonstration for peace in the nation's history (Richter Videos 2006). And George W. Bush encountered similar skepticism toward his approach to dealing with terrorism, especially when he initiated military action against Iraq. There were large peace rallies against Bush's policies, in the United States and Europe, especially after the war in Iraq was under way. Nonetheless, considering all the opposition faced by Reagan, Bush's natural reaction might have been, So what?

Reagan had great faith in the appeal of democracy on a wide scale, and in the ability of American power to exploit that appeal ultimately to bring about dramatic changes in autocratic, anti-American countries. The younger President Bush displays a similar ideological conviction, and he has had, arguably, a better opportunity to implement policies stemming from that conviction. When President Reagan launched his campaign to undermine the Soviet empire, many seasoned observers calculated that that adversary possessed military strength at least the equal of that of the United States. In addition, the United States faced severe economic problems, including the worst recession (in 1982) since World War II, massive budget and trade deficits, and stiff economic competition from Japan. As President George W. Bush inaugurated his war on terror, however, the United States was indisputably the most powerful and influential state in the world; its economy had just experienced a very impressive period of economic growth, erasing budget deficits and supporting a military force that no state in the world could match.

Surely, if Reagan could, from the relatively disadvantageous position in which the United States found itself in the early 1980s, manage to bring about the end of Communist rule in the Soviet Union and its satellites in Eastern Europe, then President Bush, with similar optimism and vigor, could undermine Islamic fundamentalism in the Middle East and help to install a series of democratic governments in the region to replace the various authoritarian regimes that have dominated it since the states there achieved independence. As one obviously sympathetic analyst of the Bush presidency (Wallison 2003) put it in March of 2003:

> The similarities between Bush and Reagan ... are so striking that it is hard to escape the thought that George W. Bush learned some important things about being president from observing Ronald Reagan. Is it only a coincidence that Bush referred to the Axis of Evil, while Reagan called the Soviet Union an evil empire? Would Bush have been as willing as he has seemed to confront foreign opposition—in withdrawing from the Kyoto Treaty, the International Criminal Court, and the ABM treaty, as well as acting against Saddam Hussein without UN backing—if Reagan had not been willing to do essentially the same thing with his policies in Afghanistan, Poland, a military buildup despite strong public sentiment for a nuclear freeze, and the emplacement of Pershing missiles in Europe? ... There is reason to hope that he [Bush] will build a record of success of the kind that made President Reagan one of the most important and consequential presidents of the 20th century.[j]

However, in July of 2006, another, much less sympathetic observer (Lieven 2006) asserted: "The Bush administration's plan to bring democracy to the Middle East is now in ruins.... Now that the U.S. dream of combining democratization of the region with submission to Washington's policies is dead, the U.S. too is faced with a stark choice: seek genuine compromise with key regional actors, or be prepared to fight repeated wars."[k] Clearly, the "key regional actors" referred to here would be either autocratic regimes such as those in Saudi Arabia and Syria, or the revolutionary Islamic fundamentalist regime in Iran.

It is possible that this conclusion is too pessimistic—that President Bush's foreign policy record will, at some point in the future, be considered as successful as that of President Reagan. After all, Reagan, too, went through some periods of tremendous unpopularity, and he encountered at least temporarily effective opposition both at home and abroad. (Also, as we have seen, some analysts believe that the link between his attempts to subvert the Soviet Union and that nation's demise is a mere coincidence.) It may be useful to recall, in considering this point, that when President Reagan left office in 1989, the Soviet Union still existed, the Berlin Wall was still in place, and, in fact, the Soviet empire was still intact. Thus it is possible to imagine that President Bush, too, will someday be credited with some foreign policy success. Perhaps, ten years after he has left office, there will be a substantial number of democratic governments in the Middle East, Islamic fundamentalism and terrorism will have subsided, and the Bush policies aimed at undermining al-Qaeda and autocratic regimes in the Middle East will be compared favorably with the anti-Communist strategies of Ronald Reagan.

---

j. "Almost everywhere in the press one reads that President [George W. Bush] sounds an awful lot like [Ronald Reagan]. Commentators and politicians alike have drawn the comparison between Mr. Bush's 'muscular' foreign policy and the Reagan doctrine" (Diggins 2004).

k. On the same day, well-known Middle Eastern scholar John Esposito (2006) asserted that "President Bush finds himself today looking at a potential legacy that includes a world in which anti-Americanism will have increased exponentially among America's friends and foes alike, terrorism will have grown rather than receded, and America will be enmeshed in Iraq and Afghanistan."

As the Bush presidency nears its end, however, Iraq remains plagued by domestic political violence that kills some 100 Iraqis every day, and Israel has again become involved in violent skirmishes with militant insurgents based in Lebanon, leading to bombing raids and rocket attacks that inevitably victimize civilians on both sides. In other words, no truly democratic or even functioning government seems likely to emerge in Iraq at any time in the foreseeable future, while promoting a democratic election in the territory controlled by the Palestinian Authority seems only to have made a tense situation considerably worse for Israel and its Arab neighbors. Why have George W. Bush's policies relating to terrorism and autocratic governments in the Middle East not met with anything like the success often credited to Ronald Reagan's policies vis-à-vis Communism and autocratic governments in the Soviet Union and Eastern Europe?

There are so many differences between the issues faced by these two presidents, and the policies they adopted in response, that it is impossible to stipulate definitively which differences may account for the divergent outcomes achieved in each case. One obvious difference is that Communism and the Soviet Union had been in existence for several decades when Reagan came into office, while Islamic fundamentalism and al Qaeda have only recently appeared on the scene. Perhaps Communism and the Soviet Union, in other words, were both spent forces, ripe for a fall, while Islamic fundamentalism, and the terrorism adopted by radical Islamic elements, are simply too fresh and full of energy to be similarly vanquished.

Then, too, Reagan may have been more subtle, more flexible, and less reliant on overt military force than Bush has been. John Patrick Diggins, a history professor writing in the *New York Times* argues, for example, that, at a crucial juncture in his second term, President Reagan ignored neoconservative advisers in his administration and approached Mikhail Gorbachev with a number of conciliatory proposals. Diggins (2004) recalls: "Not only did the neocons oppose Mr. Reagan's efforts at rapprochement, they also argued against engaging in personal diplomacy with Soviet leaders. Advisers like Richard Perle, Paul Wolfowitz, and Donald Rumsfeld ... held that America must escalate to achieve 'nuclear dominance' and that we could only deal from a 'strategy of strength'." Admittedly, President Reagan did rely on covert military strategies in Afghanistan and Nicaragua, but, unlike President Bush, who has so far engaged in two prolonged wars, President Reagan initiated overt military force only once during his term, in Grenada in 1983.

In the end, perhaps the Reagan administration's attempt to subdue or subvert the Soviet empire (and Communism) achieved whatever success it can be credited with because its target populations constituted more effective allies than the Bush administration has encountered in its confrontation with Islamic fundamentalism and autocratic regimes in the Middle East. In the Soviet Union itself, and certainly in Eastern Europe, there were important elements that had long been bitterly anti-Soviet, and even vigorously anti-Communist. When the Soviet system began to weaken—whether because of Reagan's strategies or not—these elements stood ready to take advantage of the situation, to declare independence from the Soviet center, as well as from Communist rule, and to establish democratic, or at least functioning, governments.

The situation that the Bush administration has encountered in the Middle East is quite different—to some extent because of past U.S. policies in the area. There are factions and social groups throughout many Middle Eastern states that are opposed to the status quo, and to current regimes. But many of those regimes, including those in Egypt, in Saudi Arabia, and even in Iraq, have been supported by the United States in the past. In countries such as Iran, Iraq, and Egypt, authoritarian regimes have effectively dealt with most opposition or subversive elements, eliminating them from any important political influence. Often, however, the exceptions to that rule have found refuge within religious institutions. Autocratic regimes have been unable to control what goes on in mosques, or within the ruling institutions of Islam. The result is that in state after state, the only effective, anti-regime, anti–status quo elements and organizations are religious in character and origin. In large part, they are, in other words, Islamic fundamentalists.

George W. Bush's rhetoric and some of his actions may have weakened secular, autocratic regimes in several Middle Eastern states. (Ironically, considering all the abuse that was heaped on him at the time by Republican critics, President Carter's rhetoric about human rights helped, in a similar way, to weaken the regime of the shah in Iran, producing an impact that ultimately favored Islamic fundamentalism.) The most dramatic example of this pattern has been in Iraq. Since the United States removed the regime of Saddam Hussein by direct military action, the most effective elements standing ready to move into the power vacuum have not been democratic in orientation, however. Far more effective and influential than any democratic, moderate, or liberal elements have been Islamic fundamentalists of either the Shia or the Sunni variety. The result in Iraq has been that the future seems more likely to bring the dissolution of Iraq into Shia, Sunni, and Kurdish portions, or to feature a dictator of some type—probably fundamentalist and almost certainly anti-American—with the power to hold the bitterly opposed factions together.

Similarly, in the nascent Palestinian state, the Bush administration refused to deal with Yasir Arafat, and called for democratic elections within the territory controlled by the Palestinian Authority. The result was a resounding victory for the Islamic fundamentalist group Hamas. And, although the United States has successfully utilized its influence to help bring to power a reasonably democratic government in Lebanon, that government's influence is very limited in some parts of the country, especially in southern Lebanon, and into that breach has leapt the Shi'ite paramilitary organization, Hezbollah, which has responded to Israeli bombing raids by firing Katusha rockets into Northern Israel. The United States has pressed Egypt's President Hosni Mubarak to allow his country's political system to move toward more pluralistic representation, but every step that Mubarak takes in that direction, however limited and hesitant it may be, seems to increase the probability that Islamic fundamentalists (such as the Muslim Brotherhood) will be the primary beneficiaries of any weakening of the autocratic Mubarak regime. Similarly, the Saudi regime faces increasingly important domestic opposition, but not from democratic, liberal, or pro-American elements.

PRIORITIES FOR THE FUTURE IN THE MIDDLE EAST

One of the notable features of the American invasion of Iraq in 2003 and the occupation that ensued is that academic analysts of foreign policy and international politics were almost universally agreed from the beginning that the Bush administration's project in Iraq was unfortunate, and/or a mistake. Radicals, for example, believed that it was motivated primarily by the desire of the United States to dominate, or at least increase its influence in, a geographic area containing such a large portion of the world's oil reserves. In this view, the invasion of Iraq was not a mistake, but a predictable and likely result of the capitalist economic and political structure of the United States, and it is the type of foreign policy action that will continue to be likely as long as the United States maintains its capitalist system.

At the other end of the ideological spectrum, realists felt that the attack on Iraq in 2003 was a serious miscalculation and a mistake. From their point of view, the United States should not concern itself, as a rule, with the internal political structures of the states with which it interacts, and it should certainly not become involved in extensive, expensive, and probably futile attempts to spread democracy. From the realist point of view, Saddam Hussein never posed as serious a threat as was claimed by many in the Bush administration, simply because the United States was always so much more powerful than Iraq. In the realist view, the United States should have relied on that superiority in military-industrial capabilities to deter Saddam's regime from any actions or policies that might have proved harmful to the United States.

As was argued in an advertisement placed in the *New York Times* (2002) in advance of the U.S. invasion of Iraq (and signed by such prominent realists as Kenneth Waltz, Stephen M. Walt, Robert Jervis, and John Mearsheimer), "even if Saddam Hussein acquired nuclear weapons, he could not use them without suffering massive U.S. or Israeli retaliation."[1] The group of scholars represented in that ad also predicted, in a seemingly prescient manner, that "even if we win easily, we have no plausible exit strategy. Iraq is a deeply divided society that the United States would have to occupy and police for many years to create a viable state." The message concluded that "we should concentrate instead on defeating al Qaeda."

At least some liberals would have felt some sympathy for the ostensible goal of bringing democracy to Iraq, and for relying on that example to evoke admiration and emulation throughout the Middle East. But to pursue that goal by circumventing the United Nations and skirting international law—by launching a military intervention not justifiable in terms of self-defense or sanctioned by the UN—was seen as a violation of important liberal principles. In general, and in this case in particular, from the liberal point of view, the ends do not justify the means. And in the case of the recent U.S. policy toward Iraq, the means used to pursue the admirable goals of spreading democracy and encouraging human rights there and throughout the Middle East have entirely corrupted and compromised those admirable goals. While neither scholars nor political figures of the liberal persuasion have unified behind a coherent strategy for dealing with the situation in Iraq and in the Middle East in general, in the future they will certainly recommend that the United States put a higher priority on utilizing the United Nations, on abiding by and encouraging respect for international law, and on avoiding unilateral military action, or at least military action that is not clearly in self-defense or authorized by the UN Security Council.

What lessons should be learned from the war in Iraq, and what priorities should be established in its wake, from a social constructivist point of view? Constructivists may well be too diverse to allow a simple answer to that question, but their response might likely be something as fundamental as "Change the manner in which you perceive yourself, the international sys-

---

1. The ad was also signed by a number of scholars who are not realist in orientation, but its title, "War With Iraq Is <u>Not</u> in America's National Interest," conveys the basically realist tenor of the message.

tem, and your role within it." Two ostensibly constructivist critiques of the U.S. war in Iraq actually come up with prescriptions that are rather surprisingly traditional in a liberal sense. Brian Frederking (2003, 363), relying on a constructivist theory of global security, recommends the "gradual construction" of collective security rules, modifying such rules so that they can more explicitly deal with human rights abuses, terrorism, and the proliferation of weapons of mass destruction, in addition to traditional forms of military aggression. Similarly, Richard Falk (2003, 598) expresses regret about the extent to which the Bush administration undermined the United Nations in pursuit of its goals in Iraq and the rest of the Middle East, concluding that "my legal constructivist position is that the United States (and the world) would benefit from a self-imposed discipline of adherence to the UN Charter system governing the use of force." [m]

The rational political ambition approach to U.S. foreign policy reveals some sympathy for one ostensible goal of the U.S. war in Iraq—the establishing of democracy there and elsewhere in the Middle East. There is, for example, support within this approach for the idea that democratic states will not fight wars against each other (Bueno de Mesquita et al. 2003). There is also substantial support for the idea that democratic (or large selectorate) systems are more likely to provide important benefits to their citizens. According to Bruce Bueno de Mesquita and Hilton Root (2002, 32): "Across the board, the data show that more inclusive systems generally do a better job at producing safe drinking water, expanding public education, offering access to medical care, encouraging free trade, avoiding corruption and black marketeering, attracting investors and so forth."

Nevertheless, there is also, within the rational political ambition approach, profound skepticism about the U.S. intervention in Iraq. Theoretical and empirical analysis based on rational political ambition theory suggests that democratic states are only rarely going to be able or likely to promote democracy by military intervention. It is easier for leaders of democratic states to win policy concessions from nondemocratic leaders by means of monetary or other kinds of awards. Historical evidence shows quite clearly that neither the United States nor other like-minded interlopers have, since World War II, successfully promoted democracy in the wake of their interventions. In fact, states that have been the target of such interventions have subsequently become less democratic than they might have been expected to be, all else being equal (Bueno de Mesquita and Downs 2006).

Consider the history of interventions by the United States in its own hemisphere during the twentieth century. Many of them—including those in Cuba, Nicaragua, the Dominican Republic, and Haiti early in the twentieth century, as well as those in Guatemala, the Dominican Republic, and Haiti again in the post–World War II period—have ostensibly been motivated by a desire to preserve or extend democracy. The results have more often been quite repressive and corrupt dictatorships, such as those headed by Rafael Trujillo in the Dominican Republic, by Anastasio Somoza in Nicaragua, and by François ("Papa Doc") Duvalier in Haiti. And all these dictatorships have come about in places that are much closer, geographically as well as culturally, to the United States, than are the Islamic countries of the Middle East.

---

m. Falk also argues that "it is … leading states, and above all the United States, that need to be persuaded that their interests are served and their values realized by a more diligent pursuit of a law-oriented foreign policy."

The emphasis of rational political ambition theory on the priority that political leaders place on staying in power also creates an interest in the impact of the war in Iraq on the fates of political leaders who have advocated and carried out that policy. It is no secret that public support for the war, and the approval ratings of President Bush, have declined steadily in the United States since the early days of the war. But the Iraq disaster may also have reinforced or augmented skepticism in the electorate about the policy of spreading democracy as an American foreign policy goal. In fact, as we discussed in chapter 5, the American public has for several decades now been more likely to support American military interventions aimed at resisting aggression than those aimed at regime change (Jentleson 1992; Jentleson and Britton 1998; Oneal, Lian, and Joyner 1996).

A survey of a representative sample of American citizens taken in January 2006 sought opinions about what the goals of American foreign policy should be (Yankelovich 2006, 121–122). Large majorities supported such goals as offering support to other nations struck by natural disasters, cooperating with other states in attempts to improve the environment or disease control, and even supporting UN peacekeeping. The goal that received the *least* support of any of the goals about which respondents were asked was "actively creating democracies in other countries"—only 20 percent of the respondents believed that should be an important goal of American foreign policy. In contrast, 58 percent of respondents felt that "democracy is something that countries only come to on their own." These results suggest that political leaders who want to remain in power (as almost all do) may be well-advised to think again whenever they are tempted to emphasize spreading democracy as a high priority for American foreign policy, or to embark upon vigorous, especially military, efforts in pursuit of that goal.

Such second thoughts about spreading democracy may be further reinforced by an analysis of the Iraq War's impact on opinions about the United States among the citizens of other countries, as we discussed earlier in this chapter. Leaders of all countries want to stay in power; even in undemocratic countries, the political leaders are dependent, to some extent, on support from the public. So, to the extent that public opinion is less favorable to the United States in those countries, it will be more difficult to persuade their leaders to support U.S. foreign policy goals. And public support may be particularly important in pursuit of goals such as combating or deterring terrorist attacks.

Furthermore, according to Robert L. Gallucci (2005, 129), "it is becoming common for government officials, members of Congress, national security commentators and the media in general to identify a terrorist attack on an American city with a nuclear weapon as the most serious threat to our national security today." That threat probably had *something* to do with the decision by the Bush administration to attack Iraq in the first place.[n] Ironically, however, that attack, and the ensuing occupation, have quite possibly made it more difficult for the United States to deal with the original threat. For example, Graham Allison (2006, 63) points out, "while [the Bush administration's] attention was consumed by Iraq, Iran advanced from years to only months away from completing the infrastructure for its nuclear bomb."

---

n. "The Bush administration used the danger that Saddam might supply WMD to terrorists as its decisive argument for war" (Allison 2004a, 68).

So, events in the Middle East during the first decade of the twenty-first century have discredited the goal of spreading democracy, as well as President Bush's tendency to seek unilateral solutions to various problems. Those events have also heightened concern about dependency on foreign sources for oil, even though that concern has been felt to varying degrees since the energy crisis of the 1970s. Still, those events and the reactions to them should not obscure the fact that alternatives to spreading democracy are not themselves free of problems and unfortunate consequences. The United States has for years supported autocratic governments, and even helped many to assume power, as in the case of the shah of Iran. Continued U.S. support for Hosni Mubarak may provoke a reaction in Egypt that looks, ultimately, like that against the shah. U.S. ties to the Saudi government were a factor in spawning al Qaeda. In the Middle East and elsewhere, when the United States establishes close ties to autocratic governments, or simply maintains normal relations with them, that policy, too, can lead to serious problems.

And while George W. Bush's unilateralism is now distinctly out of favor in the United States—and passionately opposed in most countries around the world—multilateralism is no panacea, either. Insisting on a multilateral approach, through the UN Security Council, for example, may well result, more often than not, in nothing being done at all to deal with such problems as the genocide in Darfur or the frequent conflicts between Israel and its many foes in the region. It must be admitted, also, that multilateral efforts to deal with nuclear proliferation threats from Iran (and North Korea) have so far been less than successful. Nevertheless, if the goals of "no loose nukes," "no new nascent nukes," and "no new nuclear weapons states" (see Allison 2004a, 2004b) are to be achieved, surely they will have to be pursued by means of multilateral strategies involving the cooperation of large numbers of states concerned about the threat of nuclear terrorism.[o]

In short, the lessons to be learned from the U.S. experience in the Middle East during the first decade of the twenty-first century suggest that, as the century progresses, American foreign policy makers would do well to make greater efforts to act in concert with international institutions and in conformity with international law (such as the Geneva convention regarding the treatment of enemy combatants), and to eschew efforts to spread democracy, at least by means of military interventions. It may even be reasonable to hope that future presidents will come to understand that such policies and strategies would make them more likely to retain power.

PRIORITIES FOR THE FUTURE OUTSIDE THE MIDDLE EAST

The wars in Afghanistan and Iraq, the continuing conflict between Israel and the Palestinians (and their proxies), as well as the escalating price of oil, have all conspired to make the Middle East the primary focus of U.S. foreign policy so far in the twenty-first century. But there are,

---

o. There are, however, some important steps toward controlling nuclear proliferation that the United States could implement unilaterally. One would be reducing its vast nuclear arsenal. "The Bush administration should drop its current plans to conduct research for the production of new 'mini-nukes'" (Allison 2004a, 74).

of course, vital problems and issues facing the United States in other parts of the world.

As usual, the problems in Africa do not receive a high priority in American foreign-policy-making circles. President Bush has made a potentially important financial commitment to combating AIDS in Africa by pledging in his 2003 State of the Union address to provide $15 billion to fight the disease in Africa (and the Caribbean) over the next five years. The problem is certainly serious in sub-Saharan Africa, where, in 2004, there were 24.5 million people infected with the HIV virus, and there were 2.7 new infections during that year (Kanabus and Frederiksson-Bass 2006). Now, however, there are doubts about how much of these funds Congress will actually provide.

Also, the United States tends to take with one hand more than it gives with the other in the case of Africa (as well as in many other developing areas of the world). For example, the 2002 Farm Bill allocated $3.4 billion in subsidies to American cotton farmers, at a time when the average cotton farmer is already quite wealthy. Meanwhile, in Mali, for example, where cotton is the chief and nearly the only export, cotton farmers will find their incomes reduced by 10 percent by the combination of such U.S. and European farm subsidies. According to Radley Balko (2003): "Economists estimate that U.S. cotton subsidies take a quarter of a billion dollars from African farmers every year." And this is just one example. Overall, the United Nations estimates that American and European agricultural subsidies cost African farmers $50 billion annually.

One of the most important steps that the United States could take to help Africans deal with AIDS, in particular, and poverty, in general, would be to eliminate, or at least drastically reduce, these agricultural subsidies. But the agricultural lobbies in both the United States and Europe successfully instill fear in their political leaders that such reductions will substantially harm their chances of staying in power; as a result, poor Africans are not likely to see such reductions made.

As we discussed in chapter 11, what was almost certainly the bloodiest military conflict in the world during the past ten years took place in sub-Saharan Africa, in the Democratic Republic of the Congo. Starting in 1998, and involving interventions by at least nine of its neighbors, the ongoing war has resulted in the deaths of some 4 million people (Lewis 2006). Although the UN has sent a peacekeeping force, the problem has received scant attention from American foreign policy makers. It is clear that because of its current preoccupations in the Middle East, the United States can hardly afford to send military forces to sub-Saharan Africa. Yet failed states in Africa may be breeding grounds for significant additions to the ranks of those inclined to engage in terrorist attacks on American people and/or property, in Africa or elsewhere (Lyman and Morrison 2004).P

Latin America is another region of the world receiving scant attention from American foreign policy makers in recent years. The exception to that rule involves immigration to the United States, mostly from Mexico (though not only by Mexicans). As discussed in chapters

---

p. "Africa may not rank with Iraq or Afghanistan as a top priority in the war on terrorism, nor with the Middle East or Southeast Asia as a primary focus of U.S. antiterrorism programs. But if Washington continues to underplay the terrorist threat in Africa, its worldwide strategy against terrorism will falter—and the consequences may be dire indeed" (Lyman and Morrison 2004, 86).

5 and 10, Samuel Huntington (2004) contends that these immigrants pose a serious threat to the national integrity and identity of the United States. Nonetheless, Congress, and perhaps the American people, are currently so divided on this issue—on one side are those who would like to deport all illegal immigrants to their home countries and build a wall along the entire U.S.-Mexican border to stem the flow of such immigrants in the future, and on the other side are those who want to give amnesty to the immigrants who are already here, as well as the right to find employment wherever they can—that it seems unlikely that any decisive action will be taken.

As we also discussed in chapter 10, there is, in the early twenty-first century, a pronounced drift to the left in much of Latin America, spearheaded by President Hugo Chavez of Venezuela. Shortly after the welcome (from Chavez's point of view) election of Socialist Evo Morales as president of Bolivia, left-leaning candidates lost presidential elections in Peru and Mexico. Nevertheless, according to Peter Hakim (2006, 47): "Anti-Americanism has surged in every country in Latin America.... A recent Zogby poll of Latin America's elites found that 86 percent of them disapprove of Washington's management of conflicts around the world." One specialist in foreign policy with respect to Latin America (Naim 2006) suggests that Chavezism could be countered if the United States would lift the embargo on Cuba and offer Brazil much freer access for its exports of steel, shoes, orange juice, and ethanol than it now enjoys. Certainly, the course of events and the growth of anti-U.S. sentiments in Latin America suggest that it may be time to try some new ideas.

The focus of global politics in the twenty-first century will almost certainly shift substantially toward Asia, thanks to the meteoric rise of China and India in recent decades. Perhaps the most pressing current crisis in the area involves the apparent determination of North Korea to develop its nuclear weapons arsenal, as well as its ability to deliver them on missiles, perhaps as far away as the United States. Whereas, at the beginning of George W. Bush's presidency, Allison (2006, 64) notes, "North Korea had two bombs-worth of plutonium.... At the end of his first term, according to CIA estimates, North Korea's nuclear arsenal had grown to eight bombs-worth of plutonium."

President Bush's efforts to deal with this particular problem have been uncharacteristically multilateral. He has long insisted that the matter be dealt with in the context of six-party talks, involving North Korea and the United States along with South Korea, Japan, Russia, and China. But these talks have demonstrated that while unilateralism has many costs, multilateralism is no guarantee of success. Still, it is promising that China appears to share with the United States the goal of curbing North Korea's nuclear ambitions—perhaps because it understands that if North Korea becomes a full-fledged nuclear power, South Korea and Japan may both move in a similar direction.

In the long run, most American foreign policy issues with respect to Asia are likely to focus on the relationship between China and the United States. As Kishore Mahbubani (2005, 50) puts it: "The history of the twenty-first century will largely be determined by the relationship that emerges between the world's greatest power and the world's greatest emerging power. History teaches that such transitions are inherently fraught with danger...." One specific issue that may provoke dangerous conflict is the future of Taiwan, as we discussed in chapter 12. Chen Shui-bian, Taiwan's president, has expressed his intention to draft a new constitution that would make Taiwan independent. According to Robert S. Ross (2005, 85): "Chinese leaders know that should there be a war in the Taiwan Strait, the U.S. Navy would intervene and the cost to China would be intolerable." But the costs to the Communist Party of China were Taiwan to become independent might be even more intolerable. For the moment, shared interests between China and the United States with respect to North Korea's nuclear ambitions, common concerns about Islamic fundamentalism, and striking degrees of economic interdependence between the two nations—involving a huge trading relationship, as well as Chinese investments in U.S. Treasury bonds—may serve to ameliorate any trend toward serious conflict.

U.S. relations with Europe have grown increasingly problematic in recent years. Europeans sympathized with Americans in the wake of the 9/11 attacks, and NATO has supported the U.S. effort to root out the Taliban in Afghanistan. However, several key European states, including France and Germany, did not support the American invasion and occupation of Iraq. Meanwhile, Gerard Baker (2003/04, 38) notes: "As European nations themselves split apart on whether to support the U.S.-led military action, the Bush Administration happily highlighted the distinctions between 'Old' and 'New' Europe." The implication was that Old Europe failed to support the American effort in Iraq, while New Europe and, preferably (from the American point of view), the wave of the future on the continent, favored it.

From a realist perspective, the tensions between the United States and Europe were simply a reflection of traditional, even timeless, balance-of-power politics. Christopher Layne (2003, 24) comments: "America still asserts its hegemony, and France and Germany still seek … to create a European counter-weight. As has been the case in the past, too, Washington is employing a number of strategies to keep Europe apart." By 2005, however, the Europeans were beginning to come apart without much help. Laurent Cohen-Tanugi (2005, 55) explains: "After the French and Dutch voters rejected the draft treaty establishing a constitution for Europe last spring, there was no doubt that a crisis of unprecedented seriousness confronted the European Union." Some Europeans still believe that the treaty will ultimately be ratified in some modified form. In the meantime, the United States needs to decide how it would like this crisis resolved.

In the immediate aftermath of the Cold War, there was hope in some circles that Russia would ultimately become a fully European state—it might join NATO, and perhaps even the EU. Those hopes now seem unwarranted, says Dmitri Trenin (2006, 87): "Until recently, Russia saw itself as Pluto in the Western solar system, very far from the center, but still fundamentally a part of it. Now it has left that orbit entirely: Russia's leaders have given up on becoming part of the West and have started creating their own Moscow-centered system." Tensions between Russia and the United States may be expected to escalate in 2008, when both states have presidential elections. The United States is unlikely to view the election in Russia as legitimate, while the Russians, in turn, can point to certain doubts about the legitimacy of the U.S. election of 2000. Should the United States, in the wake of its Iraqi experience, go from military attacks aimed at uprooting autocracy and spreading democracy, to a point at which it will not even lodge vigorous protests against a rigged election in such a vital state as Russia? Perhaps.

THE GLOBAL ENVIRONMENT

A book on American foreign policy should not end without some comment on **global warming** and **climate change**, which are possibly the most serious foreign policy problems facing the United States. And this is one more issue on which U.S. policy has disenchanted many observers and national leaders outside the United States.

The debate about climate change has become increasingly one-sided in the United States. Hurricane Katrina, a very hot summer in 2006, and melting glaciers in the North Pole as well as Antarctica and many other places, along with apparently rising sea levels, have provided persuasive evidence that global warming is, indeed, taking place. In addition, the evidence that rising carbon emissions correlate with increasing levels of carbon dioxide in the atmosphere, which, in turn, correlate with warming temperatures around the world, has left critics of global warming theory increasingly isolated. At one point, that theory's most vocal critic in the United States was novelist Michael Crichton, who wrote a novel, *State of Fear* (2004), replete with footnotes citing articles and evidence from scientific journals, to express his skepticism. But by the summer of 2006, his official Web page gave notice that "Michael has completed all interviews/speaking engagements regarding *State of Fear* and related themes and will not be revisiting those subjects in the future."

Not all critics have gone into retreat. In Canada, a Carleton University paleoclimatologist testified in 2005 to the Commons Committee on Environment that "there is no meaningful correlation between CO^2 levels and Earth's temperature.... When CO^2 levels were over ten times higher than they are now, about 450 million years ago, the planet was in the depths of the absolute coldest period in the last half billion years" (Harris 2006). In April of 2006, sixty "accredited experts in climate and related scientific disciplines" wrote an open letter to Canadian Prime Minister Stephen Harper, arguing that "observational evidence does not support today's computer climate models," and that "global climate changes all the time, due to natural causes, and the human impact still remains impossible to distinguish from this natural 'noise'" (Clark et al. 2006).

Perhaps not coincidentally, Canada is among the signatories to the **Kyoto Protocol** that will fall far short of meeting their commitments to reduce emissions of greenhouse gases. In 2002 Canada agreed to cuts its emissions by 6 percent from a 1990 base, but, by the following year, it had instead increased its emissions by 24.2 percent. But Canada is not alone. Japan has also increased rather than decreased its emissions since 1990, and most of the fifteen members of the European Union, which ratified the protocol together in 1997, have been increasing rather than decreasing their emissions as well (AFX News 2005).

Most of the states that are failing to meet their commitments under the Kyoto treaty acknowledge that the costs of meeting them are not acceptable.[q] In addition, even the scientists who support the Kyoto approach admit that if the signatories were to meet their commitments (which they will not), that effort would "at best, avert a temperature increase of less than 0.1 degrees Celsius by 2050"—an amount that is probably "too small to matter or even verify" (Lieberman 2005). In addition, in 2006 the states that have signed on to Kyoto tried and failed to persuade developing countries such as China and India to join in post–2012 commitments to reduce emissions. Both China and India have "soaring emissions" (Saunders and Turekian 2006, 79).

---

q. For example, Spain's environmental minister conceded in 2005 that Spain will not meet its commitment to reduce greenhouse gas emissions, citing costs that were proving to be "astronomical" (Lieberman 2005).

So, perhaps it is true that "the target and timetable approach" of the Kyoto Protocol is "politically flawed," as reported by Paul Saunders and Vaughn Turekian (2006, 80). Even so, the United States should probably have ratified it. The worldwide antagonism aroused by its failure to do so has been both considerable and unnecessary, as it could simply have ratified the treaty and then failed to meet its commitments, as many other signatories have done. More importantly, the evidence in favor of global warming theory—not to mention wide-spread political support for taking action against possibly catastrophic global climate changes in the future—surely suggest that the United States should take the lead in formulating a post-Kyoto approach to the problem.

It would not be necessary to say about Kyoto, "I told you so," nor to take any steps to dis-mantle the Kyoto process. A U.S. president (even George W. Bush) could make a commit-ment to achieve a zero-emissions economy by the end of the century, and then focus on efforts at deploying "available energy efficiency technologies now and developing cutting-edge tech-nologies for the future," in the words of Saunders and Turekian (84). This is the approach of the Asia-Pacific Partnership on Clean Development and Climate, a U.S.-initiated organization involving Australia, China, India, Korea, and Japan. In April of 2006, Canada also expressed an interest in joining in this partnership (CBC News 2006).

On this issue, in fact, it does appear that any U.S. president could take considerably more vigorous steps to combat climate change than have been taken so far without endangering his or her hold on power. For that reason, and because evidence in support of the idea that human behavior is contributing to ever more obvious changes in the climate at widely varied spots around the globe, we may reasonably expect U.S. policies on this issue to move in a direction that will bring it more in line with polices of other industrialized countries.

CONCLUSION

Among the more pressing foreign policy issues facing the United States toward the end of the first decade of the twenty-first century are these: (1) international terrorism and Islamic fun-damentalism; (2) the wars in Iraq and Afghanistan, as well as the conflict between Israel and its Arab neighbors; (3) escalating oil prices and dependence on foreign sources in unstable places; (4) possible nuclear proliferation, especially in Iran and North Korea; (5) failed states and serious conflicts in Africa, which may become breeding grounds for terrorists; (6) increas-ing flows of undocumented workers into the United States, and an accelerating trend toward leftist, and anti-American governments in Latin America; (7) China's increasing clout in both economic and military terms, and a possible conflict over Taiwan; (8) global warming and cli-mate change; (9) a drift toward autocracy in Russia, and a European Union that may be floun-dering; (10) sagging support for and admiration of the United States in the public opinion of an ever-growing list of countries; and (11) some crisis of which few experts are even aware. How many analysts in 2000, for example, anticipated that a global war on terrorism would be the defining foreign policy issue during the Bush administration's tenure?

And, looming over the United States and its ability to deal with all of these problems is a potential financial crisis fueled by budget deficits, which, in turn, may be exacerbated as the U.S. government incurs ever-heavier obligations under entitlement programs such as Social Security, Medicare, and Medicaid. The U.S. government may have to cut back drastically, in the not-too-distant future, on the resources it devotes to foreign policy issues, in order to cope with domestic problems. And it surely will make those cuts if political leaders feel that they must do so in order to stay in power. In fact, it is safe to anticipate that all of the issues enumerated in the previous paragraph will be dealt with in a way that maximizes the probability that the current leaders of the country will stay in power. Needless to say, this motive may not always lead to the most rational or effective solutions.

But the United States has faced one potentially catastrophic crisis after another ever since 1776, while its leaders have always had, as their highest priority, staying in power. Yet, it has resolved most of those crises successfully. Or, at least, it has dealt with them in such a manner that, for the most part, the country has become larger, more powerful, and wealthier with every passing decade (with some possible exceptions that were ultimately overcome). Perhaps that pattern will be broken in the twenty-first century, although the list of challenges facing the United States in the past has often seemed equally overwhelming. On one point, however, there is no doubt: U.S. foreign policy decisions in the remainder of the twenty-first century will have a profound impact on Americans, and on the world.

KEY CONCEPTS

climate change   372

containment   355

glasnost   354

global warming   372

Kyoto Protocol   373

perestroika   354

rollback strategy   356

RATIONAL POLITICAL AMBITION AND . . .
U.S. FOREIGN POLICY IN THE TWENTY-FIRST CENTURY

LESSONS LEARNED

☑ Under Gorbachev in the 1980s, the Soviets adopted policies intended to preserve their Communist regime, as well as the Soviet Union itself. Yet both disintegrated. Rational political ambition theory suggests that leaders seek to stay in power; it does not predict that they will always succeed.

☑ The Reagan administration often seemed to focus on undermining the Soviet Union to the extent that it endangered its hold on power by generating vigorous domestic opposition to its policies. Rational political ambition theory would account for this risk-taking by emphasizing the extent to which the administration's leaders saw international competitors as particularly threatening, causing them to be less concerned than is typical about domestic competitors.

☑ Because it also saw international competitors as particularly threatening, the administration of George W. Bush apparently sought to emulate what it saw as the Reagan administration's successful policies for winning the Cold War in its own attempt to deal with Islamic extremism and global terrorism.

☑ Rational political ambition theory is quite pessimistic about the ability of democratic states to promote democratic transitions in other states by means of military intervention.

☑ Political leaders of the United States who focus on staying in power may not consistently select the policy options best suited to dealing with the serious problems facing the United States. But American leaders in past generations were similarly motivated, and they often faced crises and problems at least as serious as those facing the United States today.

BIBLIOGRAPHY

Acheson, Dean. 1969. *Present at the Creation: My Years in the State Department.* New York: Norton.

Ackerman, David M., and Richard F. Grimmett. 2003. "Declarations of War and Authorizations for the Use of Military Force: Historical Background and Legal Implications." *Report for Congress* (Order Code RL31133). Updated January 14. www.ndu.edu/library/docs/crs/crs_rl31133_14jan03.pdf#search='CRS%20Report%20RL3 1133,%20Declarations%20of%20War\' (accessed August 16, 2005).

AFX News. 2005. "Canada, Japan, Europe Failing on Kyoto Greenhouse Gas Targets." *Forbes.com,* November 18. www.forbes.com/finance/feeds/afx/2005/11/18/afx2345473.html (accessed August 12, 2006).

Aids in Africa. 2004. "Comprehensive Up-to-Date Information about HIV/AIDS in Africa." www.afronets.org/linkview.php/104 (accessed January 23. 2005).

AIPAC. 2005. "AIPAC Issues: Who We Are." www.aipac.org/documents/ (accessed May 24, 2005).

Albright, Madeleine. 1997. "Enlarging NATO: Why Bigger Is Better." *Economist* 342 (February).

Alexander, Klinton W. 2000. "NATO's Intervention in Kosovo: The Legal Case for Violating Yugoslavia's 'National Sovereignty' in the Absence of Security Council Approval." *Houston Journal of International Law* 22: 404–449.

Allen, Mike, and Jonathan Weisman. 2003. "Steel Tariffs Appear to Have Backfired on Bush." *Washington Post,* September 19. www.washingtonpost.com/ac2/wp-dyn/A31768-2003Sep18?language=printer (accessed May 22, 2005).

Allen, Richard. 1974. *Imperialism and Nationalism in the Fertile Crescent: Sources and Prospects of the Arab-Israeli Conflict.* New York: Oxford University Press.

Allison, Graham. 2004a. "How to Stop Nuclear Terror." *Foreign Affairs* 83: 64–74.

———. 2004b. *Nuclear Terrorism: The Ultimate Preventable Catastrophe.* New York: Times Books/Henry Holt.

———. 2006. "A Nuclear Terrorism Report Card." *National Interest* 83: 63–65.

Allison, Graham, and Philip Zelikow. 1999. *Essence of Decision: Explaining the Cuban Missile Crisis.* 2nd ed. New York: Longman.

Almond, Gabriel A. 1960. *The American People and Foreign Policy.* New York: Praeger.

Alperovitz, Gar. 1965. *Atomic Diplomacy: Hiroshima and Potsdam.* New York: Vintage Books.

———. 2005. "Hiroshima after Sixty Years: The Debate Continues." *Common Dreams News Center,* August 3. www.commondreams.org/views05/0803-26.htm (accessed June 8, 2006).

Amanpour, Christiane. 2004. "Looking Back at Rwanda Genocide." CNN.com. www.cnn.com/2004/WORLD/africa/04/06/rwanda.amanpour/ (accessed January 22, 2005).

Ambrose, Stephen E., and Douglas G. Brinkley. 1997. *Rise to Globalism: American Foreign Policy since 1938.* 8th rev. ed. New York: Penguin Books.

Anderson, Scott. 2004. "How Did Darfur Happen?" *New York Times Magazine,* October 17, 54–63.

Andres, Richard B., Craig Wills, and Thomas E. Griffith Jr. 2005. "Winning with Allies: The Strategic Value of the Afghan Model." *International Security* 30: 124–160.

Angell, Norman. 1913. *The Great Illusion: A Study of the Relation of Military Power to National Advantage.* New York: Putnam.

Assassination Archives and Research Center. 1976. "Church Committee Reports." *Public Library Contents.* www.aarclibrary.org/publib/church/reports/contents.htm (accessed July 8, 2005).

Atkins, G. Pope. 1977. *Latin America in the International Political System.* New York: Free Press.

Ayittey, George B.N. 2002. "The Myth of Foreign Aid." *The Free Africa Foundation.* www.freeafrica.org/features5.html (accessed September 21, 2006).

Baker, Gerard. 2003. "Does the United States Have a European Policy?" *National Interest* 74: 37–42.

Baker, Peter. 2005. "Bush Faults WWII Legacy in E. Europe." *Washington Post,* May 8. www.washingtonpost.com/wp-dyn/content/article/2005/05/07/AR2005050701232.html (accessed June 12, 2006).

Balko, Radley. 2003. "President Bush's $15 Billion Package to Fight AIDS in Africa." *Capitalism Magazine,* June 23. www.capmag.com/article.asp?ID=2875 (accessed August 6, 2006).

Barba, Monica, Martha Carias, Aimee Dehbozorgi, and Kasey McCarthy. 1999. "Slavery in British America: The Colonial Era." http://cghs.dade.k12.fl.us/slavery/british_america/colonial_era.htm (accessed October 14, 2004).

Bard, Mitchell. 2005a. "The Hussein-McMahon Correspondence." *Jewish Virtual Library.* www.jewishvirtuallibrary.org/jsource/History/hussmac.html (accessed December 27, 2005).

———. 2005b. "The Lebanon War." *Jewish Virtual Library.* www.jewishvirtuallibrary.org/jsource/History/Lebanon_War.html (accessed February 21, 2005).

Barton, David. 1999. "Were All of America's Founding Fathers Racists, Pro-Slavery, and Hypocrites?" *ChristianAnswers.net.* www.christiananswers.net/q-wall/wal-g003.html (accessed October 17, 2004).

Baum, Matthew A. 2002. "Sex, Lies, and War: How Soft News Brings Foreign Policy to the Inattentive Public." *American Political Science Review* 96: 91–109.

BBC News Online. 2001. "Embassy Bombs: The FBI Trail," May 30. http://news.bbc.co.uk/1/hi/world/americ as/1359752.stm (accessed January 23, 2005).

———. 2007. "Sudan's Darfur Conflict," May 29. http://news.bbc.co.uk/1/hi/world/africa/3496731.stm (accessed May 31, 2007).

Becker, Eddie. 1999. "Chronology on the History of Slavery and Racism, 1790–1829." http://innercity.org/ holt/slavechron.html (accessed November 23, 2004).

Bender, Lynn Darrell. 1975. *The Politics of Hostility: Castro's Revolution and United States Policy.* Hato Rey, Puerto Rico: Inter American University Press.

Bennett, D. Scott, and Allan C. Stam III. 2000. "EUGene: A Conceptual Manual." *International Interactions* 26: 179–204. http://eugenesoftware.org.

Benson, Brett, and Emerson Niou. 2002. "The U.S. Security Commitment to Taiwan Should Remain Ambiguous." In *The Rise of China in Asia: Security Implications,* edited by Carolyn W. Pumphrey. Carlisle, Pa.: Strategic Studies Institute.

Benson, Michael T. 1997. *Harry S. Truman and the Founding of Israel.* Westport, Conn.: Praeger.

Bergsten, C. Fred. 1972. "The New Economics and U.S. Foreign Policy." *Foreign Affairs* 50: 199–222.

Bernstein, Barton J. 2000. "Understanding Decisionmaking, U.S. Foreign Policy, and the Cuban Missile Crisis: A Review Essay." *International Security* 25: 134–164.

Bernstein, Carl. 1992. "The Holy Alliance." *Time,* February 24. www.mosquitonet.com/~prewett/holyalliance1 of2.html (accessed July 19, 2006).

Beschloss, Michael, and Strobe Talbott. 1993. *At the Highest Levels: The Inside Story of the End of the Cold War.* Boston: Little, Brown.

Beveridge, Andrew. 2006. "Undocumented Immigrants." *Gotham Gazette,* April. www.gothamgazette.com/article/ demographics/20060406/5/1809 (accessed August 8, 2006).

Beyan, Amos J. 1991. *The American Colonization Society and the Creation of the Liberian State: A Historical Perspective, 1822–1900.* Lanham, Md.: University Press of America.

Bhagwati, Jagdish. 2004. "Don't Cry for Cancún." *Foreign Affairs* 83: 52–63.

Bin Laden, Osama. 2002. "Statement: Jihad against Jews and Crusaders. (February 23, 1998)." In *Anti-American Terrorism and the Middle East,* edited by Barry Rubin and Judith Colp Rubin. New York: Oxford University Press.

Blecker, Robert A. 2005. "U.S. Steel Import Tariffs: The Politics of Global Markets." In *Contemporary Cases in U.S. Foreign Policy,* edited by Ralph G. Carter. Washington, D.C.: CQ Press.

Bobbitt, Philip. 2002. *The Shield of Achilles: War, Peace, and the Course of History.* New York: Anchor Books.

Boot, Max. 2004. "Think Again: Neocons." *Foreign Policy* 140: 20–28.

———. 2005. "Q&A: Neocon Power Examined." *Christian Science Monitor.* http://csmonitor.com/specials/neo con/boot.html (accessed June 25, 2005).

Boulding, Kenneth. 1963. *Conflict and Defense: A General Theory.* New York: Harper and Row.

Blitzer, Wolf. 1997. "Clinton Defends 'Constructive Engagement' of China." *CNN/Time:Allpolitics,* October 24. www.cnn.com/ALLPOLITICS/1997/10/24/clinton.china/ (accessed February 20, 2005).

Brams, Steven J. 1975. *Game Theory and Politics.* New York: Free Press.

Bremer, Stuart A. 1992. "Dangerous Dyads: Conditions Affecting the Likelihood of Interstate War, 1816–1965." *Journal of Conflict Resolution* 36: 309–341.

Brinkley, Alan. 2006. "The Making of a War President." *New York Times Book Review,* August 20, 10–11.

Brinkley, Joel. 2005. "Japan Said to Support U.S. on Security of Taiwan." *New York Times,* February 19, A6.

Brooks, David. 2003. "Cynics without a Cause." *New York Times,* November 11. www.nytimes.com/2003/11/11/ opinion/11BROO.html?ex=1116993600&en=0967b45531174889&ei=5070&oref=login (accessed May 23, 2005).

Brown, Michael E. 1999. "Minimalist NATO: A Wise Alliance Knows When to Retrench." *Foreign Affairs* 78: 204–218.

Brzezinski, Matthew. 2004. "Red Alert." *Mother Jones.com,* September–October. www.motherjones.com/news/fea ture/2004/09/08_400.html (accessed August 12, 2004).

Brzezinski, Zbigniew. 2000. "Living with China." *National Interest* 59: 5–21.

Bueno de Mesquita, Bruce. 1981. *The War Trap.* New Haven, Conn.: Yale University Press.

———. 2003. *Principles of International Politics: People's Power, Preferences, and Perceptions.* Washington, D.C.: CQ Press.

Bueno de Mesquita, Bruce, and George Downs. 2006. "Intervention and Democracy." *International Organization* 60: 627–649.

Bueno de Mesquita, Bruce, and Hilton Root. 2002. "The Political Roots of Poverty: The Economic Logic of Autocracy." *National Interest* 68: 27–37.

Bueno de Mesquita, Bruce, and Randolph M. Siverson. 1995. "War and the Survival of Political Leaders: A Comparative Study of Regime Types and Political Accountability." *American Political Science Review* 89: 841–855.

Bueno de Mesquita, Bruce, James D. Morrow, Randolph M. Siverson, and Alastair Smith. 1999. "An Institutional Explanation of the Democratic Peace." *American Political Science Review* 93: 791–807.

Bueno de Mesquita, Bruce, Alastair Smith, Randolph M. Siverson, and James D. Morrow. 2003. *The Logic of Political Survival.* Cambridge, Mass.: MIT Press. Data available at www.nyu.edu/gsas/dept/politics/data/bdm2s2/Logic.htm.

Bureau of European and Eurasian Affairs. 2002. "NATO: Coalition Contributions to the War on Terrorism." *Fact Sheet,* October 31. www.state.gov/p/eur/rls/fs/14627.htm (accessed April 10, 2005).

Bureau of Public Affairs, U.S. Department of State. 2001a. "Department Organization." www.state.gov/r/pa/ei/rls/dos/436.htm (accessed July 1, 2005).

———. 2001b. "Diplomacy: The State Department at Work." www.state.gov/r/pa/ei/rls/dos/4078.htm (accessed July 2, 2005).

Burke, Edmund. 1774. "Speech to the Electors of Bristol." *The Online Library of Liberty: Select Works of Edmund Burke* (1999). http://oll.libertyfund.org/Texts/LFBooks/Burke0061/SelectWorks/HTMLs/0005-04_Pt02_Speeches.html#hd_lf5-.head.005 (accessed April 24, 2005).

Burkhart, Ross E., and Michael S. Lewis-Beck. 1994. "Comparative Democracy: The Economic Development Thesis." *American Political Science Review* 88: 903–910.

Buschini, J. 2000. "The Boxer Rebellion." Small Planet Communications. www.smplanet.com/imperialism/fists.html (accessed January 29, 2005).

Bush, George W. 2002a. "The President's State of the Union Address." January 29. www.whitehouse.gov/news/releases/2002/01/20020129-11.html (accessed April 13, 2005).

———. 2002b. *The National Security Strategy of the United States of America.* www.whitehouse.gov/nsc/nss.html (accessed April 11, 2005).

———. 2002c. "President's Remarks at the United Nations General Assembly." September 12. www.whitehouse.gov/news/releases/2002/09/20020912-1.html (accessed April 11, 2005).

Calleo, David P. 1982. *The Imperious Economy.* Cambridge, Mass.: Harvard University Press.

Calvocoressi, Peter. 1991. *World Politics since 1945.* 6th ed. London: Longman.

Caplan, Gerald. 2004. "AfricaFiles: Rwanda Ten Years after the Genocide." www.africafiles.org/article.asp?ID=4501 (accessed January 22, 2005).

Carpenter, Ted Galen. 2003/2004. "Living with the Unthinkable." *National Interest* 74: 92–98.

———. 2006. *America's Coming War with China: A Collision Course over Taiwan.* New York: Palgrave Macmillan.

Carroll, James. 2001. *Constantine's Sword: The Church and the Jews.* Boston: Houghton Mifflin.

Cardoso, Fernando Henrique, and Enzo Faletto. 1978. *Dependency and Development in Latin America.* Berkeley and Los Angeles: University of California Press.

Casey, Lee A., and David B. Rivkin Jr. 2005. "Double-Red-Crossed." *National Interest* 79: 63–72.

Catledge, Turner. 1941. "Our Policy Stated: Welles Says Defeat of Hitler Conquest Plans Is Greatest Task." *New York Times,* June 24, 1, 7. *Proquest Historical Newspapers.* http://proquest.umi.com/pqdweb?RQT=309&VInst=PROD&VName=HNP&VType=PQD&pv=1&sid=2&index=344&SrchMode=3&Fmt=10&did=87632849 (accessed June 4, 2006).

CBC News. 2006. "Canada Supports Six-Nation Climate Change Pact: Ambrose." www.cbc.ca/story/canada/national/2006/04/25/ambrose060425.html (accessed August 12, 2006).

Central Intelligence Agency. 1992, 2000, 2002, 2003, 2004. *World Factbook.* Washington, D.C. www.odci.gov/cia/publications/factbook/index.html.

Challenor, Herschelle Sullivan. 1977. "The Influence of Black Americans on U.S. Foreign Policy toward Africa." In *Ethnicity and U.S. Foreign Policy,* edited by Abdul Aziz Said. New York: Praeger.

Chatterjee, Pratap. 2003. "Halliburton Makes a Killing on Iraq War: Cheney's Former Company Profits from Supporting Troops." *Corpwatch: Holding Corporations Accountable.* March 20. www.corpwatch.org/article.php?id=6008.

Chomsky, Noam, and Edward Hermann. 1988. *Manufacturing Consent.* New York: Pantheon.

CIESIN Thematic Guides. 2003. "General Agreements on Tariffs and Trade." www.ciesin.org/TG/PI/TRADE/gatt.html (accessed August 13, 2003).

Cimbalo, Jeffrey L. 2004. "Saving NATO from Europe." *Foreign Affairs* 83: 111–120.

Clark, David H. 2003. "Can Strategic Interaction Divert Diversionary Behavior? A Model of U.S. Conflict Propensity." *Journal of Politics* 65: 1013–1039.

Clark, Ian, et al. 2006. "Sixty Scientists Call on Harper to Revisit the Science of Global Warming." *Open Letter to Canadian Prime Minister Stephen Harper.* April 15. www.citizenreviewonline.org/april2006/15/warming.html (accessed August 11, 2006).

Clarke, Richard A. 2005. "Building a Better Spy." *New York Times Magazine,* May 22. www.nytimes.com/2005/05/22/magazine/22ADVISER.html?ex=1123819200&en=acf1cea1a7791a81&ei=5070&oref=login (accessed August 10, 2005).

Clarke, Walter, and Jeffrey Herbst. 1996. "Somalia and the Future of Humanitarian Intervention." *Foreign Affairs* 75: 70–85.

CNN.com. 2002. "U.S. Policy on Assassinations." http://archives.cnn.com/2002/LAW/11/04/us.assassination.poli cy/ (accessed August 8, 2005).

———. 2004a. "Woodward: Tenet Told Bush WMD Case a 'Slam Dunk'." www.cnn.com/2004/ALLPOLI TICS/04/18/woodward.book/ (accessed August 8, 2005).

———. 2004b. "Young America's News Source: Jon Stewart." www.cnn.com/2004/SHOWBIZ/TV/03/02/ apontv.stewarts.stature.ap/ (accessed May 9, 2005).

Coffman, Edward M. 1991. "John J. Pershing." In *The Reader's Companion to American History*, edited by Eric Foner and John A. Garraty. Boston: Houghton Mifflin.

Cohen, Bernard C. 1963. *The Press and Foreign Policy: Principles, Problems, and Proposals for Reform.* Princeton, N.J.: Princeton University Press.

Cohen, Stephen D. 2000. *The Making of United States International Economic Policy.* 5th ed. Westport, Conn.: Praeger.

Cohen-Tanugi, Laurent. 2005. "The End of Europe?" *Foreign Affairs* 84: 55–67.

Collier, Ellen C. 1993. "Instances of Use of United States Forces Abroad, 1798–1993." Department of the Navy— Naval Historical Center. www.history.navy.mil/wars/foabroad.htm (accessed September 8, 2005).

Collins, Gabe, and Carlos Ramos-Mrosovksy. 2006. "Beijing's Bolivarian Venture." *National Interest* 85: 88–92.

Congressional Budget Office. 2001. *The Budget and Economic Outlook: Fiscal Years 2002–2011.* www.cbo.gov/show doc.cfm?index=2727&sequence=0 (accessed December 26, 2003).

Connell-Smith, Gordon. 1974. *The United States and Latin America: An Historical Analysis of Inter-American Relations.* New York: John Wiley.

Conquest, Robert. 1968. *The Great Terror: Stalin's Purge of the Thirties.* New York: Macmillan.

———. 1986. *The Harvest of Sorrow: Soviet Collectivization and the Terror-Famine.* New York: Oxford University Press.

Coombs, Leonard A. 1988. *Polar Bear Expedition Digital Collections.* http://polarbears.si.umich.edu/index.pl?node= Polar+Bear+History&lastnode_id=272 (accessed May 27, 2006).

Corwin, Edward S. 1957. *The President: Office and Powers, 1787–1957.* New York: New York University Press.

Council on Foreign Relations. 2004. Brochure. www.cfr.org/pdf/Council_brochure.pdf (accessed May 26, 2005).

Coutsoukis, Photius. 2003. *Countries of the World—19 Years of World Facts.* http://theodora.com/wfb/#CURRENT.

Cox, Robert W. 1986. "Social Forces, States, and World Orders: Beyond International Relations Theory." In *Neorealism and Its Critics,* edited by Robert O. Keohane. New York: Columbia University Press.

Crichton, Michael. 2004. *State of Fear.* New York: Avon Books.

Dahrendorf, Ralf. 1959. *Class and Class Conflict in Industrial Society.* Stanford, Calif.: Stanford University Press.

Dalton, Russell J., Paul A. Beck, and Robert Huckfeldt. 1998. "Partisan Cues and the Media: Information Flows in the 1992 Presidential Election." *American Political Science Review* 92: 111–126.

Dean, Jason. 2005. "Taiwan's Premier Supports Reforms to Constitution." *Wall Street Journal: Interactive Edition,* January 28. www.taiwandc.org/wsj-2005-01.htm (accessed March 11, 2005).

DeConde, Alexander. 1963. *A History of American Foreign Policy.* New York: Scribner's.

Delli Carpini, Michael X., and Scott Keeter. 1996. *What Americans Know about Politics and Why It Matters.* New Haven, Conn.: Yale University Press.

DeLong, J. Bradford. 1997. "Federal Reserve Weekly Letter: The Budget Deficit." www.j-bradford-delong.net/ Comments/1997_deficit_weekly.html (accessed September 18, 2003).

Department of Homeland Security. 2005. "Homeland Security Act of 2002: Department of Homeland Security." www.dhs.gov/xabout/laws/law_regulation_rule_0011.shtm (accessed August 11, 2005).

Department of the Navy. 2000. "The Boxer Rebellion and the U.S. Navy, 1900–1901. www.history.navy.mil/ faqs/faq86-1.htm (accessed January 29, 2005).

Department of the Treasury/Federal Reserve Board. 2006. "Major Foreign Holders of Treasury Securities." www.treas.gov/tic/mfh.txt (accessed July 2, 2006).

de Riencourt, Amaury. 1968. *The American Empire.* New York: Dial Press.

Desch, Michael C. 2002. "Democracy and Victory: Why Regime Type Hardly Matters." *International Security* 27: 5–47.

Deutsch, Karl W. 1974. "Imperialism and Neocolonialism." *Peace Science Society (International) Papers* 23: 1–25.

Deutsch, Karl W., et al. 1966. "Political Community and the North Atlantic Area: International Organization in Light of Historical Experience." In *International Political Communities: An Anthology.* Garden City, N.Y.: Anchor Books.

Dickson, David A. 1985. *United States Foreign Policy towards Sub-Saharan Africa.* Lanham, Md.: University Press of America.

Diggins, John Patrick. 2004. "How Reagan Beat the Neocons." Op-ed. *New York Times,* June 11, A27. http://pro quest.umi.com/pqdlink?did=649829661&sid=1&Fmt=3&clientId=2335&RQT=309&VName=PQD (accessed July 26, 2006).

Digital National Security Archive. 2004. "South Africa: The Making of U.S. Policy, 1962–1989." http://nsarchive.chadwyck.com/saintro.htm (accessed January 17, 2005).

Dodds, Paisley. 2005. "Amnesty Takes Aim at 'Gulag' in Guantanamo." Associated Press, May 26. http://tomweston.net/amnestygulag.htm (accessed July 26, 2006).

Dos Santos, Theotonio. 1970. "The Structure of Dependence." *American Economic Review* 60: 231–236.

Doyle, Kate, and Peter Kornbluh. 2004. "CIA and Assassinations: The Guatemala 1954 Documents." *National Security Archive Electronic Briefing Book No. 4.* www.gwu.edu/~nsarchiv/NSAEBB/NSAEBB4/ (accessed June 6, 2004).

Doyle, Michael W. 1997. *Ways of War and Peace: Realism, Liberalism, and Socialism.* New York: Norton.

Duignan, Peter, and L. H. Gann. 1984. *The United States and Africa: A History.* Cambridge: Cambridge University Press.

Durant, Will, and Ariel Durant. 1968. *The Lessons of History.* New York: MJF Books.

Eberstadt, Nicholas. 2004. "Power and Population in Asia." *Policy Review* 123: 3–27.

Economist. 2003a. "Cancún's Charming Outcome." 368 (September 20): 11–12.

———. 2003b. "AIDS: A Mixed Prognosis." 369 (November 29): 77–79.

———. 2003c. "The Not-So-Mighty Dollar." 369 (December 4): 9

———. 2003d. "Rolled Over." 369 (December 4): 28.

———. 2003e. "A Faded Green." 369 (December 4): 65–66.

———. 2003f. "Free Trade on Trial—Ten Years of NAFTA." 370 (December 30): 13–15.

———. 2004. "Is This the World's Least Effective UN Peacekeeping Force?" 373 (December 2): 45–46.

Eisenhower, Dwight. 1961. "Farewell Address." January 17. www.eisenhower.archives.gov/speeches/farewell_address.html (accessed July 20, 2005).

———. 1963. *Mandate for Change: The White House Years, 1953–1956.* Garden City, N.Y.: Doubleday.

Elshtain, Jean Bethke. 1987. *Women and War.* New York: Basic Books.

"Empire Builders: Neoconservatives and Their Blueprint for U.S. Power." 2005. *Christian Science Monitor.* http://csmonitor.com/specials/neocon/ (accessed June 25, 2005).

Enloe, Cynthia. 1989. *Beaches, Bananas, and Bases: Making Feminist Sense of International Politics.* Berkeley: University of California Press.

———. 1993. *The Morning After: Sexual Politics at the End of the Cold War.* Berkeley: University of California Press.

E&P Staff. 2004. "Pew Survey Finds Moderates, Liberals Dominate News Outlets." *Editor and Publisher,* May 23. www.freerepublic.com/focus/f-news/1141012/posts (accessed May 10, 2005).

Erlanger, Steven. 2002. "Europe Seethes as the U.S. Flies Solo in World Affairs." *New York Times,* February 23, A8.

Esposito, John. 2006. "Lebanon Crisis: The Moment of Truth Has Come for Bush." *Arab News,* July 26. www.arabnews.com/?page=7&section=0&article=84397&d=26&m=7&y=2006 (accessed July 26, 2006).

Fagen, Richard R. 1975. "The United States and Chile: Roots and Branches." *Foreign Affairs* 53, no. 2. www.foreignaffairs.org/19750101faessay10135-p10/richard-r-fagen/the-united-states-and-chile-roots-and-branches.html (accessed June 27, 2004).

Falcoff, Mark. 1999. "Guatemala's Troubles Weren't Made in the USA." *Wall Street Journal,* March 3, A18.

Falk, Richard. 2003. "What Future for the UN Charter System of War Prevention?" *American Journal of International Law* 97: 590–598.

Fanton, Jonathan, and Kenneth Roth. 2001. "U.S. Policy on Assassinations, CIA: Human Rights Watch Letter to President George W. Bush." *HRW World Report 2001: United States,* September 20. www.hrw.org/press/2001/09/bushlet0920.htm (accessed August 6, 2005).

Farhi, Paul. 2003. "Everybody Wins." *American Journalism Review,* April. www.ajr.org/Article.asp?id=2875 (accessed May 8, 2005).

Feaver, Peter D., and Christopher Gelpi. 2004. *Choosing Your Battles: American Civil-Military Relations and the Use of Force.* Princeton, N.J.: Princeton University Press.

Federman, Josef. 2006. "Israel's Olmert Doesn't Rule Out Peace Talks Despite Hamas Election Victory." *CBC News/World,* February 21. www.cbc.ca/cp/world/060221/w022152.html (accessed February 26, 2006).

Feith, Douglas J. 2006. "On the Global War on Terrorism." In *Taking Sides: Clashing Views on Controversial Issues in World Politics,* 12th ed., edited by John T. Rourke. Dubuque, Iowa: McGraw-Hill/Dushkin.

Ferguson, Niall, and Laurence J. Kotlikoff. 2003. "Going Critical: American Power and the Consequences of Fiscal Overstretch." *National Interest* 73: 22–32.

Fischer, Conan. 2003. *The Ruhr Crisis, 1923–1924.* Oxford: Oxford University Press.

Fischer, Fritz. 1975. *War of Illusions: German Policies from 1911 to 1914.* New York: Norton.

Fischer, Markus. 1992. "Feudal Europe, 800–1300: Communal Discourse and Conflictual Practices." *International Organization* 46: 427–466.

Fisher, Ian, and Norimitsu Onishi. 2000. "Many Armies Ravage Rich Land in the 'First World War of Africa.' " *New York Times,* February 6. http://proquest.umi.com/pqdweb?did=49221738&sid=2&Fmt=3&clientId=2335&RQT=309&VName=PQD (accessed January 4, 2005).

Floyd, David. 1963. *Mao against Khrushchev: A Short History of the Sino-Soviet Conflict.* New York: Praeger.

Fonte, John. 2004. "Democracy's Trojan Horse." *National Interest* 76: 117–127.

Fordham, Benjamin. 1998a. "Partisanship, Macroeconomic Policy, and U.S. Uses of Force, 1949–1994." *Journal of Conflict Resolution* 42: 418–439.

———. 1998b. "The Politics of Threat Perception and the Use of Force: A Political Economy Model of U.S. Uses of Force, 1949–1994." *International Studies Quarterly* 42: 567–590.

Foreign Affairs Council. 2003. *Secretary Colin Powell's State Department: An Independent Assessment.* Chapel Hill, N.C.: American Diplomacy Publishers. www.unc.edu/depts/diplomat/archives_roll/2003_04-06/fac/fac_task.html#summary (accessed July 8, 2005).

Forney, Matt. 2003. "Tug-of-War over Trade." *Time,* December 22, 42–44.

Foster, Richard. 2003. "Why The U.S. Can't Count on China." *JSOnline:Milwaukee Journal Sentinal,* March 16. www.jsonline.com/news/editorials/mar03/125698.asp?format=print (accessed February 20, 2005).

Frank, Andre Gunder. 1967. *Capitalism and Underdevelopment in Latin America.* New York: Monthly Review Press.

Frederking, Brian. 2003. "Constructing Post–Cold War Collective Security." *American Political Science Review* 97: 363–378.

Freedom House. 2005. "Freedom in the World 2005." www.freedomhouse.org/template.cfm?page=363&year=2005 (accessed January 9, 2005).

Friedberg, Aaron L. 2000a. "Will Europe's Past Be Asia's Future?" *Survival* 42: 147–159.

———. 2000b. "Will We Abandon Taiwan?" *Commentary* 109: 26–31.

Frieden, Jeffrey A., and David A. Lake. 1995. "Introduction: International Politics and International Economics." In *International Political Economy: Perspectives on Global Power and Wealth,* edited by Jeffrey A. Frieden and David A. Lake. New York: St. Martin's.

Friedman, Norman. 2000. *The Fifty Year War: Conflict and Strategy in the Cold War.* Annapolis, Md.: Naval Institute Press.

Friedman, Thomas L. 1995. *From Beirut to Jerusalem.* New York: Anchor Books.

Fukuyama, Francis. 2004. "The Neoconservative Moment." *National Interest* 76: 57–68.

Gaddis, John Lewis. 1986. "The Long Peace: Elements of Stability in the Postwar International System." *International Security* 10: 99–142.

———. 1972, 2000. *The United States and the Origins of the Cold War, 1941–1947.* New York: Columbia University Press.

———. 1992. *The United States and the End of the Cold War: Implications, Reconsiderations, Provocations.* New York: Oxford University Press.

———. 2005. *The Cold War: A New History.* New York: Penguin.

Gaiduk, Ilya V. 1996. *The Soviet Union and the Vietnam War.* Chicago: Ivan R. Dee.

Gallagher, Mary E. 2002. " 'Reform and Openness': Why China's Economic Reforms Have Delayed Democracy." *World Politics* 54: 338–372.

Gallucci, Robert L. 2005. "Preventing the Unthinkable." *National Interest* 81: 129–131.

Garde, Paul. 1996. "An Expert's Overview: Yugoslavia's History." *Frontline Online,* WGBH Educational Foundation. www.pbs.org/wgbh/pages/frontline/shows/karadzic/bosnia/history.html (accessed March 30, 2005).

Gardinier, Kurt A. 2003. "Clinton Calls for Change to 22nd Amendment." *U.S. Term Limits.* www.termlimits.org/Press/Press_Releases/20030529.html (accessed September 23, 2005).

Garthoff, Raymond L. 1994. "Looking Back: The Cold War in Retrospect." *Brookings Review* 12: 10–13.

Gaubatz, Kurt Taylor. 1991. "Election Cycles and War." *Journal of Conflict Resolution* 35: 212–244.

Gilboy, George J. 2004. "The Myth behind China's Miracle." *Foreign Affairs* 83: 33– 48.

Gilens, Martin. 2001. "Political Ignorance and Collective Policy Preferences." *American Political Science Review* 95: 379–396.

Gilley, Bruce. 2004. *China's Democratic Future: How It Will Happen and Where It Will Lead.* New York: Columbia University Press.

Gilpin, Robert. 1981. *War and Change in World Politics.* Cambridge: Cambridge University Press.

———. 1987. *The Political Economy of International Relations.* Princeton, N.J.: Princeton University Press.

———. 2001. *Global Political Economy: Understanding the International Economic Order.* Princeton, N.J.: Princeton University Press.

Girardet, Edward, ed. 1995. *Somalia, Rwanda and Beyond: The Role of the International Media in Wars and Humanitarian Crises.* Geneva: Crosslines Global Report.

GlobalSecurity.org. 2006. "World Wide Military Expenditures." www.globalsecurity.org/military/world/spending.htm (accessed January 29, 2007).

Gokhale, Jagadeesh, and Kent Smetters. 2003. *Fiscal and Generational Imbalances: New Budget Measures for New Budget Priorities.* Washington D.C.: AEI Press. www.aei.org/docLib/20030723_SmettersFinalCC.pdf (accessed January 2, 2004).

Goldstein, Joshua S. 1988. *Long Cycles: Prosperity and War in the Modern Age.* New Haven, Conn.: Yale University Press.

———. 2001. *War and Gender: How Gender Shapes the War System and Vice Versa.* Cambridge: Cambridge University Press.

Goodman, Amy. 2006. "Interview with Stephen Kinzer: *Overthrow: America's Century of Regime Change from Hawaii to Iraq.*" *Democracy Now,* April 21. www.democracynow.org/article.pl?sid=06/04/21/132247 (accessed May 18, 2006).

Gowa, Joanne. 1983. *Closing the Gold Window: Domestic Politics and the End of Bretton Woods.* Ithaca, N.Y.: Cornell University Press.

Grau, Lester W., and William A. Jorgensen. 1998. "Handling the Wounded in a Counter-Guerrilla War: The Soviet/Russian Experience in Afghanistan and Chechnya." *U.S. Army Medical Department Journal* (January–February). http://fmso.leavenworth.army.mil/documents/handlwnd/handlwnd.htm (accessed March 11, 2006).

Grimmett, Richard F. 2004. "War Powers Resolution: Presidential Compliance." *CRS Issue Brief for Congress* (Order Code IB81050). www.fas.org/man/crs/IB81050.pdf#search="The%20War%20Powers%20Resolution%20and%20the%20War%20in%20Iraq (accessed August 17, 2005).

Griswold, Daniel T. 1999. "Counting the Cost of Steel Protection." Hearing on Steel Trade Issues, House Committee on Ways and Means, Subcommittee on Trade. *Cato Congressional Testimony.* www.freetrade.org/pubs/speeches/ct-dg022599.html (accessed May 22, 2005).

Groeling, Tim, and Samuel Kernell. 1998. "Is Network News Coverage of the President Biased?" *Journal of Politics* 60: 1063–1086.

Gunaratna, Rohan. 2002. *Inside Al-Qaeda: Global Network of Terror.* New York: Cambridge University Press.

Hakim, Peter. 2006. "Is Washington Losing Latin America?" *Foreign Affairs* 85: 39–53.

Halberstam, David. 1972. *The Best and the Brightest.* New York: Random House.

———. 2001. *War in a Time of Peace: Bush, Clinton, and the Generals.* New York: Simon and Schuster.

Hale, David, and Lyric Hughes Hale. 2003. "China Takes Off." *Foreign Affairs* 82: 36–53.

Halloran, Richard. 2006. "Guam a Focal Point for U.S. Military Plans." *HonoluluAdvertiser.com,* May 14. http://the.honoluluadvertiser.com/article/2006/May/14/op/FP605140307.html (accessed September 22, 2006).

Handel, Michael I. 1996. "The Weinberger Doctrine." In *Reader's Guide to Military History,* sponsored by The Society for Military History. Boston: Houghton Mifflin. http://college.hmco.com/history/readerscomp/mil/html/ml_057800_weinbergerdo.htm (accessed August 17, 2004).

Hargreaves, John D. 1988. *Decolonization in Africa.* London: Longman.

Harris, Katherine. 1985. *African and American Values: Liberia and West Africa.* Lanham, Md.: University Press of America.

Harris, Tom. 2006. "Scientists Respond to Gore's Warnings of Climate Catastrophe." *Canadafreepress.com,* June 12. www.canadafreepress.com/2006/harris061206.htm (accessed August 8, 2006).

Hendrickson, David C., and Robert W. Tucker. 2005. "The Freedom Crusade." *National Interest* 81: 12–22.

Herring, Hubert. 1972. *A History of Latin America from the Beginnings to the Present.* 3rd ed. New York: Knopf.

Hersh, Seymour. 2005. *Chain of Command: The Road from 9/11 to Abu Ghraib.* New York: Harper Perennial.

Herz, John H. 1957. "The Rise and Demise of the Territorial State." *World Politics* 9: 473–493.

Hinsley, F. H. 1967. *Power and the Pursuit of Peace: Theory and Practice in the History of Relations between States.* New York: Cambridge University Press.

Hinton, Harold C. 1966. *Communist China in World Politics.* Boston: Houghton Mifflin.

History Net. 2004. "The Korean War: A Fresh Perspective." www.historynet.com/magazines/military_history/3030186.html (accessed February 4, 2005).

Hogan, Matthew. 2002. "The 'Hoax' Hoax: Kosovo's Racak Massacre at the Mercy of Partisanship." *The Ethical Spectacle.* www.spectacle.org/1202/hogan.html (accessed April 7, 2005).

Holsti, Ole R. 1992. "Public Opinion and Foreign Policy: Challenges to the Almond-Lippmann Consensus." *International Studies Quarterly* 36: 439–466.

Hook, Steven W., and John Spanier. 2004. *American Foreign Policy since World War II.* 16th ed. Washington, D.C.: CQ Press.

Horne, Alistair. 1990. *Small Earthquake in Chile: A Visit to Allende's South America.* 2nd ed. London: Macmillan.

Hudson, Michael. 1998. "The Historical Evolution of U.S. Involvement in the Middle East." *The United States and Canada: Political Systems, Policy-making and the Middle East.* Jerusalem: Palestinian Academic Society for the Study of International Affairs. www.passia.org/seminars/98/US&Canada/day-eight.htm#part3-1 (accessed December 22, 2005).

Hunt, Michael H. 1987. *Ideology and U.S. Foreign Policy.* New Haven, Conn.: Yale University Press.

Hunter, Robert. 1999. "Maximizing NATO: A Relevant Alliance Knows How to Reach." *Foreign Affairs* 78: 190–203.

Huntington, Samuel P. 1991. *The Third Wave: Democratization in the Late Twentieth Century.* Norman: Oklahoma University Press.

———. 2004. "The Hispanic Challenge." *Foreign Policy* 141: 30–45.

Hurst, Steven. 2005. *Cold War U.S. Foreign Policy: Key Perspectives.* Edinburgh: Edinburgh University Press.

IISS. 1990. *The Military Balance, 1989–1990.* London: International Institute of Strategic Studies.

Immerman, Richard H. 1982. *The CIA in Guatemala: The Foreign Policy of Intervention.* Austin: University of Texas Press.

Infoplease. 2004. Mozambique: History. *Columbia Electronic Encyclopedia,* 6th ed. (c) Publishing as Infoplease. New York: Columbia University Press. www.infoplease.com/ce6/world/A0859810.html (accessed January 11, 2004).

Institute for International Economics. 1999. "Case Studies in Sanctions and Terrorism: UN v. South Africa; U.S., Commonwealth v. South Africa." www.iie.com/research/topics/sanctions/southafrica.htm#chronology (accessed January 19, 2005).

Intriligator, Michael, and Dagobert Brito. 1984. "Can Arms Races Lead to the Outbreak of War?" *Journal of Conflict Resolution* 28: 63–84.

Irons, John S. 2003. "Beyond the Baseline: 10 Year Deficits Likely to Reach $5.9 Trillion." *OMB Watch,* August 26. www.ombwatch.org/article/articleview/1768/1/18/ (accessed December 28, 2003).

Jentleson, Bruce. 1992. "The Pretty Prudent Public: Post Post–Vietnam American Opinion on the Use of Military Force." *International Studies Quarterly* 36: 49–74.

Jentleson, Bruce, and Rebecca L. Britton. 1998. "Still Pretty Prudent: Post–Cold War American Public Opinion on the Use of Military Force." *Journal of Conflict Resolution* 42: 395–417.

Jett, Dennis. 2005. "The Failure of Colin Powell." *Foreign Service Journal,* February. www.afsa.org/fsj/feb05/Jett.pdf (accessed July 9, 2005).

Johnson, Paul. 1983. *Modern Times: The World from the Twenties to the Eighties.* New York: Harper and Row.

Johnson, Richard A. 1971. *The Administration of United States Foreign Policy.* Austin: University of Texas Press.

Kanabus, Annabel, and Jenni Fredriksson-Bass. 2006. "HIV and AIDS in Africa." *Avert.org,* July 21. www.avert.org/aafrica.htm (accessed August 6, 2006).

Kane, Tim. 2004. "Global U.S. Troop Deployment, 1950–2003." *Heritage Foundation, Policy Research & Analysis: Issues—Defense.* Center for Data Analysis Report #04-11. October 27. www.heritage.org/Research/National Security/cda04-11.cfm (accessed March 13, 2005).

Kayal, Alawi D. 2002. *The Control of Oil: East-West Rivalry in the Persian Gulf.* London: Kegan Paul.

Kean, Thomas H., and Lee H. Hamilton. 2004. The National Commission on Terrorist Attacks upon the United States, *The 9/11 Report.* New York: St. Martin's.

Kegley, Charles W., Jr. 1994. "How Did the Cold War Die? Principles for an Autopsy." *Mershon International Studies Review* 38: 11–41.

Kehr, Eckart. 1965, 1977. *Economic Interest, Militarism and Foreign Policy: Essays on German History.* Berkeley: University of California Press.

Keller, Morton. 1991. "Spanish-American War." In *The Reader's Companion to American History,* edited by Eric Foner and John A. Garraty. Boston: Houghton Mifflin.

Kennan, George F. ("X"). 1947. "The Sources of Soviet Conduct." *Foreign Affairs* 25: 566–582.

———. 1993. "Somalia: Through a Glass Darkly." *New York Times,* September 30.

Kennedy, Paul 1987. *The Rise and Fall of the Great Powers: Economic Change and Military Conflict from 1500 to 2000.* New York: Random House.

Keohane, Robert. 1980. "The Theory of Hegemonic Stability and Changes in International Economic Regimes, 1967–1977." In *Change in the International System,* edited by Ole R. Holsti, Randolph M. Siverson, and Alexander L. George. Boulder, Colo.: Westview.

———. 1983. "Theory of World Politics: Structural Realism and Beyond." In *Political Science: The State of the Discipline,* edited by Ada Finifter. Washington, D.C. American Political Science Association.

———. 1984. *After Hegemony: Cooperation and Discord in the World Political Economy.* Princeton, N.J.: Princeton University Press.

Keohane, Robert O., and Joseph S. Nye. 1989. *Power and Interdependence.* 2nd ed. Glenview, Ill.: Scott Foresman.

Kessler, Glenn, and Colum Lynch. 2004. "U.S. Calls Killings in Sudan Genocide." *Washington Post Online,* September 10. www.washingtonpost.com/wp-dyn/articles/A8364-2004Sep9.html (accessed January 17, 2005).

Keylor, William R. 1996. *The Twentieth Century World: An International History.* New York: Oxford University Press.

Khalilzad, Zalmay, et al. 1999. "The United States and a Rising China," A RAND Corporation Report, MR-1082-AF. www.rand.org/publications/MR/MR1082/ (accessed March 9, 2005).

Khouri, Fred J. 1968. *The Arab-Israeli Dilemma.* Syracuse, N.Y.: Syracuse University Press.

Kim, Woosang. 1989. "Power, Alliance, and Major Wars, 1816–1975. *Journal of Conflict Resolution* 33: 255–273.

———. 1992. "Power Transitions and Great Power War from Westphalia to Waterloo." *World Politics* 45:153–172.

Kindleberger, Charles P. 1973. *The World in Depression, 1929–1939.* Berkeley: University of California Press.

———. 1978. *Manias, Panics, and Crashes.* New York: Basic Books.

———. 1981. *Power and Money: The Economics of International Politics and the Politics of International Economics.* New York: Basic Books.

———. 1986. "Hierarchy versus Inertial Cooperation." *International Organization* 40: 841–847.

Kinzer, Stephen. 2006. *Overthrow: America's Century of Regime Change from Hawaii to Iraq.* New York: Times Books.

Kirkpatrick, Jeane. 1979. "Dictatorships and Double Standards." *Commentary* 68: 34–45.

Kissinger, Henry A. 1979. *The White House Years.* Boston: Little, Brown.

———. 1982. *Years of Upheaval.* Boston: Little, Brown.

Klare, Michael T. 2005. "Mapping the Oil Motive." *TomPaine.common sense,* March 18. www.tompaine.com/arti cles/mapping_the_oil_motive.php (accessed May 14, 2006).

Knickmeyer, Ellen. 2005. "Darfur Toll Could be 200,000, Study Finds." *Miami Herald.com.* www.miami.com/mld/miamiherald/news/world/10696237.htm?1c (accessed January 23, 2005).

Knowlton, Brian. 2006. "Global Image of the U.S. Is Worsening, Survey Finds." *New York Times,* June 14. www.nytimes.com/2006/06/14/world/14pew.html?ex=1307937600&en=a94e96e038de0fe7&ei=5090&part ner=rssuserland&emc=rss (accessed July 3, 2006).

Korb, Lawrence J. 1997. "The Department of Defense: The First Half Century." In *U.S. National Security: Beyond the Cold War,* edited by D. Stuart. Carlisle, Pa.: Clarke Center.

Kralev, Nicholas. 2004. "China Hits U.S. Sales to Taiwan; Power Defends Arms Policy." *Washington Times,* October 1, 1.

Krauthammer, Charles. 2004. "In Defense of Democratic Realism." *National Interest* 77: 15–25.

———. 2006. "A Calamity for Israel." *Washington Post.com,* January 6. www.washingtonpost.com/wp-dyn/con tent/article/2006/01/05/AR2006010501901.html (accessed February 26, 2006).

Kugler, Jacek. 1996. "Beyond Deterrence: Structural Conditions for a Lasting Peace." In *Parity and War: Evaluations and Extensions of "The War Ledger,"* edited by Jacek Kugler and Douglas Lemke. Ann Arbor: University of Michigan Press.

Kugler, Jacek, Lewis Snider, and William Longwell. 1994. "From Desert Shield to Desert Storm: Success, Strife or Quagmire?" *Conflict Management and Peace Science* 13: 113–148.

Kugler, Jacek, and Frank C. Zagare. 1990. "The Long-Term Stability of Deterrence." *International Interactions* 15: 255–278.

Kull, Steven. 2003. "Misperceptions, the Media, and the Iraq War." *The PIPA/Knowledge Networks Poll: The American Public on International Issues.* www.pipa.org/OnlineReports/Iraq/Media_10_02_03_Report.pdf#search='Surveys%20of%20Public%20Knowledge%20About%20Foreign%20Affairs (accessed April 23, 2005).

Kumar, Sehdev. 2001. "Africa's First World War: Guilt, Duplicity and Blood." *Convention des Institutions Democratiques et Sociales.* www.cides-congo.org/fre/view.asp?ID=783 (accessed January 4, 2005).

Kuperman, Alan J. 2001. *The Limits of Humanitarian Intervention: Genocide in Rwanda.* Washington, D.C.: Brookings Institution Press.

———. 2004. "Humanitarian Hazard: Revisiting Doctrines of Intervention." *Harvard International Review* 26: 64–68.

Lake, David. 1993. "Leadership, Hegemony, and the International Economy: Naked Emperor or Tattered Monarch with Potential?" *International Studies Quarterly* 37: 459–489.

———. 1992. "Powerful Pacifists: Democratic States and War." *American Political Science Review* 86: 24–37.

Lake, David, and Matthew Baum. 2001. "The Invisible Hand of Democracy: Political Control and the Provision of Public Services." *Comparative Political Studies* 34: 587–621.

Layne, Christopher. 2003. "America as European Hegemon." *National Interest* 72: 17–29.

———. 2006. "Impotent Power: Re-Examining the Nature of America's Hegemonic Power." *National Interest* 85: 41–47.

Lebow, Richard Ned, and Janice Stein. 1994. *We All Lost the Cold War.* Princeton, N.J.: Princeton University Press.

Leebaert, Derek. 2002. *The Fifty Year Wound: The True Price of America's Cold War Victory.* Boston: Little, Brown.

Lefebvre, Jeffrey A. 1993. "The U.S. Military Intervention in Somalia: A Hidden Agenda?" *Middle East Policy* 2: 44–62.

Leiby, Richard. 2001. "Terrorists by Another Name: The Barbary Pirates." *Washington Post.com,* October 15. www.washingtonpost.com/ac2/wp-dyn?pagename=article&node=&contentId=A59720-2001Oct14 (accessed August 23, 2005).

Lemke, Douglas. 1993. *Multiple Hierarchies in World Politics.* Ph.D. diss., Vanderbilt University.

———. 1997. "The Continuation of History: Power Transition Theory and the End of the Cold War." *Journal of Peace Research* 34: 23–36.

Lemke, Douglas, and Jacek Kugler. 1996. "The Evolution of the Power Transition Perspective." In *Parity and War: Evaluations and Extensions of "The War Ledger,"* edited by Jacek Kugler and Douglas Lemke. Ann Arbor: University of Michigan Press.

Leng, Russell J. 1984. "Reagan and the Russians: Crisis Bargaining Beliefs and the Historical Record." *American Political Science Review* 78: 338–355.

LeoGrande, William M. 1998. "From Havana to Miami: U.S. Cuba Policy as a Two-Level Game." *Journal of Interamerican Studies and World Affairs* 40: 67–86.

Levinson, Jerome, and Juan de Onís. 1970. *The Alliance That Lost Its Way: A Critical Report on the Alliance for Progress.* Chicago: Quadrangle Books.

Levitsky, Steven, and María Victoria Murillo. 2003. "Argentina Weathers the Storm." *Journal of Democracy* 14: 152–166.

Levy, Jack. 1989. "The Diversionary Theory of War: A Critique." In *Handbook of War Studies,* edited by Manus I. Midlarsky. Boston: Unwin Hyman.

Levy, Philip I. 1999. "Sanctions on South Africa: What Did They Do?" Center Discussion Paper no. 796. Economic Growth Center, Yale University.

Lewis, David. 2006. "Congo Election Shows Worrying East-West Divide." *Reuters,* August 4. www.redorbit.com/news/international/602514/congo_election_shows_worrying_eastwest_divide/index.html (accessed August 8, 2006).

Lian, Bradley, and John R. Oneal. 1993. "Presidents, the Use of Military Force, and Public Opinion." *Journal of Conflict Resolution* 37: 277–300.

Library of Congress. 1987. "China: The Militant Phase, 1966–1968." *Library of Congress Country Studies.* http://workmall.com/wfb2001/china/china_history_the_militant_phase_1966_68.html (accessed February 9, 2005). Republished in Coutsoukis 2003.

———. 1989. "Angola: Emergence of UNITA." *Library of Congress Country Studies.* http://workmall.com/wfb2001/angola/angola_history_emergence_of_unita.html (accessed January 6, 2005). Republished in Coutsoukis 2003.

———. 1991a. "Philippines: Spanish-American War and Philippine Resistance." *Library of Congress Country Studies.* http://workmall.com/wfb2001/philippines/philippines_history_spanish_american_war_and_philippine_resistance.html (accessed January 28, 2005). Republished in Coutsoukis 2003.

———. 1991b. "Philippines: War of Resistance." *Library of Congress Country Studies.* http://workmall.com/wfb2001/philippines/philippines_history_war_of_resistance.html (accessed January 28, 2005). Republished in Coutsoukis 2003.

———. 2004. *The African American Mosaic: A Library of Congress Resource Guide for the Study of Black History and Culture.* www.loc.gov/exhibits/african/afam002.html (accessed November 24, 2004).

Lieberman, Ben. 2005. "Kyoto Lite: A Potential Deal Breaker in the Senate Energy Bill." *Heritage Foundation: Policy Research and Analysis: Issues—Energy and Environment,* WebMemo #768. www.heritage.org/Research/EnergyandEnvironment/wm768.cfm (accessed August 12, 2006).

Lieven, Anatol. 2006. "Bush's Middle East Democracy Flop." *Los Angeles Times,* July 23. http://fairuse.100webcustomers.com/fairenough/latimes290.html (accessed July 23, 2006).

Lipset, Seymour Martin. 1959. "Some Social Requisites of Democracy: Economic Development and Political Legitimacy." *American Political Science Review* 53: 69–105.

Livingston, Steven, and Todd Eachus. 1995. "Humanitarian Crises and U.S. Foreign Policy:Somalia and the CNN Effect Reconsidered." *Political Communication* 12: 413–429.

Lowenkopf, Martin. 1976. *Politics in Liberia: The Conservative Road to Development.* Stanford, Calif.: Hoover Institution Press.

Lowenthal, Abraham F. 1972. *The Dominican Intervention.* Cambridge, Mass.: Harvard University Press.

Lyman, Princeton N., and J. Stephen Morrison. 2004. "The Terrorist Threat in Africa." *Foreign Affairs* 83: 75–86.

MacAskill, Ewen, and Julian Borger. 2004. "Iraq War Was Illegal and Breached UN Charter, Says Annan." *Guardian,* September 16. www.guardian.co.uk/Iraq/Story/0%2C2763%2C1305709%2C00.html (accessed April 12, 2004).

Machiavelli, Niccolò. 1532, 1996. *The Prince.* Translated by George Bull. New York: Penguin Books.

Mack, Andrew. 1975. "Why Big Nations Lose Small Wars: The Politics of Asymmetric Conflict." *World Politics* 27: 175–200.

Macomber, William B. 1975. *The Angels' Game: A Handbook of Modern Diplomacy.* New York: Stein and Day, 1975.

Maechling, Charles, Jr. 1990. "Washington's Illegal Invasion." *Foreign Policy* 79: 113–131.

Mahbubani, Kishore. 2005. "Understanding China." *Foreign Affairs* 84: 49–60.

Malan, Rian. 2003. "Africa Isn't Dying of Aids." *The Spectator,* December 13. www.lewrockwell.com/spectator/spec192.html (accessed May 29, 2007).

Manchester, William. 1974. *The Glory and the Dream: A Narrative History of America, 1932–1972.* New York: Bantam Books.

Mandelbaum, Michael. 1999. "A Perfect Failure: NATO's War against Yugoslavia." *Foreign Affairs* 78: 2–8.

Mansfield, Edward D., and Jack Snyder. 2002. "Democratic Transitions, Institutional Strength, and War." *International Organization*56: 297–337.

Manzella, John. 2004. "The Congressional Guide to International Trade." http://manzellatrade.com/_pdfs/Congressional_Guide.pdf#search='Worldwide%20costs%20of%20Protectionism (accessed September 13, 2005).

Martin, Lisa. 2003. "The United States and International Commitments: Treaties as Signaling Devices." Manuscript.

Marx, Karl, and Frederick Engels. 1848. "Manifesto of the Communist Party." www.anu.edu.au/polsci/marx/classics/manifesto.html (accessed May 18, 2005).

May, Ernest R. 1961. *Imperial Democracy: The Emergence of America as a Great Power.* New York: Harcourt, Brace.

———. 1975. *The Making of the Monroe Doctrine.* Cambridge, Mass.: Harvard University Press, 1975.

Mazrui, Ali A. 2004. *The African Predicament and the American Experiment: A Tale of Two Edens.* Westport, Conn.: Praeger.

McCormick, James M. 2005. *American Foreign Policy and Process.* 4th ed. Belmont, Calif.: Thomson-Wadsworth.

McDonald, Joe. 2005. "India, China to Form Strategic Relationship." *New York Times,* April 11. www.nytimes.com/aponline/international/AP-India-China.html?pagewanted=print&position (accessed April 15, 2005).

McGeary, Johanna. 2001. "Odd Man Out." *Time.* (Posted September 3, published September 10). www.rediff.com/search/2001/oct/17atr4.htm (accessed July 9, 2005).

McPherson, James M. 2002. "Causes and Results of the Civil War." Posted by Jeff Smith. *Free Republic.* www.freere public.com/focus/f-news/621892/posts (accessed February 18, 2007).

Mead, Walter Russell. 1990. "On the Road to Ruin: Winning the Cold War, Losing the Economic Peace." *Harper's* 280: 59–64.

———. 2001. *Special Providence: American Foreign Policy and How It Changed the World.* New York: Knopf.

———. 2002. "The American Foreign Policy Legacy." *Foreign Affairs* 81: 163–176.

Mearsheimer, John J. 1990. "Back to the Future: Instability in Europe after the Cold War." *International Security* 15: 5–56.

———. 1994–1995. "The False Promise of International Institutions." *International Security* 19: 5–49.

———. 2001a. *The Tragedy of Great Power Politics.* New York: Norton.

———. 2001b. "The Future of the American Pacifier." *Foreign Affairs* 80: 46–61.

———. 2005. "Better to Be Godzilla than Bambi." *Foreign Policy* 146: 47–48.

Mearsheimer, John, and Stephen Walt. 2006a. "The Israel Lobby and U.S. Foreign Policy." Working Paper, March. http://ksgnotes1.harvard.edu/Research/wpaper.nsf/rwp/RWP06-011/$File/rwp_06_011_walt.pdf#search='Walt%20and%20Mearsheimer,%20The%20Israeli%20Lobby' (accessed May 21, 2006).

———. 2006b. "The Israel Lobby." *London Review of Books* 28 (March 23). www.lrb.co.uk/v28/n06/mear01_.html (accessed May 21, 2006).

———. 2006c. "Letters: The Israel Lobby." *London Review of Books* 28 (May 11). www.lrb.co.uk/v28/n09/letters.html#1 (accessed May 22, 2006).

Meernik, James, and Peter Waterman. 1996. "The Myth of the Diversionary Use of Force by American Presidents." *Political Research Quarterly* 49: 573–590.

Metz, Helen Chapin, ed. 1991. *Jordan: A Country Study.* Washington, D.C.: Federal Research Division, Library of Congress. http://countrystudies.us/jordan/ (accessed December 22, 2005).

Milner, Helen V. 1997. *Interests, Institutions, and Information: Domestic Politics and International Relations.* Princeton, N.J.: Princeton University Press.

Minority Staff, Committee on Government Reform, U.S. House of Representatives. 2003. *Fact Sheet: The Bush Administration's Contracts with Halliburton.* http://why-war.com/files/pdf_admin_contracts_halliburton_fact-sheet.pdf (accessed May 21, 2005).

Mintz, Alex. 2004. "How Do Leaders Make Decisions? A Poliheuristic Perspective." *Journal of Conflict Resolution* 48: 3–13.

"Missouri Compromise." 2004. *The Columbia Electronic Encyclopedia.* (c) 2004 Pearson Education, publishing as Infoplease. New York: Columbia University Press. www.infoplease.com/ce6/history/A0833427.html (accessed October 19, 2004).

Modelski, George. 1964. "Kautilya: Foreign Policy and International System in the Ancient Hindu World." *American Political Science Review* 58: 549–560.

Modelski, George, and William R. Thompson. 1987. "Testing Cobweb Models of the Long Cycle." In *Exploring Long Cycles,* edited by George Modelski. Boulder, Colo.: Lynne Rienner.

Morgan, T. Clifton, and Christopher J. Anderson. 1999. "Domestic Support and Diversionary External Conflict in Great Britain, 1950–1992." *Journal of Politics* 61: 799–814.

Morgan, T. Clifton, and Kenneth N. Bickers. 1992. "Domestic Discontent and the External Use of Force." *Journal of Conflict Resolution* 36: 25–52.

Morgenthau, Hans J. 1948. *Politics among Nations.* New York: Knopf.

———. 1967. *Politics among Nations.* 4th ed. New York: Knopf.

Morgenthau, Hans. J., and Kenneth W. Thompson. 1985. *Politics among Nations.* 6th ed. New York: Knopf.

Morris, Richard B. 1972. "Revolution in the Western World: The American Revolution." In *The Columbia History of the World,* edited by John A. Garraty and Peter Gay, 753–763. New York: Harper and Row.

Morris, Stephen J. 2003/2004. "Averting the Unthinkable." *National Interest* 74: 99–107.

Mueller, John. 1973. *War, Presidents and Public Opinion.* New York: John Wiley.

———. 1995. *Quiet Cataclysm: Reflections on the Recent Transformation of World Politics.* New York: HarperCollins.

Naim, Moises. 2006. "The Good Neighbor Strategy." *Time,* July 17, 34–35.

Nathan, James A., and James K. Oliver. 1994. *Foreign Policy Making and the American Political System.* 3rd ed. Baltimore: Johns Hopkins Press.

National Security Council. 1950. "NSC 68: United States Objectives and Programs for National Security." *A Report to the President Pursuant to the President's Directive of January 31, 1950.* www.fas.org/irp/offdocs/nsc-hst/nsc-68.htm (accessed July 13, 2006).

Needler, Martin C. 1970. "Mexico: Revolution as a Way of Life." In *Political Systems of Latin America,* 2nd ed., edited by Martin C. Needler. New York: Van Nostrand Reinhold Company.

New York Times. 2002. Advertisement, "War with Iraq Is Not in America's National Interest," September 26. www.bear-left.com/archive/2002/0926oped.html (accessed July 31, 2006).

Nicolaidis, Kalypso. 2004. " 'We, the Peoples of Europe . . . ' " *Foreign Affairs* 83: 97–110.

Nincic, Miroslav. 1992. *Democracy and Foreign Policy: The Fallacy of Political Realism.* New York: Columbia University Press.

Niskanen, William A. 1993, 2002, 2006. "Reaganomics." In *The Concise Encyclopedia of Economics,* edited by David R. Henderson. Liberty Fund, Inc., Library of Economics and Liberty. www.econlib.org/library/Enc/Reaganomics.html (accessed July 6, 2006).

Nixon, Richard M. 1962. *Six Crises.* New York: Doubleday.

North Atlantic Treaty Organization. 2005a. "NATO in Afghanistan." *NATO Fact Sheet,* February 21. www.nato.int/issues/afghanistan/040628-factsheet.htm (accessed April 10, 2005).

North Atlantic Treaty Organization. 2005. "NATO Update." www.nato.int/docu/update/index.html (accessed March 13, 2005).

NPR. 2005. "Poll: Bush's Second-Term Rating Lags behind Others." *PollingReport.com.* www.pollingreport.com/iraq.htm (accessed May 4, 2005).

Nuruzzaman, Mohammed. 2006. "Beyond the Realist Theories: 'Neo-Conservative Realism' and the American Invasion of Iraq." *International Studies Perspectives* 7: 239–253.

Nye, Joseph. 2002. *The Paradox of American Power: Why the World's Only Superpower Can't Go It Alone.* New York: Oxford University Press.

Odom, William E. 2004. "Retreating in Good Order." *National Interest* 76:33–36.

O'Donnell, Guillermo. 1973. *Modernization and Bureaucratic-Authoritarianism: Studies in South American Politics.* Berkeley: University of California, Institute of International Studies.

OECD. 2003. *Trends and Recent Developments in Foreign Direct Investment.* www.oecd.org/dataoecd/52/11/2958722.pdf (accessed December 27, 2003).

Office of the Historian. 2004. "Foreign Relations, Guatemala, 1952–1954)." U.S. Department of State. www.state.gov/r/pa/ho/frus/ike/guat/20171pf.htm (accessed June 5, 2004).

Office of U.S. Trade Representative. 2002. "U.S. Proposes Tariff-Free World to WTO." http://usgovinfo.about.com/library/weekly/aatariff_free.htm (accessed May 22, 2005).

Offner, John L. 1992. *An Unwanted War: The Diplomacy of the United States and Spain Over Cuba, 1895–1898.* Chapel Hill: University of North Carolina Press.

Oksenberg, Michel, and Elizabeth Economy. 1999. "China Joins the World." In *China Joins the World: Progress and Prospects,* edited by Elizabeth Economy and Michel Oksenberg. New York: Council on Foreign Relations Press.

Olson, Mancur. 1968. *The Logic of Collective Action.* New York: Schocken Books.

Oneal, John R., Brad Lian, and James H. Joyner Jr. 1996. "Are the American People 'Pretty Prudent'? Public Responses to U.S. Uses of Force, 1950–1988." *International Studies Quarterly* 40: 261–280.

Oneal, John R., Bruce Russett, and Michael L. Berbaum. 2003. "Causes of Peace: Democracy, Interdependence, and International Organizations, 1885–1992." *International Studies Quarterly* 47: 371–393.

Operation Enduring Freedom. 2006. "Coalition Military Fatalities." http://icasualties.org/oef/ (accessed March 10, 2006).

Oppenheimer, J. Robert. 1953. "Atomic Weapons and American Policy." *Foreign Affairs* 31: 525–535.

Organski, A. F. K. 1958. *World Politics.* New York: Knopf.

———. 1968. *World Politics.* 2nd ed. New York: Knopf.

Organski, A. F. K., and Jacek Kugler. 1980. *The War Ledger.* Chicago: University of Chicago Press.

Packer, George. 2005. *The Assassin's Gate: America in Iraq.* New York: Farrar, Straus, and Giroux.

Pakenham, Thomas. 1991. *The Scramble for Africa: White Man's Conquest of the Dark Continent from 1876 to 1912.* New York: Random House.

Page, Benjamin I., and Jason Barabas. 2000. "Foreign Policy Gaps between Citizens and Leaders." *International Studies Quarterly* 44: 339–364.

Page, Benjamin I., and Robert Y. Shapiro. 1992. *The Rational Public: Fifty Years of Trends in Americans' Policy Preferences.* Chicago: University of Chicago Press.

Parsons, Craig. 2002. "Showing Ideas as Causes: The Origins of the European Union." *International Organization* 56: 47–84.

PBS Online and WGBH/*Frontline*. 1998. "Ambush in Mogadishu: U.S. Charges Relating to Osama Bin Laden's Connection to the 1993 Mogadishu Attack." www.pbs.org/wgbh/pages/frontline/shows/ambush/readings/indict ment.html.

Pei, Minxin. 2003. "Contradictory Trends and Confusing Signals." *Journal of Democracy* 14: 73–81.

Pelletiere, Stephen. 2004. *America's Oil Wars*. New York: Praeger.

Perkins, Dexter. 1927. *The Monroe Doctrine, 1823–1826*. Cambridge, Mass.: Harvard University Press.

———. 1963. *A History of the Monroe Doctrine*. Rev. ed. Boston: Little, Brown.

Peruzzotti, Enrique. 2004. "Argentina after the Crash: Pride and Disillusion." *Current History* 103: 86–90.

Peterson, V. Spike, ed. 1992. *Gendered States: Feminist (Re)Visions of International Relations Theory*. Boulder, Colo.: Lynne Rienner.

Pevehouse, Jon C. 2005. *Democracy from Above: Regional Organizations and Democratization*. Cambridge: Cambridge University Press.

Pipes, Daniel. 2005. "What Do the Terrorists Want? [A Caliphate]." *New York Sun,* July 26. www.danielpipes.org/article/2798 (accessed March 8, 2006).

Pipes, Richard. 1991. *The Russian Revolution*. New York: Vintage Books.

Plischke, Elmer. 1999. *U.S. Department of State: A Reference History*. Westport, Conn.: Greenwood.

Podhoretz, Norman. 1998. "Israel and the United States: A Complex History." *Commentary* 105: 28–43.

Polk, William R. 1975. *The United States and the Arab World*. 3rd ed. Cambridge, Mass.: Harvard University Press.

PollingReport.com. 2005a. "Iraq." www.pollingreport.com/iraq.htm (accessed May 5, 2005).

———. 2005b. "President Bush: Job Ratings." www.pollingreport.com/BushJob.htm (accessed May 3, 2005).

Pollins, Brian M. 1996. "Global Political Order, Economic Change, and Armed Conflict: Coevolving Systems and the Use of Force." *American Political Science Review* 90: 103–117.

Pollins, Brian M., and Kevin P. Murrin. 1999. "Where Hobbes Meets Hobson: Core Conflict and Colonialism, 1495–1985." *International Studies Quarterly* 43: 427–454.

Porter, Adam. 2005. "British Lawmaker: Iraq War Was for Oil." *Aljazeera.net,* May 21. http://english.aljazeera.net/NR/exeres/AC9B68BD-9853-494D-AB7D-A5EF74C46694.htm (accessed May 14, 2006).

Porter, Russell. 1944. "World Bank Urged by Keynes as Vital." *New York Times,* July 4, 1, 15.

Powell, Colin L. 1992. "U.S. Forces: Challenges Ahead." *Frontline.* www.pbs.org/wgbh/pages/frontline/shows/military/force/powell.html (accessed August 21, 2004).

Power, Samantha. 2002. *"A Problem from Hell": America and the Age of Genocide*. New York: Harper Perennial.

Powlick, Philip J., and Andrew Z. Katz. 1998. "Defining the American Public Opinion/Foreign Policy Nexus." *Mershon International Studies Review* 42: 29–61.

PPI. 2003. "Trade Fact of the Week: Foreign Investment in the United States Has Fallen by 90 Percent since 2000." June 25. www.ppionline.org/ndol/print.cfm?contentid=251817 (accessed November 22, 2004).

Przeworski, Adam, and Fernando Limongi. 1997. "Modernization: Theories and Facts." *World Politics* 49: 155–183.

Purifoy, Lewis McCarroll. 1976. *Harry Truman's China Policy: McCarthyism and the Diplomacy of Hysteria, 1947–1951*. New York: New Viewpoints.

Putnam, Robert D. 1988. "Diplomacy and Domestic Politics: The Logic of Two-Level Games." *International Organization* 42: 427–460.

Rajaee, Bahram. 2004. "War, Peace, and the Evolution of U.S. Policy in the Middle East." In *Security, Economics, and Morality in American Foreign Policy: Contemporary Issues in Historical Context,* edited by William H. Meyer. Upper Saddle River, N.J.: Pearson/Prentice Hall.

Rappaport, Armin. 1967. "Review of *Atomic Diplomacy: Hiroshima and Potsdam; The Use of the Atomic Bomb and the American Confrontation with Soviet Power,* by Gar Alperovitz." *American Historical Review* 73: 624–625.

Ray, James Lee. 1995. *Democracy and International Conflict: An Evaluation of the Democratic Peace Proposition*. Columbia: University of South Carolina Press.

———. 1998. *Global Politics*. 7th ed. Boston: Houghton Mifflin.

Ray, James Lee, and Juliet Kaarbo. 2005. *Global Politics*. 8th ed. Boston: Houghton Mifflin.

Reagan, Ronald. 1982. "U.S. National Security Strategy." *National Security Decision Directive Number 32.* http://fas.org/irp/offdocs/nsdd/23-1618t.gif (accessed July 15, 2006).

———. 1983a. "U.S. Relations with the USSR." *National Security Decision Directive Number 75.* http://fas.org/irp/offdocs/nsdd/nsdd-075.htm (accessed July 17, 2006).

———. 1983b. "Partial Text of President Reagan's October 24 Statement on Lebanon." *Washington Report on Middle East Affairs.* October 31, 6. www.wrmea.com/backissues/103183/831031006b.html (accessed February 23, 2006).

Record, Jeffrey. 2000. "Weinberger-Powell Doctrine Doesn't Cut It." U.S. Naval Institute *Proceedings,* October. http://pqasb.pqarchiver.com/proceedings/access/62318539.html?dids=62318539:62318539&FMT=ABS&FMTS=ABS:FT&date=Oct+2000&author=Jeffrey+Record&pub=United+States+Naval+Institute.+Proceedings&edition=&startpage=35&desc=Weinberger-Powell+doctrine+doesn%27t+cut+it (accessed August 21, 2004).

Reischauer, Edwin O. 1964. *Japan: Past and Present*. 3rd ed., revised. New York: Knopf.

Reiter, Dan. 1995. "Exploding the Powder Keg Myth: Preemptive Wars Almost Never Happen." *International Security* 20: 5–34.

———. 2001. "Why NATO Enlargement Does Not Spread Democracy." *International Security* 25: 41–67.

Reiter, Dan, and Allan C. Stam. 2002. *Democracies at War.* Princeton, N.J.: Princeton University Press.

Remmer, Karen. 1990. "Democracy and Economic Crisis: The Latin American Experience." *World Politics* 42: 315–335.

Renner, Michael. 2003. "The Other Looting." *FPIF Special Report.* www.fpif.org/pdf/reports/SRlooting2003.pdf (accessed May 21, 2005).

Republican Party Platform. 1952. www.presidency.ucsb.edu/showplatforms.php?platindex=R1952 (accessed July 13, 2006).

Reuters. 2006. "North Korea Vows 'Annihilating Strike' If Attacked." http://defensenews.com/story.php?F=1925727&C=asiapac (accessed July 3, 2006).

Reuveny, Rafael, and Aseem Prakash. 1999. "The Afghanistan War and the Breakdown of the Soviet Union." *Review of International Studies* 25: 693–708.

Riccards, Michael P. 2000. *The Presidency and the Middle Kingdom: China, the United States, and Executive Leadership.* Lanham, Md.: Lexington Books.

Rice, Condoleezza. 2000. "Promoting the National Interest." *Foreign Affairs* 79: 45–62.

Rice, Susan. 2005. "U.S. Foreign Assistance to Africa: Claims vs. Reality." Brookings Institution. www.brookings.edu/views/articles/rice/20050627.htm (accessed May 29, 2007).

Rich, Frank. 2005. "Karl and Scooter's Excellent Adventure." *New York Times,* October 23, 13.

Richter, James G. 1994. *Khrushchev's Double Bind: International Pressures and Domestic Coalition Politics.* Baltimore: Johns Hopkins University Press.

Richter Videos. 2006. "In Our Hands." www.richtervideos.com/InOurHands (accessed July 24, 2006).

Rieff, David. 2006. "America the Untethered." *New York Times,* July 2. www.nytimes.com/2006/07/02/magazine/02wwln_lede.html (accessed July 3, 2006).

Riker, William. 1962. *The Theory of Political Coalitions.* New Haven, Conn.: Yale University Press.

Risen, James. 2000. "Secrets of History: The C.I.A. in Iran." *New York Times.* www.nytimes.com/library/world/mideast/041600iran-cia-index.html.

Rivkin, David B., and Lee A. Casey. 2003. "Leashing the Dogs of War." *National Interest* 73: 57–69.

Roberts, Adam. 1999. "NATO's 'Humanitarian War' over Kosovo." *Survival* 41: 102–123.

Robinson, Piers. 1999. "The CNN Effect: Can the News Media Drive Foreign Policy?" *Review of International Studies* 25: 301–309.

Rockman, Bert A. 1981. "America's Department of State: Irregular and Regular Syndromes of Policy Making." *American Political Science Review* 75: 911–927.

Rodman, Peter W. 1994. *More Precious than Peace: The Cold War and the Struggle for the Third World.* New York: Scribner's.

Rosen, Steven. 1972. "War Power and the Willingness to Suffer." In *Peace, War, and Numbers,* edited by Bruce M. Russett. Beverly Hills, Calif.: Sage Publications.

Rosenau, Pauline Marie. 1992. *Post-Modernism and the Social Sciences: Insights, Inroads, and Intrusions.* Princeton, N.J.: Princeton University Press.

Ross, Robert S. 2000. "The 1995–96 Taiwan Strait Confrontation: Coercion, Credibility, and the Use of Force." *International Security* 25: 87–123.

———. 2005. "Assessing the China Threat." *National Interest* 81:81–94.

Rotberg, Robert, and Thomas Weiss, eds. 1996. *From Massacres to Genocide: The Media, Public Policy, and Humanitarian Crises.* Cambridge, Mass.: World Peace Foundation.

Rothkopf, David J. 2005. "Inside the Committee That Runs the World." *Foreign Policy* 147: 30–40.

Rummel, R. J. 1975. *The Dynamic Psychological Field.* Vol. 1 of *Understanding Conflict and War.* New York: Sage Publications.

———. 1976. *The Conflict Helix.* Vol. 2 of *Understanding Conflict and War.* New York: Sage Publications.

———. 1977. *Conflict in Perspective.* Vol. 3 of *Understanding Conflict and War.* Beverly Hills: Sage Publications.

———. 1979. *War, Power, and Peace.* Vol. 4 of *Understanding Conflict and War.* Beverly Hills: Sage Publications.

———. 1981. *The Just Peace.* Vol. 5 of *Understanding Conflict and War.* Beverly Hills: Sage Publications.

———. 1990. *Lethal Politics: Soviet Genocide and Mass Murder since 1917.* New Brunswick, N.J.: Transaction.

Russett, Bruce. 1990. "Economic Decline, Electoral Pressure, and the Initiation of International Conflict." In *Prisoners of War?: Nation-States in the Modern Era* edited by Charles Gochman and Alan Sabrosky. Lexington, Ky.: Lexington Books.

———. 1993. *Grasping the Democratic Peace: Principles for a Post–Cold War World.* Princeton, N.J.: Princeton University Press.

Russett, Bruce, and John Oneal. 2001. *Triangulating Peace: Democracy, Interdependence, and International Organizations.* New York: Norton.

Russett, Bruce, and Allan C. Stam. 1998. "Courting Disaster: An Expanded NATO vs. Russia and China." *Political Science Quarterly* 113: 361–382.

Salinger, Pierre. 1989. "Gaps in the Cuban Missile Crisis Story." *New York Times,* February 5, 1989, 25. http://proquest.umi.com/pqdweb?index=0&did=961116061&SrchMode=1&sid=1&Fmt=3&VInst=PROD&VType=PQD&RQT=309&VName=PQD&TS=1154782710&clientId=2335 (accessed June 17, 2004).

———. 1995. *P.S.: A Memoir.* New York: St. Martin's.

Sarkees, Meredith Reid. 2000. "The Correlates of War Data on War: An Update to 1997." *Conflict Management and Peace Science* 18: 123–144.

Saunders, Paul J., and Vaughan C. Turekian. 2006. "Warming to Climate Change." *National Interest* 84: 78–84.

Sbragia, Alberta M. 1993. "Asymmetrical Integration in the European Community: The Single European Act and Institutional Development." In *The 1992 Project and the Future of Integration in Europe,* edited by Dale L. Smith and James Lee Ray. Armonk, N.Y.: M. E. Sharpe.

Schattschneider, E. E. 1960. *The Semisovereign People: A Realist's View of Democracy in America.* New York: Holt, Rinehart, and Winston.

Schlesinger, Arthur, Jr. 1967. "Origins of the Cold War." *Foreign Affairs* 46: 22–52.

———. 1973. *The Imperial Presidency.* Boston: Houghton Mifflin.

Schraeder, Peter J. 1994. *United States Foreign Policy toward Africa: Incrementalism, Crisis, and Change.* Cambridge: Cambridge University Press.

Schweizer, Peter. 1994. *Victory: The Reagan Administration's Secret Strategy That Hastened the Collapse of the Soviet Union.* New York: Atlantic Monthly Press.

———. 2002. *Reagan's War: The Epic Story of His Forty-Year Struggle and Final Triumph over Communism.* New York: Anchor Books.

Schweller, Randall L. 1992. "Domestic Structure and Preventive War: Are Democracies More Pacific?" *World Politics* 44: 235–269.

Sciolino, Elaine. 2000. "Eccentric Nationalist Begets Strange History." *New York Times,* April 15. www.nytimes.com/library/world/mideast/041600iran-cia-mossadegh.html (accessed July 28, 2005).

Sek, Lenore. 2001. "Fast Track Authority for Trade Agreements." *CRS Issue Brief for Congress.* www.ncseonline.org/NLE/CRSreports/Economics/econ-128.cfm?&CFID=14869688&CFTOKEN=59856116 (accessed September 9, 2005).

Sempa, Francis P. 2004. "Ronald Reagan and the Collapse of the Soviet Empire." *American Diplomacy.* www.unc.edu/depts/diplomat/archives_roll/2004_07-09/sempa_reagan/sempa_reagan.html (accessed July 14, 2006).

Senate Historical Office. n.d. "Treaties." www.senate.gov/artandhistory/history/common/briefing/Treaties.htm (accessed September 6, 2005).

Servan-Schreiber, Jean-Jacques. 1968. *The American Challenge.* Translated by Ronald Steel. New York: Atheneum.

Shah, Anup. 2006. "Arms Trade: A Major Cause of Suffering." *Global Issues.* www.globalissues.org/Geopolitics/ArmsTrade.asp (accessed January 28, 2007).

Shain, Yossi. 1994–1995. "Ethnic Diaspora and U.S. Foreign Policy." *Political Science Quarterly* 109: 811–841.

Shambaugh, David. 2004. "The United States and East Asia." In *Divided Diplomacy and the Next Administration: Conservative and Liberal Alternatives,* edited by Henry R. Nau and David Shambaugh. Washington, D.C.: The Elliott School of International Affairs.

Shick, Tom W. 1980. *Behold the Promised Land: A History of Afro-American Settler Society in Nineteenth Century Liberia.* Baltimore: Johns Hopkins University Press.

Shifter, Michael. 2004. "The U.S. and Latin America through the Lens of Empire." *Current History* 103: 61–67.

Shirer, William L. 1990. *The Rise and Fall of the Third Reich: A History of Nazi Germany.* New York: Simon and Schuster.

Shirk, Susan. 1993. *The Political Logic of Economic Reform in China.* Berkeley and Los Angeles: University of California Press.

Shulman, Marshall D. 1987–1988. "The Superpowers: Dance of the Dinosaurs." *Foreign Affairs* 66: 494–515.

Sigmund, Paul E. 1974. "The 'Invisible Blockade' and the Overthrow of Allende." *Foreign Affairs* 52, no. 2. www.foreignaffairs.org/19740101faessay10095/paul-e-sigmund/the-invisible-blockade-and-the-overthrow-of-allende.html (accessed June 26, 2004).

Simpkins, John. 2001. "European Immigration to the United States." *Virtual School.* www.eun.org/eun.org2/eun/en/vs-history/content.cfm?lang=en&ov=10335 (accessed March 12, 2005).

Singer, J. David, Stuart Bremer, and John Stuckey. 1972. "Capability Distribution, Uncertainty, and Major Power War, 1820–1965." In *Peace, War, and Numbers,* edited by J. David Singer. Beverly Hills, Calif.: Sage Publications.

Sivard, Ruth Leger. 1977. *World Military and Social Expenditures.* Leesburg, Va.: WMSE Publications.

Skidmore, Thomas E., and Peter H. Smith. 1992. *Modern Latin America.* 3rd ed. New York: Oxford University Press.

Slater, Jerome. 1970. *Intervention and Negotiation: The United States and the Dominican Revolution.* New York: Harper and Row.

Small, Melvin. 1999. "The Domestic Course of the War." In *The Oxford Companion to American Military History,* edited by John Whiteclay Chambers II. New York: Oxford University Press. www.english.uiuc.edu/maps/viet nam/domestic.htm (accessed August 20, 2003).

Small, Melvin, and J. David Singer. 1982. *Resort to Arms: International and Civil Wars, 1816–1980.* Beverly Hills, Calif.: Sage Publications.

Smele, Jonathan. 2004. "War, Revolution, and Civil War in Russia: The Eastern Front 1914–1921." *BBC History: World Wars: World War One.* www.bbc.co.uk/history/war/wwone/eastern_front_01.shtml (accessed May 26, 2006).

Smith, Alistair. 1996. "Diversionary Foreign Policy in Democratic Systems." *International Studies Quarterly* 40: 133–154.

———. 1998. "International Crises and Domestic Politics." *American Political Science Review* 92: 623–638.

Smith, Dale L., and James Lee Ray. 1993. "European Integration: Gloomy Theory versus Rosy Reality." In *The 1992 Project and the Future of Integration in Europe,* edited by Dale L. Smith and James Lee Ray. Armonk, N.Y.: M. E. Sharpe.

Smith, Peter H. 1996. *Talons of the Eagle: Dynamics of U.S.-Latin American Relations.* New York: Oxford University Press.

Smith, Stanley E. n.d. "Winston Churchill and Eastern Europe." *Finest Hour,* vol. 85. www.winstonchurchill.org/i4a/pages/index.cfm?pageid=91 (accessed June 13, 2006).

Smith, Wayne S. 1998. "The United States and Latin America: Into a New Era." In *Latin America: Its Problems and Its Promise,* 3rd ed., edited by Jan Knippers Black. Boulder, Colo.: Westview.

Snetsinger, John. 1974. *Truman, the Jewish Vote, and the Creation of Israel.* Stanford, Calif.: Hoover Institution Press.

Sobel, Richard. 2001. *The Impact of Public Opinion on U.S. Foreign Policy since Vietnam: Constraining the Colossus.* New York: Oxford University Press.

Soroka, Stuart N. 2003. "Media, Public Opinion, and Foreign Policy." *Harvard International Journal of Press/Politics* 8: 27–48.

Spero, Joan E., and Jeffrey A. Hart. 1997. *The Politics of International Economic Relations.* 5th ed. New York: St. Martin's.

———. 2003. *The Politics of International Economic Relations.* 6th ed. Belmont, Calif.: Thomson-Wadsworth.

Steele, Bruce. 2000. "Historians Debunk Some Popular Myths about the War." *University Times,* June 22. www.pitt.edu/utimes/issues/32/000622/17.html (accessed February 3, 2005).

Stein, Janice Gross. 1992. "Deterrence and Compellence in the Gulf, 1990–1991: A Failed or Impossible Task?" *International Security* 17: 147–179.

Steinberg, James B. 1999. "A Perfect Polemic: Blind to Reality in Kosovo." *Foreign Affairs* 78: 128–133.

Stephens, Mitchell. 1994. "History of Newspapers." www.nyu.edu/classes/stephens/Collier%27s%20page.htm (accessed May 8, 2005).

Stoessinger, John. 2001. *Why Nations Go to War.* 8th ed. Belmont, Calif.: Thomson-Wadsworth.

———. 2005. *Why Nations Go to War.* 9th ed. Belmont, Calif.: Thomson-Wadworth.

Strange, Susan. 1996. *The Retreat of the State: The Diffusion of Power in the World Economy.* New York: Cambridge University Press.

Stuart, Douglas T. 2003. "Ministry of Fear: The 1947 National Security Act in Historical and Institutional Context." *International Studies Perspectives* 4: 293–313.

Sylvester, Christine. 1994. *Feminist Theory and International Relations in a Postmodern Era.* New York: Cambridge University Press.

Szulc, Tad. 1986. *Fidel: A Critical Portrait.* New York: Avon Books.

Talbott, Strobe. 2003. "U.S.–China Relations in a Changing World." In *U.S.–China Relations in the Twenty-First Century,* edited by Christopher Marsh and June Teufel Dreyer. Lanham, Md.: Lexington Books.

Tate, Merze. 1965. *The United States and the Hawai'ian Kingdom: A Political History.* New Haven, Conn.: Yale University Press.

Time. 1953. "After the Shock," December 28. www.time.com/time/archive/preview/0,10987,858401,00.html (accessed March 14, 2005).

———. 1967. "The American Challenge," November 24. www.time.com/time/archive/preview/0,10987,844150,00.html (accessed March 16, 2006).

Tocqueville, Alexis de. 1835, 1840. *Democracy in America.* http://xroads.virginia.edu/~HYPER/DETOC/toc_indx.html (accessed June 30, 2006).

Train, Brian R. n.d. "The Great Proletarian Cultural Revolution." www.islandnet.com/~citizenx/cultrev2.html (accessed February 9, 2005).

Trask, David F. 1981. *The War with Spain in 1898.* New York: Macmillan.

Trenin, Dmitri. 2006. "Russia Leaves the West." *Foreign Affairs* 85: 87–96.

Trofimov, Yaroslav. 2005. "Latvia's Divide Poses Political Risks" *Wall Street Journal,* March 10, A9.

Tuchman, Barbara W. 1966. *Stillwell and the American Experience in China, 1911–45.* New York: Macmillan.

UNAIDS. 2006. "Report on the Global AIDS Epidemic 2006: Uniting the World against AIDS." www.unaids.org/en/HIV_data/2006GlobalReport/ (accessed May 29, 2007).

"U.S. Army Will Raise Troop Levels by 30,000." 2004. *International Herald Tribune,* January 30. www.iht.com/articles/127307.html (accessed August 26, 2004).

U.S. Bureau of the Census. 1998. *Statistical Abstract of the United States, 1998.* Washington, D.C.: U.S. Government Printing Office.

U.S. Census Bureau. 2004. "Historical Poverty Tables." www.census.gov/hhes/poverty/histpov/hstpov2.html (accessed November 22, 2004).

U.S. Department of State. 2003a. "Acquisition of Florida: Treaty of Adams-Onis (1819) and Transcontinental Treaty (1821)." Bureau of Public Affairs. www.state.gov/r/pa/ho/time/jd/16320.htm (accessed June 16, 2003).

———. 2003b. "Annexation of Hawaii, 1898." Bureau of Public Affairs. www.state.gov/r/pa/ho/time/gp/17661.htm (accessed June 23, 2003).

———. 2003c. "The Oregon Territory." Bureau of Public Affairs. www.state.gov/r/pa/ho/time/dwe/16335.htm (accessed June 18, 2003).

U.S. Intelligence Community. 2005. "Members of the Intelligence Community." www.intelligence.gov/1-members.shtml (accessed July 26, 2005).

"U.S. to Move Troops . . . " 2006. *BigNewsNetwork.com,* September 21. www.bignewsnetwork.com/index.php?sid=7be31edfc0d0ef77 (accessed September 22, 2006).

Vanderbush, Walt, and Patrick J. Haney. 1999. "Policy toward Cuba in the Clinton Administration." *Political Science Quarterly* 114: 387–408.

Van Evera, Stephen. 1990–1991. "Primed for Peace: Europe after the Cold War." *International Security* 15: 7–57.

Walesa, Lech. 2004. "In Solidarity: The Polish People, Hungry for Justice, Preferred 'Cowboys' over Communists." *WSJ.com: Opinion Journal,* June 11. www.opinionjournal.com/editorial/feature.html?id=110005204 (accessed July 19, 2006).

Wallerstein, Immanuel. 1983. "Three Instances of Hegemony in the History of the World Economy." *International Journal of Comparative Sociology* 24: 100–108.

Wallison, Peter J. 2003. "Is George W. Bush Following the Reagan Model? A Lecture at the Ronald Reagan Library." *American Enterprise Institute for Public Policy Research.* www.aei.org/publications/pubID.16713,filter.all/pub_detail.asp (accessed July 26, 2006).

Walt, Stephen M. 1998. "International Relations: One World, Many Theories." *Foreign Policy* 110: 29–46.

———. 1998–99. "The Ties That Fray: Why Europe and America are Drifting Apart." *National Interest* 54: 3–11.

Waltz, Kenneth N. 1959. *Man, the State, and War: A Theoretical Analysis.* New York: Columbia University Press.

———. 1979. *Theory of International Politics.* New York: Random House.

Washington, George. 1796. "Farewell Address." The Avalon Project at Yale Law School. www.yale.edu/lawweb/avalon/washing.htm (accessed June 8, 2003).

Watkins, Thayer. n.d. "The Great Proletarian Cultural Revolution in China, 1966–1976." www2.sjsu.edu/faculty/watkins/cultrev.htm (accessed February 9, 2005).

Weber, Max. 1904, 1958. *The Protestant Ethic and the Spirit of Capitalism.* New York: Scribner's.

Weinberger, Caspar W. 1984. "The Uses of Military Power: Remarks Prepared for Delivery to the National Press Club, Washington, D.C., November 28th." www.pbs.org/wgbh/pages/frontline/shows/military/force/weinberger.html (accessed August 17, 2004).

Weiner, Tim, and Barbara Crossette. 2005. "George F. Kennan Dies at 101: Leading Strategist of Cold War." *New York Times,* March 18. www.nytimes.com/2005/03/18/politics/18kennan.html?ex=1268802000&en=5dae89b825d1ec5e&ei=5088&partner=rssnyt&pagewanted=all (accessed July 12, 2006).

Wendt, Alexander. 1992. "Anarchy Is What States Make of It: The Social Construction of Power Politics." *International Organization* 46: 391–425.

———. 1999. *Social Theory of International Politics.* New York: Cambridge University Press.

West, Thomas G. 1997. *Vindicating the Founders: Race, Sex, Class, and Justice in the Origins of America.* Lanham, Md.: Rowman and Littlefield.

Wiarda, Howard J., and Harvey F. Kline. 1979a. "The Context of Latin American Politics." In *Latin American Politics & Development,* edited by Howard J. Wiarda and Harvey F. Kline. Boston: Houghton Mifflin.

———. 1979b. "The Pattern of Historical Development." In *Latin American Politics & Development,* edited by Howard J. Wiarda and Harvey F. Kline. Boston: Houghton Mifflin.

Wildavsky, Aaron. 1966. "Two Presidencies." *Transaction* 3: 7–14.

Williams, William Appleman. 1991. "Expansion, Continental and Overseas." In *The Reader's Companion to American History,* edited by Eric Foner and John A. Garraty. Boston: Houghton Mifflin.

Winter, James P. 1997. *Democracy's Oxygen: How Corporations Control the News.* Montreal: Black Rose.

Wittkopf, Eugene R. 1990. *Faces of Internationalism: Public Opinion and American Foreign Policy.* Durham, N.C.: Duke University Press.

———. 1994. "Faces of Internationalism in a Transitional Environment." *Journal of Conflict Resolution* 38: 376–401.

Wood, Bryce. 1985. *The Dismantling of the Good Neighbor Policy.* Austin: University of Texas Press.

Woods, Randall B. 2006. *LBJ: Architect of American Ambition.* New York: Free Press.

Woodward, Bob. 2004. *Plan of Attack.* New York: Simon and Schuster.

World Association of Newspapers. 2004a. "Newspapers: A Brief History." www.wan-press.org/article2821.html (accessed May 8, 2005).

———. 2004b. "World's 100 Largest Newspapers." www.wan-press.org/article2825.html (accessed May 8, 2005).

World Bank. 2005. *WDI Online.* http://devdata.worldbank.org/dataonline/ (accessed March 9, 2005).

World News Digest. 1997. "Facts on Mobutu," May 22. www.facts.com/wnd/mobutu2.htm (accessed February 1, 2005).

Wright, George. 2003. "Wolfowitz: Iraq War Was about Oil." *Guardian/UK,* June 4. www.commondreams.org/head lines03/0604-10.htm (accessed May 14, 2006).

Wyszynski, Ed. 2002. " 'I Shall Go To Korea': Ike's October Surprise." *The Political Bandwagon.* www.thepolitical bandwagon.com/articles/2002October.html (accessed February 4, 2005).

Yankelovich, Daniel. 2006. "The Tipping Points." *Foreign Affairs* 85: 115–125.

Yergin, Daniel. 1992. *The Prize: The Epic Quest for Oil, Money, and Power.* New York: Simon and Schuster.

Young, D. Lindley. 2005. *The Modern Tribune: Online Edition.* January 14. www.themoderntribune.net/iraq_war_violating_the_war_powers_act.htm (accessed August 23, 2005).

Zaller, John R. 1992. *The Nature and Origins of Mass Opinion.* Cambridge: Cambridge University Press.

accommodationists   *See* doves. (Chapter 5)

Africa's First World War   In August 1998, Rwandan forces, soon followed by forces from Uganda, invaded the Democratic Republic of the Congo (DRC). The conflict escalated until no fewer than six outside states had some 35,000 troops involved in the military action within the DRC. (Chapter 11)

American Colonization Society   Founded in 1816 by Bushrod Washington, the society founded a colony in Liberia, on the coast of West Africa, in 1820 and transported free black people there in an effort to remove them from the United States. The society closely controlled the development of Liberia until 1847, when the nation was declared an independent republic. (Chapter 11)

apartheid   A policy of racial segregation, particularly in South Africa. (Chapter 11)

Arab League   An international organization of independent Arab states formed in 1945 to promote cultural, economic, military, political, and social cooperation. (Chapter 13)

Asia-Pacific Economic Cooperation (APEC)   A forum for facilitating economic growth, cooperation, trade, and investment in the Asia-Pacific region beginning in 1989. (Chapter 12)

Association of South-East Asian Nations (ASEAN)   A political, economic, and cultural organization of countries located in Southeast Asia. Founded in 1967, its aim is to foster cooperation and mutual assistance among members. (Chapter 12)

bandwagon effect   The joining of the threatening (and usually stronger) of two sides in a dispute to gang up on the threatened (and usually weaker) side. (Chapter 8)

Bay of Pigs   The site of a failed 1961 attempt during John F. Kennedy's presidency at a U.S.-backed invasion by Cuban exiles intent on overthrowing Fidel Castro; site is at a beach near Havana called Playa Giron. (Chapter 10)

beggar-thy-neighbor devaluations   Competitive economic policies to reduce imports by tariffs and lowering the value of currencies, with the result that the global market shrinks. (Chapter 4)

Boxer Rebellion   An uprising against Western commercial and political influence in China during the final years of the 19th century. By August 1900 more than 230 foreigners, thousands of Chinese Christians, an unknown numbers of rebels, their sympathizers, and other Chinese had been killed in the revolt and its suppression. (Chapter 12)

Bretton Woods system   In response to the tariff wars of the Great Depression, representatives of forty-four countries met in Bretton Woods, New Hampshire, in 1944 to create a new international economic system that revised the former international monetary system. Its fundamental principle was that exchange rates should be fixed in order to avoid the "beggar-thy-neighbor" policies of the 1930s and the ensuing economic anarchy. They did so by linking currency to gold, and creating the IMF (International Monetary Fund) to maintain this new monetary order, and the World Bank. (Chapter 4)

Brezhnev Doctrine   A Soviet Cold War policy stating that, "When forces that are hostile to socialism try to turn the development of some socialist country towards capitalism, it becomes not only a problem of the country concerned, but a common problem and concern of all socialist countries" (Wikipedia). (Chapter 12)

Central Intelligence Agency (CIA)   One of many government bureaus engaged in foreign intelligence generation and interpretation. Recently put under the authority of the director of national intelligence. (Chapter 6)

CNN effect   The alleged ability of the news media to motivate the U.S. government to engage in foreign policy initiatives. (Chapter 5)

Cold War   The half century of competition and conflict after World War II between the United States and the Soviet Union (and its allies). (Chapter 7)

Colombian Revolutionary Armed Forces (FARC)   A guerrilla group in opposition to the reigning government. (Chapter 10)

Comprehensive Anti-Apartheid Act   An act that severely limited trade with and foreign investment in South Africa in response to its government-launched military raids against the headquarters of the African National Congress in Botswana, Zambia, and Zimbabwe. (Chapter 11)

critical theory   Argues that the orthodox theories of foreign policy and international politics are products of, and serve the interests of, currently predominant states and their rulers. (Chapter 3)

Cuban American National Foundation   A nonprofit organization dedicated to overthrowing the Cuban government of Fidel Castro; the largest Cuban organization in exile (Wikipedia). (Chapter 10)

Department of Defense   The executive department charged with managing the country's military personnel, equipment, and operations. (Chapter 6)

Department of Homeland Security   Created by the Homeland Security Act of 2002, and under the authority of the director of national intelligence, its stated mission is to prevent terrorist attacks within the United States, reduce the vulnerability of the United States to terrorism, and minimize the damage, and assist in the recovery, from terrorist attacks that do occur within the United States. (Chapter 6)

Department of State   The department that coordinates the large number of agencies within the U.S. government that become involved in the development and implementation of U.S. foreign policy, manages the foreign affairs budget, oversees all U.S. embassies and consulates abroad, conducts international negotiations, and concludes agreements and treaties on a range of issues, from international trade to nonproliferation of nuclear weapons. (Chapter 6)

dependency theorist   Someone who claims that less-developed countries are poor because they are exploited by developed countries through international trade and investment. (Chapter 3)

domino theory   The widespread view within the U.S. government early in the Cold War that a Communist victory in one country would lead to a succession of additional victories in neighboring states. (Chapter 8)

doves   People who believe that the foreign policy of the United States should focus more consistently on cooperation, conciliation, and compromise. (Chapter 5)

economistic explanations   The basic assumptions that hold that people are generally fundamentally motivated by their economic interests. (Chapter 5)

encirclement   A military term for the situation when one state is isolated and surrounded by several other antagonistic states. For instance, Germany in 1914 with Russia to the east and the powerful French and British to the west felt it needed to "defend" itself before enemies in all directions became too powerful to be dealt with successfully. (Chapter 12)

epistemic communities, or knowledge-based experts   A set of interest groups that play an important role in the foreign policy making process, made up of intellectuals and academics. (Chapter 5)

European Coal and Steel Community (ECSC)   A group that combined the separate coal and steel markets of France and Germany—and those of other nations if they wished to join—under a political authority that would monitor and supervise the market once tariffs and quotas had been eliminated. Foundation for the European Union that initially included France, Germany, Italy, and the Benelux nations. (Chapter 9)

European Community   Established by the Treaty of Maastricht (1992), this was the first of three pillars of the European Union; called the Community (or Communities) Pillar and established qualified majority voting. (Chapter 9)

European Defense Force (EDF)   A proposal for an integrated European military force comprised of the members of the ECSC. (Chapter 9)

European Economic Community (EEC)   Created in 1957 by the Treaty of Rome; created a customs union throughout Europe known as the Common Market. (Chapter 9)

European Union   An intergovernmental and supranational organization that superceded in 1993 the various institutions of the European Communities to which most European democracies belong. (Chapter 9)

executive agreements   Agreements with the governments of foreign countries made without submitting the documents for Senate approval, avoiding the constitutionally specified role of the Senate to provide advice and consent with a two-thirds majority for ratification. (Chapter 6)

failed states   Characterized by large areas of anarchy and political disorder resulting from the national governments' incapability to maintain order or provide even minimal services to their citizens. (Chapter 11)

fast track authority   An arrangement in which Congress expedites the review and possible approval of trade agreements reached by U.S. presidents and foreign governments. (Chapter 4)

feminist Advocate and source of anti-establishment theoretical approaches to foreign policies and international politics stemming from an individuals beliefs in regards to gender, sexuality, and the rights of women. (Chapter 3)

foreign policy The decisions of governments that are designed to influence how they relate to individuals, groups, and nations outside their own borders. (Chapter 1)

Foreign Service An elite corps within the Department of State who "conduct administrative and diplomatic tasks in foreign embassies and consulates" (second part provided by Hook). (Chapter 6)

free riders Those who enjoy the benefits of collective action by others without bearing any of the costs of producing the collective outcome. (Chapter 5)

free trade Economic exchange between nations unencumbered by tariffs, quotas, or other rules and procedures designed to limit the flow of goods from one country to another. (Chapter 4)

globalization The increasingly interdependent status of national economies. (Chapter 3)

Goldwater-Nichols Department of Defense Reorganization Act of 1986 A legislative initiative created to overcome what critics saw as the debilitating effects of competition for resources and influence among the several branches of the military. The act centered the duty to provide military advice to the president in the hands of the chair of the Joint Chiefs of Staff, making all the branches of the military responsible to a single commander within specific regions or responsible for different functions, such as transportation, space, or special operations. (Chapter 6)

Good Neighbor policy The policy promulgated by President Franklin D. Roosevelt in relation to Latin America in 1933–1945 when the active U.S. intervention of previous decades was moderated in pursuit of hemispheric solidarity against external threats. (Chapter 10)

grand coalitions Those consisting of almost all states against no really formidable opponents. (Chapter 7)

Great Leap Forward A 1958 domestic economic reform campaign in China launched by Mao and based on agricultural communes and backyard iron-smelting operations. Ultimately, a tremendous disaster that led to economic turmoil and starvation. (Chapter 12)

great power politics Interactions among the largest, most important, and most powerful states in the international system that focus on matters of security, distribution of wealth, interstate conflict, and war. (Chapter 1)

Gulf of Tonkin resolution A 1964 congressional resolution that authorized Johnson to "take all necessary measures" to protect U.S. forces in Vietnam in the wake of the alleged attack of American ships by the North Vietnamese. (Chapter 8)

Hamas A Palestinian Islamist militant organization closely related to the Muslim Brotherhood, with the stated goal of conquering all of the State of Israel, the West Bank, and Gaza, including any secular Palestinian state that may come into formal existence, and replace it with an Islamic theocracy. (Chapter 13)

hawks People who support an aggressive, militant foreign policy. (Chapter 5)

hegemonic stability theory The notion that a free trade, market-based global economic order requires a predominant and willing leader to preserve itself and its stability. (Chapter 4)

Hussein-McMahon Correspondence A 1915–1916 exchange of letters between the Sharif of Mecca, Husayn bin Ali, and Sir Henry McMahon, British High Commissioner in Egypt, concerning the future political status of the Arab lands of the Middle East; the United Kingdom was seeking to bring about an armed revolt against the Ottoman Empire, a German ally during World War I. (Chapter 13)

imperialism The policy of extending the rule or authority of one state over foreign countries, or of acquiring and holding colonies and dependencies. (Chapter 2)

intelligence community The agencies and bureaus responsible for obtaining and interpreting information for the government. (Chapter 6)

Inter-American Development Bank A regional economic organization established by President Eisenhower, it is the main source of multilateral financing for economic, social, and institutional development projects and trade and regional integration programs in Latin America and the Caribbean. It is the oldest and largest regional development bank. (Chapter 10)

interest groups, or special interests Specific sets of people within the general public who advocate and promote particular ideas or policies. (Chapter 5)

internationalists People who hold the opinion that it is important for the nation to regularly play an active role on the stage of world affairs. (Chapter 5)

interventionism A type of foreign policy based on active engagement in the affairs of other nations in an attempt to shape events in accordance with a nation's interests. (Chapter 2)

Iran-*contra* project Secret negotiations between the Reagan administration and the Iranian government that offered U.S. weapons in return for the Iranians' help in securing the release of hostages then being held in Lebanon. It generated funds that were used to support the "contra" rebels in Nicaragua. (Chapter 13)

isolationism The policy of not participating in or withdrawing from international affairs, especially as practiced by U.S. governments during the first half of the twentieth century. (Chapter 2)

kleptocracy The outright theft of a nation's income by its leaders. (Chapter 11)

leftist A person who believes in and/or supports the tenets set forth by radicals. (Chapter 3)

liberalism A theory of foreign policy and international politics based on beliefs regarding the beneficent impact of market forces and the virtues of democracy. (Chapter 3)

Liberia A state in sub-Saharan Africa created by the United States, likely thought up by the American Colonization Society. More than 22,000 black Americans emigrated to this nascent country from 1821–1900. (Chapter 11)

loss-of-strength gradient The principle that holds that the power of a state decreases as the locus of any military contest moves farther from its home. (Chapter 8)

manifest destiny An ideology of expansion popularized as a campaign slogan; characterized by a belief that the huge portion of the North American continent ultimately designated the United States would inevitably emerge as one unified state as if through predetermination. (Chapter 2)

Marshall Plan 1947 program initiated by the United States; formally known as the European Recovery Program; extended significant U.S. foreign aid to Europe after WWII. (Chapter 9)

Marxist theory The basic idea set forth by Karl Marx (1818–1883) that capitalism as a social-political system had inherently self-destructive tendencies. Capitalism would therefore give birth to socialism, in which market forces would be brought under political control, to the benefit of everyone in the society except the small minority of capitalists. (Chapter 3)

Missouri Compromise This 1820 agreement established the precedent stipulating that slavery would be prohibited in the remainder of the Louisiana Purchase north of 36°30' latitude. (Chapter 11)

Monroe Doctrine The 1823 declaration to Congress by President Monroe warning the European community against any intervention in the Western Hemisphere. This declaration was a clear anti-colonialist message to the European nations, and it served as an initial expression of the U. S. intention to achieve regional hegemony. (Chapter 2)

moral hazard Kuperman (2004, 68) argues, "each instance of humanitarian intervention raises expectations of further interventions and thus encourages additional armed challenges that may provoke still more genocidal retaliation—further overwhelming the international capacity for intervention." (Chapter 11)

most-favored nation principle An economic principle aimed at fostering non-discrimination, or equal rather than privileged treatment, that stipulates that any advantage, favor, privilege, or immunity granted by any country shall be accorded immediately and unconditionally to the like product originating in or destined for the territories of all other contracting parties. In recent years, the U.S. Congress prefers to refer to this as "normal trade status." (Chapter 4)

national interest The set of objectives that enhances the welfare of the state. Usually the national interest is thought of in terms of protecting sovereignty, maximizing security or power, and improving national wealth. When two or more issues are linked together there may be many conflicting views of the national interest. (Chapter 3)

National Security Council (NSC) The principal forum for the consideration of national security and foreign policy matters, established by the National Security Act of 1947. Advises and assists the president in formulating policies to deal with those matters and to coordinate the implementation of those policies by the multiple governmental agencies that become involved in the foreign policy process. (Chapter 6)

nation-building The process by which an external government, intergovernmental organization, or nongovernmental organization attempts to create the conditions necessary for a nation to gain internal cohesion and solidarity. (Chapter 11)

neoconservatism A U.S. foreign policy perspective holding that the nation should freely use its immense power to change the world order in ways that reflect U.S. economic and political principles. (Chapter 3)

neorealism A theory of international relations emphasizing the impact of the anarchic character of the international system, the resulting requirement for states to seek security, and the great importance of the distribution of power in the international system to an understanding of international interactions. (Chapter 3)

new imperialism Europe's 1884 partitioning of Africa amongst various nations; allocated the whole of the continent to European control with the exceptions of Liberia and Ethiopia. (Chapter 11)

nongovernmental organizations (NGOs) Organizations comprising individuals or interest groups from two or more states focused on a special issue. (Chapter 5)

North Atlantic Treaty Organization (NATO) A multinational organization formed in 1949 to promote the Cold War defense of Europe from the Communist bloc (Barbour and Wright). (Chapter 9)

offensive realism A perspective that holds that "states that gain regional hegemony have a further aim: to prevent other geographical areas from being dominated by other great powers" (Mearsheimer). (Chapter 11)

Olney Corollary Predating the Roosevelt Corollary to the Monroe Doctrine, Secretary of State Richard Olney affirms "[the U.S.'s] infinite resources combined with its isolated position render it master of the situation and practically invulnerable as against any and all other powers," as a justification for U.S. regional hegemony. (Chapter 10)

Open Door policy A policy adopted by the U.S. government in 1899 that called for free trade access to China and discouraged other trading states from dividing China into spheres of influence. (Chapter 12)

Operation Pan America A policy to inaugurate a new era of political and economic cooperation between the United States and its Latin American neighbors. (Chapter 10)

Organization of American States (OAS) A hemispheric alliance; arguably the world's first and oldest regional international organization. Its charter was adopted at the Ninth International Conference of American States held in Bogota, Colombia, in 1948. The charter, stating the Latin American nations' desire "to achieve an order of peace and justice, to promote their solidarity, to strengthen their collaboration, and to defend their sovereignty, their territorial integrity, and their independence," reflects the determination of the Latin American states to restrain the United States from taking advantage of its superior military (as well as economic) power in its relations with the neighbors to the south. (Chapter 10)

Oslo Accords A series of agreements reached in 1993 between the Palestinian Authority and Israel that called for Israel to withdraw troops from Gaza and areas of the West Bank and for Israel and the PLO to recognize one another. (Chapter 13)

Palestine Liberation Organization (PLO) A political and paramilitary organization of Palestinian Arabs dedicated to the establishment of an independent Palestinian state. (Chapter 13)

Panama Canal Zone The 553-square-mile territory inside Panama that consists of the Panama Canal and an area generally extending five miles on each side of the centerline; controlled from 1903 to 1979 by the United States, which built and financed the construction of the canal. (Chapter 10)

Partnership for Peace (PFP) A NATO auxiliary that provides for mutual consultations and the sharing of resources among its members, as well as possible future NATO membership. (Chapter 9)

peaceful coexistence A Soviet doctrine emphasizing the possibility for peaceful relations between socialist and capitalist states. Purported that war—particularly nuclear—could be avoided while the ideologically opposed nations continued to compete politically and economically. (Chapter 12)

Platt Amendment offered as a "rider" to an army appropriation bill in 1901 and then incorporated into a treaty with Cuba in 1903; stipulated the conditions for the withdrawal of U.S. troops remaining in Cuba since the Spanish-American War and defined the terms of Cuban-U.S. relations until 1934. (Chapter 10)

poliheuristic A two-step approach to foreign policy decision making wherein having eliminated all options that seem too risky to their own individual political futures, leaders then choose among the remaining alternatives according to each option's perceived relationship to the national interest. (Chapter 3)

postmodernists Those who attempt to read between the lines of political, cultural, and social debates in order to uncover their deeper meanings. (Chapter 3)

Powell doctrine   A quasi-official statement reflecting a post-Vietnam sense of caution; emphasized that U.S. troops should not be deployed in foreign conflict situations unless a clear national interest was involved, unless support from the government and the public was assured, and unless military force was the last remaining option. And, even then, according to Powell, the size of the force in question should be decisive, even "overwhelming." (Chapter 8)

power transition theory   A theory of great power wars based on the idea that war is most likely when a challenger rises in power to equal and overtake the dominant state. In this theory the focus of attention is on the authority to set the rules and norms of international interactions. (Chapter 12)

protectionism   A trade policy designed to insulate or protect domestic industries from foreign competition. (Chapter 5)

proxy war   When two superpowers sponsor conflicts elsewhere—in third-party states or through terrorists—as a substitute for direct conflict. (Chapter 8)

radical   An analyst or advocate who believes that market forces have mostly unjust impacts and that the only effective manner of alleviating these impacts is to bring them under political control. (Chapter 3)

rally round the flag effect   Idea that the public will support almost any forceful, even military, action that a president undertakes, at least in the immediate aftermath of a military crisis. Generally attributed to a patriotic sense among citizens that national unity must be maintained in times of crisis. (Chapter 5)

Rape of Nanjing   Phrase that refers to what many historians recognize as widespread atrocities including rape, looting, arson, and the murder of an estimated 300,000 non-enemy combatants by the Japanese army in and around Nanking (now Nanjing), China, after the capital's fall to Japanese army in 1937. (Chapter 12)

rational political ambition theory   A theory of decision making that considers the effects of both external and internal political competitors on leaders; stems from the basic assumption that leaders want to stay in power and will make decisions perceived to be most consistent with this aim. (Chapters 1 and 3)

Reagan Doctrine   A policy that called for active efforts to subvert Communist or leftist regimes; replaced the more passive policy of "containment" that had merely tried to combat its spread to new areas and countries. (Chapter 6)

realism   A decision-making theory positing that policymakers base their choices on what is best for the states they lead, defined in terms of power. *See also* national interest. (Chapter 3)

Roosevelt Corollary   President Theodore Roosevelt's 1904 expansion of the Monroe Doctrine that proclaimed that the United States had authority to act as an "international police power" outside its borders in order to maintain stability in the Western Hemisphere. (Chapter 2)

selectorate   The group of people within any political system who choose the government's leadership and from whom members of the winning coalition can potentially be recruited. (Chapter 3)

Single European Act   A 1986 agreement to create a better-integrated market by abolishing many of the obstacles to the freer movement of capital and labor within and among the member states. (Chapter 9)

Sino-Japanese War   Conflict between China and Japan that began in 1937 and resulted in the deaths of 1 million military personnel (250,000 Japanese and 750,000 Chinese); the war ended on December 7, 1941, when, according to at least one authoritative data set, it became part of World War II. (Chapter 12)

size principle   A principle asserting that, in a variety of social and political settings, "participants create coalitions that are just as large as they believe will ensure winning and no larger." (Chapter 7)

Smoot-Hawley Tariff Act   Protectionist tariff law passed by Herbert Hoover in the wake of the stock market crash of 1929 and the onset of the Great Depression; considered a significant catalyst in the ensuing tariff wars of the interwar period. (Chapter 6)

social constructivists   Adherents to an anti-establishment approach to foreign policy and international politics that affirms there is no automatic link between the anarchical international system and national policies that seek power and security through the traditional policies of arms buildups, military alliances, and if necessary, military action. Rather, states and their leaders develop interpretations about the meaning of anarchy in the course of interactions with each other. (Chapter 3)

special economic zones   Geographical regions that have economic laws different from a country's typical economic laws; usually the goal is an increase in foreign investment. Special economic zones have been established in several countries, including the People's Republic of China, India, Jordan, Poland, Kazakhstan, the Philippines, and Russia. North Korea also has attempted this to a degree. (Chapter 12)

sphere of influence   The set of countries whose foreign (and perhaps domestic) policies are dominated or even determined by a foreign power. (Chapter 2)

stagflation   The theoretically anomalous combination of high inflation and slow economic growth. (Chapter 4)

states   The only political entities endowed with the sovereign authority and the absolute right to use force to enforce agreements or contracts within their borders and to protect the actions within their borders from external threats or incursions. (Chapter 3)

tariff wars   The protectionist governmental economic intervention policies, including currency devaluation and increased tariffs, in response to the economic crisis of the Great Depression. (Chapter 4)

Teller Amendment   An 1898 agreement pledging that the United States would not annex Cuba. (Chapter 10)

Tet Offensive   Vietcong military campaign in January 1968 during Tet, the lunar new year, that resulted in a much higher death count for the Vietcong than for the Americans, but which is seen by many as the turning point in the Vietnam War, as it exposed the Vietcong's "willingness to suffer" for the cause. (Chapter 8)

think tanks   Groups of individuals dedicated to high-level synergistic research on a variety of subjects, usually in military laboratories, corporations, or other institutions. Usually this term refers specifically to organizations that support theorists and intellectuals who endeavor to produce analysis or policy recommendations. (Chapter 5)

Treaty of Friendship, Alliance and Mutual Assistance   The 1950 agreement between Mao Zedong of the People's Republic of China and Joseph Stalin of the Soviet Union. (Chapter 12)

Treaty of Ghent   The treaty that brought the War of 1812 to an end; the United States pledged to cooperate with Great Britain in the suppression of the trans-Atlantic slave trade. (Chapter 11)

treaty ratification   Constitutional provision that requires a two-thirds majority of Senate approval. (Chapter 6)

United Nations Special Committee on Palestine (UNSCOP)   A UN committee organized in 1947 to resolve the dispute of rightful ownership of Palestine between the Jews and Arabs. (Chapter 13)

Vance-Owen Plan   Divided Bosnia into a patchwork of separate enclaves for different ethnic groups. (Chapter 9)

War Powers Resolution   A legislative measure approved by Congress in 1973 that required presidents to inform Congress in order to bring the troops home after sixty days if a majority of legislators oppose the deployments. Rarely invoked and routinely dismissed by presidents as unconstitutional. (Chapter 6)

wars of national liberation   Conflicts fought by indigenous military groups against an imperial power in the name of self-determination. (Chapter 13)

Washington Consensus   A shared understanding among other industrialized countries regarding the development strategies of smaller economies that emphasizes the developing nations' need to promote private enterprise and open markets while restricting state intervention. (Chapter 10)

winning coalition   A group of individuals that controls sufficient resources to defeat rival combinations. (Chapter 3)

Zionism   An international political movement established in the late nineteenth century that supported a homeland for the Jewish people in the Land of Israel, a goal achieved in 1948. (Chapter 13)

ONLINE RESOURCES

General

CIA *World Factbook.* https://www.cia.gov/library/publications/the-world-factbook/index.html
Foreign Affairs. www.foreignaffairs.org/

Government

Central Intelligence Agency. https://www.cia.gov/
Congressional Budget Office. www.cbo.gov/
Department of Defense. www.defenselink.mil/
Department of Homeland Security. www.dhs.gov/index.shtm
Department of State. www.state.gov/
National Security Council. www.whitehouse.gov/nsc/
United States House of Representatives. www.house.gov/
United States Senate. www.senate.gov/
White House. www.whitehouse.gov/

Interest Groups and Nongovernmental Organizations

American Enterprise Institute. www.aei.org/
American Friends Service Committee. www.afsc.org/
American Israel Public Affairs Committee. www.aipac.org/
Amnesty International. www.amnesty.org/
Brookings Institution. www.brook.edu/
Carnegie Endowment for International Peace. www.carnegieendowment.org/
Council on Foreign Relations. www.cfr.org
Cuban American National Foundation. www.canf.org/
Freedom House. www.freedomhouse.org/
Greenpeace. www.greenpeace.org/usa/
Heritage Foundation. www.heritage.org/
Human Rights Watch. www.hrw.org/
International Committee of the Red Cross. www.icrc.org/
National Council of Churches. www.ncccusa.org/

Presidential Addresses or Official Publications

Bush, George W. 2002a. "The President's State of the Union Address." January 29. www.whitehouse.gov/news/releas es/2002/01/20020129-11.html.

2002b. *The National Security Strategy of the United States of America.* www.whitehouse.gov/nsc/nss.

2000c. "President's Remarks at the United Nations General Assembly." September 12. www.whitehouse.gov/news/releases/2002/09/20020912-1.html.

BOOKS, JOURNALS, MAGAZINES, AND OTHER RESOURCES

Africa

Challenor, Herschelle Sullivan. 1977. "The Influence of Black Americans on U.S. Foreign Policy toward Africa." In *Ethnicity and U.S. Foreign Policy,* edited by Abdul Aziz Said. New York: Praeger.

Clarke, Walter, and Jeffrey Herbst. 1996. "Somalia and the Future of Humanitarian Intervention." *Foreign Affairs* 75: 70–85.

Dickson, David A. 1985. *United States Foreign Policy towards Sub-Saharan Africa.* Lanham, Md.: University Press of America.

Digital National Security Archive. 2004. "South Africa: The Making of U.S. Policy, 1962–1989."

Duignan, Peter, and L. H. Gann. 1984. *The United States and Africa: A History.* Cambridge: Cambridge University Press.

Hargreaves, John D. 1988. *Decolonization in Africa.* London: Longman.

Kuperman, Alan J. 2001. *The Limits of Humanitarian Intervention: Genocide in Rwanda.* Washington, D.C.: Brookings Institution Press.

Lyman, Princeton N., and J. Stephen Morrison. 2004. "The Terrorist Threat in Africa." *Foreign Affairs* 83: 75–86.

Mazrui, Ali A. 2004. *The African Predicament and the American Experiment: A Tale of Two Edens.* Westport, Conn.: Praeger.

Metz, Helen Chapin, ed. 1991. *Jordan: A Country Study.* Washington, D.C.: Federal Research Division, Library of Congress. http://countrystudies.us/jordan/.

Pakenham, Thomas. 1991. *The Scramble for Africa: White Man's Conquest of the Dark Continent from 1876 to 1912.* New York: Random House.

PBS Online and WGBH/*Frontline.* 1998. "Ambush in Mogadishu: U.S. Charges Relating to Osama Bin Laden's Connection to the 1993 Mogadishu Attack."

Schraeder, Peter J. 1994. *United States Foreign Policy toward Africa: Incrementalism, Crisis, and Change.* Cambridge: Cambridge University Press.

Americas

Allison, Graham, and Philip Zelikow. 1999. *Essence of Decision: Explaining the Cuban Missile Crisis.* 2nd ed. New York: Longman.

Bernstein, Barton J. 2000. "Understanding Decisionmaking, U.S. Foreign Policy, and the Cuban Missile Crisis: A Review Essay." *International Security* 25: 134–164.

Bhagwati, Jagdish. 2004. "Don't Cry for Cancún." *Foreign Affairs* 83: 52–63.

Cardoso, Fernando Henrique, and Enzo Faletto. 1978. *Dependency and Development in Latin America.* Berkeley and Los Angeles: University of California Press.

Doyle, Kate, and Peter Kornbluh. 2004. "CIA and Assassinations: The Guatemala 1954 Documents." *National Security Archive Electronic Briefing Book No. 4.*

Hakim, Peter. 2006. "Is Washington Losing Latin America?" *Foreign Affairs* 85: 39–53.

LeoGrande, William M. 1998. "From Havana to Miami: U.S. Cuba Policy as a Two-Level Game." *Journal of Interamerican Studies and World Affairs* 40: 67–86.

Naim, Moises. 2006. "The Good Neighbor Strategy." *Time,* July 17, 34–35.

O'Donnell, Guillermo. 1973. *Modernization and Bureaucratic Authoritarianism: Studies in South American Politics.* Berkeley: University of California, Institute of International Studies.

Offner, John L. 1992. *An Unwanted War: The Diplomacy of the United States and Spain Over Cuba, 1895–1898.* Chapel Hill: University of North Carolina Press.

Peruzzotti, Enrique. 2004. "Argentina after the Crash: Pride and Disillusion." *Current History* 103: 86–90.

Remmer, Karen. 1990. "Democracy and Economic Crisis: The Latin American Experience." *World Politics* 42: 315–335.

Salinger, Pierre. 1989. "Gaps in the Cuban Missile Crisis Story." *New York Times,* February 5, 1989, sec. 4, p. 25.

Shifter, Michael. 2004. "The U.S. and Latin America through the Lens of Empire." *Current History* 103: 61–67.

Skidmore, Thomas E., and Peter H. Smith. 1992. *Modern Latin America.* 3rd ed. New York: Oxford University Press.

Smith, Peter H. 1996. *Talons of the Eagle: Dynamics of U.S.-Latin American Relations.* New York: Oxford University Press.

Smith, Wayne S. 1998. "The United States and Latin America: Into a New Era." In *Latin America: Its Problems and Its Promise,* 3rd ed., edited by Jan Knippers Black. Boulder, Colo.: Westview.

Szulc, Tad. 1986. *Fidel: A Critical Portrait.* New York: Avon Books.

Vanderbush, Walt, and Patrick J. Haney. 1999. "Policy toward Cuba in the Clinton Administration." *Political Science Quarterly* 114: 387–408.

Wood, Bryce. 1985. *The Dismantling of the Good Neighbor Policy.* Austin: University of Texas Press.

Asia

Benson, Brett, and Emerson Niou. 2002. "The U.S. Security Commitment to Taiwan Should Remain Ambiguous." In *The Rise of China in Asia: Security Implications,* edited by Carolyn W. Pumphrey. Carlisle, Pa.: Strategic Studies Institute.

Brzezinski, Zbigniew. 2000. "Living with China." *National Interest* 59: 5–21.

Carpenter, Ted Galen. 2003/2004. "Living with the Unthinkable." *National Interest* 74: 92–98.

———. 2006. *America's Coming War with China: A Collision Course over Taiwan.* New York: Palgrave Macmillan.

Collins, Gabe, and Carlos Ramos-Mrosovksy. 2006. "Beijing's Bolivarian Venture." *National Interest* 85: 88–92.

Dean, Jason. 2005. "Taiwan's Premier Supports Reforms to Constitution." *Wall Street Journal: Interactive Edition,* January 28. www.taiwandc.org/wsj-2005-01.htm.

Eberstadt, Nicholas. 2004. "Power and Population in Asia." *Policy Review* 123: 3–27.

Floyd, David. 1963. *Mao against Khrushchev: A Short History of the Sino-Soviet Conflict.* New York: Praeger.

Friedberg, Aaron L. 2000a. "Will Europe's Past Be Asia's Future?" *Survival* 42: 147–159.

———. 2000b. "Will We Abandon Taiwan?" *Commentary* 109: 26–31.

Gallagher, Mary E. 2002. " 'Reform and Openness': Why China's Economic Reforms Have Delayed Democracy." *World Politics* 54: 338–372.

Gilboy, George J. 2004. "The Myth behind China's Miracle." *Foreign Affairs* 83: 33–48.

Gilley, Bruce. 2004. *China's Democratic Future: How It Will Happen and Where It Will Lead.* New York: Columbia University Press.

Hale, David, and Lyric Hughes Hale. 2003. "China Takes Off." *Foreign Affairs* 82: 36–53.

Khalilzad, Zalmay, et al. 1999. "The United States and a Rising China," A RAND Corporation Report, MR-1082-AF.

Mahbubani, Kishore. 2005. "Understanding China." *Foreign Affairs* 84: 49–60.

Oksenberg, Michel, and Elizabeth Economy. 1999. "China Joins the World." In *China Joins the World: Progress and Prospects,* edited by Elizabeth Economy and Michel Oksenberg. New York: Council on Foreign Relations Press.

Pei, Minxin. 2003. "Contradictory Trends and Confusing Signals. *Journal of Democracy* 14: 73–81.

Riccards, Michael P. 2000. *The Presidency and the Middle Kingdom: China, the United States, and Executive Leadership.* Lanham, Md.: Lexington Books.

Ross, Robert S. 2000. "The 1995–96 Taiwan Strait Confrontation: Coercion, Credibility, and the Use of Force." *International Security* 25: 87–123.

———. 2005. "Assessing the China Threat." *National Interest* 81: 81–94.

Shambaugh, David. 2004. "The United States and East Asia." In *Divided Diplomacy and the Next Administration: Conservative and Liberal Alternatives,* edited by Henry R. Nau and David Shambaugh. Washington, D.C.: The Elliott School of International Affairs.

Shirk, Susan. 1993. *The Political Logic of Economic Reform in China.* Berkeley and Los Angeles: University of California Press.

Talbott, Strobe. 2003. "U.S.–China Relations in a Changing World." In *U.S.-China Relations in the Twenty-First Century,* edited by Christopher Marsh and June Teufel Dreyer. Lanham, Md.: Lexington Books.

Tuchman, Barbara W. 1966. *Stillwell and the American Experience in China, 1911–45.* New York: Macmillan.

Branches of Government

Halberstam, David. 1972. *The Best and the Brightest.* New York: Random House.

———. 2001. *War in a Time of Peace: Bush, Clinton, and the Generals.* New York: Simon and Schuster.

Kissinger, Henry A. 1979. *The White House Years.* Boston: Little, Brown.

———. 1982. *Years of Upheaval.* Boston: Little, Brown.

Minority Staff, Committee on Government Reform, U.S. House of Representatives. 2003. *Fact Sheet: The Bush Administration's Contracts with Halliburton.*

Rice, Condoleezza. 2000. "Promoting the National Interest." *Foreign Affairs* 79: 45–62.

Rothkopf, David J. 2005. "Inside the Committee That Runs the World." *Foreign Policy* 147: 30–40.

Schlesinger, Arthur, Jr. 1973. *The Imperial Presidency.* Boston: Houghton Mifflin.

Wallison, Peter J. 2003. "Is George W. Bush Following the Reagan Model? A Lecture at the Ronald Reagan Library." *American Enterprise Institute for Public Policy Research.*

Woods, Randall B. 2006. *LBJ: Architect of American Ambition.* New York: Free Press.

Cold War

Friedman, Norman. 2000. *The Fifty Year War: Conflict and Strategy in the Cold War.* Annapolis, Md.: Naval Institute Press.

Gaddis, John Lewis. 1992. *The United States and the End of the Cold War: Implications, Reconsiderations, Provocations.* New York: Oxford University Press.

———. 2005. *The Cold War: A New History.* New York: Penguin Press.

Garthoff, Raymond L. 1994. "Looking Back: The Cold War in Retrospect." *Brookings Review* 12: 10–13.

Hurst, Steven. 2005. *Cold War U.S. Foreign Policy: Key Perspectives.* Edinburgh: Edinburgh University Press.

Kegley, Charles W., Jr. 1994. "How Did the Cold War Die? Principles for an Autopsy." *Mershon International Studies Review* 38: 11–41.

Lebow, Richard Ned, and Janice Stein. 1994. *We All Lost the Cold War.* Princeton, N.J.: Princeton University Press.

Leebaert, Derek. 2002. *The Fifty Year Wound: The True Price of America's Cold War Victory.* Boston: Little, Brown.

Rodman, Peter W. 1994. *More Precious than Peace: The Cold War and the Struggle for the Third World.* New York: Scribner's.

Schlesinger, Arthur, Jr. 1967. "Origins of the Cold War." *Foreign Affairs* 46: 22–52.

Schweizer, Peter. 1994. *Victory: The Reagan Administration's Secret Strategy That Hastened the Collapse of the Soviet Union.* New York: Atlantic Monthly Press.

———. 2002. *Reagan's War: The Epic Story of His Forty-Year Struggle and Final Triumph over Communism.* New York: Anchor Books.

Conflict and Security

Andres, Richard B., Craig Wills, and Thomas E. Griffith Jr. 2005. "Winning with Allies: The Strategic Value of the Afghan Model." *International Security* 30: 124–160.

Bobbitt, Philip. 2002. *The Shield of Achilles: War, Peace, and the Course of History.* New York: Anchor Books.

Brown, Michael E. 1999. "Minimalist NATO: A Wise Alliance Knows When to Retrench." *Foreign Affairs* 78: 204–218.

Bueno de Mesquita, Bruce, and George Downs. 2006. "Intervention and Democracy." *International Organization* 60: 627–649.

Clark, David H. 2003. "Can Strategic Interaction Divert Diversionary Behavior? A Model of U.S. Conflict Propensity." *Journal of Politics* 65: 1013–1039.

Collier, Ellen C. 1993. "Instances of Use of United States Forces Abroad, 1798–1993." Department of the Navy—Naval Historical Center. www.history.navy.mil/wars/foabroad.htm.

Feaver, Peter D., and Christopher Gelpi. 2004. *Choosing Your Battles: American Civil-Military Relations and the Use of Force.* Princeton, N.J.: Princeton University Press.

Frederking, Brian. 2003. "Constructing Post–Cold War Collective Security." *American Political Science Review* 97: 363–378.

Friedman, Norman. 2000. *The Fifty Year War: Conflict and Strategy in the Cold War.* Annapolis, Md.: Naval Institute Press.

Gaddis, John Lewis. 1986. "The Long Peace: Elements of Stability in the Postwar International System." *International Security* 10: 99–142.

Gaubatz, Kurt Taylor. 1991. "Election Cycles and War." *Journal of Conflict Resolution* 35: 212–244.

Gilens, Martin. 2001. "Political Ignorance and Collective Policy Preferences." *American Political Science Review* 95: 379–396.

Hendrickson, David C., and Robert W. Tucker. 2005. "The Freedom Crusade." *National Interest* 81: 12–22.

Hersh, Seymour. 2005. *Chain of Command: The Road from 9/11 to Abu Ghraib.* New York: Harper Perennial.

Hunter, Robert. 1999. "Maximizing NATO: A Relevant Alliance Knows How to Reach." *Foreign Affairs* 78: 190–203.

Kane, Tim. 2004. "Global U.S. Troop Deployment, 1950–2003." *Heritage Foundation, Policy Research & Analysis: Issues—Defense.* Center for Data Analysis Report #04-11. October 27.

Kugler, Jacek. 1996. "Beyond Deterrence: Structural Conditions for a Lasting Peace." In *Parity and War: Evaluations and Extensions of "The War Ledger,"* edited by Jacek Kugler and Douglas Lemke. Ann Arbor: University of Michigan Press.

Kugler, Jacek, Lewis Snider, and William Longwell. 1994. "From Desert Shield to Desert Storm: Success, Strife or Quagmire?" *Conflict Management and Peace Science* 13: 113–148.

Kugler, Jacek, and Frank C. Zagare. 1990. "The Long-Term Stability of Deterrence." *International Interactions* 15: 255–278.

Mansfield, Edward D., and Jack Snyder. 2002. "Democratic Transitions, Institutional Strength, and War." *International Organization* 56: 297–337.

Meernik, James, and Peter Waterman. 1996. "The Myth of the Diversionary Use of Force by American Presidents." *Political Research Quarterly* 49: 573–590.

North Atlantic Treaty Organization. 2005. "NATO Update." www.nato.int/docu/update/index.html.

Operation Enduring Freedom. 2006. "Coalition Military Fatalities." http://icasualties.org/oef/.

Organski, A. F. K., and Jacek Kugler. 1980. *The War Ledger.* Chicago: University of Chicago Press.

Pollins, Brian M. 1996. "Global Political Order, Economic Change, and Armed Conflict: Coevolving Systems and the Use of Force." *American Political Science Review* 90: 103–117.

Powell, Colin L. 1992. "U.S. Forces: Challenges Ahead." *Frontline.* www.pbs.org/wgbh/pages/frontline/shows/military/force/powell.html.

Ray, James Lee. 1995. *Democracy and International Conflict: An Evaluation of the Democratic Peace Proposition.* Columbia: University of South Carolina Press.

Reagan, Ronald. 1982. "U.S. National Security Strategy." *National Security Decision Directive Number 32.* http://fas.org/irp/offdocs/nsdd/23-1618t.gif.

Record, Jeffrey. 2000. "Weinberger-Powell Doctrine Doesn't Cut It." U.S. Naval Institute *Proceedings,* October.

Reiter, Dan. 1995. "Exploding the Powder Keg Myth: Preemptive Wars Almost Never Happen." *International Security* 20: 5–34.

Reiter, Dan. 2001. "Why NATO Enlargement Does Not Spread Democracy." *International Security* 25:41–67.

Reiter, Dan, and Allan C. Stam. 2002. *Democracies at War.* Princeton, N.J.: Princeton University Press.

Rivkin, David B., and Lee A. Casey. 2003. "Leashing the Dogs of War." *National Interest* 73: 57–69.

Rosen, Steven. 1972. "War Power and the Willingness to Suffer." In *Peace, War, and Numbers,* edited by Bruce M. Russett. Beverly Hills, Calif.: Sage Publications.

Rummel, R. J. 1975. *The Dynamic Psychological Field.* Vol. 1 of *Understanding Conflict and War.* New York: Sage Publications.

———. 1976. *The Conflict Helix.* Vol. 2 of *Understanding Conflict and War.* New York: Sage Publications.

———. 1977. *Conflict in Perspective.* Vol. 3 of *Understanding Conflict and War.* Beverly Hills: Sage Publications.

———. 1979. *War, Power, and Peace.* Vol. 4 of *Understanding Conflict and War.* Beverly Hills: Sage Publications.

———. 1981. *The Just Peace.* Vol. 5 of *Understanding Conflict and War.* Beverly Hills: Sage Publications.

———. 1990. *Lethal Politics: Soviet Genocide and Mass Murder since 1917.* New Brunswick, N.J.: Transaction.

Russett, Bruce, and Allan C. Stam. 1998. "Courting Disaster: An Expanded NATO vs. Russia and China." *Political Science Quarterly* 113: 361–382.

Sarkees, Meredith Reid. 2000. "The Correlates of War Data on War: An Update to 1997." *Conflict Management and Peace Science* 18: 123–144.

Shulman, Marshall D. 1987–1988. "The Superpowers: Dance of the Dinosaurs." *Foreign Affairs* 66: 494–515.

Woodward, Bob. 2004. *Plan of Attack.* New York: Simon and Schuster.

Eastern Europe and Russia

Conquest, Robert. 1968. *The Great Terror: Stalin's Purge of the Thirties.* New York: Macmillan.

———. 1986. *The Harvest of Sorrow: Soviet Collectivization and the Terror-Famine.* New York: Oxford University Press.

Gaiduk, Ilya V. 1996. *The Soviet Union and the Vietnam War.* Chicago: Ivan R. Dee.

Kennan, George F. ("X"). 1947. "The Sources of Soviet Conduct." *Foreign Affairs* 25: 566–582.

Leng, Russell J. 1984. "Reagan and the Russians: Crisis Bargaining Beliefs and the Historical Record." *American Political Science Review* 78: 338–355.

Mandelbaum, Michael. 1999. "A Perfect Failure: NATO's War against Yugoslavia." *Foreign Affairs* 78: 2–8.

Pipes, Richard. 1991. *The Russian Revolution.* New York: Vintage Books.

Reagan, Ronald 1983a. "U.S. Relations with the USSR." *National Security Decision Directive Number 75.*

Richter, James G. 1994. *Khrushchev's Double Bind: International Pressures and Domestic Coalition Politics.* Baltimore: Johns Hopkins University Press.

Roberts, Adam. 1999. "NATO's 'Humanitarian War' over Kosovo." *Survival* 41: 102–123.

Steinberg, James B. 1999. "A Perfect Polemic: Blind to Reality in Kosovo." *Foreign Affairs* 78: 128–133.

Trenin, Dmitri. 2006. "Russia Leaves the West." *Foreign Affairs* 85: 87–96.

Walesa, Lech. 2004. "In Solidarity: The Polish People, Hungry for Justice, Preferred 'Cowboys' over Communists." *WSJ.com: Opinion Journal,* June 11. www.opinionjournal.com/editorial/feature.html?id=110005204.

Economics

Bergsten, C. Fred. 1972. "The New Economics and U.S. Foreign Policy." *Foreign Affairs* 50: 199–222.

Blecker, Robert A. 2005. "U.S. Steel Import Tariffs: The Politics of Global Markets." In *Contemporary Cases in U.S. Foreign Policy,* edited by Ralph G. Carter. Washington, D.C.: CQ Press.

Bueno de Mesquita, Bruce, and Hilton Root. 2002. "The Political Roots of Poverty: The Economic Logic of Autocracy." *National Interest* 68: 27–37.

Burkhart, Ross E., and Michael S. Lewis-Beck. 1994. "Comparative Democracy: The Economic Development Thesis." *American Political Science Review* 88: 903–910.

Cohen, Stephen D. 2000. *The Making of United States International Economic Policy.* 5th ed. Westport, Conn.: Praeger.

Ferguson, Niall, and Laurence J. Kotlikoff. 2003. "Going Critical: American Power and the Consequences of Fiscal Overstretch." *National Interest* 73: 22–32.

Fordham, Benjamin. 1998a. "Partisanship, Macroeconomic Policy, and U.S. Uses of Force, 1949–1994." *Journal of Conflict Resolution* 42: 418–439.

———. 1998b. "The Politics of Threat Perception and the Use of Force: A Political Economy Model of U.S. Uses of Force, 1949–1994." *International Studies Quarterly* 42: 567–590.

Gokhale, Jagadeesh, and Kent Smetters. 2003. *Fiscal and Generational Imbalances: New Budget Measures for New Budget Priorities.* Washington D.C.: AEI Press.

Goldstein, Joshua S. 1988. *Long Cycles: Prosperity and War in the Modern Age.* New Haven, Conn.: Yale University Press.

Gowa, Joanne. 1983. *Closing the Gold Window: Domestic Politics and the End of Bretton Woods.* Ithaca, N.Y.: Cornell University Press.

Kindleberger, Charles P. 1973. *The World in Depression, 1929–1939.* Berkeley: University of California Press.

———. 1978. *Manias, Panics, and Crashes.* New York: Basic Books.

———. 1981. *Power and Money: The Economics of International Politics and the Politics of International Economics.* New York: Basic Books.

———. 1986. "Hierarchy versus Inertial Cooperation." *International Organization* 40: 841–847.

Mead, Walter Russell. 1990. "On the Road to Ruin: Winning the Cold War, Losing the Economic Peace." *Harper's* 280: 59–64.

Servan-Schreiber, Jean-Jacques. 1968. *The American Challenge.* Translated by Ronald Steel. New York: Atheneum.

Strange, Susan. 1996. *The Retreat of the State: The Diffusion of Power in the World Economy.* New York: Cambridge University Press.

Wallerstein, Immanuel. 1983. "Three Instances of Hegemony in the History of the World Economy." *International Journal of Comparative Sociology* 24: 100–108.

Weber, Max. 1904, 1958. *The Protestant Ethic and the Spirit of Capitalism.* New York: Scribner's.

Yergin, Daniel. 1992. *The Prize: The Epic Quest for Oil, Money, and Power.* New York: Simon and Schuster.

Environment

CBC News. 2006. "Canada Supports Six-Nation Climate Change Pact: Ambrose." www.cbc.ca/story/canada/national/2006/04/25/ambrose060425.html.

Clark, Ian, et al. 2006. "Sixty Scientists Call on Harper to Revisit the Science of Global Warming." *Open Letter to Canadian Prime Minister Stephen Harper.* April 15. www.citizenreviewonline.org/april2006/15/warming.html.

Crichton, Michael. 2004. *State of Fear.* New York: Avon Books.

Harris, Tom. 2006. "Scientists Respond to Gore's Warnings of Climate Catastrophe." *Canadafreepress.com,* June 12. www.canadafreepress.com/2006/harris061206.htm.

Saunders, Paul J., and Vaughan C. Turekian. 2006. "Warming to Climate Change." *National Interest* 84: 78–84.

Europe

Baker, Gerard. 2003. "Does the United States Have a European Policy?" *National Interest* 74: 37–42.

Bernstein, Carl. 1992. "The Holy Alliance." *Time,* February 24.

Cimbalo, Jeffrey L. 2004. "Saving NATO from Europe." *Foreign Affairs* 83: 111–120.

Cohen-Tanugi, Laurent. 2005. "The End of Europe?" *Foreign Affairs* 84: 55–67.

Deutsch, Karl W., et al. "Political Community and the North Atlantic Area: International Organization in Light of Historical Experience." In *International Political Communities: An Anthology.* Garden City, N.Y.: Anchor Books.

Erlanger, Steven. 2002. "Europe Seethes as the U.S. Flies Solo in World Affairs." *New York Times,* February 23, A8.

Falk, Richard. 2003. "What Future for the UN Charter System of War Prevention?" *American Journal of International Law* 97: 590–598.

Fischer, Conan. 2003. *The Ruhr Crisis, 1923–1924.* Oxford: Oxford University Press.

Fischer, Markus. 1992. "Feudal Europe, 800–1300: Communal Discourse and Conflictual Practices." *International Organization* 46: 427–466.

Layne, Christopher. 2003. "America as European Hegemon." *National Interest* 72: 17–29.

Mearsheimer, John J. 1990. "Back to the Future: Instability in Europe after the Cold War." *International Security* 15: 5–56.

Morgan, T. Clifton, and Christopher J. Anderson. 1999. "Domestic Support and Diversionary External Conflict in Great Britain, 1950–1992." *Journal of Politics* 61: 799–814.

Nicolaidis, Kalypso. 2004. " 'We, the Peoples of Europe . . . ' " *Foreign Affairs* 83: 97–110.

Sbragia, Alberta M. 1993. "Asymmetrical Integration in the European Community: The Single European Act and Institutional Development." In *The 1992 Project and the Future of Integration in Europe,* edited by Dale L. Smith and James Lee Ray. Armonk, N.Y.: M. E. Sharpe.

Shirer, William L. 1990. *The Rise and Fall of the Third Reich: A History of Nazi Germany.* New York: Simon and Schuster.

Smith, Dale L., and James Lee Ray. 1993. "European Integration: Gloomy Theory versus Rosy Reality." In *The 1992 Project and the Future of Integration in Europe,* edited by Dale L. Smith and James Lee Ray. Armonk, N.Y.: M. E. Sharpe.

Van Evera, Stephen. 1990–1991. "Primed for Peace: Europe after the Cold War." *International Security* 15: 7–57.

Walt, Stephen M. 1998/99. "The Ties That Fray: Why Europe and America are Drifting Apart." *National Interest* 54: 3–11.

Genocide

Anderson, Scott. 2004. "How Did Darfur Happen?" *New York Times Magazine,* October 17, 54–63.

Caplan, Gerald. 2004. "AfricaFiles: Rwanda Ten Years after the Genocide." www.africafiles.org/article.asp?ID=4501.

Girardet, Edward, ed. 1995. *Somalia, Rwanda and Beyond: The Role of the International Media in Wars and Humanitarian Crises.* Geneva: Crosslines Global Report.

Rotberg, Robert, and Thomas Weiss, eds. 1996. *From Massacres to Genocide: The Media, Public Policy, and Humanitarian Crises*. Cambridge, Mass.: World Peace Foundation.

Media and Public Opinion

Baum, Matthew A. 2002. "Sex, Lies, and War: How Soft News Brings Foreign Policy to the Inattentive Public." *American Political Science Review* 96: 91–109.

Cohen, Bernard C. 1963. *The Press and Foreign Policy: Principles, Problems, and Proposals for Reform*. Princeton, N.J.: Princeton University Press.

Dalton, Russell J., Paul A. Beck, and Robert Huckfeldt. 1998. "Partisan Cues and the Media: Information Flows in the 1992 Presidential Election." *American Political Science Review* 92: 111–126.

E&P Staff. 2004. "Pew Survey Finds Moderates, Liberals Dominate News Outlets." *Editor and Publisher*, May 23.

Groeling, Tim, and Samuel Kernell. 1998. "Is Network News Coverage of the President Biased?" *Journal of Politics* 60: 1063–1086.

Holsti, Ole R. 1992. "Public Opinion and Foreign Policy: Challenges to the Almond-Lippmann Consensus." *International Studies Quarterly* 36: 439–466.

Jentleson, Bruce. 1992. "The Pretty Prudent Public: Post Post-Vietnam American Opinion on the Use of Military Force." *International Studies Quarterly* 36: 49–74.

Jentleson, Bruce, and Rebecca L. Britton. 1998. "Still Pretty Prudent: Post–Cold War American Public Opinion on the Use of Military Force." *Journal of Conflict Resolution* 42: 395–417.

Knowlton, Brian. 2006. "Global Image of the U.S. Is Worsening, Survey Finds." *New York Times*, June 14.

Lian, Bradley, and John R. Oneal. 1993. "Presidents, the Use of Military Force, and Public Opinion." *Journal of Conflict Resolution* 37: 277–300.

Mueller, John. 1973. *War, Presidents and Public Opinion*. New York: John Wiley.

Oneal, John R., Brad Lian, and James H. Joyner Jr. 1996. "Are the American People 'Pretty Prudent'? Public Responses to U.S. Uses of Force, 1950–1988." *International Studies Quarterly* 40: 261–280.

Page, Benjamin I., and Jason Barabas. 2000. "Foreign Policy Gaps between Citizens and Leaders." *International Studies Quarterly* 44: 339–364.

Page, Benjamin I., and Robert Y. Shapiro. 1992. *The Rational Public: Fifty Years of Trends in Americans' Policy Preferences*. Chicago: University of Chicago Press.

Powlick, Philip J., and Andrew Z. Katz. 1998. "Defining the American Public Opinion/Foreign Policy Nexus." *Mershon International Studies Review* 42: 29–61.

Rieff, David. 2006. "America the Untethered." *New York Times*, July 2.

Robinson, Piers. 1999. "The CNN Effect: Can the News Media Drive Foreign Policy?" *Review of International Studies* 25: 301–309.

Russett, Bruce. 1990. "Economic Decline, Electoral Pressure, and the Initiation of International Conflict." In *Prisoners of War?* edited by Charles Gochman and Alan Sabrosky. Lexington, Ky.: Lexington Books.

Sobel, Richard. 2001. *The Impact of Public Opinion on U.S. Foreign Policy since Vietnam: Constraining the Colossus*. New York: Oxford University Press.

Soroka, Stuart N. 2003. "Media, Public Opinion, and Foreign Policy." *Harvard International Journal of Press/Politics* 8: 27–48.

Winter, James P. 1997. *Democracy's Oxygen: How Corporations Control the News*. Montreal: Black Rose.

Wittkopf, Eugene R. 1990. *Faces of Internationalism: Public Opinion and American Foreign Policy*. Durham, N.C.: Duke University Press.

———. 1994. "Faces of Internationalism in a Transitional Environment." *Journal of Conflict Resolution* 38: 376–401.

Yankelovich, Daniel. 2006. "The Tipping Points." *Foreign Affairs* 85: 115–125.

Middle East

Benson, Michael T. 1997. *Harry S. Truman and the Founding of Israel*. Westport, Conn.: Praeger.

Bin Laden, Osama. 2002. "Statement: Jihad against Jews and Crusaders. (February 23, 1998)." In *Anti-American Terrorism and the Middle East*, edited by Barry Rubin and Judith Colp Rubin. New York: Oxford University Press.

Friedman, Thomas L. 1995. *From Beirut to Jerusalem*. New York: Anchor Books.

Hudson, Michael. 1998. "The Historical Evolution of U.S. Involvement in the Middle East." In *The United States and Canada: Political Systems, Policy-making and the Middle East*. Jerusalem: Palestinian Academic Society for the Study of International Affairs.

Kayal, Alawi D. 2002. *The Control of Oil: East-West Rivalry in the Persian Gulf*. London: Kegan Paul.

Khouri, Fred J. 1968. *The Arab-Israeli Dilemma*. Syracuse, N.Y.: Syracuse University Press.

Krauthammer, Charles. 2006. "A Calamity for Israel." *Washington Post.com*, January 6. www.washingtonpost.com/wp-dyn/content/article/2006/01/05/AR2006010501901.html.

Lieven, Anatol. 2006. "Bush's Middle East Democracy Flop." *Los Angeles Times*, July 23.

Mearsheimer, John, and Stephen Walt. 2006a. "The Israel Lobby and U.S. Foreign Policy." Working Paper, March. http://ksgnotes1.harvard.edu/Research/wpaper.nsf/rwp/RWP06-011/$File/rwp_06_011_walt.pdf#search= 'Walt%20and%20Mearsheimer,%20The%20Israeli%20Lobby'.

———. 2006c. "Letters: The Israel Lobby." *London Review of Books* 28 (May 11).

Nuruzzaman, Mohammed. 2006. "Beyond the Realist Theories: 'Neo-Conservative Realism' and the American Invasion of Iraq." *International Studies Perspectives* 7: 239–253.

Odom, William E. 2004. "Retreating in Good Order." *National Interest* 76: 33–36.

Packer, George. 2005. *The Assassin's Gate: America in Iraq.* New York: Farrar, Straus, and Giroux.

Pelletiere, Stephen. 2004. *America's Oil Wars.* New York: Praeger.

Porter, Adam. 2005. "British Lawmaker: Iraq War Was for Oil." *Aljazeera.net,* May 21. http://english.aljazeera.net/NR/exeres/AC9B68BD-9853-494D-AB7D-A5EF74C46694.htm.

Rajaee, Bahram. 2004. "War, Peace, and the Evolution of U.S. Policy in the Middle East." In *Security, Economics, and Morality in American Foreign Policy: Contemporary Issues in Historical Context,* edited by William H. Meyer. Upper Saddle River, N.J.: Pearson/Prentice Hall.

Reagan, Ronald. 1983b. "Partial Text of President Reagan's October 24 Statement on Lebanon." *Washington Report on Middle East Affairs.* October 31, 6.

Reuveny, Rafael, and Aseem Prakash. 1999. "The Afghanistan War and the Breakdown of the Soviet Union." *Review of International Studies* 25: 693–708.

Risen, James. 2000. "Secrets of History: The C.I.A. in Iran." *New York Times.*

Stein, Janice Gross. 1992. "Deterrence and Compellence in the Gulf, 1990–1991: A Failed or Impossible Task?" *International Security* 17: 147–179.

Wright, George. 2003. "Wolfowitz: Iraq War Was about Oil." *Guardian/UK,* June 4.

Nuclear War

Allison, Graham. 2004a. "How to Stop Nuclear Terror." *Foreign Affairs* 83: 64–74.

———. 2004b. *Nuclear Terrorism: The Ultimate Preventable Catastrophe.* New York: Times Books/Henry Holt.

———. 2006. "A Nuclear Terrorism Report Card." *National Interest* 83: 63–65.

Alperovitz, Gar. 1965. *Atomic Diplomacy: Hiroshima and Potsdam; The Use of the Atomic Bomb and the American Confrontation with Soviet Power.* New York: Vintage Books.

———. 2005. "Hiroshima after Sixty Years: The Debate Continues." *Common Dreams News Center,* August 3.

Gallucci, Robert L. 2005. "Preventing the Unthinkable." *National Interest* 81: 129–131.

Morris, Stephen J. 2003/2004. "Averting the Unthinkable." *National Interest* 74: 99–107.

Political History and Historical Documents

Beschloss, Michael, and Strobe Talbott. 1993. *At the Highest Levels: The Inside Story of the End of the Cold War.* Boston: Little, Brown.

Calvocoressi, Peter. 1991. *World Politics since 1945.* 6th ed. London: Longman.

Carroll, James. 2001. *Constantine's Sword: The Church and the Jews.* Boston: Houghton Mifflin.

Dahrendorf, Ralf. 1959. *Class and Class Conflict in Industrial Society.* Stanford, Calif.: Stanford University Press.

DeConde, Alexander. 1963. *A History of American Foreign Policy.* New York: Scribner's.

Delli Carpini, Michael X., and Scott Keeter. 1996. *What Americans Know about Politics and Why It Matters.* New Haven, Conn.: Yale University Press.

Durant, Will, and Ariel Durant. 1968. *The Lessons of History.* New York: MJF Books.

Hook, Steven W., and John Spanier. 2007. *American Foreign Policy since World War II.* 17th ed. Washington, D.C.: CQ Press.

Huntington, Samuel P. 1991. *The Third Wave: Democratization in the Late Twentieth Century.* Norman: Oklahoma University Press.

Immerman, Richard H. 1982. *The CIA in Guatemala: The Foreign Policy of Intervention.* Austin: University of Texas Press.

Johnson, Paul. 1983. *Modern Times: The World from the Twenties to the Eighties.* New York: Harper and Row.

Kennedy, Paul 1987. *The Rise and Fall of the Great Powers: Economic Change and Military Conflict from 1500 to 2000.* New York: Random House.

Keylor, William R. 1996. *The Twentieth Century World: An International History.* New York: Oxford University Press.

Kim, Woosang. 1989. "Power, Alliance, and Major Wars, 1816–1975." *Journal of Conflict Resolution* 33: 255–273.

———. 1992. "Power Transitions and Great Power War from Westphalia to Waterloo." *World Politics* 45: 153–172.

Kinzer, Stephen. 2006. *Overthrow: America's Century of Regime Change from Hawaii to Iraq.* New York: Times Books.

Kirkpatrick, Jeane. 1979. "Dictatorships and Double Standards." *Commentary* 68: 34–45.

Machiavelli, Niccolò. 1532, 1996. *The Prince.* Translated by George Bull. New York: Penguin Books.

Marx, Karl, and Frederick Engels. 1848. "Manifesto of the Communist Party."

May, Ernest R. 1961. *Imperial Democracy: The Emergence of America as a Great Power.* New York: Harcourt, Brace.
———. 1975. *The Making of the Monroe Doctrine.* Cambridge, Mass.: Harvard
Morris, Richard B. 1972. "Revolution in the Western World: The American Revolution." In *The Columbia History of the World,* edited by John A. Garraty and Peter Gay, 753–763. New York: Harper and Row.
Nixon, Richard M. 1962. *Six Crises.* New York: Doubleday.
Oneal, John R., Brad Lian, and James H. Joyner Jr. 1996. "Are the American People 'Pretty Prudent'? Public Responses to U.S. Uses of Force, 1950–1988." *International Studies Quarterly* 40: 261–280.
Plischke, Elmer. 1999. *U.S. Department of State: A Reference History.* Westport, Conn.: Greenwood.
Pollins, Brian M., and Kevin P. Murrin. 1999. "Where Hobbes Meets Hobson: Core Conflict and Colonialism, 1495–1985." *International Studies Quarterly* 43: 427–454.
Republican Party Platform. 1952. www.presidency.ucsb.edu/showplatforms.php?platindex=R1952.
Salinger, Pierre. 1995. *P.S.: A Memoir.* New York: St. Martin's.
Small, Melvin, and J. David Singer. 1982. *Resort to Arms: International and Civil Wars, 1816–1980.* Beverly Hills, Calif.: Sage Publications.
Stuart, Douglas T. 2003. "Ministry of Fear: The 1947 National Security Act in Historical and Institutional Context." *International Studies Perspectives* 4: 293–313.
Tocqueville, Alexis de. 1835, 1840. *Democracy in America.*
Washington, George. 1796. "Farewell Address." The Avalon Project at Yale Law School. www.yale.edu/lawweb/avalon/washing.htm.
Weinberger, Caspar W. 1984. "The Uses of Military Power: Remarks Prepared for Delivery to the National Press Club, Washington, D.C., November 28th."
West, Thomas G. 1997. *Vindicating the Founders: Race, Sex, Class, and Justice in the Origins of America.* Lanham, Md.: Rowman and Littlefield.
Wildavsky, Aaron. 1966. "Two Presidencies." *Transaction* 3: 7–14.
Williams, William Appleman. 1991. "Expansion, Continental and Overseas." In *The Reader's Companion to American History,* edited by Eric Foner and John A. Garraty. Boston: Houghton Mifflin.

Terrorism and Homeland Security

Feith, Douglas J. 2006. "On the Global War on Terrorism." In *Taking Sides: Clashing Views on Controversial Issues in World Politics,* 12th ed., edited by John T. Rourke. Dubuque, Iowa: McGraw-Hill/Dushkin.
Gunaratna, Rohan. 2002. *Inside Al-Qaeda: Global Network of Terror.* New York: Cambridge University Press.
Kean, Thomas H., and Lee H. Hamilton. 2004. The National Commission on Terrorist Attacks upon the United States, *The 9/11 Report.* New York: St. Martin's.
Leiby, Richard. 2001. "Terrorists by Another Name: The Barbary Pirates." *Washington Post.com,* October 15. www.washingtonpost.com/ac2/wp-dyn?pagename=article&node=&contentId=A59720-2001Oct14.

Theoretical Perspectives

Boot, Max. 2004. "Think Again: Neocons." *Foreign Policy* 140: 20–28.
———. 2005. "Q&A: Neocon Power Examined." *Christian Science Monitor*
Bremer, Stuart A. 1992. "Dangerous Dyads: Conditions Affecting the Likelihood of Interstate War, 1816–1965." *Journal of Conflict Resolution* 36: 309–341.
Bueno de Mesquita, Bruce. 1981. *The War Trap.* New Haven, Conn.: Yale University Press.
———. 2006. *Principles of International Politics: People's Power, Preferences, and Perceptions.* 3rd edition. Washington, D.C.: CQ Press.
Bueno de Mesquita, Bruce, and Randolph M. Siverson. 1995. "War and the Survival of Political Leaders: A Comparative Study of Regime Types and Political Accountability." *American Political Science Review* 89: 841–855.
Bueno de Mesquita, Bruce, James D. Morrow, Randolph M. Siverson, and Alastair Smith. 1999. "An Institutional Explanation of the Democratic Peace." *American Political Science Review* 93: 791–807.
Bueno de Mesquita, Bruce, Alastair Smith, Randolph M. Siverson, and James D. Morrow. 2003. *The Logic of Political Survival.* Cambridge, Mass.: MIT Press. Data available at www.nyu.edu/gsas/dept/politics/data/bdm2s2/Logic.htm.
Chomsky, Noam, and Edward Hermann. 1988. *Manufacturing Consent.* New York: Pantheon.
Cox, Robert W. 1986. "Social Forces, States, and World Orders: Beyond International Relations Theory." In *Neorealism and Its Critics,* edited by Robert O. Keohane. New York: Columbia University Press.
Desch, Michael C. 2002. "Democracy and Victory: Why Regime Type Hardly Matters." *International Security* 27: 5–47.
Dos Santos, Theotonio. 1970. "The Structure of Dependence." *American Economic Review* 60: 231–236.
Doyle, Michael W. 1997. *Ways of War and Peace: Realism, Liberalism, and Socialism.* New York: Norton.
Elshtain, Jean Bethke. 1987. *Women and War.* New York: Basic Books.

"Empire Builders: Neoconservatives and Their Blueprint for U.S. Power." 2005. *Christian Science Monitor.* http://csmonitor.com/specials/neocon/.

Enloe, Cynthia. 1989. *Beaches, Bananas, and Bases: Making Feminist Sense of International Politics.* Berkeley: University of California Press.

———. 1993. *The Morning After: Sexual Politics at the End of the Cold War.* Berkeley: University of California Press.

Gilpin, Robert. 1981. *War and Change in World Politics.* Cambridge: Cambridge University Press.

———. 1987. *The Political Economy of International Relations.* Princeton, N.J.: Princeton University Press.

———. 2001. *Global Political Economy.* Princeton, N.J.: Princeton University Press.

Goldstein, Joshua S. 2001. *War and Gender.* Cambridge: Cambridge University Press.

Hunt, Michael H. 1987. *Ideology and U.S. Foreign Policy.* New Haven, Conn.: Yale University Press.

Huntington, Samuel P. 2004. "The Hispanic Challenge." *Foreign Policy* 141: 30–45.

Johnson, Richard A. 1971. *The Administration of United States Foreign Policy.* Austin: University of Texas Press.

Keohane, Robert. 1980. "The Theory of Hegemonic Stability and Changes in International Economic Regimes, 1967–1977." In *Change in the International System,* edited by Ole R. Holsti, Randolph M. Siverson, and Alexander L. George. Boulder, Colo.: Westview.

———. 1983. "Theory of World Politics: Structural Realism and Beyond." In *Political Science: The State of the Discipline,* edited by Ada Finifter. Washington, D.C. American Political Science Association.

———. 1984. *After Hegemony: Cooperation and Discord in the World Political Economy.* Princeton, N.J.: Princeton University Press.

Keohane, Robert O., and Joseph S. Nye. 1989. *Power and Interdependence.* 2nd ed. Glenview, Ill.: Scott Foresman.

Krauthammer, Charles. 2004. "In Defense of Democratic Realism." *National Interest* 77: 15–25.

Kuperman, Alan J. 2004. "Humanitarian Hazard: Revisiting Doctrines of Intervention." *Harvard International Review* 26: 64–68.

Lake, David. 1993. "Leadership, Hegemony, and the International Economy: Naked Emperor or Tattered Monarch with Potential?" *International Studies Quarterly* 37: 459–489.

———. 1992. "Powerful Pacifists: Democratic States and War." *American Political Science Review* 86: 24–37.

Lake, David, and Matthew Baum. 2001. "The Invisible Hand of Democracy: Political Control and the Provision of Public Services." *Comparative Political Studies* 34: 587–621.

Layne, Christopher. 2006. "Impotent Power: Re-Examining the Nature of America's Hegemonic Power." *National Interest* 85: 41–47.

Lemke, Douglas. 1993. *Multiple Hierarchies in World Politics.* Ph.D. diss., Vanderbilt University.

———. 1997. "The Continuation of History: Power Transition Theory and the End of the Cold War." *Journal of Peace Research* 34: 23–36.

Lemke, Douglas, and Jacek Kugler. 1996. "The Evolution of the Power Transition Perspective." In *Parity and War: Evaluations and Extensions of "The War Ledger,"* edited by Jacek Kugler and Douglas Lemke. Ann Arbor: University of Michigan Press.

Levy, Jack. 1989. "The Diversionary Theory of War: A Critique." In *Handbook of War Studies,* edited by Manus I. Midlarsky. Boston: Unwin Hyman.

Lipset, Seymour Martin. 1959. "Some Social Requisites of Democracy: Economic Development and Political Legitimacy." *American Political Science Review* 53: 69–105.

Mead, Walter Russell. 2001. *Special Providence: American Foreign Policy and How It Changed the World.* New York: Knopf.

———. 2002. "The American Foreign Policy Legacy." *Foreign Affairs* 81: 163–176.

Mearsheimer, John J. 2001a. *The Tragedy of Great Power Politics.* New York: Norton.

Milner, Helen V. 1997. *Interests, Institutions, and Information: Domestic Politics and International Relations.* Princeton, N.J.: Princeton University Press.

Modelski, George, and William R. Thompson. 1987. "Testing the Cobweb Models of the Long Cycle." In *Exploring Long Cycles,* edited by George Modelski. Boulder, Colo.: Lynne Rienner.

Morgenthau, Hans. J., and Kenneth W. Thompson. 1985. *Politics among Nations.* 6th ed. New York: Knopf.

Mueller, John. 1995. *Quiet Cataclysm: Reflections on the Recent Transformation of World Politics.* New York: HarperCollins.

Nye, Joseph. 2002. *The Paradox of American Power: Why the World's Only Superpower Can't Go It Alone.* New York: Oxford University Press.

Olson, Mancur. 1968. *The Logic of Collective Action.* New York: Schocken Books.

Organski, A. F. K. 1958. *World Politics.* New York: Knopf.

Peterson, V. Spike, ed. 1992. *Gendered States: Feminist (Re)Visions of International Relations Theory.* Boulder, Colo.: Lynne Rienner.

Pevehouse, Jon C. 2005. *Democracy from Above: Regional Organizations and Democratization.* Cambridge: Cambridge University Press.

Przeworski, Adam, and Fernando Limongi. 1997. "Modernization: Theories and Facts." *World Politics* 49: 155–183.

Putnam, Robert D. 1988. "Diplomacy and Domestic Politics: The Logic of Two-Level Games." *International Organization* 42: 427–460.

Ray, James Lee, and Juliet Kaarbo. 2005. *Global Politics.* 8th ed. Boston: Houghton Mifflin.

Rosenau, Pauline Marie. 1992. *Post-Modernism and the Social Sciences: Insights, Inroads, and Intrusions.* Princeton, N.J.: Princeton University Press.

Russett, Bruce, and John Oneal. 2001. *Triangulating Peace: Democracy, Interdependence, and International Organizations.* New York: Norton.

Schattschneider, E. E. 1960. *The Semisovereign People: A Realist's View of Democracy in America.* New York: Holt, Rinehart, and Winston.

Smith, Alistair. 1996. "Diversionary Foreign Policy in Democratic Systems." *International Studies Quarterly* 40: 133–154.

———. 1998. "International Crises and Domestic Politics." *American Political Science Review* 92: 623–638.

Spero, Joan E., and Jeffrey A. Hart. 1997. *The Politics of International Economic Relations.* 5th ed. New York: St. Martin's.

———. 2003. *The Politics of International Economic Relations.* 6th ed. Belmont, Calif.: Thomson-Wadsworth.

Stoessinger, John. 2005. *Why Nations Go to War.* 9th ed. Belmont, Calif.: Thomson/Wadsworth.

Sylvester, Christine. 1994. *Feminist Theory and International Relations in a Postmodern Era.* New York: Cambridge University Press.

Walt, Stephen M. 1998. "International Relations: One World, Many Theories." *Foreign Policy* 110: 29–46.

Waltz, Kenneth N. 1959. *Man, the State, and War: A Theoretical Analysis.* New York: Columbia University Press.

———. 1979. *Theory of International Politics.* New York: Random House.

Wendt, Alexander. 1992. "Anarchy Is What States Make of It: The Social Construction of Power Politics." *International Organization* 46: 391–425.

———. 1999. *Social Theory of International Politics.* New York: Cambridge University Press.